PSYCHODYNAMICALLY BASED PSYCHOTHERAPY

PSYCHODYNAMICALLY BASED PSYCHOTHERAPY

LEON J. SAUL, M.D.

Emeritus Professor of Psychiatry,
Medical School of the University of
Pennsylvania; Honorary Staff,
Institute of the Pennsylvania
Hospital; Emeritus Training Analyst,
Philadelphia Psychoanalytic Institute

SCIENCE HOUSE
NEW YORK

Library of Congress Catalog Card Number: 72-85158
Standard Book Number: 87668-054-6

Designed by Jennifer Mellen

Manufactured in the United States of America

To My Patients and My Students

Table of Contents

Psychoanalysis is not, like philosophy, a system starting out from a few sharply defined basic concepts, seeking to grasp the whole universe with the help of these and, once it is completed, having no room for fresh discoveries for better understanding. On the contrary, it keeps close to the facts in its field of study, seeks to solve the immediate problems of observation, gropes its way forward by the help of experience, is always incomplete and always ready to correct or modify its theories.

Sigmund Freud

PREFACE

Psychodynamics is the science of the interplay of all the emotional forces in relation to the past, the present, and the future. It studies the essential nature of man much as physics explores the nature of matter. Psychodynamically based psychotherapy is the most direct and indispensable method for learning what makes us what we are. It is only in seeking relief from suffering that any person will or can reveal himself, and even then special techniques such as free association and the analysis of dreams are needed in trained, experienced, and qualified hands. It is from the study of persons with emotional problems that we learn what health is, and it is already evident beyond question that health is an ideal that rarely, if ever, is fully attained.

The laboratory in which the analyst acquires his knowledge of the human heart and mind and lusts is the office. Here he has the opportunity, if he is prepared to use it, to face more directly than is done probably anywhere else in life the basic forces of human nature. The situation is unique because the patient is motivated to reveal himself and the analyst has special techniques for exposing what the patient himself does not know. How the analyst achieves his insight, how he can understand the individual patient, and how this understanding can be used toward cure—that is, toward freeing the spirit and reopening the emotional development—it is the purpose of this book to describe.

It should be noted and emphasized here at the outset that this book speaks only of the neuroses. It does not refer to the psychoses in which an individual loses in large degree his self-control and his sense of reality; nor does it deal with those disturbances that result from physical or chemical interference with the workings of the brain; nor is it concerned with analysis for training.

Knowledge of man, like that of matter, can be used to destroy us or to help us at long last toward achieving a good life for all, a life in which man is not his own greatest enemy, as all history testifies. Analytic therapy that rests on psychodynamics learns as it helps, furthering sound observations and formulations in the very process of treatment. It draws on all the behavioral sciences of man and animals and then in turn makes contributions of new data to those fields. Thereby it becomes part of behavioral science and a foundation for all other psychotherapies.

Psychodynamics derives directly from psychoanalysis. The latter has been disappointing as theory and as therapy. Dissatisfactions have existed from its beginnings, within its own ranks and among other professionals. Much of the dissension within the field and the failure to progress seems the result not of resistance but of a basic misapprehension of Freud's major contributions. These contributions were not metapsychology, most of which I believe could be and in fact is being abandoned, and this is freeing the field so that analysts do not feel constrained by the libido theory and can become more open-minded observers. Freud's great contributions are the recognition of: the dynamic unconscious, with dreams as the royal road to the unconscious, and the methods for interpreting them; free association as a tool for insight and treatment; transference and its theoretical and therapeutic uses; the permanent conditioning effects of childhood emotional experiences; fixation and regression; the emotional etiology of symptoms and of all psychopathology; and psychic trauma. It is these discoveries of Freud and not his theories (although the concept of ego, id, and superego is a valuable tool) that have opened up the investigation of the interplays of emotional forces in the mind, those which make for maturity, adjustment, and health, and those which lead to disorders of all kinds. In his *New Series of Introductory Lectures* Freud said, "The theory of instincts is, as it were, our mythology." And, about theory he claimed that "it is a superstructure."

A brilliant young analyst to whom I recently expressed some of these views replied that if there were no metapsychology, there would be no psychoanalysis. Now this seems to be a rather extreme statement that overweighs theory at the expense of fact. But even so, something might be said for this point of view if you were to adopt a very broad definition of metapsychology; that is, one that would include almost all of Freud's concepts and generalizations, such as conscious, unconscious, ego, superego, id, conflict, repression, and other indispensable formulations. In my experience, and I believe a survey of the literature would support this, those who stress metapsychology tend to describe patients by means of such generalities and with such technical jargon that very little idea is given of the patient as a human being. And, when something specific about the particular life, makeup, and problem of the patient does come through, it is apt to be a fragment of the libido theory. The following briefly told incident should illumine the point.

One of the patients of an analyst of considerable reputation was transferred to this city, where he resumed treatment. The patient was suffering from guilt, which this first analyst had told him was from masturbating as a child. The patient was helped to some extent by this for why should he feel so guilty for so minimal a reason? But he still suffered from guilt and he still sought treatment. The real reasons underlying his complaint were never understood or dealt with in his two years of treatment with this analyst. Work with his new analyst in this city quickly revealed that his guilt stemmed from hostility, and this hostility was derived from two main sources: (1) feelings of inferiority, inadequacy, and weakness because he had been the youngest of the family and had been consistently overprotected and treated as a dependent baby; and (2) feelings of protest against all the responsibility which he now carried in his adult life.

This volume demonstrates what it means to offer treatment based upon psychodynamic understanding of each individual patient rather than on a set of generalizations and theories. To be sure, theories are needed, but the analyst must *follow* the patient's material and reach understanding from observational data rather than by applying fixed preconceptions that he has learned and which have gradually become dogma. All treatment, physical or psychological, if it is rational and not simply the application of preconceived notions, must rest on as thorough as possible an understanding of the general and local psychological condition of the patient and of what the treatment aims to do. For psychotherapy this means understanding the total psychic reality, the interplay of motivations and impulses, and the interreactions of these with each other and with the environment. The analyst must also gain a clear understanding of the individual's history and pattern of conditioning and how these form the patient's personality, including his sense of reality, controls, standards, and judgment, and how these casually relate to the symptoms and to his capacity for cure and maturing.

I do not start treatment without a thorough diagnosis, that is, until I have understood to my satisfaction the basic emotional forces that cause the patient's complaints and problems, and until I have discussed these with him and he, too, understands them. Also, before beginning I want to be clear in my own mind on just how psychotherapy can be expected to help. I discuss this with the patient also, so that he clearly understands what we are trying to do and how we are going to approach working out his problems in treatment. In this way, the entire procedure of treatment can then transpire in the full light of observation, reason, criticism, and co-operation of patient and analyst. Of course, this requires a certain security in his work on the part of the analyst.

Although psychodynamics is a development of psychoanalysis first and foremost, not all analysts have used it to full advantage. This is probably due, at least to some extent, to the fact that the term "psychoanalysis" is also used to describe certain preconceptions as to mechanics of procedure, such as five meetings a week and use of the couch. Various formulae are also implied in the term, for example, the libido theory, libidinal levels, erogenous zones, and invariable complexes which are to be discovered. This is all in unfortunate contrast to the completely openminded approach of psychodynamically based treatment, which requires an understanding of the particular, individual patient and an adaptation of the treatment to meet his particular and individual personality, problem, and needs. If the analyst, through accurate insight into the interplay of the particular patient's singular emotional forces, concludes that treatment is contraindicated, then he is rational, realistic, and also dynamic in his work. If the balance of forces in a patient is such that the analyst, through understanding them and the process of his own intervention, can tilt the balance and help the patient in one hour or ten hours or thirty hours, then he is operating analytically, that is, dealing with the underlying causative, component forces. To me, thorough psychodynamic understanding is the *sine qua non* of all proper, reality-oriented, rational, scientific therapy, as opposed to intuition or formulae. It is treatment based on understanding the major underlying causes in that specific, individual person.

The technique of a psychodynamically based treatment might, with reasonable correctness, be distilled to this quintessence: the analyst must understand and bring the patient to understand as quickly, accurately, and thoroughly as possible the patient's present emotional life and problems as related to and as an outgrowth of his past, particularly but not exclusively of the patterns shaped during his most formative years (roughly from birth to about age six) by the influences on him. Then in the individual sessions, the analyst discerns and repeatedly shows the patient, through the common element of the associations, and especially as seen in the dreams, the central, presenting motivational point of each hour and the disordered childhood emotional pattern that is repeating in life, especially and consistently as this pattern is transferred from the childhood figures to the analyst. The goal of so doing is to recondition the patient in order to correct the disordered parts of the pattern. This goal is approached, with a success contingent on several factors, by repeatedly helping the patient to see and experience emotionally—especially in the transference of his feelings toward the analyst, this being a sample human relationship—the fact that he is no longer a child in disturbed relations to his parents and siblings. Once the patient can grasp this, he will be able to see that he need not repeat this pattern unconsciously toward others in his current life, and then he can start securely to outgrow these disordered infantile patterns in favour of mature ones. It should be the analyst's aim to achieve secure progress on this path with a minimal number of sessions and in the shortest period of time. All this is my concept of good psychoanalysis but it has been attacked because it does not stress a minimum number of times per week on the couch and formulation by the libido theory.

The essential tragedy of human life lies in the fact that individuals react to one another with such overpoweringly intense feelings. And, they sustain unrelieved inner conflict because they are only part adult while still, underneath, part children and in a grip, far beyond their realization, of childish motivations that are usually seriously disordered ones. It is with this center of mankind's tragedy that psychodynamically based psychotherapy, of all human endeavors, deals most directly.

For the well-being and now even the existence of humanity, nothing is so vital in the long run as the use for prevention of what can be learned from treatment. This book is concerned with the psychodynamic treatment of individual persons. However, emotional disorders are so prevalent that it would seem that almost everyone has some problem. In fact, the basic problem of mankind is the high percentage of emotional disorders, particularly those that take the form of hostile acting out against others. These result primarily from the anger and hate generated in children toward their parents or others in reaction to faulty childrearing with abuses of omission or commission. The warped emotional patterns that were formed in early childhood cause hostility and destructiveness which, when repressed, cause neurosis and masochism, and if acted out they are displaced from the psychopathogenic parents and situations to the self as masochism and to others (individuals, groups, authorities, or underdogs) as crime, tyranny, revolution, and aggressive war. Therefore, the analyst has a wider responsibility than his primary one to his patients. He, more directly than any other specialist, is brought face to face with the ultimate sources of these worldwide problems in the rearing of children, especially from conception to about the age of five, six, or seven. He must know that a better world can be achieved only through rearing children with loving feelings toward their parents so that they mature emotionally; for the great finding of our time is not nuclear energy but that emotional disorders and all their results in social disorders, in all manner of cruelty, and in personal sufferings, all over the world, are caused by warpings in the child's emotional development because of improper upbringing. And it is these warpings that cause the constant arousal to fight and flight, hostility and escapism. Conversely, the emotionally mature adult who was reared with love, understanding, and respect, is an individual of good will, a good, strong, secure, and satisfied spouse, parent, and citizen who enjoys the exercise of his constructive powers and a balanced life.

Hence the practicing analyst has an enormous responsibility. He should provide a model of maturity in his personal living and should search professionally for ways of helping the millions of people who can never be reached for individual treatment. His goal is like that of all medicine—prevention. And in this field the prevention of emotional disorders means not only the prevention of personal neurosis but also of hostile acting out of man against man, and also leadership toward the goal of every person maturing toward the realization of his full human nature.

Leon J. Saul
Media, Pennsylvania
June 1972

ACKNOWLEDGMENTS

The writing of a serious book makes demands not only on the author but also on those who are close to him. My greatest debt is to my wife, Rose, not only generally for her patience and support, but for her extraordinary perceptiveness and intuition, from which I have learned so much about myself, about others, and about life.

It is a pleasure to thank my good friends, Dr. Peter Bennett and his wife, Leena, for their unselfish contributions and stimulating insights. Thanks are also due Nicholas and Anne Sclufer for their constant interest and unfailing willingness to help in any way. Susan Bender, my secretary, did all the typing and much more besides, taking over all sorts of problems of every kind and acting as a personal bosun, who well knows my weaknesses, faults, and foibles, and provides practical judgment and know-how. My sincere gratitude to June Strickland, Librarian of the Institute of the Pennsylvania Hospital, for her indefatigable assistance to me with the bibliography.

Especial thanks are due an old friend, Walter Kahoe of Lippincott, for his part in arranging the publication of this revision of *Technic and Practice of Psychoanalysis.* To Dr. Silas Warner, who co-authored Chapter 21, my grateful appreciation for his originality and help with the pertinent current references.

I also wish to express appreciation collectively to many of my colleagues of the Philadelphia Psychoanalytic Institute, with their refreshing combination of individuality, friendliness, and cooperation.

My thanks also to Dr. Jason Aronson and to those excellent members of the staff of Science House who were so willing, pleasant, and efficient to work with on this book, Marcia Guthrie, Jennifer Mellen, and particularly Barbara Wrubel, for her outstanding job as editor.

Certain of the content of this book has grown out of researches that have been supported in part by the Willard Foundation, the Strick Foundation, the Roger Williams Strauss Memorial, and the United States Public Health Service.

The *Psychoanalytic Quarterly, the Journal of the American Psychoanalytic Association,* and Vantage Press have given their kind permission to use material, particularly in Chapters 3, 4, 5, 10, 11, 18, 19, 20, 21, and the appendix, that appeared originally in some part as articles.

Part 1

Approach to Psychodynamically Based Psychotherapy

1 / NATURE AND GOALS OF TREATMENT

We are and must remain far from any tendentiousness except for the one aim of investigating and helping.
—*Sigmund Freud*

THE GOALS OF TREATMENT

"If the patient puts the analyst in the place of his father (or mother), he is also giving him the power which his superego exercises over his ego, since his parents were, as we know, the origin of his superego. The new superego now has an opportunity for a sort of after-education of the neurotic; it can correct blunders for which his parental education was to blame" (Freud, 1940). This statement by Freud on the technique of psychoanalysis expresses the essence of the therapeutic process and goal. The analyst who fails to grasp this with complete security and who does not see how it operates in every person he treats can only fumble in the dark. I say "person" instead of "patient" to emphasize their interchangeability.

To use psychoanalytic therapy with sureness, we must understand thoroughly not only the patient but also how the therapy operates. The unsatisfactory results of psychoanalytic therapy are due perhaps most basically and most often to lack of accuracy in understanding the patient and the process (Oberndorf, 1950, 1953; Wolman, 1972) and only secondarily to other reasons, such as mild symptoms masking unsuitable cases.

An understanding of the analytic process demands an unfettered comprehension of its goals. Both the process and the goals evolved with Freud's explorations of the mind and personality. His studies gradually expanded from preoccupation with what is repressed to investigation of the total personality interacting with other persons and the whole outside world (A. Freud, 1937). Freud (1917) soon saw that the problem is not the ideational content or the memories and the fantasies themselves but rather the difficulty is with the dynamic drives of the emotional forces that produce the ideas and operate to distort and repress them. He came to see neurosis as primarily a disorder of the ego that resorts to exaggerated defense reactions, for example, the person who sees in exaggerated form the hostility in others as a defense against seeing it in himself. In *Civilization and Its Discontents,* Freud expressed amazement at himself for having overlooked for so many years the central import of hostility in the neuroses and human affairs. He concluded that all guilt derives from hostility, even when it seems to come from a libidinal desire. He saw the universality of the oedipal relationships, which he formulated narrowly as an attachment-rivalry problem and broadly as the pattern of the child's feelings toward the members of his family (Freud, 1928). He also saw the fact that each individual's own special emotional problem is the result of how he in particular was reared as a child, and that it is this which determines the specific form of the oedipus. Therefore, the goal of therapy expanded beyond only the recovering of repressed memories (Breuer and Freud, 1893) and beyond only making the unconscious conscious (Freud, 1923). Some analysts, after reaching these goals, disclaimed any further therapeutic responsibility for their patients, but Freud (1940) enlarged the objective of treatment to include after-education to correct the blunders of the parents. This means understanding what these warping influences are and the effects that they produce—what childhood emotional patterns persist unconsciously, how they operate currently, and what is needed therapeutically to correct them. The technique is only the means to the end and was never sacrosanct to Freud, who emphasized the fact that it was developed in connection with hysteria and would be altered for other conditions, even those so closely related as phobias (1919), and that it was related to the personality of the particular analyst. Today we are less concerned with the nature of the symptom and focus rather upon the basic dynamics, that is, on the specific patterns of emotional interplay between the child and those responsible for and close to him. It is this which shapes his underlying personality and determines how he reacts to feeding, toilet training, sibling rivalry, and differences between the sexes.

The goals of psychoanalysis are several and can be expressed in various ways in terms of the analytic process. They are not armchair ideas but the observable results of proper and successful treatment. It is toward these that analysis helps the patient to move. The psychoanalyst works in alliance with the patient's rational conscious ego, the organ of adaptation; hence, the great tools of analysis are insight and understanding. Highly as these are to be prized for themselves, and indispensable as they are as immediate objectives, they are, nevertheless, means rather than ends. They open the mind to unrealized ways of its own operation, and this furthers one great goal of psychoanalysis: to free the mind from the grip of the outmoded childish patterns of thinking, feeling, and behaving, which are so disordered by warping, intensity, imbalance, or fixity that they impair mature functioning and adjustment (Zilboorg, 1951).

Each person tends to repeat toward others the attitudes he had as a child toward the members of his family. He also tends to identify with them and to take out on others, often spouse and children, what was done to him during childhood. One man's mother killed herself before his very eyes when he was a child. Years later he married and became dangerous toward his wife, but before she could get him into treatment, he identified with his mother and killed not his wife but himself.

Predominance of childhood emotional patterns usually means narrow limitation of choice. A girl with no father and a very dominating mother later saw her husband and society only in terms of submitting or dominating. A young woman whose needs for prestige and money were instigated and intensified by her mother, hounded her husband for more and more income and larger homes, and she yearned for either these or, as rebellion and punishment, the opposite—a life of poverty and drudgery. By freeing the mind, analysis opens new choices and thus increases an individual's adaptability and flexibility. Insofar as a person progresses in handling his drives and in reducing his frustrations and conflicts, he (1) increases his free energy by releasing what has been bound up, burned up, and dissipated in emotional struggles and (2) moves toward diminishing emotional tension and increasing his capacity for relaxation.

All persons have their "specific emotional vulnerabilities" (Saul, 1971). The above examples show one being sensitive to domination, another to financial prestige, and so on. Psychoanalysis desensitizes these "emotional allergies." Softening the grip of the childhood pattern is, as Freud put it, a form of correcting the harmful effects of the parents or of circumstances and, as such, is after-education. It is also, as such, a corrective emotional experience (Alexander and French, 1946). In the terms of Pavlov, it is a process of deconditioning and reconditioning. Clinically, the patient is turned from the way in to the way out of his emotional difficulties.

Insofar as the analyst replaces the figure of the parent and helps the patient to move from the underlying childish attitudes to more mature ones toward himself, the analyst, and others, he is, so to speak, taking the patient's superego, reconditioning it, and returning it. The patient's view of himself and others is thereby less colored and distorted by the attitudes, the feelings, and the expectations he has toward his parents and siblings. He need not see every relationship in terms, for example, of being dominated or dominating. Thus, as Sullivan (1947) has pointed out, his human relations (or personal and interpersonal relations) are freed and matured. One girl never could be well-groomed because her mother then would tell her that any girl who dressed so well must be having promiscuous affairs with men. She took over her rejecting mother's very low opinion of herself. By loosening these superego patterns, analysis corrects and strengthens the sense of reality toward self and others. One of the great accomplishments of psychoanalysis occurs when it sucessfully changes a person's view of himself and thus improves the whole inner emotional climate in which that individual lives out his life. The patient's view of himself as a weak, guilty child in a world of adults is diminished and he can then move toward being and feeling like an adequate, mature adult. As a person becomes more aware of his childhood reactions, he no longer responds with such naive automaticity; in other words, he becomes capable of learning from experience.

We may make a first expansion of Freud's dictum: Where id and superego were, there shall ego be.

The patient is given a more mature superego, and the mature motivations of his id are released. As the childhood patterns of id and superego are softened and loosened, the patient's ego is expanded and freed; it is less at the mercy of the relentless automaticity of the unconscious patterns and is less tyrannized by infantile impulses and purposeless guilt and compulsion. The patient can make his decisions and live his life more with his ego, the organ of reason, of adaptation, of grasp of reality, and of unemotional objective thinking (Rado and Daniels, 1956). A man had been so dominated during childhood by his mother that his every view and decision was an almost fixed reflex of her too intensive and encompassing training. His life was lived for him by this rigid, ingrained, maternal pattern (superego). A girl and her sister were raised in relative isolation from other people by an overly devoted mother. Because of the mother's attitude and closeness, the competition between the sisters for her attention was intensified, and it was undiluted by the presence of other adults or even of playmates as outlets. The girl's life was dominated by this id pattern of painfully violent and sometimes paralyzing competitiveness toward others. Neither she nor the young man previously mentioned were adequately free in their egos—in their views, judgments, adaptability, and flexibility; their lives were lived too much under the fixed dictatorship of the superego pattern in the former and the id pattern in the latter rather than through the higher human capacities of their egos.

We can now further expand Freud's statement: Where immature id and superego patterns were, there shall mature id and superego forces as well as mature ego be.

Every patient feels frustrated by the childhood feelings and desires, whether conscious or unconscious, which he transfers to the analyst. The analyst can help satisfy the analysand's wishes to be understood but he himself cannot gratify the childish demands made upon him—for example, those for love and dependence. Further, unlike the parents, he charges money for what he gives and thereby sets up a mature relationship as between two adults—a value for a value. The very nature of the childish demands, the means by which the patient tries to satisfy them, and the ever-present guilt and masochistic self-punishment combine in varying degrees to doom the patient to frustration. Insofar as analysis ameliorates this inner frustration, it also increases the patient's satisfactions in real life. At the same time it helps to increase the pleasure of living by showing clearly and explicitly the nature of the mature drives, which are also in the id, and how to enjoy the exercise of them. It reopens the emotional development to maturity and its satisfactions. No child can enjoy prematurely the responsibilities of the adult, and no adult can forego the exercise of his mature functions and gain all his pleasure from childish impulses. Both all work and all play make Jack neurotic. From his analysis the patient should learn healthy, mature emotional attitudes and ways of thinking and be started on the way to achieving these.

It is said that when Freud was asked what he considered mental health to be, he replied, "The capacity to work and to love." Perhaps we could amplify this definition by saying that it is the capacity to enjoy loving and being loved and also the participation, in proper balance, in responsible working and harmless recreation. This is a good formulation of the nature of emotional maturity. It is toward this that analysis strives to help every patient, even though in some cases it is necessary to rest satisfied with the lesser goal of improved adjustment which, when not a mature one, is at least workable.

In any case, it is only practice in living that can complete the analytic process and be the test of its effectiveness. The patient's present life, as he lives it, must be thoroughly understood in terms of his motivations and feelings—it is his continuing childhood patterns that produce the difficulties and are consequently the central concern of the analyst.

A highly talented girl who had been in painful emotional turmoil and who was seen during critical periods from age fifteen to eighteen wrote a letter that poignantly expresses some of the goals of analysis.

> As time goes on I rejoice more and more in the priceless understanding gained from our work together. It has literally illuminated my days, which now are filled with self-forgetting work and joy in all human relationships. I feel that we have been able to achieve a precious freedom that is valid only when its roots exist in the individual person and from there must be reflected in the social structure as a whole. This is expressed poorly, but what I am realizing is: no inner peace, no social peace.
>
> But I am also finding that this understanding of self, far from being a static thing, is dynamic and radiant and grows stronger and deeper with experience.

Another patient, a hard-bitten man of the world in his early fifties, summed it up in a different way. He wrote, "Now I can pray again."

Every physician has letters of gratitude, and these are quoted here only to indicate how the goals may be felt and expressed by the patient.

PROCESS

To clarify the goals of psychoanalysis, we have already stated the essence of the process of achieving these goals: after-education, corrective emotional experience, and reconditioning. The analyst's daily work in the office is also, in a narrower sense, a form of psychological surgery and should have the same precision of understanding and procedure as that of the skilled surgeon. Freud repeatedly used the analogy with surgery. For example, a young man suffers from inferiority feelings because of his overly close, prolonged dependence on his mother and reacts with excessive drives for prestige, mostly in athletics and with women. He represses almost entirely his rage that results from the constant irritation of his pride by the feelings of inferiority. On the surface he is conspicuously mild-mannered, while underneath his rage causes him guilt and anxiety. Analysis, making the unconscious conscious, must show him the source of his feelings of inferiority in his attitudes of dependence. Furthermore, the dependence must be demonstrated so clearly that the patient can reduce it and shift his attitudes to expect less of others while at the same time learning to take and enjoy more responsibility for himself. He must come to see how his exaggerated demands for prestige only expose him to inevitable frustration and burn up energies that would be better spent in enjoying the exercise of his mature interests and powers. And, meanwhile, he must see that awareness of his inner rages and hostilities is a step toward understanding their sources and diminishing them and the consequent anxiety and other baleful effects that they have on himself and others.

In all this, analysis does not hesitate to discuss all possible solutions and the nature of the mature ones which the analyst himself must know thouroughly from his profession and his own life. To this extent, the analyst must, in fact and in all humility, discuss with the patient certain fundamentals of living while realizing that the patient knows far more about many aspects of life than he himself does.

This intervention by the analyst with mental and emotional processes is not so different from the intervention by the surgeon or the internist on the physiologic level. It is not unlike a complex orthopedic or gastro-intestinal operation that is done in several stages and is designed for example, to remove obstructing adhesions or to correct deformities in order to set the conditions for nature's healing processes to operate and to restore gradually more healthy structure and functioning. The analyst cannot quite do a dependectomy or a hostilectomy or a guiltotomy, but he does strive to reduce the pathologic intensities and forms of these forces.

Well-executed psychoanalysis is probably one of the most delicate types of surgical procedure. Operating on the highest psychological levels means dealing with emotional forces which, although relatively abstract, are no less real than the tissues of the body—any more than electricity is less real than a chair, although it cannot even be comprehended directly and can be dealt with only though its effects (Saul, 1972).

Because emotional forces, however chemical they may be in their origins, are abstract and known psychologically only through their effects, the analyst must beware of treating his patient as a disembodied psyche. Great care must be taken against becoming lost in a sea of symbols, of losing sight of the patient and thereby analyzing the symptoms instead of the person. These are no idle warnings; they are sounded with all sympathy. It has not been unusual to hear students of this field make astute, penetrating remarks about an anonymous patient, only to flounder in the actual analysis, losing sight of the patient as a person. No doubt this is due, at least to some extent, to the difficulty of the field and of teaching it. There has been some progress of late toward formulating the currently established fundamentals, as is done in all other fields, and in teaching them more from clinical material.

Certain principles in the analytic process seem to be so well tested and established that probably no analysts would disagree about them. One of these is that what carries the analysis is the transference. Freud once defined analysis as any treatment that is based on analyzing the transference and the resistance. Since the person being analyzed, the analysand, transfers to the analyst emotional patterns that he had toward the members of his family, he repeats to the analyst his original human relationships.

The essential of psychoanalytic therapy then is a human relation. In the office the analyst isolates a laboratory sample of the analysand's interpersonal relations, sees what his most important feelings are, and "analyzes out" what is infantile, disturbing, and does not work, showing him what one good mature relationship can be and getting him well on the way to it. This is like a vaccination (to use Franz Alexander's simile) in that riddance of the neurotic (disordered infantile) elements in this one relationship establishes relative immunity to them in other relations.

For example, an analysand, never having met the analyst before treatment, is soon plunged into a struggle of submissiveness and rebellion. He may become so dependent that he seeks from the analyst answers and decisions to every problem of his life. Or, the patient may develop almost overpowering hatred toward the analyst out of envy or because the analyst cannot satisfy his insatiable demands. He may mobilize such guilt that he punishes himself by all sorts of mistakes in life, or he may project his own wishes onto the analyst and then accuse the physician of exploiting him. The patient may worship the analyst as his own desired ideal, or he may reveal a too extravagant identification with the analyst by aping his mannerisms and dress, believing that his kind of car and house are the best, and so on.

As the roots of the disturbing reactions in the childhood

pattern are exposed, the analysand sees ever more clearly and with increasing emotional awareness how they cause trouble in his relationship to the analyst and to persons in his life. The patient comes to realize how the power of these feelings generates so much emotional tension that symptoms result that affect his whole life. As the analysand works this through, he sees that he will avoid this psychic pain and gain inner peace and satisfaction from life as he relinquishes these childhood patterns in favor of easy, mature, friendly give-and-take, value-for-value, live-and-let-live relationships as between equals.

This is not achieved easily or rapidly—there is always resistance to change—and the infantile patterns toward the analyst persist for years after analysis, although with ever-lessening power. But the forces of development, of gaining peace and pleasure and of avoiding pain all work constantly toward cure and maturity and gain the ascendency as the infantile patterns are softened and analyzed out. This is achieved in large part by repeatedly confronting the patient with and helping him to discriminate between the past patterns of childhood and the present realities of his adult life.

"I bandage, nature cures" quoted Freud. Not only can't the analyst gratify the patient directly, but he also cannot actually help him directly either. He can only help him to help himself. The patient must realize this and have a sense of taking the responsibility for himself and thus recognize his part in the treatment. Many an analysis has run on for unnecessary months because the patient felt that he did his part merely by free-associating and the analyst did the rest and the cure would simply arrive. But this never can be. On the lower physiologic levels the surgeon can intervene even better while the patient is unconscious. The analyst, however, must work with the patient's ego, and so it is the patient in the end who has the ultimate responsibility for himself, whether or not he knows it. This is one of the great facts of living. No matter how much the infant is a part of its mother and continues an identification with her, nevertheless, as it matures, it must eventually rely on itself (McDevitt and Settlage, 1971); no matter how close the companionship and the interdependence between husband and wife, no matter how intimately understood by his analyst the patient may feel, yet in his soul the adult is alone, able in the long run to rely and depend only on himself, "for the race is run by ones and ones, and never by twos and twos," as Kipling put it.

No matter what the seeming, no matter how much a herd animal, no matter how much a part of family and friends, each human being must go through life as he goes through death—alone. Yet he is not fully alone, for if he had from conception loving and wise parents, then he has a loving and wise superego in his own mind and he can face both life and death with confidence and faith and without loneliness.

One's unconscious is part of oneself, and the patient must take the responsibility of utilizing the analyst's help and the transference experience for understanding his unconscious and learning to handle it. This is not easy because of the tendency to repeat toward the analyst the infant's dependence on its parents—but analysis is only possible in persons who have a certain minimum of healthy mature ego that can work with the analyst.

The physician intervenes to affect the conditions so that the developmental and curative forces within the organism can better operate. In treating a human, or even a tree for that matter, you are dealing with a living organism that has its own inner drives toward healthy growth of maturity and toward the healing of injuries and warpings. The therapist only frees the healing and developmental tendencies already inherent in Nature. Therefore, he must know not only the forms of illness and pathology but also the course of development to healthy maturity. This he can learn, even if there are few ideally mature persons, from his own practice. He can note what this or that patient would be like without the partial fixations in childhood patterns, he can confirm this by seeing the course of the patient's progress as these are relieved, and he can extrapolate as to what the patient would become ideally. He can arrange his patients in a series from the most infantile and regressed to the least so (Saul, 1971). Biographies of such men as Jefferson and Lincoln also reveal the nature of emotional maturity.

It must now be evident that the depth of understanding and treatment is a function of the extent to which the effects of the early warpings are comprehended and corrected. It is not a matter of awesome semimystical discovering of fecal penises dangling from breasts and other intriguing bizarre symbolizations. It is not a matter of remoteness of fantasy but of penetrating understanding of the basic human motivations in the individual patient.* The goal of treatment is not to reduce the highest intellectual reality-testing functions of the ego to the dream processes of the unconscious; quite the contrary the purpose is to translate the language of unconscious processes into that of very realistic, down-to-earth comprehension by the person of his own motivations so that the ego can learn to master, to alter, and to outgrow the disordered infantile ones. If the child is congenitally healthy, and if the treatment that he receives by the members of his family, especially up to the age of five, is basically benign, there will be no warping in his emotional growth and in his later personality. If, on the other hand, the treatment is in any way extreme, then exaggerated reactions are apt to be aroused in the child, and these may become fixed as either open or hidden, but nevertheless permanent, traits of his personality. Or, they may develop only as vulnerable points for regressions, in which case they will be unmasked only by special stresses.

This is like growing a tree. If the seed is healthy, then the tree will grow straight in meeting the normal vicissi-

*The term "depth" is used in many ways, among which are: power and effectiveness, pervasiveness, remoteness from consciousness, earliness in the existence of the organism, e.g., prenatal, oral, etc.

tudes—the soil, the heat and the cold, the storms, and the winds. It is shaped by Nature to meet these and to adjust to them as it grows. Thus is the child formed for adjusting, as it grows, to the members of its family and to the typical parental and brother-sister (oedipal and sibling) relationships. The young tree reaches its mature beauty through the normal stages of its development. But, if the soil is too barren, the heat or the cold too extreme or inconsistent, or the storm winds too violent, then it is "shown by slant and twist which way the wind has blown."

The results of injurious influences on the child during the earliest years, that is, the warpings of the actual symptoms, are no longer of primary interest. Psychoanalysis developed out of investigating neurotic symptoms, that is, symptoms that were of emotional origin. It succeeded in penetrating to the interplay of forces that generated them. It is now this interplay of emotional forces, the psychodynamics, that is centrally significant. However important in certain ways is the form of the outcome, that is, the symptoms, it is another way only of secondary interest whether they eventuate as headaches, social insecurity, obsessive ideas, spells of anxiety, or other symptoms or personality characteristics. For it is in the interplay of the underlying motivational forces that the problem and the source of the symptoms lie, and it is this that must be understood and corrected. It is with these forces that analytic treatment deals to achieve cures, and it deals with them more directly than does any other approach.

There is no technique apart from solid, realistic understanding of the goal and purpose, of the analysis—understanding what is wrong, what needs to be corrected, and what healthy mature functioning is. The technique is only the means to the end. As in surgery, it is hollow, empty, and meaningless except as dictated by understanding of what is healthy and what is to be corrected. It is no blind dredging operation. It has become the more precise procedure that

Freud hoped for and predicted. It still rests upon understanding the patient.

The psychoanalytic therapeutic process can perhaps be illustrated very briefly here. A young woman grew up with parents who kept her extremely dependent. They restricted her natural growth into a life of her own by making her feel that her only great obligation was to them, that any step out of the home was disloyalty, that they needed and were dependent on her, that she should enjoy only being with them and not traveling or visiting, and that any expression of rebellion or resentment was unthinkable. There was enough love, however, and the parents were so busy with their own interests that the patient did manage to marry and soon had a daughter and then a son to make a happy, pleasant family. Then gradually, however, she developed such severe anxiety and depression that she feared a breakdown; the family life was in jeopardy, and she sought analytic help.

After three years she achieved security in her mind, harmony with her husband and children after a difficult period, and emancipation from her parents plus reestablishment of a loose but friendly relationship with them. How was this accomplished? Very briefly it was achieved (1) with transference to the analyst of the pattern of feelings toward her parents described above, (2) with insight, and (3) with help in correcting and resolving the childhood pattern. At first she became desperately dependent on the analyst but proportionately less so on her parents, which, at her age of thirty, was appropriate, not to say long overdue. She clung to the analyst in dread of breakdown but gradually saw that this fear came in large part from rebelliousness and hostility against her parents which, for all these years, was repressed far from awareness and, because of their attitudes, generated almost insufferable guilt. The dependence on the analyst could be discussed openly and freely with him, as her dependence on her parents could not be discussed with them. Where the parents' very attitudes caused guilt for any breath of resentment toward them, the analyst encouraged the direct talking out of any such feeling toward him. Where restrictiveness was the price of parental approval, the analyst was pleased to see progress toward freedom. So precise was the transference that the patient even felt toward him as she had toward her parents, that is, that her devotion to her husband and children was disloyalty. Gradually freed of guilt and then by taking steps to develop her own life, she began to experience a significantly lessened dependence on the analyst. She grew able to feel that she gained rather than lost approval by loving and being loved in her own home and in a growing circle of friends. In addition, her submissiveness and thereby her reasons for rebelliousness and hostility were also diminished. She began to test herself out in life, meeting new people, facing new situations, and taking trips.

Thus what had so troubled her in her pattern of feelings toward her parents, but had been throughly repressed from her consciousness, was transferred to the analyst where it could gradually emerge and be discussed frankly. Once this was achieved, what had bothered her could be exposed to her own knowledge and experience as an adult and then reconditioned by the difference of the analyst's attitude toward her as an adult from what the parents' attitude had been during her childhood and unfortunately still was. Her possibilities for growth we reopened so that she could move from a dependent, restricted, hostile, guilty, fixated child to a responsible, loving mate and parent. And she progressed by testing herself out in meeting life as it came.

Because of the analyst's intimate dealing with human motivation, one might even say with the human spirit, he carries a special responsibility not only to his patients but also to his students, his colleagues, and to mankind. And this responsibility calls for certain intellectual and emotional attitudes and capacities in the analyst.

REFERENCES AND SOME RELATED READINGS

Alexander, F. (1963), *The Fundamentals of Psychoanalysis*, 3rd ed. New York: Norton.

——— (1961), *The Scope of Psychoanalysis.* New York: Basic Books.

——— (1956), *Psychoanalysis and Psychotherapy.* New York: Norton.

——— (1925), A metapsychological description of the process of cure. *Internat. J. Psychoanal.*, 6:13–34.

Alexander, F., and French, T. (1946), *Psychoanalytic Therapy: Principles and Application.* New York: Ronald.

Balint, M. (1950), Changing therapeutic aims and techniques in psychoanalysis. *Internat. J. Psychoanal.*, 31:117–124.

Bergler, E. (1937), Symposium on the theory of therapeutic results of psychoanalysis. *Internat. J. Psychoanal.*, 18:146–160.

Bibring, E. (1937), Symposium on the theory of therapeutic results of psychoanalysis. *Internat. J. Psychoanal.*, 18:170–189.

Brenner, C. (1969), Some comments on technical precepts in psychoanalysis. *J. Am. Psychoanal. A.*, 17:333–352.

Breuer, J., and Freud, S. (1893), *Studies in Hysteria.* New York: Nerv. and Ment. Dis. Pub., 1936.

Bromberg, W. (1962), *The Nature of Psychotherapy.* New York: Grune & Stratton.

Chessick, R. (1969), *How Psychotherapy Heals.* New York: Science House.

Engel, G. (1968), Some obstacles to the development of research in psychoanalysis. *J. Am. Psychoanal. A.*, 16:195–229.

Fenichel, O. (1941), *Problems of Psychoanalytic Technique* (monograph). New York: Psychoanal. Quart.

——— (1937), Symposium on the theory of therapeutic results of psychoanalysis. *Internat J. Psychoanal.*, 18:133–138.

Freud, A. (1954), The widening scope of indications for psychoanalysis. *J. Am. Psychoanal. A.*, 2:607–620.

——— (1937), *Ego and the Mechanisms of Defense*, 1–3. London: Hogarth Press.

Freud, S. (1940), *An Outline of Psychoanalysis*, 67. New York: Norton, 1949.

——— (1930), *Civilization and Its Discontents*, 131. London: Hogarth Press.

——— (1928), Dostoevsky and parricide. In *Collected Papers*, 5:22–242. London: Hogarth Press, 1950.

——— (1923), *The Ego and the Id.* London: Hogarth Press, 1935.

——— (1919), Turnings in the ways of psychoanalytic therapy. In *Collected Papers*, 2:392–402. London: Hogarth Press, 1924.

——— (1917), *Delusion and Dream.* London: Allen & Unwin.

Fromm-Reichmann, F. (1954), Psychoanalytic and general dynamics conceptions of theory and therapy; differences and similarities. *J. Am. Psychoanal. A.*, 2:711–721.

Galdston, I., ed. (1969), *Psychoanalysis in Present-Day Psychiatry.* New York: Brunner/Mazel.

Glover, E. (1954), Therapeutic criteria of psychoanalysis. *Internat. J. Psychoanal.*, 35:95–101.

Greenacre, P., *et al.* (1953), The traditional psychoanalytic technique. *J. Am. Psychoanal. A.*, 1:526–574.

Holzman, P. (1970), *Psychoanalysis and Psychopathology.* New York: McGraw-Hill.

Kaiser, H. (1955), The problems of responsibility in psychotherapy. *Psychiatry*, 18:205–211.

Klein, M. (1955), The psycho-analytic technique: Its history and significance. In *New Directions in Psychoanalysis.* New York: Basic Books.

Kubie, L. (1950), *Practical and Theoretical Aspects of Psy-*

choanalysis. New York: Internat. Univ. Press.
Little, M. (1957), "R"— the analyst's total response to his patients' needs. *Internat. J. Psychoanal.*, 38:240–254.
Mahrer, A. (1967), *Goals of Psychotherapy.* New York: Appleton.
Marmor, J., ed. (1968), *Modern Psychoanalysis.* New York: Basic Books.
——— (1955), Validation of psychoanalytic techniques. *J. Am. Psychoanal. A.,* 3:496–505.
Masserman, J. (1961), *Principles of Dynamic Psychiatry.* Philadelphia: Saunders.
McDevitt, J., and Settlage, C., eds. (1971), *Separation-Individuation.* New York: Internat. Univ. Press.
Mullahy, P. (1970), *Psychoanalysis and Interpersonal Psychiatry.* New York: Science House.
Oberndorf, C. P. (1953), *A History of Psychoanalysis in America.* New York: Grune & Stratton.
——— (1950), Unsatisfactory results of psychoanalytic therapy. *Psychoanal. Quart.*, 19:393–407.
——— (1913), The scope and technique of psychoanalysis. *Med. Rec.*, 84:973.
Rado, S. (1939), Developments in the psychoanalytic conception and treatment of neuroses. *Psychoanal. Quart.*, 8:427–437.
Rado, S., and Daniels, G. (1956), *Changing Concepts of Psychoanalytic Medicine.* New York: Grune & Stratton.
Reik, T. (1933), New ways in psychoanalytic technique. *Internat. J. Psychoanal.*, 14:321–334.
Saul, L. (1972), *Basis of Human Behavior.* Westport, Conn.: Greenwood Press.
——— (1971), *Emotional Maturity*, 3rd ed. Philadelphia: Lippincott.
Stone, L. (1954), Widening scope of indications for psychoanalysis. *J. Am. Psychoanal. A.*, 2:702–710.
Strachey, J. (1937), Symposium on the theory of therapeutic results of psychoanalysis. *Internat. J. Psychoanal.,* 18: 139–145.

——— (1934), The nature of the therapeutic action of psychoanalysis. *Internat. J. Psychoanal.,* 15:127–159.

Sullivan, H. S. (1947), *Conceptions of Modern Psychiatry.* Washington, D.C.: William Alanson White Psychiatric Foundation.

Wolman, B., ed. (1972), *Success and Failure in Psychoanalysis and Psychotherapy.* New York: Macmillan.

Zilboorg, G. (1951), *Sigmund Freud.* New York: Scribner.

2 / ATTITUDES OF THE ANALYST

INTELLECTUAL ATTITUDES

Ideally, the analyst's attitudes and procedures should be scientific intellectually and mature emotionally. Research is the lifeblood of science, and science is the basis of treatment. The free, enquiring spirit of Freud will yield far greater security through understanding than will strivings for purity through rules and rituals. Freud described psychoanalysis as a science, and as such he meant it to be a research tool and a form of therapy.

Difficulties in psychoanalysis arise from several sources. The problems of proof are particularly troublesome because the data consist of the patient's necessarily subjective reporting of his own observations and because there is so very large an element of interpretation on the part of the analyst, who is himself swayed by his own fantasies and subjective influences. These latter presumably are minimized by the analyst's personal analysis; but indispensable as the personal analysis is for acquainting the student with his own unconscious processes and motivations, the suggestibility toward the training analyst and the identification with him limit its effectiveness unless the training analyst himself has had experience in science and can conduct the training analysis in a highly accurate scientific fashion with scrupulous regard for validity of procedure, evidence, logic, conclusions, and proof.

It is to be expected that the three aspects of psychoanalysis will separate more and more until we have flexible therapeutic methods applying scientifically established knowledge, which is coming to be referred to as psychodynamics. Then such currently controversial matters as numbers of hours per week and whether the patient should or should not lie on a couch will be seen in proper perspective and will not be confused either with essential knowledge of the human mind and spirit or with the essentials of research and therapeutic method.

Every phase of psychoanalysis must be subjected to continuing questioning and research. In the end, validity and proof must be generated from such sources and criteria as (1) predictability of the patient's utterances, feelings, and behavior; (2) predictability from the current, disturbed behavior and the emotional pattern that underlies it of what will be found in the history—this can then be verified by interviews with those who knew the patient during childhood; and (3) predictability from the way a child is reared of the sort of adult he will become. (4) Further proof will come from reproducing experimentally in animals the disorders seen in human beings. (5) Quantitative estimation of emotional forces has been attempted (Saul *et al.,* 1954; Saul and Sheppard, 1956, 1958). It can be hoped that this type of work will increase the range of observations and experimentation. (6) Recordings of interviews are now being made and should help analysts to learn and to improve what is done in the sanctum of the office. (7) Meanwhile, we can increase our understanding of the patient and of the therapeutic process to the point of judging analytic results on the basis of the actual underlying shifts in motivation and of the reopening of the emotional development to maturity.

It is not the mechanical incidentals that differentiate the psychoanalytic process from the more superficial techniques. Rather, what distinguishes it is the fact that it deals with the major motivations that underlie all the symptoms and shape the patient's personality. The analytic process also involves confrontation with the central issue of how the patient succeeds in the living of his life and with the questions of how the individual chooses his career, his wife, his friends, and his standards.

In the office an enormous responsibility for another human being is in the analyst's hands: the patient's success or failure, marriage or divorce, happiness or misery, and even life or death. Clearly this responsibility extends beyond just the patient and necessarily includes his family and intimates as well. The analyst must utilize all that he knows and be prepared for this responsibility intellectually and emotionally.

Analytic training often has been in the form of first learning the theory and then later applying it. There is some evidence that this is changing, hopefully, to basing procedures on an understanding that is grounded in a critical examination of the clinical facts. Reality is the only authority, and Freud's and all other writings can serve only as guides to what to look for in reality in the patient. This mature attitude toward reality and the student's grasp of it may be influenced by the student's own residual infantile orientation, which makes a tendency to accept the author of the printed page as an authority, such as the parent is to the child. The force of this is especially strong in psychoanalysis where the material is abstract and the prestige of Freud so overriding. One man of forty-five said to me, "If Freud says it, it's true; it's good enough for me." The trouble is, of course, that Freud himself did not feel this way. He constantly searched and then revised his material so that it is not unusual to find that what he says at one point is later altered in the light of new observations and points of view. But analytic students sometimes learn the *Studies in Hysteria* so well that afterward they cannot master Freud's later writings or use them adequately to understand their patients. The focus must be on the reality of what is going on in the patient as a human being. All grain must be grist for this mill—reading, observing, and living. All must help; no preconceptions should hinder. The analyst must be able to rid himself of notions that are not demonstrably valid. He must cleave to reality as the only authority and keep a truly open mind toward new developments in a young and growing field.

Independence of thought is indispensable since the analyst, in dealing with his patient, is alone. Although mutual feelings of warm friendliness may spring up, and although the analyst works with the patient's ego by eliciting interpretations and help from him, yet the ineluctable fact remains that the patient's unconscious is really unconscious. Asking the patient's opinion is laudable technically at many points, but the patient cannot describe or understand what is unconscious to him. Whatever glimmerings the patient may have, whatever clues, intuitions, or intellectual insights, the analyst still sits totally alone with no one to turn to or to rely on but himself in his task of understanding the patient and of using this understanding therapeutically.

EMOTIONAL ATTITUDES

What shall be the analyst's emotional attitude toward the patient? In a word, mature; in several words, a genuine, easy, natural, and friendly interest combined with the wish to help. Cool objectivity is necessary for complete security in handling technically the powerful emotional forces under whose merciless pressures the patient suffers and which will be loosed on the analyst if he is competent. Appropriate to the analyst is the sage formula of Kipling's Spurstow (in *At the End of the Passage*): "Lay low, go slow, keep cool."

We all operate, putting it broadly, on two levels—the infantile and the mature. As Freud never tired of remarking, the child an individual once was lives in every adult and lives on "almost unchanged in the dreamer and the artist and in the sick person too" (1925). However realistically the analyst is perceived by the mature part of the patient's personality, the childish part sees him in some degree as the bogeyman or witch or other nightmare character that never has been fully outstripped. For although the patient unconsciously slips the analyst into some kind, helping image, he also feels toward him like a hostile, guilty, needy, and ashamed child before its parents.

Hence, the analyst must be as supporting and tolerant as he would be with a small child, while at the same time he must strive to maintain a realistic and adult-to-adult relationship. The patient unconsciously puts the analyst in such a position that sometimes the analyst could crush the patient's self-esteem. The analyst must be wary of this hazard since his goal is to work with and strengthen the patient's ego and help him to handle and outgrow his infantile feelings. Therefore, it is vitally important that the analyst unwaveringly show his respect and regard for the patient and his faith and confidence in him. This will help enormously to sustain the patient through difficult periods, especially when very disturbed childhood patterns are mobilized.

Probably the best attitude to exhibit toward a child, at least after its babyhood, is the same as toward an adult—a friendly interest and identification, with full respect for its individuality and reasonableness. At the same time, of course, it is necessary to be prepared to make allowance, as need be, for its being a child. Then, the analyst, himself part child, will have no great problem in his attitude toward the childish and the mature side of his patients. Throughout he will keep a kind, friendly, natural, easy, mature adult-to-adult relationship, while making allowances for the child, that is, the neurotic motivations. While using all gentleness and flexibility in dealing with the disturbed child that operates below the patient's mature ego, the analyst must not allow the relationship to be pulled down to the level of the child. The patient must learn to outgrow this disordered childishness in favor of establishing mature adult relationships.

The patient cannot progress well in analysis if he is too

much in the child position, with the analyst all-giving and the patient all-receiving. It has been my experience, for example, that except in the most extraordinary circumstances it is a serious mistake to forgo the analytic fee or set only a negligible one. There are some excellent analysts who would disagree (see, for example, Fromm-Reichmann, 1950), but I maintain that even if this is done out of the most humane motives, it vitiates the treatment or makes it considerably more difficult by playing into the childish needs of the patient. It forsakes the value-for-a-value relationship between equals, which is the basis of democracy and society as well as of friendship. The relationship between patient and analyst comes into balance only if the values given and received are commensurate—that is, so to speak, help to the patient with his life, help to the analyst with his livelihood.

The analyst naturally feels a friendly identification with his patient, but this must not become extreme or too close. For example, one young married woman so embroiled her inexperienced analyst in her hatred of her family that he soon came to hate them and consequently lost his analytic perspective on the patient. This is countertransference in the more narrow sense of the term.

Often a patient sounds so plausible about wife or husband that it is very difficult to discern and evaluate the interrelationship. Sometimes the spouse actually is as difficult as the analysand describes and may even have an emerging emotional disorder of severity.

Emotional reality is indeed difficult to know. The patient tends to put the analyst into the flattering position of an all-knowing, all-wise parent. The analyst must not yield to this temptation and should maintain instead a cautious skepticism of the reality of what he observes. His sympathetic ear (as we shall mention again) may be taken by the patient to mean agreement with his angry criticism of, say, a spouse. This hostility may then mount as the patient feels that the analyst is justifying it. A wife complained about her husband's absorption in his profession to the exclusion of herself and the children. It turned out that while this was in part true, the reality of the situation was that the husband's behavior was actually a withdrawal and defense against the excessive demands and hostility of the wife. These were a continuation of her childhood feelings of frustration, which were intensified by rejection. Apparently the woman had depriving parents who were too preoccupied with their own interests to have much to give to their two children.*

Of value in discerning psychic reality is intimate knowledge of animals, even pets, provided that, first, there is more than one so that their interrelationships can be observed and, second, there is opportunity to identify with each. To be sure, no speech, no dreams, and no free associations are available, but to compensate for these drawbacks there is little repression—the feelings are mostly expressed freely in eloquent behavior. I realize that living with a few animals as part of your emotional life is a privilege that is not always available to therapists, city-bound as most are (Saul, 1962).

The basic attitude of the analyst, as we have said, is the same as that of any good physician: a mature, friendly, genuine interest in the patient combined with both a wish to cure and the objectivity needed for any technical medical procedure. All doctors realize this. But occasionally there can be found in medicine some remnant of the old authoritarian tradition. This approach, we may surmise, has certain sociologic roots in the old feudal class stratification of Europe and is transmitted and perpetuated basically by the attitudes of the parents toward their children. It may be reminiscent of the vain nobleman lording it over what he considered to be the utterly inferior peasant. While this kind of attitude is generally offensive to anyone in a democratic

*For a further discussion of this point, see L. Saul, *Fidelity and Infidelity* (Philadelphia : Lippincott, 1967). This book is a clinical study of the psychodynamics of the marital relationship.

society, it should be especially disturbing to the analyst. He can be expected to understand how such infantile egotistic tyranny over the mind of man is one of the great sources of the human suffering that his life is devoted to combating. Such an attitude of superiority and depreciation toward patients should be unthinkable in an analyst. Apart from the sociologic reasons for such an orientation, it is likely that the child-parent relationship is again the key, as doubtless it is to the social phenomenon also. The patient, by unconsciously assuming toward the analyst the position of dependence, submissiveness, and awesome deference, as of the small child to the parent, invests the analyst with an aura of omniscience and omnipotence. This is balm to the analyst if he has not come to terms with the inadequate child that persists within his own self. If he has done so, at best through fortunate upbringing and at second best through being helped by his training analysis, then there is no problem. But if he has not done so, then he may enjoy too well this coronation by the patient and unconsciously accept it too readily.

The child lives in the analyst as in everyone else; only one anticipates that the child will be a little less fractious, unruly, and disruptive in those whose profession it is to help others in life's journey. Because of the very nature of the mind, complete maturity can never be expected. The mind operates, at least in part, on the principle of saving of energy by making automatic those patterns of behavior that work. When you first drive a car, every operation must be consciously thought out, but after a while they become automatic and are performed quite unconsciously. Suppose you had always driven a car that had a conventional gearshift. If you were then to drive one with an automatic shift, no doubt you would find your left foot going through the old motions for a while as though there were a clutch pedal. Similarly, the patterns of childhood, ingrained during the formative years of helplessness, are never entirely dissolved. Despite the biologic thrust to maturity, childhood is never fully outgrown.

Some analysts believe that in the majority of cases the student cannot really master analytic therapy without spending some years in the tempering fires of private practice. It is here that he is paid directly by the patient himself for what he gives and accomplishes; his security and that of his family depends directly and solely on his therapeutic ability (Kubie, 1950). Thereby he is brought by necessity into seeing his patient's motivations, not academically, but with realistic closeness. Certainly this question is of great practical importance relative to the integration of psychoanalysis with medical education. My own experience has fully confirmed this view that intensive psychotherapy can only be learned thoroughly in the atmosphere of private practice and rarely, if ever, is it mastered, except theoretically, by one who is on full-time salary.

Life being what it is, private practice has its own complications. One of these is financial. The analyst is paid by the hour. The more hours he works, the more money he makes. He is in middle life, with wife and children, and perhaps in debt because of his long years of training. He is insecure about filling his time and is not sure when a patient finishes treatment whether the hour coming available will be filled promptly by another patient. Therefore, he works all the hours he can and risks slipping into the mire of equating hours and income. Of course, this equation is true, but if not properly balanced and separated, the result is entrapment and slavery. He can no longer take time for lunch, because, although the lunch itself may be inexpensive, whatever fee he would be losing must be added to its cost. It can get to the point where he feels he can no longer take a day off—obviously, as his fees grow higher the more is to be lost. And so the dance of the hours begins. The hours have become too intimately associated with the analyst's own receptive needs. Time off is no longer a legitimate, wholesome respite from work, the satisfaction of his proper receptive needs; it has become a frustration of these needs because he is not receiving, in the form of money, when he is not working. This is a trap in which the young analyst would do well to avoid ensnarement. Practice satisfies both the mature and the infantile, hence its virtue and charm. But unless the infantile is healthy, therein too lies its siren danger. While it lures the analyst, he is pushed in the same direction by the pressures of a civilization in which money is a means to security, pleasure, prestige, romance—well-nigh everything.

The solution takes some maturity on the part of both the analyst and his wife. She will see that he never will have the income of the financially successful surgeon, obstetrician, radiologist, or various other specialists. However, a discerning woman will also recognize that her husband can devote himself to his patients and to his academic and community work and soon have an adequate livelihood and, if he has learned psychodynamics at all well, a clear conscience. A little calculation will reveal what he will earn by working a reasonable number of hours per day, allowing for breaks for meetings, illnesses, and vacations. He then can set his income and have a good life if he and his wife are not greedy. Even young men who work conscientiously with their patients tell the author that they cannot see more than six or seven patients a day without becoming fatigued.

They are fatigued in part because of the sustained intellectual effort of an hour of penetrating through the patient's associations to the unconscious meanings. A ten-minute break between patients well repays him who has the courage to take it, especially the less-experienced analyst. While he struggles with "reading" the material, the analyst is never quite sure whether his difficulties in understanding arise from the patient's resistance or from his own failings. This groping can be a constant frustration that causes wearing irritation and also feelings of guilt, conscious or unconscious, for not doing the job for the patient that should be done. These three tributaries to fatigue—the effort, the uncertainty, and the guilt—are apt to be strongest in the best students and weakest in those who can look the other way.

The latter, enveloping themselves in a protective coat of egotism and projection, blame the patient rather than learn this difficult field with humility. Finally mastering his speciality makes the greatest difference to the analyst and compensates him for all the struggle. It is not unlike a long, hard climb up a mountainside, with occasional glimpses out through the trees—glimpses that become more frequent, revealing an increasingly inspiring vista. Still, all is not seen; climbing remains. But now, as the analyst works, he sees what he is doing, his conscience is clear, and his confidence is based on comprehension of the realities of his patient's emotional life.

The mind is a reflection of the biologic motivations of the body, and the body is subjected to more strain in a day of analyzing than the beginner may realize. Sitting all day is a strain that injures, perhaps not in days or even months, but certainly over a number of years it can be damaging unless balanced with adequate exercise. After a million years of living by vigorous physical battle with the soil and in the hunt, the human machine cannot readily withdraw to the analytic chair without this affecting the heart, the blood vessels, the muscles, the spine, and so on. In the long run, sociability and large muscle activity seem to be essential to the mental and physical hygiene of the wholesome analyst.

This issue of the wholesomeness of the analyst is no personal incidental matter. The very neurotic analyst, so many of whom were attracted to this field in its early days, may indeed have certain advantages to offer to the patient. This would be so because this individual's neuroticism may give him a special sympathy and understanding and may drive him to making his profession his whole life. On the other hand, his own problems may create reactions other than sympathy for his patients, which in turn may make him more perceptive here but less so there. Whatever the advantages of neuroticism may be for understanding the patient, it can hardly be anything but a drawback when it comes to helping the patient to resolve his own morbid pathologic processes in favor of healthy thinking, feeling, and living. Essentially, it is a question of how far an analyst can be expected to help a patient to solve life problems that he himself has not been able to solve.

Poor human relations have characterized a certain group of analysts. There are obvious reasons for this, among them the fact that many analysts were, and often still are, attracted to this field predominantly because of their own personal problems, and by this I mean problems in personal relationships. It has also been noted that this had certain advantages in the early development of the field, for the students who were first drawn to it had few outside interests to distract them and soon became a cohesive band of devotees, although not, of course, without their dissensions (Knight, 1953; Saul and Watson, 1955). Perhaps this total absorption of their lives into analysis, with patients as their chief human contacts, was advantageous or even necessary for founding the field. But creation is not development. In historical perspective, it seems safe to say that personal problems in analysts with difficulties in human relations, especially egoism and hostility, have caused serious trouble in the development of the field and cause difficulties in the office with patients.

While the very essence of psychoanalysis is that it establishes for the patient a sample human relationship, this should not obscure the fact that it creates what is still a very real human relationship for the doctor. It may be that he has bad interpersonal relationships in life with family, friends, colleagues, and others, but in the office with his patients he does very well. On the other hand, however, his relation to the patient may be no such salutary exception. More often it would seem that poor human relations in life extend to poor underlying relationships in the office. This may disturb understanding and therapy and make take the form of the analyst fearing (1) the transference and the countertransference, (2) the patient's feelings, and (3) his own feelings toward the patient. Hence, these analysts are apt to be the most strict about procedural rules in the office and also about ever seeing a patient outside of the office, however accidentally, for they are usually too ill at ease.

If the analyst is, although no paragon, reasonably healthy and mature and has solved his major life problems reasonably well and has generally good personal relations, then he has the emotional base upon which to build his professional knowledge, skills, and experience. Such a person will have, in addition, a genuine confidence and security that will give him the inner strength for an easy, natural, sympathetic, and mature attitude toward those who come to him for help with their confusions, inferiorities, insecurities, and tensions.

With a mature human attitude, the analyst naturally focuses on the patient, not on the symptom. He may have an opinion about the patient, but it will be easy for him to follow the analytic principle of directing it to the patient's ego. His regard for the patient will depend not on the patient's underlying motivations but on the patient's capacity for emotional honesty, on his ability to face, understand, and handle his own inner forces. The analyst will not blame the patient for his psychopathology, and his reactions to it will be minimal. He will be realistically optimistic, and because he is sincere, the patient will respond.

He will have compassion and love. Once, while on vacation in the mountains, a surgeon, who was truly a fine man, went to see an aged woman because the local doctor was not then available. The woman's family was exceedingly poor, and the surgeon knew he would receive no fee. The old woman herself was disagreeable, bloated, and repugnant. The surgeon saw through her ego and its suffering to what it must be like to dwell in that mind and that body. He spoke to her tenderly, calling her "dear," but still was completely professional. And so too must the analyst remain—friendly, yet imperturbably analytic in the face of the full force of the transference. His reward is one of the great thrills of his profession and his life—to see the liberation of the human spirit from inner tyranny.

We have been discussing the intellectual and the emotional attitudes of the analyst, the effects of his practice, and the health of his own personality. It should be unnecessary to state that these, however perfect, are only prerequisites; they provide the necessary setting for the technical procedure. Alone, they no more substitute for a proper analysis than for a surgical operation. That this is not always so obvious, the following example will perhaps demonstrate.

A gifted woman of superior sensitivity, breadth, and liberality was treated by a female therapist of maternal warmth and recognized ability. In early childhood the patient had lost her father. Her mother, taking over the support of the family, was always too exhausted and resentful of the burden to have enough energy left to give affection and easy tolerance to the patient and her brother. It was because of this childhood of emotional deprivation that the patient was referred by a perceptive friend to this woman therapist, the lovingness of whose personality might be expected to fill the patient's need.

At first, unfortunately, this did occur. The patient's desires and expectations mounted, and she became bound ever more closely to the therapist with increasingly intense, intimate, and intricate involvement. The therapist lacked skill in seeing and handling the hostilities. Naturally, since every frustration, threat, or irritation stimulates the fight-flight reaction, the child in this adult patient was as angry as she was needy. Throughout her childhood she had had to repress the least inkling of resentment against her mother who, while strict, puritanical, and depriving, nevertheless worked and sacrificed for her children. The child's anger became bottled-up bitterness and a wellspring of guilt. It sought outlet, in the clinical form of depression, only toward the patient herself.

More and more she began living out this childhood drama, transferred now in her middle years to the therapist.

She could not show the palest hint of displeasure with the woman, who was warm and friendly and to whom she repeated her sense of obligation. Nor, however, could the patient free herself from her, and consequently, she began to feel herself sinking into an emotional morass. She tried to struggle, but all that resulted was ever-heightening guilt and with it self-directed rage, until she finally experienced all but irresistible impulses to suicide.

Catastrophe was averted by getting her with an analyst who well knew the central role of hostility in emotional disorders. Some of the things this analyst showed her were: (1) that in spite of her childhood training and experiences, it is no sin to have hostile impulses, which, in fact, everyone has; (2) that she would find relief by reducing these hostilities, but that this would be impossible for her to do until she faced them; and (3) that facing these impulses psychologically was not the same thing as acting on them and could be interpreted as a protection against doing so. Not even in the woman's dreams had there appeared the least suggestion of the mildest harm ever occurring, certainly to no person but herself. Even this, however, would be no more than spilling a bit of sauce or getting a drop of ink on her dress. Then, one night, she dreamed that her mother fell downstairs and died. This she reported to the analyst the following day with uncontrollable paroxysms of hysterical laughter. It was the turning point. The pressure passed floodtide and began to ease. The suicidal danger abated, and her relations with her mother began to improve. She was beginning to move from the way in to the way out—however long and hard it might prove to be—toward freedom from the pressures of a childhood pattern that, with a little unskilled love, had nearly killed her. Of course, the second analyst was male.

This experience has been related because it illustrates, besides our immediate point, some preceding statements about the nature of the psychoanalytic process which, in turn, shapes the technique. That love without skill can be a mortal danger in an analytic therapeutic situation is demonstrated by this example. An interesting question is whether skill without love can be equally threatening. It would seem to be safer by far. Is it lack of skill rather than lack of love when a patient, years after an analysis, complains that the analyst never could unbend enough to acknowledge that there was anything special about a relationship in which one human being bares his soul to another? Is sympathetic rather than cold clinical understanding only a childish expectation? Should the reliving of the childhood drama occur in a modulated atmosphere characterized by the kind of interest that the parents should have had in the child's welfare? Can the after-education, the corrective experience, be effected without this ingredient? Even to begin to answer such questions requires sound understanding of the process of the psychoanalytic cure.

But of one fact we can be sure—one great gift of the analyst to the patient is understanding. For the patient to realize that he is correctly and reasonably understood is usually an enormous relief, reassurance, and gratification. If understanding of the major motivations and feelings that underlie the difficulty can be achieved in the first or the first few interviews, then the wish for analytic treatment is usually consolidated. The facing of unpleasant truths as well as other difficulties is compensated for in large degree by the sense of being understood accurately.

REFERENCES AND SOME RELATED READINGS

Freud, A. (1971), *The Writings of Anna Freud,* vol. 7. New York: Internat. Univ. Press.

Freud, S. (1925), Psychoanalysis and delinquency. In *Collected Papers,* 5:98. London: Hogarth Press, 1950.

Fromm-Reichmann, F. (1950), *Principles of Intensive Psychotherapy.* Chicago: Univ. of Chicago Press.

Galdston, I., ed. (1969), *Psychoanalysis in Present-Day Psychiatry.* New York: Brunner/Mazel.

Gitelson, M. (1952), The emotional position of the analyst in the psychoanalytic situation. *Internat. J. Psychoanal.,* 33: 1–10.

Holt, R., ed. (1971), *New Horizon for Psychotherapy—Autonomy as a Profession.* New York: Internat. Univ. Press.

Kaiser, H. (1955), The problem of responsibility in psychotherapy. *Psychiatry,* 18: 205–211.

Knight, R. (1953), Present status of organized psychoanalysis in the U.S. *J. Am. Psychoanal. A.,* 1: 197–221.

Kubie, L. (1950), *Practical and Theoretical Aspects of Psychoanalysis.* New York: Internat. Univ. Press.

Saul, L. (1962), Psychosocial medicine and the observation of animals. *Psychosomatic Medicine,* 24: 58–61.

Saul, L., and Sheppard, E. (1958), An approach to the ego functions. *Psychoanal. Quart.,* 27: 237–246.

——— (1956), An attempt to quantify emotional forces using manifest dreams. *J. Am. Psychoanal. A.,* 4: 486.

Saul, L., Sheppard, E., Selby, D., Lhamon, W., Sachs, D., and Master, R. (1954), The quantification of hostility in dreams with reference to essential hypertension. *Science,* 119: 382.

Saul, L., and Watson, A. (1955), Milestones in psychoanalysis. In *Present-Day Psychology,* ed. A. A. Roback, 563–591. New York: Philosophical Library.

Thompson, C., *et al.* (1956), The role of the analyst's personality in therapy. *Am. J. Psychotherapy,* 10: 347–367.

3 / THEORETICAL BASE OF TREATMENT*

The rationale of psychoanalytic treatment has been foreshadowed in the previous chapters. In the simplest terms psychoanalysis can be said to be a method of correcting the aftereffects on the personality that have resulted from the injurious influences that warped the child's development during its most formative years. In reactive cases, current external stresses that are unusual cause regressions to infantile patterns. To paraphrase the statement from Freud that was cited earlier: Correction of the permanent aftereffects of early injurious emotional influences is the essence of psychoanalytic treatment. However, to see this in perspective and in relation to the rest of psychanalytic theory, we must take a broader view and also delve deeper into detail.

Although psychoanalytic theory is not free from controversy, perhaps the broad, basic concepts can be stated in terms with which all analysts would agree in principle. Our concern here with theory is only as a common basis for

*Some of the material in this chapter on the ego meaning of dreams of flying is drawn from a paper prepared in collaboration with Burton Fleming, M.D.

understanding the essentials of the psychoanalytic method of treatment. This book is an outgrowth of Freud's instinct theory, including the oral, anal, phallic, and oedipal phases, constellations, and accustomed representations. This theory, like his papers on technique, is so well known that I shall assume the reader's familiarity with it and therefore not review it here.

GENESIS OF EMOTIONAL PROBLEMS

Six main factors can be distinguished in the genesis of the patient's emotional problem. All of these involve the basic motivations that make up his personality, and they assume a pattern that is already well formed in its essentials by the time the child is five or six years old.

1. The child comes into the world with certain innate needs, drives, and reactions.

2. These involve as objects other human beings, particularly those responsible for the child: the parents, the brothers, and the sisters, and the substitutes for them.

3. The result is the development from birth of certain typical patterns of feelings toward these family members—the oedipal and the sibling constellations.

4. From birth, the child, with its motivations, responses, and feelings in these emotional patterns toward the parents and the siblings, is reacted to by all the emotional forces of these specific individual personalities in the particular family into which he happens to be born. These forces (i.e., how the child is felt toward, treated, and trained by these particular family members) condition the child during its very early and most formative weeks, months, and years, shaping its personality and emotional life for the rest of its existence. Since humanity and its conditions of life are what they are at present, many of these forces usually do not help the child's development but hinder and warp it.

5. The warpings—the results of this faulty condition-

ing of the infant and the young child—persist for life as the essence of mental and emotional disorders.

6. Each adult's place in life evokes from him various reactions in accord with his nuclear pattern, for example, a much-loved child who grows up to face a community which, because of class or caste, is hostile to him.

It is the task of psychoanalytic treatment to correct the warpings that occurred as the personality was developing. Now let us take a closer look at the six factors outlined above, which contribute so directly to the patient's emotional problem.

THE CHILD'S INNATE NEEDS

At birth, and even before it, a child has certain inborn drives, instincts, impulses, and mechanisms of reaction. These develop as the child grows. Among the requirements of the total organism are its needs for mother love, for demonstration of affection, for sense of security with the mother, and for confidence in her and in the whole environment. Examining the infant's drives and needs, we can distinguish the following: physical dependence; a need for love; the fight-flight reaction; a drive toward activity; sensual satisfactions; curiosity; and a capacity for identification.

Physical dependence. The child depends upon the mother for the satisfaction of all its needs for physical care that are necessary for survival. This would include such things as being kept adequately warm, clean, and fed.

Need for love. In addition to the actual physical dependence, there is the child's need for love, affection, and being valued. These are the child's guarantee of security. They are the libidinal aspect of dependence. Freud noted repeatedly that the child behaves as though these dependent love needs were sexual in nature and that, therefore, the term sexual should be expanded to include them. Just how powerful they are has been amply demonstrated by much recent work in this area. Of particular note here is the film by Rene Spitz which graphically depicts the fate of babies who are left by their mothers in a home for foundlings when barely five months of age. In this institution the babies are given far better food and surroundings and medical care than they had in their usually poverty-stricken homes. Nonetheless, when their mothers depart, most of the babies deteriorate pitifully, often becoming emaciated. A considerable percentage of them die.

Fight-flight reaction. Besides these libidinal desires toward the mother, there is the fight-flight reaction, which is evident from birth and is probably also present even before that. When frustrated, threatened, or irritated, the child manifests its rage although it is yet too tiny and uncoordinated to be able to flee or to fight. There is no question, however, of the intent of this animal reaction.

Drive toward activity. In addition, there are present in larval form the drives toward activity, in the kernel of which lie the capacity for mature, productive, and responsible effort.

Sensual satisfaction. There are other impulses and reactions also. Sensual satisfactions, which Freud considered basically sexual, seem to be centered chiefly in the mouth, with suckling at the breast as the chief point of focus in relation to the mother. They are also evident in the skin in the enjoyment of being stroked, bathed, petted, caressed, and fondled (Saul, 1950b).

Curiosity. In addition, there is the reaction of curiosity, which is probably not exclusively in the service of sexuality. For example, it is important for seeking and testing food, and perhaps it also serves the ego in its explorations of the world. Curiosity is a reaction seen in all animals at early ages. In nonhuman creatures there is no such restriction on the sexuality as that which drives human sexuality into sublimations and into perverse channels. Hence, there would be no reason for the curiosity to operate in other directions unless it were in its nature to do so in order to serve a variety of needs. Indeed, as the biologists point out, an animal without curiosity would not long survive.

Capacity for identification. The child's capacity for identification is of profound psychological importance. It probably derives, at least in part, from the biologic fact that the child was at the very beginning of its existence within the mother and in a way a part of her. At any rate, the child has the capacity of considering itself to be sufficiently in another person's place so that if, for example, someone is harsh to the mother, the child, because of a deep attachment to her, may cry as though the harshness were directed toward itself. This identification is another way of relating to other persons.*

THE CHILD'S RELATION TO OTHERS

These drives, needs, and reactions of the infant and the small child are largely in relation to other human beings. At the very beginning of life they are aimed primarily at the mother. We are speaking throughout of those biologic motivations and reactions that are common not only to all humans but also to at least the higher mammals. Normally, the relationship to the mother is the first and most important one for the newborn child, and we may remark immediately that a good mother during the early years is the best guarantee of a healthy pattern for relationships to other people throughout life. In our culture the father usually has less contact with the child during its first weeks and months after birth. Relations to brothers and sisters, if any, are determined by the relative ages and sexes, but most critically by the parental attitudes, and treatment. In any event, so long as the mother carries, bears, and suckles the child, the relation to her is primary, central, and paramount and strongly influences the child's emerging and developing relations with father and siblings.

*For a discussion of the evolution and development of these and other needs and responses as the infant grows up, see Saul, 1971.

OEDIPAL AND SIBLING CONSTELLATIONS

The relationships of the needs, the drives, and the reactions to other human beings involves the child in certain typical situations, which may vary to some extent in different cultures. Typically, there is the sibling relationship, the interplay of motivations with brothers and sisters, especially in relation to the parents. This is generally referred to as pre-oedipal while it is mostly a very early infantile, suckling, and protective relationship to the parents. But a little later, even by the age of two or three, the feelings toward mother and father in particular are termed oedipal, in that they now involve attachment, longing, rivalry, and hostility that has an erotic coloring or overtone as described by Freud. These typical situations are the inevitable consequences of the nature of the drives and of the child's attachments to other persons. We have said that the child needs its mother's love as a guarantee of its very existence. One guarantee of security is love, as demonstrated by affection, attention, and being valued. Since the child is attached to the mother and needs her love, any other person on the scene is bound to be viewed as a rival and, consequently, tends to stir up the child's fight-flight reaction. This takes the form of fleeing to be alone with the mother and fighting off with hate and hostility any rival, be it brother or sister or father. So far as the needs for love attach to any other member of the family, still other individuals, even the mother, can become rivals. At this stage of development, the focus of the relationship is, in preliminary larval form, more at the genitalia, as in adults, rather than at the mouth, as during the oral suckling stage. Hence, it is called oedipal.

By the time the child is two, three, or four, it is already a personality and has the capacity for more developed feelings toward other persons than it had as a suckling baby. It is nearer to being a miniature adult. As such, there is an increased capacity for love, even in the erotic sense with some connection to genital sensations. Because of this and the fact that the personality is formed to such an extent by this age, the child must already have achieved considerable identification with its own sex. It has achieved the position from which, normally, the boy will develop to mature masculinity and the girl will develop to mature femininity.

CONDITIONING INFLUENCES ON THE CHILD

There is another factor of enormous importance, namely, the ways in which the child is treated (the conditioning influences, the traumatic forces). Understandably, the child does not have its every wish and impulse satisfied sympathetically, and so its needs for security may not be met. Clearly, the deprivation and lack of satisfaction will be more serious in some cases that it is in others. For example, the child's sex may displease the parents, who reject it for a long period on this account. Or, the child may, from birth, be unwanted. Perhaps it is only partially welcome and basically resented as another mouth to feed, another bottom to diaper, another drain on the energies and the resources of those responsible for it. It may be set upon and secretly tormented almost from birth by a jealous brother or sister. It may be neglected or overprotected or made into a plaything. It may not even be respected as a miniature human being. It may be subjected to all sorts of abuse—by omission and commission. Indeed, perhaps it will be fortunate if it receives half such good care as most other mammals provide for their young. The child may be subject to every type of misunderstanding, abuse, and lack of regard as a human being: overprotection, underprotection, domination, undersocialization or oversocialization that is imposed too early or too late or too rapidly or too inconsistently, neglect, overindulgence, weakness, harshness, impatience, and lack of respect.

It is not usually a single event which is injurious to the child's development, unless this is of overwhelming violence and power. Rather, it is the protracted traumatic emotional influences to which he is subjected during his very earliest days, weeks, months, and years that prove so damaging ultimately. He cannot solve the inevitable problem of competition with brothers and sisters if, for example, his parents show gross favoritism to his rival, or if they hold the children so close and so exclusively to themselves that the children are driven into an intensified jealousy, or if the normal competition is met only with violence from the parents so that every normal impulse to it awakens only guilt, shame, and terror.

The child's relationships to the parents cannot develop normally if the mother so mistreats the child that he hates and fears her instead of loving her, or if a father is so seductive toward his son, sensually or psychologically, that the boy turns toward him and against his mother, or if the mother is so seductive that the attachment to her and rivalry with the father becomes too intense for the child to handle. Then the oedipal relationships, normally manageable in an emotionally healthy family, become pathologic. In fact, the normal oedipus, in the narrow definition, is a luxury in the sense that the child who has only to solve a normal, healthy attraction to his mother and rivalry with his father is fortunate indeed (Freud, 1924).

The danger lies in misunderstanding the child's nature and the typical emotional problems of attachment and rivalry in his relation to parents and to brothers and sisters. Abusing his nature in this regard can prevent the child from growing through these difficulties, coming to terms with them, and achieving good human relations with the members of his family.

EFFECTS OF WARPING THE NORMAL DRIVES

These warping influences act on the child's needs to form in his mind an emotional pattern of attitudes and feelings toward other persons which will persist for life. These influences, in concert with the ways in which the child has been treated and conditioned, form the individual's superego. Throughout his life he will carry in his mind the images of the emotionally significant figures of his childhood: those who loved and understood him and those who abused him (however unintentionally). He will project these images onto other persons; in other words, he will transfer to others the emotional patterns formed toward the members of his family. Thus, his difficulties in human relations in childhood will be continued toward other persons for the rest of his life. Psychoanalysis is a method for correcting these lasting effects on the normal drives and reactions of early trauma.

THE NUCLEAR PATTERN AND THE ADULT'S EXPERIENCE

Each person shows a certain deep-seated pattern of motivations, a pattern remarkably constant, that distinguishes him from all other persons. This basic, underlying, constant pattern can properly be called the nucleus of his personality. This nuclear pattern results from few motivations stemming from the id and the superego with the ego functioning as receptor, integrator, mediator, and executive.

Ernest Jones (1957) suggests that an important aspect of Freud's personality lay in his having been a much-loved child who met with no such welcoming warmth as an adult. However, apparently because of this early love, he reacted to rejection and hardship with inner self-confidence and heroic independence. What Jones is describing could be called the nuclear pathogenetic dynamic pattern or the nuclear pathodynamic pattern. The total nuclear pattern, as was suggested above, also contains the mature motivations with all their defenses, compensations, sublimations, and other efforts to control and outgrow the psychopathological, the disordered and infantile.

SOURCES OF INDIVIDUAL DIFFERENCES

In the matter of the specific features of each individual human personality, it can be said that the basic drives, needs, urges, and impulses with which the normal baby is born are approximately the same in every child. There are two broad classes of interactive variables that determine the pattern of motivations (personality) in each individual: maturational factors and external events. Maturational factors are the potentials for development. Assuming that the fetus and the newly born infant are physically and mentally healthy in all ways, it is expected that development will proceed to adequate, or superior, physical and emotional maturity unless acted upon by adverse external forces. There is at present no substantial evidence that hereditary factors have any importance in impairing the normal course of emotional development and the achievement of emotional maturity. (It must be emphasized that organic conditions, mental retardation, and idiopathic psychoses are excluded from our discussion.)

Some correlations between body types and personality have been reported, and these findings suggest that there may be hereditary factors that predispose to corresponding temperament and personality (Sheldon and Stevens, 1942); but these have not been demontrated to be appreciably causal in the development of psychopathology. Occurrence of neuroses in families is usually demonstrably by transmission, the neurotic parent making the child neurotic, just as the tubercular or syphilitic parent transmits these diseases, which once were thought to be inherited because they "ran in families."

There might be a tendency, a diathesis, to psychoses and maybe even to neuroses. But this predisposition is probably not greater than, for example, the possibly increased susceptibility to tuberculosis in very thin persons. The fact remains that a person does not get tuberculosis unless he has tubercle bacilli. Studies of identical twins provide imposing data, but they do not establish that the causes of similarity of psychopathology lie in heredity rather than in similarities of early environmental influences. Psychoanalysis has demonstrated that characteristics are transmitted from parent to child through the child's treatment by and identification with the parents. Therefore, the routine family history is no longer valued by the analyst as more than slightly suggestive.

Recent studies (Fries and Woolf, 1971) have indicated that there do exist individual differences in the degree of motility and other reactions from birth. However, it has not yet been established that these differences are inherited rather than a result of the mother's way of life before the child was born, including such contributing factors as drugs, alcohol, emotional state, and others. Nor do they suggest that the variations in the infants studied are wider than differences in temperament within the bounds of normal healthy emotional development.

There is historically a strong prejudice, not only among laymen but also in psychiatric tradition, in favor of considering hereditary factors to be the causes of psychopathology. But, on the evidence as we know it, the thrust of the healthy human infant to mature is like that of the pine seedling to grow straight and strong. Whether inherited aberrations exist that can warp is not established; but there is no doubt that external influences can crush any seedling and any psyche. No infant, no matter what his heredity, can withstand being driven into a psychosis if sufficiently abused psychologically by omission or commission.

Maturational factors are the forces that lead to the development of physical and social maturity. A good deal is known about these from psychoanalytic and other studies (Saul, 1971). The analyst in daily clinical work observes what has impeded or otherwise distorted each patient's emotional development, and he learns how each individual would presumably have matured had there not been injurious influences. He sees over the years the course of development of those patients who have been able to resolve and become free of the conditioning effects of early traumatic influences.

All patients tend to move and, with help, do indeed

move strongly toward a certain common motivational pattern. Discovering the sources of a patient's problems helps to engender certain positive motivations. For example, relinquishing pathological extremes of dependence and need for love, hostile competitiveness, and rages of the small child helps the patient to develop the capacities of a parent for responsibility, giving, and social cooperation (Saul, 1971).

Regression—the tendency to retain or return to infantile attitudes—is present in everyone. This leads to the conclusion that an individual can achieve only relative emotional maturity because, as Freud concluded, of the very long period of dependence that is characteristic of the human young. The analyst reconstructs what his patient could be like had his fixations and regressions not been abnormally intensified and thus, by simple extrapolation, can clearly discern the nature and degree of the patient's emotional immaturity. Maturation is a powerful, unidirectional combination of biological forces that acts best under ideal conditions but is capable of continuing against disadvantages. The healing of emotional as well as physical injuries may be considered part of the maturational process.

It follows as a consequence of these considerations that the environment need only provide an approximation to ideal conditions for development and maturity will ensue naturally. Nothing need be done to stimulate or promote it; indeed, any such attempts, in so far as emotional development is concerned, are apt to be deleterious.

External influences on development of personality involve certain broad hypotheses. Time relations are of great importance. In *An Outline of Psychoanalysis,* Freud points out that the essential features of an individual's personality, that is, his nucleus of motivations, is established at approximately six years of age. Although there may be certain vulnerable periods, in general the earlier the external influence is exerted, the greater will be its effects upon the developing personality. After about the age of six, though growth and development continue for life, their directions have for the most part been set, and the nuclear pattern remains on the whole fairly constant. One or another aspect of the pattern will be brought to the fore by circumstances, whether special strengths or specific vulnerabilities.

How early influences operate can be shown in the following example. A young couple wanted a child but when the baby girl arrived the mother did not want her because of her own emotional complexities. Feeling guilt for rejecting the child, she overcompensated by giving her daughter incessant attention. By four months, the child was so demanding of the mother's presence and attention that she could not be separated from her without crying in rage. There was already a disturbance in this baby's personal relations; she was "an unpleasant child," not "appealing," and self-induced rejections could confidently be anticipated unless the mother's feelings changed toward her.

The way an individual's drives, impulses, and reactions become attached to persons is approximately the same in every child. They can become attached to animals as well, and even to things such as dolls, houses, and neighborhoods. Basically, however, the tendency for the newborn child is to be attached primarily to its mother or to substitutes for her and then to slowly spread these attachments to other persons.

When it comes to the common constellation of people to whom the growing child is attached, there is some variation from family to family. Although usually there is a father and a mother, we must recall that approximately one-third of all marriages end in divorce or separation. Other parents are separated by death. Sometimes parent substitutes are added in the way of grandparents, aunts and uncles, and nurses. Similar variations, perhaps even greater ones, are seen in the constellations of siblings. The child may be the only one or it may have older or younger siblings, the numbers vary and so do the sex differences. There may be all sisters or all brothers or any combination of these. Thus, the combination of persons to whom the young child must adjust varies considerably, both in regard to the parents and their substitutes and to siblings or the lack of them.

The really enormous variation that comes into play has to do with the emotional influences that are brought to bear on the child. It is obvious that these are going to vary, first of all, simply by virtue of the particular culture in which the child is raised. But even within the same culture, in the same country, different emotional climates are created because of the vast socio-economic, educational, and even geographic differences that exist. By far the greatest differences in terms of the emotional influences on the child come from the personalities of those who rear him and those to whom he must adapt during his earliest years. The personalities of those who rear him and those who are emotionally significant to him are highly specific and individual for every child and determine in a highly specific and individual way the treatment that this child receives—the emotional influences to which he is subject.

The pattern of the emotional relationships that are formed in the child toward those who are close to him persists throughout life toward others, not merely in a general way but very precisely in terms of the major features and often in great detail. Very realistically, the child we once were lives on in all of us. For instance, a man was so overindulged during early childhood that he never could rebel; he remained in middle life a petulant, demanding, irresponsible bachelor. Another man who in early childhood was too much dominated by his mother was also given considerable freedom by her and by his father. In later life he rebelled against all authority (Saul, 1971).

Among individuals, the differences in personality and disorders of personality are expressions of the unique combination of influences that acted upon each of them in childhood. Why an emotional disorder takes one form rather than another—the "choice of neurosis"—becomes understandable on this basis. Different individual outcomes result primarily from the qualitative and quantitative variations in the emotional forces that acted during infancy and childhood to produce the variations in motivational patterns.

The child who during his first six years has had favorable relations with those responsible for his rearing, has a stable core of good relations toward others and can withstand a good deal of injurious influence thereafter. Circumstances can also be important, but it is remarkable what the small child can tolerate if it is loved and secure with its parents. For example, during the bombings of London in World War II, those small children who felt secure with their parents, and whose parents did not show fear, did not betray signs of fear themselves (Freud and Burlingham, 1943). This has also been shown experimentally in animals by the fundamental researches of Liddell (1956). He demonstrated with twin kids, for example, how the one separated from its mother broke down under stress while the one that remained with its mother did not.

A child treated badly during his first six years will never become adequately mature. Babies are easily driven into psychotic, prepsychotic, and other seriously disordered states (Liddell, 1956, 1961; Spitz, 1945). Parental hatred, abuse, and neglect are introjected by the child as his superego. For example, if a mother is punitive and rejecting, through a process of conditioning the child comes to associate this behavior with the mother and to expect it each time the mother appears. This can result in the child's expecting such treatment from everyone, or at least especially from women; or he may treat himself badly, as his mother treated him. Thus the traumatic treatment is taken over in the child's mind with the image of the parent and persists through life. Both the image and the reactions to it may be unconscious.

Injurious external influences producing psychopathology can be grouped into two broad categories: first, various forms of "doing too little" (neglect, rejection, cruelty, coldness); second, "doing too much" (overindulgence, domination, seduction). Both, which Freud (1940) so charitably called parental blunders, give undue stimulation to the fight-flight response in the child. Physical flight being impossible, its psychological counterparts, repression and withdrawal, occur. The fight response becomes hostility, which Freud (1930) considered to be the prime source of guilt. Regression and hostility play a central role in all psychopathology.

Thus, traumatic influences act on the child's inborn drives and reactions through the constellations of persons to whom he is attached and to whom he must adapt. And it is this that produces a certain pattern of personality, which is characteristic for every individual human being. Hence, in every patient we must find out as soon as possible the nature of these traumatic influences in his particular case and the aftereffects of these on him. These aftereffects, specific for each individual, are what we can properly call the main emotional pattern at the core of his personality. In every patient there is an individual emotional pattern which is the key to his psychopathology, to his symptoms, and to his personality. Indeed, as we now know, neurosis really means the excessive persistence in the adult of disturbed emotional patterns of his childhood. These too greatly affect his emotional life as an adult and produce symptoms, tensions, or character traits that are disturbing to himself, to his intimates, and to society.

Since each person has such a main emotional pattern, it is this which the analyst must uncover. Insofar as he succeeds in doing this, he is able to find the formula for that particular individual's emotional problem. For example, the key may be depreciation and rejection by both parents during childhood, which causes insecurity and an excessive clinging to them. There are also feelings of inferiority which the patient tries to compensate for by great strivings for strength, toughness, and independence. At the same time he shuns close relationships to people lest they awaken his overly intense but underlying needs for love and place him in a position of too great vulnerability. Hostility, generated by frustration and inferiority feelings, is repressed lest he estrange others and lose still more love, and it is turned, instead, largely against himself to produce severe guilt feelings and other effects. This information that the analyst uncovers can be written almost like a mathematical or a chemical formula. It can certainly be readily diagramed, and, perhaps before too long, methods for estimating these emotional forces quantitatively will enable us to write a rough mathematical formula (Saul, 1971; Saul and Sheppard, 1956).

It is this nuclear emotional pattern of childhood that is transferred to the analyst with such incredible intensity. This is the reason that the transference is what "carries" every psychoanalytic treatment and is central to the therapeutic method.

RECENT PROGRESS IN PSYCHOANALYSIS

In psychoanalysis, as in all other fields, the technique of treatment can be expected to change with expanding knowledge in the field. Most of the recent advances were initiated by Freud. Before proceeding to discuss the technique in detail, it may be useful to list briefly, even though somewhat repetitively, some of the outstanding advances.

1. The importance of the dynamics, the interplay of emotional forces, which earlier intrigued the attention of analysts, is becoming better recognized as being distinct from the content.

2. The central importance of dependence, so often emphasized by Freud as being fatefully significant for human development and for neurosis, is becoming better realized.

3. Hostility is claiming its just attention since Freud's formulation of the death instinct. The whole relationship of the fight-flight response to hostility and to regression is also now being recognized.

4. Freud's pioneering clinical studies of sex are now being amplified by biology and ecology. We are better able

to distinguish sensual feelings from mating tendencies and from feelings of love (in both the romantic and the broad senses of the term). Loving is seen to be not the same as wishes to be loved (Saul, 1950a). There is also increasing understanding of the fact that while sex is often masked by the seemingly nonsexual, the converse of this is also true. That is, the sexual can also mask the nonsexual. An example of this would be a girl whose sexual misbehavior was motivated chiefly by hostility to her parents. Any emotion can have a sexual coloring or take a sexual form. Further, sex is a great drain, escape, and diversion as well as a basic drive in itself. Thus, sex itself must be analyzed carefully and not taken either as an indivisible atom or at its face value. It can have various contents and meanings and can be only a coloring for other motivations.

5. The ego has been the subject of increasing studies which have broadened psychoanalysis in many ways, made it more realistic, and deepened it. Even indisputable sexual material and symbols are often seen to have ego meanings.* In some dreams of flying, for example, the sexual meaning is relatively unimportant compared with the ego meaning of release and freedom (see also Chap. 11).

In one such instance a patient had been struggling with

*Anna Freud states in *Ego and the Mechanisms of Defense:* "From the beginning, analysis as a therapeutic method was concerned with the ego and its aberrations : the investigation of the id . . . was always only a means to an end.

"When the writings of Freud . . . took a fresh direction, the odium of analytic unorthodoxy no longer attached to the study of the ego . . . we should probably define the task of analysis . . . to acquire the fullest possible knowledge of all three institutions . . . and to learn what are their relations to one another and to the outside world. That is to say : in relation to the ego, to explore its contents, its boundaries and its functions and to trace the influences of the outside world, the id and the super-ego by which it has been shaped and, in relation to the id, to give an account of the instincts, i.e., of id-contents, and to follow them through the transformations which they undergo."

an anxiety about her parents that was so strong that for several years it had been impossible for her to bring herself to visit them although she much wanted to do this because of their advanced age. What she struggled against was the fear of the childhood pattern of dependence upon them, hostile rebellion against them, and consequent guilt. While ostensibly encouraging her to be independent, the parents had actually exerted and continued to exert—even now when the patient was far from home, married, and with children of her own—strong pressure to bind her to them and keep her dependent and subservient. As this whole emotional constellation toward her parents, which underlay her anxiety about visiting them, was worked through, she decided one weekend to take the plunge, mustered her husband and children together, and made the trip. The actual time with her parents was brief, lasting only several hours, but it was successful in that she remained in control of her emotions. She returned feeling greatly relieved, believing that because she had handled this situation she could probably handle any other. That night she dreamed that she was flying. Her spontaneous associations to the flying in the dream were her feelings of being unburdened, of being liberated, of "a wonderful sense of freedom." Throughout her very severe neurosis there had been no disturbance in her sexual relationship with her husband.

A second patient, a young man, was making an adequate adaptation to reality but unconsciously protested with anger against the burden of responsibility imposed by his job and by his large family. He dreamed:

> I was taking a flight as a co-pilot, against regulations, in which I would get to pilot the plane. Before the flight I was anxious, but this feeling gave way to serenity and peacefulness when we actually became airborne. The flight was momentarily marred by a close brush with treetops and telephone wires, forcing the pilot to pull up sharply to avoid collision. This resulted in going into a spin, but my anxiety abated when I observed that

this was a controlled maneuver, confidently executed by the pilot of the plane.

In his associations, the idea of flying emphasized the regressive wish to return to the pleasures of the "carefree" latency period. Flying was characterized as pleasant because "all of the problems and hazards are the pilot's responsibility, and as a passenger you give yourself over into his hands . . . It means being above the congestion and hustle and bustle below. It is a means of effortless travel." There is evident, of course, the struggle between the more mature aspects of the ego and the regressive wish, which, along with the hostility account for the anxiety. There is also protest against the dependency; the patient was going to pilot the airplane himself, utilizing muscular activity and skill as a denial of helplessness and passivity.

The patient had a second dream the same night that represented the further success of the protest—this dream was of skiing admirably. Here the protest is more active. Muscular activity with exhibitionistic features combined with the pleasurable aspect of a soaring sensation and the passive dependence on gravity for power. The operation of the fight-flight mechanism is evident in this dream pair; fight is connoted by the anxiety from hostility and guilt, while flight is quite literal in both dreams.

That the dynamics of the transference should reflect this struggle between passive-receptive-dependent wishes and the more mature protest is to be expected. Actually the circumstances are quite similar: the analyst is represented as the pilot and the flight of the airplane depicts the analysis itself. Insofar as the analysis is represented by airplane flight, one can see the degree to which the patient accepts a passive-dependent relation to the "pilot" or the degree to which he feels involved with the "pilot" in the actual task of conducting the "flight." A less overt theme is competitiveness. This was alluded to in the first dream in the idea of who will pilot the plane, and in associations to the second dream about the patient having skied competitively.

No doubt since everyone has strong sexual feelings with infantile as well as mature content, all unconscious productions can be expected to have sexual meaning. However, in certain cases more central and prominent, there may be an ego meaning which must also be understood.*

6. Freud's remarks that reality could also cure have been fully confirmed by the war neuroses and by the studies of cultural anthropologists as well as psychoanalysts. The external realities of every individual's existence are a vital part of his emotional life and, conversely, each person, to a considerable extent, makes his own place in the world. His inner feelings shape and color his grasp and handling of his reality situation.

7. Cognizance of the ego and of the realities of a freely competitive civilization are finally obviating the importance in life of strivings for status and prestige while also demonstrating the pain of inferiority feelings and loneliness.

8. One of the great central discoveries of psychoanalysis is being more sharply illumined, namely, the operation of injurious emotional influences on children from birth to the age of about six and the shaping by these influences of warped emotional patterns. The oedipus complex and the sibling rivalry and how they are resolved are affected by the specific emotional influences, e.g., whether one or both parents is seductive or harsh, whether the patient is an only child or one of many, and the like. Mention should be included here of increasing recognition of the vital importance of the mother-child relationship and also of the relationship with siblings.

9. Even as, in Freud's language, psychoanalysis progressed from occupation with the repressed to study of the repressing forces, so its increasing attention to the ego and reality parallels its concern not only with the infantile but also with the development to maturity. The very nature of

*For further discussion of dreams of flying, see Bond, 1952; Freud, 1916-1917, 1900; Gatto, 1954; Saul and Curtis, 1967.

human maturity itself has come under increasing scrutiny. The focus has shifted to concern over its significance for mental health, for the sort of world of people in which we now live, for the future of humanity, and perhaps, for survival.

Psychoanalytic attention has gradually enlarged and shifted focus: from sex alone to other repressed forces, such as dependence and hostility; from what is repressed to the repressing forces themselves—the ego and the superego; from the symptoms and the contents to the causal dynamics; from the universal childhood problems of relationships with parents and siblings to the specific warpings of personality; from these warpings to what caused them, namely, the trauma—the injurious influences on the child; from the unconscious alone to reality and adjustment; from the subject matter of treatment to the goals of treatment; from the sole study of the infantile to the whole course of development to maturity.

THE BASIC MOTIVATIONS

Psychoanalysis is becoming less difficult than it was because the fluid unconscious processes, the many detailed dynamic mechanisms, and the variable constellations and complexes are now seen to be the results of a relatively small number of basic biologic motivations. The endless details that emerge during treatment are no longer chaotic and confusing when seen as the manifestations of these few basic motivations. Just as the apparently senseless pieces of a jigsaw puzzle are actually the closely interrelated fragments of a single pictorial conception, so too the innumerable details in dreams and in the uninterrupted associations of each hour are seen to be patterns shaped by the relatively few underlying forces. The complexities of personality and of the psyche derive not only from the varied combinations of the few fundamental biologic motivations but also from the many defenses and reactions of the ego (Saul and Sheppard, 1958).

What are the basic motivations in human beings, the fundamentals with which the analyst deals? Separating them out of the combinations and complexes in which we are accustomed to seeing them and considering them apart from their objects, they are, as our discussion of recent development suggests, (1) the child's elemental dependence on its mother and its libidinal needs for love; (2) the drive to mature, adult independence and its libidinal component of giving love; (3) the derivatives of the dependent-love needs—frustration, shame, inferiority feelings, competitiveness; (4) the genital sexual drive—as a mechanism in itself and as a pathway for other impulses, including the pregenital; (5) the fight-flight response to any frustration, threat, or irritation—primarily as hostility and as regression; (6) the derivatives of hostility—chiefly fear, anxiety, guilt; (7) the effects of early conditioning; (8) anxiety, a subjective signal from the fight-flight reaction.

Perhaps there are other truly elemental motivations, but those that are outlined above will show that there is a limited number which, operating in the framework that we know as id, ego, and superego, make intelligible the core of the personality and its problems. The interplay of these motivations forms in each person a characteristic nuclear emotional pattern that is usually discernible and comprehensible.* It is each person's subjective perception of the basic motivations and reactions of his psychophysiological organism as a unit that is the foundation of his emotional life, of his feelings and thoughts, and of his behavior. It is this perception, be it conscious, preconscious, or unconscious that constitutes the psyche. It is one of the great discoveries of modern times that the preconscious and unconscious can be made conscious by the most direct and effective method yet available, namely, by psychoanalytic techniques for clinical study of selected persons, chiefly those who can reveal themselves for therapeutic purposes.

*See Saul, 1971 for a study of these forces, their interplay, and their effects.

APPLICATION TO TREATMENT

From the foregoing theoretical discussion, the rationale of psychoanalytic treatment should now be clear; it is precisely as stated by Freud in *An Outline of Psychoanalysis.* That is, the goal of the procedure is to correct those injurious influences on the child which, because he was so conditioned, still persist in his mind. This is achieved primarily through the transference: the patient's disordered patterns of emotional reaction to other human beings, which had their source toward the figures of childhood, repeat themselves toward the analyst as the patient free associates. Thus, the analyst comes to stand in the patient's mind in the place not only of those persons who were kind toward him but also of those who grossly mistreated him. The analyst now has the opportunity to point out to the patient the unreality of his present reactions to the analyst and the fact that they are repetitions of the childhood patterns. This reopens the patient's capacity for outgrowing these reactions, thus enabling him to become more adaptable and to achieve more mature relationships. If the analyst does not clearly understand the disturbed emotional pattern of childhood, then, obviously, he cannot recognize or comprehend the transference, which is a repetition of it toward himself. Only by consistently understanding, analyzing, and working through this transference of his patient's conflicting infantile attitudes and feelings can the analyst recondition the patient and effect what Freud called "emotional after-education."

It is because of the fact that the patient comes to see and feel toward the analyst as he saw and felt toward those who mistreated him in childhood that hostility against the analyst is bound to develop. This also accounts for the patient's attempts to flee from him. The analysis of the "negative transference," or, in other words, this hostility toward the analyst, is of central importance in achieving a therapeutic result. Because the hostility is the most immediate force behind the symptoms, analysis of it leads most directly to the understanding of those libidinal impulses that were frustrated and still persist in the patient in infantile and insatiable form.

Thus, for the analyst, the theoretical basis for psychoanalytic therapy lies in understanding the infantile pattern of emotional reaction which is troubling his patient and producing the complaints and the symptoms. The analyst's task also involves deconditioning and reconditioning the patient by guiding him with this insight through the corrective emotional experience of the analysis, especially in the transference.

The student must learn systematic, scientific procedure for penetrating to the major, central, traumatic influences and their permanent results in the disturbed childhood emotional pattern. He must learn to do this in the first diagnostic interviews. He must perceive these influences constantly in the patient's reactions and in the transference. Equally important as recognizing these is the ability to analyze them clearly, thoroughly, and consistently as they appear throughout the analysis in the transference. He must not be misled into all sorts of peripheral mechanisms and details, however intriguing. It is well to miss none of these, but it produces only confusion to be led hither and yon by them to the neglect of the central, major forces. This results in a fragmentation in which the analyst sees various bits of mechanisms but does not come to grips with those key forces that give rise to the patient's problem. This happens not infrequently in highly intuitive students whose intuition, however correct for certain material, is not yet sufficiently disciplined and scientifically systematized to serve them in penetrating to the main issues. Nowhere is it more important than in analysis to discriminate invariably between the peripheral and the central.

These difficulties are, in part, the result of the state of the psychoanalytic literature. Freud's writings were the very first studies in a new and pioneering field, and they extend in many different directions. His observations were of many different kinds—clinical, formulative, theoretical—which he himself was constantly changing and revising. Hence, they can be confusing to the student, especially if he is taught them chronologically. In such an unhappy instance, the student must learn much at the beginning of his training, which represents Freud's thoughts around 1900, only to have to struggle later to replace this with Freud's own revisions, especially evident in his writings after 1920.

It is essential for the student to be material-oriented, patient-oriented, and reality-oriented rather than theory-oriented. Complete agreement on theory and technique cannot be expected at this stage of psychoanalytic development (and in a young field this is healthy). If there is general agreement with the above statement, then all that follows about the method of treatment will be the more readily intelligible.

Because the analyst is called on by the patient to correct those factors that cause the emotional difficulties, it will be worthwhile to review these factors systematically, moving from the present backward. The patient is an organism of a certain heredity whose development has been affected and conditioned by his past. A relatively constant core pattern of motivation and responses has been shaped by early influences, and it is this pattern that is interacting with his current environment, emotional and otherwise.

1. The extreme reactive cases are those in which the healthiest personality breaks down because the stress is too severe, prolonged, and unrelieved. This was demonstrated by experiences in World War II (Appel, 1946).

2. Where the personality is relatively healthy, the individual breaks down or becomes sufficiently upset quantitatively to be considered emotionally disturbed only when great enough stress over a long enough period strikes his specific emotional vulnerabilities (Saul, 1971).

3. If the first six years of life have provided a healthy environment with good, warm, easy, loving human relations, then injurious influences occurring even soon after this age, although able to warp the personality while it is still mal-

leable, nevertheless will usually leave unscathed the secure core that formed during the earlier years.

4. If only the first two or three years have afforded the emotional climate, warmth, and security for healthy growth, a sturdy core may still withstand later traumatic influences if these are not too severe and unremitting.

5. If the injurious influences come to bear upon the child in its very first days, weeks, and months after birth, then even the core may be warped, and psychosis may be the result, depending on what comes later.

6. Pushing back still further, it is now known that the development of the fetus can be affected during pregnancy, and the principle continues to hold good that the younger and more immature the organism, the more deleterious the effect of a given injury. The mother's fatigue or nervousness, drugs, alcohol, or other conditions or behavior can affect her unborn child. There is mounting evidence that anxiety and other emotional states in the mother during pregnancy can also produce harmful effects (Montague, 1950).

7. There is also evidence that the condition of the parents preceding and at the time of conception can affect the development of the fertilized ovum. The germ plasm is well insulated from the rest of the body but not completely, and exhaustion, illness, drugs, and possibly emotional states may well have their effects on the new being at its very inception.

8. The germ plasm may be damaged long before fertilization by such a factor as radioactivity.

9. Only after exhausting all these possibilities, starting with the adult and working back through its development to the sperm and the egg cells, do we rightly come to possible aberrations of heredity. In considering these, the analyst does well to bear in mind two distinctions. The first is between neurosis (in the broad sense of emotional disorders), in which the evidence for the effects of early conditioning is so overwhelming that it is extremely unlikely that heredity plays a major role, and psychosis, in which the evidence for

hereditary factors may be more serious (Kallman, 1953). The other distinction is between prophylaxis and treatment. If a young couple, each partner with an extensive family history of mental disorder, ask about the possibility of such disorder in their children, or if a couple ask about adopting a baby that has such a family history, the psychiatrist must indeed ponder the evidence. But, in office practice, it is best for the analyst to forget heredity as a factor in all cases that he finds suitable for treatment, for he devotes his energies and skills primarily to correcting the early faulty conditioning and cannot allow himself to excuse his failures by attributing them to factors that he cannot positively establish. He cannot change heredity, physical damage, or the patient's environment. He must try to help the patient to mature and to adapt; this includes aiding the patient in expanding his own control of his environment.

It goes without saying that the analyst never can depart from his basic attitude of sympathetic help based on understanding. It is for help alone that the patient legitimately comes, and it is to this alone that the analyst will be devoted, however the patient may try, consciously or unconsciously, to manipulate the relationship into socializing, direct advice, refuge, or anything else.

The analyst will be alert to all of the above factors diagnostically, but therapeutically his own techniques limit his competence chiefly to influencing the major motivations that underlie the emotional disorder. In practice, this means mostly correcting the aftereffects of injurious pressures, usually those which were operative during the formative years. Correcting these aftereffects probably can tilt the balance therapeutically even if other factors, including hereditary ones, are causally important. It is a quantitative matter of the relative weight of each factor. At least in ambulatory office practice, with psychoses excluded, the author's evidence points to the vast majority of patients developing fully from birth and resolving satisfactorily the oedipal and sibling constellations, provided that injurious influences have not interfered. For example, a mother who loves her first child too well, too adoringly, too overprotectingly may create such closeness to herself that the child's later sibling and oedipal relations are too intensified for the child to handle.

REFERENCES AND SOME RELATED READINGS

Alexander, F. (1961), *The Scope of Psychoanalysis.* New York: Basic Books.

——— (1956), *Psychoanalysis and Psychotherapy.* New York: Norton.

——— (1935), The problem of psychoanalytic technique. *Psychoanal. Quart.,* 4:588–611.

——— (1925), A metapsychological description of the process of cure. *Internat. J. Psychoanal.,* 6:13–34.

Alexander, F., and French, T. (1946), *Psychoanalytic Therapy.* New York: Ronald.

Appel, J. (1946), Preventive psychiatry. *J.A.M.A.,* 131:1469.

Bergler, E. (1937), Symposium on the theory of therapeutic results of psychoanalysis. *Internat. J. Psychoanal.,* 18: 146–160.

Bibring, E. (1937), Symposium on the theory of therapeutic results of psychoanalysis. *Internat. J. Psychoanal.,* 18: 170–189.

Bond, D. D. (1952), *The Love and Fear of Flying.* New York: Internat. Univ. Press.

Bromberg, W. (1962), *The Nature of Psychotherapy.* New York: Grune & Stratton.

Chessick, R. (1969), *How Psychotherapy Heals.* New York: Science House.

Fenichel, O. (1941), *Problems of Psychoanalytic Technique* (monograph). New York: Psychoanal. Quart.

——— (1937), Symposium on the theory of therapeutic results of psychoanalysis. *Internat. J. Psychoanal.,* 18: 133–138.

Ferenczi, S. (1936), *Further Contributions to the Theory and Technique of Psychoanalysis.* London: Hogarth Press and Instit. of Psychoanal.

French, T. (1945), Ego analysis as a guide to therapy. *Psychoanal. Quart.,* 14: 336–349.

Freud, A. (1937), *Ego and the Mechanisms of Defense,* 4–5. London: Hogarth Press.

Freud, A., and Burlingham, D. (1943), *War and Children.* New York: Medical War Books.

Freud, S. (1940), *An Outline of Psychoanalysis,* 67; 31; 83. New York: Liveright, 1949.

——— (1930), *Civilization and Its Discontents,* 131. Garden City, N. Y.: Doubleday, 1958.

——— (1924), The passing of the oedipus complex. In *Collected Papers,* 2: 269–277. London: Hogarth Press, 1924.

——— (1916–1917), *A General Introduction to Psychoanalysis.* New York: Liveright, 1935.

Fries, M.. and Woolf, P. (1971), The influence of constitutional complex on development phases. In *Separation-Individuation,* ed. J. McDevitt and C. Settlage. New York: Internat. Univ. Press.

Fromm-Reichmann, F. (1954), Psychoanalytic and general dynamics conceptions of theory and therapy; differences and similarities. *J. Am. Psychoanal. A.,* 2: 711–721.

Gatto, L. E. (1954), Understanding the fear of flying syndrome. *U.S. Armed Forces Med. J.,* vol. 5.

Glover, E. (1954), Therapeutic criteria of psychoanalysis. *Internat. J. Psychoanal.,* 35: 95–101.

——— (1937), Symposium on the theory of therapeutic results of psychoanalysis. *Internat. J. Psychoanal.,* 18: 125–189.

Guntrip, H. (1971), *Psychoanalytic Theory, Therapy and the Self.* New York: Basic Books.

——— (1961), *Personality Structure and Human Interaction.* New York: Internat. Univ. Press.

Holzman, P. (1970), *Psychoanalysis and Psychopathology.* New York: McGraw-Hill.

Jones, E. (1957), *The Life and Work of Sigmund Freud,* vol. 3. New York: Basic Books.

Kallman, F. (1953), *Heredity and Mental Disorders.* New York: Norton.

Kubie, L. (1950), *Practical and Theoretical Aspects of Psychoanalysis.* New York: Internat. Univ. Press.

Lampl-de Groot, J. (1969), Reflections on the development of psychoanalysis, technical implications in analytic treatment. *Internat. J. Psychoanal.,* 50:567–572.

Lichtenberg, P. (1969), *Psychoanalysis: Radical and Conservative.* New York: Springer.

Liddell, H. (1961), Sheep. In *Lectures on Experimental Psychiatry,* ed. H. W. Brosin. Pittsburgh: Univ. Pittsburgh Press.

——— (1956), *Emotional Hazards in Animals and Man.* Springfield, Ill.: C. C. Thomas.

Little, M. (1957), "R"—the analyst's total response to his patient's needs. *Internat. J. Psychoanal.,* 38: 240–254.

Lowenstein, R. (1969), An historical review of the theory of psychoanalytic technique. *Bull. Philadelphia A. Psychoanal.,* 19:58–60.

Mahrer, A. (1967), *Goals of Psychotherapy.* New York: Appleton.

Montague, A. (1950), Constitutional and prenatal factors in infant and child health. In *Symposium on the Healthy Personality,* ed. M. Senn. New York: J. Macy.

Mullahy, P. (1970), *Psychoanalysis and Interpersonal Psychiatry.* New York: Science House.

Oberndorf, C. P. (1913), The scope and technique of psychoanalysis. *Med. Rec.,* 84:973.

Payne, S. (1956), Notes on developments in the theory and practice of psychoanalytic technique. *Internat. J. Psychoanal.,* 37:12–19.

Rado, S. (1939), Developments in the psychoanalytic concep-

tion and treatment of neuroses. *Psychoanal. Quart.*, 8:427–437.
——— (1925), The economic principle in psychoanalytic technique. *Internat. J. Psychoanal.*, 6:35–44.
Redlich, F., and Freedman, D. (1966), *The Theory and Practice of Psychiatry*. New York: Basic Books.
Saul, L. (1971), *Emotional Maturity*, 3rd ed. Philadelphia: Lippincott.
——— (1950a), On the distinction between loving and being loved. *Psychoanal. Quart.*, 19:412–413.
——— (1950b), Physiological systems and emotional development. *Psychoanal. Quart.*, 19:158–163.
Saul, L., and Curtis, G. (1967), Dream form and strength of impulse in dreams of falling and other dreams of descent. *Internat. J. Psychoanal.*, 48:281–287.
Saul, L., and Sheppard, E. (1958), An approach to the ego functions. *Psychoanal. Quart.*, 27:237–246.
——— (1956), An attempt to quantify emotional forces using manifest dreams. *J. Am. Psychoanal. A.*, 4:486–502.
Searle, M. N. (1936), Some queries on principles of technique. *Internat. J. Psychoanal.*, 17:471–493.
Sheldon, W., and Stevens, S. (1942), *Varieties of Temperament*. New York: Harper & Row.
Spitz, R. A. (1945), Hospitalism: An inquiry into the genesis of psychiatric conditions in early childhood. In *The Psychoanalytic Study of the Child*, vol 1. New York: Internat. Univ. Press.
Strachey, J. (1937), Symposium on the theory of therapeutic results of psychoanalysis. *Internat. J. Psychoanal.*, 18:139–145.
——— (1934), The nature of the therapeutic action of psychoanalysis. *Internat. J. Psychoanal.*, 15:127–159.

4 / PSYCHODYNAMICS AND THE LIBIDO THEORY

As Freud pointed out, the marks of their early histories are left upon groups as well as upon individuals. Perhaps it is just because of the great initial impact of his own first insights that the evolution of psychoanalytic theory has, in some respects, not kept pace with rapidly expanding observations and, to some extent, with practice. This seems more true of the libido theory and of the exclusively sexual etiology of neurosis than of other areas in the field of psychoanalysis. There have been a number of critical reviews of this part of psychoanalytic theory, and one of the most searching of these has been done by Franz Alexander in *The Scope of Psychoanalysis.* Freud (1940) himself questioned whether the sexual etiology was an exclusive one, and most analysts, I believe, recognize other traumatic factors in childhood which they seek to correct in their therapy. I shall not attempt a thorough review of this situation; however, because of its great practical consequences, I should like to present some facts and thoughts about the problem.

Alexander points out that in the natural sciences there is a continuous discarding of older views and a replacing of them with new ones that seem better adapted to the natural course of the development of the science. While this process of continuous change keeps the theory as close as possible to its observational base, it is not at all easy to do. This is especially true in a new field in which a great number of followers have laboriously learned certain ideas that they accept from authority. Naturally, then, there is a tendency to defend the old views emotionally and to feel confused if a critic, however accurate and constructive, undermines these views. Freud's own work throughout his life, however, consisted in just this kind of continuous struggle for the adjustment of his theoretical concepts to the increasing factual material that he kept discovering. He never left off revising even his most fundamental concepts. In comparison, physics, as Alexander says, started out with the idea of a mechanical substance, and this developed into the concept of an energy that appears in different forms. Physicists then arrived at a field theory in which the energy quantities were no longer dealt with in isolated systems; instead, they were seen in relation to each other. This is not unlike what has happened in the last ten or twelve years in our field. In what has become ego psychology, interest has focused on the individual tendencies in the complex interrelationships of these energies to each other and to the environment. And, as in *The Evolution of Modern Physics* by Einstein and Infeld, there is no tendency to minimize the older concepts, but rather there is a concerted effort to show their beauty and accomplishments, and to show how later observations gradually led to the evolution of the new ideas.

One wonders how many analysts still maintain the early views of the libido theory according to which the bodily pregenital activities are considered the basis of fundamental emotional tendencies, dependence being the manifestation of an oral libido; cruelty, stubbornness, or independence as manifestations of anal libido; ambition the sublimation of urethra libido; and so on. But Alexander deplores the fact that new developments have been advanced as a polemical attack on the libido theory, rather than offered as further data that needs to be considered in modifying and advancing the theory. He does praise Horney, however, for attempting to understand patients in terms of detailed psychological realities instead of theoretical abstractions; Alexander notes (and this is certainly my experience) that in our field there is a temptation to replace with theory a real understanding of the living person. Alexander believes that there are many excellent psychoanalytic practitioners who, in their clinical work, represent the most advanced practice while, theoretically, they might still adhere to the earlier libido concepts. Nevertheless, a well-formulated theory becomes more and more valuable for practice, if not actually imperative. Naturally, further advance in the field will depend upon well defined, well established theory.

A chapter on motivation, energy, and cognitive structure in psychoanalytic theory by Louis Breger (1968) covers a great variety of disciplines and approaches, and thereby puts psychoanalytic theory in perspective. He states that psychoanalytic theory, while dealing with many aspects of human thought and action, is above all a theory of motivation, with emphasis on the basic forces and urges that underlie human psychology. But, the conceptual underpinning—the concepts of psychic energy of libido, of the life and death instincts—has long been its weakest aspect. In fact, he says the evidence from a variety of sources now makes it clear that a theory based on these concepts is no longer tenable. Those officially committed to it, he says, can only defend it by a series of rear-guard actions that seem increasingly ineffectual. Several writers, among them Apfelbaum (1965) and Loevinger (1966), have pointed out that this conceptual underpinning, which is frequently referred to as Freud's metapsychology, has long lived an isolated life from the "clinical" theory, that is, the observations and hypotheses with which the analyst is concerned in his actual work with patients. Consequently, this has become unnecessary. Colby (1955) presents an excellent analysis of this problem and outlines an alternative model. More recently, Klein (1967) and

Loevinger (1966) have presented new ideas for dealing with the problems to which metapsychological theory has been applied, ideas which may more adequately encompass the observations on which the theory is based. Breger goes on to outline historically the origins of Freud's ideas. Therefore, instead of attempting to repeat this, I will discuss here only a few ideas that represent conclusions that I have reached based on my own clinical experience as well as extensive reading in the literature. However, for a perspective on Freud's thinking and the development of modern critiques on libido theory and metapsychology, the student is strongly urged to read the Breger material. It is excellently written, non-polemic, and scholarly. For other very competent but different types of critiques, see Knapp (1966), Rosenblatt and Thickstun (1970), and Kestemberg (1970).

First and foremost, the formulation of an exclusive sexual etiology is of fundamental importance for therapy, determining much of the orientation, approach, and procedure of the analyst in treating his patients. Secondly, it is an area of controversy that contributes, on the academic level, to tensions among psychoanalysts. Thirdly, it is responsible for much of that criticism of psychoanalysis, which does not necessarily come into being only from emotional resistance. The hypothesis of an exclusive sexual etiology is that all neurotic symptoms are disguised returns from repression solely of infantile sexual impulses and of no others. Freud (1940) wrote, "our observation shows us invariably, so far as we can judge, that the excitations that play this pathogenic part arise from the component instincts of the sexual life." Waelder (1960) writes, "Psychoanalytic therapy stands and falls with the psychoanalytic theory of the neuroses. . . . The neurotic process consists of three steps—conflict over a sexual urge, (unsuccessful) repression, and return of the repressed. The psychoanalytic treatment attacks the second of these steps only . . ." We are interested here in the libido theory not per se as a theory of sexual development, but only in its relationship to the etiology of neurosis.

To keep close to observation, let us sketch very briefly a common clinical vignette and then quote two passages from Freud that make the dynamics intelligible and also raise questions about the determinants of personality and neurotic disorders.

A married woman of forty-five complains of anxiety. It appears that for fifteen years she has had a lover; she thinks she has been successful in keeping this secret. If her husband, who is a rigid martinet with a violent temper, found her out, the consequences would be dire if not dangerous. It turns out that her greatest pleasure in the affair centers upon this deception of her husband, which is her secret rebellion and revenge for his cruel, egotistic domination of her.

Now why did a charming, beautiful, and intelligent woman choose such a husband, and why did she evolve this particular pattern of response? As is usual, the pattern traces back to her early childhood. Her father died when she was one year old. Her mother, who had very high standards, loved her but was shrewish, overly strict, and controlling. These traits were not expressed toward the child during babyhood but built up from about age three or four, as the infant became a small person. The quantitative balance of forces were such that the child was not crushed: overtly she would defy her strict mother by picking her nose, masturbating, and occasionally pilfering. Thereafter, she repeated this pattern of defiance toward harsh authority figures. Unconsciously, she selected such a one as a husband and repeated the pattern toward him, feeling that his cruel domination justified her behavior.

How do we understand this woman? Does this understanding provide a basis for rational, causal treatment? Could her unhappy pattern and her symptoms have been prevented? The answers, or the key to them, are contained concisely in the following two passages from Freud's *An Outline of Psychoanalysis*.

> . . . the superego continues to act the role of the external world to the ego, although it has become part of the internal world. During the whole of a man's later life, it represents the influence of his childhood, of the care and education given to him by his parents and of his dependence on them . . . not only the personal qualities of these parents, but also everything that produced a determining effect upon them themselves, the tastes and standards of the social class in which they live and the characteristics and traditions of the race from which they spring.

> If the patient puts the analyst in the place of his father (or mother), he is also giving him the power which his superego exercises over his ego, since his parents were, as we know, the origin of his superego. The new superego now has an opportunity for a sort of after-education of the neurotic; it can correct blunders for which his parental education was to blame . . . In all his attempts at improving and educating the patient, the analyst must respect his individuality.

In the light of these statements, the patient's pattern of living results from internalizing her attitudes and feelings toward her mother. Throughout her life she has carried the image of a loving but over dominating mother and, in response, she has always felt hostile rebellion and because of the love and the high standards, guilt. Not only did the patient project this pattern onto authority figures, but also, and more importantly for her life's design, she would find people to fit the pattern; most fatefully, her husband. So the external became internal, and the internal then dictated the external: the needs for love, the hostile rebellion and the guilt, and fear of discovery and punishment. Guilt and fear were the most immediate forces behind the anxiety symptoms.

The aforementioned treatment, as quoted from Freud, should correct this superego, this blunder of too harsh domination by the mother which existed in the place of a gentle, gradual, sympathetic understanding and socialization which would never have given rise to these pathologic dynamics. Where in this description can the sexual basis of personality and of neurotic symptoms be found?

If we insist that the anxiety must derive solely or in appreciable extent from penis envy or the oedipus complex, we are in danger of forcing the clinical facts into a preconceived formula. This may fit and be correct, but it does not allow for and cannot pass off the patient's rebellious hostility and guilt toward her mother as a direct reaction to her mother's domineering treatment of the patient. However, if this reaction accounts adequately for the dynamics and the symptom, then what of the infantile sexual etiology of neurosis, this being, presumably, a typical neurotic hysterical anxiety? True the symptom is intimately related to the sex life, and the sex life causes conflict and guilt. But obviously the sexuality is only one form in which the hostile rebellion has expressed itself, rather than the fundamental basis of the neurotic pattern. In another patient, a young man with a highly satisfactory marriage and sex life, a similar rebellion takes the form, because of his specific early conditioning, of overt difficulties with superiors. Doubtless, sexual abuse in early childhood would have produced aftereffects, but other kinds of abuse also can produce pathologic aftereffects, as these and countless other examples illustrate. Then why try to force every case into the libido theory and then base treatment upon this?

Sexuality—or perhaps better, sensuality (a term Waelder suggests)—is a powerful force in early life. On this point, I believe, there is no disagreement. But sexuality and sensuality are used and handled very differently in different persons, and in actual cases it usually is easy to demonstrate that this is an expression of the different personality make-ups. Whether a man loves, marries, and is true to one woman, or whether he is a libertine usually is determined chiefly by the kind of human relations he had with those who reared him, just as this was the case in the examples given above. Of course there are reactive cases in which current pressures—whether of war, occupation, or of a shrewish wife or depriving husband—alter personality patterns, including sexual behavior. If abused in childhood, sexuality can indeed produce lifelong psychopathology; but other, entirely nonsexual abuses, also can generate psychopathology. Where nonsexual abuses warp the personality, sexuality almost always is secondarily involved. In the woman in our example, sexuality is being used in various ways to serve other dynamic forces. Sexuality is a fundamental force and it is so powerful that it probably causes some conflict, frustration, and guilt in everyone. However, the facts do not, by any definition, support it as the exclusive force. Deeper than the sexuality and determining how it is handled, are other forces that are shaped by the reactions of the child (especially before age six) to the feelings, attitudes, and treatment accorded it (see Chap. 3).

The question must be raised as to whether these other forces are not themselves essentially sexual, as Freud initially thought, although he later recognized unerotized hostility. Is imprinting basically sexual? Is the dependence of the young on the mother basically or exclusively sexual, or is it part of some kind of "instinctual response system" (as John Bowlby (1960) uses the term), which may or may not have a sensual aspect or component? We simply do not have the answers yet, but it is the virtue of the libido theory to have raised the questions. Today we know that the answers will require decades of study, not by analysts alone but by other investigators of behavior as well. Only after realizing how little we know, even of the attachment of the young to the mother, shall we be in a position to learn by our own clinical observations and from advancing knowledge in related fields.

The libido theory, in the final form given it by Freud, is a theory of the development of sexuality. However, it is rather commonly used as a theory of the development of the personality. This raises the question: Is the development of the personality to be understood only in terms of the sexuality, that is, the sensuality, or is this part of a larger picture? Furthermore, it must be noted that of itself the libido theory has nothing to do with psychopathology. Psychopathology appears only if fixations or regressions are present, or if the "component sexual instincts" are for other reasons too strong in the later stages of development. But what causes this? Attributing it to the strength of component instincts, to too powerful a sucking reflex, or to over-strong orality, for example, is pure speculation. In his early writings Freud attributed disorders to trauma during early childhood; then, curiously, he all but abandoned consideration of the effects of traumatic influences on the child, only to return to the concept sharply and clearly in his last formulation, wherein he states that psychoanalysis is "after-education of the neurotic to correct the blunders for which the parental education was to blame." He makes the same statement broadly, by implication, in portraying the superego as the internalization of the treatment received during childhood.

Freud (1940) wrote that "analytic experience has convinced us of the complete truth of the common assertion that the child is psychologically father to the man, and that the events of his first years are of permanent importance for his whole subsequent life." Freud then searches for "a central experience" as traumatic, considers sexual misadventures but finds the oedipus complex to be the culprit.

In Freud's (1940) description the mother recognizes that the sexual excitement of her son refers to herself, thinks this is wrong and that it must be stopped, and therefore forbids him to manipulate his genitals. When this demand proves ineffective, she threatens castration, reinforcing this threat by delegating its execution to the father. Thus, again, it is essentially a matter of how the child is treated by the parents. In this instance the trauma is the anxious forbidding of sexual feelings by crude threats of mutilation. Furthermore, there is evidence that the child's oedipal reactions are determined in large part by how his personality has been shaped during his pregenital years. The traumatic influences upon him during this earlier period can consist of all manner of mistreatment, not only sexual. This mistreatment may arise from within the parent or, like the child's sexuality (as described by Freud), other behavior of the child may also provoke the parents into threats and into all forms of punishment. From the time a child crawls he gets into drawers, pulls over lamps, refuses to eat, throws his food on the floor, cries at night and disrupts his parents' sleep, and in other ways can drive even tolerant parents to exasperation, threats, and violence—unless the parents are well-educated as to the behavior of children and mature enough to take it in stride and remain loving and sweet-tempered. If it is maintained that the child's anxiety derives from hostility to his father because of sexual rivalry, then the broader principle is that fear of father can result from hostility to him. But the child can be hostile to his father for many reasons besides sexual rivalry, and he can be hostile to his mother also.

Thus, just as children do all sorts of things in addition to activities having a sexual nature, which provoke threats and punishments from their parents, so too do parents behave in all sorts of ways which provoke hostility and anxiety in the child. Parents behave thus because of their own immature warped patterns.

Considered in this light, the oedipus complex appears as a special case only—one in which the sexuality provokes threats from the parents and reactions of anxiety in the child. The oedipus complex fits a broader picture if the sexual element is not overemphasized to the neglect of the child's other needs for the mother, or for both parents. The most powerful needs of the infant and young child are for care and affection from the mother. These needs are the fundamental; the sexual element is essentially a coloring of these basic dependent love needs. This is not meant to deny the doubtless valid notion that sex, in conflict with repressive parental attitudes and later with cultural mores, is one of the forces that causes rebellion, guilt, and neurotic symptoms. Perhaps this was especially evident in the Victorian era.

The broader principle, which is not restricted or necessarily more appropriate to any age or phase, runs as follows: functions other than sex provoke threats and punishments from the parents; parents often behave punitively toward the child because of their own personality problems and not only in reaction to the child's behavior, thus stimulating hostility and fear in the child; parental threats and punishments concerning any function, not only sex, and parental behavior that arouses hostility and anxiety in the child result in disturbances in any function that may be involved and in the emotional interrelations between parent and child. Thus are formed patterns of disorder for physiologic and psychologic functions and for emotional relations with the parents. And, if the mistreatment is sufficiently severe and prolonged, these patterns become permanent and operate in some degree toward persons other than the parents.

Thus, in the light of all available evidence, what is fundamental is the personal emotional interrelationship between child and parents and others close to the child. It is this emotional relationship that facilitates or warps the maturing of the child's personality by shaping patterns of emotional reactions that will be repeated toward others. The importance of oral, anal, and genital activities in the child is proportional to the disturbance they introduce into the relationships with the parents. It is this disturbance in relationship and its aftereffects that are the essential causes not only of neuroses but of all types of emotional disorder. No doubt other factors exist, but this is the crucial one, upon which rational, causal treatment must be based. Focus on the libidinal impulses without full recognition of the emotional pattern as warped by the influences of the parents upon the child cannot correct the warping, the psychopathology, and can only produce confusion and more severely negative therapeutic responses in the patient.

There is no question but that the sexual etiology is only one dynamic, part of a broader picture that includes emotional relations with the parents and functions in addition to the sexual, such as those activities that are open to parental intervention (e.g., eating, sleeping, speaking, motor behavior). Out of the sexual etiology and oedipus, the still embryonic science of psychodynamics has developed. The essential comes down to this: Persons responsible for the child and emotionally important to him exert profound effects for good or ill—for maturing or for fixation and warping—upon the child's development. Parental blunders and mistreatment are not sexual alone, but take innumerable forms.

This statement is fully consonant with Freud's position in *An Outline of Psychoanalysis,* and probably few analysts would take exception to it. As a corollary, it could be said that a person's attitudes, feelings, motivations, and reactions toward other human beings are essential to the roots of emotional health and illness.

The two excerpts from Freud that were quoted above are well supported by observation, and they show how impossible it is to understand psychic processes in purely intrapersonal terms, for psychic processes are inextricably interrelated with interpersonal reactions and motivations. Even the fetus has a relation to the mother. What was external is internalized and then projected ever afterward onto others.

In 1937 Anna Freud wrote:

> . . . the term "depth psychology" certainly does not cover the whole field of psycho-analytical research . . . we should probably define the task of analysis as follows: to acquire the fullest possible knowledge of all the three institutions of which we believe the psychic personality to be constituted and to learn what are their relations to one another and to the outside world . . . to trace the influences of the outside world . . .

Yet in 1962, the report of Group I for Study of Curriculum and Didactic Teaching claimed that, "The task in analysis is to understand the patient, intrapersonally, not interpersonally, and to give him, in so doing, an opportunity to understand himself, and therefore greater freedom to choose." To try to understand the mind, psyche, or personality of a human being without regard to his feelings toward others and toward himself places a strangling limitation upon psychoanalytic investigation, if it does not actually make such investigation impossible. We seek to understand the patterns of reaction to others and to the self that are formed in childhood and repeated ever after. How can these patterns be understood without reference either to their origins or to their current operation? Each person lives in a psychologic field, not in a vacuum, so to try to understand a person's patterns of reaction, healthy or pathologic, without reference to their objects is like trying to understand the physiology of the stomach without reference to food.

It is possible that students of our field would be better observers if they began their training with Freud's last words—the last three pages of his *Outline*—and if the libido theory were omitted so far as possible from teaching of basic discoveries until the libido therapy can be reviewed critically in the perspective of other data and formulations. Then, the student would have a concept of the total personality development in relation to the outer world before pursuing the place in it of sexuality and its development.

It is obvious that mistreatment upsets and disturbs the child's human relations or feelings toward others, and that prolonged mistreatment produces long-lasting, even permanent, aftereffects. No matter what his heredity, any child can be driven into severe disorder, even psychosis, if treated badly enough emotionally. But, on the other hand, I do not think there is any direct evidence that hereditary alterations in oral erotism can produce any such effects.

If, as was pointed out in the previous chapter, the child's personal relations with those close to him and responsible for him are good, his feelings toward them will be satisfactory, and the child will mature emotionally in a healthy fashion and will not suffer from emotional disorders. This, as shown by clinical observation and animal studies, is the critical factor. The theoretical structure of psychoanalysis, so well grounded in other respects, may be overweighted by the libido theory in explaining development, personality, and psychopathology. As we move from the era of great discoveries into an era of systematic observation and more rigorous research design, the validity and place of the libido theory will become apparent.

Freud searched for universal patterns of inner development, concentrating on sexuality. If the therapist does not balance this approach with his knowledge of psychopathology and of individual differences among his patients and among all persons, he might neglect the specific influences during childhood that affect development, and the detailed ways the effects are brought about. The therapist may carry this thinking over into his treatment of individual patients, and note among the patient's highly specific dynamics only what fits the theory of sexuality. If the analyst is preoccupied with ideas about inner sexual development and does not see the reactions to childhood traumata, it is easy for him to conclude that all is ontogenetically and phylogenetically determined. Out of this reasoning has come an unfounded pessimism, both about the effectiveness of psychoanalysis as treatment and about human personality. Could it also be that some of this reasoning has stemmed from emotionally-based pessimism? The essential in psychoanalysis is to apprehend the psychic realities and the underlying emotional forces, motivations, and reactions. Theory is valuable only if it helps in this grasp of the realities of the dynamics; if theory hinders understanding of underlying motivation, then the theory must be altered, for, as Freud has said, the theory is only the superstructure.

In science, not logic but fact is the authority. What facts establish the role of heredity in the neuroses and in other emotional disorders? I know of no conclusive factual evidence that heredity plays any role whatsoever in neuroses and other emotional disturbances other than psychoses. In sharpest contrast, when you focus on early chronic traumatic influences, that is, upon the ignorant and hostile rearing of children that blunts natural parental instincts and transmits emotional disorders down the generations, a different situation exists. As we study the strengths of our patients in handling the injurious omissions and commissions to which they were subjected during their earliest years, the probability emerges that physically healthy babies mature in healthy fashion with good human relations unless acted upon by injurious external forces, that they grow strong emotionally unless subjected to powerful emotional threats and injuries. The evidence suggests that heredity is relatively as important for emotional disorders as physical strength is in a man who is hit by an automobile going fifty miles an hour. Breed the most powerful horse or the toughest oak, but mistreat it when young, and deformity will follow. There is not a scrap of evidence that the same is not true for emotional disorders.

Preoccupation with infantile sexual impulses, rather than acknowledgement that external influences can impair total normal development, may lead to unrealistic conclusions. For example, we have seen little emphasis in the literature that hostility, like perverse sexual impulses, is repressed and can return to produce or contribute to symptoms. Nor have we seen much published about differences among people in the amount and expression of hostility. This is true despite alarming increases in crime and violence and their obvious relationships to extremes of neglect and harshness in the earliest years. Surprisingly little attention has been paid to the very notable contrast between the overt brutality of some persons and the obvious good will of others. Children raised with good will grow up with good will; children so treated as to hate their parents continue to hate others.

Man is unique among all animal species in his excess of hostility to his own kind, and in the intensity and extent of his resulting cruelty, brutality, and murder. However, this is an over-simplified generalization—not all men are overt sadists and killers. Although all men have the fight-flight mechanism of reaction, men and women raised with love grow up loving and with good will, whereas makers of violence, the leaders of organized violence, are probably without exception persons who were treated with violence in early childhood. Individuals raised in violence grow up with inner fear, inferiority feelings, and frustrations, which keep their fight-flight reaction mobilized, making them blood-thirsty egotists rather than mature, responsible persons with kindly feelings toward spouse, children, and fellow men. Because of the general atrociousness of child rearing, men of cruelty seem to far outnumber the men of good will.

Thus, we now know how to prevent neurosis and the other manifestations of hostility that plague and endanger humanity. The generally pessimistic views about prevention are derived, I believe, largely from the libido theory and an overly endopsychic concept of pathogenesis. But the clinical facts we have today show clearly that the inclined tree was bent as a twig, and never grew twisted of its own nature.

Failure to achieve good results with psychoanalytic treatment is another source of pessimism. However, failure seems inevitable if the analyst concentrates too exclusively upon making the patient conscious of his infantile sexual impulses, and fails to give due weight to other powerful motivations, especially as parts of the childhood emotional pattern. The problems of very few patients seen in a private office practice stem primarily from their infantile sexuality. The analyst who bases treatment exclusively upon the hypothesis that all psychic ills stem from infantile sexuality will not understand his patients broadly and deeply enough to achieve thoroughgoing therapeutic results. Such an analyst may well feel frustrated, become pessimistic, and consider man's problems as essentially inaccessible to influence. The facts are opposite: if the analyst utilizes current knowledge —free from preconceptions—then, as Freud predicted, he will comprehend the aftereffects of parental blunders and help toward correcting them.

The concept of an exclusively sensual etiology has practical effects upon the efficacy of psychoanalytic treatment. Several years ago, in a seminar, I heard an analyst of national standing describe a patient with observations that were impressively keen, astute, and realistic. The analyst described the dominating, depriving, demanding mother of the patient's childhood; detailed how the patient reacted to her in ways that made clear his present dynamics and his symptoms; and demonstrated with numerous examples how, as an adult, the patient now fought against the pattern formed in his earliest years. However, when the analyst discussed his treatment of the patient, no mention was made of using psychoanalysis as after-education in correction of parental blunders. Instead, the analyst lost the patient in a sea of oral, anal, and phallic symbols, levels, and erotisms. Although the analyst saw clearly that as a child the patient had wanted but not received love, tolerance, understanding, freedom to grow and explore, gradual socialization, and education with respect for his own individuality; although the analyst noted the patient's reactions of repressed rage and his efforts to reach a *modus vivendi* with this well-meaning but dominating, depriving, demanding mother, once the patient was in treatment, the analyst confined his efforts to reconstructing the history of the patient's infantile sensuality. The basic problem, however, was not sensuality. The sensuality was only one area affected by the child's needs versus the mother's mistreatment. Its disturbance was secondary, a result rather than a cause.

Sensual behavior of the child is only one factor among others that can disturb the emotional interrelations with the parents. This is internalized, as Freud has described, and makes the psychopathology, involving id, ego, and superego in varying degrees. Infantile sexuality can be disordered by excessive prohibitions and threats, and by seductions such as kissing too fervently on the lips, too much fondling, stimulation of the anal region or the genitals, etc. Very often the disturbed sexuality is a consequence of disordered feelings, motivations, and reactions that are a result of poor child-rearing, with poor personal emotional relationships. In turn, these disturbed relations derange many other functions and areas of the personality. Sexuality is one area that suffers. The key lies in the feelings that are generated in the child toward emotionally important persons. The early conditioning persists in some degree for life. Because childrearing is generally so atrocious, most personalities are warped in considerable degree and the world is the neurotic, criminal place we know, with a variety of disorders produced by an equal variety of abuses in childrearing.

Id, ego, and superego comprise the total personality. Disorders in these structures are by definition disorders of personality. Disorders of ego and supergo are bound to permeate the total personality, which they affect in many ways. The modern concept of neurosis as a disorder involving ego and supergo obliterates the distinction between neurosis and personality disorders, and neurosis becomes one particular form of personality disorder. The personality disorder is primary. The specific nature of the symptoms, whether neurosis, perversion, behavior disorder, or whatever, is secondary, resulting from the specific balance (or rather imbalance) of forces. The libido theory alone is not an adequate scientific conceptual model for comprehending the realities of an individual patient's psychopathology and for helping to correct this. Freud's later interpersonal model, psychoanalysis as after-education to correct parental blunders incorporated as supergo, is effective.

Knowledge from all related fields supports the broader dynamic concept of the life-long effects in animals and humans of personal relationships during the earliest part of life. The evidence clearly supports the thesis that if early relationships are good, sexuality is handled without neurotic difficulties. More fundamental for the infant than the difference between the sexes of its parents is its need for loving care, and these dependent love needs are among the deepest motivations. Important though sensuality is, personality cannot be understood in terms of erotic impulses alone, but only can be comprehended through appreciation of the major emotional forces and their interplay, that is, through the main dynamics. Out of the initial formulations of infantile sexual etiology of neuroses and of the oedipus complex has developed the new science of psychodynamics, in which setting these appear in perspective. The external influences are so overwhelmingly powerful compared with the resistance of the organism that these influences upon the child, and not any hereditary strength or weakness of instinct nor any endogenous intrapsychic instinctual process, constitute the critical factor in determining psychopathology of any and all kinds in a sound, healthy organism. Further, these influences are not upon the sensuality alone nor in response to the sensuality alone, but upon the security, attitudes, dependent love needs, and whole pattern of feelings, reactions, and motivations toward the parents and others emotionally important to the child. These influences condition the child, are internalized as superego, and hence affect large areas of its personality for the rest of its life. Psychoanalysis is much more than merely making conscious repressed, infantile, sexual impulses; it is essentially what Freud called it: after-education—a way of correcting the aftereffect of early injurious influences that have been internalized. If this is not done, if the aftereffects of all the major injurious influences are not dealt with but only the sexuality, then psychoanalytic treatment can harm instead of help.

REFERENCES AND SOME RELATED READINGS

Alexander, F. (1961), *The Scope of Psychoanalysis.* New York: Basic Books.

Allee, W. (1951). *Cooperation Among Animals.* New York: Schumann.

Apfelbaum, B. (1965), Ego psychology, psychic energy, and the hazards of quantitative explanation. *Internat. J. Psychoanal.,* 46: 168–181.

Astley, R. (1962), Group I for the study of curriculum and didactic teaching. *J. Am. Psychoanal. A.,* 10: 152.

Bowlby, J. (1960a), Ethology and the development of object relations, *Internat. J. Psychoanal.,* 41: 313–317.

——— (1960b), Separation anxiety. *Internat. J. Psychoanal.,* 41: 89–114.

Breger, L. (1968), Motivation, energy and cognitive structure, 44–65. In *Modern Psychoanalysis,* ed. J. Marmor. New York: Basic Books.

Colby, K. M. (1955), *Energy and Structure in Psychoanalytic Theory.* New York: Ronald.

Einstein, A. and Infield, L. (1938), *The Evolution of Physics.* New York: Simon and Schuster.

Freud, A. (1937), *Ego and the Mechanisms of Defense,* 4–5. London: Hogarth Press.

Freud, S. (1940), *An Outline of Psychoanalysis,* 85; 122; 87. New York: Norton, 1949.

Horney, K. (1925), New ways in psychoanalysis. *J. Nerv. Ment. Dis.*

Kestemberg, E. (1970), Discussion of 'Towards a basic psychoanalytic model'. *Internat. J. Psychoanal.,* 51: 183–193.

Klein, G. S. (1967), Peremptory ideation: structure and force in motivated ideas. In *Motives and Thought: Psychoanalytic Essays in Memory of David Rapaport,* ed. R. Holt. *Psychol. Issues,* 5,6: 80–128.

Knapp, P. (1966), Libido: a latter-day look. *J. Nerv. Ment. Dis.,* 142: 395–417.

Liddell, H. (1956), *Emotional Hazards in Animals and Man.* Springfield, Ill.: C. C Thomas.

Ostow, M. (1960), Psychoanalysis and ethology. *J. Am. Psychoanal. A.,* 8: 526–535.

Rosenblatt, A. and Thickstun, J. (1970), A study of the

concept of psychic energy. *Internat. J. Psychoanal.*, 51:265–278.

Saul, L. (1971), *Emotional Maturity*, 3rd ed. Philadelphia: Lippincott.

Tidd, C. (1960), Symposium on psychoanalysis and ethology. *Internat. J. Psychoanal.*, 41:308–312.

Waelder, E. (1960), *Basic Theory of Psychoanalysis*, 212. Internat. Univ. Press.

Part 2

Practice of Psychodynamically Based Psychotherapy

5 / DIAGNOSING THE NUCLEAR DYNAMICS*

No moment of time is so favorable for the understanding of a case as its initial stage.
—SIGMUND FREUD

"In the field of observation," wrote Claude Bernard, "the rewards go only to him who is prepared." The analyst with a mastery of psychodynamics is in a position to make an accurate, rapid, and penetrating diagnosis of the nature and the extent of the patient's disorder and the major forces that underlie and cause it. The situation is basically the same as it is in cases presented for physical diagnosis. Only the physician who is thoroughly grounded in the basic medical sciences is adequately prepared to make physical diagnoses. His acumen increases with experience as he learns to apply to one patient what he has learned from others who manifest similar symptoms and conditions. However knowledgeable and experienced he may be, an outline or a form for history-taking is just as valuable a guide for him as it is for the novice. The same is true for the psychiatric history and the psychoanalytic history.

These forms are, of course, only guides; they are no

*This chapter is based in part on a paper written by the author in collaboration with Drs. Thoburn Snyder, Jr., and Edith Sheppard (1956), *Psychoanalyt. Quart.*, 25:228-237.

substitute for knowledge and experience and astuteness of understanding. By no means is it intended that they be followed scrupulously and in every detail. But, for the analyst who has the basic knowledge and knows what to look for, they do provide a systematic method of procedure that has evolved out of the experiences of others who have devoted so much of their professional lives to achieving the objectives of psychoanalysis.

We have stressed the fact that psychoanalytic treatment is much more than a process of repeated sessions of free association and interpretation. It is analogous less to a hydrotherapeutic procedure, such as daily immersion of a limb for a certain period in water of a certain temperature and swirling at a certain rate, than it is to major surgery, wherein the pathology must be thoroughly understood and skilfully corrected without damage. As Freud put it in his *Outline of Psychoanalysis:* "It can correct blunders for which his parental education was to blame." Psychoanalytic treatment cannot be carried out intelligently unless the analyst first penetrates diagnostically to the main issues: the major parental blunders, other major traumatic influences, and the main effects of these. If he does not succeed in discerning the central emotional forces that need correction, preferably in the very first interview or in the next few, he may find himself beginning an analysis without knowing exactly what he is trying to correct. Surely this situation is as potentially dangerous as that of a surgeon not knowing clearly what he is doing. To master the psychoanalytic technique and to achieve results rationally and scientifically, the analyst must first be able to diagnose the main central dynamics, what is wrong, and what he seeks to correct; what is awry among what Gamaliel Bradford calls "the essential, permanent, and vitally characteristic strands out of the continuous texture of man's entire life" (quoted in Maugham, 1943).

It would seem that in the earlier days of psychoanalysis, relatively little attention was paid to the initial history and to securing a rapid diagnostic penetration to the central dynamics. In certain instances, there would be only a brief determination of whether the patient seemed to have a neurotic problem, that he was not psychotic, and that he was suitable for a trial of psychoanalysis. Very often, a psychiatrist without any psychoanalytic training actually learned much more about the patient in one hour that did an analyst who had been working for many weeks. Even today there is need for increasing realization of the necessity of gaining during the first diagnostic hours thorough and accurate psychodynamic understanding of every patient—instinctually, structurally, and in relationship to the strength and the functioning of the ego and the entire life situation. Some systematizations have already appeared (see Menninger, 1952). Following are certain points and features which, so far as I know, have not been included heretofore and may prove to be of some general use.

The history, which focuses on gaining some understanding of the patient's central dynamics in one single interview, if possible, is divided into three parts. Needless to say, depending on the patient, the purpose of the interview, and the circumstances, more time may be necessary or advisable. The three parts are: (1) anamnestic data, (2) conscious emotional attitudes, and (3) unconscious associative data. It is true that these are not sharply differentiated; the grouping is for convenience, and supplementary information may also prove to be useful. From a practical point of view, it is sometimes a bit easier to consider the history in only two aspects, the anamnestic and the associative. Throughout, the interviewer is attempting to "read" the material and penetrate to the essential underlying motivations as rapidly and surely as possible. He seeks insight into the core of the major current motivations (the dynamics), as well as insight into the early conditionings, (the historics). The most effective therapy will depend on seeing how the patient's life is dominated by disordered patterns of childhood—for this is the essence of neurosis. A clear perspective on the casual forces, if not gained in the very first interviews, is usually exceedingly difficult to obtain once treatment is underway and may not emerge sharply until after the end of the analysis.

INTERVIEW MATERIAL

ANAMNESTIC DATA

The conscious, descriptive anamnestic part of the history includes statements by the patient of his reasons for seeking help, his current life situation, his chief interests, his libidinal investments, etc.

Current reality situation

The patient lives in a real external world. The interviewer will do well to construct a picture of that world by establishing what the patient's present life pattern is—how he lives behavioristically, motivationally, and emotionally. A thorough grasp of each patient's current reality situation is usually vital for understanding the patient's basic dynamics and his present emotional problem as these interact with his environment. Each patient's situation must be seen from two critically important points of view. First, it is a *result* of the ways in which his personality functions. Second, it is a *source* of pressures and stimuli to which he reacts in accordance with his particular dynamic make-up. Is the patient a woman of middle age with two small children and a sadistic elderly husband who refuses divorce? Is it a person of great wealth or one in dire poverty? Is it someone struggling under an unshiftable load? How are the patient's immediate emotional problems and his nuclear dynamics interrelated with such realities? What are his external and internal resources, flexibilities, and other potentialities for handling these realities of his life. Responses to this last question will be pertinent later in the history-taking.

In married persons it is most often very useful to learn something about the spouse. This is important, not only in order to estimate the emotional interrelations but also, more revealingly, because most people unconsciously choose someone who is in some fundamental way very much like themselves or else somehow fits their own childhood emotional pattern.

Are his human relationships good, bad, few, many, close, gratifying, frustrating? How are they with men, women, peers, older and younger people, etc.? In *The Interpretation of Dreams* Freud noted that, "For all practical purposes in judging human character, a man's actions and conscious expression of thought are in most cases sufficient."

The history must determine how much of his problem is internal and how much reactive to his environment. This is extremely important to know even though he may be largely responsible for creating this environment or for finding himself in it. The basic principle is to recognize that the patient can only be understood as an individual human being, with his total personality, id, ego, and superego, operating and interacting with his environment (A. Freud, 1937). Id, ego, and superego are simply convenient and useful ways of grouping the many psychic forces. In simplest terms, under id are grouped the instinctual, biological drives and reactions; the superego connotes all the effects, particularly the early ones, of identification, conditioning, and training, and includes ideals, standards, and conscience; the ego covers the consciousness, judgment, memory, intellectual power, and sense of reality—it is the chief integrator and executor of the impulses from id, superego, and the outside world. How all of these forces operate within the particular individual must be comprehended, for the patient can only be understood in terms of all of his motivations, of his total psychodynamics. The interviewer must value him and give him mature responsible interest as a person. He is not a depersonalized psyche; he comes as a patient, but as A. A. Brill used to say, "We are all patients."

Habits

As part of the current life situation, the patient's habits should be reviewed. Usually, it is a good idea to try to get a picture of a typical twenty-four hour day.

The complaint

The analyst then, of course, is interested in the development of the patient's complaints and symptoms, the circumstances of their onset, and their course. Furthermore, he wants to know why the patient comes to the psychiatrist at precisely this time. The circumstances of onset are usually best discovered without directly asking the patient who rarely can describe them and, if asked about them, might well tend not to divulge them. It is usually more effective to question him about the date and the manner of the onset of the symptoms and then later, without any reference to this, find out as part of the history what was going on in his emotional life at that time. The circumstances surrounding the onset of symptoms may reveal the specific emotional vulnerabilities which, under pressure, led to the emotional problem (Saul, 1971).

History of emotional relationships

The interviewer can trace the history of the patient's emotional relationships either by beginning with the present and working back or, as is usually more convenient, by leaping back to the patient's earliest childhood relationships and working on through to the present. The history can be divided into three groups: the earliest years (from birth to the age of four, five, or six); the latency period (from the age of six to ten); adolescence and maturity. Naturally, it is most difficult to learn the outstanding relationships prior to the age of five, the truly critical period, for this is usually before continuous memory. However, something can usually be learned, if only by asking the patient for his "feel" or "sense" or guess as to what the major emotions were (or were not) in the family, especially in relation to himself, during that preoedipal and oedipal period.

In all relationships the elements of identification and object relationship must be very carefully watched for. For example, a child may identify with his father and unconsciously behave like him; he may also be dependent on him, hostile to him, or otherwise feel toward him as an object.

It is also interesting to learn as much as possible about the period from immediately before conception to birth, both emotionally and physically, regarding the parents and the fetus, even though as yet we do not know much about how to choose and use this information precisely. Evidence from varied sources strongly suggests that emotional states in the mother can produce affects in the unborn child that influence its reactions for the rest of its life (Thompson, 1957).

The impression gained of the outstanding emotions that were at play in relation to the patient from his birth until the age of four, five, or six is of utmost importance because it is during this period that the basic pattern of emotional reactions, the core of his motivations, is formed. This impression is contributed to by all the other data also. It is essential for understanding the central features of the case, the strengths as well as the weaknesses, and for the plan of treatment and prognosis. If there are no good relationships during childhood or no elements of goodness in them, if the person therefore has no good images into which to slip other persons or the analyst, then the prognosis is not so favorable. In such a case the analyst, instead of beginning as a good image, must provide something new in adult life. He must build in a good image almost *de novo* against the faulty conditioning that took place during early childhood. Hence, an evaluation of the patient's imagoes is of great significance for prognosis.

The effects of the early emotional influences depend on their (1) intensity, (2) consistency or inconsistency, (3) duration, (4) relation to age—usually the earlier the age the greater the effect, and (5) relation to possible vulnerable points in the libidinal development. The central symptoms may be a guide to the degree of development; for example, sexual symptoms in an otherwise relatively healthy personality probably indicate adequate development to the oedipal period of the age of three to six, while schizophrenic symptoms strongly suggest traumatic influences much earlier in life.

The patient's emotional investments of the past, of childhood, provide the key to the present dynamic. For example, a strong and able man of twenty-five says he is merely keeping up a front and that in reality he can barely keep going and fears a breakdown. He is afraid that he might lose control of himself in a public place and begin to throw things or yell obscenities. Everything he relates comes back to a single source: he starts talking about his interest in girls, how inhibited he is with them, and recalls that Bob, his closest friend since age three, used to try to shame him for being with a girl, calling him "sissy." Then he tells of how shy he is about bathroom functions, how he could not provide the doctor with a urine specimen at a routine physical examination. Then we find him talking of Bob and how Bob would watch him go to the bathroom, laughing at him, teasing him, so that he became self-conscious of elimination. Sports, studies, work, everything he began speaking of quickly led into a flood of associations about Bob. The patient's family lived in a neighborhood in which the only playmate of his age was in the family next door. At age three the patient and Bob were inseparable. Bob was a little older and much bigger and stronger, and often beat up the patient, whose enormous attachment to Bob and his identification with him kept the friendship from collapsing. The competition between the two was intense, Bob always being the superior. Bob was jealous and threatened to beat up the patient and any other boy he might go with, and he shamed him out of friendly association with little girls. The point here is not to present an analysis of the relationship, but only to show that, whatever the emotional components, it was so strong and penetrating (it lasted from age three to about age thirteen) that now in adulthood all associations led back to it and it provided the key to all the symptoms. So intense was it, in all its complexity, that only the stability, love, and understanding of the patient's parents prevented the young man from having a breakdown. By contrast, other patients never develop such intense relationships. Either they were given enough emotional support from others to develop defenses against them, or they were never subjected to such extreme closeness to any one person, whether parent, sibling, friend, or anyone else, that they were emotionally engulfed to this degree. The excessive involvement during childhood, like emotional distance, can seriously impair normal, enjoyable ease and closeness to others in adult life.

The patient's attitudes in describing the earliest years, his "feel" about the period that he cannot even remember, is a guide to whether that period was pleasant or otherwise. In addition, there are specific cultural factors that should be noted, since the analyst is apt to see persons of different national, racial, and socio-economic backgrounds. In evaluating the patient's motivations, these factors must be neither neglected nor overvalued, but given their proper weight.

Medical history

A medical history is obviously necessary and revealing. Enough is now known about many symptoms, both physical and psychological, for the symptom itself to be at least suggestive of some aspect of the dynamics. A thorough medical history of all physical symptoms is not only a safeguard (relative to organic illness) for the psychiatrist but also affords important clues to the emotional dynamics. It is essential for every patient. Knowledge of psychosomatic medicine provides a biologic grasp of emotional reaction which is perhaps not otherwise obtainable.

CONSCIOUS EMOTIONAL ATTITUDES

The conscious emotional attitudes are obtained by conscientiously asking the patient for them. The analyst, instead of plunging the patient into free associating and himself into a position of passively waiting, can get many essentials of attitude and feelings initially by simply asking.

Feelings toward others and himself

We are interested in his feelings toward others and toward himself, currently and for the periods from age zero to about six and thereafter. One ounce of feeling is worth many pounds of cold external facts.

Opinion of himself

It is especially important to ask the patient for his own opinion and understanding of himself and of his complaints. It is he who has lived with these and is suffering with them, so that he is apt to have observations that are of value to the interviewer.

View of the future

Also illuminating is the patient's view of the future, his expectations, ambitions, fears, and the like.

Mental status

The routine mental status as used for borderline and psychotic patients is usually not practicable as such with the majority of patients seen in a private, ambulatory practice. Nevertheless, even here, it is well to have it in mind and to adapt it as needed.

Major motivations.

Since the analyst works with the major motivational forces in the patient, obviously, it is important and revealing to include these in the history. This must be done with skill and tact. The patient will be relatively conscious of some of these emotional forces and will have some awareness of their operation. Of other forces he will have only a dim glimmering; of others, and of the processes connected with them, he will be unconscious. The therapist should form an idea of all this during the history-taking and not wait many hours to learn what the patient could have told in the first interview.

In reviewing these major forces, Freud's original horizontal description of libidinal levels may be followed. Or, you may prefer to think more in accord with his later more vertical description of these forces as they "persist side by side with, and behind, later organizations and obtain permanent representation in the economy of the libido and in the character of the individual" (Freud, 1933). Such a presentation of the major forces in the mind follows. I have attempted this after a systematic evaluation of the major dynamics of each of a series of analysands over a ten-year period (Saul, 1971). The forces observed in this way correspond to the libidinal levels but, following Freud's statement, are presented side by side, the presence of one drive not excluding another. It is probably a matter of personal choice at the stage of history-taking. The important point is to cover each major motivation explicitly:

1. No doubt a sexual history is taken by every analyst, since Freud made his first observation in this sphere of the human emotional life.

2. One great force underlying neurosis is dependence. In *An Outline of Psychoanalysis,* Freud repeatedly attributed the human propensity to emotional disorders to the long years of dependence on the parents. Hence, the history should cover, as explicitly as is psychologically indicated, the interplay between the forces toward dependence and those toward independence.

3. The same applies to the patient's needs for love (oral and otherwise) and to his receptivity and demands as

opposed to his capacity for giving energy, love, interest, and sympathetic understanding to others.

4. Also vital are the feelings of inferiority and their sources. Certainly not to be neglected is the egotism, the narcissism, and the competitiveness toward parents and siblings and their derived figures.

5. Usually, the superego situation can also be tactfully explored—the kind of training and how the patient adapted to it, the state of shame and guilt, the kinds of imagoes the patient has. This, as noted above, is of immeasurable importance for prognosis as to the course of the tranference, the treatment, and the final outcome. For example, as noted above, a person with almost no good imagoes is apt to require long and difficult treatment, often with risks.

6. That the hostile motivations are as important as the libidinal ones was recognized by Freud in his later publications, such as *Civilization and Its Discontents.* The history of the patient's hostility is as indispensable as the various aspects of the libidinal history. Asking the patient about his temper, his anger, his resentments from earliest childhood to the present time usually is most rewarding in that it brings out highly significant material. Freud's grouping of drives and impulses as erotic and destructive is eminently useful in history-taking and in clinical thinking.

7. Flight mechanisms, including regressive trends, should be explored. One of the most basic biologic reactions for meeting life is the fight-flight response. Hostility is one direction of this and flight is the other. Psychological flight takes many forms, the best-known analytically being return to earlier, more or less fixated patterns. This will overlap somewhat with previous topics.

8. For neurotic symptoms to be present, the nuclear emotional pattern must have been warped to some extent by injurious influences during childhood. We seek the nature of these traumatic influences and their effects on the core of the patient's dynamics. The success of analytic treatment will depend very largely on the understanding of this infor-

mation since the essence of psychoanalytic treatment lies in correcting these after-effects. This is the case whether one calls the process of deconditioning and reconditioning after-education and correction of parental blunders (Freud) or corrective emotional experience (Alexander).

Needless to say, all of the motivational forces covered in the history are not on the same level, as is pointed out above. They are not discrete nor even all strictly comparable, but they are empirically derived and cover, it seems, the major motivations of the personality. How far each can be gone into in these first hours depends on the patient and on the skill, the judgment, and the tact of the interviewer. They should be in the analyst's mind and not neglected in taking the initial history even though it is quite correct to think that not all will emerge by the one hundredth or even the two hundredth hour. The perspective obtainable in the first interview, if once missed, is usually never again so clearly attainable, except possibly long after the analysis.

9. Throughout the history-taking, the interviewer does well to notice explicitly the ego functions, the ego's relation to id and superego forces, its sensitivity, most prominent defense mechanisms, grasp of reality, aesthetic and intellectual capacities, judgment, will, strength, and so on.

The positives

Psychoanalysis developed, as Freud stated, from a study of symptoms. It has progressed from study of the repressed to understanding of the repressing forces. Through investigations of the pathologic it has begun to learn the nature of the healthy (Saul, 1971). To understand the positives in the patient is as essential for a true view of his total personality as is an understanding of his problems. The positives have a direct and vital influence on the prognosis as well as on the goals and even the nature of treatment. An artist may be far better off with less analysis and with leaving untouched those forces that do not interfere with his art but which might indeed be the wellsprings of it. Any condescension in the feeling of the analyst toward patients can only impair analytic understanding and treatment. The hopeless epileptic or the gambler with a disordered family life yet may have the most superior potentialities in other ways. An excellent example of this can be seen in Freud's (1928) discussion of Dostoevsky and parricide. No matter how deep the analyst may go in understanding and treatment, he will not do a proper job if he does not evaluate quickly and accurately the ego in all its functions. Successful analysis is possible only with a clear view of the total personality, its resources as well as its problems, as it interacts with other persons and with the total environment.

UNCONSCIOUS ASSOCIATIVE DATA

The unconscious associative material makes use of much that has gone before, using everything that can provide insight to the interviewer. It also includes at least the following.

Memories

It is always important to get to the patient's earliest memories, the very first one, and one or two or more others, if possible. These are most revealing, since the adult personality retains only those which fit it, distorting them if need be (Saul, Snyder, and Sheppard, 1956). Unconscious associative data also includes the first part of the content of the continuous memory.

Dreams

As far as this material is concerned, the interviewer needs to gain information about (1) the first and earliest childhood dreams; (2) repetitive dreams in childhood and later; (3) common types of dreams throughout life and currently; and (4) some current dreams. (5) Of special significance here is the dream of the night preceding the interview and/or the night after the appointment was made. This one is usually very revealing in regard to the patient's whole attitude toward his illness and toward treatment and the therapist.*

Conscious fantasies and daydreams

Childhood, current, and repetitive fantasies are filled with vitally important clues, but it is not always possible to get this data in the first interview. The patient may have reservations about revealing some of his daydreams at once. Should this reticence occur, frequently success will reward gentle persistence and repeating the request later in the interview, if this can be done without awakening too much anxiety.

Personal style

The patient's facial expression, voice, mode of dress, posture, carriage, mannerisms, and the like are clues that should not be missed by the analyst when taking the history.

Transference

This includes clues from the material expressed by the patient, not only as to how the transference *will* develop, but also observation of what his attitudes, conscious and unconscious, *are* toward the analyst from the very beginning of the contract. This is very important for the purpose of understanding the patient's current motivations. For example, one patient very evidently uses the first diagnostic interview as a confessional and a plea to relieve his feelings of guilt; another, with very strong dependent needs, makes the termination of the interview difficult with his intense needs to prolong it.

---

*For further discussion of dreams, see Saul, L., Snyder, T., and Sheppard, E. (1956), A guide to the understanding of dreams and other unconscious material (a report of the panel on the dream in the practice of psychoanalysis), *J.Am. Psychoanalyt.A.*, 4:125–127.

Associations

Everything the patient says can also be reviewed as though it were associations. Of course, it is not adequate associative material because it is given in response to specific questions by the interviewer and, as such, is not free. Nevertheless, all the verbalizations are, at least in part, associations to the questions and often contain passages which, treated as associations, are revealing. It is well to be assured of such passages by letting the patient ramble a bit several times during the interview.

Countertransference

The countertransference, as has been recognized, is usually an excellent guide in understanding the patient. For example, the analyst may react with feelings that he considers to be too strong within himself, and how he reacts is a clue to what motivations in the patient are evoking this. Things may look well, but the analyst may feel anxious; or they may look alarming, but the analyst feels easy about them. These are all useful accessory guides.

NONINTERVIEW MATERIAL

SUPPLEMENTARY DATA

The patient's family

Although the focus in analytic therapy is rightly on the patient himself, yet there are no completely rigid rules about seeing the relatives concerned. In some cases there is a great advantage in meeting them. Often it does not hinder treatment, and in fact is very useful to see the spouse. It is often especially necessary to consider the relatives when treating not only children but adolescents and postadolescents, for example, college students. Young people of this age group usually are not earning money for themselves and cannot finance the treatment. Moreover, their parents still have a strong interest in them as children, and, in reality, these young people are not yet out on their own. It is not infrequently of benefit to such a person for the analyst to meet one or both of the parents. Then the parents do not feel as though they are being pushed out or excluded, as though their child were now confiding solely in the psychiatrist while they are being relegated to the status of merely bill payers. This may also help to relieve anxiety, guilt, and shame in the patient for being in treatment.

Social service data

Social service data becomes increasingly important as analysts more and more undertake the treatment of seriously disturbed patients. Today many a patient is treated in the analyst's office who twenty years ago would doubtless have been quickly institutionalized. Since the patient can be understood only as an individual operating in and interacting with his environment, parts of this environment must be the concern of the analyst. The one basic rule is to understand the patient so that the analyst knows what he is doing. Indeed, just as electric convulsive treatment, when used on the basis of thorough psychodynamic understanding, can be considered to be an adjunct to psychoanalytic treatment, so too can outside data, if needed, be considered to be an adjunct to the psychoanalytic diagnostic interview. For example, when the dynamics of a neurotic depressive or passive regressive reaction are well analyzed for a long period without improvement or even with a negative therapeutic response, then, in selected cases, a few shocks may serve to bring relief. The same applies to the analyst's consideration of using drugs in the treatment of certain patients.

Psychological and other special tests

Psychological tests such as the Rorschach, the Thematic-Apperception, and others are used by some analysts to obtain supplementary insight. The patient's intelligence is usually evident from the history, but intelligence, reading, and other special tests may be indicated.

Needless to say, the above suggested outline for a psychoanalytic diagnostic interview is meant only as a guide. Its chief use lies in helping the interviewer to have clearly in mind the essential points that need to be covered. How it is used is a matter of the analyst's knowledge, experience, skill, and art; and it is a matter of tact. If the patient is antagonized or does not have confidence in the psychiatrist, the task of rapidly understanding him becomes very difficult. One of the key points to remember in interviewing is making certain that the experience is no threat to the patient. The art of interviewing lies in not making him feel that he is forced to reveal anything, in not offending him but rather in giving him a sense of the therapist's sympathy, understanding, and potential helpfulness. The only way to achieve this properly is, of course, for the physician actually to feel sincerely sympathetic and understanding. What the data that he obtains mean to the interviewer and what use he can make of them depend on his own capacity for understanding.

The great goal is to try to understand the essential dynamics of the total personality in one single interview if possible (Alexander and French, 1946). If not, then in as few as possible. For many years I have made formulations of the central dynamics after the first interview or first few interviews, and my experience has been that the dynamics as understood in these very first hours are usually borne out by the long-range analysis. Naturally, in the full analysis, many more facts appear and new light is shed in many areas. And, it might turn out that quantitative differences in the emphasis and in the strength of various emotional forces may be unlike what was formulated originally. It is extremely rewarding to make these initial formulations in every case, then to repeat them after perhaps six months of analytic work, at the end of the analysis, and again a year or more after treatment has terminated. At these times usually it can be done in open discussion with the patient.

The better the patient is understood at the outset, the more the analyst and the patient work in the light and with a perspective that is hard to achieve thereafter once the transference conflicts develop. Moreover, the first interview usually unfolds like a powerful short story—the various clues accumulate and develop to a climactic revelation of the essential motivations of the personality and of the emotional problem. This climactic burst of insight is usually highly therapeutic for the patient and confirmatory for the analyst's impression. It usually clinches the patient's interest in analytic treatment, and it provides a kind of illumination and perspective that are probably attainable in no other way.

Of course, all interviews, both diagnostic and therapeutic proceed in an atmosphere of absolute confidentiality. The whole basis of understanding and of treatment is emotional honesty. The analyst requires of the patient entire frankness, for this is essential to his method of helping him; the analyst cannot ask this unless he provides the conditions for it, namely, utter confidentiality. This, as we shall remark later (see Chap. 8), should be mutual, because the analyst must be equally honest with the patient within the limits of the technique and because the patient may talk indiscreetly as a form of acting out that which is injurious to his progress. Possibly the patient has some slight latitude, but certainly the analyst has none. The analyst will convey this by the very atmosphere that he creates and will make it explicit as soon as he can do so appropriately.*

---

*For further discussion of the diagnostic interview, consult the reference materials listed at the end of this chapter for the following authors: Appeland Strecker (1936); Deutsch (1939); the Diagnostic and Statistical Manual (1952); Gill, Newman and Redlich, (1954); Preu (1943); and Whitehorn (1944).

SUMMARY

To master the analytic technique and to achieve therapeutic results that are rational and scientifically based, the analyst first must be able to penetrate diagnostically to the major traumatic influences and the effects of these so that he knows from the outset what is wrong and what he intends to try to correct. Psychoanalysis is analogous to major surgery.

OUTLINE

A psychoanalytic history form can be a valuable guide in penetrating quickly and surely to the essentials in each patient—his total personality with his assets as well as his problems—as he functions in his environment.

I. Interview Material

A. Anamnestic Data

1. Chief complaints; current life situation with emotional involvements.
2. Habits; routine; a typical twenty-four day.
3. Onset and course of complaints and symptoms.
4. Emotional interrelationships; birth to about six, six to ten, and adolescence to maturity; nature of period from conception to birth.
5. Medical history; symptoms, psychological and physical, themselves often revealing.

B. Conscious Emotional Attitudes

1. Attitudes toward others, past (especially during earliest years) and present.
2. Attitudes toward and understanding of himself, his symptoms, and his problems.
3. View of the future, expectations, ambitions, etc.
4. The routine mental status when indicated and modified as advisable.

5. Major forces in the personality (categories which are not all on the same level and involve some overlap).

   a. Sexuality, affectional and sensual.
   b. Dependence and independence.
   c. Needs for love and object-interest.
   d. Inferiority feelings, egotism, narcissism, competitiveness toward parents and siblings and toward parent and sibling figures.
   e. Superego—shame and guilt—imagoes.
   f. Hostility.
   g. Flight mechanisms, including regressive trends.
   h. The nuclear emotional constellation; the childhood motivational pattern at the core of the personality which is a fundamental that the interviewer is trying to understand.
   i. Ego functions and interrelations with id and superego, grasp of reality, prominent defense mechanisms, aesthetic and intellectual capacities, judgment, will, and strengths.

6. The positives. A perspective on not only the crucial psychodynamics underlying the patient's problems but also on his assets, capacities, talents, and potentialities.

C. Unconscious Associative Material

1. Memories.
   a. Earliest; very earliest; plus others available.
   b. First part of continuous memory.
2. Dreams.
   a. From earliest childhood.
   b. Repetitive, in childhood and later.
   c. Common types of dreams throughout life and currently.
   d. Some current dreams
   e. Dreams of the night preceding the interview

and of the night after the appointment was made.

3. Conscious fantasies and daydreams—past, present, and long-continued ones.

4. Facial expressions, mode of dress, mannerisms, etc.

5. Transference.

6. The whole course of the interview can be surveyed as though it were associations for drift and main themes.

7. Countertransference.

II. Noninterview Material

A. Supplementary Data.

1. Interviews with relatives and others if indicated.

2. Social service information when indicated.

3. Psychological tests if needed.

REFERENCES AND SOME RELATED READINGS

Alexander, F., and French, T. (1946), *Psychoanalytic Therapy: Principles and Application.* New York: Ronald.

Appel, K. E., and Strecker, E. A. (1936), *Practical Examination of Personality and Behavior Disorders.* New York: Macmillan.

Cantor, M. B. (1957), The initial interview, pt. 1. *Am. J. Psychoanal.,* 17:39–44.

Deutsch, F. (1939), The associative anamnesis. *Psychoanal. Quart.,* 8:354.

Diagnostic and Statistical Manual: Mental Disorders (1952). Washington, D.C.: Am. Psychiat. A.

Freud, A. (1971), *The Writings of Anna Freud,* vol. 7. New York: Internat. Univ. Press.

——— (1937), *Ego and the Mechanisms of Defense,* 1-3. London: Hogarth Press.

Freud, S. (1940), *An Outline of Psychoanalysis,* 67; 16; 85; 88. New York: Norton.
——— (1933), *New Introductory Lectures on Psychoanalysis,* 137. New York: Norton.
——— (1930), *Civilization and Its Discontents.* London: Hogarth Press.
——— (1928), Dostoevsky and parricide. In *Collected Papers,* 5:222–242. London: Hogarth Press, 1950.
——— (1900), *The Interpretation of Dreams,* 570. London: Allen & Unwin, 1933.
Gill, M., Newman, R., and Redlich, F. (1954), *The Initial Interview in Psychiatric Practice.* New York: Internat. Univ. Press.
Maugham, S. (1943), *Introduction of Modern English and American Literature,* 424. Philadelphia: Blackiston.
Menninger, K. (1952), *A Manual for Psychiatric Case Study.* New York: Grune & Stratton.
Novey, S. (1968), *The Second Look, The Reconstruction of Personal History in Psychiatry and Psychoanalysis.* Baltimore, Md.: Johns Hopkins Press.
Preu, P. W. (1943), *Outlines of Psychiatric Case Study,* 2nd ed. New York: Hoeber.
Saul, L. (1971), *Emotional Maturity,* 3rd ed. Philadelphia: Lippincott.
——— (1940), Utilization of early current dreams in formulating psychoanalytic cases. *Psychoanal. Quart.,* 9:453–469.
Saul, L., Snyder, T., and Sheppard, E. (1956), On earliest memories. *Psychoanal. Quart.,* 25:228–237.
Thompson, W. (1957), Influences on prenatal maternal anxiety or emotionality in young rats. *Science,* 125:698.
Whitehorn, J. C. (1944), Guide to interviewing and clinical personality study. *Arch. Neurol. & Psychiat.,* 52:197.

6 / THE FIRST INTERVIEW

There are roughly five main hurdles in the course of phychoanalytic treatment. First, there is the difficulty in understanding the patient's nuclear emotional constellation, the main elements of the formula for his problem, be it simple or complex. A second hurdle involves getting the patient to understand these central dynamics. Third, there is the difficulty in perceiving the chief emotions toward the analyst that are difficult for the patient. Fourth, there is the problem of getting the patient to see these main transference difficulties. The fifth main obstacle has to do with the patient becoming able to live through these intense emotions toward the analyst and to understand and learn to handle them. Once these main hurdles are met, both patient and analyst can feel that the major difficulties are over and only working through remains.

Diagnostically, in the first interview or so, the analyst is concentrated unswervingly on understanding the patient and is interested only secondarily in descriptive diagnostic classification. He never will reason, "This patient is schizoid; therefore, analytic treatment is contraindicated." Instead, he will steadfastly endeavor to understand the patient and his major dynamics. Therefore, his reasoning would go something like this: Is he so withdrawn and schizoid because of guilt for hostility to a wife on whom he is excessively dependent? What pattern do these dynamics repeat—rage against a mother who permitted no expression of anger and took to bed whenever she was needed most so that the child was enraged at being alone but could not express it for fear of estranging his mother still further and making himself even more alone? What is the present pattern that needs to be corrected? What is its history? How deep-seated is it? How long has it incapacitated the patient? Is the masochism not so sinister, and is there enough healthy ego to work with to provide a reasonable chance of correcting the pathologic dynamics?

If the analyst understands the dynamics (including always the ego, its functioning and strength), then he forms an idea of what is wrong and what is needed to correct this. Then he can proceed to the practical questions of how this can best be achieved in view of the patient's proximity to analysts, financial status, time available, and so on, and what the first choices of the analyst would be. In summary, the steps are (1) understanding the problem (dynamic diagnosis); (2) formulating what is needed to correct it; (3) deciding how best to achieve this; and (4) considering who is the best therapist for this particular problem and person.

Often the patient complains only about one or more symptoms, but the analyst must inquire about others while he searches beneath them for the underlying causal dynamics, the emotional forces that are making the trouble. What the patient complains about is only symptomatic and therefore, however important, of only secondary interest. Analgously, it may be central to the patient that he has fever, nausea, and pain, but these are secondary to the surgeon because they are only symptomatic of the underlying physiologic dynamics, the inflamed appendix or whatever is the pathology that must be treated. The student of psychoanalysis must learn, as in physical diagnosis, when he has adequate information to understand the patient. And, if he needs more, he must be able to formulate some idea of what he wants to know.

Some disturbances are more reactive than they first seem, especially those that are widespread sociologically. Take a businessman, a physician, a lawyer, or anyone who is, let us say, irritable, a bit depressed and anxious, difficult with his family, and suffering from insomnia, ulcers, headaches, and perhaps a phobia or two. Sometimes the chief complaint is real anxious depression which threatens the patient's ability to carry on. The man works himself beyond his physical and emotional means. The dynamics reveal the greediness, the pride, the competitiveness, the masochism, and so on, which make him drive himself. Yet, he does so largely because of the sociologic factor, the setting in which all his colleagues and competitors also overwork. It is undoubtedly true that he might be very different, without benefit of psychoanalysis, if only he dwelt in a part of the world where prestige attached to leisure.

As in other medical specialties, the underlying condition is sometimes readily evident while at other times it is obscure. Here too, the student must learn when the opaqueness is in himself and when it is in the patient. And he must learn every skill and trick of the trade. For example, when the patient reports the onset of anxiety as having occurred fourteen months previously, the analyst will not usually ask at once what was then transpiring in the patient's life; instead he will carefully get the patient's story, keeping his own mind alert as to what might have precipitated the anxiety at that time.

The student will also learn when he should persevere and doggedly continue to hunt for the dynamics and when this will be futile or generate resistance or even be downright dangerous. I once saw a very schizoid young woman who had made a suicidal attempt. During treatment, however, the rapport seemed good enough for me to think that the risks of not bringing the morbid motivations into the open were greater than the risks of insistent exploration. It took two solid hours of ceaseless effort before a clue finally appeared—this interesting and brilliant girl had been reared in social and psychological isolation, alone with her mother, without playmates, on a remote farm. While only a clue, the young woman experienced some immediate relief, for she now felt for the first time that her suffering sprang from intelligible, treatable sources, dimly as we could then discern them.

In rare instances not even a clue is forthcoming. For example, I saw a boy who was so blandly pleasant that no real underlying forces could be perceived to account for his symptom, which happened to be stuttering. However, his mother gave a story of his childhood that revealed the main issues. Apparently, her restrictiveness, domination, and carping so enraged the child that the most extreme obscenities and profanities against her sprang to his lips. The stuttering began as he struggled to check them. This understanding became an effective catalyst for the analysis. (This is not meant to imply that all stuttering is psychogenic.)

Once, when treating an adolescent girl, a long interview with the mother revealed nothing to account for the child's condition, and there was no doubt whatever of the sincerity and the psychological percipience of this cultured and intelligent woman. I insisted that because the disorder was so schizoid it must be the result of injurious influences in the girl's very early years, probably well before the age of three and possibly even before two. The mother was equally insistent that only good feelings had ever existed in the family, which was an unusually harmonious one. Finally, I asked about other possible persons. She told of a nurse who cared for the child from birth until the age of two and a half. It was the familiar story of the nurse, recommended for her efficiency, whose cruelty is so subtle that it is barely even noticed except in retrospect when its true magnitude is horrifyingly grasped.

Everything depends on the dynamics, the current balance of forces in the person, including his ego strengths and weaknesses, and on how deep-seated these are, how ingrained, how early, and how thoroughly the injurious influences conditioned the growing infant and child.

The symptoms and the descriptive diagnosis are by no means without value prognostically, but only as guides to be used with care. This is especially true now that psychoanalysis is becoming a more accurate and flexible procedure. Freud once believed the psychoses to be utterly out of reach of analytic therapy; nor was the outlook at all encouraging for the neurotic character, the homosexual, the exhibitionist, the ambulatory schizophrenic, the depressed patient, and the person with a psychosomatic symptom such as, for example, high blood pressure. But, in recent years, experience has shown that if the patients are selected on the basis of accurate dynamic understanding, and if the therapy is conducted with skill and precision, very favorable results can be obtained even with symptoms and conditions like these. We have already noted that today many a person is in analytic treatment who twenty years ago would have been placed in an institution. It is not even unusual any more to treat persons who are psychotic enough to be hallucinating. Some even continue to carry on their lives, often on a high level and as pillars of the community.

Requisites for analyzability have broadened greatly over the years as understanding of the patient and the process has expanded. The age of forty used to be considered somewhat advanced for a person to enter psychoanalytic treatment. However, my experience would seem to indicate that I have been of thoroughgoing help to men and women in their sixties, and I am quite certain that other analysts can say the same. No blanket rule applies. It is a matter of considering first of all, the patient's life expectancy, flexibility, particular problem, kind of ego, and balance of forces. Then it is a question of estimating the probable duration and intensity of the experience for him. If an elderly person has based his living largely on illusions about himself, an analyst would undoubtedly hesitate to disturb these. If the problem is largely reactive to illness, aging, or external stresses, it may be that much can be accomplished without very great investment, while still dealing with the main motivations.

Similar comments can be made about intelligence, physical condition, and other qualifications. For the most part, the analyst will get the answers from understanding the patient as well as possible in the first interviews and during the trial period. Decision may be difficult in certain cases of peptic ulcer, colitis, coronary symptoms, hypertension, and similar conditions. These are especially problematic when the analyst is sure that emotional tensions are important factors in causing them. The analyst may know that he can help to diminish these tensions but fears what may result if they increase for even a brief time in the course of the treatment. The risk is not dissimilar to that encountered in treating borderline psychoses or patients with serious suicidal trends or other kinds of dangerous acting out. Of course, in cases involving patients with physical conditions the analyst will rely on the medical specialists and probably will arrange to be in regular communication with the physician in charge of the patient. All medical treatment, of course, should be left to the appropriate physician in order to keep the transference to the analyst free of any such extraneous participation by the analyst.

Obviously, the patient's motivations for treatment, his "therapeutic urge," are important for the prognosis. They are part of the main issue—the total balance of forces—and as such they are significant for the whole dynamics of analytic therapy. In the foreground there is usually a conscious wish for release from suffering. Therefore, painful symptoms (such as acute anxiety, headaches, depression, or self-defeatism) are apt to stimulate the therapeutic urge more than a pleasurable symptom (such as promiscuity or overeating). There may also be the entirely justified expectation of more satisfaction from life as a result of treatment. And, more or less unconsciously, the wish for the analyst's approval can be a powerful motive.

The forces of development toward maturity impel the patient toward cure. If a person sees that mature attitudes will help win the love, the security, the inner peace, and the satisfactions that he wants, then he has added impetus to mature. Sometimes the demands are so great that satisfaction can be achieved only if they are reduced, and the patient will accept this if he sees the real possibility of a half a loaf of real gratification in life instead of a whole loaf in fantasy only. One man grew into a high degree of independence as he realized that his dependence on his wife and others actually yielded him only insecurity, frustration, and depression. Sometimes the need can be satisfied by changing its form. For example, this might be done by sublimation. One patient reduced his demands for direct emotional support and satisfied his revised expectations quite well through membership in social and professional organizations, which gave him a sense of belonging. The problem of living is largely how to enjoy the present realities rather than pine in constant frustration for potentialities.

Some patients themselves do not know what they mean or want when they ask for help. And some want it for quite neurotic reasons, as did one young man who wanted help with a speech inhibition in order to lead women on only to then turn around and tell them off. The analyst needs to assess what help and cure mean to the patient as well as his motivations for wanting these.

Having concluded that the patient is treatable, some questions still remain. Should everyone be taken for treatment, and should this treatment be psychoanalytic? Perhaps in theory the answer is yes, but in actuality there may be reservations. One view is that if a patient wants help, this shows that he can in fact be helped. This is true, I think, only to a degree, for some patients come for help who are not really helpable; analytic treatment is by no means universally successful. When a patient comes, the analyst never shuts the door to him but deals with the problem in some way, always trying first to understand him and from this deduce what treatment might help, how to obtain this, and from whom it should come. Every patient may be dealt with, but what is needed may not be psychoanalysis. As a simple example, many of the derelicts who come to clinics, psychiatric or otherwise, want the warmth of the building in winter and the air-conditioning in summer, the attention of the doctor and the nurse, and the actual little pills, no matter what they are. These men and women settle for this emotional support and could not be analyzed out of it.

At present, psychoanalysis is a luxury item. There are not nearly enough analysts, there being, at this writing, 1,287 members of the American Psychoanalytic Association and 562 members of the American Academy of Psychoanalysis. Most of the established analysts seem to have waiting lists, and it is not long before the beginners do too. Hence, the analyst must consider whether he should be selective in choosing patients, for here he has a serious responsibility to his patients and to society. There can never be enough analysts, and, as I pointed out in an earlier book, *The Hostile Mind,* the only hope lies in using our knowledge for prevention.

Obviously, it is only fair to the individual patient not to undertake his treatment unless the analyst is convinced that what the patient will derive from the work will much more than compensate for the sacrifices of money, time, and possible upset. From the first interview, the analyst has responsibility for the patient's unconscious. He must, let us say, protect the patient against the patient's own masochism and, for example, not allow him to sink long-accumulated savings into years of five-day-a-week analysis when the prognosis is dubious. Long-continued analysis does not help every patient. Negative therapeutic reactions, wherein the patient gets worse, not better, are well known and may last for years, in the course of which the patient sinks thousands of dollars into the attempt. Although not always avoidable, these tragedies are on the heads of those who have any motivations except the sole good of the patient.

For an analyst to sink limitless hours into work with an aged, dissolute roué, when he could spend them helping, say, a father or a mother on whom a whole family depends, or a physician, or a key man in a business, or a fine artist, or a whole series of youngsters with their lives before them, is patently wasteful in terms of his obligations. It would seem evident that the responsible analyst, to some extent at least, will select his patients so as to make the maximum contribution to human welfare. If he sets a proper fee for the patient and then doesn't give it any more thought and instead devotes his full interest and technical professional skills to the job of seeing to the patient's welfare, then he will have a secure income. It might not be quite so large as if his sole aim were to line his pocket, but what is more important and beyond any doubt, he will have a better life and will help to make better lives for others.

The analyst, because he deals professionally with the wellsprings of human living, has a very special responsibility, even beyond that of other medical specialists, not only toward his patients but also toward society. He is a parent image to his patients, who tend to model themselves upon him, after the child's imitation of its parents. He must be worthy in his professional and personal life of being a parent image to society as well, and, as a good and mature parent, he must devote his major energies responsibly and productively to human welfare.

Our society is neurotically sick, rife with crime, poverty, alcoholism, broken homes, prejudice, hate, wars, and ceaseless threats of impending calamity. The basic reason is that the characteristics of the individuals are reflected in the society. Or, to put it differently, it would seem that because of their warped infantile patterns (neuroses), adults, lacking enough true love, enough real mature object-interest, even for their own spouses and children, certainly do not seem to have enough for other persons and for society. Capacity for love must extend beyond one's immediate family, for that is the very basis of human relations and of social organization. If the analyst helps his patient to mature, then he is helping him toward this social end. And it should be clear, if he is to help the patient to it, the analyst himself must have achieved an attitude of social responsibility.

This raises the topic of the choice of analyst. It has been maintained that all good analysts do the same thing. This, however, is hard to establish. In the first place, how do we know that an analyst is good? National and international reputation is a poor guide, especially because it can be acquired by politicians, as in other professional fields. Perhaps, if the vogue spreads, recordings of interviews may be possible so that other analysts can hear what actually goes on in the sessions; it is chiefly secrecy and discretion that are the problems in the way of this highly important educational device.

Apart from not knowing precisely what the analyst actually does in the hours with his patients, the whole field is far from standardized. If you were to try the experiment of having the anamnesis and an analytic session reported blind to four analysts, you would see considerable differences in their approaches. Agreement in this young field will be reached in a scientific and healthy fashion only out of mutual free discussion. In the past fifteen years I have seen more than fifty patients in consultation for other analysts, and well over half of my practice has come to consist of patients who have been in treatment, usually intensive and prolonged, with other analysts. This would seem to demonstrate that by no means do all analysts do the same thing. They have different personalities, interests, approaches, knowledge of dynamics, and countertransference feelings toward their patients. In fact, it may be that no full standardization will ever be possible. Certainly at present the choice of analyst involves some very pertinent considerations and remains of first importance. An analyst's professional as well as personal qualifications must be brought into question, for in this field these aspects of the man are not separable.

Professionally, the overinsistence on orthodoxy seems in the past to have impaired some analysts' appreciation of modern developments in the field. This lack of open-mindedness hindered their skill and experience in handling the forces of dependence and independence, inferiority feelings, hostility, maturity, ego relationships, and similar motivations.* It is not possible to help a patient analytically without mastery of these motivations, and such mastery requires an open mind. The analyst who has been so absorbed in the infantile that he does not fully understand the nature of the mature cannot possibly comprehend the process of analytic cures. Consequently, he is certainly in no position to show the patient the way out and onto the path of development.

Furthermore, the analyst probably cannot understand these forces in his professional experience if he does not grasp them in his personal life. We can only assume that if he himself has not resolved them into reasonably well-balanced mature living, then his ability to help his patients to do the same is limited. There are always exceptions, but ordinarily it would be almost impossible, with full confidence, to refer an attractive woman in her early thirties, who complains of an inhibition against marrying, to a female analyst of forty who herself never succeeded in marrying. This would apply no matter how exceedingly well the woman analyst might do with other problems. One feels easier if, in addition to the open mind, a sound sense of psychic reality, and professional ability, the analyst has solved fairly well his motivational problems and his life problems and as such represents a reasonable model of maturity and adjustment.

At least a few analysts have carefully observed the differences in the reactions of patients to themselves as compared with the reactions of these same persons to an analyst

*See quotation from Anna Freud, in footnote on page 75, concerning "the odium of analytical unorthodoxy no longer [attaching] to the study of the ego."

of the opposite sex. A patient may be seen once or several times and then be referred; or, for various reasons, a patient in analysis for some time may be seen by another analyst, either a few times or to continue treatment. In the author's experience with this, there is no doubt whatever that the sex and also the age of the analyst do make a difference in the material in many cases and might be expected to have some effect on the course and the duration of the analysis.

The reasons are usually apparent. Some patients have very sharp, fixed imagoes, while those of other patients are much broader and looser and consequently are much more easily transferred from one person to another. A bubbly woman craves attention without discrimination and rambles on, little influenced by the age, the sex, or other characteristics of the analyst. She feels as toward her good mother to whomever will listen. One man was raised in a houseful of grandparents, aunts, and uncles, in addition to his parents and siblings. He had no sharp imagoes and only loose and shifting relationships. In one analysis the patient reacts to the analyst with old patterns toward mother and father in shifting fashion so that there is never any fixed, prolonged mother or father or sibling transference. However, in another analysis the imago may be fitted to the analyst in the most immovable fashion. A young married woman had been won over by her mother against her father, whom the mother saw as so preoccupied with his books that he never provided his family with enough money for a fine home and social position. Keeping mother's love meant identifying with this attitude, and this young woman's hostilities were channeled against her father and fixated upon her imago of him. Naturally, she attached this imago to her husband and bedeviled him with the identical complaints that her mother had launched against her father. In the analysis she projected this father imago onto the analyst, and nothing could shake or soften the pattern really effectively except changing to a woman analyst. This imago, too, was so rigid that the pattern toward her mother sprang up full-blown toward the woman analyst. The patient's pattern could finally be mollified by the analyst convincing her that she could be loved by mother without hating father and that she could even work out her hostilities in the mother pattern.

Certain principles are readily evident, as these illustrations will demonstrate. A young man who never had a father with whom to identify probably would profit most from the transference experience with a male analyst. If, however, he lacked good relations with women during childhood, a woman analyst might be preferable, other things being equal. A woman who is unconsciously homosexual because of an overcloseness to her mother probably would emancipate more readily through a heterosexual transference and should be with a man. This arrangement will better provide her with the model of good relations with a man, which should help her in marrying and in marriage.

This is only to indicate that what could be deduced logically from the essentials of analytic therapy is in fact true. What carries every analysis is, as we have said, the transference, the repetition to the analyst of human relations of childhood. As part of this experience there is, more or less, an erotization and "falling in love" with the analyst. The imagoes into which the analyst is fitted, whether or not the transference is sexualized (whether hetero or homo) and to what extent, and similar considerations, are very influential on the course and the duration of the analysis and even on its outcome and the effects that it has on the rest of the patient's life.

It is necessary then, in eliciting the childhood pattern, to evaluate the characteristics of the imagoes insofar as these bear on the choice of analyst. The intensity of reaction and feeling is often critical. For therapy this should be optimal, not too weak nor too strong. A young woman had intense conflict with her mother, and the results of this affect all her other personal relations. She, of course, cannot abide the idea of a woman analyst. But this must be explored with all diagnostic care because it is very possible that if she can stand a woman initially that the analysis may go very much faster. This was indeed the case with this patient who, with a woman analyst, had her chief conflict mobolized immediately but was then denied the refuge and gratification of a man. And, for this patient, a man represented the kind but ineffectual father to whom she tried to escape.

These are basic considerations, but sometimes unforeseen details are potent. A girl of twenty was referred to a charming, sympathetic, able woman analyst of nearly forty. The girl liked her but fled and could give no reason for her compulsive, unreasonable flight. Fortunately, very shortly thereafter, her married sister came to visit, and the resemblance of this sister to the analyst was unmistakable. As discussion with the patient forthwith revealed, this was the key. Her envy of her sister was strong but deeply repressed. She went to the woman analyst unconsciously expecting a mother imago and was unconsciously shocked by the unanticipated, sudden arousal of the sibling envy through the accident of her resemblance to the older sister.

This borders on the subject of the patient's intuition in the choice of analyst. Sometimes this intuition is a result of the childhood pattern and imagoes, as in the case of an entertaining, sophisticated young lady who felt that her analyst must be a man under thirty-five or over fifty-five, and under no circumstances was he to be like her father, who was within this age range.

The intuition, however, may also represent an objectively realistic feeling about the analyst and must be considered with the greatest respect. Freud pointed out that the patient is always right, even though some translation of his meaning may be needed. This statement seems to hold for the patient's intuition also. It is not unusual to see patients who have gone to an analyst against their inner sense later bog down in treatment or otherwise rue the move. Experience probably will confirm how unwise it is to refer a patient to any analyst toward whom the patient feels serious reservations unless these reservations are explainable completely and satisfactorily to the patient on the basis of his own childhood patterns. Otherwise, it may well be something in the analyst that does not go well with this patient—some residual immaturity or pattern or imago of his own.

At the other extreme is the procedure of giving a patient a long list of names and exposing him to the ordeal of shopping for an analyst and enduring repeated rejections. The referring analyst usually can find out who has time available or, especially if the patient is in a distant city, who will see the patient and help place him properly. Even if a patient comes for only one interview, for evaluation and referral, reactions following childhood patterns can be expected. For example, the referral may be taken as being sent from one parent to another, or to a sibling, and so on. Therefore, it is well to look for this in the interview and perhaps discuss it by way of saving some wear and tear on the patient and on the receiving analyst.

If some time must intervene before the receiving analyst can begin treating the patient, then it is usually well for him to meet with the patient before the wait. The advantages of so doing, to both the patient and the analyst, are obvious. The analyst is seen more as a real person and less as an imago about whom fantastic anxieties can cluster in anticipation.

Of course, this whole matter of choice of analyst is out of necessity independent of making referrals and applies with equal impartiality to each one of us. If the patient would do better with an analyst of different age, sex, or whole background in life, then, regardless of our own wishes, he must be sent to the analyst who can best meet his particular needs.

7 / A DIAGNOSTIC INTERVIEW

The nuclear dynamics could be discerned in the first interview in, at a rough guess, 85 percent of the patients that I have seen. For the purposes of this chapter, it was necessary to select an instance in which the original notes on the initial interview were complete enough to convey a reasonably adequate description of what transpired. Furthermore, for the sake of discretion, the case to be used here had to be one from many years ago. The following notes, only slightly edited, appear as they were written. It is to be hoped that their verity compensates for their lack of literary form. It is unfortunately true that without this literary form there is lost the unfolding of dynamics from the foreshadowing hints to the dramatic impact of the denouement, the revelation of the core of motivation underlying the complaints and the whole emotional disorder. Perhaps I would handle this interview somewhat differently today than I did at the time, which was shortly before the Second World War.

"An unusually pretty girl is waiting to see you," said the telephone operator. She was right. This twenty-one year-old girl, whose name was May, smiled pleasantly but briefly as we met. She was fresh, pert, well-dressed, and somewhat silent as we entered the office. I sensed a certain distance in her, with a feeling about it that might be haughtiness, coldness, hostility, or perhaps only anxiety. What conveyed itself in the few seconds was not easy, warm rapport. However, without too much difficulty, she said that her problem was shyness, that she did not feel at ease with people, that it was difficult to describe, and that perhaps the whole thing was too trifling to tell me. Others, she said, have much worse problems. As though trying to justify her coming, she said that she was engaged to a young man, Ralph, and, therefore, all the more did she want to have an interview to see whether or not everything was really all right.

I asked her what she meant by shyness. She said that she was uneasy, especially when with many people and also when with people who mattered to her. She gave me an example, Ralph and his family. She goes to his home to dinner; he is very funny and gets much attention. She does not, she believes, compete with him but becomes silent. Yet it is the esteem of these people that she wants the most; therefore, she seems to be the most ill at ease with them.

She is also a little uneasy about the meeting of the two families. "When you plan to marry," she said, a bit acidulously, "it seems that the families have to meet each other."

She is an only child, and up to six months ago, when she came to this area, she lived with her father in a small house in the suburbs of a city in a nearby state. Her father is with a manufacturing firm. He drinks too much, sometimes having five or more at lunch, then perhaps some before dinner, and highballs after dinner. He is pouring his life down the drain. Sometimes she feels that she actually hates him.

The father and the mother are separated. The mother had a breakdown at about that time, and now she lives in a different city, nearer to the girl than the father is. The patient may go to see her mother every few weeks. Here that guarded lack of facial expression becomes evident as she goes on to say that her mother now makes a great fuss over her and tries to hug and kiss her. It is as though she tries too late to behave as she should have eighteen or twenty years ago. The girl does not resent her so much as she pities her.

Asked what she meant about making up for years ago, May says that she was turned over by her parents to nurses. Everything was all right, she said, because she liked them and they liked her. But, as she told her story, her underlying bitterness about being turned over to nurses was evident in spite of the impassive expression and tonelessness of her voice in speaking about this. Replying to my question, she said that the nurses all left and none maintained any contact with her. She has never seen them since they left. In saying this she showed no emotion, but I suspected that it was not far beneath the surface.

When she had some difficulty in describing what she meant by her shyness and expressing why she had come to see me, I said that I would help her in any way that I could and would ask questions if it made it easier for her. She seemed to respond to this offer of helpfulness and told all of the above, guided only lightly by an occasional question. I now asked what she did after the age of eleven, and she told of her schooling, of her difficulties with other students and the faculty, and of her eventual graduation from college. The details must be omitted. At present she is doing well as a secretary in a small industrial company.

We were still close to what she was saying about her childhood, so it was easy to bring up the matter of her first memories. I said that I would now ask her a rather difficult question, namely, to tell the very first things that she remembered in her whole life from even before her continuous memory. After a little reflection, she said that her very first memory was of riding in an automobile; she was seated next to her mother, and they were on their way to get Mrs. Q., who was coming to be her nurse. This must have been when May was three, because that was when Mrs. Q. came.

The next memory, she said, must have been at about the same time or very shortly afterward. She was sitting in a car outside their house and was furious at her mother for taking so long in the house and leaving her waiting alone in the car.

She also remembers a situation that repeated itself at other times in her life. She was closely attached to an older girl; then a third girl, also a little older than herself, appeared, and she, May, became enraged.

After this time, and as she grew up, she believes that she was an awful bully and frequently cruel to other children. She remembers, for example, that a girl fell and cut her nose so badly that she lay on the ground weeping in in pain while the patient and another girl stood over her making scathing remarks about her rather than offering sympathy or help.

At this time, she could not remember a dream either current or from childhood.

I now asked her if she had any idea, after telling all this, as to the reasons for her shyness and why she had come to see me. "Some lack of stability," she said, but was not able to carry this much further. I asked if she would like to try further or would like to have me put it together as I saw it. She was eager for the latter course.

Therefore, I said that I thought that perhaps her pride was hurt by her parents, by the mother with her breakdown, the father with his alcoholism, and the two with their separation, so that she did not look forward happily or securely to their meeting her fiancé's family. To this she responded quickly by saying that it did not strike her as being fundamental. With this I fully agreed and told her that I would try to point out what I thought was really fundamental. I thought that there was a basic pattern and that this showed clearly in her memories. I then reviewed these, as follows.

In the first memory she is with her mother, but her mind is on meeting the nurse. The whole scene is a sort of anticipation of being turned over by her mother to the nurse, so that this memory alone tells in one flash almost the whole story. The second memory confirms this. In this one she is openly extremely angry at her mother, and the reason for it is that the mother has left her alone while going to attend to her own affairs. Here we also see that however she feels about her mother today, there was certainly anger at that time. It probably still persists, the reason for it being the feeling that she did not get as much love and affection from her mother as she wanted and felt that she was turned over to nurses while mother did other things. This ties in with the feeling that mother now makes a great fuss over her as belated compensation for apparent neglect during her childhood.

This anger, I said, is pointed out because it, in turn, explains much that comes later, particularly the next memory. She must have had a continuous anger at her mother, and this came out toward other girls. Because of her longings for closeness to her mother, intensified by frustration, she probably transferred these longings to the older girl, developed a very close dependent attachment to her, and then became very angry when a third girl appeared and she again felt pushed out.

She was now listening with rapt attention.

This, I continued, probably is also the hostility that she described in connection with her bullying and cruelty to the girl who fell and cut her nose. Moreover, her present reaction is obviously one of shame and guilt for this bullying and cruelty.

The pattern then was that the patient felt that she was turned over to nurses by her mother and perhaps also by her father, and then the nurses themselves left and she never saw them again. What were the effects of this? We could easily imagine that one result was that she did not grow up feeling secure in being loved. Moreover, there was resentment, especially against her mother, and this was displaced to other people, particularly to the other girls mentioned in her memories. This resentment caused much guilt and shame. We know, I pointed out, that most of us tend to think that others will feel about us as we feel about ourselves and as our parents have felt about us.

To all this she had a strong emotional reaction. "This is striking," she said intensely, "but will just talking correct it?"

"No," I said agreeing with her, "just talking will not, but the kind of talking we have been doing has not been that simple; it has been a way of communicating feelings and insight. In this sense, the talking, if it gives insight, is designed to help you to be able to learn from experience so that you do not continue forever feeling about yourself as you do and then thinking that others feel the same way about you, even if they do not."

"I see what you mean," she said. "That is why I've feared I'd spoil everything in relation to Ralph and his family!"

"Precisely," I said. "Let us assume that Ralph is potentially a completely true, devoted husband and father who really loves you and that his family is similarly devoted. Then you would have to be able to accept this, although underneath, because of the pattern that we have discussed, the effects of your insecurity may make you insecure even in this situation." She nodded knowingly, and I went on to say that if she has Ralph's continuing stability and devotion, then perhaps insight alone would be enough to help her to correct her inner insecurity. However, even if she does not, it is still possible to provide this continuity in what is called the transference relationship. In this case she would see me or someone else, work out these insights, and continue the relationship over a long period so that if she felt, through a cancelled appointment or any incident, that she was rejected, she would be able to vent her anger and all her feelings. In this way she could work to correct the old pattern against the present reality, and see that she could receive continuous, long-sustained interest in her welfare, which is the essence of love.

I also pointed out that her initial anxiety about the interview was largely a fear of what I would think of her. This was similar to her fear of what others will think in that it reflects her own opinion of herself, both the insecurity about getting love and the guilt and the shame for her hostilities. If your own parents do not accept, value, and approve of you, how can you expect anyone else to? You anticipate from others the feelings from your parents.

"This is exactly it," she said, "I see what you mean for I already want to work it out. I doubted the engagement and talked about breaking it, not believing that I could really be loved and be secure. When I talk that way, I know something is wrong, and Ralph says, 'How can a girl like you be like that?' " She went on to say how she realized the truth of what we had been saying, namely, that even though she was sure of the love of Ralph and his family, yet she felt with them the same old insecurity that she had had toward her own parents and nurses. She was afraid that she would reveal it and do something to spoil everything. Therefore, she was eager for us to meet again to pursue this further.

The above interview shows in actuality the following typical features, which should be perceptible even from this brief and sketchy summary.

1. The gradual building up of insight to a climax of understanding the main issues. In this the patient discerns his or her key motivations and sees how they fit the overall picture. The sort of climax of insight that is reached in one interview rarely occurs if the insight must be achieved over several interviews, for then the continuity is lost. For this reason it is well to allow an hour and a half for the initial interview in case more time is needed.

2. The confirmation of the correctness of the initial formulation by the patient bringing new instances to confirm its truth.

3. The melting of the initial defensiveness under the effects of the growing insight. This immediately puts the

analyst in a position to interpret, if it seems to be indicated, even in the first interview, the transference resistance.

4. Also demonstrated is the fact that there is no better way to win a patient to a wish for treatment where treatment is really needed than to gain at least some insight into the central dynamics during the first interview and to discuss it tactfully with the patient.

8 / BEGINNING TREATMENT

On occasion the initial interview is also the beginning of treatment. Some patients are seen for one or for a few interviews, and then arrangements are made to go ahead with a trial of analytic treatment or else to start it at a future time, either with the interviewer or with someone else. But the analyst must ever be on guard lest the initial interview uncork such an effervescence of emotion that there is no choice except to handle it. The diagnostic probing must be light and sensitive as well as penetrating until the analyst feels sure of the balance of forces in the patient.

A college student was doing poorly in his studies and dates and sustained a sense of futility and mild depression. In the first interview he began to sense the intensity of the hostility that he felt toward his father. The man was narrow, demanding, restrictive, and overambitious for his son, who reacted with unconscious hate and impotent impulses of rebellion. At the same time, however, there is no doubt but that the father was also loving. And, ever since the mother's death, he had done his best to rear the boy and labored hard to send him to college. The boy loved and appreciated all this genuine devotion, so that as insight into his repressed rebellious hostility dawned on him, he was overwhelmed with guilt. This left the analyst no choice but to help him abreact it. In this particular instance, circumstances were such that therapeutic advantage could be taken of this eruption of emotional forces that were so pointed and so near the surface. Consequently, in the course of a few sessions the boy felt much relieved: the acute abreaction was over and the main issue was in the open. The working through could be done at relative leisure and not necessarily with the same analyst, for this was not primarily a transference phenomenon, there being no special emotional involvement with the analyst at this point.

Such an incident illustrates, besides the need to probe cautiously, the analyst's responsibility for a patient who, though he may come for what is intended to be only a diagnostic interview, may unexpectedly suffer an acute outburst. This happenstance can and should be turned to therapeutic advantage to give insight, relieve the patient, and win him or her to systematic treatment, if this is indicated.

Unusual transient acting out, as well as other symptoms or exacerbations of them, is seen not infrequently as a reaction of the patient to beginning treatment or only to his decision to begin. These reactions, some examples of which follow, must be especially guarded against when the person has had a first interview with one analyst and then is referred by him to another analyst for treatment.

A rather puritanical young woman of high standards decides to start regular treatment and thereupon allows herself to become involved in a situation, previously unheard of for her, in which she is not sure whether or not she has lost her virginity and possibly become illegitimately pregnant. She then settles down in treatment and in behavior and progresses well with no further aberrant episodes. A schizoid young man with homosexual trends makes arrangements for treatment and then, before beginning, indulges in a single, isolated, overt experience. An engaged girl suffers from rather severe anxiety because of repressed anger at her parents for their attempts to control and dictate her choice of husband. She is greatly relieved by one interview in which she sees this. Then she feels that she wants a period of systematic help and develops almost unbearable anxiety.

After a few such observations, an analyst should learn to do everything he can to forestall them with future patients. Forewarned is forearmed—and the patient too must be forewarned so far as this is possible to do without alarming him and thus precipitating what the analyst wants to avoid. The key is, as always, understanding the patient. Symptoms are defenses against feelings. The idea of being analyzed is apt to mobilize the whole childhood pattern of feelings and motivations and the defenses against these. The patient, following this pattern, often is frightened by his decision to start analytic work and seeks to escape by flight from the analyst into some other relationship. To guard against this, it should be understood and discussed so far as possible. Referring the patient, even after only a single interview, may introduce further problems. If the analyst who is first consulted is not sure that he himself can take the patient for treatment, it is usually best to let the patient know this when making the appointment. Even though this contingency is made clear to the prospective analysand, this analyst can expect the initial transference and hence a sense of rejection in the patient when he is referred. It is important to know if the referral plays into any specific emotional vulnerabilities. For example, this might well be the case in a patient who, in childhood, was turned over by mother or father to the care of relatives or nurses. Or, if a patient is referred to a younger analyst, this may be a wound to his egoism. To sum up, while concentrating on understanding the central dynamics, a weather eye must be kept open for the patient's reactions to his decision to be analyzed and to any specifics in the situation, such as referral.

The older view that the analyst (1) need not take a history, (2) need not make a dynamic diagnosis, and (3) can not know anything that is really worthwhile about his patient for one hundred or two hundred hours, reflected the state of the analytic understanding of that time. Note, for example, in Freud's penetrating report on Little Hans, how the parents' divorce is barely mentioned. Today, of course, we and he certainly would wonder if the tensions between the parents, which led up to the divorce, were not a critical factor in causing the child's phobia. Today we would follow out the lines of Freud's own progression of observation and thought and try not only to understand the main forces in the very first interview but also to communicate to the patient as much as he could tolerate of what we discern.

There are three very cogent reasons for this. First, the patient's sense that he can be and is understood usually brings satisfaction and interest. Further, if it is imparted tactfully and egosyntonically, it is one of the most potent ways of demonstrating to him the rationale and the advisability of treatment and enlisting his interest and desire for it.

Second, one of the soundest, most necessary therapeutic steps is to isolate the emotional problem, to distinguish for the patient as soon as possible what is neurotic (the disordered pattern) and what is healthy ego. The college boy mentioned before felt enormous relief and new hope when he saw that what was casting a pall over his whole life was a very specific dynamic, namely, his guilt for unconscious, unexpressed hostility toward his loving and loved father. This could be isolated, seen at a distance in perspective, and separated from the rest of his ego. As soon as it was defined and circumscribed, though not worked through or resolved, the rest of his ego was relatively freed.

Third, as the problem is discerned, so usually is the nature of its solution. The college boy became a normal person with a distressing problem—no longer a mind enveloped and engulfed by unknown forces.

For the future of the treatment, this starts the process of distinguishing between what is neurotic and what is healthy maturity, so that the patient can deal with the former and develop toward the latter.

To move rapidly and accomplish much from the first moment requires good communication between patient and analyst. Because, basically, this interaction is probably emotional, the analyst with a natural, easy capacity for warm and sensitive human relations, doubtless will understand the patient more quickly. And, the patient will respond readily to the analyst who is himself secure and keenly and genuinely interested in him. The patient, in his way, must also understand the analyst; and patient and analyst, in order to work together most effectively on the patient's problem, must understand each other in this sense.

It is not necessary here to go into much detail about the role of technical language in communicating with the patient. Usually, but not always, it is best to avoid technical terms. Sometimes, however, their coldness, remoteness, and broad meaning make them useful for touching only lightly on a sensitive topic. Psychoanalytic technical terms seem to be almost the opposite of other scientific terms in that most of them are broad and general rather than narrow, rigid, and precise. The oedipus complex, narcissism, oral and phallic levels, and other terms came into use through searching for the broad, fundamental concepts that underlie human motivation. Hence, they have very general meanings, covering many specific phenomena, which must be described concretely and exactly. It is almost meaningless to describe a person as having an oedipus complex and being narcissistic or to talk with him about his feelings in these terms without very much more precise definition and explanation. For not only does everyone have an oedipus complex and narcissism, but the form and the content, as well as the quantities differ radically from person to person.

As the patient's problem comes to light diagnostically, the patient and analyst will discuss it in its various aspects, including the direction of its solution and the undertaking of analytic treatment for it. There seems to be a natural tendency for the patient to talk freely and unreservedly and, because of this inclination, he can be eased into free associating smoothly and without delay. If, instead of recognizing and delicately following this natural tendency, the analyst bluntly demands that the patient tell everything, the patient may become anxious and resistant, and much time may be lost. Even the announcement that now or at the next visit the patient is to "free associate" is apt to awaken unnecessary anticipations and anxieties. Such an announcement suggests that a very sharp distinction exists in the character of the patient-analyst communication, and the introduction of this notion is quite disadvantageous. At all times, throughout treatment, the patient is expected to tell of his problem and his history unreservedly. The whole point being to establish an atmosphere in which all can be told. Today most people who reach this point have read or heard of the fundamental rule of free association. They can be eased into complying with it simply by letting them know that nothing that comes to mind is to go unmentioned once they begin talking.

There are no rigid rules or formulas, only guiding principles. The patient may soon run out of anamnestic material and have difficulty talking, at which point the analyst can discuss free associating. The patient may block, and the analysis can then be on its way to dealing with this resistance. Each patient is different, but usually the initial frankness can be almost imperceptibly bridged into free associating (with all the needed explanations) if the analyst watches the trend and the timing. However, it may be that in training analyses bolder discussion is indicated earlier.

The natural easing into free associating also includes the introduction of dream material. Freud became interested in dreams only because the patients brought them and often insisted on interpretations. Patients bring dreams naturally and they usually can be guided smoothly, casually, and conversationally into analyzing them without pomp or fanfare.

Of course, not all beginnings are smooth and easy. For our purposes here, I'll not catalogue the innumerable special problems but only mention two key points. First, the patient may be resistant to the interviews from the beginning, in which case it is well to discuss with him as soon as possible what bothers him. Often it is something quite conscious—he is afraid of being seen at a psychiatrist's office; he feels that it is a weakness to tell of his difficulties with his work, and, he is ashamed to do so; he thinks he should be handling his unconscious himself; he fears becoming dependent; he is guilty for expressing complaints about his wife; and so on. Much time can be saved and progress speeded by dealing with these obstructions with as little delay as possible.

Second, sometimes an individual may be resistant even before a beginning can be initiated. What of the patient who will not come for even an initial interview and yet desperately needs to begin treatment, both for himself and his dependents? Even in such a contingency it may be possible to get quite a good dynamic diagnostic and prognostic impression from the relatives. From this you may then be able to estimate the practicability of trying to initiate treatment even in the face of seemingly impenetrable initial resistance to it.

In one such situation, I went to the person's home on a Sunday, with the warning that the door might be shut in my face. It was not. After four and a half hours of discussing why this gentleman hated doctors in general and psychiatrists in particular, and its connection with how and why he was ruining himself and his family, the patient was won over to the idea of having another talk. He eventually agreed to treatment and even to referral to another analyst, since my schedule was filled at the time. He was placed with an analyst who was carefully selected to meet the needs of this patient's particular make-up and problem, and he progressed well. It is usually good to have the anxieties and the resistances come out early in treatment—if they are not so powerful as to preclude it. As always, it is a matter of optimum intensities of the forces.

Modern analytic knowledge seems to confirm thoroughly the importance of the very beginning of treatment. Today persons coming to an analyst are usually beset by double anxieties. First, there is the fact that the prospective analysand now typically knows in advance that to go for treatment involves revealing himself utterly. Second, there is the fact that in childhood there is much less distinction between awareness of an impulse and acting on it. Thus, the patient fears what he will find out about himself and about his feelings for others, and he worries about what he may become or do or what may happen to his mind if he gets to be conscious of these forces: Am I homosexual underneath? Do I really love my mate? Do I hate my children? Will I lose my drive? Will I cease to enjoy my hobbies? The patient must be helped to see that consciousness of the forces operating within him is the path to increased power of the ego over them—the very opposite of his fears that mere recognition will unleash them.

At the same time, it should be noted, there is some truth in his fears. Free associating in the presence of another person does mobilize actual feelings—passions from the id and stern reactions of the superego. Therefore, the initiation of treatment means mobilization of motivation and emotion and threats to the defenses, the automatic controls. Hence, the analyst must be alerted to struggles against dependence, to strivings to make a good impression, to hostile defensive reactions, to the arousal of guilt with masochistic tendencies, to self-punishing acting out, and so on. The violence of the reactions of human beings to each other is ceaselessly amazing.

The point here is that the beginning of treatment, and sometimes even just the prospect of beginning, is apt to catalyze a potent emotional ferment, and this must be made the most of analytically at once. It is a therapeutic opportunity that knocks loudly, and the door must be opened. You can read and hear reports by students in which the initial clarity and intensity of the material is not utilized by the analyst; he does no take the tide at the flood, and, as a result, the patient's enthusiasm wanes, his material muddies, he becomes bogged down and confused, and the whole remaining task of the analysis is immeasurably more difficult, longer, and less effective. It cannot be emphasized too strongly that the beginning of treatment is a therapeutic moment of the greatest importance. The analyst must understand this, see the interplay of aroused emotional forces, know what is going on, and make the most of this opening opportunity which, once lost, means so much more time and trouble.

We have already noted the importance of the patient's assuming, as early in treatment as possible, a sense of responsibility for himself. His utilization of the whole experience is vital so that he will not slip into feeling that so long as he follows the technique the rest is all up to the analyst. We come hereby to a few miscellaneous points but will not attempt an exhaustive survey of other relevant ones. Certain others were covered in the discussion earlier of the diagnostic interview (Chap. 5).

If the patient, although not a child, is still not financially independent, as is the case with most college and graduate students, then the parents need to be considered. Analysts almost always like to deal with the patient exclusively, and this is a sound guiding principle. However, where the parents pay the bills, they are apt to feel very much left out of everything. Again, since each case is different, there is no general rule beyond understanding all that is going on well enough to do what is best for all concerned. This often involves meeting the parents, who want to see the person who is entrusted with such influence over their son or daughter. Usually, this can be done in a way that does not disturb the analytic relationship, by enlisting the patient's understanding and permission.

To keep the analytic field as psychologically aseptic as possible, experience has validated a number of precautions, mostly covered in Freud's papers on technique. We need not discuss here those which are well-known and relatively mechanical. Again, because of the endless variety of human personalities and situations, it is always a matter of guiding principles.

In general, it is easier if the analysand and the analyst do not know each other.

Then there is the matter of a patient discussing his analysis with others. To want to talk about one's experiences in treatment is natural to many persons. However, even if it is not done as an outlet or leak or some form of acting out but only in brief response to questions, it is apt to make difficulties. Psychoanalysis deals with emotional material, and others react emotionally to any such highly charged material. Hence, experience shows that it is well for a patient not to discuss his analysis in any way with others, especially with other persons who are in analysis. This includes and perhaps even applies especially to candidates in training, since all are in analysis and are associated with each other.

The patient must be relatively naive in actual living and human relations in the sense of behaving as he feels and judges without probing every act or decision for its unconscious meanings. All the insights of analysis can and should be used, but to be preoccupied with the mechanisms of your unconscious processes or to reveal them to others almost always makes trouble in human relations. This comes up in marriages.

Marriage presents a special situation relative to analysis in that the husband or the wife often feels that the mate suddenly no longer gives exclusive confidences to him or to her but now tells all to the analyst. Of course, this "all" is rarely of any such nature, detail, or consequence as the mate or anyone else imagines, the content only serving the work of the sessions. In addition to this are all the unconscious transference reactions of both analysand and spouse. A wife often feels that she has won her husband away from his family; then, his going into analysis feels to her like his returning to his father or mother and giving confidences to them rather than to her.

Reading is sometimes a very important issue. Generally, the analysand is advised not to read at first because the analysis stirs up his feelings and is apt to distort his perspective on what he reads. And, the reading may in turn stir up material out of sequence and disturb its orderly emergence in treatment. It may also influence the patient to overintellectualizing about interpretations. However, many persons have read widely before coming for analysis.

To read or not to read is probably of considerably less importance than *how* the individual reads. Analysands sometimes read Freud, not in the spirit in which he wrote, to be sure, but rather in the emotional atmosphere of regression to childhood and submission to authority. This, of course, is encouraged by the fact of their being in analysis and developing the transference relationship to the analyst—in other words, unconsciously putting themselves in the position of the child to the parents. Hence Freud, with his enormous reputation, recognition as a renowned authority, and compelling style of writing, is, in particular, read by patients as a form of dictate and dogma rather than as a guide to the world of reality. It is essential to read with thoroughgoing scepticism and a healthy unwillingness to take anything on faith. The best approach is to use what is read as a Baedeker or a guidebook that shows the reader what to look for in himself and, in the case of the analyst, in his patients. Reality, to reiterate, is the only authority. Of course, if a young analyst in training fails to see in his patients what important authorities write about and what is described in the developments in his field, then he must also question his own capacities for observation and consider whether he has certain resistances or blocks. Naturally, these will come up in his training analysis. Nevertheless, he must never abandon his critical faculty, one of the highest functions of the ego.

Freud continually changed his views of reality. Theory and formulations can obfuscate thought and confuse simple realities as well as clarify them. A good principle is this: Don't believe anything you read; believe only what you see in reality, but use the reading as a guide to observing reality.

REFERENCES AND SOME RELATED READINGS

Ekstein, R., and Wallerstein, R. (1972), *The Teaching and Learning of Psychotherapy*. New York: Internat. Univ. Press.

Freud, S. (1922), Two encyclopaedia articles. In *Collected Papers,* 5: 107–135. London: Hogarth Press, 1950.

9 / FREE ASSOCIATION

Free association is the very heart and core of the psychoanalytic method. Freud, when he was frustrated in attempts to make patients recall certain memories directly, reversed himself with a stroke of genius and told them to tell anything they wanted to, but to omit nothing. Free association has been called simply "thinking out loud." You might assume that this method has been so mastered over the years that a chapter about it would be superfluous. But this device is curiously difficult: while so apparently uncomplicated that everyone can use it, not everyone will see the same thing or get a complete and ordered picture or be able to interpret accurately what is presented.

Each patient's daily associations are different in character—recital of the events of the day, preoccupation with historical data, manic flight of ideas, complaints about this and that, endless questions, passionate tossings on waves of emotion, rarified intellectualizations, and so on. It is a tangled and pathless psychological jungle. To thread his way, the young analyst must rely heavily on his reading and on what he has learned from his own analysis. However, both are hopelessly inadequate. No amount of theory fits the particular patient. Freud kept revising his views, and this kind of flexibility has characterized the growing body of analytic literature to the present. Because it is expanding so rapidly, it is already vast, kaleidoscopic, and rather confusing. This is healthy—a young growing field is far better kept fluid until, out of free academic discussion, testable facts and theories emerge. However, this does make the field harder to learn as it provides less solid ground

The beginner's training analysis is not a secure guide either, because it biases his view of his patients' dynamics. He cannot go through such an emotional experience himself, working with his own motivations, without this influencing his perspective on his patients. It may be a few years before his own analysis shakes down and subsides far enough so that it does not distort his capacity for well-balanced psychological vision.

Faced daily with floods of associations, with few fixed stars for guidance, the beginner is apt to grasp eagerly at anything that seems to be familiar: "Ah-hah, that sounds like homosexuality"; "There is anal material"; "That is sex, good, can't go wrong on that." In this way, disjointed fragments of associations are yanked out of the context, and as a result, the continuity of the hour and the flow of the patient's associations are disrupted and diverted. Continuing this process is a fairly certain way to produce confusion in the train of associations and in the mind of the patient. Most seriously, this way is contrary to the basic theory of obtaining the unconscious meaning from the conscious associations.

The fundamental principle that an understanding of unconscious meaning can be gained from the train of associations depends on the fact that, in Freud's words, "an internal connection which is still undisclosed will announce its presence by means of a contiguity—a temporal proximity—of associations" (Freud, 1905). Therefore, the very essence of the method lies in listening for the internal connections between the associations. To do this, the sharpest possible demarcation must be drawn between dynamics and content, between the motivating emotional forces and the ideas that the patient uses to express them. In *Delusion and Dream,* Freud put this as follows:

> We remain on the surface so long as we treat only of memories and ideas. The only valuable things in psychic life are, rather, the emotions. All psychic powers are significant only through their fitness to awaken emotions. Ideas are repressed only because they are connected with liberations of emotions which are not to come to light; it would be more correct to say that repression deals with the emotions but these are comprehensible to us only in connection with ideas.

The patient tells ideas, and through this ideational content shines the light of the underlying emotions, which dictate the ideas and their sequence. This light can be discerned by completely ignoring the content of the associations and focusing on their common elements. The undisclosed internal connection lies in what the contiguous individual associations have in common. The secret lies in the central similarity of the whole hour-long chain of associations.

The analyst listens, then, with what Freud called "evenly hovering attention"; and, this kind of concentration is to be focused on delineating the internal connection in *all* the associations. The analyst cannot fish up two or three associations because he likes them or recognizes something in the content or because he sees a connection among these few but not between them and all the other associations of the hour. The analyst should not show partiality to one association over another because it seems to be a familiar face in the crowd or for any other reason whatever, because all associations are free and equal. Freud is emphatic on the dangers involved:

> For as soon as attention is deliberately concentrated in a certain degree, one begins to select the material before one; one point will be fixed in mind with particular clearness and some others consequently disregarded, and in this selection one's expectations or one's

inclinations will be followed. This is just what must not be done, however; if one's expectations are followed in this selection, there is danger of never finding anything but what is already known, and if one follows one's inclinations, anything which is to be perceived will most certainly be falsified (Freud, 1924-1950).

First and foremost, then, the element that is common to *all* of the associations of the hour must be discerned. The analyst who has not mastered this principle simply does not know or employ the basic technique of psychoanalysis. It is inconceivable that a smooth swift effective analysis can be conducted without first gaining this foundation. Of course, this does not mean that content is of no importance. We have discussed it in connection with the diagnostic interview, relative to the patient's history, life situation, and early memories. However, it is not essential in the use of free associations. In reading the patient's unconscious, content cannot be substituted for the common element (or the red thread, the drift, the undercurrent, as it has been variously called).

The analyst listens. He hears content—ideas, facts, fantasies, history, current problems—and by no means does he ignore these. Much of this material is probably significant and revealing. For example, there may be a memory of feeling that father was always busy and mother always ill so that neither could be counted on, and this memory may give the key to the transference and to the patient's current anxieties. This is very important, but still not enough. The analyst who knows his craft will not settle for it until he also sees what the role of this content is in the whole chain of associations, of which it is but a single link. He simply cannot ask the patient to associate freely, to reveal, on the basis of contiguity, the undisclosed connection and then select what he wants and ignore this connection throughout the associations. The drift never can be ignored, for it is the essential.

At the very beginning of treatment a woman tells of a doctor who missed the correct diagnosis; of another doctor who forgot to tell her to discontinue using a certain medication; of how her father forgot to pick her up at school one day; of how her husband had to be reminded of their wedding anniversary; of a movie she saw in which a child was neglected; of a dream in which a small boat was left unpainted. The analyst listens to this content, but at the same time, in a certain sense, he disregards it. He considers what she has said only as a series of associations, each of which can be numbered one, two, three, and so on. He focuses on the emotional element that these have in common, that is, on the dynamics, regardless of the content. Focused at this level, the analyst cares not one whit whether the association is a memory, a current experience, a complaint about himself, a tall story, a motion picture, a dream (which, however, brings in other considerations), or any other form whatever. They are nothing but free associations, and, at this point, the interest is solely in the red thread, in what they have in common.

In regard to the first two associations in the above simplified example, the analyst would think of complaints and about the patient feeling abused or neglected. With only these two associations he could draw no sure conclusions. However, the third association extends the theme of neglect, now not by a doctor but by the patient's father. Association number four involves this same notion of neglect, this time directed toward the husband. In number five there is a bit of a movie, but the theme is the same. In the sixth association the patient offers a dream, but there is still the same recurring theme. Since this last association remains consistent with all the previous ones, the competent analyst will begin to judge that the main theme is the feeling of being neglected, that this is directed toward father figures, and that there is some hostile reproach against them for the neglect.

First, the analyst will isolate and define the emotional forces alone—the feelings of being neglected and the implied reproach—without reference to their objects. Second, he will note the objects, that is, the father figures. Third, he will look for the operation of these forces in (1) childhood (toward father), (2) current life situation (toward husband), and (3) transference (probably implied toward analyst in frank reference to doctors). Of course, the pattern is always operative in these three situations; it is only a matter of quantitive evaluation of prominence at the time. The basic emotional pattern is formed by the conditioning influences of early childhood and emerges in life situations and in the transference to the analyst, which is also part of the patient's life. One might call the basic dynamics of the patient the "macrodynamics" and what goes on in each hour, that is, the specific facet or edition of the basic dynamics, the "microdynamics."

Our example presents a simplification of an unusually transparent series of associations, but even in such a case the analyst must be wary of jumping in prematurely with an interpretation. Even though the main theme is, to all appearances, quite obvious after the fourth and fifth associations, the analyst would do well to keep silent, his mind open to be changed with further material. If the patient reveals the red thread so clearly by these first consistent associations, will the rest be the same—or what? If they are the same, will he not soon tell a dream as is usual when the unconscious is expressing itself clearly, for the dream is in very fact what Freud called it—the royal road to the unconscious—and, as such, can never, or almost never, be allowed to pass. It invariably expresses the main theme of the session, which otherwise is expressed by the red thread of the associations.

If the analyst's understanding of the main theme is correct, then his interpretation regularly stimulates a confirmatory response from the patient.

A charming young woman, engaged to be married, gives the following associations. The four episodes related here are not presented verbatim; they have been summarized for our purposes. For strict accuracy, of course, associations cannot really be summarized, but the aim here is neither to present a particular session with the young woman in exacting detail nor to evoke the characteristic features of associations in general. Instead, the point of the following is to illustrate the analyst's approach to arriving at an interpretation of a series of associations.

> 1. Del, my fiancé, was driving from out of town with two other boys to come to see me. But instead of coming directly, he stopped with them for beers. Is that any way to behave when one is in love? Isn't he more eager to be with me than that?
>
> 2. Father says he will take care of certain matters [deleted for discretion] when I have a date. Then he doesn't. He doesn't have enough regard for me to keep his word.
>
> 3. Del's family is so large, close, and jolly. He has had so much love and security in the family. I must envy him that—what an awful childish thought.
>
> 4. I don't want to be a quiet little wife while Del is the center of the stage, as he always is when we go out; but isn't that selfish of me?

The hour was nearing its end. The analyst, judging that the associations, condensed here as four themes or sections, revealed the undercurrent in a consistent fashion, expressed what he understood. Interpretations are in two stages: First, the analyst must understand; and second, he must judge what to discuss with the patient and when.

In this case, the analyst said that it seemed to him that the main theme in all of these associations was the need for love. This was expressed as being frustrated (by Del and father) and leading to envy and jealousy (of Del). But the patient was a generous, loving person who could not feel easy about her demands for attention and love nor for her hostilities to her father and fiancé. Consequently, she blamed herself for having such childish reactions; she was angry but turned this feeling on herself as blame.

To this interpretation the patient responded with alacrity and feeling. "Yes! Del says his only great fear in our marriage is that if he harmlessly helped a man with his car I would be jealous and furious. You know, I can't stand even talking to a girl that I know Del has ever gone out with." Thereby, with a new series of associations, she confirms, clarifies, and sharpens what the analyst has said.

Although the dynamics in this example are clear, it was not indicated in this particular hour to relate them to the two essentials: the childhood pattern (actually, they were shaped primarily in reaction to her mother) and the transference. At this point, with this particular patient, it was best only to point out the major forces and let the patient apply her dawning insight to them as she would.

In every single session, by tracing the common element in all the associations, the analyst must try to see the main theme. And this (with certain reservations, which are taken up in Chap. 12) he must discuss, with all analytic judgment and tact, with the patient. If he is unable to see the main undercurrent, then he will discuss this fact too, for, if it is not the analyst's own faulty perspicacity, it signifies powerful resistance in the patient, and this must be analyzed. However, only rarely can the main drift not be seen.

Interpreting each session has been deprecated by some analysts as "giving the patient a package." However, I am not sure that Ferenczi meant it that way, but I am sure that the best way to make every hour count is by making conscious to the patient the unconscious central theme of every single session. The analysis then moves far more swiftly, smoothly, surely, and effectively.

Freud (1912a) stated: "[It] is of the greatest importance for the cure that the analyst should always be aware of what is chiefly occupying the surface of the patient's mind at the moment, that he should know just what complexes and resistances are active and what conscious reaction to them will govern the patient's behavior." The analyst must keep dealing with the central, presenting, major material. If this is done consistently, the deeper material keeps emerging, and, as we have said, every hour is made effective, with resulting smoothness, speed, and effectiveness in the whole analysis. From this basic principle many corollaries follow. To begin with, the analyst cannot see the common element in all the associations if he speaks during their recital. Doing so not only interrupts the flow but also stimulates reactions to what is said, and this means a collection of broken chains of associations. Of course, sometimes the analyst must ask questions, and, of course, he will have remarks. But he must know exactly what he is doing when he breaks in with them lest he destroy the very web of connections that he seeks to discern.

Another corollary is this: If the analyst sees the major central theme, then he knows what to interpret. He must not be led or seduced off the main track by content or by secondary or tertiary themes. When the patient free associates he turns over the direction of his thinking to emotional forces within him. We are after these forces which, now responsible for directing all the associations of a session, are sure to be central and presenting. If they are near enough to consciousness to affect the whole train of associations, then they are almost invariably near enough to interpret to the patient. Hovering his attention over those major motivations, which all the associations have in common, the analyst learns what is going on most centrally, what is most presenting, and also, therefore, what to interpret. The session with the engaged girl summarized above illustrates this. When the forces of expression are stronger, it is usually easier to see through to the forces that direct the associations; when the forces of repression are stronger, it is harder but then the analyst focuses on the resistance, insofar as it becomes the central feature of the associations.

Another vitally important corollary is that the technique of analysis requires a double attitude on the part of the analyst. This fundamental split involves holding in abeyance the knowledge of background and nuclear dynamics while listening uninfluenced to the associations and integrating them only after the main theme revealed by the associations is understood. The analyst must see the main issues, the core of the dynamics, the central emotional constellation, the essential problem, the total personality and its history. But, at the same time and with the perspective of this insight, understanding, and knowledge, he must approach each session completely afresh, completely without preconception, listening with gentle curiosity to hear what will come up today, as though he never had seen the patient before.

Everything the patient says is free association if it is offered freely without control or censorship and if nothing is omitted (unquestionably a very difficult task for the patient). One patient is reported as having said: "I don't like to free associate because then I can't tell the important things." He meant, in part, that when he thought of abandoning conscious control, his resistances welled up. Such distinctions between associations and real thoughts need to be watched for. In this sense the example of the above patient illustrates one of the advantages of easing into associations in most cases. Another is that between the associations and the casual unrelated remarks made "before" the sessions, the key to the hour is usually, even regularly, first sounded, simply but clearly.

A further differentiation that patients sometimes naively introduce is between associations and reality, telling, perhaps "apart from the hour," certain facts and realistic comments. But why are only these selected out of reality? It makes no difference to the listening analyst whether what the patient tells is fact, fantasy, or fiction, because, in looking for the common emotional element, everything is only associations, nothing else. All else, such as the content, comes later (with rare exceptions). No doubt the analyst pays attention to many matters simultaneously, and certainly later on his recognition of *what* the patient's associations are (entirely fantasies, only dreams, only daily incidents, and so on) will be extremely significant in many ways, especially as an indicator of the nature, the health, and the strength of the ego.

Of course, it takes practice and experience to perceive the main theme. The material may be poorly integrated, the resistance may have the upper hand, frequently there are subsidiary themes in addition to the main theme and so on.

In one hour, for example, the main theme, that became evident throughout a young man's associations was rejection of women with an expressed but very conflictful preference for men. This was coupled with a secondary theme of feeling rejected himself which led to feelings of depression. Guilt also ran through enough of the associations to be considered a theme, but a tertiary one. A subsidiary theme related to foreign girls and reflected his inhibited heterosexual desires. The more accurately the main presenting forces were understood and discussed, the less complicated and confused the hours usually became. Simple hours can be badly messed up and complicated material never clarified unless there is accurate understanding of the red thread, the major, central, presenting forces.

This session was reported by a young analyst. The associations are summarized and numbered as follows.

1. I ended the relationship with A (girl).
2. Just nothing there; I didn't enjoy it.
3. I spent some time lying nude in the sun, and this gave me homosexual feelings.
4. I had no sex with that girl.
5. She said that I was cold.
6. When I broke off with her, she cried.
7. She had a friend whose engagement was broken by her boy friend and she became depressed and went to a mental hospital.
8. How the boy friend must feel.
9. Discussion of alcoholism and homosexuality, attractions but dangers.
10. There was another girl I went with, but I ended that also.

11. Discussion of a poet who was considered to have homosexual tendencies.

Such a brief summary gives a bit of the flavor of the session, but at the same time it can be very misleading. Indeed, as we have remarked, it is highly doubtful that associative material can be summarized, except, as here, for the singular purpose of illustrating a point. If a student wants to learn psychoanalysis, he must drill in presenting complete sessions and in discerning the central dynamics. If he only summarizes a whole week's material, he never will learn to come to grips with the individual sessions. He will be talking *about* psychoanalysis rather than being trained in doing the actual operation of each session.

Some previously described points are illustrated, by the example of the session outlined above. The patient's identification with the girls and his depression because of feelings of rejection are only alluded to, but every analyst will suspect them. The analyst will seek the operation of the dynamics in the childhood pattern (not explicit in this example), in the life situation (the girls and the homosexual problem), and in the transference. The conflictful homosexuality, with its attractions and dangers, probably has a transference reference, but it is not open enough to interpret at this time. All references to breaking off relationships are transference unless proved to be otherwise. The secondary theme comes out more prominently in the summary. The patient probably feels rejected, like the girls, and reacts with depression and identification with the aggressor. He rejects others as revenge—the girls in his life situation and, potentially, the analyst in the transference application of the pattern.

Besides the major and the subsidiary themes, the associations during a session often occur in sections or blocks, such as those summarized in the above illustration. In addition, some associations can be considered to be compound. An example of this would be an instance in which a patient relates a whole narrative that makes only one point.

Throughout this chapter the fact has been emphasized

repeatedly that the analyst must comprehend the fundamentals thoroughly and that these yield basic, guiding principles but, because of the diversity of personality, not rigid rules. The principle of discerning the most central and presenting unconscious forces, must be mastered, but even this, although it always must be tried, cannot be employed rigidly.

One possible exception, for example, is where the patient recounts events of the day and current problems, all of which have no genuinely common element between them. The reason for this is that the common motivating force lies not in similarity of theme but in the fact that they are all pleas for help and emotional support. Such associations are of the reporting type and, in a sense, are a form of acting out. Instead of expressing his dependent needs for sympathy, understanding, and help verbally, though indirectly, in the content and flow, the patient acts these out toward the analyst.

Another possible exception occurs in the following circumstances. If the patient relinquishes conscious censorship, his thoughts will flow under the influence of unconscious forces. If, however, the resistance prevents these forces from directing the flow, then the forces themselves cannot be recognized. Like electricity, the forces are only comprehensible in terms of their effects. Here the resistance is the central, presenting force, and usually why and what it is against will show through. A keen eye must be kept out for it because the emergence may come in the form of flashes; that is, for example, in a slip of the tongue or through a casual but revealing offguard remark or opinion.

The process of free associating can itself be caricatured through apparent conscientiousness in order to serve the resistance. A patient, sincerely meaning to be conscientious, can start to tell an emotionally important thought or experience but never actually relate it because of getting off into endless details. For example, a young man started an hour by saying that he felt bogged down in his work recently and that this seemed to be related to his visit to his parents. He then told about the problems of getting to see them, all about the train and the plane schedules, what connections could be made, what was easiest for him, what was most convenient for his parents, and so on. By the end of the hour his account had not yet reached the meeting with his parents. Thus he shunned the emotionally significant essentials by preoccupation with endless emotionally irrelevant details. The content did not reveal the dynamics; he did not even tell the actual first association, that is, his thought of the relation of his effectiveness in working to his feelings toward his parents during the visit. His associations, under the guise of overly conscientious freedom and inclusiveness, by-passed the essentials for a mass of peripheral incidentals, which only means that the resistance took this particular form and, being central, called for being analyzed.

We have already remarked that a dream coming into the associations creates a special situation because of the particularly revelatory nature of dreams. In fact, hours may be usefully divided into two kinds, those without dreams and those with them.

Those without dreams are basically understood, with certain exceptions, as we have noted, through perception of the internal connection, the red thread. Those hours that have dreams are dealt with in the same way as those that do not, with the exception, however, of the way in which analysis of the dream is handled. This involves a special form of application of the same procedure. For, as we shall see, the dream itself selects and presents the major points of the session. Because of the basic principle that contiguous associations are internally related, all associations of the hour apply somehow to the dream and the dream to them. Nevertheless, this nexus method is usually not precise enough for dream interpretation. In fact, only one method is really reliable for accuracy and effectiveness, namely, the one described by Freud in *The Interpretation of Dreams.**

*Freud later reported some variations in approach (see *Collected Papers*, vol. 5), but these are essentially supplementary and are not to be taken as substitutes for his original method.

The original procedure formulated by Freud is, to the present, the standard one. It must be followed to the letter: break up the dream into its conceptual elements and get free associations to each of these; discern the common elements for each chain and reassemble the whole as the original manifest dream. This is done in order to reach the latent emotional meaning of the dream, just as we reach the latent emotional meaning of the hour's associations. The processes by which the unconscious forces form the dream are analogous to the processes by which they summon up and influence the flow of the waking free associations in the session. In both cases the unconscious motivations affect what comes to conscious awareness—in the dream during sleep, in associating while awake. Put technically, the analytic task is to uncover the emotional forces that empower the primary processes to dictate and influence the secondary processes.

This, as Freud suggested, is not unlike translating a foreign language or deciphering hieroglyphics. The patient presents dreams and associations. The associations in particular have a conscious content meaning, which is a secondary process and of secondary significance at the moment. The analyst is after the unconscious forces and the primary processes that underlie them. Beneath the surface conversation is this underlying emotional expression. The jumble of apparently unrelated associations or the utterly fantastic impossibilities of a dream are like the seemingly unintelligible hieroglyphs; they are in the language of the unconscious, and the analytic task is to translate them into the ordinary speech of everyday life.

This is another point of utmost importance and one that is often misunderstood and abused: The actual dynamics, the emotional forces, which Freud, in *Delusion and Dream*, designated as "the only valuable things in the psychic life," cannot be very complicated or difficult to understand, for they are fundamentally the emotional reactions of the child which persist in the adult. The adult's ego, and even the child's, is capable of extreme complexity, especially in content. But ideas, as Freud said, are valuable only to help us understand emotions, which have not yet come to light. These emotions, in their essence, are direct, uncomplicated reactions of early childhood. Hence, the motivations that we are after are not in themselves difficult to comprehend; it is a matter of how disguised they are. (In this book, psychoses will not be discussed.)

The analyst must learn the language of the unconscious so that he can read the material and translate it into our usual speech. Where the id and its language are, there must the ego with its language be. However, it is not unusual to encounter the misconception that the analyst's job is the opposite, but a patient so treated can become sorely confused. Analytic therapy must help the patient to free himself from these childhood fixations and to expand and strengthen his ego. This, of course, involves enhancing his grasp of reality and his ability to live out his mature motivations in the present real world. "Where id was, there shall ego be" (Freud, 1923). The unconscious infantile must be translated into the conscious, realistic mature, not vice versa. The patient must be helped to develop out of and not be driven deeper into his unconscious infantile thinking.

In analyzing the dreams, the single-track continuity of the associations must be interrupted for the hour because the patient is asked to use each conceptual element of the dream as the starting point of a new train of associations. Thus, free associations are used, but, instead of following on uninterruptedly from the beginning of the session, fresh, smaller trains are started from each dream element. However, this does not interfere at all with reaching the red thread, the presenting central dynamics of the session. Paradoxical though it may seem at first, quite the contrary is true. The dream contains the very same unconscious forces that also direct the associations, and it exposes them more frankly and nakedly than any other psychological phenomenon. The dream is very special. It is like a hole in the wall of the resistance through which the analyst can see with incomparable directness into the unconscious, into the very heart of the dynamics that are responsible for creating not only the dream but also the person's pattern of living. The dream expresses in disguised, sleep-preserving form this core of motivation as it operates at the time in relation to what is uppermost in the patient's mind. And it is precisely this core, in relation to the day's problems, which directs the free associations of the hour. Thus, the dream serves the analyst well; it picks out for him the central theme of the session, the undercurrent of the associations, which it epitomizes.

REFERENCES AND SOME RELATED READINGS

Freud, S. (1923), *The Ego and the Id.* London: Hogarth Press, 1935.

——— (1922), Two encyclopedia articles. In *Collected Papers,* 5:107–135. London: Hogarth Press, 1950.

——— (1917), *Delusion and Dream,* 159; 119. London: Allen & Unwin.

——— (1912a), The employment of dream-interpretation in psychoanalysis. In *Collected Papers,* 2:305–311. London: Hogarth Press, 1924.

——— (1912b), Recommendations for physicians on the psychoanalytic method of treatment. In *Collected Papers,* 2:323–333. London: Hogarth Press, 1924.

——— (1905), Fragment of an analysis of a case of hysteria. In *Collected Papers,* 3:13–146. London: Hogarth Press, 1925.

——— (1900), *The Interpretation of Dreams.* London: Allen & Unwin, 1933.

La Forgue, R. (1937), Exceptions to the fundamental rule of psychoanalysis. *Internat. J. Psychoanal.,* 18:35–41.

Marmor, J. (1970), Limitations of free association. *AMA Arch. Genl. Psychiat.,* 22:160–165.

Zilboorg, G. (1952), Some sidelights on free associations. *Internat. J. Psychoanal.,* 33:489–495.

10 / UNDERSTANDING UNCONSCIOUS MATERIAL

If we can now formulate some useful guidelines as to how the analyst reads and interprets associative material for unconscious meaning, for the forces that bring it to mind and speech, then we will have emerged upon a high and broad plateau and will have less arduous going.

Understanding of unconscious meaning by intuition alone is obviously treacherous since it depends to such an enormous extent on the observer's unconscious. And even if it turns out to be correct, it is a personal talent and not a scientific procedure that can be analyzed, systematized, tested, and taught. Intuition and psychological capacity are essential, but alone they are not sufficient for they are not yet science.

This chapter presents a series of guides that probably all good experienced analysts use to some extent, consciously or unconsciously, in understanding the unconscious meaning of psychic production. In fact, these points probably should be so intrinsic to the analyst's processes of observing and thinking that he uses them unconsciously and simultaneously. But this ability to utilize them without giving the process much thought stems from learning and experience. This is not unlike the example of driving an automobile: at first it is a complex, conscious procedure but before long, following the adaptive principle of saving energy, it becomes automatic, and the coordination operates unconsciously as it serves the will of the experienced driver. Examining the processes of understanding the unconscious from the material, we come out with the following points as guides (Saul, Snyder, and Sheppard, 1956).

1. Keep very close to the material; do not introduce your own associations; do not swing wide and away from the material by getting involved with your own ideas about it.

2. Look for the big, major, central themes first instead of becoming preoccupied with details, with subsidiary themes.

3. Keep to the level of consciousness and repression of the manifest dream and associative material. The depths descend indefinitely. Do not mix levels. This is especially important for interpreting to the patients.

4. Distinguish the dynamics from the content. No matter how unintelligible the associations or the dream may be, at least the main topics and tendencies, the emotional forces and something of their interplay, are usually discernible (e.g., hostility, receptivity, striving, passivity, genital sexuality, etc.).

5. Keep separate what is current. Carefully distinguish the motivations in the present life situations and those in the transference from what is past, that is, the sources of these motivations in the emotional patterns formed in childhood. In the case of dreams, perhaps the favorite device of these childhood patterns is to say to the dreamer: "It is not this unpleasant reality that is troubling you; no, it is only this in the dream with which you are occupied." Interpretation reverses this process.

6. Be alert to note the effects on dreams, associations, and behavior of any special current stimuli in the patient's life and particularly in the transference.

7. Following Freud's dualistic instinct theory, review

the material for (a) the libidinal motivations directed toward self or others and (b) the hostile motivations directed toward self or others and arising from the id and from the superego. Also, watch for the manifestations of fight and flight.

8. Review the material in terms of Freud's original differentiation of the ego motivations and the sexual motivations. For example, let us take this dream element: "A man is standing at the top of a flight of steps on a level above me." As this patient's associations showed, this represented, from the point of view of the ego, social feelings of inferiority to the father figure, who was represented as being on a higher level professionally, financially, and socially. In addition, the stairs led to sexual associations regarding his superiority in the sexual sphere also, with passive homosexual tendencies toward him.

9. Pay close attention to the sequence of associations and of dream elements. The secondary elaboration used in dreams is not accidental, it is very revealing. Usually the repressed impulses emerge more and more frankly as the associations progress and, in the case of dreams, as the dream progresses. The beginning of the hour and of the dream is of special importance in expressing the topic, the emergence of the disturbing motivation. In dreams, the end shows the result of the interplay of forces, the kind of solution or lack of solution that the dreamer reaches.

10. In the parts of the manifest dream and also in non-dream hours, watch for those associations that are connected with the greatest emotional response. Pay especially careful attention to just what the affects are. Freud (1900) states: "In a psychic complex which has been subjected to the influence of the resisting censorship, the affects are the unyielding constituent, which alone can guide us to the correct completion. This state of affairs is revealed in the psychoneuroses even more distinctly than in dreams. Here the affect is always right, at least as regards its quality." Freud goes on to point out that, "Wherever there is an affect in the dream, it is to be found also in the dream-thoughts."

11. Look for the positive progressive forces as well as for the regressive ones.

12. Examine the types of interpersonal relations for (a) object relations, such as persons whom one loves, hates, is dependent on, etc., and (b) identifications (and projections). Freud (1900) indicated that all figures in a dream usually represent to some extent parts of the patient's own personality and desires. "In cases where not my ego but only a strange person occurs in the dream-content, I may safely assume that by means of identification my ego is concealed behind that person." This is also true to a considerable degree in the associations of nondream hours (see the examples in Chap. 9).

13. Use symbols, as advised by Freud (1916–1917), only with a great caution, only in context, and only when associations to them are not forthcoming. As noted under point 8, take both the ego and the sexual meanings into account, that is, climbing a mountain may be both sexual striving and ambition.

14. Look for what the patient himself (that is, in his own ego) accepts and acts on in the associations and in the dreams. This is a prognostic guide to what the dreamer is capable of accepting and acting on in real life.

To demonstrate the workings of all of these points in a complete hour of associations would be too lengthy. Instead, here is a summary of a session that took place years ago, which should serve our purpose. In addition, what follows can also be used first, to illustrate the reading of associations for their unconscious meaning and second, to show something of the attitude of the analyst. In a later chapter we shall exemplify the use of these points in understanding a dream. Here are the associations of an early hour in the analysis of a quite open and frank young woman. The red thread running through these associations, that is, the elements common to all of them, appears in rather transparent fashion.

The patient begins the hour by saying that she seems to

have some difficulty in getting started talking. She does not know what to start with. The analyst responds that she should start with anything just so long as she omits nothing once she begins. She still hesitates somewhat, and the analyst points out to her that the understanding of why she hesitates is of itself of the greatest importance in regard to the speed and the effectiveness of the treatment. He suggests that perhaps she is a little concerned about what he will think of her if she reveals certain of her real motivations. She said that she understood this and recalled that a few hours back she had produced extremely significant material and obtained great insight although she had at that time also felt considerable resistance against getting started. She then went on without difficulty as follows.

> I had a dream. It was a few days ago. That day I received a letter from mother saying that Josie's sister, Laura, had gotten married. Josie is twenty-seven, and Laura is twenty-two. In the dream my mother entered the room and told me that Josie had married. I asked, "To whom?" Mother mentioned the name of a boy who I consider to be rather nondescript.

Asked for associations, the patient goes ahead with the following.

> I have always felt that in a family of girls, the oldest should marry first. I feel badly about Josie not being married although Laura is married. My husband used to date Josie. Josie had been shocked when she learned that he was dating me, but I was perfectly innocent in the matter. I did not realize the situation until I saw Josie's expression; I had never done anything to win him away from Josie.

Here we see clearly the theme of sibling rivalry as between the younger and the older sisters.

Thus far in the analysis, no mention has been made of the patient's own sister, who is three years older. Of course, the analyst says nothing and waits to see what theme the next association will reveal.

> I am friendly with two girls. Sally is quite proper. Perhaps this is due in part to the fact that she lives in her mother's house. Everything there is always neat and orderly. Somehow it seems that when I talk to her I always tell about all sorts of difficulties and how awful things are. Janie, my other neighbor, is easier to talk to. I feel at home in her house because she does not keep it very orderly. Things can lie around, and it makes everything very informal and easy. I have something of a time keeping my house the way it ought to be. I am afraid I really don't pick up things the way I should. It certainly never looks like Sally's house, but perhaps Sally's mother really takes care of it. Sally is a very beautiful girl. She is difficult, but she certainly is good-looking; all the men remark about it.

Here again the theme involves comparison between two other girls and then a view of the patient herself in contrast with them. The relationship to the mother is also mentioned.

The analyst remains silent, waiting for the next association. Naturally, he wonders whether she will mention her own sister and her own mother or whether this sibling rivalry has been repressed and will come out at this time only in the form of being transferred to other young women of her own generation. Realistically, the patient, with her beauty, charm, intelligence, and maturity of ego had little need to worry about competition.

> You know, mother stayed here with us a few weeks ago. After she returned home, I got a letter from my sister saying how rested mother looked. Of course, she said that to make up for what she said after mother's previous visit. At that time she was angry because mother did not stay near her and help with her house and children but left to come and spend a few weeks with me. After mother returned, sister wrote that she looked worn out.

Now the sibling rivalry emerges frankly in relation to getting direct help from mother, as well as in connection with how the house looks, how good a housekeeper one is, etc., as in the previous associations.

The analyst watches the time carefully throughout the hour for he wants to be sure to leave time for discussion of the theme that is common to all the associations. Now that the main current has emerged into the open, he has a good opportunity to discuss it in connection with the patient's actual rivalry with her sister in relation to her mother. Nevertheless, it is always better for the analyst to wait if he possibly can. Now that she has brought this out so openly, what will she go on to say next? Fifteen minutes remain to the hour; the analyst gauges that he can wait another five minutes and still leave five minutes for discussion of his interpretation and another five minutes to see how the patient reacts, unconsciously as well as consciously, to the interpretation. Therefore, he remains silent.

> We do have some help in the house now. It is a mother's helper. She does not like to baby-sit. She says too many girls get killed baby-sitting. I laughed; but, actually, where we live the street is very dark, and I am sometimes frightened myself.

Here a new theme appears—a direct expression of anxiety about hostility. It follows the consistent theme of sibling rivalry and again has to do with a young girl.

> My husband and I expect to get away in a week for a short vacation of five days. Two years ago before my younger child was born, I never would have dreamed of going off and leaving the older one alone, but I seem to have no anxiety about the younger one. She is only a baby, but I always seem to feel quite at ease with her. I am never afraid that she is going to hurt herself or that anything is going to happen. I still have much more anxiety about the older one. The younger one is certainly always cheery and happy.

The analyst has now waited as long as he possibly can to discuss the unconscious meaning of the associations. He is certainly pleased that he has not rushed in prematurely for now the theme of anxiety, which ties up with the patient's original resistance to getting started, has appeared. In addition, the sibling rivalry theme has recurred in relation to her own two small children.

At this point the analyst very casually and tentatively says that the possibility of this material being related to the patient's own rivalry in relation to her own sister should be discussed. He then quickly reviews the associations to show how this theme is in each one of them. Since this theme has emerged so clearly, the analyst is not surprised to find that the patient reacts very positively and with a real sense of insight to this brief discussion of her own sibling rivalry. Consciously she accepts it, but what does her unconscious say?

> My husband told me an amusing incident yesterday. He was walking along the street and saw a beautiful girl waiting at the doorway of a building. Turning his head to look at her, he walked smack into another man whose head was also turned to look at the girl. He said: "Some looker," and they both laughed.

This is good, but the sibling rivalry is not so clear as it might be.

There is no alternative; the analyst must wait for another association to reveal a little more of what the patient's unconscious is saying.

> My husband mentioned Sally. He told me he saw a woman on the street the other day who looked the way Sally would look in twenty years. I waited for him to say that this woman was big and fat and sloppy. Instead, he said she was one of those women who keeps her figure and is still beautiful and striking.

At this the patient laughs because she herself clearly sees that she is still on the same theme of rivalry. In the light of this last association, the analyst can feel that his interpretation is well confirmed.

Laughter, like tears, unerringly reveals a sensitive emotional spot. It is a common response to insight. The rivalry with sister in relation to mother has been discussed openly; its current edition, both toward her two friends and her neighbors, has appeared clearly. Now it is also revealed in the form of narcissistic competition with other women in relation to men and to her own husband in particular. Its operation is also clear in her identification with the younger of her two children. All this was discussed openly with the patient in this hour.

The patient's initial resistance and also the association concerning fears appeared in this setting of sibling rivalry. Therefore, it would seem that they have to do with the patient's hostility and guilt toward her older sister out of competition with her in relation to the mother, narcissistically, and in relation to men. It is the hostility to her sister that is more repressed than the actual fact of the competition, which has been close to consciousness. In all probability, it is this hostility to the sister, transferred also to the patient's friends, which, through being repressed and generating guilt, brought up the association of the dangers of baby-sitting and also the initial resistance. She very much wanted the analyst's esteem and preference for her, just as she had wished for her mother's esteem and preference for her over her older sister. Correspondingly, on an unconscious level, she feared what the analyst would think if he heard about this rivalry and the hostility involved in it. No doubt, she herself did not wish to face these hostile feelings because of guilt and shame. The wish to excel over sister figures specifically in the eyes of the analyst did not come out yet, nor, if present, did any sibling rivalry directly with the analyst. All of this was discussed openly with the patient before terminating the hour.

Of course, the main theme of the hour and its relationship to the transference, the resistance, and the anxiety was also discussed in connection with the dream. In the dream the patient absolves her own guilt toward Josie by correcting the reality. She no longer need feel badly about marrying the man whom Josie used to date—poor Josie, who even to this day at the age of twenty-seven is not yet married—for mother says in the dream that Josie really is married. Of course, the man she married is rather nondescript, so that the patient, with her own husband, is still ahead in the competition.

He who has mastered the principles to this point is on the plateau. He has a base for the expansions and the applications to come. Without the fundamentals, his professional experience cannot even begin.

REFERENCES AND SOME RELATED READINGS

Freud, S. (1922), Two encyclopaedia articles. In *Collected Papers,* 5: 107–135. London: Hogarth Press, 1950.

——— (1916–1917), *A General Introduction to Psychoanalysis,* 124. New York: Liveright, 1920.

——— (1900), *The Interpretation of Dreams,* 426; 432; 308. London: Allen & Unwin, 1933.

Saul, L., Snyder, T., and Sheppard, E. (1956), Report of the panel on the dream in the practice of psychoanalysis. *J. Am. Psychoanal. A.,* 4: 125–127.

11 / DREAMS

The interpretation of dreams is the
via regia to a knowledge of the unconscious
element in our psychic life.
—SIGMUND FREUD

The interpretation of dreams is a cornerstone of the psychoanalytic technique. Freud (1900) evaluated it thus: "The physician who cannot explain the origin of dream-images will strive in vain to understand the phobias and the obsessive and delusional ideas, or to influence them by therapeutic methods." It must never be forgotten that Freud did not start out with an interest in dreams. This developed because patients insisted on telling him their dreams and demanded interpretations. This is a general phenomenon in psychotherapy. For example, during World War II, nightmares were one of the constant symptoms of combat fatigue—the men told them spontaneously, urgently, hoping for relief through understanding (Saul, 1971).

The basic principles of understanding the unconscious underlie the interpretation of dreams. In addition, dreams show certain particular characteristics—or perhaps they are only the same fundamental characteristics of unconscious processes, but appear here in clearer, more visual, and often more exquisite form. To be understood fully, the dream's meaning must be revealed in the usual three aspects—childhood pattern, current reality, and transference. The dream preserves sleep by taking our minds off reality. We have noted that the dream says: It is not this unpleasant reality that is troubling you; no, it is only this in the dream with which you are occupied. Interpretation reverses this process. It finds the real problem for which the dream, to preserve sleep and rest, is a substitute, screen, and change.

The more naive the dream, the more openly are id and superego impulses apt to be portrayed and gratified in it. For example, a young woman's husband loses his job (a serious matter for a family with three children), and that night she dreams of a magazine with something missing, something cut out of it. The castrativeness is her anger at her husband. But we wish here to indicate only the main trends and not to go beyond these and work out the precise thought processes in detail. The latter is the therapeutic goal. It can be reached in many dreams during a single session.

Dreams are invaluable in many ways. If a patient is not progressing well enough or if the core of the dynamics, the nuclear emotional constellation, is difficult to understand, then focus and perspective can often be achieved by reviewing the first ten dreams of the analysis and a series of current dreams in isolation from any other material (Saul, 1940). This is useful mostly for beginners, but probably no analyst, however experienced, will fail to get fresh insight, focus, and perspective if he takes the time to review the dreams in this way. It is rarely advisable for students to study their near-verbatim notes of the analytic sessions, if they keep any. However, the dreams select out the presenting unconscious material, and reading through a series of six to ten seldom fails to illumine the peaks.

The dream as the royal road to the unconscious is so revealing that it is not necessary to have ponderous verbatim records of a psychoanalysis to reveal the essential dynamics. The central dynamics that shape the person's life usually are disclosed by the early dreams, and progress in treatment usually shows in samples of dreams taken at intervals. The dreams at the end of treatment are also especially revealing, as are samples taken postanalytically. We have already noted that although associations to the dream elements are essential to full understanding, we must not blind ourselves to the fact that often much can be learned from manifest dreams themselves, especially if a series of them is available. Usually, examining a series of at least ten will disclose the major emotional pattern that is common to all these dreams, although each shows different facets and has different forms and emphasis. The underlying pattern is usually discernible despite the great fluidity of dream images if one looks for it in an adequate series.

Sample dreams can also be supplemented profitably by a few sample nondream hours of associations. Here, too, the very first few hours and the ending hours are apt to be especially revealing, while others show what is happening in midstream.

LATENT CONTENT

EGO-SYNTONIC INTERPRETATIONS

In general, analytic hours with dreams are more revealing while those without them are less so. This is the case primarily because the dream is a barometer of the ego's relation to the unconscious, of the balance between the forces of *ex*pression and those of *re*pression. The fact that a patient tells a dream usually means that he is revealing something and wants it interpreted; and, always with certain reservations, the analyst should respond by interpreting, following the basic principle of keeping the insight at a level and in a form acceptable to the patient, that is, ego-syntonic. The dream demands interpretation—the only question is how to interpret it.

These considerations raise the question of how soon in treatment the analyst can begin interpreting dreams. The answer is as soon as the patient brings a dream, provided that the interpretation can be tactful and ego-syntonic. Any rule specifically indicating how soon or late, in what day, week, or month, dream analysis can begin is of necessity false because of the variety of patients. Some are very near to their unconscious and are already acquainted with their dreams, while others are not. On the other hand, the analyst need not wait for a fully developed transference if he makes his interpretations correctly and in accordance with the basic principle of feeling his way along as far as the patient can understand and accept. This does not mean that he systematically gets associations to every element of a dream in the first or the second hour and stirs up too much too soon—but neither does it mean that he should always avoid any mention of this material early on in treatment. Depending on the kind of material and the relation to the ego, it may be indicated to discuss at least some aspect of a dream in the first anamnestic interview. Much can be accomplished immediately by the astute use of dreams.

The following example is the third dream (notes were not recorded in detail for the first two) in the analysis of a talented and psychological young man who obviously was rather unusually close to his unconscious. He dreamed: "I was playing softball and hit a marvelous home run which everybody admired. Tom R. was there." The young man's associations ran like this (in summary form): "Discussion with a group of my friends at the plant about where to have the picnic. Being admired—mother, and perhaps father too, always wanted to have me get very high grades. In high school I set out to be president of every organization in the school. Another fellow and I finally did occupy all these positions. However, once I was elected, I lost interest. I recognize that this is all showing-off." Asked to associate to Tom R., the patient says, "I think of a fellow who was something of a friend of Tom R., Bob H. When he was an officer in the fraternity during the war, he was able to get meat, but he sold some of it on the black market, paid half the money to the fraternity, and kept the other half for himself. Because of this he was asked to leave school. Later he joined a public relations firm where he signed a contract in which it was agreed that if he ever left he would not set up a similar business nearer than fifteen miles. He managed to get himself fired and then set up his own similar business just down the street, where he did very well."

The dream illustrates the patient's showing-off tendencies, his needs for prestige, and the origin of these in relation to his mother in particular. He also became quite hostile to his mother because she made him study for grades and then he discovered that many of the things he learned his mother did not know. Thus, his need for prestige caused hostility and also feelings of inferiority since he senses that there is something infantile in living with this as such a central motivation.

What are the main dynamics? The needs for prestige are fundamentally plays for mother's love, which he gets by being very successful, particularly intellectually. However, his rebellion against mother and against the dependence on her and against her authority, which had shown in the previous hours, comes out here in the associations about Bob H., who represents a person who fools the authorities. Of course, the naive narcissism, orality, and other impulses are also evident; but central for this hour is the matter of winning mother's love and rebellion against her authority. This was turned to therapeutic advantage by showing the patient that all of these reactions were those of a child to his mother or parents and were no longer necessary or even consonant with attitudes of a person who is now a parent with responsibilities toward his family, community, and occupation. This was clarified in considerable detail by discussion; it gave a new insight and a great amount of relief and answered the question that the patient raised when he stated that he had felt keenly that he had a problem but did not know what it was or what to do about it.

A young married woman in analysis related the following pair of dreams (Alexander, 1961). These examples demonstrate how very clearly dreams can depict the main dynamics. The first dream reveals the major problem, the patient's dependent attachment to and hostility toward her mother; the second shows the retaliatory guilt, the source of her chief symptom—anxiety.

She reports them this way: "In the first dream I was home and was angry with mother. I told her she gave me no love and attention but was always sick in bed when I needed her. In the second, I dreamed that I had cancer and probably would die."

Dreams come up spontaneously in the associations, and the patients of today usually know their importance. If they do not appear, there is no longer any call to treat them as novel and mysterious. Like free association, dream analysis can be introduced easily, casually, and conversationally. In those rare instances in which the patient does not initiate discussion of them, their importance usually can be conveyed, and the analyst can solicit them with a few simple words of explanation.

Even the patient who scoffs at dreams is apt to accept them and perhaps be impressed by them if no great issue is made and if the analyst quietly uses this powerful instrument of insight. One young man was totally impervious to dream analysis, laughing down the notion that they could mean anything at all. Of course, no arguments were brought by the analyst; no attempt was even made to analyze the resistance, for it was not clear at this point that it was of any lasting importance. Instead, the analyst simply waited a week or so for a dream. It came and was to the effect that the patient was being photographed. The analyst worked in the casual comment that this probably signified some exhibitionistic trend. The patient literally jumped in startled surprise. This hit home. From that point he began a lively interest in dreams, which he learned to use very effectively in his analysis.

In sharp contrast, it must be noted that some patients can also be frightened off from dreams when they realize what penetrating insights they provide. However, if this creates resistance, then the resistance is analyzed, and this speeds the analysis. Of course, the more acceptably (ego-syntonically) the dream is interpreted to the patient, the less fear and resistance are aroused.

Questions often arise as to how to handle dream material in the very early stages of analysis. Should any associations be asked for at this point? If so, what can be interpreted helpfully? Should the analyst, instead, use the dream at this stage mostly for his own understanding? Look at the following example, which is the first dream of an attractive girl, emotional but rather repressed.

She is in a room where smoking is forbidden because the building is an old, ramshackle firetrap; but she is smoking. The firewarden comes in, and the patient flips her cigarette out of the window. The warden asks if anyone is smoking there; the girl says no, and he leaves, apparently satisfied.

Now, will it increase the patient's anxiety or relieve it to interpret this dream, to let her see her feeling that she is secretly hiding an infraction but doing so successfully? The transference implication is clear. Will it relieve her to discuss the fact that the analyst is no firewarden, makes no rigid rules or prohibitions, and that she need not hide anything from him? Or, since the cigarette probably symbolizes more serious infractions, will she flee in fear from revealing what she feels guilty about? The analyst, being in doubt, decided to wait rather than risk an interpretation at this point. Toward the end of the hour she told how she sometimes felt crushed by her father. She remembered that once, when he smiled, she thought it was in approval of herself but then realized that it was at his own witty remark. With this, it became possible to chat very lightly and casually about her need for her father's approval, her anger at not getting it, and her fear that she would not get it unless she hid her smoking, which to her meant secret defiance of her father and secret hostility to her sister, who lived in a building like that in the dream. Her defiance was also acted out in part by secret masturbation, but this was not touched on at this point; it came up later as simply one form of acting out her defiant resentment. The main thrust of this illustration is that there is no point in discussing symptoms, which themselves provoke guilt and shame, when the analyst can instead deal with the forces that underlie and produce these symptoms.

PERSPECTIVE ON DREAM INTERPRETATION DURING TREATMENT

Some analysts are extremely cautious about showing any interest in dreams in the early stage of analysis and may even refrain from asking for any associations to them lest they betray their interest. The fear is that thereafter the patient will dream only to please the analyst. But this need not cause trouble. If the patient's extreme need to please the analyst is a problem and a source of resistance, then it will show, not only in bringing dreams but in the dreams themselves and in the associations. This, in turn, must be recognized, interpreted, and dealt with directly. The truth is that the analyst *is* interested in his patient's dreams for the reason that they are the royal road to the unconscious. Freud's word of caution, written in 1912, is certainly to be heeded: "One must generally guard against displaying special interest in the meaning of dreams, or arousing the idea that the work would come to a standstill if no dreams were forthcoming; otherwise there is danger of resistance being directed against the production of dreams and a risk of bringing about a cessation of them.

As discussed above, the better the analyst understands the dream and the presenting material, including the resistance, and the more ego-syntonic his interpretations, the less the risks of provoking resistance, and the fewer the blocks on the royal road to the unconscious. As Freud goes on to say, "The patient must be brought to believe that material is always on hand for analysis, regardless of whether or not he has dreams to report or what measure of attention is bestowed upon them." Certainly; but if the patient does not bring dreams, moreover, intelligible dreams, then the resistance is too great for proper progress in the analysis. Empirically, when the forces of expression overbalance those of repression, the patient brings dreams. If the resistance is not weakened sufficiently for dreams to appear, then the analysis is not moving satisfactorily. It is still true: No dreams, no analysis. But if there are dreams and if they are used as resistance, then it is imperative that they be analyzed and the roadblocks removed, without sacrificing the use of this royal road.

Considering dreams in relation to treatment, it is well to remember that analytic treatment produces effects that are very different in different people, depending, of course, on their individual problems and personalities. Furthermore, these effects are produced in varying lengths of time as the person uses the analytic experience in living his life. The basic therapeutic effect of analytic treatment usually does not take place during the treatment itself but in a varying period of time from months to many years after the patient has stopped seeing the analyst. Moreover, the effects of treatment are complicated during treatment by immediate reactions, particularly the reactions to being in analysis itself. This is somewhat like the dilemma of modern physics as expressed in the principle of indeterminism, namely, that the method of observing the position and the behavior of electrons itself disturbs the behavior of the electrons that are observed. Hence, the early dreams in treatment do not show the patient as he regularly has been but show him in his initial reaction to the treatment situation. Later on they show him in a state of intense transference reaction to the therapist. Then, for a considerable time after analytic treatment, the patient is apt to be in a state of deprivation, reacting to the giving up of the analyst and the treatment situation. This post-analytic period may be very long—months, even years. Only toward the end of this does the patient begin to make use of the total analytic experience in the living of his own life again, as a person independent of the treatment situation and the relationship to the analyst. Hence, it is to be expected that the amounts and the patterns of the main motivational forces could vary greatly with these different stages of the relationship to the analyst and to the treatment situation, and, of course, this would be reflected in the dreams.

All dreams refer to the analyst unless proved otherwise, and it is well to watch for the application of this general principle in all details about leaving. We have remarked previously that unless this is positively ruled out any leaving, however minor or tucked away, means a wish to leave the analysis.

This also applies to complaints. Usually such dreams refer to the analysis, and they may even refer to something that is justified, at least in some part. Freud said that the patient is always right in some way about what he expresses. A woman dreams that she is in a bookshop where a man is trying to sell her a book, to foist it upon her. The book is above the patient's comprehension. She becomes angry and wants to argue but cannot. A doctor comes in to see what the man is doing but doesn't understand it. The sense of this is self-evident. Historically, the patient tried to win her father's love by intellectual success, through books, but she could not talk easily with him, and he tended to pass off her problems when she came to him with them. In the analysis, the analyst had not made any interpretation because he did not understand the material. The patient complains about this in the last scene of the dream and wants a more experienced man to check on the analyst.

Special attention must be paid to the status of the motivations. Taking hostility as an example, first the patient may hide it from himself and from the analyst. It may partially disappear, both because of the gratification of treatment and also because the patient represses it. Later, its appearance may not indicate a true increase of hostility but rather an increasing capacity to face it and an augmented ability to experience and handle it. It may well be that the most significant change in the course of therapy is the changed status, that is, the changed relationships of the hostility to the person's ego and superego. That is, what is important is not so much the changes in total amount and intensity as the changes in insight and relationship to the hostility. The same holds for other motivations and for complexes of them. Nothing shows the actual psychodynamic shifts within each patient so clearly and pointedly as dreams.

Although certain symptoms occasionally are relieved in a single interview or in a short period of treatment, yet where it comes to changes in the total personality, these cannot be expected to take place until some time after the analysis through practice in life. The analysis, as we have said, reopens the capacity for growth and development, and the fundamental changes within the personality generally take place only through practice in living and in the utilization of the whole analytic experience. Thus, during the period of treatment symptomatic relief or seeming adjustment in life is almost no indication at all of what changes actually have taken place or are taking place in the patient. But, the true state of affairs is rather certain to be represented in the dreams.

Hence, any studies of the dreams of patients before, during, and after treatment must take into account the essential nature of the analytic treatment, which is not at all analogous to the meaning of the word treatment in ordinary medical and surgical procedures. Moreover, special attention must be paid to the fact that different therapists with differing amounts of analytic training, experience, and skill work somewhat differently with patients.

IMPORTANCE OF EGO-REALITY MEANINGS

In the previous chapter, fourteen guides to understanding the unconscious meaning of material were outlined. They apply without alteration to dreams, the epitome of unconscious productions. However, the guideline having to do with a review of the material in terms of Freud's differentiation of the ego motivations and the sexual motivations warrants some elaboration here.

Interest in the ego emphasizes the narrowness of concentrating too exclusively on the deep symbolic meaning of dreams. "A body does just the same in a dream as he'd do if he was awake," says Tom Sawyer's aunt. And there is a humorous story about a woman who in a dream is abducted by a powerful man. He drives her into a deserted woods. He takes her off the road into a small clearing in a thicket and throws a blanket on the ground in the moonlight. "Oh dear," says the woman, "What are you going to do with me?" "That, lady," replies the man, "is up to you—it's your dream."

Usually, as pointed out in a previous chapter, it is much easier to make a deep symbolic interpretation than it is to find the meaning of the dream in current reality as done by Freud in *The Interpretation of Dreams* and in the *Introductory Lectures.* A young man dreams of sex with a prostitute who resembles his mother. Ah—deep material! This young man, who is very attached to and spoiled by his mother, got as far as law school on his own. Now, up against a variety of problems including difficult studies, rooming alone, and friction with some other students, he reacts with spiteful unconscious wishes for escape through running home to his mother. In the dream the relationship is erotic in form. In life he struggled against underlying impulses to return home and be supported without the responsibilities even of being a student. The main point is not the sex alone, but the escape. True, it takes an erotized form and does relate to avoiding marital as well as other responsibilities, and the pattern is the erotized extreme dependence on his mother. This deep material with its manifold facets and significance, can be understood only in the perspective of current reality.

That ego-reality meanings must be understood as well as sexual meaning can be illustrated again by the following.

A young man suffered from having to feel his testes to find out if they were gone. This appeared in his dreams. The castration, as is usually the case, was only a special form of hostility, which regularly fuses with the sexual drives, that is, it becomes erotized. The form of the symptom is now of secondary academic interest. The essential point here is that the patient's anxiety was a guilt reaction and an expectation of punishment because of his hostility to his two-year-younger sister. This arose out of sibling rivalry and was intensified by the way the mother reared them. The symptom took this form because his own hostility to the sister became mixed with his sexual impulses as sexual attack. In the midst of these drives the patient came down with the mumps and was kept in bed for a considerable time for fear of "losing" his testes. Here again, the castration is only a special form of the major motivations. These are the really deep, pervasive forces that generate the symptom and shape the personality—the childish needs for love, the rivalry, the genital sexual feelings, the hate, the guilt, the dread of retaliatory punishment.

Following is a particularly revealing example that demonstrates the extreme importance of understanding dream material in the perspective of current reality. A man dreams that he is being shot up in an elevator in a building; he has great anxiety because he cannot stop the elevator and anticipates going right out of the building. The patient said that he was sure that the elevator, running in a shaft, must mean the shaft of the penis. He concluded that the dream must show that he has an overstrong sex drive. Of course, it took no dream to tell him of his excessive sexual drive, for he knew that very well already and suffered under its impulsion. The ego meaning of the dream stemmed from the fact that it occurred the night before the analysis was interrupted for the summer vacation. He felt ejected from the analysis, shot out of the building, and was enraged at this; he sought to drain his rage by sexuality, which, to him, meant attack. It was because of the pressure of this hostility seeking expression in attacking women that he was oversexed. His sexual drive had the elements of a compulsive symptom.

The point we come to is that the ego-reality aspect of the dream, as of all the material, must always be understood. Searching out sexual meaning alone, or depth alone, is misleading—the whole picture must be seen so that the parts are in perspective. We live, feel, and experience our lives through our egos mediating between inner desires and inner restraints on the one hand, and outside reality on the other. These essential ego functions are indispensable to understanding dreams and other unconscious productions.

Even the most flagrant sexual representations usually also symbolize ego meanings, which must always be sought even if only to rule them out. The child normally identifies with both father and mother. A bisexual picture, such as the common one of a woman with a phallus, is sometimes a condensation of the two parents. It can have different meanings in different patients and in the same patient at different times. It may reflect a man's feeling that he is too feminine; therefore, he tries to show off his masculinity, symbolized by the phallus. The phallus itself is usually a symbol of strength, toughness, and masculinity. A young man dreams that he is a child, cared for by his mother, but that he has a huge penis—a sop to his masculine pride. A girl, frightened by her own hostility and guilt, which conjure up fantasies of being attacked, tries to be tough and dreams of herself as having a penis. This is her defense against a too masochistic feminity which, as far as she is concerned, means exposure to dangerous sexual onslaught.

METHOD OF INTERPRETATION

The best basic method of dream interpretation for therapy is, as previously noted, the one originally described by Freud. This should be standard and others used only as especially indicated. The patient himself soon learns to break the dream into elements and to associate to each of them. Often, however, the analyst must use his own discretion, in which case the following points are usefully borne in mind.

Where there is a choice of dreams of different nights, it is usually best to hear them all. If one of them seems to be especially clear, it is apt to be a good one to start with. However, remember that the chief goal is to understand the most recent one. This is usually the most difficult, the resistance and repression being greater—possibly this is one reason for the patient telling the dreams of previous nights also.

If all the dreams of a night cannot be analyzed during an hour, then the ones of the deeper sleep are preferable to those that occur while awakening. This is the case because the latter usually have much more secondary elaboration and sometimes even semiconscious fantasy.

The first and last elements of the dream are particularly important. The first shows the sleep-disturbing stimulus (or stimuli) at its emergence. Then the mind deals with it (or them). The last element shows the solution or the effort at solution—the final resolved or unresolved status.

If the patient associates spontaneously to certain elements, usually it is best to let him proceed freely. If he does not, it is frequently best to accustom him to doing so. If the elements are associated to in sequence, from the first to the last, this has the advantage of following systematically the unconscious thought processes as they deal with the sleep-disturbing feelings and impulses (with due regard to secondary elaboration).

Sometimes, however, the analyst sees some of the dream clearly and wants to get associations to the elements that he does not understand before the patient becomes suspicious of what the dream is saying and perhaps unconsciously becomes defensive and no longer able to associate as naively as when he was totally in the dark about it. For example, a young lawyer dreams that an associate in the same office dies of a heart attack while giving a demonstration. The analyst would suspect that the dying is a frank death wish, that the precise form the heart attack is probably incidental or historical, and that the colleague has aroused hostility for some reasons that would not be too hard to seek since he and the patient are of about the same age and are in the same office. But what can be the meaning of "giving a demonstration"? Here the analyst would want to ask for associations to this element first, to get naive associations before the patient gets an idea of what this probably transparent dream is expressing.

The sequence of the elements of a dream, the way in which the drama unfolds and progresses, is of great significance and therapeutic usefulness. It cannot be dismissed as secondary elaboration, as only the weaving of inchoate elements into a story by the ego. Even if this were true, why would the ego do it exactly this way and why does it choose one sequence rather than another?

The secondary elaboration, as described by Freud in *An Outline of Psychoanalysis,* is the form given to the unconscious material by the ego to make it less unacceptable. We are interested in precisely this—for the form given the material by the ego is exactly what we must understand in order to grasp the relationships of the deeper material to the ego and to know what and how to interpret.

If the analyst observes very carefully the story of the dream, obtaining associations to every element, he will find that almost always the repressed impulses emerge more and more prominently through the defenses. This is why nightmares often begin quite innocuously. Gradually, the defenses weaken, the repressed motivation comes close to awareness, and the dreamer's anxiety mounts until often, as a last defense, he awakens to escape it.

However, in some dreams or dream series, the forces of repression rally their strength and conquer the emerging emotional forces, and the dreamer quiets down into a less disturbed or even peaceful sleep. Even here, however, the repressed impulse rarely if ever bursts out in full force at the outset of the dream then to become more and more repressed. Usually, if not always, it pushes up against the controls only slowly at first. Then it gains power but may be forced under control again by the automatically operating defenses.

Often the patient escapes the repressed impulse by psychological regression to a child-parent relationship or situation—the escape after the struggle. The following is an example. A woman patient dreams: "I am riding with my husband in an automobile. At some little distance there is a terrible accident. I look away and do not see it. Then my husband and I go there. He acts as a doctor and I as a nurse. It turns out to be two men, Englishmen. One of them has a forked tongue. Then the scene changes. I am at a dining table with two women, drinking coffee. One of these women is the daughter of wealthy parents and can have everything she wants. The other woman is a physician."

The associations to the individual dream elements revealed tension with her husband that could be traced back to hostility toward her father and the fact that she never had had good relations with men. In fact, she had at one time entered a convent. However, she found this alternative impossible, left the convent, and on the way back from it stopped in at a hotel and had a sexual relationship with a man whom she had met. The accident and the two Englishmen apparently represent repressed hostility against her husband and against other men. The forked tongue reminded her of a snake, and this led directly to fellatio fantasies in relationship to her husband. In the last scene, drinking coffee is what she did when she visited her mother and talked with her about the troubles she had with men. To the two women she directly associates her envy. First, there is her wish to be like the girl who has wealthy parents and can thus have everything she wants. Second, there is her wish to be like the other girl, who is a physician.

The dream sequence reveals her efforts to solve her

basic problem. The dream starts off with her riding with her husband. She tries to go along and make a go of the marriage with him. However, the hostilities mount up and are defended against by projecting them—the accident involving the two Englishmen. Still, the association of fellatio with her husband to the tongue of the Englishman shows that the Englishman, whatever else he may refer to, also represents the husband. Thus, the conflict with her husband is such that she is unable to resolve it. She tries to do so in part by putting herself in the position of a nurse in relation to the husband who, in the dream, is a doctor. The dream work is successful in that she does not awaken in anxiety from the part about the accident. Instead, unable to solve the problem in relation to her husband and to other men, she changes the scene to one in which she is with women. This shows how in life she has tried to solve her disturbed relationships with men. First, she wishes to be the daughter of a wealthy family and simply indulge herself through money, thus substituting parental wealth for a good relationship with a man. The second girl, who in the dream is a physician, represents her efforts to solve her problem through doing good for others who suffer, that is, projecting her own suffering and trying to help others who represent her own need. The third attempt at solution is by directly turning to her mother, the more regressive oral relationship. (Other aspects, such as the masculine connotation of the woman physician, as well as the whole transference meaning, we will not discuss here.) The pattern that shapes her life is reflected in this dream.

DREAMS OF INSIGHT AND OF RESOLUTION

Dreams, revealing as they do the balance of motivational forces, including the ego's relations to them, reflect delicately the dawning insights that occur as the analysis progresses. At the same time, they also reveal the person's (more narrowly, the ego's) efforts to resolve the problems.

It is unnecessary to illustrate these dreams of dawning insight in detail as this very term is already rather graphically explanatory, and furthermore, the dreams themselves are widely recognized. A simple one is transparent, without background or associations: "I was looking through some of my wife's papers, found a photograph of myself and thought it very good. Then I suddenly thought, 'Surely I can permit myself *some* exhibitionistic pleasure'." Needless to say, some of this patient's narcissism had emerged in the previous hour.

A very superior young woman describes another dream of dawning insight. "I am in a room. There are holes in the ceiling. Someone is able to watch everything I do through these holes. I am angry and anxious because of this. Then someone looks in through the window. Then they manage somehow to enter the room, and I hit them over the head."

The patient's associations all dealt with her relationship to her mother, whom she felt knew about everything she did. The mother used this information in order to control her, to separate her from her brothers, sisters, and friends, and to try to keep her entirely dependent and submissive. The mother did the same thing with the other brothers and sisters and used all the information she could get in this way. For years the patient was extremely dependent on and submissive to her mother. Only after treatment began did she dare face the fact that underneath she was rebelling against her mother and deeply resentful of this treatment. She realized then that much of her life, in fact, the central portion of her emotional life, had been devoted to escaping from her mother's influence.

She now realizes that this is what she has been acting out in the transference, feeling that the analyst has been trying to control her, that he cannot be trusted, that she really cannot tell him everything because he will use it for some sort of ulterior motive. She also sees this as the reason she has felt so strongly that she must go to a different analyst; however, she lost this feeling as soon as her own analyst said that if she insisted on doing so he would help her to locate the right person.

She also recognized this pattern in her life situation, seeing that when she meets other people, at first they like her and she likes them, but soon she feels as though they are hanging on to her and that she must free herself and break off the relationship. Because of this she is defensive about making friends with anyone and feels that down underneath she does not get close to a single person. Now she understands that this is because she fears to do so because of an aversion to repeating this pattern toward her mother.

Here is another simple example of a dream of dawning insight. A housewife whose good relations with her husband and children are disturbed by her childish, hostile, guilty attachment to her mother dreams as follows. "I am back at my parent's home. There is a bed that becomes a child's crib. I say, 'I can't possibly fit in that any more.' "

The dream of dawning insight can also reflect an isolation in the sense of separating out or sequestration of the neurotic motivations and a placing of them in improved perspective. A very masochistic, self-defeating girl began to see that her self-punishment resulted from guilt for hostility to her sister. This had arisen out of envy and rivalry and had spread to other girls. She reported: "In the dream I committed some crime. As a punishment I was given a choice between flight to a swamp, which would mean certain death, or taking some torturing path like running a gauntlet, which meant torment but held out a chance of surviving. Some other girl chose the swamp and ran to it, but I took the path. Then, I was surprised to find myself on a train with happy people. I awoke feeling that I could have a happy life after all. I never had believed it to be possible. I have always lived awaiting catastrophe." In this dream the patient expresses the new realization that her suffering in life is largely self-made. Therefore, it can be relieved by a shift in her own attitudes. Reducing the hostile competitive orientation will reduce the guilt and the self-punishment and thereby put her on the track of happiness.

This dream represents the possibility of solution of the problem, the self-injuring trend, but only hints at how this can be done. Dreams that go beyond insight and deal centrally with how to solve the problem have been called dreams of resolution. They reflect the patient's grasp of the problem, the kinds of solutions he struggles with, and something of his degree of success in achieving a solution.

It sometimes works out well to ask selected patients, at certain stages of their analyses, to write down a key hour or a key dream soon after the session, preferably the same day. Not infrequently, this helps the patient to clarify and consolidate his intellectual insight by reviewing the main issues and by doing so alone. The following notes were made in this way by an ambitious, energetic young husband and are edited only slightly for reasons of discretion.

> [The Dream] I visit Bill S. who has a sprawling solid brick house with much fancy equipment. He shows me around and is preparing some food, but I go to the place where I am to sit. I pass some tables where some other people are resting. One of them is Dad. He looks up and smiles. I am afraid I'm late and will get only leftovers, but, to my surprise, there is plenty of food and my plate is heaped up.
>
> [Associations and Dynamics] Competition with Bill S., with my analyst, and also with other men to try again to be first so as to win love and get plenty to eat—figuratively speaking, to get a lot of everything, fancy equipment, food from mother, therapy. It really is not necessary to compete to receive enough (in golf, work, therapy). Seems that my unconscious is beginning to accept the idea of trailing along behind.

Toward the end of a successful analysis, as resolution progresses, this type of dream tends to reflect the solution more clearly and usually more realistically; there is less disguise and distortion, and the analyst and other emotionally charged persons appear more and more openly. For example, a young physician, whose problem stemmed from competition for prestige, dreams that he and his analyst are together in a medical clinic discussing a medical problem. Sometimes the patient is right, sometimes the analyst is right. Thus he can dream of himself and his analyst in their own persons; both can be in the clinic together and both can be right. This is a very far point from his original, intensely hostile, intolerant competitiveness.

MANIFEST CONTENT

When Freud pioneered in this field, he had to militate for recognition of the manifest dream as a façade manufactured by the dream work out of the latent thoughts and feelings, which were the true underlying, disguised meaning. Some fervid followers continue to fight this battle today, and they go to such lengths as would seem to betoken a wish to abolish manifest dreams entirely, certainly as a topic for psychoanalytic study. But the battle was won years ago, and analytic students can be given credit for the ability to study and use manifest dreams without being corrupted by them.

Freud's own writings are solidly objective and balanced on this subject. While insisting that the manifest dream is a condensed, more or less disguised expression of the underlying unconscious impulses, he was still interested in this form of expression and in the dream work that shaped it. With the shifting of attention from what is repressed to the repressing forces, Freud (1940) pointed out that dreams may arise from the ego as well as from the id. The danger in psychoanalysis today is not that students will neglect the latent dream content, but that they will tend, in their conscientious striving for depth, to see the sexual motives and symbolisms to the relative neglect of the reality and the ego meanings.

Let us review very briefly here some observations of Freud on the subject of dreams. He emphasized the point that no dream can be reliably understood without detailed associations to its elements and a reconstruction of the dream work and the latent dream thoughts. He also pointed out that the manfest dream tells something of the interplay of forces, and it does so at a very important level of awareness. In his *New Introductory Lectures on Psychoanalysis,* Freud suggests that "There must be a force present which is trying to express something and another which is striving to prevent its expression. What comes into being as a manifest dream may, therefore, be regarded as comprising all the solutions to which the battle between these two opposing forces can be reduced." A bit later on he states that the manifest dream ". . . allows to a repressed impulse the satisfaction which is possible in these circumstances in the form of an hallucinatory wish-fulfillment." In his work, *On Dreams,* he states further, "Thus the dream façade may show us directly the core of the dream, distorted through admixture with other matter." Since the basic concept of the dream is that it is a more or less distorted expression of wishes and impulses, it thereby follows that its intelligibility depends on the degree of distortion. Moreover, however great the distortion, the chief underlying topics that find expression in the manifest dream are almost always evident. Of course, the kind and the degree of distortion are also important in understanding the dynamics.

This can be seen not only in the dreams of every analysand but also in Freud's own dreams, which he reported in the *Introductory Lectures* and in *The Interpretation of Dreams.* Freud's dream of the botanical monograph did deal with his writing a book and with his botanical discoveries, even though the details could not have been deduced from the manifest dream alone. In fact, about this dream Freud (1900) said explicitly, "Even the dream's apparently indifferent form of expression at once acquires a meaning." His dream of digging in a grave dealt with defense against anxiety about death. His dream of sitting at a dinner table and having a lovely lady admire his eyes expressed, as his associations and interpretations show, his wishes for love for his own sake and not only as reward for years of hard work and accomplishment.

In his *New Introductory Lectures on Psychoanalysis,* Freud wrote: Naturally this manifest dream displays all sorts of characteristics to which we are not completely indifferent. It may be coherent, smoothly composed like a literary work, or unintelligibly confused, almost like a delirium; it may have absurd elements or jokes and apparently brilliant inferences; it may seem clear and well-defined to the dreamer, or it may be dim and indefinite; the pictures in it may have the full sensuous force of a perception, or they may be as shadowy and vague as a mist. The greatest variety of characteristics can be found distributed in the various parts of the same dream. Finally, the dream may be attended by an indifferent feeling tone, or by a very strong pleasurable or a painful affect. You must not think that we regard this endless variety as a matter of no importance; we shall come back to it later and shall find in it much that is useful for our interpretation.

The manifest dream then, even when considered independently of anything else, is far from valueless. Although it is so much more illuminating to have the associations and to do a thorough analysis, this does not mean that the manifest dream alone is not of great significance and of great practical use in understanding the patient.

THERAPEUTIC VALUE

The manifest dream exquisitely reveals the whole interplay of motivations. What of the id comes through and the form of distortion imposed by superego and ego are there evidenced for the discerning eye. It portrays the upshot, the solution for the ego, what the person is really like, what he wants, and what he will allow himself to do. In general, the daydream visualizes what a person wants consciously, while the manifest dream during sleep represents what he permits himself to have.

We have remarked that what is lacked in not having associations to the elements can often be made up partially by having a series of manifest dreams. By comparing these, the major themes begin to emerge in different forms. Since, for practical use in understanding patients in their first visits, the life history, the earliest memories, the present life situation, and other data are usually also available, the manifest dreams can also be of indispensable value for the initial diagnostic understanding of the essential psychodynamics.

A manifest dream can, in very frank terms, state the main dynamics, as seen, for example, in reaction to beginning treatment. The night before beginning in analysis, one person dreams of having a brain operation, another of losing his clothes, another of a long and expensive cab ride, another of exploring underground caverns, and so on. How accurate this dream material can be prognostically as far as behavior and transference are concerned can readily be illustrated. A woman who was involved in some questionable business practices dreamed the night before coming for the first appointment with the analyst that she was going on a trip to a distant country, and when she went for the tickets, the agent presented them to her gratis, saying they were with the compliments of the firm. Despite analytic efforts, this dream warning was acted out: she never really started treatment; she left after a few hours and was one of the rare persons who never paid.

If a manifest dream is remarkably frank, the analyst must be suspicious as to whether this is really so transparent or if it hides something else. It is safest to lean over backward to be doubly conscientious and careful and to be sure that the patient is not unconsciously drawing a red herring across the trail. Probably, if it is a genuine insight dream, the patient will understand it readily, and if it is, he deserves praise and encouragement for his ego's ability to accept and express the motivations so openly.

Sometimes an important motivation is tucked away as an inconspicuous or seemingly irrelevant detail in a dream but will be picked up by making certain that every single element is noticed. An attractive woman, self-frustrated internally, dreams that she is with a man; a woman is also present somewhere. The man declares his love to the patient, proposes marriage to her, kisses her, and then abruptly stops. She feels that he thinks she is no good and she becomes furious. Associations to the detail of another woman's presence, which all the rest of the dream has by-passed, lead to the reason for the patient's masochistic self-frustration. The woman refers to the patient's sister, toward whom she is extremely hostile unconsciously because of rivalry and envy toward her which date from earliest childhood. This hostility creates guilt and the self-punishing tendency. In this dream the rivalry related to marriage; therefore, since "the punishment fits the source" (Saul, 1956), the punishment for envying the sister her man and her marriage is that the patient shall not have or enjoy this domestic happiness herself.

The coming of a dramatic turning point in treatment may well be forecast in dreams. For example, one acutely suicidal patient literally could not dream of any hostility at all. Then a little glimmer of it appeared in a dream. Soon thereafter, she dreamed of her mother breaking her neck, and this first dream of open extraverted hostility marked the turning point in treatment and the subsidence of the suicidal drive. A young man with strong paranoid trends had dreams in which the hostility, usually in the form of derision, was always directed by others at him. The breakthrough in treatment came when he dreamed of verbally attacking someone, after which his projecting diminished.

The manifest dream, however effectively it may disguise the content, is usually franker in representing the dynamics. Hostility in certain elements of the manifest dream usually is confirmed as hostility by the associations to these elements. Similarly, overcompensatory kindness in the manifest dream usually represents this same reaction in the associations and in the person's motivations. But whether or not this distinction between content and dynamics helps to explain the nature of the manifest dream cannot be indisputably ascertained. Thus, the only sound course is to proceed, not by rules alone, but by exploration. Only increasing knowledge about the manifest dream, only observation and testing, will reveal more of the reality of its nature and thereby of its potential usefulness.

BLIND ANALYSIS

Testing how correctly dynamics can be read from manifest content (blind analysis) is a most illuminating exercise. As an example, a manifest dream is presented from a patient about whom no other information whatever is given. "I am in an automobile at the base of a mountain. Someone is with me. We proceed with great difficulty because of ice and snow, often slipping back. Also, the motor is not operating properly. Then we get out and struggle up the mountain on foot. I straddle a ridge. I feel utterly exhausted by the effort. My companion seems to be on the mountain top. Up there I see a professor refereeing a football game."

Solely from this dream, having in mind the fourteen guiding points for the understanding of unconscious material given in Chapter 10, the following was deduced. The dreamer is a man, probably young, as evidenced by the predominance of postadolescent masculine activities (e.g., automobiles, mountain climbing, and football games). His central problem is ambition—he feels forced to struggle upward in the world but actually underneath he is very resistive to this. This resistance arises from protest against the effort involved and also probably from the guilt because of the competition. The guilt is indicated by the fact that the only real hostility in the dream is directed against the patient himself; he is the only figure in the dream who really suffers. The instigation to this excessively ambitious effort would seem to be his mother, because it is a mountain that he is climbing. This is probably a representation of his close attachment to his mother and of his needs for her love. This is sexualized to some degree as suggested by the straddling of the ridge, which seems to be a reference to masturbation or coitus because straddling is frequently used in this way. The relationship of the patient to the big mountain also suggests the regressive wish of the patient to give up the struggle and return to the small child relationship to his mother.

His feelings of inferiority are also shown by his representation of the professor on the mountain top. He strives upward to identify with him, and the football game shows the strong competitive feelings that he harbors, which seem to be directed mostly toward his colleagues. Probably at a lower level they are aimed at the professor, who very likely represents his father. That his father should be represented as a professor shows that the dreamer has academic ambitions. He wants to be not only an athlete, as seen in the football game and the mountain climbing, but also a professor, that is, prominent in the academic field.

The patient's second manifest dream in treatment is now presented with no further data whatever. It is as follows. "I am with a girl, going up a hill toward my home to meet her parents. There is a dinner party going on there with many notable people present. I must behave properly and make the right impression. Actually, I am riding up the hill on the back of an old truck."

It is immediately apparent that this dream is built on the same basic plan as the first. It expresses the same essential dynamics. Going up the hill with the goal at the top is now expressed in terms of social superiority with the oral element clear. The companion is now a girl, suggesting that this is, in part, the patient's alter ego, that is, representing the feminine part of the patient. He attempts to relieve his tensions by directing them in sexual form toward women of his own age with whom he closely identifies. At the end of the dream, he is again the only person who fares badly in that he puts himself at the back of an old truck rather than achieving the social height.

The salient facts about this patient and his associations to the elements of the dream, as obtained from his therapist, confirmed the interpretation in every detail. The dreamer turns out to be a young man who comes from a poor background and is a member of a minority group. His parents, especially his mother, have impressed upon him their own ambitions—to achieve great success and distinction in the field of law. He is driven by this need, implanted by his parents, that he must become a notable. At present, he is in law school, where he drives himself incessantly and is chronically fatigued and somewhat depressed. He has been very active sexually with prostitutes and with depreciated girls, who are objects for draining hostility by sexuality and with whom he also identifies. In reality, he is a most attractive, intelligent, likeable, and capable young man but is miserably unhappy because of the feelings of inferiority. These result, in part, directly from the excessive, unachievable ambition of the parents for him and also, in part, from his close, childish attachment to his mother. He torments himself with his upward strivings, as represented in the first dream, longs to regress and, out of guilt and self-directed hostility, blocks his own climbing. With his excellent endowment, he should be enjoying his student days to the full. Instead, he is in a torment, reminiscent of Sisyphus of mythology, who perennially struggles to push a boulder to the top of a mountain, only, at the moment of achievement, to have it slip and roll back down.

It is a rewarding exercise to reconstruct as much as possible about a person from one or two manifest dreams alone and then to hear the main facts and the associations in order to see the extent to which those predictions are correct. The interpretation is usually amazingly accurate if it is based on the actual evidence of the manifest dream. The analyst must be scrupulously careful to use only the conceptual elements of the manifest dream and to avoid introducing any of his own associations.

GUIDES TO UNDERSTANDING

How are manifest dreams to be understood? This is only a special case of the more general problem of learning to interpret unconscious forces and the processes that shaped them. We have already discussed fourteen points to keep in mind as guides. Let us review them here in abbreviated form.

1. Keep very close to the material.
2. Look for the major central themes first.
3. Keep to the level of consciousness and repression of the manifest dream and associations.
4. Distinguish the dynamics from the content.
5. Keep separate what is current. Carefully distinguish the motivations in the present life situation and those in the transference from what is past, i.e., the sources of these motivations in the emotional patterns formed in childhood.
6. Be alert to note the effects of current stimuli on dreams and associations from life and transference.
7. Review the material for the libidinal and the hostile motivations and for fight and flight.
8. Review the material for the ego motivations and the sexual motivations.
9. Pay close attention to the sequence of the dream elements.
10. Watch for the material connected with the greatest emotional response.
11. Look for the positive progressive forces as well as for the regressive ones.
12. Look for the object relationships and also relationships by identification and projection.
13. Use symbols only with great caution and only in context.
14. Note what the dreamer's ego accepts and acts on in the dream, for this is an important guide to what the

patient will accept as interpretation in analysis and as behavior in life.

THE EGO AND UNCONSCIOUS MEANINGS

We have so often stressed the importance of appreciating the ego in understanding unconscious meanings that it is worth showing how it operates in dreams. The overall problem is highly complex; the scales that we are developing for gauging ego functions have some forty-eight categories (Saul and Sheppard, 1958). But the essential phenomenon can be illustrated by the following simple example (reprinted from Saul, 1953).

A male patient, well advanced in his analysis, reported a pair of dreams that reveal with crystal clarity how effectively the ego, even in sleep, can deal with disturbing stimuli. The "psychic situation," as Freud called it, was, in barest outline, as follows. The patient was in a hospital, his leg scrubbed and bandaged in preparation for the surgical removal of an exostosis the following afternoon. He understood that the operation was to be performed under local anesthesia, although he recalled that a surgeon once told him that local anesthesia does not work well in operations on bones and joints. Moreover, on admission, a physician who had stopped in to see him felt sure that a general anesthetic would be used and expressed surprise that the patient had been told otherwise. Nevertheless, that evening the patient was not aware of more than minimal anxiety. Although a private room had been reserved, the facilities were so crowded that it was necessary for him to share a double room. This was a considerable disappointment, as he had hoped to luxuriate for the few days in the leisure of well-controlled privacy relieved by reading, writing, and a few pleasant visits. This wish for a transient, mellow semi-seclusion was frustrated further by noises of the corridor, the elevator, and a ward just outside the door—a confusing, distracting cacophony that forestalled sleep until a small dose of Seconal induced it. During the evening he thought: "What kind of dream does one have the night before such a minor but possibly discomforting operation?" His curiosity was satisfied on awakening by recalling vividly a pair of dreams. "In the first one, I am all alone, viewing a pleasant but faintly somber landscape. A dead tree stands out on the skyline, rather marring it. In the second dream, there are many people of all ages about a pond which is used in winter for ice skating. A large smooth boulder and a few small ones protrude above the surface. I think: These are hazards for skating, but one can skate around them, and they even make it interesting."

The first dream fully satisfies the wishes for solitude and silence and corrects the disappointing reality of having a roommate and enduring nightlong noise. The dead tree is a replica of one that mars his view at home, which he is planning to cut down. Thus the exostosis is transformed into the tree. Cutting down the tree will improve appearances and provide fine firewood. There is only pleasure connected with its removal, no anxiety at all. The dream is almost completely successful. Only the faintly somber landscape suggests a possible allusion to anxiety.

The second dream brings in many people, but the noisy workers and the sufferers of the hospital are no longer disturbing—they have become the jolly, sonant crowd of the skating pond. Ice skating is a sport that the patient deeply enjoys, especially now that he takes and teaches his children. But it was doing this that irritated his foot and made necessary the operation. The dream transforms this unpleasantness into the boulders. Now the overgrowth of bone (the result of an old injury) appears as a boulder that makes the skating interesting. Thereby the anxiety vanishes except for the slight reference that one must be careful to avoid the boulders when skating. But this is no threat to even an average skater like the patient if he exercises reasonable care. Forgotten is the exostosis, the operation, the shattered privacy, the noisy corridor—all are corrected, replaced by situations of pleasure, thereby permitting the dreamer to sleep happily and awake refreshed.

The remarks about this patient's dream are limited to the functioning of the ego, omitting mention of id impulses, some of which are obvious in the manifest content of the dreams.

SUMMARY

In the use of the dream for treatment, it is essential to obtain associations very conscientiously in order to reach the fullest understanding and to achieve the maximum therapeutic effect. Thus, a manifest dream may seem quite obvious to the analyst and therefore may tempt him to interpret it forthwith. This, however, is not the most effective technique therapeutically. If the analyst will obtain detailed associations, almost inevitably he will obtain unexpected material and insight, and the patient, through this associative work, will further himself more rapidly and securely.

Yet, even in treatment and after carefully reaching an understanding of the dream through associations to its elements, the manifest dream is the best possible guide for making the interpretation itself. The manifest dream represents, as we have noted, a certain level of psychic activity—not libidinal level, but level of consciousness and of repression. It is deep enough to be infallibly revealing and yet not so deep that the unconscious processes are unintelligible or unacceptable to the patient. The manifest dream tells with great accuracy the level or depth at which the interpretation should be made (see Chap. 13).

The manifest dream is the product of many much deeper forces, but if these are dealt with simply as they appear, undue resistances are not mobilized. And the analysis proceeds in a smoother, faster fashion than it does if the analyst is not careful to follow the manifest dream as exactly as possible in making his interpretation to the patient. In most cases, what the ego represents and accepts in the manifest dream it will accept in interpretation without being greatly disturbed; if the ego accepts and acts on an impulse in the dream, then it is close to being able to do so in waking life. Since the manifest dream is the form given the unconscious forces and material by the ego in order to make them more acceptable, it tells the form in which the interpretation will be more acceptable.

Surely by this time, the danger of wild analysis has sufficiently diminished for us to study and make maximal use of the manifest dream for research, for rapid diagnostic understanding of the patient's dynamics, to show us the level at which to interpret, and as an indicator of his progress in treatment. It cannot be emphasized too strongly that for treatment, full associations to the dream elements must be obtained.

REFERENCES AND SOME RELATED READINGS

Alexander, F. (1961), *The Scope of Psychoanalysis,* 31–36. New York: Basic Books.

Altman, L. (1969), *The Dream in Psychoanalysis.* New York: Internat. Univ. Press.

Eder, M. D. (1930), Dreams as resistance. *Internat. J. Psychoanal.,* 11:92–94.

Erickson, E. H. (1954), The dream specimen of psychoanalysis. *J. Am. Psychoanal. A.,* 2:5–56.

French, T. (1970), *Psychoanalytic Interpretations.* Chicago: Quadrangle Books.

——— (1939), Insight and distortion in dreams. *Internat. J. Psychoanal.,* 20:287–298.

——— (1937), Reality and testing in dreams. *Psychoanal. Quart.,* 6:62–77.

French, T., and Fromm, E. (1964), *Dream Interpretation.* New York: Basic Books.

Freud, S. (1940), *An Outline of Psychoanalysis,* 51; 48. New York: Norton, 1949.

——— (1933), *New Introductory Lectures on Psychoanalysis,* 26; 32; 19-20. New York: Norton.

——— (1914), *On Dreams,* 71. London: Heinemann, 1924.

——— (1912), The dynamics of the transference. In *Collected Papers,* 2: 307. London: Hogarth Press, 1924.

——— (1900), *The Interpretation of Dreams,* 15; 75. London: Allen & Unwin, 1933.

Kanzer, M. (1955), The communicative function of the dream. *Internat. J. Psychoanal.,* 36: 260–266.

Krishna, D. (1952), Some Indian dream theories; a study and a comparison with western views. *Indian J. Psychol.,* 27: 27–37.

Lewin, B. D. (1952), Phcbic symptoms and dream interpretation. *Psychoanal. Quart.,* 21: 295–322.

——— (1948), Inferences and the dream screen. *Internat. J. Psychoanal.,* 29: 224–231.

Masserman, J., ed. (1971), *Dream Dynamics, Science and Psychoanalysis,* vol. 19. New York: Grune & Stratton.

McElroy, W. A. (1952), The frequency of dreams. *Quart. Bull. British Psychol. Soc.,* 3: 91–94.

Mittelman, B. (1949), Ego functions and dreams. *Psychoanal. Quart.,* 18: 434–448.

Saul, L. (1971), *Emotional Maturity,* 3rd ed., chap. 16. Philadelphia: Lippincott.

——— (1966), Embarrassment dreams of nakedness. *Internat. J. Psychoanal.,* 47: 552–558.

——— (1956), *The Hostile Mind,* 102. New York: Random House.

——— (1953), The ego in a dream. *Psychoanal. Quart.,* 22: 257–258.

——— (1940), Utilization of early current dreams in formulating psychoanalytic cases. *Psychoanal. Quart.,* 9: 453–469.

Saul, L., and Curtis, G. (1967), Dream form and strength of impulse in dreams of falling and other dreams of descent. *Internat. J. Psychoanal.,* 48: 281–287.

Saul, L., and Fleming, B. (1959), A clinical note on the ego meaning of certain dreams of flying. *Psychoanal. Quart.*, 28: 501–504.

Saul, L., and Sheppard, E. (1958), An approach to the ego functions. *Psychoanal. Quart.*, 27: 237–246.

Winget, C., and Kramer, M. (in preparation), *Dimensions of Dream Content*. Los Angeles, Calif.: Brain Infor. Service, Univ. of Calif., Los Angeles.

12 / SOME FEATURES OF CONDUCTING THE ANALYSIS

The tactics of conducting the individual hour depend on the basic strategy just as the individual plays in, for example, bridge or chess are devoted and coordinated to the overall goal. Therefore, the basis for dealing with the separate sessions is what we have already surveyed—the handling of the fundamental dynamics as they emerge in many forms and facets in each hour. What remains is, as in the matter of transference, special applications of eliciting the central dynamics and correcting them. The general principles of so doing have been covered already, but it will be well to review them briefly before discussing some special features of conducting the analysis.

Psychoanalysis is not hedonistic, as it has been popularly misconstrued as being. Because of the child-parent transference, it is basically authoritarian in setting. The analyst must, however lean over backward to avoid influencing or directing the always highly suggestible patient, while yet showing him the nature of his emotional development, life cycle, and relations to himself and others. Therefore, the analyst will do more than make the unconscious conscious and do more than focus exclusively on the infantile. The latter is exposed for the purpose of demonstrating how it impairs the mature functioning and for pointing to the directions in which solutions lie to the problems that it creates. The analyst always looks to the positive, healthy, normal, and progressive as the base to work from and toward.

The analyst will work with the presenting material from the top down, distinguishing the essential from the incidental, realizing how he would feel were he in the patient's ego, and using all data and content to comprehend emotion and motivation. He knows that the patient reacts to the analyst as he did in early childhood to his parents and as he now does to his superego, with object relations, identifications, and projections. The analyst uses his position to analyze out the disturbing forces, to overhaul the superego, and so to free and expand the mature development and the ego. Generally, the analyst follows the fourteen points that were described earlier (see Chap. 10) to guide him in understanding the unconscious meaning of the material. He works with the patient, with the patient's ego, and the mature parts of his personality. The analyst analyzes the person, not the symptom, and helps the patient to see how his childhood pattern of emotional forces affects his relations toward other persons, toward the analyst in particular, and toward himself. The patient must feel responsibility for himself—his unconscious is part of himself, and he must learn to take responsibility for it.

The analyst likes his patients and respects them. He realizes that many of the people that come to see him are not deeply neurotic but only mistaken in using infantile methods to reach their goals (e.g. in trying to win respect by exhibitionism rather than by accomplishment). The analyst remains incorruptibly analytic, helping the patient, however clinging and urgent he may be, toward getting his supports and satisfactions from real life.

Every patient has a central problem and a unique individual dynamic constellation. The analyst has this and the whole background in mind, yet, as we have noted, he observes the patient and the material of each session afresh, with an open mind, as though he never had seen the patient before.

He knows the analytic meaning of the term "to express" —not to act out, but to bring into awareness, to verbalize, discuss, and understand, to deal with, and solve.

He translates the meaning of the material from the language of the unconscious to that of the conscious, raising the level by keeping to the mature and analyzing the infantile, contrasting the infantile pattern of the past with the present reality. Unconscious psychoanalytic problems become raised to conscious psychological problems.

The analyst knows that he must especially handle the patient's dependent needs for love and his hostilities and their derivatives of inferiority and shame, guilt and masochism. And, he knows that in the end he must still bear some of the patient's resentment because the unconscious infantile wants not maturity but gratification. He will not be distressed by hostility or resistance, realizing that the distress that these cause the patient is precisely what he is called on to relieve. The analyst will simply deal with whatever is central and presenting, knowing that the more accurately he understands and can interpret this, the more clear the material will become and the more will the emotions become of optimal intensity. Usually the emotions are too strong, and the sooner the hostilities and the resistances come out, usually the sooner they can be analyzed.

The analyst's own feelings about the patient, his countertransference reactions, are typically a sensitive indicator of what is going on in the patient. The patient must feel that the analyst's opinion of him is directed, as it should be, not to the infantile feelings but to his ego's courage and maturity in facing and handling these childish feelings.

Thus, gradually, the analyst will learn when the obscurity is in the patient's material and when it is in his own inexperience.

The procedures of elucidating the core of the dynamics and interpreting what is central and presenting in each session are complementary and interrelated; together they constitute a cornerstone of the techniques of understanding, interpretation, and therapy.

It is usually essential therapeutically not only to see the main issues from the very beginning but also to acquaint the patient with them. Freud's reputed remark states the guiding principle: "You know it, why doesn't the patient know it?" The patient can know what he can accept, assuming it is imparted to him with skill and tact. He usually needs to know what is central and presenting. Once the patient knows the main issues, (1) his ego has a forewarning and thereby even a certain control over them, and (2) interpretations can be made more easily and more ego-syntonically. A patient becomes confused if his analysis is only a series of sessions dealing with this and that but without perspective on the central problem, rather like, perhaps, the pieces of a jigsaw puzzle that are never fitted together. By contrast, a patient's grasp on the main issues alone often can turn the tide.

A girl who was under such emotional pressure as to be in danger of a psychotic break responded rapidly with excellent development to discussion of her main problem in the very first few visits. What was involved in her case was simple but profound narcissistic competition—the uncompromising necessity to be the best in everything. It was an extension into every current relationship of the pattern toward her brother, which was intensified in earliest childhood by exaggerated closeness of both children to their mother. This was the result of the mother's ambition and a prolonged absence of the father. The girl's reaction to comprehending this was relief and the immediate beginning of progress.

In this girl, as in many instances, insight alone produced a strong and favorable initial effect. Of course, insight alone does not solve the problem, but it does give the ego the opportunity to see it openly and grapple with it rather than grope in darkness with an invisible foe. Some persons already have insight, and while this is probably good to some extent, it also can be, in part, disadvantageous. The effect of fresh insight in beginning analysis is lost, and it is evident that the patient, even though he knows the problem, has been unable to benefit from his life experience in solving it. However, this may only mean that a transference relationship is needed. In other persons the balance of forces is such that insight alone seems to be sufficient to tip the see-saw, and with it they are apparently able to go ahead, resolving the problem in life without having to go through the reconditioning correcting process of the transference. If this is tried first in doubtful cases, and if it then proves not to work, the patient is apt to return with good therapeutic urge for an analytic job.

It was with considerable difficulty that the historic pattern was discovered in the girl mentioned above. The dynamics were evident—the competitiveness with boys and girls of her own generation—but not its historic origin. The analyst can discuss the importance of this, probe tactfully for it, test the patient's responses to trial reconstructions of it from the current pattern in life and transference, but he cannot "ring in" what is not in the material. If, as is most unusual, the historic origin, the pattern in childhood, is not even vaguely discernible from the diagnostic interview, it probably will reveal itself as specific memories in the associations. This will prove true especially in response to accurate interpretations of the presenting dynamics and to continued searching for it on the parts of both patient and analyst. In rare instances, it is not only permissible but also advisable to see a parent or other person who can illumine the matter. On occasion, confronting the patient with information about his childhood pattern, which is gained from interviews with his relatives, might provide all the starter that is needed.

Focusing on the central dynamics and the presenting material yields the smoothest, fastest, most therapeutic analysis, because it always deals with what is uppermost and at the time most important. In addition, it also obviates many problems. For example, some patients make quite a point of their religious beliefs and may be chary about analysis because of them. Some beginners feel called upon to analyze these beliefs when they come up in the material. Clearly, in the light of all that we have said, this would be very poor technique indeed. It is the whole patient as a person who is being analyzed; he does not complain of the beliefs as a symptom, and even if he did, they are part of the content of the associations. The analyst should be focused not on parts of the content but on the common element that reveals the presenting dynamics. He usually can analyze the patient without even discussing the religious beliefs.

The same principles hold true for the arts and other forms of sublimated, delicately balanced creativity. In general, these talents should not be analyzed as such or even touched at all if it can be avoided. This can be achieved by adhering to a technique that focuses on the bull's-eye—the underlying disturbed emotional forces that produce the difficulties—while at the same time it is flexible and looks to observe the whole picture.

As in surgery, the pathology can be dealt with while leaving the healthy tissues as untouched and unmolested as possible. The principle is to do no harm—*primum non nocere.* Precious talents, sublimations, abilities, and capacities should be recognized, appreciated, valued, and above all, respected. Usually it is best to avoid tampering with them unless absolutely necessary. (This point will be taken up in more detail in Chap. 13.)

Dealing with the major, underlying forces not only makes it possible to avoid disturbing that which should be preserved, but it also often undercuts the symptoms of which the patient wishes to be rid. Not infrequently a symptom, such as headache for example, will disappear as the main emotional problem is resolved, even though the symptom never has been discussed and analyzed as such. Conversely, if the analyst goes after the symptom, it may persist stubbornly because the fundamental forces that produce it have not been dealt with successfully.

Cognizance of the positives in the patient also usually establishes a justifiably optimistic atmosphere for treatment and gives legitimate emotional support. A borderline schizophrenic young man, after some months of marked progress, commented with deep appreciation, "Why you never treated me as though I were very sick." Moreover, this attitude made it harder for him to use his illness for secondary gains, such as special consideration and indulgence from others, escapes from responsibility, and so on. Expecting the mature and dealing with the mature, helped the patient to achieve it. And, very significantly, it made him ashamed of regressing and thereby being less respected.

A woman had had an acute psychotic episode, but the underlying dynamics were clear. The analyst adopted this attitude toward the patient: "Yours is not a terribly unusual problem at all. You have a little more resentment toward your father and your husband than you are fully aware of, and you take your resentments too hard because your ideals for being all-loving are so high. Just relax; let's look at this a bit more closely and you'll soon be on the way out."

Sometimes this puts the analyst in a difficult professional position. For instance, a winsome young wife is patently a barely compensated, severely schizoid personality. However, the tendency to regress and behave like a small child is quite near to consciousness and is analyzable. Her young husband is very able, energetic, and boyish but he is not at all psychological. Through careful analyzing of the extreme regressiveness, totally unconscious hostility, and almost insupportable guilt, the prospects of development toward maturity and secure stability are reasonably good. Of key importance in this strategy is to give the wife confidence and support, expecting the best from her. But, of course, there are very considerable risks. Suppose a psychotic break is not successfully prevented. To protect himself, the analyst should discuss these risks with the husband. The physician's duty, however, extends to more than just forewarning; he must also share the responsibility with the young man. However, to do so will jeopardize the chances of helping the patient, for one can easily picture how this thoroughly unpsychological, eager young husband will be dashed by hearing that his wife may have a psychotic episode even if she is treated and that the outlook is unquestionably bleaker if she is not. With what strange, distant expressions will he thereafter view his wife? How will her own loving and being loved equilibrium with him be upset? To what extent will their anxieties be aroused? Will her marital security and her self-confidence be shaken or shattered? The analyst cannot put the patient's relationship with her husband in jeopardy, for this provides the very setting and security that cure requires.

Some potentially suicidal patients present the same dilemma. Some wives and husbands simply cannot tolerate the knowledge that their mates are suicidal or verge on breakdown, and they react so strongly that there is risk of precipitating what the analyst is called on to prevent. In such a spot, the analyst may find that he has no choice but to risk his own professional reputation rather than the patient's chances of cure. However, if his lodestar consists in doing his best for the patient, then, come what may, he will sleep nights.

While on the topic of families, certain other points deserve mention. Even sympathetic listening can be destructive if the analyst is not everlastingly aware of what is going on. For example, a husband may come because of domestic difficulties and, in describing them, express himself about his wife, warming to the subject under the analyst's sympathetic ear and feeling more and more justified in his resentment. If the wife finds an equally benevolent listener, she too may vent more and more criticism, and the rift between the two is widened. In situations like this, I have seen friendships between analysts become very strained. Both husband and wife sought help in the hope of saving their marriage, each going to a different analyst. In theory these two analysts were free to communicate, which they did. But each over-identified with his own patient. As often happens, the husband spoke mostly of his wife and she of her husband, each justifying their frustrations and hostilities to their respective analysts. Each analyst seemed to understand the other analyst's patient better than his own, was drawn into the rift, and unintentionally widened it instead of closing and thereby healing it. This not too uncommon pitfall applies, of course, to other relationships as well, such as that of parent and child.

Wives of psychoanalytic candidates and, of course, husbands of female candidates have the same reactions as spouses of analysands in straight treatment, but what is unique about them is that they have an enduring relation to the field and the profession.

The wife (or, *mutatis mutandis*, the husband) is apt to experience (1) jealousy of her husband's confidential relation and transference attachment to his analyst; (2) fear of what her husband will find out about his feelings for her; (3) fear that he will change too much or in the wrong ways; (4) concern over the household skeletons that he may reveal; and (5) envy of him for a relationship to the analyst that she would like to have. The wife's hostility to analysis may mask a desire to replace her husband with the analyst, out of childish sibling or oedipal rivalry. For example, a very well-balanced wife whose husband was in analysis told him this dream. "You (the husband), the analyst, and I were on the moon. I sent you to get some bread. Then I was embarrassed to find that I was alone with the analyst. Then he put diapers on me. I permitted it but then was surprised and shocked."

Of course, there are many other reactions besides the common ones listed above. For example, here are two less typical but certainly not rare attitudes: (1) some wives and husbands feel that since the analysand is getting emotional support from the analyst, it is permissible to beat on him or her; and (2) there may be resentment because of the time and the expense involved.

Whether or not to see the spouse often merits judicious consideration. In my experience, doing so in carefully selected instances is almost always helpful. The spouse feels less left out and more in on the whole, long, time-consuming, and expensive undertaking. The desire to belong is one of the powerful human motivations, stemming probably from the child's need for acceptance by its family. Its relation to exclusiveness, cliques, and the like warrants more special study than has yet been accorded to it.

By meeting the analyst, the spouse sees him as a real person, and usually some of the unconscious feelings about him can be palliated, sometimes even by frank discussion. And in most instances, the spouse gives valuable sidelights on the patient, of whom the analyst, after all, has only an office-eye view, seeing him through his free associations but not through his actual intimate behavior during everyday experience.

Reconciliation with the parents may be of special importance in the case of younger persons. The parents provide the natural biologic emotional support for children, and for a person to feel this support is critical. It is devastating to feel unloved by one's own parents or to experience the pain that invariably arises from unresolvable discords. Contrastingly, what is critically necessary to emotional development is to feel secure and confident from having the love of harmonious parents. Each adult's primary job, domestically, is good relations with mate and children so that the latter can develop in emotional health. The relation to the parents remains powerful throughout a person's whole life because of his introjection of them in early childhood as his main superego figures.

An eighteen-year-old girl was becoming distraught and anxious to the extent of withdrawing from all of her friends. Her history revealed that her family was constantly moving from one place to another. These repeated uprootings and new adjustments—new homes, schools, teachers, friends—made her irritable as a child. The parents, themselves, frustrated, reacted with impatience; this, of course, made the child feel more insecure and less loved, and she became still more irritable. This common vicious circle increased the hostilities between child and parents until they were quite alienated from each other. The child, now a young woman, was so upset by the friction and the estrangement that her other human contacts were disrupted. This upset her further, setting up another vicious circle—friction with people increased her isolation, and this caused more anxiety and even greater difficulties in making and holding friends. Few persons can stand extreme isolation; it is when the last libidinal bond is threatened or severed that breakdowns occur.

Early in treatment the girl realized the nature of the vicious circles in which she was trapped. However, the thought of having it out openly and frankly with her parents was enough to make her quite hysterical with anxiety and weeping. Nevertheless, she went to them. She told them outright that they were her natural supports and that she needed their love. To her astonishment, her mother replied that they had tried to give it but that she would not accept it! They found each other again. The girl had gained enough insight from the analysis to effect this. Thus reunited, feeling loved by her parents, the vicious circles were broken; she quieted down and felt enough assurance to mend her friendships and move gradually toward healthy interpersonal living. The mother always had tried to impose excessively high social and scholastic standards; this had created a serious problem of rebellion and conflict in the girl, but it could now be worked out along with other problems in a setting of basic filial-parental rapport. Thus, it is often important to get the patient not only to see the nature and meaning of the relationships to the parents but to learn to handle them and to improve them.

Needless to say, good relations with parents are best

established for grownups on an increasingly mature adult-to-adult level and less and less as child-to-parent. It is essential to recognize this. Gradually the child becomes the mid-generation, with the strength of biologic maturity, while the parents weaken in the inexorable course of the life cycle. Yet, a man of sixty-five remarked to a friend when he lost his father, aged ninety, with whom, moreover, he had had almost no rapport, "I always felt that no matter what happened I could go to my father—now I am like a child, naked and alone in the world." It is not so easy to relinquish having parents and to accept the biologic destiny of being one.

We can now deal with a few points that would have diverted us had we touched on them previously.

Even effective, accurate insight into the presenting dynamics, while clarifying and usually relieving, often produces some legitimate confusion. It shakes the patient's accustomed reactions of a lifetime, without immediately providing new, better, more realistic attitudes and adaptions. And the new attitudes, even with the forces of maturity behind them, can be developed only slowly, by practice in life. Strength comes, as in the muscles, through use. The interim is often confusing, difficult, and painful. However, this is the wholesome confusion of change and growth, to be distinguished sharply from the confusion that results from failure to focus on the essentials and on the central presenting material.

A young analyst remarked that he felt rather self-conscious because as he looked for the main issues it seemed that "the same conflict keeps coming up." His patient was a law student who struggled with such dependence on his mother that he was in constant conflict over leaving law school to live in her apartment with her. Now one facet, now another, showed in the associations. The various adult masculine strivings toward responsible productive independence (RPI), marriage and children, professional success, and the like, mingled with passive receptive dependence (PRD). The latter was usually directed toward mother but sometimes it was aimed at substitutes and in different forms such as being given money and automobiles, going to prostitutes, relinquishing all responsibilities by leaving law school, and being supported.

By penetrating deeply enough to the core of the problem, the basic constellation was seen again and again, with different aspects coming uppermost, like a revolving crystal whose facets successively catch a ray of light and thus reveal themselves. This recurrence of the basic constellation of emotions is not sterile repetition. It is a growth process. It is the patient revolving the core of the problem in his mind, seeking solutions, trying to move to the mature against the undertow of the infantile. It is part of the working through, the deconditioning and reconditioning. For this purpose, in addition to the insight, much talking over is needed. Insight alone, as we have emphasized, is indispensable, but it is only the first step. For the patient to understand something about himself by solitary introspection, that is, only intrapsychically, is very different from discussing it with the analyst. It is largely by talking it over that the patient learns that, despite his underlying feelings, he is not a child and that the analyst is not his parent. This young law student would see that the analyst, instead of repeating his mother's tendency to coddle him into dependence, wants to see him become mature and responsible; and when this angers the patient, he need not be secretly sadistic but can discuss it forthrightly. Gradually, he feels the deconditioning and reconditioning effects of this different attitude, this after-education, this corrective emotional experience. He is now exposed to those attitudes under which, had he been reared properly, he would have grown up from birth without this problem.

A very able but inhibited man was surprised that, unlike his father, the analyst did not always show him that he could not do a thing, nor try to show him how to do it, nor do it for him. Often the analyst has to say things that the parents never said, and the patient must express what never could be mentioned to his parents.

A patient may gain insight into handicapping infantile

needs only to react so vigorously against them that he goes to an opposite extreme. The law student mentioned above, for example, began to feel that to escape dependence on his mother, with all its consequent sense of weakness, femininity, and inadeqaucy, he must do nothing but slave-drive himself. He felt that to relax and read a magazine or go to a concert was feminine.

Here the talking over must clarify the direction of the solution, namely, a life in which the mature responsible-productive-independent (RPI) activities are in balance with the infantile passive-receptive-dependent ones (PRD), and both are enjoyed. A man may yearn for vacation, but when he is on one he may feel uneasy and that he should be at work—he enjoys neither, instead of enjoying both. We have mentioned Freud's remark that mental health is the capacity to love and to work. We can expand this to the capacity to enjoy responsible loving and working in proper balance with the enjoyment of legitimate respite, recreation, and relaxation (Saul, 1956).

In regard to the femininity mentioned above, even to the extent of becoming unmistakable latent homosexuality, usually it is best not to discuss it too openly or too much until it is thoroughly understood. This, of course, is not to say that it should not be dealt with in the most effective way. The point here is that there is great danger in interpreting it prematurely because this is more apt to mobilize than to cure it. For it is itself only symptomatic, the result of something else, of some ten or more different possible dynamic mechanisms (Saul and Beck, 1961). In the law student it was one expression of his excessive infantile dependence on and identification with his mother. If it is overt, it is mentioned by the patient, being already mobilized. But if it is latent, it is patently far better to remove the causes without mobilizing it, as can be done with other symptoms and feelings. For example, one man had lost both parents when he was a small child. A maiden aunt took him into her home. He was deeply afraid of feeling any hostility whatsoever toward her, let alone expressing it, because of his insecurity about being loved. He developed intensified needs to be loved by her to cover this anxiety and insecurity in relation to her, and these desperate needs for love made him feel overly submissive, childish, and weak, and this enraged him. It was not necessary to mobilize his hostility in order to analyze it for it diminished as the causes of it were analyzed and decreased. Of course, if the ability to express hostility is an issue, or if there are feelings of weakness and rage over the hostility being inhibited and not available, then it may be necessary for the patient to test the analyst by verbally expressing some hostility directly to him to prove that it can be done without loss of love or dire punishment. This is similar to the phobias in which, usually, the patient must test himself in the anxiety situation, for example, entering the water if this is what he fears to do.

What has been said about latent homosexuality is part of another principle also, namely, that the analyst not be sucked into the patient's own defenses, especially that of flight by regression. Just as it is often easier to be occupied with the latent homosexuality than to remove its sources, so also with other trends. Thus, a businessman with serious financial difficulties and much masochistic competitiveness escapes in his dreams to infantile situations, mostly oral and anal. The unwary analyst may be led off into analyzing his infantile feeding and toilet habits, without realizing that this is the essence of the dream's defense—to flee in fantasy to these situations in order to escape the sleep-disturbing problems of the pressures, demands, and complexities of current life. Not that the oral and the anal trends are not important, but, as always, they must be seen not as irreducible and unanalyzable entities in themselves, but in the perspective of the childhood constellation and the presenting dynamics in the current life situation. Otherwise, the analyst may mistake for the real problem what is actually defense and escape (Alexander, 1961).

Another interesting type of defense to be alerted to is

that of the patient doing everything himself. This is, in part, independence and responsibility and, as such, mature and excellent. But one day the explosion may burst forth as an angry attack by the patient, who vehemently proclaims that the analyst has done nothing and done it all wrong, that he has got nothing from the analysis and can do everything and do it better, and so on.

Some patients bring up floods of infantile memories to escape from current irritations; others flee to immediate matters to avoid childhood patterns and deeper feelings, as did a young woman who could not stand facing her feelings of having been unwanted by her parents. Some flee into the past, some into the present (Deutsch, 1932).

Of course, the patient's resistance may be aroused. It may be turned against facing something in himself or in his feelings toward parents or siblings or the analyst or anyone at all, for that matter. A wife, for example, may shy off any analyzing because she vaguely senses that her marriage is not so idyllic as she leads herself to picture it. She fears that she actually has more hostility to her husband than she could stand, and that were she analyzed she might turn irretrievably against him. One woman had been forced by her parents for empty, snobbish reasons to relinquish the man she had long loved. Forced to marry her parents' choice, she had to believe that she loved him and that she still loved her parents. Would a properly conducted analysis actually disrupt marriages such as these? Are all concerned better off with their illusions? Or will the repressed frustration, the inner lie, the unacknowledged hostility, always return and find expression, however disguised? Could analysis, without destroying, build better upon the truth, upon emotional honesty? Psychoanalysis is emotional honesty combined with corrective, reconditioning after-education.

The analyst must ever be alert to the forms of regression and hostile aggression. These are the two forces of the fight-flight reaction, which is the deep-seated, automatic, reflex, primitive form of adaptation. It is in fundamental contrast and opposition to mature cooperation. Interpreting flight, escape, and dependence frequently hurts the patient's pride and arouses hostility, and interpreting the patient's hostility often stimulates escape by flight through regression. The patient may feel trapped and anxious because of this. It is usually relieving for him to be shown the way out.

A patient talks of suicide, rambles on about gay nothings, or vituperates bitterly, but, whatever the content, the analyst, while noting what the patient says consciously, looks through it for the red thread. What is his unconscious saying? There are exceptions to all rules, but the most reliable guide is to understand the patient, see the childhood pattern, read each session's material for what is most central and presenting unconsciously, and make every hour count by discussing this understanding with the patient in a therapeutic way and insofar as he can accept it. This brings us to the matter of making interpretations.

REFERENCES AND SOME RELATED READINGS

Alexander, F. (1961), Two forms of regression and their therapeutic implications. In *The Scope of Psychoanalysis,* 290–304. New York: Basic Books.

——— (1954), Some quantitative aspects of psychoanalytic technique. *J. Am. Psychoanal. A.*, 2: 685–701.

Bion, W. R. (1965), *Transformations, Changes From Learning to Growth.* New York: Basic Books.

Brodsky, B. (1968), Working through: Its widening scope and some aspects of its metapsychology. *Psychoanal. Quart.*, 36: 485–531.

Deutsch, H. (1932), *The Psychoanalysis of the Neuroses*, 23. London: Hogarth Press.

Dunbar, F. (1952), Technical problems in the analysis of psychosomatic disorders with special reference to precision in short term psychotherapy. *Internat. J. Psychoanal.*, 33: 385–396.

Ekstein, R., and Wallerstein, R. (1972), *The Teaching and Learning of Psychotherapy.* New York: Internat. Univ. Press.

Ferenczi, S. (1936), *Further Contributions to the Theory and Technique of Psychoanalysis.* London: Hogarth Press and Instit. of Psychoanal.

——— (1931), Child analysis in the analysis of adults. *Internat. J. Psychoanal.,* 12:468–482.

French, T. (1937), A clinical study of learning in the course of a psychoanalytic treatment. *Psychoanal. Quart.,* 5: 148–194.

Freud, S. (1910–1919), Papers on technique. In *Collected Papers,* vol. 2. London: Hogarth Press, 1924.

Giovacchini, P., ed. (1971), *Psychoanalytic Treatment.* New York: Science House.

Glover, E. (1955), *The Technique of Psychoanalysis.* New York: Internat. Univ. Press.

Greenacre, P. (1956), Re-evaluation of the process of working through. *Internat. J. Psychoanal.,* 37:439–444.

Greenacre, P. *et. al.* (1953), The traditional psychoanalytic technique. *J. Am. Psychoanal. A.,* 1:526–574.

Greenson, R. (1967), *Technique and Practice of Psychoanalysis.* New York: Internat. Univ. Press.

Guntrip, H. (1971), *Psychoanalytic Theory, Therapy and the Self.* New York: Basic Books.

Haley, J. (1963), *Strategies of Psychotherapy.* New York: Grune & Stratton.

Hallender, M. (1965), *The Practice of Psychoanalytic Psychotherapy.* New York: Grune & Stratton.

Horney, K. (1956), The technique of psychoanalytic therapy. *Am. J. Psychoanal.,* 16:26–31.

Kelman, H. (1969), What is technique? *Am. J. Psychoanal.,* 29:157–169.

Masserman, J., ed. (1971), *Techniques of Therapy.* New York: Grune & Stratton.

——— (1955), *The Practice of Dynamic Psychiatry.* Philadelphia: Saunders.

Oberndorf, C. P. (1913), The scope and technique of psychoanalysis. *Med. Rec.,* 84 : 973.

Redlich, F., and Freedman, D. (1966), *The Theory and Practice of Psychiatry.* New York: Basic Books.

Saul, L. (1956), *The Hostile Mind.* New York: Random House.

Saul, L., and Beck, A. (1961), Psychodynamics of male homosexuality. *Internat. J. Psychoanal.,* pts. 1 & 2.

Schmideberg, M. (1938), The mode of operation of psychoanalytic therapy. *Internat. J. Psychoanal.,* 19 : 310–320.

Simmel, E. (1929), Psychoanalytic treatment in a sanatorium. *Internat. J. Psychoanal.,* 10 : 70–90.

Waelder, R. (1936), The problem of freedom in psychoanalysis and the problem of reality testing. *Internat. J. Psychoanal.,* 17 : 89–108.

Wolman, B., ed. (1967), *Psychoanalytic Techniques, A Handbook for the Practicing Psychoanalyst.* New York: Basic Books.

13 / MAKING INTERPRETATIONS

UNDERSTANDING THE PATIENT

Interpretation is always the second of two steps, the first of which is understanding what is going on in the patient. Only on the basis of this understanding can the analyst know what to interpret and how and when to do so. Interpretations must be made only as a skilled, careful, precise technical procedure, as uninfluenced as possible by any personal interests or subjective feelings of the analyst. Beginners especially sometimes feel urged to make interpretations because of their own inner reactions; because it is far easier to talk than to read the unconscious silently; because they may feel impelled to give the patient a response and thus demonstrate understanding; and so on.

What we have said about the nature of psychoanalytic therapy and the reading of the unconscious has laid down the basic general principles for making interpretations. For orientation to the context of this chapter, let us skim over them here before going on to more specific points.

Ever in the analyst's awareness will be the dynamics, the historics, the transference, the resistance, and what is essential and central and currently presenting rather than the peripheral, incidental, off-center associations, for almost everything is in every hour, but not everything is in the very center of the limelight. With the background and the dynamics and all the other hours in the back of his mind, the analyst will view each hour afresh as though he never had seen the patient before. He will refer to what he knows only after understanding, without preconception, the present hour. If he sees the main topic of an hour and the patient is far enough along, he may ask the patient if he can recognize any childhood pattern behind it, for he will constantly confront the internalized past with the current reality.

All sorts of contents of associations can reveal the main dynamics. Needs for love, revenge, rivalry, identification, dependence, and the like, can be expressed in the associations through such contents as the events of the day, opinions on various topics, professional or domestic problems, gossip of all sorts, books read or plays or motion pictures seen, memories, dreams, and fantasies. The analyst, as we have pointed out previously, is seeking the main unconscious dynamic forces that have brought forward and directed these associations, but he is by no means uninterested in what telltale contents are used to unveil them. One person, rather schizoid, may be unable to face these forces in his life and will tell mostly fantasies and stories; another can speak of childhood but not of his present feeling; another can do nothing except complain about her husband.

It is most instructive and illuminating and often yields a fresh perspective to pass in review the different contents that characterize the associations of a series of patients. This shows what they have on their minds consciously, regardless of what their unconscious forces may be. And this content reveals much about the ego and its relations to the rest of the personality and to the outer world, especially to other persons. In the proper broad sense of the term, this is also part of the dynamics, which includes the interplay of all forces in the personality.

However, the analyst will not be misled by conscious utterances alone but will use everything to discern the unconscious forces, for what the patient's unconscious says is far more important than what his conscious says. He may even say one thing consciously and mean another unconsciously. The analyst works through the conscious ego, the great organ of adaptation, but through it he converses with the unconscious, all the while bringing it to consciousness. A man verbally flayed the analyst for an interpretation, but at the end of the session, as he was stalking out of the door, turned and dropped his voice to quiet friendly tones to say, "Of course, you are perfectly right."

Usually there is no trouble if the analyst keeps to the level of the common elements and the manifest dreams and makes interpretations as closely as possible in their language. The fourteen guides to understanding unconscious material (see Chap. 10) apply also, for the most part, to interpreting.

INTERPRETING THE MATERIAL

The analyst wants the patient to feel understood, but he does not want to give interpretations that are threatening to him, except in special circumstances wherein this would be done very deliberately and for well-considered reasons. Of course, whether or not an interpretation is threatening depends on when and how it is given. The analyst should not strive to be deep or in any way artificial. The depth comes if he sticks to understanding that part of the interplay of unconscious forces that is most direct, simple, and uppermost, always working from the top down.

To discover this presenting interplay, the analyst should be silent almost the whole session for any remarks, questions, or off-center interpretations of secondary issues will invariably throw into disorder the unfolding chain of associations. Rarely is it a mistake to wait until near the end of the session to remark, question, and deal the big punch squarely on target. Another reason for this is the fact that very often the unconscious emerges more and more frankly as the associations go on, developing, taking more definite shape, and appearing more directly. Undoubtedly, there are several reasons for this. There are inner ones such as the progressive emergence of underlying feelings, as seems to occur in so many dreams. There are also more reactive reasons such as the pressure of the ending of the hour, which can, for example, either spur wishes to make the most of the time or impel the patient to bring revealing material in order to please the analyst. It is not impossible to keep a conversational tone and atmosphere without actually speaking. In occasional instances an exception must be made, and the analyst must ease the tension, if it is too great, by actual conversation—the principle here is one of keeping emotional intensities optimal. It is far easier to converse, but his job is to analyze.

TIMING INTERPRETATIONS

The guiding principle in timing interpretations, relative to the whole treatment and to individual sessions, is that of readiness. This usually boils down to the question: can it be done ego-syntonically and almost unnoticeably? What is central and presenting is usually, ipso facto, close enough to consciousness to require interpretation if the interpretation is communicated ego-syntonically. If dreams come up spontaneously in the associations, this is usually because the patient consciously or unconsciously wants them interpreted, and most often the main theme can be discussed in a way that is acceptable to the patient. Anxiety in dreams and associations is not helped by ignoring it or waiting; it can be alleviated only by understanding and discussing it.

Fear of making an interpretation because of possible extreme reactions of the patient is usually groundless, prodeded that the analyst sees the major, presenting issue clearly. Emotions are usually stronger and more dangerous when unconscious. Thus, a properly made interpretation relieves rather than increases the patient's anxiety. In fact, anxiety and dangers increase if the material is ripe and *not* interpreted. It is more dangerous to delay when the patient is ready for an interpretation than not to.

Although there has been much discussion about maintaining the patient's anxieties in order to speed treatment, this seems to refer only to exceptional situations. For example, a threat to cut down the number of visits of a patient who cannot see his dependence is a move intended to keep the intensity of feeling at an optimum. However, since most patients are handicapped and threatened by overly intense childish drives, most analyses progress best as they reduce the anxiety and so reclaim ego—"Where id was, there shall ego be."

The sooner the patient is understood and is made acquainted with the drives and the feelings that trouble him, the sooner these threats will be reduced. He will be able more freely to associate and reveal himself and learn to handle these forces. Further, the sooner he recognizes his problem, the sooner will he have advance preparation and perspective to forearm himself against the impacts of future insights. Early interpretation diminishes dramatic moments in favor of smoothness, swiftness, and effectiveness.

The necessity of seeing the pattern of the whole hour and of shunning part, peripheral, and off-center interpretations dictates the postponement of interruptions and interpretations until near the end. Only rarely are exceptions indicated. It is often not easy to maintain silence, especially if a patient wants to discuss certain content, but the analyst almost invariably is rewarded if he explains that he can be of more help if he listens further and comments later. It is nearly always better for the analyst to think it and postpone saying it. If he waits, he will usually find that he has something different to say.

There are always exceptions—what we are describing here are guiding principles, not inexorable rules. We must recognize, for example, that free association can be extremely difficult for some patients. Some start the hour by being relatively calm; then, as they free associate, there is no mistaking the mounting of tension, anxiety, and hostility. The emotions build up as the patient free associates, and sometimes this is accompanied by regressive thinking, feeling, and behavior. Therefore, in order to keep the transference at an optimal intensity, the analyst may have to break in and usually interpret, if possible, before the transference exceeds this optimum.

Making every hour count does not necessarily mean that an interpretation must be given at the end of every hour, even though this is usually the best way to make the hour effective. However, by way of example, if the analyst gauges that in a particular patient at a particular time there is some increasing frustration in the transference and that for very good reasons it would be better to continue this frustration, then he may say nothing at the end of the hour, feeling that the whole issue will emerge more clearly in the next hour or so if he remains silent. However, such a procedure is part of the broader question of manipulation. Should the analyst go still further and be late to hours or cancel hours or resort to other methods outside of strict analytic understanding in order to influence the development of the patient's feelings?

More specifically related to interpretations themselves is the question why the main point of the hour is not intelligible. If the analyst is sure that this is because of the patient's material and not because of his own lack of discernment, then is it best to discuss this obscurity of the material with the patient? Or is it better to remain silent in order not to reward the patient with any discussion for an hour of undecipherable material? No doubt, the answer depends on the individual patient and circumstance.

Almost every hour can be made to count, and with rare exceptions, this means interpreting or eliciting an interpretation of its central presenting unconscious meaning. In the past, long periods of weeks and months without movement were sometimes explained by the analyst as having been necessary for certain feelings to develop or certain material to be expressed. It is true that the transference develops and that further key material emerges. There is usually an initial spurt, followed by the slower working through, with a terminal spurt under the pressure of ending. But the main issue in almost every hour must be discerned and discussed if the session is to be of maximal effect. This means allowing a little time near the end of the period for the patient to react to the interpretation. The analyst will, first of all, want to hear the analysand's conscious reaction. Then, he will want to let the patient go on with enough associations to learn from their common theme how his unconscious is responding.

GENERAL PRINCIPLES OF INTERPRETATION

How to make interpretations is largely an art, but the principles can be formulated, as the foundations of all arts can be formulated and taught. The art probably lies largely in the personality of the analyst and in his feelings for the patient, in his basic countertransference attitudes, as well as in his professional knowledge and experience. If he has genuine interest, sympathy, and a sincere desire to help, then these will be reflected in all that he does and says. Tact, sensitivity, and consideration are the attitudinal bases of interpreting. And if the analyst is reasonably secure and free in his own personality and in his interpersonal relations, then he can be easy and natural in discussing all matters with the patient.

Following is a description of the general principles underlying the making of interpretations.

Total interpretation. The student often gingerly advances a partial interpretation with the correct and laudable purpose of making it simple and acceptable for the patient. However, frequently it is far easier for the patient to understand this bit in relation to the overall than it is for him to comprehend an isolated motive or feeling. The ego integrates. The total interpretation of the major feelings and their relationship often facilitates comprehension and integration. Naturally, this refers to the major emotional forces and not to an intricate mass of detail. Sometimes it is indicated to interpret only certain details, but as a general principle, these are digested much better if they are brought into their relationships to the major emotional forces and the total situation.

Realistic interpretation. It is easier to interpret symbols in the "dreambook" fashion that Freud warned against than it is to translate the language of the unconscious into the ego's conscious way of verbalizing feelings. Much time is saved if the analyst can see the unconscious meaning in very practical, ordinary, realistic terms and interpret it in a friendly, matter-of-fact way. As a rule, all elements of the dramatic, the mystic, the wonderful, and the awesome should be entirely eliminated. They make it interesting for the analyst but they are apt to arouse unnecessary anxieties in the patient. To fascinate him and to provide him with a dramatic element tends to allow the patient to focus on unconscious forms without realizing their connections with the everyday realities of his life. Such reactions slow the analysis. The unconscious feelings are basically those of childhood and are simple and direct in nature, however disguised by the defenses. To shear from them these defenses and also the unconscious language and the excess of intellectualization and express them in a simple and realistic form is a great help, a timesaver, and a prophylactic against rationalizations. This form of conversational and easy-going discussion helps the patient with his troubles, allays his anxieties, and often makes it possible to get across with ease alarming interpretations in borderline cases.

Usually it is best to ease over interpretations so casually that the patient hardly realizes the speed and the importance of his deepening insight. This too helps eliminate any tendencies toward the exotic that might be present, and as such, it serves the goal of realistic interpretation.

Allying with the ego. Of great help in making interpretations is the technique of allying with the ego. The patient comes to the analyst for help, and so the tone and slant of the interpretations should be designed to acquaint the patient with the unconscious motivations that cause his troubles. Expressed technically, the analyst sides with the ego and acts as its friend and supporter. Thereby, the analyst also undermines the threatening, accusing, punishing concept of himself that the patient unconsciously almost always has. Furthermore, it is usually well to ally with the progressive, developmental forces in the patient, showing the role of the masochistic and infantile reactions in impairing mature, well-balanced management and enjoyment of life.

Focusing on the main issues. All of the above presumes, of course, the ability to understand accurately the patient's unconscious and to keep always in mind the central emotional forces and not to be misled into side issues, now here, now there, which only confuse the analysis.

Focusing on the main issues is perhaps the most important single technical principle. If the resistance is the central material, it will be brought out into relief, and then, of course, it is this which must be focused on. The patient must see the main issues quickly and consistently so that he can integrate the endless details rather than flounder in them.

Concentrating on dream material. Interpretation usually should be narrowed down to the presenting material, particularly to that which shows in the dreams. Dreams reveal most openly the presenting forces and the defenses against them; and this means that what is necessary is an accurate interpretation of the manifest dream in the light of the latent dream thoughts. If there are no dreams, the resistances against them must be resolved, for the dream is, as Freud said, the via regia, the royal road, to the unconscious. Unquestionably, the most revealing hours are those with dreams. No penetrating analysis is possible without dreams.

Supporting evidence. Interpretation usually should be backed up by plenty of evidence. There should be the common element in the associations, the representation in the manifest dream, and what of the dream-work can be constructed. A mass of cogent material should be marshaled to bear down on the narrow, limited, highly focused point of the hour. In other words, the interpretation should be narrowed down to the very point of the presenting material and should be backed up by ample evidence. This accuracy is one of the truly legitimate methods for shortening analysis.

An important exception is where the analyst wants to throw out only vague suggestions to help a patient gain his own insights. This would be particularly appropriate in a case where the analyst wanted to prepare a patient for a shocking one. For example, a woman who could tolerate no hint of hostility to anyone had to be prepared to recognize her rage at her own mother, which was keeping her seriously depressed.

Patient participation in interpretation. Freud (1910) stated:

> Every advance in our knowledge means an increase in the power of our therapy . . . the more we understand the more we shall achieve. At its beginning, psychoanalytic treatment was inexorable and exhaustive. The patient had to say everything himself, and the physician's part consisted of urging him on incessantly. To-day things have a more friendly air. The treatment is made up of . . . what the physician infers and tells the patient, and of the patient's . . . "working through" what he hears . . . We give the patient the conscious idea of what he may expect to find and the similarity of this with the repressed unconscious one leads him to come upon the latter himself.

Except for potent reasons, interpretations should not be made in a dogmatic way. An authoritarian attitude toward the patient will prove hopelessly ineffective. It is much more convincing and incisive to convey interpretations by eliciting them from the patient. When the analysand is asked what he makes of the dream, his attention is called to the chain of associations. In an effort to elicit the central point from the patient himself, he may be asked what this might refer to in his daily life, what its application is to the transference, and what the childhood pattern might be.

Asking the patient what he makes of the hour (1) encourages independence of thought; (2) trains him for future ability to understand himself; (3) provides the analyst with more ideas as to the meaning of the associations; (4) shows the status of the ego—what the material means to the ego; and (5) provides a good starting platform upon which the analyst can build and modify what the patient already sees. This is an important technical device. Often the patient can help the analyst understand obscure material, and much is gained through the patient's interest and responsibility in participating in his treatment in this way. Nevertheless, the analyst is alone basically; only he can understand what is unconscious to the patient, and, in this, on him alone rests the ultimate responsibility.

Revealing the whole process. The patient usually gains much greater insight by quickly being let in on the whole process and on the evidence by which the analyst reaches his conclusions. The patient should be told about the red thread, his manifest dreams, and the relationship of his associations to the elements of the dream in connection with the total interpretation. He should understand the whole method by which an accurate interpretation is reached.

Interpreting in perspective. It is usually well for the patient to see his own problems in perspective, against the biologic and sociologic nature of living and in relation to the emotional problem of others. No doubt, different analysts convey this in individual ways. Rather than discuss these possible variations at length, here is a simple example.

I have a slogan that most of my patients seem to find amusing and useful, and it usually seems to strike home. It consists of three letters: GDM. This grew out of observing again and again the reactions of parents to the presence of their parents—that is, the grandparents—in the household, whether for brief visits or for long periods. Sometimes the grandparents do not live in the household but only exert their influence from a distance, succeeding nevertheless in playing an important part in the lives of the married couple and their children. Perhaps sometimes the three generations really are able to make a harmonious go of it, but, in my experience in treating patients, that would be the rare exception. GDM means "generations don't mix." Usually the effect of using this slogan is to give the parents of the young children some perspective on the difficulty of having the grandparents exert any appreciable influence in their lives. After all, probably it is only in human beings among all animals that the individual can grow up, pass adolescence, marry, and have his own family without being thoroughly separated physically and psychologically from his parents.

The above principles are not advanced as fixed rules but only as helpful guides. Everything depends on understanding what is going on in the patient, not only in the deeper levels but also in the ego, in its operating relationships to the instinctual impulses, to the superego, and to the entire relevant environment. In other words, we must observe and fully understand the total personality as it functions in the total life situation. In practice, as in theory, everything depends on understanding the patient.

SOME EXAMPLES—SOME CAUTIONS

Illustrations of concepts of ego-syntonic interpretations and of elicitation, which would have interrupted the above discussion of the principles of interpreting, can now be given.

A young woman who had much guilt and fear toward her mother dreamed that she (the young woman) was seen nude in a theater and that she had some sex-play with a boy when her mother appeared. The associations, confirming the manifest dream, unmistakably revealed a sexual transference, which, in a relatively young girl, was, quite naturally, conflictful. She was not told, "You have a sexual transference," but, siding with her ego, the analyst gradually brought out the following in discussion. "Being seen without clothes often refers to analysis where one reveals one's thoughts to the analyst. In the dream it is mother in particular who sees you and makes you anxious about her. Perhaps you fear to reveal things that would be thought embarrassing or naughty by your mother. The analyst is not your mother and does not have such attitudes. Disturbing, conflictful feelings should be dealt with by discussing them frankly, which apparently you could not do with your mother. Or could you? What do you think?"

It is often indicated to interpret material at first only in sublimated form and ego meaning so as not to disturb the defenses too early or too much and perhaps risk precipitating excessive anxiety or regression. For example, a cultured, childless young married woman gave associations that dealt chiefly with revulsion against breasts and suckling babies, although breasts nonetheless fascinated her; but all this she found revoltingly animalistic. The force behind her associations was her persisting dependence on her mother from whom she was never emancipated. The young woman continued in close intimacy with her mother, whom she still saw almost daily despite her marriage. She could accept seeing and discussing the dependence in this ego aspect, although she was repelled by the unsublimated oral libidinal form of it. The analyst allies with the ego, not threatening it with the id. He works through the ego to help the patient understand, accept, and learn to deal with the id.

A courageous, frank, tense young man began to express open hostility to his wife and child and to friends and colleagues. As soon as he glimpsed this hostility, he reviled himself for having such feelings, adding, "I hope you won't think ill of me, doctor." As usual, what the ego does and feels in the dreams in relation to the rest of the dream content tells the analyst what it accepts and hence how and what he can expect to interpret ego-syntonically. This man's dreams might almost have been predicted. He dreamed of violence to others and of wrestling with a lion. Here, in this latter more characteristic dream, he himself, in his own ego, is wrestling with the dangerous beast, and the analyst sides with him, not with the lion, helping him in this struggle with his own hostilities.

Frequently, it is well to compliment a patient on bringing out underlying feelings clearly. This implicitly demonstrates to him the analyst's identification with his ego and the needlessness for shame and guilt over unconscious content. In fact, the worse the content is in the patient's view, the higher is the analyst's opinion of the patient for declaring it and dealing maturely with it. For the patient now wins progress and approval by revealing that which hitherto he has won love by hiding.

Especially when a patient is not ready for an insight, it is usually best to work by eliciting it rather than telling it, regardless of how tactfully you think this can be done. An attractive, able young woman created for herself a situation that threatened her position, but she was unaware of her masochistic, self-injuring tendencies or of their sources in her guilt for underlying hostilities. She dreamed of struggling through a thorny thicket to a pleasant cave. All she could see was the pleasantness. The analyst would not force an interpretation of the thorns and the thicket but would wait for her associations to them to lead her to discovering their meaning. If it is not forthcoming in this hour, the same theme will appear again in the dreams and the associations, although perhaps differently symbolized. In this context we can note Freud's remark (1930), "I am convinced that very many processes will admit of much simpler and clearer explanation if we restrict the findings of psychoanalysis in respect of the origin of the sense of guilt to the aggressive instincts."

It is perhaps worth giving an example of a session in slightly more detail.

An attractive, successful, easygoing young husband, in analysis for some months, enters the office, greets the analyst casually and, before officially beginning to associate, remarks that his wife would like to see the analyst, preferably next week. He then begins his free associations and soon relates a dream of the previous night: his new baby has two cuts on its back.

He goes on to associate to the elements of the dream as follows: his new baby; he now has two; his resentment of the additional work; the disturbed sleep at night; the size of this second child; the concern he had had as to whether this would be a very difficult delivery for his wife; how this younger son is almost as big as the older one already; how the patient tends to identify with the older boy and hopes that he will be able to maintain the superiority due him because of his being older. He then recalls an hour in which something about his own sibling rivalry emerged. He himself was the older of two boys but was never aware of resenting the younger one, although now that he comes to think of it, often he was asked to read to the younger one and to take care of him and he resented that. He sees that there must have been some rivalry for the mother, who devoted so much attention to the younger brother because of a long illness he had. The cuts remind the patient of injury, castration, the fact that the new baby had a large scrotal sac, and when his wife remarked about this, he jestingly asked her if she were envious. The patient's associations continued along these lines, all dealing with sibling rivalry but never as between himself and his wife.

He saw the resentment against the children because of their demands on him, the interruption of his sleep, the demands on his wife, the interference with his wife and himself being together, and so on. What he did not see was any possible connection between this dream and the fact that his wife wanted and expected an appointment to come to see the analyst. In this he identified her with his younger brother in relation to his mother (the analyst). However, this interpretation was not made directly to him. Instead it was elicited by questioning him as to what else this dream might signify. This began to awaken his suspicions. Finally, he was asked, "What could this dream have to do with the transference?" At this point he said, "Oh, you must have in mind the fact that this must have something to do with my wife's wanting to see you, which I told you about before beginning the hour." With this, the patient laughed (a sure sign that an emotional spot has been touched) and went on to discuss the material with the analyst, who had given him no hint whatsoever in the questions as to the interpretation that was in his mind. Nevertheless, he did succeed in eliciting the anticipated intepretation from him.

The example shows, among other points, how the unofficial, initial side remark made by a patient before beginning his hour and apparently without any relationship to the hour is almost invariably the key to the hour and always must be included in the analyst's mind as an association. This example also points out how eliciting interpretations can be a good procedure; and how the transference meaning invariably and unswervingly must be watched for and sought after because it carries every analysis.

When there seems to be little transference feeling because of strong emotions toward persons in life, analyzing the disturbing elements in the latter sometimes seems to drive them the sooner into the transference.

Freud's analogy between psychoanalysis and surgery is valid in many ways, as has been emphasized repeatedly. It is true that psychoanalysis is a process, a sort of unfolding organic process, and a reconditioning and educational one, but in dealing with this process the analyst must behave like a skilled surgeon (or might it be better to say obstetrician?). So much of what has been said previously and in this chapter must demonstrate this that a few brief examples should suffice.

That the analyst must stick to the material of the hour and move only cautiously from this point of departure is illustrated by the case of a woman who, as the last of several children, born just prior to the divorce of her parents, had been unwanted and given to relatives to be reared. She dreamed that her husband deserted her. To this she associated her wish to be rid of responsibility for her sister, her resentment of her husband for leaving to visit his mother, and her feelings of being held down by her own child. She could tolerate discussion of such sensitive matters but could not stand the slightest shadow of a reference to the key to it all, her own rejection by her parents. This was utterly unbearable and completely repressed.

A girl seeks help for sensitivity to authority and emotional upset caused by repressed hostility to her father. He had imposed his will on her, forcing her to do things. He beat her if she stayed up late, he had tied her left hand behind her back to force her to use her right, he had compelled her to go to the college of his choosing, and so on. Now, the analyst does not say to himself, "Psychoanalysis is making the unconscious conscious" and, therefore, say to the patient, "You hate your father." This would be naive, clumsy, and a form of wild analysis.

The approach would be for the analyst to separate out the problem for the patient to see, isolating it, sequestrating it, demarcating it from the healthy parts of the personality and of the interpersonal relationships. Thereby the girl ceases to regard herself as "a neurotic" who must go to a psychiatrist. She can begin to see herself as a good, healthy person who has an emotional problem. She is told that her good relationships to college and friends and especially to those she sees as authorities are disturbed by certain elements in her feelings toward her father. Then, as soon as she can accept such ideas, the rebellion, the hostility, and the guilt are discussed, using the most innocuous terms and the most reassuring approach. In doing this, she is also shown her mature, healthy, positive qualities and given confidence in these and in using them, as the long-time invalid must regain confidence in his body and strengthen it by exercise.

Solutions can then be worked on with the girl. For example, there can be discussion of how unnecessary this pattern to her father now is, for she no longer is a little child and no longer is at his mercy but is able to talk and reason with him. Can she not establish good, friendly rapport with him on a new, more mature, adult-to-adult basis? It can then be pointed out that even if this is not possible, she can still have a problem with her father without necessarily repeating it to all other authorities, without its disrupting all her other relationships, and without being so upset all the time by it.

To barge in with an interpretation of her hostility to her father would only heighten her guilt, shame, and anxiety. It would not be ego-syntonic and would not be dealing with the total personality in relation to the life situation and the transference.

The analyst, as we have said, does well to adopt the surgeon's motto: *Primum non nocere*—first of all, do no harm. In the previous chapter we introduced a point that we return to now to consider in further and different aspects, that is, the idea that some things must not be interpreted. This, as we said, is no problem for the analyst if he keeps close to the central and presenting unconscious forces and does not interpret individual associations, specific contents, and peripheral issues, except for the most cogent reasons. However, the matter of what not to interpret is so important for not harming the patient that a few, very brief, random examples must be given.

The first of these is an application of the principle of not disturbing the defenses too soon or too abruptly. A young man's associations during the hour very clearly revealed his excessive dependence on his mother, which made him submissive to her while also stimulating extremely hostile rebellion. His last association had to do with a drop of blood on his arm. This he took realistically and felt severely anxious about it, but the rest of the associations, with all their violence, he told as intellectual exercises. He delivered them as though they were "only associations" and thus not necessarily to be taken all that seriously. Obviously, in view of his disproportionate anxiety about the last, rather innocuous association, it would be an error to interpret to him his defense of splitting off emotion from the previous associations and thus making him, at this point, take them realistically. It must be done bit by bit with ample laying of groundwork, lest in such a person a schizoid episode be precipitated.

A good-looking, vivacious, responsible girl was nearing thirty and still was unmarried; she was unable to free herself from the effects of her guilt to her mother. She lived with her mother and was in a continuous revolt which, however, produced not freedom but only strife and guilt with needs for self-punishment. In a dream she fought with her mother and then was attacked by strangers, from whom she sought to hide in a church. It would be a mistake to interpret the church in any way that would cut off this refuge for her, because in reality it was here that she did find escape from her mother in companionship, consolation, community activities, and other very positive, constructive values. Here she could have a life of her own. Therefore, the task is to interpret and help resolve the source of her trouble, the conflict with her mother. It is important to let the patient associate to the church, which is her attempted solution. The analyst should urge her to see what she can and then clarify this in a constructive and not destructive fashion. The psychological surgery here is a "guiltectomy." The reasons for this girl's hostility to her mother were elicited, and the hostility was reduced by shifts in her attitudes away from the childhood involvement. The reduction of hostility, of course, diminished the guilt, which was its chief source. The guilt was also analyzed and further decreased. This removed the masochistic, self-punishing behavior that resulted in the girl cutting herself off from wholesome friendships with men, and a year later she married.

We have noted that it is usually risky, profitless, and

contraindicated to tamper with sublimations unless absolutely essential, unless loss of a great socially acceptable outlet be compensated for in some vital way or unless only in this way can dire illness be prevented. A young man retreated from extreme sibling competitiveness to preoccupation with painting and became a fine artist. Because of his painful human relations, he came to the analyst for help. He did not come to contribute to psychoanalytic understanding of artists, nor because of dissatisfaction with his work, nor because he wanted a "complete" or "deep" psychoanalysis for its own sake. He came for relief from suffering in his relations with people. The analyst's job is to give this help, first by analyzing the causes of the disturbed relations, and then by helping the person outgrow them. It is not the analyst's job to tamper with talent. In fact, if he sees infantile components in it, it is his job to leave them alone.

Mature, adult, responsible, productive work is at its best when it also contains all possible infantile elements, for these reinforce the drive to it, adding an atmosphere of play and enjoyment. Not only happy but effective is he who can make his work play. If he can readily see and accept the unconscious infantile motivations, so much the better. But if his pursuit is a highly delicate, subtle sublimation, some airy, buoyant, ethereal quality of acting or music or painting, then it is best to let it be while only the source of the suffering is dealt with. A talented amateur artist painted as a release and a hobby. On meeting him again, after an interval of a few years, I found, much to my surprise that he had dropped his painting completely and now regarded it with distaste. He had been "analyzed" in the meantime and had found in his analysis that painting was an escape and that it expressed infantile interest in smearing feces, exhibitionism, and latent feminine passive homosexual trends. That infants can't paint, that everyone is exhibitionistic, and that feminine trends are inevitable in every man who is raised by a mother apparently was never made clear to the man. Nor for that matter was it ever pointed out to him that it takes maturity to be productive. No doubt, this is an extreme example, but the point that it makes is obvious—*primum non nocere.*

This also applies to more primitive, less sublimated activities. A young man's favorite recreation was going on canoe trips. This pleasure developed out of trips that he had taken with his parents when he was a small child. It was an expression in his adult life, as his associations showed, of his childish dependence on them. But this dependence was now a terrible problem to him; he hated it, it jeopardized his job and his marriage, and much of his emotional life was organized to fight it. If he were told that the canoe trips were unconscious expressions of this dependence and desire to be with his parents again, he might well lose this fine source of recreation, pleasure, and health.

If the basic problem is solved, the danger of doing harm is past. The analyst who keeps focused on the presenting dynamics has little problem. But it is well to be aware of the fact that analysis can destroy as well as help and that it is no more to be used indiscriminately to attack everything in sight than is the surgeon's scalpel. We shall return to this subject again (see Chap. 22).

In a converse case, a self-made, rags-to-riches gentleman suffered from severe anxiety and tension but feared that if he were analyzed he might lose his drive and therefore his wealth and prominence. Because of the very neurotic nature of his drive, his reservations were not without a certain justification. He kept postponing treatment, kept his drive, burned himself out, and a few years later was dead.

A person's social and political outlook is usually an extension of his feelings toward the members of his family. Therefore, these attitudes are an important concern of his analysis, even though ordinarily little attention seems to be paid to it in therapy. If a patient retains love toward his family but displaces hostilities against them onto the social scene so that, from his inner inferiorities and frustrations, he is filled with hates and prejudices socially and politically but is oblivious of any problem in being so, then his analysis has neglected an area of motivation that is of great importance for society as well as for the patient. Such a person has matured to adequate object-interest in his family and immediate circle but not in the rest of his society and in humanity of which he is a transient part and without which he would not exist. Analysis should help him grow toward the mature capacity for love and sympathetic interest in others. If it stops short at the intimates, leaving a residue of hostilities deflected socially and politically, then is the job not incomplete and out of step with the times? For if society does not work with reasonable harmony, what security can anyone have?

REFERENCES AND SOME RELATED READINGS

Bion, W. R. (1965), *Transformations, Changes From Learning to Growth.* New York: Basic Books.

Dunbar, F. (1952), Technical problems in analysis of psychosomatic disorders with special reference to precision in short term psychotherapy. *Internat. J. Psychoanal.,* 33: 385–396.

Ekstein, R., and Wallerstein, R. (1972), *The Teaching and Learning of Psychotherapy.* New York: Internat. Univ. Press.

Ferenczi, S. (1936), *Further Contributions to the Theory and Technique of Psychoanalysis.* London: Hogarth Press and Instit. of Psychoanal.

French, T. (1970), *Psychoanalytic Interpretations.* Chicago: Quadrangle Books.

——— (1937), A clinical study of learning in the course of a psychoanalytic treatment. *Psychoanal. Quart.,* 5: 148––194.

Freud, S. (1930), *Civilization and Its Discontents,* 131. London: Hogarth Press.

——— (1922), Two encyclopaedia articles. In *Collected Papers,* 5: 107–135. London: Hogarth Press, 1950.

——— (1910–1919), Papers on technique. In *Collected Papers,* vol. 2. London: Hogarth Press, 1924.
Giovacchini, P., ed. (1971), *Psychoanalytic Treatment.* New York: Science House.
Glover, E. (1955), *The Technique of Psychoananlysis.* New York: Internat. Univ. Press.
Greenacre, P. (1956), Re-evaluation of the process of working through. *Internat. J. Psychoanal.,* 37:439–444.
Greenacre, P., *et al.* (1953), The traditional psychoanalytic technique. *J. Am. Psychoanal. A.,* 1:526–574.
Greenson, R. (1967), *Technique and Practice of Psychoanalysis.* New York: Internat. Univ. Press.
Haley, J. (1963), *Strategies of Psychotherapy.* New York: Grune & Stratton.
Hallender, M. (1965), *The Practice of Psychoanalytic Psychotherapy.* New York: Grune & Stratton.
Horney, K. (1956), The technique of psychoanalytic therapy. *Am. J. Psychoanal.,* 16:26–31.
Isaacs, S. (1939), Criteria for interpretation. *Internat. J. Psychoanal.,* 20:148–160.
Kelman, H. (1969), What is technique? *Am. J. Psychoanal.,* 29:157–169.
Kris, E. (1951), Ego psychology and interpretation in psychoanalytic therapy. *Psychoanal. Quart.,* 20:15–30.
Lowenstein, R. (1951), Ego development and psychoanalytic technique. *Am. J. Psychiat.,* 107:617–622.
——— (1951), The problem of interpretation. *Psychoanal. Quart.* 20:1–14.
Masserman, J., ed. (1971), *Techniques of Therapy.* New York: Grune & Stratton.
——— (1961), *Principles of Dynamic Psychiatry.* Philadelphia: Saunders.
——— (1955), *The Practice of Dynamic Psychiatry.* Philadelphia: Saunders.
Oberndorf, C. P. (1913), The scope and technique of psychoanalysis. *Med. Rec.,* 84:973.

Parens, H., and Saul, L. (1971), *Dependence in Man.* New York: Internat. Univ. Press.

Redlich, F., and Freedman, D. (1966), *The Theory and Practice of Psychiatry.* New York: Basic Books.

Rycroft, C. (1956), The nature and function of the analyst's communication to the patient. *Internat. J. Psychoanal.,* 37:169–172.

Schmideberg, M. (1938), The mode of operation of psychoanalytic therapy. *Internat. J. Psychoanal.,* 19:310–320.

Wolman, B., ed. (1967), *Psychoanalytic Techniques, A Handbook for the Practicing Psychoanalyst.* New York: Basic Books.

Wolstein, B., ed. (1971), *Psychoanalytic Techniques.* New York: Science House.

14 / MECHANICS

> *The* Recommendations on Technique *I wrote long ago were essentially of a negative nature. I considered the most important thing was to emphasize what one should* not *do, and to point out the temptations in directions contrary to analysis. Almost everything positive that one* should *do I have left to "tact," the discussion of which you are introducing. The result was that the docile analysts did not perceive the elasticity of the rules I had laid down, and submitted to them as if they were taboos.*
>
> —Sigmund Freud

Although Freud devoted volumes to understanding the patient, he wrote only paragraphs on the mechanics, that is, the use of the couch, the frequency of visits, the duration of a visit, and so on. Of course, the mechanics are only devices to serve a therapy that is based very solidly on an understanding of the patient. The more the whole treatment is conceived as a kind of mechanical procedure, like orthopedic corrective exercises of so many minutes per day for such and such periods, the more important these devices become. The more the analyst understands the patient and the psychological process of the treatment, the less is he involved with the mechanics and the more ready will he be to adapt them to the therapeutic needs of the individual patient.

DYNAMICS OF THE COUCH

The device of the couch has its origins in Freud's use of it in his work with hypnosis. This traditional carry-over offers the analyst the frequently welcome convenience of not being watched. At the same time, the couch affords the patient the advantage of being able to assume a position of relaxation in which he is withdrawn from face-to-face confrontation and can, perhaps, therefore more readily abreact emotions, recover childhood memories, and project onto the analyst. However, it would be most unscientific to believe that these advantages to analyst and patient complete the picture. The passing decades have shown that the couch is a powerful tool, the effects of which require careful study in order to determine its indications and also its contraindications. I shall sketch a few points to illustrate.

In the first place, the couch has very important unconscious meanings to different patients, and it would be utterly unanalytic to ignore these and to force every patient to assume the supine position. The very same principle of never forcing an issue without first thoroughly understanding the patient's motivations for it also applies to the implementation of the couch. For example, a man was quite anxious about lying down on the couch, and this was handled analytically, and it happens that there were very specific reasons for his reluctance. His central problem was a really dangerous rage against his extremely dominating mother, a rage so great that he sweated profusely in associating about her. The couch was a special symbol of this complex to him, for his mother had compelled him to nap daily and had regulated this by the clock, and often it was on a couch that she made him lie. She also forced him to eat spinach, and he hated spinach; she had him move his bowels every morning, and he became constipated in rebellion.

It is important to remember that times have changed, that psychoanalysis is widely known and that the variety of patients seen has broadened beyond all limits. Many, probably most, patients today do not resist the couch and many, in fact, dive for it. It would be equally unanalytic to accede automatically to this desire of the couch-divers without first understanding it. Lying down, in general, has many unconscious meanings. The infant spends much time lying down, and for many months great pleasures and sufferings are experienced thus—swaddling, cuddling, diaper changing, and nowadays often feeding. In later years, lying down is associated not only with fatigue but also with illness and sometimes with punishment. It is also the position for sex and the posture for sleep. It is usually a withdrawal.

There seems little doubt that the couch, through the withdrawal to the supine position, often with closed eyes, encourages regression. One young man enjoyed the couch but said frankly that when on it he felt like a small child with mother—which also had a historical pattern. In some patients it arouses strong sexual feelings, hetero or homo. Months and years of using the couch to encourage and play into tendencies to withdrawal dependence, and other forms of regression are not to be considered lightly. For some patients it may be indicated, but for those in whom such trends are already dangerously strong, it may be harmful. Even if some regression may be therapeutically useful, if a patient once regresses too much, it is usually considerably more difficult to get him back to more mature behavior than if this had been avoided.

The same consideration applies to the question of the couch being in a position from which the patient cannot see the analyst thus making it easier for him to project images upon the analyst. If the patient is schizoid he may tend to do this too strongly and need all possible help in discriminating between his own fantasies and imagoes of childhood and the current real relation to the analyst. He needs help in strengthening his grasp of reality at the expense of his fantasying and in tolerating and resolving the transference rather than intensifying it. The analyst must evaluate in each patient whether what he gains in possibly freer fantasy by using the couch is lost by lessening the ego's grasp of reality and the patient's ability to make use in his real life of what he learns in the analytic experience.

One man expressed very clearly his feeling that it was more difficult to associate freely when he sat up because then what he said felt more real and he had more sense of responsibility for it. When on the couch however his resistance was less because what he said was more remote and less real, and he felt more separated from life and could make less use of his insights. We know today that the attention of analysts has expanded from the repressed to the repressing forces and that treatment involves after-education. Anna Freud (1937) pointed out that psychoanalysis works through the ego in relation to the total personality and external reality. Neurosis is a distortion of the ego and cure takes place not through insight or transference alone but through the person's (ego's) capacity to make use of and integrate the analytic experience. Therefore, this capacity and activity of the ego must be carefully and continually watched and evaluated, and everything possible must be done to increase it lest the patient analyze brilliantly but not make use of it to achieve real progress in his daily living.

In some patients, lying on the couch seems to mobilize much masochism initially. Sometimes this happens more rapidly than is consonant with the fastest, smoothest progress. If the patient has much guilt, then lying down, and, as such, being nearer the child-parent position combines with the factor of not seeing the analyst to make the analyst more readily a punishing bogeyman to the patient's unconscious. Again, it is a matter of optimal intensities. If the guilt is mobilized faster than the patient can handle it, his anxiety may be so heightened as to cause too great resistance, he may be driven to escape from it into too deep regression, he may become depressed, and a negative therapeutic reaction may be precipitated. If it is ever advisable to make the patient worse in such ways, which is certainly questionable, then it must be done on the basis of thorough understanding and very cogent indications. Otherwise, everything should be done to prevent this. But either the couch is of little effect one way or the other, a mere trademark, or else it is an instrument of such power that it is not to be used without thoroughgoing comprehension of precisely what effects it is producing in each individual patient.

An exhibitionistic, ostentatious young man could not act out his sublimated desires for attention and admiration nearly so well lying on the couch as he could when sitting up and facing the analyst. Here the couch was definitely indicated for good dynamic reasons and not because of tradition, dogma, the analyst's comfort, or because it has been established by exhaustive experimentation with other positions that it is invariably best for every kind of patient.

For the analyst too, the couch has a mixture of effects. It is usually much easier for him, more relaxing, and his attention is not distracted from the associations alone. On the other hand, however, his mind can wander more easily to problems of his own, which in the course of living, he cannot help having, and sometimes they must be distressful for him. His face is not seen, but then he cannot watch the patient's expressions either. This can be a drawback for sometimes his own facial expression can be important therapeutically, for example, when it stays benign as the patient succeeds only with effort in telling what he thought would be shocking to the analyst. And possibly it is worth mentioning the subtle effect on the analyst of sitting year after year in the psychological position of a god to the infantile unconscious of his patients, without the face-to-face converse of real relationships of adult-to-adult discussion, which keeps the unconscious in perspective. The analyst, however, is first and last a physician, and the effects on the patient and not on himself must determine the use of the couch.

When some patients lie on the couch they become more on guard, not less. It may well be that slight, even distraction is the best analyzing situation for certain patients. Freud conducted sessions while walking and Ferenczi, in at least one instance, on horseback, but apparently no scientific studies were made of the effects of these settings. Today we are more careful and confine ourselves to standardized procedure in the office. But occasionally, necessity, not choice, dictates otherwise. The vicissitudes of life and practice being what they are, an analyst may have occasion to help a patient even in a situation that necessity makes highly unorthodox. If he is of an inquiring mind, an analyst will observe carefully these rare, unavoidable experiments and ask his colleagues about their experiences. In these atypical situations it is usually a choice of seeing the patient under exceptional circumstances or not at all, and the analyst must weigh the possible disadvantages against the importance of having the session. From what I have been able to piece together, excellent analytic hours can be conducted, not only in sitting positions, but also while walking or even while riding in an automobile (not driven by the patient). If these sessions are compared with hours of the same patient on the couch, the impression seems to be that the set and the power of the patient's unconscious is so great that the efficacy of the session is but little affected by the exceptional setting. It seems possible that, at least in some patients, the mild, continuing distraction of the ego might facilitate the flow of significant material and the expression of unconscious motivations. Of course, this would require systematic study to determine whether or not it is true, but the suggestion is made because science progresses only by continued questioning, observing, challenging, and testing. Independence of perceiving and thinking is, as Freud said, so rare that we should treasure it and nurture it in this new, expanding field.

FREQUENCY OF SESSIONS

In the early nineteen thirties psychoanalysis was just catching on in the big cities. Tearooms advertised free psychoanalysis with the seventy-five-cent lunch. Charlatans were jumping on the bandwagon, and there can be no question but that the public needed protection. Five times a week on the couch seemed to be a workable touchstone to distinguish those analysts who were truly conscientious and trained and willing to invest so much in real analytic therapy. After my own training, I saw my patients five times a week on the couch exclusively, just as I had been taught to do. I felt that this was the best and only way, that anything different was something less and not only could not be effective but was not really the same method. Only gradually did my experience increase with out-of-town patients whom I occasionally accepted even though they could come less often. Slowly I came to a fuller appreciation of the human mind, of the operation of the forces in it, of the nature, the power, and the scope of the psychoanalytic method. I continue to be astonished by the flexibility with which this method of treatment can be adapted therapeutically to the increasingly diverse problems and personalities that its ever-expanding applications have been encompassing.

The still controversial question of frequency of meeting is, of course, related to the goals and the processes of psychoanalytic treatment. The goal is an ambitious one, namely, the emotional development to new, more mature attitudes and better adaptation. But, granted agreement on grasping each patient's central problem and the core of its dynamics and the utilization of psychoanalysis to correct it, important questions still remain. To correct in the mid-channel of life the deep-seated effects of injurious conditionings during the earliest years is a lengthy and difficult job. I would think that all analysts would agree that this job, characterized by Freud as correcting the blunders of parents, is the essence of psychoanalysis, that it is this which is depth and this which distinguishes it from superficial therapies. It is this which should be properly prized and guarded. However, to do so, without damaging what one wishes to defend, the essential must be distinguished from the incidental.

If there is agreement on the goal, then the crucial question for technique probably is: What is the process that corrects the after-effects of the warping influences of the earliest years? Insight combined with the emotional experience of the transference, the analyst replacing and correcting the superego, and consequently the correcting of the id and the ego, is certainly the indispensable base. Now, does the after-education, as Freud called it, take place *only* in the sessions with the analyst or does the analytic experience so alert the patient to his unconscious patterns that he no longer reacts with them so automatically and blindly in life but gradually learns by practice and experience to work out of them? If the cure takes place exclusively during the meetings then the question still remains as to whether daily meetings are the optimal arrangement for speedy improvement. For curing a hysterical symptom by recovering a repressed memory, possibly only what is done with the analyst is of any help. However, how many patients today come with such a monosymptomatic hysterical complaint, and of those who do, is not the symptom always an expression of an underlying personality disorder?

Therefore, further questions must be raised. Is the optimal frequency for a monosymptomatic hysterical complaint also optimal for every other type of problem seen by the analyst? If cure takes place exclusively during the session, then why limit the meetings to fifty minutes? If quantity of time with the analyst is important, then why fifty minutes daily rather than periods of two or three hours daily? What about more time daily but fewer times per week? If daily for continuity, is the identical continuity of daily visits the very best arrangement for every patient and every problem? Is continuity completely beneficial or does it have any disadvantages for some patients?

Questions of this kind occur naturally to anyone who views the matter from a scientific background. They are not threats or iconoclasm to tradition but the normal, healthy inquiry into reality, which is the lifeblood of every science and without which it cannot thrive or even survive. Freedom of inquiry is the soul of science.

If the process of cure involves digestion of insights, working out of the sample human relationship to the analyst in the transference, and testing what is learned by applying it in current life situations, still further questions are raised. For then, we must take into account not something like the quantity of dredging but the integrative capacity of the ego. Freud (1937) recognized this and remarked, "No doubt it is desirable to shorten analytic treatment, but we shall achieve our therapeutic purpose only when we can give a greater measure of therapeutic help to the patient's ego." Anna Freud (1937) and others have stressed the fact that neurosis is a deformity of the ego and that it is the ego that is dealt with in treatment. We noted in the preceding chapter that it is not alone the insight and the transference experience that is of vital importance, but it is also a matter of how the person (his ego) is able to use this experience. The final and most critical test is how he learns to use it in life. It is in life that he had his difficulties and in life that he wants to be freed of them, to live more maturely and more harmoniously. In this view, psychoanalysis initiates a learning process, a process of after-education, which is emotional growth out of the fixity of childhood patterns and, if properly begun, goes on for years, even for the rest of the patient's life.

How frequent should the interviews be for each patient? Identically the same for all? If a patient gains insights rapidly and produces much revealing material in every meeting, will he not do better and progress faster if he has time to digest what he has learned in one session and live with it a few days before having another session? How much independence from the analysis in life is optimal in each patient as a base for the analysis? Might not some patients, by free associating every single day, produce too much material—with too much insight too continuously—to digest and integrate it? Might not such a patient become confused and the treatment become less orderly, less effective, and take more hours and be of longer duration than if he were allowed a day or a few days between meetings to make the most of each one? Must not frequency of sessions always be considered in relation to the individual, who will be dosed in accordance with his make-up and problem, especially relative to his ego's capacity for insight, integration, and progress through utilizing in life what he learns in the analysis?

On the analyst's side, it is largely a matter of making every hour count. The field is now far enough advanced so that he should be able to grasp the main unconscious point of very nearly every hour, and if he understands it, he can use it to help the patient. If he does make every hour count, then he will find, if his mind is not completely closed by prejudgment, that he can accomplish thoroughgoing analytic work with fewer visits, in properly selected patients. The same goals of producing deep reorientation within the patient's personality and alteration of his psychic life in the direction of maturity will still be achieved even though the length of treatment is diminished.

Semantic usage sometimes causes confusion. Years ago, psychoanalysis could be readily differentiated from other methodologies of treatment (then called simply "psychotherapy") by the daily sessions on the couch, for only those who dealt with the unconscious used these expedients. Therefore, a tendency has persisted to think that if a patient is seen less than five times per week, certainly if less than four times, that what is done in the session must be the same as of old—only superficial psychotherapy. But times have changed. Today, even an analyst who has had twenty or thirty years of experience in the field conscientiously seeing patients five and six days per week, may find good analytic reasons to see a patient one, two, or three times per week. He may find, for example, that what is lost in continuity is more than compensated for because the increased tension from not meeting makes the fewer hours more productive and that the interim makes more satisfactory the integration of what is learned. Such an analyst, concentrating on making every hour effective, is not "messing around" or being only supportive, nor is he "watering down" analysis. He is a far cry from the superficial therapist of yore who denied the unconscious. In fact, today the untrained nonanalysts often use the form alone, the daily meetings and the couch, without the substance, the real grasp, and the mastery of the field. The mechanics are no longer of any validity as criteria for separating the psychoanalytic from the superficial. No longer can it be said that briefer treatment is not deep enough to hold and last if by this description what is meant is fewer than four or five meetings a week. Essentially, what briefer treatment may actually signify is that the analyst proceeds with fewer meetings per week because his work is more accurate, deep, and realistic, and the patient produces more revealing material and uses it more therapeutically in this arrangement. Such brevity resembles that of the surgeon who, through mastery of the essentials of what is wrong and how to correct it, does a better job in less time. It is not unlike golf in which the better the player the fewer the strokes, because the expert makes each stroke count, makes the most of each contact with the ball. Such vital questions as have been raised above require dispassionate scientific study.

Many psychiatrists now act as consultants to colleges and universities. This is sometimes on a visiting basis of one or more days per week. If only once a week, and the demand exceeds the psychiatrist's available time, as it seems to all over the country, then any therapy that is attempted must be on an abbreviated basis. This provides a gold mine of observation and experimentation. For example, a girl came to the office in rather desperate condition, on the verge of disrupting and losing all of her human contacts, which is often a precursor of breakdown. Her father was a man who had been transferred so often from city to city that the girl had been through more uprootings than she was years of age. She was so sensitized to these moves, and her last bonds to people were so tenuous, that it would have been highly dangerous to reject her even by referring her, and she could not afford a private referral. There was no choice but to do the best we could with what we had. After the initial interview of an hour, we had regularly available one-half hour a week for two weeks and then fifteen to twenty minutes once a week; then, after the acute phase, which lasted a few months, we could meet only fortnightly. We did so with reasonable regularity for two academic years of nine months each.

This was most instructive. The patient was young, psychological, and intuitive, as well as highly intelligent, and under extreme emotional pressure with the all-out drive of desperation for therapeutic help. Impelled by this urge for treatment, what occurred was a regular psychoanalysis modified only by the infrequency and the brevity of the sessions. The childhood pattern emerged clearly and was worked through in the transference where she repeated the clinging, the panic over being uprooted by referral, the hostilities to her parents with the guilt and the anxiety over the estrangement that these caused, and so on. She gradually reestablished workable, reasonably good rapport with her parents and friends and a year after graduation married the young man she was on the verge of breaking up with when she first came in for treatment.

Of course, I am not recommending this as a procedure of choice. After the patient's marriage, I was able to refer her to a suitable analyst who could finish the job under less stringent circumstances. This experience is described here to illustrate one extreme variation in the mechanics of treatment. It suggests how enormous the power of the analytic approach can be if every session goes directly to the presenting material in a tactful, ego-syntonic fashion. This patient is only an example of one among many that an analyst will see when he consults once a week to an organization and does what therapy is required despite the restrictions and the irregularities of time. It is such necessities of circumstance that provide instructive experiences.

At the opposite extreme is a relatively young man who, because of certain pressures, wanted to devote himself wholeheartedly to treatment and to progress as rapidly as possible. He had a genuine interest in the field that extended beyond his desire for help. The schedules of analysts are not usually characterized by so much free time as to be very flexible or expandable; however, this young man made his arrangements in advance of a summer when the analyst could alter certain plans for a while. This young man was so seriously interested, in such striking need, and of such high caliber and maturity that the pros and cons of experimenting with more hours could be discussed frankly and realistically with him. It was agreed to start with all the hours that the analyst could arrange up to four a day, with the proviso that this be continued only so long as it was mutually agreed that every hour counted and was unquestionably worthwhile. During the first week the sessions totaled seventeen, with no wastage. Thereafter the frequency had to be diminished, falling in a few weeks to the standard five meetings.

Intermediate situations are probably within the experience of most analysts, for example, the patient who lives at a distance and can come to the area for only one or two days a week. The physician does not shut the door to him but does his best with some such arrangement of sessions as one or two late Friday and again Saturday morning or one or two hours in the morning, repeated the same afternoon. In my experience, it is possible to make great analytic progress within these temporal confines if, as always, the patients are properly selected and the analyst goes to the heart of the matter ego-syntonically in every period. There is repetition and working through of the disturbed childhood pattern in a strongly developed transference to the analyst. Obviously, considerable experience, accuracy, and skill are required of the analyst under such restricted circumstances, but, given these, even difficult personality problems can be analyzed successfully in selected patients. Much will be learned as seasoned analysts collect their experiences and observations in these cases, provided, of course, that they do so with objectivity and open minds.

Certainly some patients sail along while others crawl sluggishly. The tempo of progress is often faster in patients who, whether by indication or uncontrollable necessity, come less frequently, even in some cases only once a week. These patients are probably nearer to their unconsciouses and more impelled therapeutically. Furthermore, they may be able to better utilize insight and transference feelings curatively and developmentally.

A young woman, rather indulged during childhood, developed anxiety and depression and was rapidly becoming increasingly difficult, if not impossible, to live with. She was in a fury of anger at her responsibilities of home and three children, she was in financial circumstances that were much reduced from those of her childhood, and she had an average sort of husband instead of the powerful father and mother rolled into one whom she unconsciously demanded. But stronger than the anger were her impulses to regress—to escape by withdrawal to the psychology of childhood, refusing obligations and effort and behaving like a child needing to be taken care of. She wanted to throw herself on the couch and her responsibilities on the analyst.

If such a patient lies on the couch for an hour daily, abandoning her mind to associations, there is risk of her regressing into fantasies remote from the responsibilities of living. And, as was noted earlier, once she regresses and psychologically jettisons her home, husband, and children for the mothering she anticipates from the analyst, it is usually much harder to bring her back to mature, adult living than it is to prevent the regression in the first place. If frequency of visits influences regression at all, then this risk for the patient must be evaluated and the number of meetings per week adjusted to the optimum.

The same considerations hold in such cases as that of a young man who longed for the father he lost and erotized this to the point of homosexual coloring—the wonderful, loving father who would relieve him of all struggle.

The analyst, as we have noted previously, must weigh in each case whether there might be any advantages in a certain amount of regression. It certainly cannot be simply assumed that there are any at all. Usually, I think, there are none. For the infrequent instances where there are some advantages, these must be weighed against the risks and other disadvantages.

The analyst who looks will see that patients become addicted to psychoanalysis in much the same way and with equal intensity as individuals become addicted to alcohol and drugs and for the same basic reasons. Freud said at one point that at first he could not induce patients to come for psychoanalysis but later he could not get them to terminate. The advantages of the continuity of daily visits are not unalloyed. The "Sunday crust" is perhaps a small price to pay for the patient having one day a week on his own out of analysis and away from the powerful addiction to the analyst. This addiction can be called by other names but the point is that it is a real risk and a real problem. It must be mobilized to be analyzed, but its intensity must be kept optimal if the patient is to be analyzed with the most desirable effect and not have years of living made needlessly painful and unhappy. The analysis starts a process, but this process is not uninfluencable. Obviously, if it was totally immune to all exterior forces there would be no need for interpretations or any really analytic therapy. The intensity of the addiction is influencable in part through the frequency of meetings; therefore, this must be evaluated for each patient thoroughly and continuously during the treatment.

It has been customary to regard every analysis as a trial for the first few weeks. This safeguard can be strengthened by building up only gradually the number of weekly visits, while observing the strength of the ego relative to the nature and the intensity of the childhood patterns. Such precaution, when indicated, can prevent some patients from slipping in too far too soon and mobilizing too much. Speed in dynamic diagnosis and caution in analytic involvement complement each other. With many, if not most, patients, it is easier to increase than to decrease the frequency of hours. Further, beginning with the lesser number weekly provides a base for estimating both the minimal and the optimal frequency for the individual patient.

An important question is whether there is any significant difference in what is accomplished with one frequency as compared with another. An analysis goes well at three sessions per week; but there exists the possibility that it might go better at five sessions. This must be balanced against the increased sacrifices on the part of the patient. Some topflight analysts have found over the decades that three times a week is optimal for most patients (Dr. Catherine Bacon was the first to tell me about this), and they use this as a base line, increasing or decreasing the frequency from it. I have come to have no number whatever in mind; I start out with a few diagnostic hours and then begin systematic treatment at the minimum frequency, increasing as indicated. Occasionally a patient comes under such pressure and danger of breakdown that he or she must be seen daily, including Sundays, and it is a triumph and a relief to both patient and analyst when the frequency can be reduced.

It may well be that there are increased risks in having meetings more than three times per week, for then there is less time between visits for living with what is learned, for testing it in life, and for integrating it. In addition, there is more temptation to excessive regression. For all these reasons, there may be more chance of confusion, a slowed rate of progress, and less clear, satisfactory results.

It is highly improbable that there is any qualitative difference between an analysis conducted with four weekly visits and one conducted with five. But can this argument be carried further—is there any qualitative difference between one at three and one at six? If every hour is made effective, are the differences all only quantitative or are there qualitative differences also?

Some patients do better with five visits a week, such as a professional man who has so many outside interests, involvements, and reactions that he needs proportionately more continuity and intensity of transference. Some who demand more hours are unconsciously equating them with more love, attention, and dependence. It must always be kept in mind that these demands cannot be satisfied with impunity lest too great a price be paid later in the intensity of the inevitable frustration and in prolongation of the analysis through difficulty in weaning the patient from it.

This is all part of the principle of greatest economy: every analyst must seek to do the best job he can for each patient in the smoothest and fastest as well as the most thorough fashion, with the least expense to the patient of time, money, suffering, and confusion. When there is doubt as to whether more or less hours are optimal, my experience has been that it is usually best to choose the lesser—the least optimal frequency and the least optimal total number of hours—and then increase if so indicated.

DURATION OF A SESSION

If you were to gather the experiences of a large sampling of analysts on the topic of the duration of a visit, you would find a range extending from patients who can be seen for only fifteen or thirty minutes at a time, as in a consultative situation in a college or business setting, on through to those who come from distances for all the time they can get in the course of one or two days. It would seem, however, that the fifty-minute period is generally regarded as usually being the most convenient convention. The analyst can arrange a workable schedule within this time span, and the patient has a fixed period to which to adapt.

This adaptation by the patient is interesting. Most patients seem to adapt to the duration of sessions whether circumstances such as those mentioned above make these shorter or longer than the conventional fifty minutes. Most patients unconsciously equate minutes with love and feel that they are paying for the time and, if they get it, that they are getting their money's worth, for the infantile wants gratification. Actually, what they pay for is skilled help with their emotional lives.

Each analytic period runs a certain course. One patient reveals the main point of each session only slowly, although effectively, and can do best in a full hour or even more, at least for a while. One young man was so absorbed in all sorts of reality matters and problems that it would take him forty-five minutes to run out of this material and reveal the transference, the childhood patterns, and the emotional meaning of it all. Another patient who regularly reveals the central issue in twenty or thirty minutes, might do as well or even better in shorter periods. If the point of the session is expressed so early on in the session, then it is often better not to confuse what is sharp and clear by further work at that time but rather to leave what is illuminated with the patient as it is, for him to digest and integrate and live with until the next hour. Not going much beyond the main point of the session and thus not giving the ego more to integrate may save time. In other instances the further work helps the ego to integrate and is indicated. There are indeed a few patients, like the young man mentioned above, who take almost the whole session to get to the analytic material. Sometimes this can not be resolved analytically and the best course, for a while at least, is to have extended meetings of seventy, eighty, or ninety minutes. I have had a few patients who make much better progress with these longer sessions, whether or not balanced by decreased frequency.

EXTRA-ANALYTIC MEETINGS

The principle of analyst and analysand not meeting outside of the sessions in order to keep the field psychologically aseptic is well-established; but all rules are only guides to be used, and in science they must be tested constantly and modified in the light of increasing knowledge and experience. Such powerful feelings are generated toward the analyst that he does well indeed to limit seeing the patient to the strictly professional analytic visit. However, toward the end of analysis, at least in selected patients with good egos, it may not be a bad idea at all for the patient to see the analyst extra-analytically for several reasons. To see him objectively, as a real person, helps to correct the analysand's emotionally colored view of him. One of the goals of psychoanalysis is to free the patient's sense of reality about people from distortion by unconscious feelings and attitudes. If treatment is successful, these distorted feelings will be so reduced that the patient will be capable of seeing the analyst realistically, as he is. But this takes time. Once the transference is full-blown, it may be years before the patient can see the analyst at all objectively. Hence, whatever brings the infantile reactions into relief and frees mature objective judgment is apt to speed analytic progress and, therefore, must be explored.

One young woman was convinced that her analyst was a really evil person, as she felt her mother had been. To this notion she clung stubbornly in the face of all analytic efforts to show the delusional nature of the view and its historic infantile sources. Then, by accident, patient and analyst met at a theater during an intermission. The analyst did not rebuff the patient's greetings but chatted with her in a natural, friendly fashion. This was the catalyst that the patient needed. The next hour she expressed with strong emotion her realization that the analyst was really not like her mother, and she then went on to correct her view of him.

Sometimes very specific elements in the transference feelings that the patient cannot grasp become clear to him through an outside experience. A young man who was in treatment with a relatively young male analyst saw the theme of hostile competition in his material; he agreed that it was there but simply could not feel it toward the analyst despite conscientious efforts to analyze the resistance against doing so. Without warning, a situation arose in which the patient attended a community meeting where the analyst, not knowing of his presence, made a few remarks. This brief appearance in public struck an emotional vulnerability of the patient. He suddenly surged with envy of the analyst for speaking before a group and almost jumped up to speak himself. This was just the breakthrough that was needed. In the next hours, the hostility to the analyst out of envy, repeating that toward father and brother, poured out freely.

To be seen by a patient outside of the office, the analyst's own personality must be mature enough for him to feel secure; he must be at ease under the inevitable scrutiny and intense transference feelings and not feel overly self-conscious about being seen as he is. As we have noted hitherto, if an analyst, because of his own human relations, is uncomfortable with the patient's feeling toward him and with his own toward the patient, he may tend to be overly strict in this regard.

REFERENCES AND SOME RELATED READINGS

Brenner, C. (1969), Some comments on technical precepts in psychoanalysis. *J. Am. Psychoanal. A.*, 17:333–352.

Brodsky, B. (1968), Working through: its widening scope and some aspects of its metapsychology. *Psychoanal., Quart.*, 36:485–531.

Dahlberg, C. (1970), Sexual contact between patient and therapist. *Contemp. Psychoanal.*, 6:107–124.

Ekstein, R., and Wallerstein, R. (1972), *The Teaching and Learning of Psychotherapy.* New York: Internat. Univ. Press.

Freud, A. (1937), *Ego and the Mechanisms of Defense,* 3–5. London: Hogarth Press.
Freud, S. (1937), Analysis terminable and interminable. In *Collected Papers,* 5:332. London: Hogarth Press, 1950.
———(1910–1919), Papers on technique. In *Collected Papers,* vol. 2., London: Hogarth Press, 1924.
Giovacchini, P., ed. (1971), *Psychoanalytic Treatment.* New York: Science House.
Glover, E. (1955), *The Technique of Psychoanalysis.* New York: Internat. Univ. Press.
Greenson, R. (1967), *Technique and Practice of Psychoanalysis.* New York: Internat. Univ. Press.
Haley, J. (1963), *Strategies of Psychotherapy.* New York: Grune & Stratton.
Hallender, M. (1965), *The Practice of Psychoanalytic Psychotherapy.* New York: Grune & Stratton.
Horney, K. (1956), The technique of psychoanalytic therapy. *Am. J. Psychoanal.,* 16:26–31.
Karush, A. (1967), Working through. *Psychoanal. Quart.,* 36:497–531.
Lichtenberg, P. (1969), *Psychoanalysis: Radical and Conservative.* New York: Springer.
Lowenstein, R. (1969), An historical review of the theory of psychoanalytic technique. *Bull. Philadelphia A. Psychoanal.,* 19:58–60.
Masserman, J., ed. (1971), *Techniques of Therapy.* New York: Grune & Stratton.
———(1961), *Principles of Dynamic Psychiatry.* Philadelphia: Saunders.
———(1955), *The Practice of Dynamic Psychiatry.* Philadelphia: Saunders.
Redlich, F., and Freedman, D. (1966), *The Theory and Practice of Psychiatry.* New York: Basic Books.
Salzman, L., and Masserman, J. (1962), *Modern Concepts of Psychoanalysis.* New York: Philosophical Library.
Schmideberg, M. (1938), The mode of operation of psychoanalytic therapy. *Internat. J. Psychoanal.,* 19:310–320.

Wolman, B., ed. (1967), *Psychoanalytic Techniques, A Handbook for the Practicing Psychoanalyst.* New York: Basic Books.

Wolstein, B., ed. (1971), *Psychoanalytic Techniques.* New York: Science House.

15 / SOME FURTHER PRACTICAL POINTS

A few further practical points will be mentioned only briefly because the solutions to the problems that they raise will be evident from the fundamentals.

Since analysis, whatever the frequency of interviews, extends over many months, unanticipated intercurrent events of all sorts are bound to occur. If the analysand becomes ill during treatment, even in a minor way such as having a cold, the analyst will look for emotional factors; he will watch the transference with special care to see whether anything he has done or failed to do may have contributed in some way. As Alexander and French (1948) have pointed out in their *Studies in Psychosomatic Medicine,* there may be a direct correlation, as when the analyst leaves for meetings and the analysand reacts with an asthma attack because of the specific vulnerability to separation described in certain of these cases. Or, for example, the symptom or the illness may be an indirect result of poor sleep and fatigue, which are occasioned by the emotional stress of the analysis, a stress that may be avoidable or may be a legitimate unavoidable accompaniment of at least a phase of the procedure.

However, in seeking the emotional causes for the symptoms or the illness and the role that he plays in them, the analyst will not neglect the ego and reality. Except for cogent technical reasons, he will be friendly and sympathetic, since the mature part of himself works with the mature part of the patient on the patient's infantile reactions. In this joint venture there naturally should be mutual human interest and sympathy. In the happier matters such as engagement, marriage, pregnancy, and childbirth, the same considerations hold. Here, however, the roles of analyst and analysand normally have been very different ones in that the motivations for these important decisions presumably have been worked through with thoroughness well in advance. Life goes on during the period of the analysis—the patient experiences successes and failures, illnesses and deaths of close relatives and friends, and all the intercurrent happenings of living. The analyst seeks the emotional factors, while responding appropriately to the patient and reality in ways that are humanly supporting without hindering the treatment.

The principle is simply that unusual situations must be adapted to in ways that may be unusual for the routine of analytic treatment. *Primum non nocere*—if no harm will be done, the analyst offers congratulations, even attends the function, or, in the unhappy circumstance of illness, he telephones or may even visit, giving support and sympathy.

He makes allowances, including financial ones. He cannot be a true analyst without at the same time being a physician and a friend. If fate deals a patient a blow, how can the analyst, on the principle of leasing the time, still demand his fees for services not rendered. If the patient is really acting out hostilities by using time and fees, this is a different matter. But the basic attitude should be one of trust and confidence. It would be thoroughly inappropriate to fear that the patient is not as honorable in his ego as the analyst, or that his unconscious motives are such that he will always use every human situation to resist treatment and exploit the analyst. This is like the parents whose concept of their own child is that they must strike first. I think that, by and large, this dread of resistance and of exploitation is waning in today's practice of psychoanalysis. In years past, this attitude was compounded, among other factors, of the analyst's own hostility projected onto the patient and of much less understanding of the patient and the analytic process than we enjoy today. Only the analyst who well understands psychodynamics in general and the specific dynamics of each of his patients can be secure in conducting the analysis and in meeting the various intercurrent events.

On the patient's side, it is of course, evident that while he is reacting emotionally to some event, a special problem obtains in the analysis, however much he wishes to proceed routinely. It may be that the event so stirs up a part of the childhood pattern that it is seen the more clearly. Conversely, the emotional reaction to the event may fog or disrupt the analysis or even prevent it for a time and call for an interruption until the patient's feelings have settled down. Infrequent meetings may be indicated to provide support during such a period. As to the analyst's time and income and the patients on his waiting list, if any, I have never, or almost never, encountered any real difficulties in my own experience or in that of other analysts that I have known. Serious problems don't seem to arise if the patient is treated justly and reasonably and if he is just, reasonable, and reliable as well, whether this has to do with occasional missed appointments, holidays, vacations, business trips, unforeseeable events, or whatever.

On the analyst's side, if he himself must live through a difficult emotional situation, he will have to decide what is best for each of his patients. Is he too distracted by something in his own life to do his best analyzing? Does some personal problem or unhappiness encourage him to analyze as a refuge? If he is not working well, is it in the best interests of his patient for him to arrange an interruption? Or, would it be so upsetting for the patient to have his confidence in the anlyst thus shaken at this point in the analysis that it is best for the analyst to say nothing and work away as effectively as he can? Is it possible to follow one course with one patient and another course with another patient? Again, the answers depend on understanding each patient.

The patient's dependence on the analyst is usually so powerful as to be ever-astonishing and difficult to realize. Of course, other involvements, such as envy and guilt, can also be dangerously powerful. Hence, it is usually advisable to warn the patient many months in advance of any prolonged interruptions for vacations or other reasons unless there is some clearly seen, compelling technical reason for not doing so. For no rule is so perfect that it can cover every situation and can take precedence over understanding, reason, and experience.

The handling of the amenities, the greeting and the farewell to the patient, depends on understanding the patient and on a basically mature, friendly, secure adult-to-adult feeling toward him. As to handshaking, my own conclusion is that the less physical contact, the better—paralleling the rule of the least possible extra-analytic meeting and relationship. Yet, in a particular patient there may be specific reasons for exceptions.

Details that are natural for one analyst may not be for another. Whether to use first names or a more formal manner of address will derive from the personalities of the analyst and the patient as well as from local custom. It might very well be that considerations of this sort may be quite incidental. Two persons working together for months and years on intimate matters can well come into very naturally using first names. On the other hand, the style of appellation may have very significant emotional meaning to the patient. Sometimes the patient feels that it is too seductive; he wants to become too close socially, he presses on the analyst invitations to dinner, and the transference feelings become more difficult to deal with, slowing up progress. On the other hand, the use of the first name is but a detail in the overall reserve of the analyst, both professionally and personally, so that the patient can feel the friendliness of it but not be tempted to overstep the very clear line that separates him from the analyst. And as the analyst becomes, willy-nilly, a model for the patient, he should provide a prototype of easy, friendly relations, analyzing out the disturbing elements. We assume that the analyst's attitude contains nothing condescending or depreciating. With some patients, after a time, it may be artificial to shun first names. Some analysands use the analyst's first name in an overly familiar, ingratiating, egoistic, offensive way; others are unable to bring themselves to such familiarity even after several years of analysis. One such man of forty-five had been so cowed by his father that he dared not venture the slightest sign of anything except a totally submissive, overly respectful attitude. To bring him into an easy adult-to-adult relationship was an important part of the analytic goal.

Occasionally, a patient will write the analyst that he must discontinue treatment, and he may give a good reason, such as unforeseen pressure of business. This may happen at the very beginning or later in treatment. Usually, the best approach is for the analyst to use reasonable and friendly means to induce the patient to come in for a single interview. This is less alarming to the patient than asking him to continue indefinitely as he was doing. But if something were not wrong, he would not have interrupted in this way. The purpose of the single additional interview is to clarify what is wrong, to find the real reason for discontinuing treatment. Is it an escape, and if so, from what? Is it a testing of the analyst? Is it a gesture of hostility? What, exactly, is the childhood pattern for it? If the analyst can discern it accurately in the single interview, usually the patient will return. If not, then there is at least opportunity to reach a friendly agreement as to the state of affairs and the pros and cons of stopping, at any rate for a time. If the deeper reasons for leaving can be seen, even if they cannot be analyzed and corrected, then at least there is a chance that the patient may accept them and thus part from the analyst and the treatment with good feelings.

The answers to the incidentals come from adequate mastery of the fundamentals.

16 / TRANSFERENCE

> *This struggle between physician and patient, between intellect and the forces of instinct, between recognition and the striving for discharge, is fought out almost entirely over the transference manifestations. This is the ground on which the victory must be won, the final expression of which is lasting recovery from neurosis . . . for in the last resort no one can be slain* in absentia *or* in effigie.
>
> —Sigmund Freud

We have been discussing the basic dynamics of analytic therapy; in this chapter we shall consider them in relation to the analyst. Hence, little will be new except that now the focus will be on the transference.

We have said that the transference is what carries every psychoanalysis and what, more than any other methodologic feature, distinguishes it from other forms of insight therapy. Freud's well-known statement (1914) warrants quoting here, namely, "that the theory of psychoanalysis is an attempt to account for . . . transference and resistance. Any line of investigation . . . which . . . takes them as the starting point of its work may call itself psychoanalysis, though it arrives at results other than my own."

The transference is a special direction of each person's basic dynamics, which were molded by and were operative in the childhood relationships. They are operative now in the patient's current relationships in life and are also transferred to the analyst. A characteristic of the emotional forces is this transferability. A person craves love and tries to satiate this hunger with more than a single person, often hoping that every new face will have a satisfaction for his need. Or he is filled with anger and hate, and this shows through toward almost everyone with whom he comes in contact.

Some persons transfer their feelings from one person to another with great freedom and fluidity, while others are much more fixed and much more discriminating. The latter select as the objects of their feelings only such personalities as fit very closely the dramatis personae of their childhood. One young woman was so attached to her father that she could develop strong feelings for no one else. But she did have other contacts, since everyone actually does, except possibly hermits and extreme psychotics, neither one of which is discussed in this book. Every individual transfers the original basic feelings that he had toward the significant persons of his childhood onto other persons to some degree and extent.

These feelings, the deepest unconscious desires and motivations, in coming out toward others, follow the pattern that was established in childhood. As we have already noted, psychoanalysis simply takes a laboratory sample of the patient's human relations and lets the childhood pattern develop, that is, transfer itself to the analyst. He can then analyze it, not in absentia, but as it actually is manifested towards himself, in the present, with the full power of the emotions.

The process of free association, dream interpretation, and the whole work of gaining insight into these forces probably intensifies the feelings of the patient, who concentrates them on the analyst. He in turn becomes like a lightning rod, attracting these emotional thunderbolts in order to render them harmless. He does this through the fact that these feelings, directed originally to the members of the patient's family, have continued toward mental images (imagoes) of them; now they are vented on the analyst in full fury as though he were the original relative.

Therefore, the analyst can help the patient to discriminate between past and present, showing him that he is no longer a tiny child and that the analyst is not his father or mother or other relative of the childhood pattern. The analyst can show the patient how he is still dominated unconsciously by the little weak, dependent, angry, guilty child he once was. He can help the patient toward gaining insight into how this is the source of the stresses, the strains, and the tensions that he now has in his feelings toward persons in his life and toward the analyst. He can show the patient how his needs for love, his guilt and shame, and his whole pattern of early conditioning generate the resistance against knowing and feeling the infantile repressed wishes, impulses, fantasies, and ideas.

The analyst can unravel the motivations, laying each one bare in its undisguised expression of the exact reactions that the patient had in childhood to the family members. He can show the pain that this causes the patient and he can show the nature of a good mature relationship between two adults as equals, thereby indicating the solution, the way out.

He can discuss with the patient how the infantile attitudes need not be eliminated but can be altered in their direction (e.g., satisfying dependent love needs through groups, institutions, and friends rather than by looking to only one or two persons) and reduced in intensity. He can discuss how attitudes can be shifted so that they work successfully and reduce torment and turmoil in favor of satisfaction and peace. In other words, the infantile, the unworkable, the pain- and strain-producing, can be analyzed out of this sample human relationship. Freud (1912) said, "The conscious and unobjectionable component of (the transference) remains, and brings about the successful result . . ." In this way an alteration can be brought about in the patient's reactions to persons in his life where the same pattern operates.

The analyst can show that what remains when every disturbing element is analyzed out, and as the patient understands the emotional development and the nature of object-interest, genital-level, mature attitudes, is a balanced relationship between two adults as equals. It is a friendly relationship, but at the same time it must be a loose one as well. While a permanent bond is inevitable when one human being has bared his soul to another, even though for professional help, yet the patient must be free of the analyst (just as he must be freed from his parents) so that he no longer looks to him for satisfaction but only to the persons in his real life.

We have traversed familiar ground: the basic dynamics, always as interrelated with childhood, with current life reality, and with the transference, which is a particular part of the patient's life, and we are constantly alert to the resistance, which is only one aspect of the whole emotional pattern.

Some patients react to the analyst with very sharp, clearly defined imagoes, as though he were precisely mother, father, or sibling, and they continue for long periods in this set reaction. In other patients, the imagoes overlap and even fuse, and the patient reacts to the analyst as though he were a mixture. One young man was raised in a house with parents, grandparents, aunts, and uncles, so that, to him, parents meant a broad blur of kind adults. Some patients have relatively definite imagoes but shift with quick fluidity, reacting to the analyst one moment with a pattern toward father, the next with one toward mother, and so on. Some imagoes are very discrete, others more composite, others mixtures and mostly resultants. The analyst is after the same thing in the transference as he looks for in the associations, the dreams, and the behavior—the central, presenting, foremost emotional forces. This statement is almost a tautology, for the analyst seeks the presenting dynamics, and the transference is only one edition of them. Once the analyst discerns the red thread, he always looks to see how it operates in the transference and in life, as well as for the historic pattern it continues.

If the imagoes are mixed, fluid, and shifting, naturally it is apt to be more difficult to define the childhood pattern. A young man, in a single early session, reacted to the analyst as though he were mother making him go to school, grandmother sitting back and accepting him, and father who was so overworked that the patient fought against identifying with him.

The beginning analyst usually recognizes what is openly expressed in the transference and what is pleasing to him, for example, the idealization, the dependence, and the submissiveness. But he often finds special difficulty in seeing the disguised hostility that is directed toward himself and the patient's unconscious view of the analyst as a hostile, punishing, guilt-producing superego figure. One reason this is hard to recognize is that the patient tries to hide it for fear of losing the analyst's love and approval.

The understanding of the presenting dynamics in the transference is the very essence of the analytic treatment. This is not too difficult if the analyst can interpret the material, discerning the presenting motivations, and if he consistently, without exception or deviation, keeps steady watch for their meanings in the transference to himself. But it is exactly this application of these potent feelings toward the analyst that is usually the most hidden, the most resistant to insight. Therefore, the feelings toward him tend to be subtle and elusive, and the whole transference, if not kept track of and watched constantly and deliberately, with forewarnings, discussion, and interpretation, may develop insidiously.

Freud, at one point, leaned toward not troubling the transference until it troubles you. This is borne out in experience, but with reservations—for all may be calm and seemingly going quite well while sinister forces may be gathering insidiously beneath the surface. If and when these do break out, it may be with such power and turbulence that it is too late, and the opportunity for a speedy, accurate, effective analysis is lost.

The transference grows in intensity, especially if it is neglected, and if it exceeds optimal intensity, there is trouble that may be hard to correct. Although the transference grows and develops, it is by no means nonexistent at the beginning of treatment. Most patients have rather intense transference feelings mobilized by the very decision to have an interview—before even seeing the analyst. These must be detected with the utmost acuity at the very first instant, and then they must be carefully monitored as they develop.

Everything is transference unless proved to be otherwise —this is the only safe attitude. In fact, the presenting dynamics must always have some transference reference, whether expressed in associations, dreams, or behavior. (This is shown by a fact that patients often notice, that is, their flow of thought is quite different when they are associating in the analyst's presence from what it is when they are alone.) To be forewarned is to be forearmed, and this applies to the patient as well as to the analyst. Through understanding and judicious preparation and interpretation, the analyst can keep the transference edition of the dynamics out in the open, with the patient knowing in advance what is likely to come so that his ego is readied for it.

This helps to keep the emotions at optimal intensities. Rarely are they too weak—usually problems arise because of their violence. It is a fundamental of the whole analytic procedure to keep the emotional intensity optimal, and this applies to the transference edition of them as well. A young man displayed little feeling, but it was because of an intense, silent transference feeling: his overriding need to win love through repressing all feelings that were not on the highest moral plane. The patient was transferring this pattern from his mother.

Dreams are especially effectual warning signals for sinister undercurrents. A most pleasant young woman, with only a minor problem, was all gratitude, friendliness, sweetness and light in her manner and associations and partly in her dreams. That this was but a superficial condition masking a turbulent undercurrent was betrayed by close analysis of her dreams. In her first one she is newly married and idyllically happy, but in her elaborate description of the enjoyable domestic scene there is one contrasting detail, a broken place in the floor which might be dangerous. This was the characteristic pattern of her dreams—happiness, but with repressed anxiety that was invariably revealed in a detail. The moral for the analyst is that the sooner such broken floors get attention, the less the danger for the future. This girl soon revealed how much her gaiety covered desperate insecurity and fear that she would cause her marriage to break up. She then made gratifying progress.

Even if the analyst deciphers the transference and sees the storm brewing, it may be difficult for a time to get the patient to see it. This varies with how insidiously the transference develops and with how subtly the hostilities to the analyst are disguised, often under dependence, erotism, and idealizing. If the patient does not see it, then the analyst concentrates his attention on the resistance, on the question of why the patient does not see it.

A warm and friendly but anxious young matron had parents who had been neglectful of her as a child, through no great fault of their own, for one was ill and the other overworked, but they did love her. Therefore, it is not surprising that the patient's resentment against them was hard for her to recognize until her resistance to seeing this, which arose out of guilt and shame, was analyzed. Ultimately she came to recognize it, but absolutely no trace of this pattern could she acknowledge toward the analyst. Even when he had to leave town or cancel an hour, no insight-producing response was stimulated. Then her husband was transferred to another city. To the analyst's surprise, she did very well—for two years—and then the storm broke. Her anxiety was so exacerbated that she feared for her sanity. She was located in a rather remote area in which no analyst was available for many hundreds of miles. Since the transference was already developed, the logical resource was the telephone (see Chap. 19). So she resumed analytic hours with her original analyst by phone.

Under the pressure of her present anguish, she was able to apply the insights to the transference at which the analyst had hammered so relatively ineffectively two years before. She realized that she had been repressing her feelings of being alone, following the pattern toward her never-available parents, and now she saw her irrational rage at the analyst for letting her go off, for not being available, exactly like her parents. She saw the pattern of the resistance also, how she never dared express the least sign of resentment toward her terrifyingly strict father or toward her invalid mother. The latter would react to any sign of anger in her daughter by taking to her bed, so that the patient feared that a real tantrum actually might kill her mother and then she would be left truly alone. After gaining insight into the transference and into her resistance to it, the patient could discuss her past and present hostilities to the analyst, and she improved steadily. Life had intervened, and she was far enough along analytically to profit from the experience, although she was tried by it nearly to the breaking point. At first she thought herself in such imminent danger of losing her mind that she felt that even a single day without a session would strain her beyond endurance. We had seven daily sessions a week until gradually these could be reduced in number and, after many months, finally tapered off.

It seems that the central therapeutic feature of every analysis is the transference toward the analyst of dependent and more or less erotized love needs, generating frustration and inferiority feelings, and hostility, generating guilt and anxiety. It is these with which the patient struggles and seeks to rationalize and to justify. A patient may be unable to be entirely honest about his feelings because he dare not express his hostility to the analyst. This may then come out with unusual violence or with the intensification of serious symptoms because the patient cannot face the irrational reasons for it. Instead, he finds some rationalizations to use for justification—the analyst did this; he neglected to do that; he emphasized something; he overlooked something else; and so on. The patient is failing to see that the real reason for the intense hostility against the analyst is the fact that he is reacting to him with the same pattern he had toward a member of his family—father, mother, brother, or sister. Often a patient insists that the analyst's personality make-up or his treatment of the patient is exactly like the father or the mother. Because of the reactions to the parent in childhood, the patient has been conditioned and has developed a hypersensitivity to these characteristics. He singles them out in the analyst and exaggerates them, often far beyond reality, while at the same time he neglects other characteristics (Saul, 1938). This is something like the homosexual patients who are so observant of the least signs of homosexuality in other persons, whereas the average individual would never notice them. Also similar is the paranoid, who is hypersensitive to the slightest shadow of the possibility of rebuff. So, for example, if the patient had rejecting parents, he is apt to be on the lookout for signs that he is being rejected by the analyst and will react to this with rage, which is usually repressed, emerging in the form of symptoms.

It is of great importance that the analyst perceive so accurately that the patient will not have real reason for hostility against him. The damaging consequence of the patient developing such feeling is that it will mask the hostility coming out of the childhood pattern. Of course, this does not mean that there are not powerful resistances against motivations other than hostility. For example, another is shame over what a person feels are inferiorities. Moreover, hostility itself is commonly used as a defense. For instance, a patient was so frustrated during childhood by his parents in his needs for their love that he feels he can stand his own rage and hate against a person better than the anxiety lest he reveal his needs for love, which he feels will make him too abjectly dependent and expose him to intolerable pain from feeling rejected and frustrated in these needs. However, even here, the fact that hostility is used as the defense is significant. Hostility, as we have noted elsewhere, occupies a key position. Analyzing it upward, so to speak, it is a regular and vital link in forming all or nearly all symptoms. Analyzing it downward to its sources leads to what is irritating, frustrating, and threatening the patient, that is, to the underlying libidinal sources of the patient's difficulties. Hostility is one of the most difficult forces in the mind to handle, and Freud (1930) concluded that it is the greatest obstacle to social living.

Therefore, the hostile transference occupies a uniquely significant place in psychoanalytic treatment. The analysis of this tremendously significant and revealing dynamic is possibly the most important single procedure in effecting cure. For, just as mechanical friction generates heat, emotional friction generates hostility. Behind the hostility is the frustration of the libidinal wishes that generate it, but if the hostility is well worked through, it is usually not so difficult to deal with these underlying libidinal wishes. The most basic of them, as we have noted, is dependent love needs—the repetition of the dependence and the needs for love that the child experiences toward the parent. The overall goal of analytic therapy remains the same: the correction in the adult of the disturbed emotional pattern he had in childhood toward those who were close to him during his formative years.

It is highly important then to understand the hostility from the very beginning and especially to watch for it toward the analyst. If it can be analyzed early, much time and labor are saved, while unnecessary pain, struggle, and danger are avoided. Freud (1930) concluded that all guilt is derived from hostility. Most anxiety also arises from this source, or, at least hostility is usually the most important intermediate link in producing it. Freud (1910a) called attention to this when he said: ". . . their apprehensive overanxiousness which is to conceal their hatred, their agoraphobia which betrays disappointed ambition, their obsessive actions which represent self-reproaches for evil intentions and precautions against them." The patient's anxieties can move the analysis along, but they are usually a prime source of resistance. Thus, in most cases, if the hostility is brought out into consciousness early, the anxiety is reduced, the patient can express his motivations more freely, and the treatment gains momentum and smoothness.

"Getting out" and "expressing," as we have noted, are often misunderstood to mean venting or even acting out or abreacting through literal verbal attack. What these terms really mean is getting the feelings into consciousness where they can be expressed verbally and discussed rationally by the mature part of the personality. To be swamped by them is no advantage. Simply to become enraged at the analyst is not the sign of progress and maturity unless it signifies some special childhood pattern. An example of this would be if the patient was proving that he could have a tantrum but still be loved. But the ideal is for the mature ego to see the childish impulses, to get them out into full consciousness, and to express them in rational discussion. The purpose of so doing is to gain perspective on them and control over them in order to learn to handle and reduce them. Understanding their sources makes possible shifts in attitude to avoid generating them, for example, by expecting less dependent or exhibitionistic satisfactons from others, diminishing inferiority feelings, and so on.

A young matron who had been adored by her parents in a very close relationship, lived in an urban area where she had an intimate circle of friends. Because of her husband's business, they and their three children moved to another town, whereupon she became anxious, agitated, and depressed. She was enraged by the separation from her neighbourhood friends but, following her childhood pattern, could not express this and was not conscious of it. Instead she suffered with the symptoms of her fight-flight reaction, a spiteful withdrawal and an "I won't play" response. The more the rage, the more the guilt and the anxiety, and the stronger became the regressive childish clinging. When she saw the rage and its sources in her unsatisfied wishes for attention and acceptance, she saw that she herself was frustrating these very desires and that she could get more attention by demanding less and being less enraged. Gradually her mysterious symptoms turned into a comprehensible, solvable life problem. The analysis of her hostility led directly to the heart of the difficulty. She learned what changes in expectations, feelings, and attitudes would relieve her emotional pain and bring her into adjustment within herself and with other persons. These changes were, as usual, in the direction of development to maturity.

Commonly, this ideal situation of seeing the problem and thereby being able, in a relatively short time, to achieve appreciable shifts in attitudes and desires toward adjustment and maturity cannot be accomplished in one jump. Usually the groundwork for it must be laid as much in advance and as efficaciously as possible. Then, if there is a period in which the hostilities are aroused too much and the patient is really angry, this will be as brief and mild as possible, and the analysis will hasten to resolve these hostilities by dealing with the underlying childish reasons for them.

Some patients begin analysis with much open antagonism. This may give the analyst a hard time at first, but, if it means dealing with the hostilities without delay, a speedy, effective progress may very well be brought about. The same is true for initial severe anxiety and strong resistance. The worst then shows itself frankly at once and can be dealt with directly early in the game. The most consistent and worst threat usually is hostility, which, as part of the fight-flight reaction, occupies a special position in the emotional life. Considered together with flight by regression, it is probably one of the two most important single forces in psychopathology (Saul, 1956). Hostility pervades the psychic life, taking myriad shapes and forms and ranging in degree from a cross look to a breath of gossip to a sadistic murder. It is always the sign of some inner difficulty. It may find expression directly or indirectly, actively or passively. Let us note for terminologic accuracy that aggression can be constructive and not hostile and that hostility can be passive as well as aggressive. Aggression can mean merely energetic or else it can mean destructive, but it always implies activity. It has two meanings, the antonyms of which are passivity and constructive activity. Hostility has no such ambiguity; the word itself is derived from the Latin *hostis*, meaning enemy. It always refers to something unfriendly, inimical, and it includes a vast range of responses from a frown to destructive action. It is a much more psychological term than aggression.

One of hostility's innumerable forms, which makes a particular transference problem for both patient and analyst, is provocativeness. This is singled out for mention here because beginners sometimes do not recognize it as a symptom and feel instead that the patient simply has an irritating, unpleasant personality. However, no patient should be blamed for his psychopathology, it being the analyst's job to detect, disclose, and resolve it. Today, analysts are concerned with pathology of personality and not only with that of specific neurotic symptoms. Provocativeness expresses hostility directly but also masochistically, that is, as self-punishment, by the patient bringing down on himself dislike, disparagement, and rejection. The analyst will not want to fall into the trap of reacting to it but will want to define it as a symptom to be cured.

A successful businessman came for help with a marital problem. He lost no time in taking over, making pronouncements about analysis, about which he knew nothing, telling the analyst how to behave, what to do, how to conduct the treatment, and so on, all in an unctuous, dictatorial manner. He was so insufferable that it was impossible not to react in some degree to him. Nevertheless, this made it very easy to see why he had a marital problem—no one could stand him, least of all his wife, who was exposed to this more constantly and intimately than anyone else. Here was his chief symptom right out in the open, in the transference. Unconsciously he was trying to provoke the same rejection in the analyst as he was provoking in his wife, whose demand for divorce brought him to treatment. Actually, he did well in treatment, and in time his visits could be anticipated pleasantly rather than with a distaste that was alleviated only by professional interest. However, he came too late to save the marriage, for his wife had already exhausted her capacity for a patient, detached analytic attitude.

Another fascinating hostile defense mechanism is indifference, but let us not be beguiled by it off our main road and into intriguing byways. We come now to some fundamental dynamics as they relate specifically to the transference.

Hostility, as one of the basic motivations, must, like the others, be fundamental in the transference relationship to the analyst. The two great poles are hostility and dependence. Almost all else is derived from these. The analyst who knows them well has two fixed stars to guide him; he who does not will ever flounder with side issues and miss the paramount and essential. The dependence as of child to parent, with its libidinal aspect, childish needs for parental love and approval,* causes feelings of weakness and inferiority along with shame and competitiveness and invariably leads the individual to frustrations. These in turn generate hostility, which arouses guilt and masochistic reactions of self-

*Freud repeatedly stressed the central importance of the human child's long dependence on its parents as a source of neurosis and as a force in living. The child behaves, he stated, as though this dependence were at its core sexual, meaning both sensual and affectional. Freud (1910a) said, "Only very few civilized persons are capable of existing without reliance on others or are even capable of coming to an independent opinion. You cannot exaggerate the intensity of man's inner irresolution and craving for authority." Freud went on to point out, "We reckon as belonging to 'sexual life' all expressions of tender feeling, which spring from the source of primitive sexual feelings, even

punishment. These, reduced to the barest essentials, are the basic forces in the childhood pattern and in later life relations; of course, they will develop toward the analyst and must be understood and watched with hawklike vigilance throughout. All these impulses generate anxiety and, in some degree and proportion, they give rise to all the symptoms, from the psychosomatic in which they are mostly repressed, through neurosis, psychosis, and acting out against self and others, to the extreme in senseless murder.

Some of the impulses appear with relative directness, while others manifest themselves in the form of resistances. For example, the superego reactions of shame and guilt usually make it difficult for the patient to confess certain other motivations; but they are themselves important motivations. If they are recognized as such, then they are analyzed the same as any other motivation would be. Conversely, the inevitable dependence on the analyst at first may be more or less openly expressed to the satisfaction of the therapist and to movement of the analysis, but later it may act as a resistance through the patient's clinging to treatment. Some patients are so anxious that they find relief only in clinging to the analyst and must always know where he is, lest they succumb to panic. This is the transference edition of the fear of being alone that is seen so often in those who never had security in childhood. These individuals lack the inner sustainment that derives from having had loving, secure, supportive, always available parents, who can now

---

when those feelings have become inhibited in regard to their original sexual aim or have exchanged this aim for another which is no longer sexual. For this reason we prefer to speak of *psychosexuality,* thus laying stress on the point that the mental factor should not be overlooked or underestimated. We use the word sexuality in the same comprehensive sense as that in which the German language uses the word *lieben (to love)*. And we have long known that a mental lack of satisfaction with all its consequences can exist where there is no lack of normal sexual intercourse." Later Freud (1910b) formulated sexuality as part of Eros, the basic tendency of protoplasm to come together and increase.

live in their minds as sustaining imagoes and superego (see Chap. 20).

The overall of the resistance is that each person thinks, feels, and acts as he was conditioned to by the influences of his childhood interacting with his congenital make-up. Actually this essential finding is merely the recognition in humans of what has long been known by those who deal with horses, dogs, and other animals. Their personalities reflect for life the ways in which they were reared—some are intractable, some fiery, some docile, some friendly, and so on. This accustomed pattern of motivation, which we call the personality, does not change readily but, once formed (in humans, over the first five or six years), it is like a colloid that has congealed and set. It resists change. This is partly the principle of inertia, and it is advisable that the reader consult the first section of Franz Alexander's *Fundamentals of Psychoanalysis* for this and other general principles. If an individual cleans his teeth or combs his hair or does this or that in a certain way, or feels in certain ways, or, unfortunately, thinks in certain ways, there is always a resistance against changing the pattern which, for the conservation of psychic energy, has become an automatic habit. The principles are those of stability, economy or inertia, and surplus energy.

The interpretive principle of focusing on the central, presenting issues in the associations and dreams applies, as do all the main dynamics, to the transference also. The analyst must not be diverted to peripheral matters or seize upon fragments but must concentrate on what is foremost and uppermost, always working from the top downward. If he does this, then resistances are dealt with as they come into the center of the arena. The analyst then need not feel frustrated in not getting the flow of material he wants, for if he is always attentive to what is uppermost and central, he will find himself dealing with the reason for this sluggishness, that is, the resistance.

And, as in the reading of any unconscious material, the

analyst must ever be aware that the patient's feelings toward him are in the form of object-relations, identification, and projection.

The easiest to see, usually, is the object-relationship. The patient is dependent on, submissive to, demanding toward, and loving or hostile to the analyst, who is the object.

Identification is apt to be more subtle and harder to grasp when it is felt toward your own self, when you are the "identifiee." If someone is loving or demanding or hostile toward us, we usually can feel and recognize these emotions and attitudes. But if someone feels himself to be identified with us, that is apt to be harder to know when it extends beyond sympathetic mutual understanding. It is undesirable when it is a childish, nondiscriminating imitativeness—the adopting of mannerisms, modes of dress, and the like—and usually betokens an excessive influencability by others, which is a symptom to be cured. The analyst should have sufficiently mature healthy attitudes and ways of thinking to provide the patient with something of a model. This is how the patient should have been helped in his emotional development—by having healthy mature parents (or substitutes) with whom to identify. How can the lack of this experience in his life be corrected without the analyst providing it in at least some degree? As a delightful and perspicacious patient once said, "One of us has to be mature." The patient who failed to reach strong identifications with a parent and lacks a solid sense of identity, who has never found himself, is very apt to seek an independent identity for himself by identifying with the analyst.

Free associating in the presence of another human being is very different from doing it alone, for every person reacts violently to every other person who comes into his emotional field. This is one significance of free association and transference. Some things are so difficult to tell that the patient may confess that he withheld them for months in the face of his best efforts at frankness and in the full knowledge that this was hindering the analysis and thus injuring himself.

The patient craves the analyst's good opinion and esteem with all the power and the compulsion of the child's need to be in the good graces of its parents. He is convinced that the analyst will react to certain confessions as his parents would have during his childhood and, therefore, as he himself has learned to. He may even expect physical assault or danger, as in childhood he feared being spanked or much worse, although his reason tells him that this is nonsensical. One man, with much repressed hostility, even feared that he would be killed.

The patient must feel, and this must be made explicit to him, that the analyst does not react to material that the patient is ashamed of or guilty about, or that the patient's parents would shame or reproach him for. On the contrary, the analyst does not blame the patient for what is in his unconscious or for anything in his feelings. The patient's resistance is diminished as the analyst is able to get him to realize that insofar as the analyst has any judgment at all of him, it is directed not to the impulses or the material but only to the ego—to the patient's capacity for emotional honesty, to his courage and strength in facing, relating, and learning to handle these forces and contents and to go on in his development toward maturity. If the patient feels that the analyst is not critical of what is in his mind, then his powerful need for approval becomes a help and not a resistance in associating freely. Now the patient can progress by verbalizing what as a child he was rewarded for repressing.

Mention should be made before concluding this chapter of the fact that some patients go so far as to wish to remain disturbed and in the grip of their infantile patterns. They do this in order to justify holding onto the analyst. This is not only the matter of getting satisfactions from real life instead of from the blind alley of a professional relationship. Improvement means, or should mean, increasing the analyst's regard, winning his love—as the child should win its parent's love by maturing properly. Also, it means relinquishing the hostility to the analyst, which masochistically balks his efforts at cure. Above all, it means winning through to the invaluable peace of mind that comes of solving and outgrowing the childhood patterns. Achieving this frees the capacities for the greatest satisfactions that life affords the adult human being, who has succeeded in gaining relative freedom from excessive hostility and dependence.

REFERENCES AND SOME RELATED READINGS

Alexander, F. (1948), *Fundamentals of Psychoanalysis.* New York: Norton.

Balint, A., and Balint, M. (1939), On transference and countertransference. *Internat. J. Psychoanal.,* 31:117–124.

Bion, W. R. (1965), *Transformations, Changes From Learning to Growth.* New York: Basic Books.

Daniels, R. (1969), Some early manifestations of transference; their implications for the first phase of psychoanalysis. *J. Am. Psychianal. A.*, 17:995–1014.

de Forest, I. (1942), The therapeutic technique of Sandor Ferenczi. *Internat. J. Psychoanal.,* 23:120–139.

French, T. (1937), A clinical study of learning in the course of a psychoanalytic treatment. *Psychoanal. Quart.*, 5: 148–194.

Freud, S. (1930), *Civilization and Its Discontents,* 102; 131. London: Hogarth Press.

——— (1914), The history of the psychonalytic movement. In *Collected Papers,* 1:298. London: Hogarth Press, 1924.

——— (1912), The dynamics of the transference. In *Collected Papers,* 2:319. London: Hogarth Press, 1924.

——— (1910a), The future prospects of psychoanalytic therapy. In *Collected Papers,* 2:286–296. London: Hogarth Press, 1924.

——— (1910b), Observations on "wild" psychonalysis. In

Collected Papers, 2: 299. London: Hogarth Press, 1924.

Glover, E. (1955), *The Technique of Psychoanalysis.* New York: Internat. Univ. Press.

Greenacre, P. (1956), Re-evaluation of the process of working through. *Internat. J. Psychoanal.,* 37: 439–444.

——— (1954), The role of transference; practical considerations in relation to psychoanalytic therapy. *J. Am. Psychoanal. A.*, 2: 671–684.

Greenson, R., and Wexler, M. (1969), The non-transference relationship in the psychoanalytic situation. *Internat. J. Psychoanal.,* 50: 27–39.

Guntrip, H. (1971), *Psychoanalytic Theory, Therapy and the Self.* New York: Basic Books.

Haley, J. (1963), *Strategies of Psychotherapy.* New York: Grune & Stratton.

Hallender, M. (1965), *The Practice of Psychoanalytic Psychotherapy.* New York: Grune & Stratton.

Heimann, P. (1956), Dynamics of transference. *Internat. J. Psychoanal.,* 31: 81–84.

Hoffer, W. (1956), Transference and transference neurosis. *Internat. J. Psychoanal.,* 37: 377–379.

Jacobson, E. (1954), Transference problems in the psychoanalytic treatment of severely depressed patients. *J. Am. Psychoanal. A.*, 2: 595–606.

Klein, M. (1952), The origins of transference. *Internat. J. Psychoanal.*, 33: 433–438.

Lowenstein, R. (1969), An historical review of the theory of psychoanalytic technique. *Bull. Philadelphia A. Psychoanal.*, 19: 58–60.

Lowenstein, R., *et al.* (1954), Defense mechanism and psychoanalytic technique. *J. Am. Psychoanaly. A.,* 2: 318–362.

Marmor, J. (1970), Limitations of free association. *AMA Arch. Genl. Psychiat.*, 22: 160–165.

Masserman, J., ed. (1971), *Techniques of Therapy.* New York: Grune & Stratton.

Nacht, S. (1957), Technical remarks on handling of the

transference neurosis. *Internat. J. Psychoanal.*, 38:196–203.

Orr, D. (1954), Transference and countertransference. *J. Am. Psychoanal. A.*, 2:621–670.

Racker, H. (1968), *Transference and Countertransference.* New York: Internat. Univ. Press.

Rappaport, E. (1956), Management of an erotized transference. *Psychonal. Quart.*, 25:515–529.

Roth, N. (1952), The acting out of transferences. *Psychoanal. Rev.*, 39:69–78.

Rycroft, C. (1956), The nature and function of the analyst's communication to the patient. *Internat. J. Psychoanal.*, 37:169–172.

Salzman, L., and Masserman, J. (1962), *Modern Concepts of Psychoanalysis.* New York: Philosophical Library.

Saul, L. (1956), *The Hostile Mind.* New York: Random House.

——— (1938), Telepathy as a neurotic symptom. *Psychoanal. Quart.*, 7:329–335.

Schafer, R. (1968), The mechanisms of defense. *Internat. J. Psychoanal.*, 49:49–62.

Silverberg, W. (1948), The concept of transference. *Psychoanal. Quart.*, 17:303–321.

Spitz, R. (1956), Transference; the analytic setting and its prototype. *Internat. J. Psychoanal.*, 37:380–385.

Thompson, C. (1938), Development of awareness of transference in a markedly detached personality. *Internat. J. Psychoanal.*, 19:299–309.

Thompson, C., *et al.* (1956), The role of the analyst's personality in therapy. *Am. J. Psychotherapy,* 10:347–367.

Waelder, R. (1956), Introduction of the discussion on problems of transference. *Internat. J. Psychoanal.,* 37:367–368.

Winnicott, D. W. (1956), On transference. *Internat. J. Psychoanal.*, 37:386–388.

Wolstein, B., ed. (1971), *Psychoanalytic Technique.* New York: Science House.

Wright, E. (1955), Transference and countertransference in relation to anxiety. *Acta Psychotherapeut., Psychosomat. et Orthopaedagogica*, 3:443–449.

Zetzel, E. (1956), Current concepts of transference. *Internat. J. Psychoanal.*, 37:369–376.

17 / COUNTERTRANSFERENCE

The countertransference is a rather complex feature of psychoanalysis, which has very many conscious and unconscious elements. It has been variously defined, but for our practical purposes here it can be taken as the analyst's private reactions and personal feelings toward a particular patient. As you would expect, his gross basic attitude is usually the same to all patients, that of the good physician; but the particular mixture of feelings that he has toward each patient will vary, depending upon his own imagoes, his own childhood patterns toward parents and siblings and substitutes, and also according to the age, sex, personality, dynamics, and transference of the patient. The variations within these limits need not concern us here. What stands out, overshadowing them all, is that the analyst's attitude toward his patients is an expression of the basic dynamics of his own personality. His personality is tested in his countertransference ability to sustain the full power of the patient's demands and hostilities, as these develop toward him in the transference, which he may not always be able to keep at optimal intensity. Needless to say, we assume complete professionalism in the analyst, that is, the unselfish devotion of all his skill and experience to the welfare of the patient.

Nevertheless, because the entire personality and emotional resources of the analyst are involved in the transference/countertransference interplay, it is conceivable, if not probable, that one patient is suitable while another is not for treatment by a particular analyst. By way of illustration we can take the example of an analyst who, deprived in his own childhood, has difficulty in relating to people. He lacks warmth toward his patients, but his reserve provides a distance that aids his objectivity and he does a fine job. To this analyst I referred a patient who had been overwhelmed with affection in childhood and now wanted and demanded more than life provides for adults. Before referring him, I explained this to him and said that he would more quickly develop his frustrated love needs in the transference with this analyst and save months of treatment. There are patients, however, who would not fare as well with this analyst. One patient, a deprived and anxious woman, complained that she could not work with him because of his lack of emotional giving.

Another analyst is intuitive far above the average, but he comes through as a brother figure for patients, as one not yet sufficiently secure and mature. He is outstanding with children and with certain adults. But again, there are many patients who would probably not do well with him.

A beautiful young girl is a sexual temptation to the male analyst, but there are other temptations as well that emerge during treatment. These can vary from just a wish to be friends with one or two patients, to the habit of building a social life largely of former patients, to using and perhaps taking advantage of a patient's knowledge and expertise, to even using patients for the purpose of social climbing. A coterie of current and/or former patients can be very pleasant, especially if considerable idealization of the analyst continues unresolved. But to help a patient analytically is very expensive for the patient in time and money, and it is difficult enough without any extraneous components and often impossible with them. If the analyst once lets social or other elements that are not strictly related to professional work enter into his relationship with the patient, he will find it extraordinarily difficult to get them out, and only rarely will he succeed in removing them at all. Also, as far as former patients are concerned, you never really know when an analysis is "finished." Any patient may need the analyst professionally in the future and find him unaccessible psychologically because the relationship is now social. And yet, the patient now may not want to start with a different analyst, so the results can be unhappy and perhaps even tragic.

Some analysts are very good because they are so parental in attitude, but if this is overdone, they find themselves patronizing and managerial, unable to resist tendencies to direct the patient's life.

Other examples of feelings in the therapist that can impair treatment are narcissism and competition. These vitiate the extremely important combination of maturity and sublimations that gives rise to and forms the professional attitude. If a child complains about his parents or if a desirable young woman expresses resentment about her husband, it is not unnatural for the analyst to feel that he is more understanding, kinder, more considerate, a better kind of parent, a more satisfactory husband. But if such impulses are allowed to develop, they can widen the patient's breach with parents or spouse and increase the dissatisfactions and hostilities. Clearly what is needed is quite the contrary: a gentle, concerned, but disinterested understanding purified of any personal psychological seductiveness.

The temptations are many and strong; for example, to let the work of understanding the basic unconscious feelings degenerate into pleasant conversation; to feel irritation, even exasperation, at the patient's resistances; to be distracted by your own personal problems; to respond with rejection or too great acceptance of the analysand's dependence, sexually and otherwise. But this is only to say that the countertransference feelings are one of the major difficulties in psychoanalytic treatment. The only goal and consideration must be the benefit of the patient, and for this the professional must be kept uncontaminated by the personal.

The weighty responsibility of the analyst for his patient extends over the years, for long after formal treatment is stopped. Once resistances are opened up and insights gained, the process of increasing insight and emotional growth continues for life, but difficulties may again occur for the patient at any time. In this sense the analysis is never completed. Consequently, during treatment and for the future, which is always unforseeable, the only responsible and conscientious way to assure the patient's welfare is for the analyst, however friendly, to maintain a fine reserve characterized by respectful distance. The analyst may, of course, be warm and interested, but he must do so in a manner such that if the patient ever needs him professionally in the future, an entirely effective treatment situation can be resumed.

The basic principle here is to keep the interrelationship between analyst and patient, the transference and the countertransference, psychologically aseptic. Sound therapy is difficult enough even under the best of conditions; it is usually impossible if any nonprofessional feelings or behavior are permitted to contaminate the emotional field.

REFERENCES AND SOME RELATED READINGS

Balint, A., and Balint, M. (1939), On transference and counter-transference. *Internat. J. Psychoanal.*, 20: 223–230.

Cohen, M. B. (1952), Countertransference and anxiety. *Psychiatry*, 15: 231–243.

Dahlberg, C. (1970), Sexual contact between patient and therapist. *Contemp. Psychoanal.*, 6: 107–124.

Gitelson, M. (1952), The emotional position of the analyst in the psychoanalytic situation. *Internat. J. Psychoanal.*, 33: 1–10.

Heimann, P. (1950), On counter-transference. *Internat. J. Psychoanal.,* 31 : 81–84.

Little, M. (1951), Counter-transference and the patient's response to it. *Internat. J. Psychoanal.,* 32 : 32–40.

Orr. D. (1954), Transference and countertransference. *J. Am Psychoanal. A.,* 2 : 621–670.

Rycroft, C. (1956), The nature and function of the analyst's communication to the patient. *Internat. J. Psychoanal.,* 37 : 169–172.

Thompson, C., *et al.* (1956), The role of the analyst's personality in therapy. *Am. J. Psychotherapy,* 10 : 347–367.

Tower, L. (1956), Countertransference. *J. Am Psychoanal. A.,* 4 : 224–255.

Wright, E. (1955), Transference and countertransference in relation to anxiety. *Acta Psychotherapeut., Psychosomat. et Orthopaedagogica,* 3 : 443–449.

18 / EROTIC TRANSFERENCE AND COUNTERTRANSFERENCE

The delicate subject of love, sexual and sublimated in the transference and countertransference, has received very little treatment since Freud's "Observations on Transference Love" (1915). This, one of his favorite essays, is perhaps not so assiduously taught and studied as it deserves, considering its practical importance for both analyst and patient. Because some excellent analysts of unquestioned integrity have had difficulties with the erotic transference, these observations are made in the hope that they will prove useful.

The analytic situation taxes the maturity of the analyst; it is highly charged emotionally, as it constantly deals with the deepest and strongest feelings of the patient. The analyst must have a proper balance between sympathetic identification with the patient, without which he cannot understand him, and full, effective objectivity, without which he cannot do the professional, scientific, therapeutic job. Toward some patients this is not a difficult countertransference because the patient's combination of expression and repression, of insight and detachment, evokes a similar balance in the analyst. But extreme transference feelings sometimes arouse less modulated countertransference responses. When the patient's hostility to the analyst takes an overtly provocative form, or when a patient is excessively demanding, most analysts will probably notice some reactions to this in themselves.

Another type of transference familiar to analysts occurs when a young woman in full sexual vigor has sexuality as a major channel of expression for her receptive desires and active impulses. One girl, under pressure of feelings, gets headaches, another scrubs the house, another overeats, and so on—and another seeks release through heterosexuality. The following may serve as an example. The girl's parents were always rather distant emotionally. She was unconsciously deeply resentful, but this hostility toward her parents was repressed for fear of even more coldness from them. She seeks to satisfy her frustrated needs for love and closeness and to quench her slow-burning resentment through falling in love with older men and having dead-end sexual affairs with them. Sex is her chief pathway of expression, satisfaction, and release of tensions of all sorts. So, when such a girl is in analysis, it is not at all surprising that her transference feelings toward the analyst are channeled in this same direction. The full heat of her strongest feelings, hostile as well as libidinal, seeks satisfaction through demands for love and sex from the analyst.

Such considerations as these help us to understand how Ferenczi was tempted to experiment with the therapeutic effects of acting the part of the mother toward a deprived child by limited expressions of affection. He was nearly seventy years of age at the time. Freud, although he was interested in sound experimentation, of course saw the folly of this and gently pointed it out (Jones, 1954). However, he did not, to my knowledge, publish anything to explain the psychodynamic reasons why it is folly. There are at least five such reasons, any single one of which is, of itself, conclusive.

The first reason is that the patient must not be encouraged, even in the most minute degree, into a blind alley into which she is already pushing herself too far. She craves gratification for her sexual and dependent needs for love. If she could obtain this in real life, she would not crave it from the analyst, she would not seek it in a professional situation. Not finding reasonable gratification in life probably means, in our culture at least and biologically at most, failure to mate satisfactorily, to make a good workable marriage. This failure is probably caused by inhibition or masochism, which, consciously or unconsciously, she wants the analyst to reduce. In other words, she looks for the gratification in the physician's office that she has been unable to obtain in life because of her inner difficulties. The only way that the analyst can help her find the satisfaction in real life that she craves is by helping her in removing the inner blocks.

It might be hypothesized that the analyst can crash through the inner blocks by himself showing love directly; but both experience and theory prove this notion invalid. All too often have I seen a patient who has been frustrated and deprived since childhood referred to a warm, giving therapist only to develop intense, frustrated transference feelings. These precisely repeat the childhood pattern toward the depriving parents and they must be accurately and thoroughly analyzed lest the patient become even more frustrated, even more in the grip of the childhood pattern. Also, the rage and guilt can pile up and increase the depression or other symptoms. The patient will be helped in the long run only by diminishing the internal problem through effective analytic treatment, not by giving love. This does not mean that a warm, yielding therapist may not provide a better countertransference setting for certain patients or even generally, than would a colder, more distant analyst. It does mean that warmth alone does not dissolve the childhood emotional pattern that keeps the patient frustrated for internal reasons.

The same thing is seen in life. To take a simple and common example, let's look at the case of the girl who, the youngest of many children, was viewed by her parents as being just another mouth to feed. The parents by this time were tired, their hopes for themselves were fading, they were becoming embittered, hostile, impatient. The older children, especially the boys, could pitch in and help; the new baby could give nothing and only demand. So this baby grew up feeling rejected, neglected, deprived, and jealous of her older brothers. She is pretty and is hungry for love and marries a man who, whatever else may be in his character, is most devoted to her. At first she basks in this love and attention. But inevitably in a few years her childhood pattern emerges. She feels toward him as she did during childhood toward her parents and older brothers: as though he does not love her enough, prefers his work, and gets more recognition and appreciation in life than she. In time her repressed hostilities press through in disguised, and then in open, reproaches to the husband. He tries everything, but still she is depressed, irritable, unhappy, frustrated. He therefore begins to get depressed himself and finally she unconsciously repeats her pattern by getting him in fact to withdraw his love and reject her. The marriage may end, or else continue for the sake of the children, but with this tragic relationship worsening or stalemated. Every analyst can think of many such cases. They show that real love in real life cannot overcome the inner causes of frustration. And the very same thing is true of an analyst's attempts to satisfy a patient's love needs in the transference. They are doomed to failure, for the needs of the adult to be loved are based upon the original dependent needs of the child toward his parents. These groove the channel through which the adult's needs for love and sexual satisfaction flow.

This brings us to a second major reason why an analyst's attempts to satisfy the love needs of a patient in the transference relationship must fail. The essence of the transference is repetition to the analyst of the emotional patterns that were formed toward the parents, especially of those parts of the pattern that persist and cause the patient's present difficulties. The basis of analytic treatment, as Freud put it, is the correction by after-education of the results of the parental blunders. Thus it is true that the analyst seeks to correct the patient's feeling of being deprived by the parents through allowing the patient, now no longer a child, to repeat these patterns toward himself. Essentially, the patient feels toward the analyst as he used to feel toward his parents and toward other significant figures in the family. By its very nature, therefore, the transference is incestuous. The kind of love the child requires is solicitude for his well-being, not anything unsublimatedly sexual. Of course the adult woman erotizes the transference and may have direct genital sexual desires—may "fall in love with her analyst"—but to her unconscious this is the child's wish for the good parent. The analytic task is to correct the images of the parents whose faults have produced the present plight. Hence to the patient's unconscious any unsublimated sexual gesture is like a similar gesture by a parent toward a very small child. What the analyst treats in the adult patient is the small child who lives on in him and who, to such an amazing degree, lives his life for him. The analyst, appearing as the parent figure to the patient's unconscious, to the little child in the patient, attracts the basic biological needs for parental love. And, these needs are enormously powerful, for that love which the child craves is his only guarantee of survival. Any sexual element, however appealing to the patient's mature ego, can only be a threat to the small child within. Analysts know too well the emotional warpings caused in children by sexually seductive or abusive parents.

Of course all adult sexual love follows to some extent the childhood patterns of love needs and loving toward parents and other family members. But the critical issue here is determining the quantitative factor; to what extent does the adult love pattern imitate the childhood pattern? The satisfactory loved one, the mate chosen for a stable, satisfying marriage usually in part resembles a parent or sibling or other figure of childhood, but also is in part different, enough different to be not incestuous but exogamic. When spouse and marital home become too much like parent and parental home, the persons usually look outward, as they did in their parental home, for some such exogamic sexual object, and infidelity occurs in fantasy if not in reality (Saul, 1967). Other powerful unconscious factors in choosing a spouse are similarity of childhood patterns and the way in which these fit together; for example, the generosity of one partner corresponding to the receptiveness of the other.

A third major reason why any hint of unsublimated expression can only hamper and not help therapy is its effect in intensifying the patient's involvement in the transference. One result of this is that the patient's interests and efforts at finding satisfaction in real life are diverted into seeking satisfaction in the analysis situation instead. Another result is that any intensification of the transference makes the analysis of it, which is at best the most difficult as well as most effective part of treatment, immeasurably more difficult, if not impossible.

A fourth reason lies in the often deeply repressed hostility and guilt, which are probably always hidden behind, but intrinsic to, the sexual desires toward the analyst. Freud began with explorations of sexuality but finally, in *Civilization and Its Discontents,* he formulated hostility as the primary, if not sole, cause of guilt. He claimed it to be coequal with eros in neuroses and in human feelings and living. The analyst may see clearly the sexual desires and love needs, but let him not for an instant doubt that behind them, behind what the patient may frankly, even flagrantly express, there will lurk hostility and guilt. It cannot be otherwise. The frustration inevitably stimulates anger and resentment and these produce guilt and masochism. This pattern was formed in childhood, continues in life, and repeats itself in the transference. The hostility is an intrinsic part of it. Were it not for the repressed hostility, there would be no guilt and little or none of the masochism that makes the patient unconsciously keep himself frustrated in life. In point of fact, this is the very thing that brings the patient to the analyst—this is what he wants cured or alleviated. (The reader will readily understand that the preceding discussion does not imply that positive feelings cannot be genuine or that expressions of them are necessarily mendacious.)

Therefore, let the analyst beware. In the face of sexual love needs, he should remember that what the patient puts forward may mask the opposite, and in fact regularly does so. If the analyst is tempted to follow Ferenczi in experimenting with eros, let him be certain that as surely as any patient comes to him for help, no matter how obvious eros may be, hostility is the inevitable middle link. Hostility arises from dependence and weakness and libidinal frustrations; repressed, it is an essential force in producing the symptoms. This is so because it is part of a primitive biological mechanism of adaptation, the fight-flight reaction. If it is carefully and effectively analyzed and reduced at its sources, the guilt and masochism will be diminished and the patient will be helped in a truly analytic fashion toward getting real love and sexual satisfaction in real life. If the fight-flight reaction, the hostility and regression, are not effectively analyzed, the patient will not be basically helped. Experimentations with eros such as Ferenczi tried can only be traumatic, as Freud pointed out. It is one of the great imperfections and ironies of human life that although the physical expression of love is one of life's culminations, yet people are so full of hostility, engendered by almost universally faulty upbringing, that there is always the threat of the latent hostility.

A fifth reason, also in itself alone sufficient contraindication, is this: Not only do any extraneous emotional elements jeopardize the analysis or make it totally impossible, but the thoroughgoing professional objectivity that is indispensible for the analyst to do his job is vitiated if not shattered beyond repair by the countertransference feelings that sexual or other experimentation must inevitably arouse.

It is a fundamental of the analyst's therapeutic task to

protect his patients against their own inexorably powerful transference feelings toward himself, whether these be dependent, hostile, or erotic, or any other.

REFERENCES AND SOME RELATED READINGS

Balint, A., and Balint, M. (1939), On transference and counter-transference. *Internat. J. Psychoanal.,* 20:223–230.

Cohen, M. B. (1952), Countertransference and anxiety. *Psychiatry,* 15:231–243.

Dahlberg, C. (1970), Sexual contact between patient and therapist. *Contemp. Psychoanal.,* 6:107–124.

Freud, S. (1930), *Civilization and Its Discontents,* 131. London: Jonathan Cape.

Heimann, P. (1950), On counter-transference. *Internat. J. Psychoanal.,* 31:81–84.

Jones, E. (1954), *The Life and Work of Sigmund Freud,* 3:163–165. New York: Basic Books.

——— (1915), Observations on transference love. In *Collected Papers,* 2:377–391. London: Hogarth Press, 1924.

Kestenberg, J. (1969), Acting out in the analysis of children and adults. *Internat. J. Psychoanal.,* 49:341–346.

Little, M. (1951), Counter-transference and the patient's response to it. *Internat. J. Psychoanal.,* 32:32–40.

Orr, D. (1954), Transference and countertransference. *J. Am. Psychoanal. A.,* 2:621–670.

Racker, H. (1968), *Transference and countertransference.* New York: Internat. Univ. Press.

Rappaport, E. (1956), Management of an erotized transference. *Psychoanal. Quart.,* 25:515–529.

Reich, A. (1951), On countertransference. *Internat. J. Psychoanal.,* 32:25–31.

Rosenfeld, H. (1966), The need of patients to act out during analysis. *Psychoanal. Forum,* 1:19–29.

Saul, L. (1967), *Fidelity and Infidelity*. Philadelphia: Lippincott.

Tower, L. (1956), Countertransference. *J. Am. Psychoanal. A.*, 4: 224–255.

Wolman, B., ed. (1967), *Psychoanalytic Techniques, A Handbook for the Practicing Psychoanalyst*. New York: Basic Books.

Wolstein, B., ed. (1971), *Psychoanalytic Techniques*. New York: Science House.

Wright, E. (1955), Transference and countertransference in relation to anxiety. *Acta Psychotherapeut., Psychosomat. et Orthopaedagogica,* 3: 443–449.

19 / SAMPLE DIFFICULTIES

A review of all the special difficulties encountered by the analyst would comprise a sizeable volume. Therefore, we shall content ourselves with a few samples and some notes about techniques that can be tried in attempts to handle these difficulties.

INTERPERSONAL "VICIOUS CIRCLES"

We have mentioned those patients in whom a little analytic intervention suffices to tilt the balance of forces strongly toward development and those in whom the tilt occurs at first in the negative direction so that the patient feels worse. There are other patients in whom the motivations are in such stable equilibrium that they resist any shift. One woman was interminably critical of her long-suffering husband but kept her guilt expiated by keeping herself miserable. The hostility was hard to diminish because she felt that it was justified by her suffering, and the masochistic suffering was hard to relieve because of the guilt from her unrelinquished hostility. This woman's reactions, like those of the patients described in the following paragraphs, can be viewed as forms of interpersonal "vicious circles."

A man or a woman may unconsciously select a mate

whose personality so fits his or her own as to establish a stable balance of forces between them. A patient, Griselda, married a dominating man and expressed her resentment against him indirectly by exhibiting her martyrdom as an appropriate reaction to her husband's cruelty.

Similar reactions sometimes occur in the transference in the form of a patient canceling hours and being otherwise inconsiderate. The guilt for such actions then makes the patient punish himself by defeating his own efforts to get well, and he does this by continuing this behavior, which is hostile not only to the analyst but also to himself.

Often "the good do indirectly what the bad do directly." Anxiety and other symptoms, as we have noted, are frequently, perhaps always, the result of guilt for actual behavior in life. This is true even though the person may not be conscious of the hostility in his behavior (Saul, 1956). A tall, good-looking, able man used up much of his wife's money and indulged in extramarital affairs that hurt her deeply; and, in spite of their three children, he divorced her. He did not realize the hostility in all that he was acting out against her, unconsciously revenging himself on his mother, according to his childhood pattern. But he developed increasing anxiety about premature aging and heart disease and acted out self-punishment by masochistically defeating himself in his potentially successful career.

SEXUALIZATION OF THE TRANSFERENCE

The sexualization of the transference can make difficulties unless it is clearly understood (see Chap. 18). How it works is shown clearly in the dream of a happily married young woman who had two children. She had been the baby of the family, certainly loved, but also somewhat neglected, in that her father was always busy and her mother always ill. Her yearnings for a good, powerful father and mother, always available and ready to help her, were frank and infantile, but nonetheless quite intense. These dependent demands developed toward the analyst in florid form. At first they were entirely unerotized—such as desires for more hours to prove the analyst's availability—always defended against for fear of disturbing him. This was precisely the way she felt toward her father. Then she brought a dream: She was in her father's automobile; he reached his arm around her and closed the window for her, but he might have patted her on the shoulder.

To this she associated her father's going out so often in his car and being unavailable; her wishes to be with him; her resentment at his not doing things for her; and her feeling that the possibility of his patting her shoulder might not be quite proper. Apparently she had to compel herself, against great shyness, to tell this dream to the analyst.

The analysis had progressed far enough, and her appreciation of her infantile dependent demands in the transference was great enough so that she could follow what was happening. She could not correct her pattern of feelings about her parents' unavailability by simply gaining more hours with the analyst. All strong emotions seek some physical expression. The parent expresses affection for the child by a cuddle. The child seeks some physical demonstration of affection. This physical element is mild in childhood, relative to the all but irresistible urgency of the full-blown sexual drive of adolescence and maturity. This drive follows the paths of the childhood pattern of desires. The dependent demands toward the analyst form a channel, wide or narrow, for the sexual feelings of the adult. The dependent desires tend to seek a sexualized gratification, to take on a sexual coloring.

These dynamics must be analyzed thoroughly and accurately, using all that is known of the childhood pattern. The analyst's uncompromising professional objectivity and reserve reinforce the interpretations in shutting off in the patient all hope of anything but a therapeutic relationship to him. This keeps the sexuality in the real relationships of life, that is, toward the patient's mate. In addition, the analyst's insistence on maintaining an exclusively therapeutic relationship prevents the sexuality from being deflected hopelessly and frustratingly into the transference to occasion grave, but avoidable, difficulties in the marriage as in therapy. The dream related above signified only a very brief, transient period in this young woman's analysis. As her dependence, hostility, and anxiety were analyzed and reduced, her whole relationship to her husband, including sexual intercourse, improved enormously, and erotic feelings in the transference never became a problem and soon diminished as a central issue.

The focus is always on reality and on achieving satisfaction in real life. Some patients try to settle for such love as they feel they get in the transference because their masochism does not permit unreserved satisfactions in real life.

A clear and sharp focus on reality, probably always essential, is especially important in patients in whom there is borderline psychosis or danger of a psychotic reaction. The patient is shown how the childhood patterns, once appropiate, now disturb the present human relations, including the transference, and how analyzing them out leads to good relationships to the self and to the analyst and in life. The patient must be brought to see what he must learn to discriminate and to handle and how the analyst can help in this.

Hostility, always to be reckoned with, can enter poignantly into the sexual transference. Sexual feelings, when thoroughly aroused, tend to stir up other feelings as well. In men, hostility often fuses with the sexual drive so that, beyond its normal aggressive, somewhat hostile component, the drive can become sadistic and even dangerous to the woman. Guilt and fear because of this hostile component are common causes of oversexuality, impotence, and other sexual disturbances.

The same dynamics are seen in women. A girl may even want to be a man, feeling that she could then more actively vent her hostility through sexuality. This is readily observable in animals. When our young female collie becomes active and energetic toward the aging female boxer, she mounts her with male copulative movements of the pelvis. Males have the active executive organ, the phallus, and it is easy to see why a female with a drive to express the hostility sexually would want to be a male.

As with the men mentioned above, it is not at all unusual to see women who become so hostile when they are aroused sexually that they become filled with murderous fantasies and impulses; therefore, they shun sex because they cannot stand these. The result is that the hostility intensifies the sexual impulses or that the inhibition of it causes some degree of frigidity and other disorders and symptoms.

In women, the hostility tends to fuse with the feminine receptive desires and be directed against the woman herself. Whether because of simple repression and turning against the self, or because of guilt, or for other, possibly biologic, reasons, the hostility is readily experienced and fantasied as turned toward the self along with the sexual wishes, that is, masochistically (Freud, 1924a).

All this must be considered in interpreting the genital sexual transference; often superficial embarrassment about it, especially in young women, can be relieved by explaining and interpreting the erotization of other feelings toward the analyst. But if genital sexual feelings mean dangerous hostility either to others or to the woman, if sex means brutal attack, the anxiety naturally will be far deeper. Then it is risky to interpret the genital sexual feelings alone; it is the hostility that must be interpreted and dealt with, showing that it is because of this hostility, however directed, that the sex is a problem.

In similar fashion, hostility can cause difficulties and symptoms in spheres other than sex, for example, in social and professional success, in grades in school, etc. The analyst must watch for it keenly and constantly in all transference feelings—sexual, competitive, dependent submissive, or whatever.

NEGATIVE THERAPEUTIC REACTIONS

We shall not review the extensive literature on the negative therapeutic reaction but only make a few comments about it. It is doubtful whether any single reason or constellation of motives causes patients to get worse instead of better in analytic treatment. Rather, there seem to be different reasons in different persons. These can be roughly grouped as libidinal and hostile.

The libidinal motives include being ill in order to hold onto the analyst, getting worse in order to justify getting greater attention, or using the analyst as an excuse for giving in to infantile feelings and impulses. These same reactions usually or regularly have hostile motivations also—getting worse can be a plea for more attention and also a gesture of hostility to the analyst as well as a result of guilt and hostilities turned upon the self. That is why so many patients, however unconsciously, like to hold on to at least one last symptom—it is too good a double-edged weapon to relinquish.

The handling of negative therapeutic reactions seems to be a matter of accurate analysis of them in each individual patient, for their roots may be different in each person, and there are always special individual features. The general principles of approach are the principles of good, dynamic, ego-syntonic psychoanalysis. For the purposes of illustration, let us look at the following example: a woman began to improve as her repressed hostility, the chief reason for her deepening depression, was analyzed. In this case there were four main points.

First, it was necessary to decrease her guilt. It came to her with the force of a revelation that those hostile feelings that are not acted out are no crime or sin but only a motivation that creates problems and symptoms. Those feelings can be analyzed, understood, handled, diminished, and otherwise dealt with. This helped her to isolate and sequestrate the greatest single emotional force behind her suffering.

Second, she was brought to see that she turned this hostility against herself so automatically that it could not even be discussed without arousing it and increasing her self-chastisement. In her dreams she might spill ink on her best dress or do something more serious to herself, but never was there the slightest hostile gesture, however faint, toward any other person. Consistently pointing out this unconscious automatic directing of her hostilities exclusively against herself helped her to turn her anger reactions outward and away from herself. Eventually the point was reached where we could see for whom they were meant and why, watching especially for those toward the analyst, and encouraging every insight into a verbal expression of them. The purpose is not to make a tigress of the patient but to get her to realize the existence of her anger, to get it into the open, to get it recognized and talked about, in order to see its effects, to deal with it maturely, and to reduce it at its source.

Third, care was taken not to increase her hostility and guilt by interpretations. For example, as the pattern toward her mother emerged, she was encouraged to recognize the hostility toward her but to see it in perspective and proportion by showing, on sound evidence, how mother loved her also and how she does have a loving superego in spite of everything else.

Fourth, the reasons why it was painful for her to discuss her feelings, her depression, and her guilt and hostility were discussed consistently and carefully in order to diminish the resistance against facing these and to prepare and strengthen her (ego) for so doing. (She had been reared by a widowed mother who sacrificed so much for her that she was overwhelmed with guilt and obligation. The patient literally dared not even dream of the faintest resentment toward her martyr mother for whose frustratingness and repressiveness she felt the extreme hostility underneath.)

These points must be sufficiently illustrative. If the worsening were a paranoid rather than a depressive reaction, the handling would be different, for the details should be individual for each patient. In every person's make-up is a mixture of a certain limited number of biopsychological mechanisms and reactions, one or more of which are of greater or lesser prominence in one individual than in another.

The above-mentioned depressive reaction was difficult because of its severity, but when examined from the point of view of structure, it was actually quite simple. However, this is not always the case; some negative reactions to treatment are very complex, being the result of many motives and thus overdetermined. For example, a talented teacher of some distinction developed in middle life a paranoid type of reaction in which his overall intent was to prove the analyst wrong in every respect. In childhood, his mother had depreciated his father as weak and as a poor provider, building up the patient as far superior. This produced much unresolved conflict in the patient, both "give-get" and prestigewise. To this man, being healthy meant being the strong, effective breadwinner that his mother wanted his father to be. This meant more effort in supporting his family and taking less support from his wife's inheritance—a change that this man thought the analyst, like mother, would try to force on him, and he fought it angrily.

Besides this, his pride was severely hurt by lack of a childhood person for a satisfying masculine identification. If he identified with father, he felt weak and depreciated in the eyes of his mother. If he identified with his mother, he felt strong but feminine. This inner sense of weakness enraged him. His analyst was a man and provided a figure to identify with, but the patient's competitiveness with men was boundlessly hostile. This was a consequence of his feelings of inferiority, coupled with the need to be superior, which his mother made him feel toward his father. He had dreams of his father and of the analyst being injured, poor, and incapacitated. He felt himself impelled to help the weak old man but did not do so because this meant not only the effort of giving when he wanted to receive, but also being feminine for helping father as mother did. Moreover, he felt that he could win the love of women (mother) only by siding with them and by showing up men (father) as weak, foolish, and inadequate. Actually, his father and mother both loved him devotedly and, as in probably all negative therapeutic reactions, he had much guilt and need for punishment because of his hostilities, especially those that he acted out unconsciously and indirectly.

The reactions of this man raise several significant points. He is only one of a considerable number of patients whose analyses present special difficulties because of the childhood pattern of one parent depreciating the other so that, as here, the child feels that he or she can win the love of the one only by taking sides against the other. This would seem especially to be the case when the mother turns the child, boy or girl, thus depreciatingly against the father. This kind of observation suggests fruitful statistical studies. How often, for example, does one see severe emotional problems in life and negative therapeutic reactions in analysis as a result of this constellation in families that are otherwise quite pleasant and "normal" (that is, in which there is no really serious mistreatment such as gross rejection, neglect, over-protection, inconsistency, domination, and so on)?

Another point in the genesis of negative therapeutic reactions is emphasized by the fact that both the woman with the depressive reaction, who was discussed earlier, and this man with the paranoid one were taken into analysis under unusual but unavoidable special circumstances. In these days in which analysts courageously and properly save many persons from institutionalization by treating them while they continue their lives, very difficult and even risky analyses are commonplace. Problematic obstacles and dangers are common, but how frequently do actual negative therapeutic reactions occur? That is, if there are no special circumstances and if the analysis is conducted properly, how often is it that patients become noticeably worse after some time in treatment? The depressive woman had had some treatment with a fine but not systematically trained psychotherapist. The man's paranoid reaction was, in a sense, not a true negative therapeutic reaction because it was completely confined to the transference, and he maintained good relationships in his life and work.

A violent early negative therapeutic reaction occurred in a young man of twenty-seven after only six meetings (held over a period of two weeks). He came for treatment because of severe anxiety, and after the two weeks he plunged precipitously into a panic state, weeping, totally unable to work or to see people, suffering intolerable rage and acute suicidal impulses. What we had learned in the first interview came to our rescue. His relationships with his parents, although not entirely smooth, were quite good, but as a small child he had been extremely close to a slightly older brother who excelled him in every area, but who also secretly beat him up, physically and verbally. The patient had hardly seen this brother for nearly ten years, avoiding him because he felt upset in his presence. Now in this hour of anguish I asked him if he might possibly feel so terrible because his feelings toward me were those he used to experience toward his brother. I was suggesting, in other words, that because I was an older person he wanted to be dependent upon me, but at the same time he feared that if he did indeed have such a relationship with me he would become too dependent, too close, and also subjected to being beaten down, as he once was by his brother. With this question the dam broke—though still in terrible psychic pain, he was able to say that this was correct. He never had any close relationship because he trusted no one; now he could see that this pattern toward his brother was the reason. He was panicked by talking to me because the same pattern was being aroused toward me and it enraged him, in defense against it and as part of his pattern of repressed hostility toward his brother. These were the essential details of his negative therapeutic response. I told him that although his suffering was indeed regrettable, it was good to get this out in the open so early, for it would unquestionably speed progress. The task was to decondition him, for him to realize that I was nothing like his brother, and to correct the pattern through learning this in the transference. He saw this, but the unconscious feels its way slowly and gradually. He could perceive intellectually what I said and even agree with it, but it would be months before the disturbing elements of this pathodynamic pattern toward his brother would be analyzed out, so that he could really trust me, and through this be open to secure, good relationships with other persons.

One of the very few instances I have seen of an apparently true negative therapeutic reaction occurred in a woman whose analyst consulted me about her over a period of months. This analyst, although lacking long experience, seemed to understand the patient and the material thoroughly and to be dealing with the central issues. Yet, for a year the patient got worse but continued fighting. In this case, too, there was an unusual situation. The patient, a superior woman, had been in treatment for two years with a psychiatrist who had no psychoanalytic training; when the patient became depressed after he left for the summer, she was given several electroshock treatments. Three points stood out in her continued worsening with the excellent analyst to whom she then went. First, more emotion seemed to be mobilized than her ego could handle, in spite of every effort to control this. She was so desperate that she was seen daily for a period. Second, the central material was intolerable hostility and guilt to her mother. Third, her mother was really a most difficult, hostile rejecting person—when she heard of her daughter's breakdown, she said, "Good! Now maybe she will stay home and cook!" The question that emerges here is this: If she had not had her emotional forces mobilized for two years by the former therapist without working through the dependence, rejection, hostility, and guilt in the transference to him, would she have had this negative reaction? Was there then a true negative therapeutic reaction after all? Here again is a special circumstance of no minor nature.

Certainly, transference troubles and difficult periods, while the full power of the emotions is aroused but not resolved, must be distinguished from true negative therapeutic reactions, but two questions remain. (1) Is the difference only one of degree? (2) How often do the latter occur except under special conditions and how avoidable are they by correct, accurate analysis from the beginning? The answers probably will require systematic pooling of experience.

TECHNIQUES AND RECOURSES FOR HANDLING DIFFICULTIES

INTELLECTUAL SYSTEMATIZATION

Any analyst, but especially a beginner, is apt to encounter difficult periods in analysis. It then sometimes helps considerably to clarify for the ego precisely what the main issues are at the moment. These should always be kept clear, but intellectual systematization in a very definite specific manner can help the patient's ego in getting control of unconscious motivations at critical periods.

For example, one patient, under emotional pressure, acted out in his work in such a way as to jeopardize his job and even to make people believe that he might require a stay in an institution. The acting out, plus the associative material, revealed enough of what was going on to make possible the following systematization, working from the top levels of consciousness down to the deeper levels and motivations. It was pointed out that (1) the patient's fears that something bad was going to happen were grounded in (2) the provocativeness of his own behavior. He did various things to spoil his work, irritate people, and make them want to discharge him from his job and even, as stated above, get him in a hospital for a while. This provocative behavior stemmed in turn from (3) guilt and needs for punishment.

These were superego reactions to (4) his own hostilities. He was filled with bitterness and resentment because (5) he felt that he did not get adequate recognition, attention, and love. But these feelings of frustration were irrational because, in reality, he was attractive and well-liked. Nevertheless, he felt depreciated and rejected because, (6) as nearly as could be reconstructed from all of the analytic material, he was, in reality, depreciated and rejected by his mother. Hence, he continued this pattern of feeling in life and in the transference. It was once true toward his mother when he was a little child; now he continued to view his other human relationships with the same underlying feelings, failing to discriminate what was once reality from what no longer remained so in his current life.

He must see this discrepancy between the past reality and the current reality and see the inappropriateness of continuing the childhood pattern in his current life. He must be helped to see the solution to this problem by correcting his superego through learning new attitudes and recognizing that he can be loved and accepted. It is often helpful to contrast for the patient his own childhood pattern with an opposite pattern. In such a case as this, we might mention the type of person who is so completely adored by his family that as he grows up he feels himself to be equally adored by everyone else. Because he has been loved, he usually gets himself loved, but this may be carried to an extreme, and he may become somewhat insufferable.

At any rate, working from the top levels of consciousness down to the deeper levels and motivations yields an accurate intellectual systematization of what is going on at a difficult period and often helps the ego's capacity for differentiation and mastery and may even save a patient from hospitalization.

READING DREAMS IN A SERIES

If an analysis is very difficult, if the patient is hard to understand, if the material of the hours themselves does not seem to be clear, it often helps for the analyst to go back and read the patient's dreams in a series, one right after the other, being alerted to the common element in each dream. Simply reading over the dreams with what Freud called "evenly hovering attention" usually will reveal the most significant, constant, and recurring themes running through them and their interrelations.

REPEATING THE DIAGNOSTIC INTERVIEW

Another very good technique is for the analyst to wait for a favorable opportunity and then, during an hour, make a fresh start on the case by repeating the diagnostic interview as though he never had interviewed the patient before. This is equivalent to endeavoring to reconstruct the dynamics from the current life situation and the past history, especially to get the early emotional constellation, the early conditioning influences. Of course, as part of this, the first memories are extremely valuable. Frequently, taking the history again reveals the main issues more clearly because the patient now gives the history after having gained some analytic experience. Even when the material is clear, the main issues may be sharpened further by such repetition of the diagnostic interview.

INTERRUPTING ANALYSIS

Occasionally, stubborn difficulties arise that do not yield adequately to consistent, sound analyzing. Facing such special difficulties, the analyst can consider certain recourses. They are only recourses, and their use must be based on the fullest understanding by the analyst and by the patient of what is going on motivationally. Any manipulation will be resorted to reluctantly and only after the most careful consideration and discussion with the patient. What must never be forgotten is the insidiousness of the transference and the central fact that psychoanalysis operates through the patient's ego. Everyone has everything in his unconscious. The dreams of psychotics differ but little from those of stable persons. There are relatively few basic id drives. The great differences, the inexhaustible individualities are in the ego (Freud, 1924b). The patient's progress depends mostly on what use he (his ego) makes of the analytic experience. Hence, the analyst must evaluate the main dynamics, particularly in regard to the ego.

These considerations apply pointedly to the use of devices such as "trial interruption," "therapeutic interruption," or "fractionation." Freud thought that for training purposes the initial period of analysis should be quite short. Life and the trials and the emotional strains of psychoanalytic practice would mobilize neurotic reactions, which then could be analyzed more effectively than they could be in the initial period. Freud also suggested later brief periods of analysis as possibly being helpful to the analyst because his own unconscious is stirred up by the nature of his work. Now these ideas were for the training of analysts. Supposedly these analysands are minimally neurotic by selection; and this book excludes consideration of analysis for training. But Freud's thinking shows a repeated emphasis on the importance of reality factors and also the notion that analysis need not be thought of as a one-shot procedure, but rather as a continuing process of growth and education in which life experience (and for the analyst, his practice) plays a very important part. This idea of fractionation is also implied by Freud (1937) in his remarks on the ineffectuality of analyzing in advance neurotic reactions that life may stir up in the future years after a person's analysis. (Of course, this does not mean that prophylaxis is not feasible to the extent of acquainting the analysand with what to expect and to look for in his own motivations and reactions.) In this same paper Freud discusses the setting of a stopping date as a device for stimulating progress under the pressure of the anticipated interruption.

A narcissistically competitive young married man, very

much at the phallic level, insisted that his analyst was an unrealistic idealist when he pointed out the connection between the patient's vicious rivalries and his symptoms and his masochistic trend. He announced his intent of surpassing his peers in income and ostentation. His ideal was the football player taking out the opposition. After over two and a half years of analysis, progress became so slow that the idea of an interruption was discussed with him. Could his way of life work for him in spite of what his unconscious said, which analytically we know to be inexorable? It seemed certain from his material that his masochism would get him into repeated trouble. It did. He was too transparently a climber, a self-promoter, with too little regard for his co-workers, whom he saw only as brothers to be surpassed. He became unpopular and, failing to gain promotions in the firm, he grew increasingly insecure. He returned to treatment two years later, and now the analysis moved swiftly. He began to understand the meaning of object interest and genital level, did well with the transference, and he has gone on to mature well.

Therapeutic interruption can also be useful with a patient who has been, for example, much overprotected and very repressed, winning mother's love by being very good and regressing to the refuge of the couch from every life problem. In the carefully selected case, if properly timed, interrupting can mobilize expression of the unconscious by pushing the patient back into facing life on his own and forcing him to realize that now he can progress only by revealing what he once won mother's love by concealing.

In long, drawn out analyses with slow movement, and in strongly schizoid patients who will need help for years, the total number of sessions may be reduced somewhat, even though the overall duration might not be lessened. Thus, the periods in which the patient must meet life on his own can be enhanced and, in the long run, this can prove stimulating for analytic progress. Freud's remarks, mentioned above, are especially interesting when connected with observations of the effects on patients of interruptions occasioned by summer vacations, by temporary transfers of businessmen to other areas, and for other reasons. Also enlightening are experiences with patients and with analysts who have returned for brief periods, usually to make excellent progress. These are apparently common, for already they are known as tune-ups or retreads.

CHANGING ANALYSTS

The procedure of changing analysts requires the greatest caution; however, when actually indicated, it can be signally successful (see chap. 6). A young woman, not long married, was seriously handicapped in her whole life by anxiety mixed with some depression. She could not pursue her interests or friendly relations and was in a constantly miserable state. Her husband had to bear the brunt of her unrelieved rage. Her nuclear constellation was not unlike that of the talented teacher previously mentioned. Her mother despised her father as a bookworm because he could not or would not provide his family with the financial standard of living that the mother felt to be her right. To this the mother attributed her sense of social inferiority. She completely won over her daughter against the father, and the daughter continued this pattern in full force against her husband and, of course, repeated it in the transference. She raged against her hard-working young husband, who was just starting his career, for not immediately earning as much as the various Joneses, and then she railed against the analyst for only talking and not somehow increasing their income. This childhood pattern fed an unwavering flame of rage and hate, and this produced such guilt for the wishes, but more so for the real suffering she caused her father and still caused her husband, that she unconsciously punished herself by cutting off all real satisfactions in life. She slowly improved in life to such an extent that the marriage was saved and she was able to bear two children and be devoted to them. But no amount of analyzing of the childhood pattern adequately softened the hostility in the transference. She was unshakably imbued with the unconscious conditioned emotional conviction that to keep mother's love she must despise father, and the male analyst could not correct this superego dictate. However, referring her to a woman analyst worked magically well. This young woman had very fixed imagoes, and the emotional pattern toward her mother gushed forth toward the female analyst. This analyst who was automatically seen by the patient as a mother image, now quickly corrected the mother's dictate. The patient felt that she could really and truly be loved by mother without conjuring up a parental battle in which she sided with her against a contemptible father. She soon was able to talk openly with the male analyst again, in a most friendly fashion, and acknowledge his help, including the salvaged marriage and her ability to bear and accept her children. This is in sharp, contrast to the fact that while she was in the grip of the childhood pattern, she could only feel, despite her intellect, that the analyst was a most neglectful, inadequate father who gave her nothing of value. This mellowing was equally effective toward her husband.

Another patient's pattern was rejection by both parents, but always with a clinging to one or the other. At first she could not tolerate the transference to one analyst but, following her pattern, had to play him off against and run to another one. She had to be carried by two analysts for a while until the intensity of her emotions subsided. While being analyzed for a few months by one analyst, she learned to realize that the other analyst was still her friend (her other parent) and gradually proved by trying it that she could turn in a rage against one and go to the other and yet have both remain friendly and available. After some months she could settle down to treatment with a single analyst.

Such changes of analysts, and even multiple analysts,

can be effective and legitimate procedures for the properly resourceful analyst, but they are so easily abused, can be resorted to so readily (for example, to pull out of a difficult transference relationship) that they must be thought of in the category of last resorts and employed only after the most careful evaluation and soul-searching. The *sine qua non*, the indispensable base, remains: understanding the patient. The main issues must be understood so far as possible, and any manipulation should be considered only as indicated by the main dynamics.

SHOCK THERAPY

Even shock therapy can be considered as an adjunctive analytic resource. If a patient is depressed or is regressed and in a withdrawal state (Saul, 1972), and if he does not improve, despite struggles against this reaction and despite persevering analytic efforts, then a time may come when shock serves as the needed stimulus. A successful businessman, devoted to his wife and three children, reacted to breaking up with his business partner by going into a withdrawal type of regression. He felt that he could not get up mornings, that he could make absolutely no efforts at anything, that he could take on no responsibilities, and that he must withdraw. These feelings terrified him because he saw as the results, collapse of his business and destitution for his family. When he could not get on his feet, even though he could see very well the childhood pattern of dependence and hostility and how losing his partner mobilized it, it was agreed to try shock. Two electroshocks were enough; they were given in a setting of psychoanalytic treatment with well-developed insight and transference and served a specific purpose. Of course, the risks of brain damage must be taken into consideration whenever the analyst contemplates recourse to shock therapy.

It is a very different matter to give shock treatment during psychoanalytic therapy for a psychodynamically well-understood purpose than it is to give it as sole treatment for a symptom of which the genesis is not known.

PERSEVERING

An extremely valuable conscious procedure of the analyst is perseverance. Like dripping water on a stone, even brittle patterns often can gradually be worn down and be made malleable. This does not mean rigid adherence to a set number of hours per week; every alteration may be tried —fewer meetings, more meetings, interruptions—with any kind or degree of flexibility that is rationally indicated by what is going on in a particular patient. The point is to stay with it, however this is done. But here, too, the patient must be understood, else the law of diminishing returns may set in, or the patient may settle into psychoanalysis as a way of life, or some other untoward effect may eventuate.

GIVING DIRECT ADVICE

Simple, realistic, and direct suggestions can sometimes have considerable beneficial effects. For example, think of the commonly seen patient who, as a consequence of early deprivation, overprotection, or other experience, has a strong distaste for responsibility. This could be the young married man who constantly complains of the demands of job and family, or it could be the forty-year-old adolescent matron for whom three children are just too much. Besides accurate analyzing and working through, it may help to point out directly, if true, that the patient acts as though only passive-receptive-dependent (PRD) play and self-indulgence were pleasurable. The analyst can then advise that in reality the use of mature powers can also be enjoyable when exercised in combination with play to create a balanced life; that the responsible, productive, independent giving can be erotized, pleasurized; that what is at first duty can, if accepted, be made the best of, rather than the worst of, and it can even become a source of enjoyment. Because the mature powers, like the muscles, become strong through exercise, the patient must be cautioned not to wait for them to grow strong and then cut the wood, but he must cut the wood and thereby contribute to the growing strength of the muscles, however sore they may be at first. So, too, the mature responsible-productive-independent (RPI) capacities of the personality develop and grow into strength.

A very intensely rivalrous young man was caught in a vicious circle. Overprotected and overadored in childhood, he was too focused on winning praise and approbation to have much object interest in persons or pursuits. Therefore, he was insecure and anxious and strove for security by winning yet more praise and approval and beating out all men as rivals. He grasped all this in his analysis, but much hostility from envy and competition persisted. He was a loved child, sincere, loving, and well-intentioned. I pointed out that these men that he constantly sought to surpass were like himself; they too had wives and children and needs for security and prestige. I then advised the patient to take an attitude of "friendly identification," of "live and let live" as between equals. He reacted to this as though he had gained a burst of insight and was helped toward this goal with diminution of his hostile envy and increase in object interest and security.

Another expression often of use with self-striving patients is "abandon your narcissism." In this instance, such a broad term covering deficient object interest and heightened devotion to self at the expense of others can make a valuable slogan. It gives the patient who can accept and use it a watchword for development out of narcissism and toward mature absorption in working and loving.

What was said earlier about shifting analysts applies also to the procedure of directly advising the patient. It has already been pointed out that it can be effective only if used in very carefully selected situations. Here the reason is that it is usually unnecessary because the change urged by direct advice is best produced as a natural result of analytic progress. A professional man of thirty three who still lives like an adolescent in the bosom of his family should see so clearly the connection between this prolongation of his childish attachment and his current problems that he emancipates himself on his own initiative. However, it might be that he requires some encouragement to change his environment. He may have to see that relations with his parents will improve if he gets them on an adult-to-adult basis and establishes himself independently. Freud (1909) said that the phobic may eventually have to be forced into the feared situation if he is to be cured—so may a man such as this need an analytic push. But any advice, interference, or maneuver is only a resource—it were better if the analysis were so conducted that the patient acted independently.

How the real power lies in analyzing is emphasized by those patients who try to draw the analyst into reality discussions. A patient may ask a series of ostensibly important practical questions, and these will continue until the real underlying purpose behind them is unmasked. A young married woman subtly involved her analyst in an urgent discussion of her semidetermination to divorce her husband until the analyst realized that he was being inveigled into a resistance against analyzing. After this he was able to penetrate to the unconscious spite against himself and against the husband, which followed the patient's pattern toward her mother.

ANALYZING ACTING OUT

Such a case raises another point. Usually, analyzing acting out helps to drive the feelings into the transference. But this patient by acting out and being involved in one vitally important pressing problem after another thereby provided an excuse to discuss these instead of analyzing.

Dynamically, a close watch must always be kept out for various possibilities—one patient is stable in his living while emotional storms rage in the transference; the next patient is the opposite, a lamb in the transference but with all manner of acting out.

Competition is often double in direction, both progressive and regressive, striving for and envying babyish passive-receptive dependence (PRD) and also mature responsible-productive independence (RPI). Failure to progress can be passive-regressive "lying back" or the blocking of proper effort at cure; usually it is both—the pull back of the desire to be cared for and other libidinal wishes and also the blocking, usually by hostility and guilt.

USING THE TELEPHONE

I remarked earlier that silence was one of the most serious forms of resistance, but certainly the very worst form of all is the patient being absent. Some twenty years ago, an extremely tense, slightly suicidal young woman could hardly talk in our meetings but took to phoning, thereby interesting me in the uses of the telephone as a technical aid. Since then, I have resorted to it for patients who have moved to areas devoid of dynamic psychiatrists and in many other special circumstances. Clearly, its effectiveness depends upon the patient and the situation. Some patients freeze on the telephone and are only able to talk in the office. For example, one patient who was almost paralyzed by anxiety, could get little or no relief by phoning and exclaimed, "It isn't personal enough." Nevertheless, when very carefully used with certain patients, in certain circumstances, at certain times, it can be of such help as to warrant a few clinical details.

A young woman who had endured a very traumatic childhood now had an almost complete amnesia for everything before the age of ten. Her human relations were so painful that she had only very few tenuous contacts with people. She feared to let herself go in any relationship lest she become so terribly dependent that she lose her freedom of action and be rendered intolerably vulnerable to the slightest rejection. These were her reactions in the transference. The idea of free association terrified her. She felt, she said, as though she would rather jump out of the window than tell her thoughts freely. With her great guilt and her fears of rejection, free association meant to her that she would be sadistically censured by her mother and rejected by her father as she had been in actuality in childhood. Daily interviews were more than she could endure, and less frequent visits did not solve the problem. She was too disturbed, the transference was too painfully anxious for her to tolerate, and this resistance could not be resolved quickly enough for treatment to progress. Being almost destitute of object libidinous relationships, she was, inevitably, suicidal. Too anxious in the presence of the therapist to talk but also desperate for help, she would, when her distress became threatening enough, telephone.

Two facts quickly became apparent. The first was that the telephone calls came at the periods of greatest distress and desperation, and therefore in timing made the maximal use of her wish for help; second, whereas the transference in personal interviews in the office was so intense and far above the optimal level that it interfered with treatment, on the telephone she was much better able to talk freely. Thus, the telephone caught the therapeutic urge at its maximum and diluted the hyperintensity of the transference to intensities that the patient could endure.

Accordingly, no restraint was put upon her use of the telephone. She by no means abused this privilege and was most considerate, and whenever possible she would make appointments to telephone if I were not immediately available. During the course of the year she came to the office once a week and telephoned about once a week. The telephone conversations usually lasted about half an hour, during which time full-fledged analytic work was accomplished. The dynamics of her neurosis, her emotional reactions, and their historic sources were analyzed. The transference was analyzed and eventually the motivations for resorting to the telephone were explored thoroughly. Subsequently, she became able to discuss her anxieties, resistances, and the transference in personal interviews. Coincidentally, her general human relations improved dramatically. The central task of the analysis was accomplished, and only the integration of her relationships in and outside the transference and consolidation of her gains remained to be worked through.

I believe that this use of the telephone, not accidentally, but deliberately, goal consciously, and systematically, not only succeeded in penetrating a resistance that might not otherwise have yielded, but succeeded in so doing in the way chosen by the patient. I think it also helped to resolve the resistance more quickly than could otherwise have been done.

Another patient, with quite a different emotional structure, had an alarming negative therapeutic reaction. This was largely the result of her total inability to express intense hostility in the transference during the interviews. This hostility accumulated and occasioned severe guilt with needs to justify it by feelings that the analysis was harmful and a terrible mistake—opinions that the patient threatened to make public. This of course followed closely a pattern of her childhood. The feelings were too intense for the patient to handle in the analytic sessions. Variation of the frequency of interviews and attempts at many other resources in interpretation or mechanics of the treatment failed to resolve this negative therapeutic reaction. Because of this the telephone was tried. Fortunately, the intensities of the emotions were again diminished by being out of the analyst's presence. The patient was able to talk with comparative freedom and the essential mechanisms of her negative therapeutic reaction were clearly revealed, after which progress was made in personal interviews. There is no doubt that much time was saved.

Apart from its use as an aid to technique, it is interesting how much can be accomplished by telephoning purely as a means of communication. For example, a mother and father who were worried by some misadventures of their only son, with whom they were deeply involved emotionally, became so upset that the mother's health was in jeopardy and the father was unable to work. This couple lived at some distance, my schedule was full, and for various reasons they refused to consult another psychiatrist. They talked at length about their problem on the telephone. Later they came once to the office, and thereafter for three strenuous months the whole matter was handled by telephone. This amounted to about two calls a week of about a half hour each. The son's problem was reactive, but acute and difficult. They were helped greatly in adapting to the traumatic reality by this means.

USING THE TAPE RECORDER

The use of the tape recorder was brought to my attention by a couple who recorded some of their discussions, usually heated, of their marital difficulties. Rather to my surprise, these proved highly illuminating. My experience with these devices, however, is much too limited to justify more than mentioning tape recorders here as having promising potential.

It cannot be emphasized too strongly that every technical procedure is only a means to an end, and its use must depend upon the basis of the rationale of all treatment—psychoanalytic accuracy in understanding the patient.

REFERENCES AND SOME RELATED READINGS

Alexander, F. (1935), The problem of psychoanalytic technique. *Psychoanal. Quart.*, 4 : 588–611.
Brenner, C. (1969), Some comments on technical precepts in psychoanalysis. *J. Am. Psychoanal. A.*, 17 : 333–352.
Brodsky, B. (1968), Working through: Its widening scope

and some aspects of its metapsychology. *Psychoanal. Quart.,* 36:485–531.

Calogeras, R. (1967), Silence as a technical parameter in psychoanalysis. *Internat. J. Psychoanal.,* 48:536–558.

Chessick, R. (1971), *Why Psychotherapists Fail.* New York: Science House.

Dahlberg, C. (1970), Sexual contact between patient and therapist. *Contemp. Psychoanal.,* 6:107–124.

Deutsch, H. (1939), A discussion of certain forms of resistance. *Internat. J. Psychoanal.,* 20:72–83.

Dunbar, F. (1952), Technical problems in the analysis of psychosomatic disorders with special reference to precision in short term psychotherapy. *Internat. J. Psychoanal.,* 33:385–396.

Fenichel, O. (1941), *Problems of Psychoanalytic Technique* (monograph). New York: Psychoanal. Quart.

Freud, A. (1971), *The Writings of Anna Freud,* vol. 7. New York: Internat. Univ. Press.

——— (1969), *Difficulties in the Path of Psychoanalysis.* New York: Internat. Univ. Press.

——— (1954), Problems of technique in adult analysis. *Bull. Philadelphia A. Psychoanal.,* 4:48.

Freud, S. (1937), Analysis terminable and interminable. In *Collected Papers,* 5:316–357. London: Hogarth Press, 1950.

——— (1924a), The economic problem in masochism. In *Collected Papers,* 2:255–269. London: Hogarth Press, 1924.

——— (1924b), Neurosis and psychosis. In *Collected Papers,* 2:250–255. London: Hogarth Press, 1924.

——— (1909), General remarks on hysterical attacks. In *Collected Papers,* 2:100–104. London: Hogarth Press, 1924.

Glover, E. (1955), *The Technique of Psychoanalysis.* New York: Internat. Univ. Press.

Grinker, R. R. (1955), Growth inertia and shame; their

therapeutic implications and dangers. *Internat. J. Psychoanal.,* 36: 242–253.

Haley, J. (1963), *Strategies of Psychotherapy.* New York: Grune & Stratton.

Hoffer, W. (1954), Defensive process and defensive organization; their place in psychoanalytic technique. *Internat. J. Psychoanal.,* 35: 194–198.

Horney, K. (1936), The problem of the negative therapeutic reaction. *Psychoanal. Quart.,* 5: 29–44.

Karush, A. (1967), Working through. *Psychoanal. Quart.,* 36: 497–531.

Kestenberg, J. (1969), Acting out in the analysis of children and adults. *Internat. J. Psychoanal.,* 49: 341–346.

La Forgue, R. (1937), Exceptions to the fundamental rule of psychoanalysis. *Internat. J. Psychoanal.,* 18: 35–41.

——— (1934), Resistances at the conclusion of analytic treatment. *Internat. J. Psychoanal.,* 15: 419–434.

Masserman, J., ed. (1971), *Techniques of Therapy.* New York: Grune & Stratton.

——— (1955), *The Practice of Dynamic Psychiatry.* Philadelphia: Saunders.

Riviere, J. (1936), A contribution to the analysis of the negative therapeutic reaction. *Internat. J. Psychoanal.,* 17: 304–320.

Rosenfeld, H. (1966), The need of patients to act out during analysis. *Psychoanal. Forum,* 1: 19–29.

Roth, N. (1952), The acting out of transferences. *Psychoanalyt. Rev.,* 39: 69–78.

Sachs, H. (1930), Behavior as an expression of mental processes during analysis. *Internat. J. Psychoanal.,* 11: 231–232.

Saul, L. (1972), *Bases of Human Behavior.* Westport, Conn.: Greenwood Press.

——— (1956), *The Hostile Mind.* New York: Random House.

——— (1951), A note on the telephone as a technical aid. *Psychoanal. Quart.,* 20: 287–290.

Schmideberg, M. (1935), Reassurance as a means of analytic technique. *Internat. J. Psychoanal.,* 16: 307–324.

Silverberg, W. V. (1955), Acting out versus insight; a problem in psychoanalytic technique. *Psychoanal. Quart.,* 24: 527–544.

Thompson, C. *et al.* (1956), The role of the analyst's personality in therapy. *Am. J. Psychotherapy,* 10: 347–367.

Waelder, R. (1936), The problem of freedom in psychoanalysis and the problem of reality testing. *Internat. J. Psychoanal.,* 17: 89–108.

Weiss, E. (1942), Emotional memories and acting out. *Psychoanal. Quart.,* 11: 477–492.

Wolman, B., ed. (1967), *Psychoanalytic Techniques, A Handbook for the Practicing Psychoanalyst.* New York: Basic Books.

Wolstein, B., ed. (1971), *Psychoanalytic Techniques.* New York: Science House.

20 / THE SUSTAINED AND THE UNSUSTAINED

THE CONCEPT

We have long known that a patient can be internally sustained or unsustained. Awareness of this is of value as it provides clearer insight for analyst and patient into the ego's strengths and weaknesses. The analyst who perceives that a patient is sustained or unsustained can better help the patient to outgrow childhood attitudes toward self and others, to build up an adequate superego, and to develop a more mature sense of his identity, ability, and value. By way of illustration, let's look at the case of a Jewish refugee from Holland. He had no home and no family; his father, mother, and sister were long since dead. He had a partial scholarship to a Midwestern college and supplemented this by working as a waiter and at other odd jobs. He was so poor that for some periods he lived only on bananas. Yet he did outstandingly well in his studies and was elected to Phi Beta Kappa. Moreover, he participated in the college theatrical group, had dates, and was popular with students of both sexes and with the faculty. He continued thus through law school. Upon graduation he married and five years later was well established in his profession and happy with his wife and two children. Where did he get his strength and confidence?

His father and sister had died in an automobile accident when he was four years old. Thereafter his mother had had to work long hours, and he helped increasingly with the housework. As soon as he was old enough he was sent on errands; he learned to tidy up, to clean, to cook, and to shop. He had playmates and friends, and visited back and forth. His mother loved him wisely. She provided unquestioning love and all the security she could, combined with safety and freedom. Therefore he felt loved and protected but still free and independent. In his mind there grew and became consolidated the image of a loving, tolerant, permissive mother who had confidence in him and in his judgment and ability to carry responsibility. This served him well; it saved his life. When he was twelve years old the Nazis overran Europe, and he and his mother were herded into a detention camp. His resourceful mother instructed him how to escape and where to go, and he obeyed her suggestions. His mother was taken to a camp in Germany and was never heard from again. The boy found persons who got him to the United States.

His symptoms from this experience were a degree of preoccupation with the Nazis and anxiety. The anxiety, which was not enough to interfere with his daily living, stemmed from anger because of a continuing sense of lack of loving support after the sudden premature loss of his mother. Clinically this looked like a traumatic neurosis; the anxiety diminished rapidly upon analysis.

He had the usual emotional tensions and problems from which few human beings are free, but he had no more than most people, perhaps even less. His inner security and confidence saw him through dangers and difficulties, and his self-image never wavered. He felt that he was a good, sound person, as able as the next, and capable of doing what needed to be done and of meeting situations as they arose.

He was sustained from within by the continuing image in his mind that was formed early by the love from his father, sister, and mother. His help with the problems of living had won his mother's admiring approval. He could escape from a concentration camp and make his way alone in a foreign land, but he was not truly alone for in his mind was the sustaining image of his loving, intelligently permissive mother. By expecting this attitude from others, he made friends. Feeling loved, he loved others; hence they responded with warmth to him. He was devoted to several older men and women who were good, admired friends.

The man's story demonstrates the fundamental importance of a good, loving, encouraging image of parents—an image formed by experience from birth through early childhood.

The opposite kind of person is the unsustained, and there are many of them. Their backgrounds in childhood vary in detail: "Father died and mother worked. She did a good job, but never let us forget that she was a martyr, that she was sacrificing herself for us"; "I felt that I was just supposed to be good and not cause any trouble, that mother would have been happier if I were not there"; "Father worked hard and wasn't around much. Mother didn't care too much for any of us, but liked me the least"; "Recently father told me I was his favorite, but he never treated me that way. I felt as though he treated me like some business associate of his"; "Father was very friendly and nice to me but was constantly being criticized and torn down by mother. I was too. Sometimes she'd let fly the most devastating criticism as though nothing I did was right. Then she'd make up and be loving again. It tore me apart. I never knew where I stood and I never could stop hoping and trying to keep her loving me"; "My parents had their troubles with each other. They sent me off to school, maybe to get me out of their hair. But then they never cared. I wrote them my problems and they never bothered to answer; or if they did, they didn't help but as much as told me to manage somehow and not bother them"; "I felt sort of loved, but dispensable"; and so on.

Some patients are quite aware of these feelings; others express them only with anguish after much analytic work. Many are intelligent, healthy, and attractive, but they feel unloved and unlovable, insecure, unsure of themselves in work and with people. One young man, a junior in college, said, "I can't study. Some kind of personal problems get in the way. I have a constant feeling of failure in academic things. And I can't get on with people. I rarely can get close to anyone and if I do, then I fight with them." Some of these people seek love and closeness through the sexual act.

A girl from a well-to-do family had every advantage, but she felt equally lost and inadequate at school, in studies, and socially. Beautiful and wealthy, she attracted many young men, and this was her one consolation, her one way of feeling that she was lovable and acceptable. She married and had two children, but her troubles deepened as she began to feel toward her husband as she felt toward her mother. Although potentially very capable, she was inadequate emotionally. If the furnace sputtered, she panicked and called in her neighbor for help. She lacked self-confidence to such a degree that she developed a common symptom—fear of being alone. It was a wrench when her husband left for work in the morning, and she tried to prevent his leaving her unless she knew where he was going to be at every moment of the day and was sure that her near neighbors would be in. When I saw her she would not drive a car. On one occasion she went to the nearby shopping center and became panic-stricken because her husband left her alone in the supermarket while he stopped in at the adjacent drugstore.

This is like the behavior of a young child. While the adult part of such people is fully capable, there is no emotional support within—no expression of love and no self-confidence. The parents' attitudes and feelings are felt about the self—feelings of being rejected, neglected, criticized, unaccepted, unsupported. Consequently, there is no feeling of being sustained from within. Such partial rejection and insufficient love and acceptance during childhood continue in the individual's inner feelings and creep into every relationship with others. The person then expects that every relationship will sooner or later become like the original one with parents. This certainty of eventual disapproval and rejection is fought off in many ways: it is often hidden under a mask of gaiety, a euphoria, to cover the inner depression at feeling unvalued.

The consequences of all this are so typical as to form an almost mathematical progression. The first reaction is the same as to any threat or frustration: solve it by flight or fight. Flight means a withdrawal from people, from closeness, from responsibilities. Fight creates anger, either open or repressed. The anger usually has two results. First, it causes guilt and thereby self-injurious behavior. Second, the chronic undercurrent of anger and guilt, and an unsupporting superego, lead to anxiety, often a nameless dread, without content.

When the two cases, that of the Jewish refugee and that of the young married woman, are compared, the implications for treatment are obvious. In the first patient, who was internally sustained, there was some problem with his dependent needs for love and with narcissistic competition, which derived from the loss of parental support before puberty, from the premature requirements for independence, and from the wish to continue as the only child in a world of competitors. But here the analysis could proceed rapidly and successfully because of the firm foundation of the personality upon the loving, giving, tolerant, confidence-imparting maternal superego. The dependence on the analyst, the identification with him, the wishes for his love and approval, the competition and hostility toward him, were all moderate in degree. The background of transference in which the analysis progressed was that of the child to his supporting maternal superego. This basic transference repeats the central dynamics, continued from childhood, and determines the atmosphere and dynamics of the treatment.

In the second case, the internally unsustained woman, there was a hollowness or softness—a feeling of being insufficiently loved and wanted; a lack of confidence in the self because there had been deficient experience during her early childhood with parents who did not provide enough love, respect, and confidence.

A person unsustained feels alone even with friends and often has agoraphobia, anthropophobia, and general fears and anxieties because of an unsupporting superego that imparts no self-confidence. This individual feels inadequate to life and its problems and challenges. Out of this insecurity and sense of inadequacy comes a desperate clinging to whomever can give acceptance, guidance, and leadership. Excessive needs for dependence and love along with inner emotional inadequacy render the unsustained person supersensitive to frustration. Any sudden problem, even a minor nuisance, or slight to self-esteem, any hint of disapproval or rejection, stirs up anxiety and therefore anger. Hence there is chronic anger and usually guilt from this. The person is demanding, clinging, and hostile and feels guilty toward those to whom these feelings come out in behavior. This anger and guilt add to the anxiety from the lack of a supporting superego, and usually causes masochistic, self-injurious behavior.

THERAPY

In treatment, the transference of the unsustained person may rise far above what is optimal in intensity because of the exaggerated needs for dependence and love. This is the case whether or not they are strongly erotized, because of hostility, guilt, and masochism, and because of envy. But this is not the main problem in therapy if one is to deal with the core of the difficulty. The analyst not only has to alter the balance of forces as with a secure person but, with the unsustained, he must try to build a personality from that which was insufficient and minimal. Of course, there is always some degree of inner sustainment, otherwise an individual would not have sufficient strength to be carrying on at all in life or to be in analytic treatment. Nevertheless therapy must build up something from a minimal amount, not just alter the balance of forces; it must build a proper, supportive superego almost from scratch.

For this task, the emotional attitude of the analyst, which is always of fundamental importance, becomes vital and crucial for treatment. The internally strong can withstand much; the unsustained are terribly vulnerable and can be seriously damaged rather than helped by analysis if it is not used supportively, ego-syntonically (see chap. 21). We now know that analysis is a potent instrument that can damage as well as heal. There is no such thing as the analyst's having no attitude. If he is formal and distant, that is an attitude. If he is silent for long periods, this is potent silence for one patient takes it as assent and support, another understands it to be censure and disapprobation, and another considers it a lack of interest. The patient with an unsustaining superego will interpret the analyst's attitude in terms of his needs, of his parental imagoes and identifications, of his superego. A young man came to see me in a pitiful state. He had been in analysis for a year and a half. "My analyst," he said, "is right in everything he tells me; but I just can't take it anymore. The analysis is beating me down. What he says is true—but it makes me feel I am a hopeless child, that I'm infantile, that I'm inadequate and full of anger. I felt this myself before seeing him. And I know I'm terribly dependent. I can't stand being alone. But hammering at all this makes me feel worse and worse."

This illustrates our point precisely. After this young man lost his father at the age of three, his mother had to work part time. It was too much for her, and she considered her son to be merely an inconvenience and a nuisance. He felt this, felt that he was only being tolerated and that his mother would have preferred it if he were not there. He was expected simply to be good and not make trouble. The dynamics were clear, but therapy was extremely difficult, for this was a hollow man, that is, a man lacking in inner sustainment. The analyst had to be accurate in reading the patient's associations, in interpreting his dreams, in understanding what the man's unconscious was saying. But he had to communicate this in an understanding, supportive, ego-building way, and not make his insight into the infantile roots of the problem come through to the patient as examples of the patient's childish qualities. His analyst had been trying, by correct interpretation of the infantile alone, to encourage the patient to drop these attitudes. But this focus on the infantile made the patient feel disparaged and rejected, just as he had been made to feel during his childhood.

For the unsustained, the analyst must provide the experience that the patient lacked in childhood: that of having an interested, sympathetic, understanding person always available in his life. Without such an attitude, technically correct interpretations may be construed by the patient to mean disapproval. Accurate interpretations also require an attitude of human understanding, of being on the patient's side, of having confidence in him. The patient must be shown his mature strengths and capacities. The analyst's confidence is partly internalized and can move even the most hollow of men in the direction of a sense of sustainment and identity, thus helping him build a good self-image and feelings of self-acceptance.

21 / IDENTITY AND A POINT OF TECHNIQUE

A vitally important point in the technique of making interpretations is the conveying to the patient of the sharp distinction between the mature part of his personality and that portion of the childhood part that causes his difficulties. An example of this is a young man who had some psychoanalytic treatment but was in a state of depression, rage, withdrawal, and severe self-depreciation. He told his new analyst that the previous treatment had showed him the kind of person he was: infantile, dependent, withdrawn, lonely, hostile, and unable to feel. It quickly turned out that all this was true, but with the very important limitation that it was true for only part of his personality. His therapist had naturally focused upon that part of the personality that made the trouble. However, by concentrating his interpretations exclusively on this part, he gave this young man the impression that his entire self—his total personality—was meant, rather than a sort of disturbed foreign body in an otherwise mature adult.

*This chapter is drawn from a paper originally prepared in collaboration with Silas L. Warner, M.D.

The first task was to make the young man see realistically, without flattery, and with complete honesty, his mature characteristics. To correct his limited image of himself as nothing at all but a guilty, shameful person ridden by infantile impulses, he needed to realize that he was mainly a person with a strong, healthy physique, good looks, intelligence, and education; in short, an individual with adequate instruments, in body, mind, and personality, for the requirements of life.

Essentially he was given a more complete picture and was shown that he had sufficient maturity, or at least capacity for maturity, to use these instruments to make his way in the world, to love and to be loved, to marry and have children, to enjoy friendship, and to contribute to society. Interference with his doing this, then, originated in the disturbed childhood part, which exists to some extent in all of us. Childhood characteristics that make trouble for the mature part must be dealt with, but the patient must never lose sight of the fact that the mature part has, indeed, perfectly adequate capacities. An individual cannot go through life with any feeling of confidence or peace unless he sees his strengths and eventually finds he can trust in them through experience in living and in handling his infantile motivations.

Besides giving the patient a realistic self-image that he can validly respect, awareness of the mature part of the patient's personality should be kept in sharp focus because of the nature of analytic treatment. The therapeutic effect of the analytic procedure depends largely upon the patient's ability to discriminate between present reality and those patterns that have been derived from the realities of childhood and which now interfere with mature functioning. Since in the course of the analysis the patient projects his superego onto the analyst, the analyst willy-nilly becomes part of the patient's superego. Insofar as the patient identifies with his parents or is seeking such identification, he will identify himself strongly with his analyst. Therefore, if in making interpretations the analyst unwittingly gives the impression of seeing the patient as an infantile personality, the patient through identification with the analyst is apt to continue this attitude toward himself, reinforced and entrenched rather than corrected.

This is one of the pitfalls of interpretation. If the analyst, focusing upon the infantile reactions, conveys to the patient that this covers the patient in toto rather than merely a part of his personality, then, even though every interpretation is correct, the patient may emerge from the analysis in a beaten-down condition. He will see himself as a disturbed, infantile individual rather than as a person whose total, otherwise-adequate personality includes the conflicting inadequacies.

The importance of the analyst not conveying any sense of criticism or depreciation in his interpretations, spoken or unspoken, cannot be exaggerated. When the analyst makes interpretations that bring to the patient an infantile image of himself, then these have behind them the full force of the analyst's authority the authority the parents originally had over the patient as a child. If the analyst implies that the patient is infantile, this must be true, for it repeats what the parents said or implied. To have and to hold the love of the parents is the most important single goal of the young child's life. This same need is the core of the transference. It must be fully recognized by the patient, and the analyst must be aware of its potential for damage.

Analysts generally agree that the patient is strongly influenced by his identification with the analyst. More narrowly, the patient's ego-identity is influenced by his identification with the analyst, as it was in childhood by the identification with his parents and others. In "The Technique of Psychoanalysis" Freud warns that the analyst should not misuse his influence. "If he does, he will only be repeating a mistake of the parents who crushed their child's independence by their influence, and he will only be replacing the patient's earlier dependence by a new one." By including interpretations of how the entire personality deals with the infantile reactions, both successfully and unsuccessfully, the analyst can give the patient a truer concept of himself and not add the weight of his authority to the patient's tendency to see himself critically.

Actually, the analyst becomes a powerful part of the patient's new superego. The patient through his need for the analyst's love and approval, his fear of the analyst's criticism, accepts the analyst's opinions and interpretations, no matter how devastating. It is unrealistic to think it possible to analyze any patient in such a way that when the analysis ends, it is as though the patient never met the analyst. As Freud clearly stated, the analyst has become part of the patient's superego, and as such he is a very influential part of the patient's personality. If he has used his role as the patient's new parent wisely and therapeutically, the residue of the transference is friendly, and the patient usually feels warm and grateful toward him. If he has used it badly, there is an undercurrent of resentment for many years and the patient may be unimproved or worse. The patient's original pattern of feelings toward the parents, repeated with the analyst, is never completely outgrown or resolved. However, a diminution may tilt the balance in the patient's life from one of neurotic distress to relative freedom. This is reflected in a countertransference atmosphere that encourages the mature to see and to learn to handle and outgrow the disturbing infantile.

The following example demonstrates the technique of assuring the patient with a realistic but non-deprecatory sense of identity while at the same time discussing possible solutions to problems. An attractive young woman who, a few years before, had completed four and a half years of full-scale, five-day-a-week analysis, came to see an analyst because of a severe state of indecision and confusion which affected all areas of her life. She was undecided as to how to handle her children at mealtime; whether or not to let them have sweets; whether to take them to shows; what to buy them to wear; what clothes to purchase for herself; whether to change the decorating of the house; and so on throughout every aspect of her life. It soon appeared that she felt compelled to do everything perfectly. This was part of her childhood pattern. It was her way of winning love. With her parents, she felt insecure and could only assure herself of their acceptance by perfect behavior. This pattern had been dealt with intensively and extensively in her analysis, but persisted uncorrected. In fact, the patient complained that she was worse now than when she first went for treatment. The situation was clear; she had the insight into her problem but was totally unable to use it for therapeutic effect.

In such an instance, shouldn't the analyst take the position that since the insight has been achieved, the central problem and therefore the main concern should now be to find inner emotional solutions to discuss with the patient? Freud took the position of helping the patient find solutions when he described psychoanalysis as a process of after-education by which the blunders of the parents can be corrected by the analyst. What is to be the nature of the after-education that analysis can offer a patient in this young woman's situation?

The analyst imparted to this patient and discussed with her, with therapeutic effect, the following ideas. He began by emphasizing that the young woman herself was not neurotic, indecisive, insecure, perfectionistic, and the like, but that this was only a part of her childhood pattern. He reassured her that this was only one part of her personality and that it was in sharp contradistinction to the mature part of her makeup. He went on to point out that her mature self had a good sense of reality, good judgment, was able to marry and have children, to take responsibility for her home, and to relate adequately to people. The first step, in other words, was to separate the pathodynamic pattern, to make clear what was the pathologically infantile and what was the mature. Several points were involved here: (1) to give her a perspective on her problem; (2) to give her a good image of her own self in maturity; and (3) to use the mature part of her ego as a basis for understanding, while keeping the infantile in perspective. In this process we could come back to Freud's original simile of the reclamation of the Zuyder Zee: the task is to build on the mature ego at the expense of the disordered childhood pattern.

The second step continues the first. In this case, the obvious realities were pointed out to her. Her husband loved her and she had friends, and not to see this was unrealistic. We understood why she did not: her childhood insecurity in relation to her parents persisted. She was told that there were dynamic reasons, as well as historic reasons, for her feelings and that guilt made her feel that she was unworthy of love. The main point that was emphasized, however, was that her feeling of being unloved was a delusion; and her ideal of perfection had in fact been attained in order to get what, all the time, she actually had.

The third issue discussed with her was the ineffectiveness of the methods that she customarily used in her attempts to get love. Others would not give her love if she was too directly demanding. In reality, the way to get love is not to demand it; this leads to frustration and rejection and hence, to anger and vindictiveness. To get love she should use the mature part of her personality to do a good job with her husband, her children, her friends, and with her community. One gets love by giving it, not by being perfect or anything else.

The three points that were discussed with the patient have been presented here in condensed, almost schematic form, to convey the essential fact that in many instances the analyst cannot depend upon insight alone for successful therapeutic results. The analyst will find it necessary in cases like the one given here to pause and consider what uses he can make of the insight he has gained. The first step would be for the analyst to make in his own mind a thoroughgoing formulation of the patient's essential problem. The second step is for the analyst to think out what the solutions to this problem may be. Naturally, these solutions are not given to the patient in any dogmatic fashion but only after, in Freud's spirit of after-education, the analyst takes stock and reviews with the patient the nature of the problem and the main dynamics, and then considers the possible solutions.

Recapitulating, every person's sense of identity stems from its nucleus in the relationships to the parents and siblings (or substitutes) in the earliest years, especially prior to age six. This occurs by object relations with the parents, for example, feeling loved or unloved, and by identification with them, taking over their attitudes, feelings, reactions. Both processes involve very largely introjection of the parents to form the superego, which continues the images and authority of the parents. Both processes determine in large degree a person's image of himself—his self-esteem and his ego-identity. This develops without problems where relationships with the parents are basically good; when they are not, the sense of identity is vague, insecure, unacceptable, or otherwise disordered in a variety of ways.

The importance of this in analytic technique is great, for the analyst comes into the position of the parents as a significant part of the patient's superego. Inevitably, therefore, the analyst influences the patient powerfully. Part of this influence is on the patient's view of himself. If the analyst implies, wittingly or unwittingly, through his interpretations that the totality of the patient's personality consists of the disordered infantile patterns that the analyst interprets, then the patient comes to see himself as only this —a depreciated, infantile, inadequate, hostile, shameful, guilty creature. Hence, it is essential that the analyst give the patient a realistic view of himself, enabling him to see clearly and in perspective his mature qualities and capacities, and to discriminate the disordered infantile patterns, that is, the psychopathology, from the mature. The mature is used as a base for dealing with the disordered infantile, the pathodynamics. In this way, the patient achieves a sound, realistic ego-identity, building up and being conscious of the mature healthy part of his personality; and his identity gives self-respect and confidence in dealing with the infantile parts in the analysis and in life. The transference and countertransference can thus correct faults in the object relations and identifications of childhood with the parents, moving these toward a more adult-to-adult relation of the patient with the analyst, with persons in life, with his parents, and with himself.

REFERENCES AND SOME RELATED READINGS

Balint, A. (1943), Identification. *Internat. J. Psychoanal.*, 24:97–107.

Brody, M. W., and Mahoney, V. P. (1964), Introjection, identification and incorporation. *Internat. J. Psychoanal.*, 45:57–63.

Devereux, G. (1966), Loss of identity, impairment of relationships, reading disability. *Psychoanal. Quart.*, 35:18–39.

Erickson, E. H. (1959) *Identity in the Life Cycle.* New York: Internat. Univ. Press.

French, T. (1945), Ego analysis as a guide to therapy. *Psychoanal. Quart.*, 14:336–349.

Freud, A. (1946), *Ego and the Mechanisms of Defense.* New York: Internat. Univ. Press.

Freud, S. (1938), The technique of psychoanalysis. In *Standard Edition,* 23:175. London: Hogarth Press, 1964.

Guntrip, H. (1971), *Psychoanalytic Theory, Therapy and the Self.* New York: Basic Books.

——— (1961), *Personality Structure and Human Interaction.* New York: Internat. Univ. Press.

Hayman, A. (1965), Verbalization and identity. *Internat. J. Psychoanal.*, 46:455–466.

Jacobson, E. (1964), *The Self and the Object World,* 24–33. New York: Internat. Univ. Press.

Koff, R. H. (1961), A definition of identification. A review of the literature. *Internat. J. Psychoanal.,* 42:362–370.

Kris, E. (1951), Ego psychology and interpretation in psychoanalytic therapy. *Psychoanal. Quart.,* 20:15–30.

Lampl-de Groot, J. (1956), The role of identification in psychoanalytic procedure. *Internat. J. Psychoanal.,* 37: 456–459.

Leites, N. (1971), *The New Ego.* New York: Science House.

Lomas, P. (1965), Passivity and failure of identity development. *Internat. J. Psychoanal.,* 46:438–454.

Lowenstein, R. (1951), Ego development and psychoanalytic technique. *Am. J. Psychiat.,* 107:617–622.

Mittelman, B. (1949), Ego functions and dreams. *Psychoanal. Quart.,* 18:434–448.

Rappaport, D. (1951), *Organization and Pathology of Thought, Selected Sources,* 724. New York: Columbia Univ. Press.

Saul, L. and Pulver, S. (1965), The concept of emotional maturity. *Comprehensive Psychiat.,* 6:6–20.

Stone, L. (1961), *The Psychoanalytic Situation. An Examination of Its Development and Essential Nature.* New York: Internat. Univ. Press.

Tabachnick, N, (1965), Three psychoanalytic views of identity. *Internat. J. Psychoanal.,* 46:467–473.

22 / FAILURES—LEGITIMATE AND ILLEGITIMATE

Primum non nocere

It is an open question whether or not harm can result from a properly conducted analysis, that is, one in which the patient is correctly selected and well understood, the frequency of meeting adjusted to his individual needs, and the presenting material of each hour accurately discerned and tactfully made to count. In my experience and observation, if these requirements are fulfilled, then, although there may be difficult periods, the long-range end result is always improvement. And in the great preponderance of cases, the improvements are so great as to be worth the sacrifices to the patient many times over. Difficulties (see Chap. 19), even prolonged ones, are distinguishable from overall development and results (see Chap. 1).

When the therapeutic outcome is poor, after years of effort, there are usually two main possibilities. Before spelling these out, mention should be made of a few pertinent facts. Erroneous selection of patients is probably an only infrequent reason. A patient with no good imagoes doubtless will suffer through protracted periods that will be very trying for the analyst as well as for the patient, but in the end the patient will usually be at least somewhat better, not worse. In rare instances a paranoid, a depressive, or other type of core may be so hidden as to escape detection in the diagnostic interview and during the few weeks of trial analysis. Then it will flower at a time when the analyst can do nothing but continue his help. Usually, however, this too will be lived through with benefit if the analysis is well conducted, and the patient probably will improve even if treatment is broken off. No longer can the analyst excuse his failures as schizophrenics whom he had failed to recognize. For even if he does identify such a core or trend in the diagnostic interview, in all likelihood he will undertake the patient for treatment anyway, so effective has analysis become as a tool of therapy, even in borderline cases.

Of the two chief possibilities, the first is that the analyst lacks personal competence for treating this kind of person and problem. Insofar as this is a matter of human frailty and inexperience, it is entirely legitimate. Not all doctors have equal therapeutic ability, and probably not every analyst is maximally effective for every patient. Thus, legitimate failures include difficulties in selection—selection of the patient for treatment and selection of the most appropriate analyst for the patient. As Freud noted, you cannot take at face value what a patient says about a previous analyst. But usually it is not difficult to determine whether the previous analyst has clearly seen the central dynamics, with origins in the childhood pattern, and helped the patient to come to grips with them in his life and in the transference. And where this has been done by dealing with the presenting material so that confusion is minimal and insight sound, the result is a pleasure to see. Any difficulties in such a situation are entirely legitimate.

But the second possibility is not legitimate—when the incompetence is a result of misconceptions about the psychoanalytic treatment itself. These misconceptions seem to fall into two main groups. The first is emphasizing the form at the expense of the substance, the psychic realities. The second is emphasizing the infantile to the exclusion of the ego and the current realities, the total psychic situation as Freud (1916) called it. In both groups the difficulty stems from a failure to see the whole picture.

When a young analyst, who is himself in the process of divorce, unconsciously influences toward divorce a young woman whose home could have been saved, this is tragically bad analysis, but the reason may be only human frailty in the analyst. However, when this results from his insistence that his patient come five days a week for four years, when he looks only for clichés and consequently misses the childhood trauma and its effects, when he fails to see that the patient is sinking into so deep a transference with daily visits that it is becoming harder for her to save her marriage, and when he ignores her desperate pleas for a consultation, then this is not a legitimate failure, for it springs from a misguided insistence on form with neglect of the realities of the patient's life and motivations.

Occasionally, an error in the use of infrequent visits is encountered. Here the therapist is so aware of the fewer sessions per week that, in trying to make the most of each, he jumps to wild analytic interpretations. In time, the whole power of the unconscious forces will be mobilized, and the transference will develop in full intensity, even if the meetings are only once a week. The arousal of these mighty emotions is not avoided nor is their power palliated by the analyst's deciding in his own mind that less than four meetings per week means that the therapy is superficial. The emotions will rise up, and the analyst must deal with them. If he does so accurately and ego-syntonically from the beginning, then he will help his patient; if he does not, he will grapple with these emotions when they have become too intensified and confused to be handled well and to be turned to the best therapeutic advantage. The analyst who cannot understand the patient or use the main presenting issues of each hour therapeutically, when he sees the patient two or three times a week, is not apt to do so any better when he sees the patient four or five times a week. This of course, does not mean that the more frequent meetings may not be indicated. The key point here is that the decision as to how often to see a patient must be grounded, not on definitions of analysis, but on an understanding of the patient.

We are in a transitional stage, and, while knowledge advances, it behooves us to be tolerant of all misconceptions and differences. However, it also behooves us to clarify the realities. Note the following examples.

When an unusually well-balanced young wife with a small child, whose main difficulties result from her mother-in-law living with them, is advised to go into full five-day-a-week analysis without mention of the mother-in-law, then the reactive elements, the external realities, have been missed.

When a dependent husband in middle age is analyzed for three years, five times a week, and his dependence is treated as a purely internal problem with no relation to his wife (even though the chief source of the marital friction is this dependency on the wife, which neither he nor she can stand), then the nature and the operation of the dependence has not been understood, nor has the whole role of his pattern toward his mother, which he was repeating unconsciously toward his wife.

When after eight years of standard psychoanalysis, a patient can hardly be spoken with because he buries his face in his hands, "free associating" and trying to relive age three and a half and feeling that if he could relive age two that there would be deeper analysis and better cure, then the nature and the dynamics of psychoanalytic treatment have not been understood by the analyst, who has allowed the patient to indulge in regressive infantile fantasying as an escape from the mature responsibilities of his life.

We have noted the increasing attention to the ego and to the person's relations to reality. But here, too, there is a lag. A young analyst, stable and realistic, has been treating a woman four to five days a week for five years, but she is not improved. He feels sure though that he does understand her central problem. What is it? He replies, "She wants my penis but is too inhibited to ask for it." At the end of the conversation he adds as an afterthought an observation that for him has no connection with the analysis. He says, "I think that she wants to unload her problems onto me."

Here we see the error that Freud (1928) described as taking as an explanation a symbol which must itself be interpreted to reach the truth. One analytic view is or, hopefully, was that this symbol is the only reality, that whatever this woman wants in real life is itself always only a symbol for her true wish, which is for the analyst's penis, a wish probably transferred from her father's organ. This can be true, especially where the father or a brother is given outstanding preference and privilege in the family. But, even here we see the ego meaning, which is lacking in the bare statement. If the sexual symbol is to be of full therapeutic effectiveness, this ego meaning must be understood and interpreted.

In our example it quickly appeared that the woman, because of her upbringing, was full of resentful protest against life's demands on her. She did, in fact, want to unload them onto the analyst and envied him the power, position, and success in life that she saw in him as compared with her own lot. It is this which must be worked through, from the top down. Is the penis envy nothing more than a symbol for these feelings? Does it express a biologic desire? Is it a sexual representation of an ego wish? Does it have direct sexual significance through early conditioning by emotional influences and experiences (such as envy of a preferred brother with whom she was bathed until the age of five, six, or seven)?

The number of meetings per week has been mentioned in connection with the cases discussed above only to show that these patients were in regular, full-scale psychoanalysis. The frequency itself is not under discussion here at all. The point is that with conscientious standard procedure, failures can occur because of misconceptions about the fundamentals, particularly form at the expense of substance and the infantile too much for its own sake rather than as the key to the current psychic realities.

To reemphasize the importance of the ego and of the central internal and external realities of the patient's present life, let us note very carefully the words of Anna Freud (1937):

> Somehow or other, many analysts had conceived the idea that, in analysis, the value of the scientific and therapeutic work done was in direct proportion to the depth of the psychic strata upon which attention was focussed. Whenever interest was transferred from the deeper to the more superficial psychic strata—whenever, that is to say, research was deflected from the id to the ego—it was felt that here was a beginning of apostasy from psychoanalysis as a whole. . . . It should confine its investigations exclusively to infantile phantasies carried on into adult life, imaginary gratifications and the punishments apprehended in retribution. . . . But this definition immediately loses all claim to accuracy when we apply it to psycho-analytic therapy. From the beginning, analysis, as a therapeutic method, was concerned with the ego and its aberrations: the investigations of the id and of its mode of operation was always only a means to an end. And the end was invariably the same: the correction of these abnormalities and the restoration of the ego to its integrity.
>
> When the writings of Freud, beginning with *Group Psychology and the Analysis of the Ego* and *Beyond the Pleasure Principle,* took a fresh direction, the odium of analytic unorthodoxy no longer attached to the study of the ego and interest was definitely focussed on the ego-institutions. Since then the term "depth-psychology" certainly does not cover the whole field of psychoanalytical research. At the present time we should probably define the task of analysis as follows: to acquire the fullest possible knowledge of all the three institutions of which we believe the psychic

personality to be constituted and to learn what are their relations to one another and to the outside world.

Some patients, as was mentioned previously, hide sexual conflicts under nonsexual problems, but others hide the real life problems by tending to regress into intriguing erotic memories and fantasies while withdrawing from responsibilities, from other human relations, and from present problems. Freud's paper dealing with "wild analysis" (1910) should be ingrained in the student to emphasize the distinction between "sexual," "genital," and "sensual" on the one hand, and needs for love in the psychological sense on the other.

Considerable confusion is resolved if one discriminates carefully the sensual from the psychological, as well as the libidinal from the ego meaning. Wishes to allay loneliness and neediness, desires for companionship and acceptance, and needs for love in the sense of being esteemed and valued, are more basic than sensuality. It is common to see inhibited people who are cut off from sensual gratifications but who, nevertheless, live fairly satisfactory lives because they are loved, accepted, and esteemed. The opposite is rarely true, if ever. The pariah is apt to be extremely disturbed emotionally, and the severing of a last tie to others may even precipitate psychosis. It seems that love can compensate for sensual deprivation, but sensuality cannot so well compensate for octracism. This is understandable socially, biologically, and historically. The baby and the small child must be loved and valued, for, helpless as they are, this kind of love is their only guarantee of survival. As Rene Spitz (1947) has shown, infants who are cut off from this love often become so disturbed that they die; Liddell (1956) has demonstrated the same principle in animals. Anna Freud and Dorothy Burlingham (1943) reported the very slight reactions to the bombings of London in small children whose mothers did not show perturbation. Without care for its needs, the infant must perish, and it can feel secure about the fulfilling of its needs only if it feels loved psychologically. As it grows older, the sensual components intensify, and certainly after the great access of genitality at adolescence, the person seeks to satisfy his needs for love most directly through sensual, physical sexuality. Of course, there are some who seek satisfactions largely through eating, some through accumulating money, some through striving for fame, and so on, but certainly the most common, regular pathway is physical sexuality. If the needs were attached in childhood to the parent, or substitute, of the same sex, the object may be homosexual, but the principle, nevertheless, is the same—it is through the sexual physiologic system that people seek to gratify their psychological needs for love (Saul, 1950). Put another way, the needs for love become strongly sexualized physically because the potent and pervasive sensual sexual drives fuse with many of these needs and, psychobiologically, they become part of the mating drives, which the genital sexuality serves. The psychic reflections of the biologic demands for love and care are fundamental from birth, if not earlier. These demands and their interrelations with the ego-instincts for self-preservation, as Freud originally called them, must be understood in their own right, with their history and conditionings by life experiences, if the patient is to be understood and helped as he lives the life he has so largely created for himself unconsciously.

There is another point to which we must return in the present context. As we have noted in a previous chapter, too much analysis can be harmful. Everything, especially every content, cannot be blindly analyzed with impunity lest essential sublimations, as in artists, and workable defenses be destroyed to no constructive purpose. A young woman through her excellent sense of humor, was able to laugh at her father's philandering and at the hostility between him and her mother. She could laugh for fear that she weep. The analyst will not recklessly strip her of this defense but will try to solve the underlying unhappiness while allowing her to maintain the protective reaction.

Nor can illusions be destroyed lightly, for who can live

without them? A fine woman, somewhat advanced in years, lived with the illusion that she had had a happy marriage. Only with great caution and for a very well comprehended purpose would one rob her of this. Things can be lost in analysis as well as gained, and the analyst cannot barge blindly ahead making conscious whatever he sees is unconscious, disclaiming further responsibility, and hoping for the best. Like the surgeon, he must see the main issues and know at every moment exactly what he is doing.

Some individuals have personalities that are so good, realistic, stable, and well-integrated that they can survive poor analysis. Some analysts can conduct the treatment so well that they obtain good results despite serious drawbacks in the patient's personality. Much remains to be learned, and premature crystallization and standardization might well impair the development of this still young field. Freud was always most liberal in his outlook and open to experimentations (even such as Ferenczi's in his later years) and to the views of others. The introductory paragraph of his recommendations on technique (1912) concludes thus: "I must expressly state that this technique has proved to be the only method suited to my individuality; I do not venture to deny that a physician quite differently constituted might feel impelled to adopt a different attitude to his patients and to the task before him."

In general, patients and prospective patients are well advised to keep confidence in their judgment regarding the analyst and the whole procedure. It is my impression that they are usually correct in what they sense. If they are not, and their views are but morbid suspicion, normally the analyst will be able to demonstrate this and show that the resistance is genuinely neurotic, that is, an expression of a disturbed childhood pattern.

REFERENCES AND SOME RELATED READINGS

Bergler, E. (1937), Symposium on the theory of therapeutic results of psychoanalysis. *Internat. J. Psychoanal.*, 18: 146–160.

Bibring, E. (1937), Symposium on the theory of therapeutic results of psychoanalysis. *Internat. J. Psychoanal.*, 18: 170–189.

Chessick, R. (1971), *Why Psychotherapists Fail.* New York: Science House.

Fenichel, O. (1937), Symposium on the theory of therapeutic results of psychoanalysis. *Internat. J. Psychoanal.*, 18: 133–138.

Freud, A. (1969), *Difficulties in the Path of Psychoanalysis.* New York: Internat. Univ. Press.

——— (1937), *Ego and the Mechanism of Defense,* 3–5. London : Hogarth Press.

Freud, A., and Burlingham, D. (1943), *War and Children.* New York: Medical War Books.

Freud, S. (1928), *The Future of an Illusion,* 78. New York: Liveright, 1949.

——— (1916), *Introductory Lectures on Psychoanalysis,* 124. New York: Liveright, 1920.

——— (1912), Recommendations for physicians on the psychoanalytic method of treatment. In *Collected Papers,* 2: 323. London: Hogarth Press, 1924.

——— (1910), Observations on "wild" psychoanalysis. In *Collected Papers,* 2: 297. London: Hogarth Press, 1924.

Glover, E. (1937), Symposium on the theory of therapeutic results of psychoanalysis. *Internat. J. Psychoanal.*, 18: 125–189.

Liddell, H. (1956), *Emotional Hazards in Animals and Man.* Springfield, Ill.: C. C. Thomas.

Marmor, J. (1955), Validation of psychoanalytic techniques. *J. Am. Psychoanal. A.,* 3: 496–505.

Saul, L. (1950), Physiological systems and emotional developments. *Psychoanal. Quart.,* 19: 158.

Spitz, R. (1947), Emotional growth in the first year. *Child Study,* 24: 68.

Strachey, J. (1937), Symposium on the theory of therapeutic results of psychoanalysis. *Internat. J. Psychoanal.,* 18: 139–145.

——— (1934), The nature of the therapeutic action of psychoanalysis. *Internat. J. Psychoanal.,* 15: 127–159.

23 / PROGRESS AND TERMINATION

PROGRESS

When a patient improves during the course of treatment, it is not enough simply to note this fact. Instead, a careful evaluation of the person's progress must be made in order to clarify whether this is incidental or fundamental, for improvement can occur in reaction to analysis without being truly analytic. As Freud repeatedly stated, life produces effects and changes. Some patients react well to the analytic situation itself and some to the free associating alone. But such improvements through living, through the mere existence of the transference, through the permissiveness of free associating, through flight into health and the like cannot be credited to the analyst. The results will be genuinely analytic only insofar as they are based on real shifts in the central motivations.

The point of genuine analytic progress probably can be expressed this way: How clearly do both the analyst and the patient see what needs to be corrected and the means for accomplishing this, and how surely is the process on its way? This can be elaborated as follows.

1. To what extent do the analyst and the patient see the central essential dynamics of the problem, the core of underlying desires, reactions, motivations, and feelings that come to expression as the difficulty? Do they see clearly the childhood traumatic warping influences, their after-effects, and the course toward correcting these after-effects?

2. Is the patient's insight mostly intellectual or has he a solid emotional grasp and realization of his motivations?

3. How is the patient using this insight and the transference experience? What shifts are noticeable in his attitudes and feelings? Does he feel that his analysis is right, solid, that it rings true and that he is grappling with what are truly the main issues, with the pathologic after-effects of the early injurious conditioning?

4. Is there progress in the following four areas: in resolving the emotional problem; toward resolution of the transference; in adjustment in life; toward achieving maturity?

If improvement is evident on the above bases, it is apt to be real and not merely a reaction to the situation of being in analysis. Furthermore, you can probably discount the possibility that it is just an act, an effort of the patient to convince himself, after all his sacrifices and perhaps those of his family, that something truly substantial has been gained. In the analysis, confirmatory evidence is to be gleaned from various sources. First, it comes in the patient's ability to understand and discuss his own dynamics freely. Second, changes in the associative material toward more mature dealing with real relationships while better understanding the infantile components will also be indicative of genuine analytic progress. Third, confirmatory evidence lies in dreams of resolution. Fourth, progress can safely be assumed when there is greater prominence in the material of good imagoes and of more satisfactory personal relations.

In life, confirmatory evidence is seen in various ways, especially in diminution of regressive, childish behavior and in improved relationships to self and to intimates, friends, and wider circles. Further evidence lies in definitive movement toward increased relaxation and free energy, greater latitude of choice and adaptability, and the other goals of psychoanalytic treatment, which were listed in the opening chapter of this book.

When a patient does not progress well the good analyst knows that the fault can lie within himself, in the way that he is conducting the analysis. Resistance exists, of course, and is an essential of the analytic process, but it must be understood in relation to other factors. However, this is no reason to go to the other extreme. A patient may understand his problem and yet not do well. We have already discussed legitimate lack of success.

Reduced to a single sentence, it is perhaps not too oversimplified to state that true analytic progress lies in seeing, appreciating, and better handling the childhood patterns in their repetitions and relationships to current human relations and living, to transference, and to the symptoms. Of course, throughout when referring to the childhood pattern we are always speaking of correcting only those parts of it that are disordered and are causing the patient's symptoms and difficulties, only the pathodynamics. All the childhood residues of enjoyable human relationships normally fuse naturally with the mature, responsible, productive drives and interpersonal feelings of the adult in a balanced life.

ENDING THE ANALYSIS

The key to proper termination of treatment is, as for all other major steps, understanding of the patient. The analyst must have a clear understanding of the basic problem and the current status of the forces as reflected in the presenting material, the symptoms, the behavior in life, and the transference. The question of ending arises seriously when the analyst judges that these major areas of motivation have been well worked through. Of course, they are never worked through with utter completeness. Moreover, the real therapy takes place in life and not in the office. This is true during the analysis and especially so after it. Then the patient is on his own and has the full responsibility for himself and for how he can use in life what he has learned through insight, intellectually, and above all, emotionally in the analytic experience. The transference is never resolved completely in the office and it is even questionable if it is ever resolved utterly. After treatment the patient's perspective on it may be greatly improved for he is less immersed in it, and consequently, he may learn more from it.

Effective progress in dealing with the major emotional forces in the transference and in life and special indicators, such as increased frankness of material and dreams of resolution, will make the analyst think of a trial ending. Just as the beginnings of analysis are trials, so too almost always, must the endings be. However, once the suggestion of interrupting or stopping is made, even tentatively, there is usually, under this pressure, an augmented flow of revealing associations. It is well to prolong treatment while this continues. However, although the foreshadowed ending stimulates this analytic progress, it should be remembered that it cannot do so for very long. In general, it is more efficacious to stop the analysis sooner rather than later, leaning toward the minimal effective amount and avoiding the temptation of too much analysis. If the patient is able to use the experience to good advantage, then he is independent the sooner. If he cannot, then a short period of analysis later, after he has been on his own for a while, usually brings out in sharp relief that which still causes trouble. It is as though the more soluble material settles, leaving the harder formations standing up like columns, more readily visible and easier to deal with in a second period of treatment. Therefore, fractionation, that is, interruption of treatment, has been experimented with (see chap. 19).

Endings vary, as do the individual personalities of patients. A brilliant professional man maintains some resistance although his life has become very satisfactory and his symptoms, migraine and depression, have disappeared. The law of diminishing returns sets in, and it seems far better to try termination than to continue indefinitely for the sake of resolving the resistance to a point of ideal thoroughness. The judgment here was correct. This man developed exceptionally well, rose to the top levels of his profession, saw the transference hostilities better after treatment, his symptoms gradually diminished to the vanishing point, and he returned occasionally for a chat, discussing his insights with warm friendliness.

Here is another case in which the analyst must carefully evaluate the risks of delaying termination against the possible advantages that might come from the patient being out on his own, at least for a while. A young woman expresses her motivations with unusual frankness but, because of her depriving, rejecting experience with both parents, she cannot tolerate any sharp breaking off of treatment because of clinging to the transference.

A man in his mid-thirties presents clear material with intelligible dreams and sees well the relations of his motivations to his life and maturing. The passive-dependent wishes in the transference, resulting mostly from overprotection in early childhood, seem not to be thoroughly worked through, but is it not better to let him struggle with these on his feet, on his own, without further help? Is there not too much risk of his regressing if held in analysis for years? On the principles stated above, preferring too little to too much, an interruption of two years was tried. He did not have to return. Now, five years later, he is well analyzed in the sense that he has achieved good emotional appreciation of his major motivations, good adjustment, and good progress toward maturity. Psychoanalysis must help patients to help themselves. The test of a successful treatment is their ability to do so.

Sometimes, if the material does not flow to freely as is desirable at the ending of the analysis, an interruption of a year or more, even of several, corrects this. Over the period of time outside analysis the patient gains perspective and, after living with these forces on his own, his ego becomes stronger, he can face his unconscious better, he associates more freely and revealingly, and he makes much better use of all aspects of the psychoanalytic experience. Thus, some patients are able to progress rapidly and effectively on their own after analysis and, because they are no longer embroiled in it, their resistances soften postanalytically. If a patient who has been quite resistive comes in for an hour's stock-taking chat a year or two after termination, he may surprise the analyst by the emotional insight that he has achieved, carrying on by himself what the analysis laboriously started.

Probably no analysis is "finished," because no matter how thoroughly it is analyzed, the infantile id desire is to be gratified, not analyzed. Hence, the patient always feels that the analysis is not complete, always feels some frustration, always nurses some resentment. And this very frustration is usually a repetition of feelings toward one or both parents. This plays a role in the problem of the frustration which is implicit in human relations in many ways. As an example, no man can have every woman he desires sensually, nor can a woman have every man, and, psychologically, no one is ever satiated in his desires for love and esteem. Men and women, with all outward success, security, and well-being, will fret, fume, and even cheat because of something so totally inconsequential as a missed stroke in golf.

Of course, the fact that all endings are frustrating does not mean that the ending is well-timed. The timing of termination rests as we have said, on understanding the patient, the status of his motivations, and the working through of them. Is the patient turned from the way in to difficulties, and is he securely on the way out toward development? But, however perfectly timed, some frustration and resentment are to be expected and need accurate analyzing. Even satisfactions in life do not look like acceptable substitutes to those patients who as children wanted not only the gratification itself but demanded it specifically from one or both parents.

Such patients desire it from the analyst himself, and it is hard to get them to accept it from persons in real life.

Moreover, as we have said, life does not yield such satisfaction as one desires, and as the child blames the omnipotent parents for its unhappiness, so the patient tends to blame the analyst. Here, too, we must distinguish neurotic blame from justified, rational blame and not allow the two to be confused or the one to mask the other.

The well-recognised flare-up of symptoms, so common under the pressure of ending, is natural insofar as frustrations and resentments are thus stimulated. We have noted that, in addition to the specific motivations of the symptoms, they serve the purposes of justifying further demands on the analyst and of serving as weapons of revenge. It is in these reactions to termination that you can see most clearly, especially in the dreams, the unbelievable degree to which the childish dependent, love-demanding attachment to the mother lives on in the full-grown adult. An able-bodied, capable, highly successful, middle-aged man, in the prime of his maturity, felt underneath like a tiny child abandoned by its mother, as his associations and his dreams showed with but little disguise.

After termination, some patients act out all too freely, although they dared not do so while in treatment. One man indulged his egotistic competitive desires so openly for some months, even though they had been well worked through, that he made some real trouble for himself during this short period. This is only a single illustration of the general advisability of shunning the abrupt ending, except for very good therapeutic reasons, and, instead, terminating by tapering off. This is a parallel to the fact that it is often well to begin gradually and cautiously.

Tapering off is usually the best technique of ending, but even if it is not in a given case, the analyst should always carefully and deliberately consider the postanalytic period for each individual patient. Usually it is best to keep watch on it more or less closely; this can be done by meeting once every two, three, or four weeks. It helps the patient to make the transition to being on his own, often keeps him on the line of excellent insights and good progress, and may prevent transient and troublesome acting out. However, in special instances and circumstances the analyst may feel that, for example, the patient's dependence is such that he should be cut off sharply and cleanly from all analytic meetings and help and be inexorably on his own for a while. In such an event, postanalytic meetings and their advantages might have to be sacrificed because the other benefits outweigh them.

We have noted in a previous chapter that it would seem to be advisable for many reasons for the patient to see the analyst as a person, as another human being who has his own unconscious, his own childhood patterns, his own virtues, vices, limitations, strengths, and frailties. Gaining this view of the analyst can oftentimes help the patient toward the resolution of the transference, the contrasting of past pattern and present reality, the dissolution of illusions, delusions, and projections, and the correcting and strengthening of a healthy sense of reality. This may very well mean that some extraoffice contact could prove helpful in some cases—this is a subject for study.

Freud went so far as to list potential later friendship with the analyst as one of the advantages for the candidate in training. He did think of the candidates as being free of neurosis in contrast with the "patients." But today we know that child rearing being what it is, everyone has problems in some degree.

Some patients do become friends with their analysts after treatment, and it works well—at least I have seen it work well in many instances for over twenty years. But this must be the exception—probably where the kernel of friendship lies in both personalities and would have flowered had their meeting been purely social. Patients cannot expect this, for it would encourage acting out at the expense of analyzing and would create feelings of rejection if the analyst's friendship were anticipated and not forthcoming and if he became friendly with some other patient. Further, the patient must work for progress for his own sake and for those to whom he is important in his life—not to win the love of the analyst. Neither should the analyst anticipate friendship for he must remain unswervingly professional lest, after official termination, the patient will at some future time require his services. However, in rare instances, the analysis is so thorough and effective, the rapport so good, and the neurotic (disturbing childhood) elements of the transference so successfully resolved that a lasting friendship eventuates. Even when it does not, the analyst must be a friend to his patient—how else could they unreservedly trust him with their inmost motivations and feelings? He must be staunchly professional but also a friend, and normally he remains so in spirit even though the patient may never see him again. Ideally, the transference is completely dissolved, although, as we have said, it probably never is in reality. But even if the neurotic, disordered, infantile elements are dissipated (which they never are entirely), the rational ego relation cannot be, for the patient has revealed himself and feels that the analyst knows him better than he knows himself, and this holds even if they never meet again.

The disordered childhood pattern, however diminished in its power, is not eliminated at the ending of the analysis. After two or three years of anlytic work, an occasional patient may deny credit to the analyst for his improvement, claiming to have been cured after the ending by one chat with a lay person. And whatever happens to the patient in life after analysis, the patient tends to hold the analyst responsible for it, to blame the analyst for all his troubles, and to resent him for not being the beneficent, omniscient, omnipotent parent almost forever after. This is inevitable insofar as it is the pattern of the young child to its parents. It is the disturbance in the child's emotional relations with the important figures of its first years of life, which is the secret of neurosis that Freud discovered. These disturbed emotional relationships condition the child during its earliest years to disordered patterns that persist for life. Psychoanalysis, when properly understood and applied, can reveal this pattern and its disorders and, as after-education through the transference experience, can alter the conditioning to correct the disordered pattern. The little child that lives on in the adult gets a new chance at more healthy upbringing, at maturing more fully, and at learning how to help itself, but the little child continues in the adult, still longing for the all-powerful, all-good parent.

We may return here to the opening paragraph of this book. Since the analyst comes to stand, in part, in the place of the patient's parent or substitute, he will ever remain in the patient's mind as a certain personality. If the analyst could be "a blank screen" then the patient would have a blank screen for his new parent, that is, for the new, presumably corrected part of his formerly traumatic superego. Obviously, this would yield an unrealistic and certainly undesirable state of affairs. The analyst as the correcting parent figure must, of course, have the qualities of understanding, interest, and respect that a good parent has toward a child. The aim is to help the individual meet life in a rational, realistic way and as little as possible through automatic, trained responses that may not fit at all his life's problems and situations. The child part of the patient should be freed as much as possible to reach decisions with a mature ego, with the highest powers of an unobstructed sense of reality. This is facilitated by the patient's transference experience with an analyst whose basic attitudes are those of interest, tolerance, understanding, and the seeking always of the psychological reality. It is these desirable after-effects of the analytic experience that are properly permanent in the patient's mind. They provide the patient with increased inner sustainment and independence and keep open the process of emotional development.

REFERENCES AND SOME RELATED READINGS

Balint, M. (1950), On the termination of analysis. *Internat. J. Psychoanal.,* 31 : 196–199.

Buxbaum, E. (1950), Technique of terminating analysis. *Internat. J. Psychoanal.,* 31 : 184–190.

Firestein, S. (1969), Problems of termination in the analysis of adults, A panel discussion. *J. Am. Psychoanal. A.,* 17 : 222–237.

Freud, S. (1937), Analysis terminable and interminable. *Internat. J. Psychoanal.,* 18 : 373–405.

Hoffer, W. (1950), Three psychological criteria for the termination of treatment. *Internat. J. Psychoanal.,* 31 : 194–195.

Klein, M. (1950), On the criteria for the termination of psychoanalysis. *Internat. J. Psychoanal.,* 31 : 78–80.

La Forgue, R. (1934), Resistances at the conclusion of analytic treatment. *Internat. J. Psychoanal.,* 15 : 419–434.

Milner, M. (1950), A note on the ending of an analysis. *Internat. J. Psychoanal.,* 31 : 191–193.

Rickman, J. (1950), On the criteria for the termination of an analysis. *Internat. J. Psychoanal.,* 31 : 200–201.

Wright, E. (1952), Contribution to the problem of terminating psychoanalysis. *Psychoanal. Quart.,* 21 : 465–480.

Part 3

Clinical Material

24 / HOW AN ANALYST THINKS

Psychodynamics is the emerging science of the interplay of emotional and motivational forces. Developing chiefly out of psychoanalysis, it is seeking to use everything that is sound and positive in the contributions of psychoanalysis and at the same time to use the basic knowledge of behavior that is derived from the related behavioral fields, including the social sciences on the one hand and experimental psychology and animal ethology on the other. Psychodynamics is obviously broader than psychoanalysis; it is not simply a tool of investigation or a method of treatment. Rather, it is the basic science of the human spirit, seeking to make explicit the laws and principles of the development of the personality and its healthy and mature functioning, and also its warpings and psychopathology.

The clinical setting is uniquely appropriate to the study of the mind. The office is indeed a laboratory in which a sample human relationship unfolds and in which processes can be observed as under a microscope. Thus what the patient says in the analyst's office becomes the basic material from which we can begin to learn about the human mental and emotional life.

Yet the knowledge that dynamic psychiatrists have gained through their years of clinical experience has for the most part remained more in their own minds than it has become part of science. Almost nowhere in the literature does there appear any of the raw data of psychoanalytic sessions. One reason for the present form of the literature is confidentiality, and another equally obvious reason is that the raw data, that is, what the patient says, is so extensive that even a single session reported verbatim outruns the conventional limitations of space. These are probably the central reasons why psychoanalytic papers are not in the usual scientific form: presentation of the data followed by the conclusions that can be drawn from them. Yet, it is what the patient says that is the very heart of the matter. It is from this that the analyst develops his concepts and comes to his conclusions. Living daily with what the patient says, he can reach a degree of certainty about his information and his conclusions. It is to begin to fill this gap, to give at least a sample presentation of raw data, of what the patient says, that is the aim of this and the following chapter. It should be noted that all the clinical material has been disguised as thoroughly as possible without omitting or altering data important for understanding the dynamics.

The case that follows is, from the vantage point of the standard mechanics of psychoanalytic treatment, somewhat unusual; but nevertheless, it does provide an excellent case record wherein to illustrate the way in which the analyst comes to an understanding of his patient. Along with the raw material of the nearly verbatim record of the patient's remarks throughout each session of her analysis, there is presented here the thought processes of the analyst as he works through each meeting with the patient.

In this particular case the sessions were brief, rarely more than thirty minutes in length, as well as infrequent. Treatment was limited to about six months. The chief technical difficulty lay in trying to combine in the very short time that was available, the full proper use of free association and dream interpretation with the amount of interpretation and information that the analyst must impart, mostly by tactful eliciting from the patient. Because of the consequently serious limitations imposed by the time factor, the analyst, to get in the points he saw, frequently had to forego listening in silence for the common emotional element to emerge in adequately long trains of associations. To some extent he also had to forego the technique of gaining sufficient systematic associations to all the elements of dreams. Therefore, this record is more a demonstration of how and what the analyst thinks than it is an example of the proper and strict use of the fundamental psychoanalytic techniques of free association and dream interpretation. The advantage of the presentation as it is given here, however, is that the reader has an opportunity to see something of the actual thought processes of the analyst as he seeks to understand the unconscious meaning of the material. Further, the analyst's use of this understanding for the therapeutic help of the patient is also revealed.

This patient's overall problem seems to be of somewhat more than average difficulty, and its derivatives are of rather more than usual complexity. The notes are reasonably full, and they are presented just as they were taken down during the visits. Some additional remarks have been inserted where necessary to clarify the analyst's interpretive commentary. Obviously, the sequence and content of the associations are too important to permit alterations or omissions, so no attempt has been made to enhance in any way the "readability" of the raw data. The reader must be prepared for considerable repetition because this is intrinsic to the material and to the analytic process. The analyst must quickly discover and ever be aware of the patient's emotional background and of "the constant and permanent strands in the texture of the patient's life." At the same time, as was stressed earlier in the chapter on technique, he must begin each session as though he were seeing the patient for the first time, being completely open-minded as to what material will come and as to what its significance will be. However new the material is, it usually presents a different facet of the same essentials.

It may seem, as I will say again in the case record that follows in the next chapter, that at times the transference was brought into the interpretations when there was insufficient supporting material. This may well be. The reason for this is that the human relation of patient to analyst is a sample of the patient's human relations and the transference is so centrally important that the analyst must watch for it like a hawk, having it always in mind lest he miss it when it appears. The analyst must always be a few steps behind the material, following it, and trying to understand the emotional forces it is revealing and defending against.

On reading this case record any analyst, myself included, will see much in the material that is not mentioned. Some of these connections and meanings were perceived at the time but were not described or interpreted to the patient because they seemed peripheral or else not certain enough or ripe enough for mention. The great deficiency here is my failure to find at once the injurious influences during childhood that produced the patient's problems. I hope that today I would be more perspicacious, accurate, and therapeutically effective. And so, it must be made clear that what follows is not intended to serve as a model of analytic technique and practice. Instead, these notes indicate the procedure that was followed, perhaps roughly and somewhat inadequately, in a single random case. Here the analyst can be seen working downward with the ego and preconscious to bring out the main issues and deepest motivations and to help the patient deal with them with minimal confusion and unhappiness.

1st hour

An arresting looking young woman in her early twenties entered my office one day some years ago, while I was in Chicago. She had made the appointment on her own initiative. Her manner was straightforward. Her directness and a certain maturity and honesty were engaging. She was very attractive with a fine face and figure and a strong personality. Because of the particular and unalterable external circumstances, she could come only once a week and after the first few weeks for only one-half hour sessions. Four visits were required to find the psychodynamic formula in this instance, although in the vast majority of cases, it can be done in a single hour interview.

She wants to see me, she says, because she is engaged to a fine young man in his middle twenties but has noticed about herself a distressing fact: when she loves and becomes close to a person, she tends to destroy that person. When asked about other complaints, she says that she also has a phobia. This thought causes her such anguish that she weeps and says that she cannot reveal it to me. Of course I do not press her with a topic so obviously intolerable to her, and instead I go on with the history.

Nothing remarkable emerges about her present life. She is twenty years of age, attends a college in a suburb of Chicago and lives in an apartment with another girl. She describes herself as popular, energetic, and responsible, well able to enjoy human relations, work, and play. This contrasts with her complaints, but then, the human personality is full of paradoxes.

She is from Denver where her parents still live. The family is extraordinarily close. The patient adored her mother but noticed that she also hated her with a resentment that apparently became very conscious by the time the patient was between nine and thirteen years of age. The reason for this hostility she does not give, but goes on to say that at about sixteen she felt disillusioned with her father and can only think that this was because he was not a super Santa Claus. She has a sister three and a half years younger with whom she fought a good deal in their younger years. She understands this is normal and now gets along very well with her.

For a time during her high school years she was away at a coeducational boarding school.

She can tell no dreams but when asked for her first memory, she says this dates back to earlier than three years of age: her mother and another woman, both of whom were pregnant, left the patient with friends for two weeks. The patient was forbidden to go in the front door but did so. She was caught and punished.

This memory suggests feelings of rejection because of pregnancy and its restriction as well as some rebelliousness and defiance of prohibition, which is specifically directed toward her mother and is in connection with her pregnancy. The memory also reveals that for this rebelliousness there was punishment. The earliest memory is like a manifest dream, and it is even more powerful in revealing unconscious motivation. No detail of it can be neglected. It can be no accident that this scene of abandonment, defiance, apprehension, and punishment occurs when the patient's mother is pregnant. This point is carefully noted mentally and no issue is made of it to the patient.

Thus far the emotional motivational content of what the patient has said is: (1) the closeness of the family; (2) the unexplained hatred of the mother, emerging especially at age nine and probably connected with the first memory; (3) the exaggerated and frustrated expectations toward her father; and (4) the fighting with her sister. This would all fit together if there were an excessively close attachment to the mother with too great dependent love needs toward her. If this were the case, these needs might cause hostility to the mother, the father, and the sister. Hostility to the mother might be aroused because the very intensity of these dependent love needs foredooms them to frustration. Also, the hostility might serve as a defense against this too strong dependent-receptive attachment, which threatens normal growth toward independence. The hostility to the mother would tend to be the greater when the sister was born because the stronger the dependent love needs toward mother, the greater the reaction to the pregnancy and the birth of a sister. Hostility to the father might arise from frustrated wishes of the patient as a child to have mother all to herself and from turning to father these demands that were originally directed toward mother. Hostility toward the sister might arise because the greater the need toward mother, the greater is sibling rivalry apt to be. Therefore, from this meager material, I suspect that excessive dependent love needs toward mother provide the core of the problem and the primary source of at least some of the emotional difficulties with father and sister. However, the reasons for this excessive attachment are not evident and the whole idea is only an airy hypothesis in my mind, a potentiality that would fit in with other experiences. The material is far too inadequate for this to be more than a notion, which I must be prepared to alter or to abandon totally in the face of more information. It is too inconclusive as yet to consider giving a formulation to the patient. This description of an initial visit does not provide a very good example of how to conduct a psychoanalytic diagnostic interview, and the notes are, lamentably, very rough indeed. Nevertheless, a beginning has been made in reaching the essential nuclear dynamics that underlie the patient's problem.

2nd hour

Two weeks go by before the patient returns for a visit. She seems courageous and clear-eyed, though it is obvious that she is deeply distressed. As she begins to tell why, she weeps. She and her fiancé, Tom, have agreed not to see each other for six months. I get the impression that this was not all her own doing and that she feels deeply rejected. Since Tom expects to leave in six months for South America, the patient feels that now analytic treatment is urgent. She says that she must get her feelings straightened out in order to hold him and go on with the plans for the marriage. This implies that when she came for the first visit, she had not resolved upon treatment but had an exploratory attitude about it and about her problems—problems that she herself had not defined sharply.

Her mother might understand analytic treatment, she says, but her father would be strongly opposed. This would also present serious difficulties in financing treatment, which she can hardly afford to do on her own. Her emotional reaction to the separation from Tom filled the hour which, consequently, could not be used for finding the key to her emotional problems.

This interview is interesting analytically. Such reactive situations as, in this case, the agreed upon six month separation from Tom, stir up emotions and disrupt analytic unfolding and even psychoanalytic history taking. But is this situation accidental, purely external, a frustration by fate? I must, on the basis of analytic experience, assume the opposite, that is, that the situation has somehow been brought on unwittingly by the patient. Was this girl attracted to a man who was bound to reject her? Or, however loyal the fiancé, did the patient unknowingly provoke him into rejecting her? Is this a masochistic, self-injuring act, stemming perhaps from guilt? More broadly, is this separation from Tom, this apparent rejection by him, this whole situation, somehow an outgrowth of or connected with the formulation I suspected by the end of the first visit?

I tentatively inferred that the patient's difficulties in human relationships in her adult life were continuations of the difficulties in her relationships to the members of her family during childhood. I thought these difficulties might be traced to excessive dependent love needs toward mother, which in turn generated hostility. Is this part of the patient's chief complaint: her tendency to destroy anyone she loves and is close to? Is she, therefore, following the pattern I suspect toward her mother, father, and sister, so strongly that she is incapable at present of a close relationship with another person and hence, despite her attractiveness, incapable of marriage with any *man? Is the separation from her fiancé for six months motivated by the forces that pre-*

serve the first memory in which she was abandoned by her mother for two weeks? All of this is only speculation on my part, and I say nothing of it to the patient. These are possibilities but the actual evidence is as yet far from conclusive. Moreover this mutually agreed upon separation from Tom may cause enough emotional reaction to disrupt more or less the eliciting of solid evidence upon which to base a formulation of the central motivational pattern.

Nothing is yet known about what went on historically to cause the patient's problems. The central emotional charge seems to be on her mother, which may make difficulties with men. But we do not know what her mother did or felt toward her to make for the excessive closeness and hostility. I know from other experience that a vicious circle usually develops between closeness, anxiety, and hostility. If a parent so treats the child as to cause resentment, the child is then usually anxious and overly clinging, which in turn results in frustration and hostile defensiveness.

3rd hour

One week later the patient returns in very nearly full possession of herself. She says she still thinks only of Tom but entirely destructively, that is, only of his shortcomings that anger her. Now she repeats her original complaint. She is always hostile to those to whom she is very close. This time I ask her whether or not this was the case in relation to her mother whom, I remind her, she said she adored during childhood but also hated. Her response is a flash of anger, which then subsides as she recounts the following:

PATIENT: I feel that mother does not entirely love and understand me. Mother is a fine person and a good mother but has a great reserve. I feel that all my life I have been looking for something in mother which I have not gotten nor have I gotten it from father. I feel that I must be something of a wife and mother to father. I feel

> that mother was not and is not. While mother was away for six weeks I cooked for father and did all sorts of little things that mother never did for him. Mother refused to go to various conventions with father, but I went with him; I met people, acted as hostess, and fulfilled for him the many things mother could not. Nevertheless, father and mother are very close to each other. Now I want to give to my own husband but can't with Tom because he reminds me of my own mother. Yet paradoxically I never get on with boys who are outgoing extroverts like father.

From this emerges the picture of a family in which the feelings are perhaps rather too close. What supports this notion is the fact that in the midst of breaking an engagement, the patient seems more emotional about her family than about her fiancé. Apparently she has been extremely close to her mother but has wanted more from the woman than she has gotten. Probably this was, in part, the reason for her turning in later years to her father with such intense attachment, becoming hostile toward her mother and viewing her as a rival whom the patient could beat.

The formula that was barely suspected at first now begins to take shape: (1) there persist in the patient too intense needs for love, originally from mother, with feelings of not getting enough love and with feelings of rivalry; (2) along with this there is possibly some deprivation and rejection and this is possibly connected with the mother's pregnancy and the subsequent rivalry with the sister; (3) these feelings result in hostility which, though not openly expressed, nevertheless creates an undercurrent of hatred; and (4) because of all the actual love and closeness in the family, what can be expected is a powerful reaction of guilt for this hostility to these close loved ones, especially mother. Taking mother's place with father is not necessarily, or even probably, simple sexual rivalry with mother. It is likely to be a derivative of the dependent love needs toward mother, perhaps a mothering of father by the patient in reaction to her own wishes to be mothered. But all this is not yet clear and sure enough to discuss it and the evidence for it with the patient.

4th hour

PATIENT: I joined my mother, father, and sister (Letty, *three and a half years younger*) for a vacation together, hiking and golfing by day and dancing evenings. At first it was very difficult because my parents wanted to hear about Tom, but I was unable to discuss the matter. Finally I told mother about our agreeing not to see each other for six months and then I told father also and felt enormously relieved. After speaking with them, I realized what was in my mind the last time I spoke with you—that my relation to Tom was an intense and unhappy one and much better terminated or at least interrupted, since I have not yet completely given up the idea that we might yet marry.

There being a brief pause, I asked if she could say anything further as to why during childhood she was hostile to her mother, whom she also adored. By asking this I interrupted the free flow of her associations. I would scrupulously avoid any disturbance whatever in the flow of associations if this were a later session; but this fourth meeting is still a psychodynamic diagnostic interview. I do not yet understand the basic motivational constellation; I have not yet elicited sufficient sound evidence to establish the central continuing motivational pattern that underlies the patient's varying current vicissitudes. For example, I still do not have a clear understanding of the choice of Tom, the difficulties in that relationship, and its present status, except as these are seen against the long-range pattern of her emotional life. Hence my question is really to be seen as being part of the history taking.

In response to my question she said she still did not understand this hostility toward her mother. The patient then veered off to tell that she is now again seeing Will, a boy she has known almost since babyhood. This is a healthy sign, this preference for talking about her present love-life rather than about her mother. However it may also be in part a resistance against facing her feelings toward her mother and others of her family. I must get the dynamic pattern, but I decide to give her a little time to see where these thoughts about Will will lead.

PATIENT: He is two years older than I. I feel very guilty toward him because I always dominated him and picked on him.

While on the vacation, a golf instructor showed such favoritism toward my sister, Letty, that I became jealous to the point of being unable to learn anything from him and almost unable to hit a ball, although I have played well for many years. When we were saying good-by to him, this instructor practically ignored me. He addressed himself almost entirely to my sister and said how sorry he was that she was leaving. This instructor was a married man with grown children, yet I could not stand this attention to my sister. In fact, I recognize within myself a terrible jealousy of Letty, who has blossomed out suddenly to be a most beautiful girl.

Here the love needs are stated with complete openness, as is the resultant jealousy and rivalry with her sister. The patient's thoughts have led right back to intense feelings toward members of her family.

PATIENT: The evening after this good-by scene, I had a dream. (*It is to be noted that previously when I asked for dreams she had none to report.*) In this dream my father was giving my sister, Letty, all sorts of presents and giving nothing to me. Then he called Letty into a room and when she came out, she had on a new,

> beautiful fur coat. But then it turned out that father spoke to Letty to tell her that he was arranging a surprise party for me. This overwhelmed me with guilt and I woke up feeling miserable.

The dream is indeed the royal road to the unconscious. This dream is reported spontaneously by the patient. This is almost invariably the case when the patient is revealing important feelings. When the forces of expression are stronger than those of repression, the patient brings dreams; and the stronger the forces of expression, the franker and the more understandable the dream. In this dream the theme reveals itself without disguise—intense childish love needs in the form of gifts and parties. The form of the dream is masochistic, self-suffering. The dream portrays what a person allows himself in real life. Even in her dream the patient cannot picture herself as the loved, preferred one. Why not? An important clue to the reason is that the patient's jealous rage is not directly expressed in the dream. The one who is passed over while sister gets all the presents is the patient herself. She awakens miserable and with conscious guilt. I suspect, therefore, that her rage is pent-up, and because of guilt, turned against herself. She cannot stand her hostility to mother, father, and sister. She feels so close to them, they love her, and she loves them.

I still say nothing by way of interpretation to the patient. I note silently that even in her sleep her mind and feelings dwell on her family, rather than on what would be the normal current interests of a healthy girl of twenty. Of course this may be stimulated in part by my interest in getting the pattern of her feelings toward the members of her family.

The patient goes on to say that in later years her sister has been very athletic and very close to the father, arousing in the patient almost intolerable jealousy. She recognizes, however, now that in earlier years the jealousy of the sister was in relationship to their mother. Then, quite spontane-

ously, the patient says her phobia (recall that in the first hour she was quite unable to talk about this at all and said she would never be able to describe it) began the night she was shown her newborn sister. (Recall that the patient's first memory had to do with her mother's pregnancy.)

PATIENT: I was then three and a half years of age and had been sent away for two weeks. I returned home and that evening was shown my new sister, who was less than a week old. I remember that after seeing her, I went into my room, which was dark, and I felt that the room had no boundaries and that I was floating in space. This began a terrible fear of open spaces and heights. I could not bear to look at even a picture of mountains, nor could I look into a magnifying mirror, nor through a telescope, or even at pictures of heights or of airplanes. It was no question of looking and standing the discomfort. I became so clutched by terror that I could not possibly face these even as pictures. The phobia seems to center about mountains, and it is in mountains that I have lived.

As she told of the phobia, she became somewhat panicky. I therefore complimented her for telling what she had hitherto found to be intolerable and went on to say that we must certainly get this cured.

These remarks of mine were designed in part to wall off what was emotionally unhealthy so that she could see herself, not as an emotionally upset individual, but as a good, normal twenty-year-old who had an emotional problem. Further, I wanted to show her that the problem could be held at a distance from the mature, realistic, healthy part of her in order to examine it, understand it, and resolve it. Another purpose of my comment was to show by implication what I would later discuss very openly at an opportune time, that is, that any judgment I had about her was not directed to her inner feelings, to the content of her thoughts and feel-

ings, but only to her ability to face and talk about what disturbed her. In other words, my opinion of her did not go down because of any feelings she might have, but on the contrary, it went up because of her emotional honesty in facing them.

At my remark, which was made quietly and almost unconcernably, she sprang up, quite excited, her eyes illumined, and a sudden conflictive smile came on her lips. She could scarcely contain herself at the incredible proposition that she might be relieved of her phobia. In the few remaining minutes of our fleeting session, I told her what I thought was the key to her problems, including her phobia.

ANALYST: The formula seems to be your great closeness, first to mother and then to father; you have had very strong needs for love in a very close, loving family. These needs for love are so strong and the closeness desired is so great that they cannot be satisfied and they brook no rivals. You wanted more from mother than she could give, and you wanted it exclusively, being unable to put up with any rival.

I realize that I must be extremely cautious and tactful in touching upon the possibility of any actual lack of interest or love from her mother during babyhood since this is usually a most upsetting idea. Generally, it must be left to the patient to bring up this idea, even if the analyst suspects it. There is some evidence for it in this patient's case, namely the first memory and also the patient's feeling of a lack of love and understanding from mother. The idea of some rejection or emotional deprivation also comes to mind because I know from other clinical experience that such intense demands for love are very often reactions not to closeness or overindulgence alone, or at all, but to some underlying rejection and emotional deprivation. The child that feels a lack of closeness often clings the more strongly. There are, to my knowledge, no statistics on this sort of observation in the psychoanalytic literature. Hence, until they are systematically and scientifically gathered, we must rely only upon such a clinical impression as I have just stated.

ANALYST: Later you transferred this to father and then your mother and sister became rivals. Father could not, as you said, be a super Santa Claus but probably you got so much in the first three and a half years of your life before your sister arrived that this is what you have continued to desire. We do not know why these wishes were intensified. Perhaps there was some overindulgence or too much closeness or perhaps mother's reserve that you spoke of made you feel you wanted more closeness than you received. At any rate, being unable to satiate these desires for exclusive closeness, attention, and gifts, you became enraged. But you are a fine person of a close, loving, devoted family; you cannot with impunity hate those who love you, upon whose love you are so dependent, and who, after all, you also love. This hatred flows beneath the surface as an undercurrent which you have recognized, and it is also projected as your phobia where you have not recognized it. Your phobia is probably nothing more than the reflection of this hostility.

It was also pointed out during the discussion with the patient that as she described her pattern of dominating and picking on Will, this sounded rather like a replica of the same feelings and behavior toward her sister during childhood. Perhaps she tended also to repeat toward Tom this pattern of hostility toward her sister in addition to the hostility that followed the pattern toward her mother.

I had achieved, through the dream and her spontaneous associations to it, a good glimpse of the current interplay of motivations that generated the troubles. A view of their history was also to be seen, although the particular injurious treatment of the patient as a small child, which produced these aftereffects, was not yet clear. It would be justifiable to suspect that it involved a problem of excessive desires for closeness to the mother during the very early years, prior to the birth of the sister. Possibly this is derived from early overcloseness, possibly from some deprivation or rejection or insecurity, as mentioned above. Usually a reasonably good picture can be obtained in the first diagnostic interviews of how the patient was treated during babyhood and early childhood (that is, from birth to six years of age). Were the attitudes, feelings, and motivations molded in such ways as to cause difficulties? This can be found out from what the patient tells, from attitudes, and from unconscious material; of special significance in this regard are the early memories and dreams (see Chap. 5). But occasionally it is contraindicated to go into this question very far until the analyst is sure that it can be explored in a way that is entirely ego-syntonic and helpful to the patient. The more that is known of the injurious influences, the parental blunders, the better can the analyst and patient correct their aftereffects.

Poor as this illustration is of a proper psychodynamic diagnostic interview and of adequate evidence for determining the central emotional pattern, and disturbed as the history was by the break with Tom, nevertheless enough of the dynamics were now seen to enable me to give the patient a rough preliminary formula. Where this can be done accurately, which is in the great majority of cases, the emotional impact is powerful, as though a sudden light illumines what has so long lain in darkness so that what has controlled the patient can now be subjected to control. The patient's whole expression was lighted up by this insight and by the promise of relief that it held. Only now could I see clearly in her relief and hope what pressure of anxiety she had been controlling beneath that poised and pleasant expression.

PATIENT: This is unbelievable. It is really possible to be rid of this phobia? What can I do?

ANALYST: If the phobia bothers you, remember that it is the result of hostility and guilt. If you recognize these feelings in yourself, and if you know to what you are hostile or guilty or both, I think your phobia will begin to diminish noticeably.

Of course the phobia may well be the product of other forces also, but only these had emerged clearly thus far as the immediate causal links. I would, of course, be alertly watching for other motivations to emerge. Probably every psychic product has sources in both libidinal and hostile impulses. Also I wanted to reassure her about the phobia which so terrified her and I felt it was necessary to interpret the forces that seemed most dangerous in order to palliate them by bringing them into consciousness.

5th hour

The patient's reaction to the insight of the preceding hour was classic. She began with some inconsequential remarks about a bit of work she had to do which she disliked. This quickly petered out, and she asked if she should continue.

PATIENT: Much has happened. Shall I tell it?

ANALYST: This is quite unlike your preceding hours when you had so much to tell that you just poured out the material.

PATIENT: Actually there is so very much tell that it is hard for me to tell it. What you said last hour clicked. I feel great. Now it feels as though what I was not aware of has become conscious. It makes sense. That's why I now seem able to understand many things and can see how they fit together. This gives me a feeling of being clear instead of the fog and confusion I was in.

This is not necessarily superficiality. If the essential dynamics are seen and are discussed in a way that is acceptable to the patient, there is usually a sense of relief and an improved state of mind plus stronger will to treatment. To be understood is no small matter.

PATIENT: All week I thought of how things fit together and wanted to tell you. For example, I never thought anything of the fact that I have in my room a picture of my sister, who is so gorgeous. It stands in a position where I can see it from every angle. *(Her associations now poured out in a flood.)* My jealousy of my sister must originally have been greatest in relation to my mother rather than to my father, for I remember clearly that from the age of seven to about ten I thought my mother gave more attention to other girls, even though I am sure she actually did not. Nevertheless I used to complain to her that she loved them more than she did me. Another thing occurred to me. When I was left alone with my sister at the same age of about seven to ten as a baby-sitter, I would be in a near panic even though my parents were just up the street. Once I telephoned father and mother and told them sister was up and around and in terrible shape; I lied to them just to have an excuse to call them. Next morning sister, of course, denied that she had misbehaved in any way. Now from what you said last time, do you think that this fear when I was alone with my sister could be fear of my own wanting to harm her?

I agreed with the patient that it could and complimented her on her insight.

This material is pretty good confirmation of the correctness of the interpretations I had given her during the last hour. The idea that an accurate interpretation muddies the following associations, thereby making their unconscious meaning unintelligible, has never seemed true to me. The analyst can discuss the patient's deeper feelings as they show through the associations as a presenting central theme, but he must be certain to do so in a tactful way, making them as little anxiety-producing as possible. In other words, if he understands the associations, their common elements, and their central theme, and if he makes this clear to the patient in the form of the patient's own thinking, then the patient is usually relieved and intrigued and what resistances are aroused are usually intelligible and not too difficult to deal with. The patient clearly demonstrated the validity of this approach and technique. She was under severe emotional pressure and was openly seeking help and relief through understanding. Consequently, she was not distressed by the interpretations but felt that she was understood and that she had been given permission to vent feelings and ideas that were deeply troubling her. These reflections were confirmed at once by a dream.

PATIENT: Two days ago I had a terrible nightmare. I was in my room, sister was coming up a ladder to the window to kill me; I was not simply anxious, I was deathly afraid. Now again, could this nightmare be a projection of my own hostility on to my sister?

This question shows considerable insight and psychological capacity. I again agreed with her, pointing out that she would have to sense which way this felt the most correct, whether as projection of her hostility, or as guilt for her hostility, or as fear of retaliation for the hostility. She seemed to follow this line of reasoning quite readily.

Of course every dream in treatment has a transference meaning of some sort, so it can be suspected that the sister might represent the analyst. Her coming to the window might represent the patient's fear of his seeing, and perhaps also of her seeing, what feelings and thoughts are in her mind. But I say nothing about this at this point and wait for more associations to reveal the main emotional trend.

PATIENT: I always liked closed places; I feel safe in them. I like to be shut up in the room, to pull the blankets over my head, but I fear anything open. I even fear having a door open.

Can this connect with the first memory of mother's pregnancy and sister? If so, this would mean, in terms of physiological organ systems, preference for the intrauterine rather than, for example, the oral pathway. This relates to the detail in the first memory of going to the front door of the house, apparently to go outside against orders.

PATIENT: I used to test myself, trying to train myself to look at pictures of mountains in books and magazines. Once when we were going to the Canadian Rockies, I could not sleep for fear of the mountains, but it turned out that the pictures were worse than the real thing, and I was not so afraid of the mountains themselves as the pictures. This seems to be partly because I have had the funny idea that the pictures magnify.

One of my earliest memories is at age four when at grandmother's I picked up a mirror and looked at myself.

Very early memories, like dreams, appear when the deeper feelings are coming to expression. As the patient comes to face them, she thinks of incidents and memories connected with them. The very first memories reveal the basic patterns of motivation that shape the person's life. Hence the emergence of earliest memories signifies analytic progress. Probably just these fragments are remembered because, like dreams, or even more so, they fit the emotional make-up.

PATIENT: It was a magnifying mirror and when I saw myself, I became panic stricken and screamed and even today I cannot stand seeing myself in a magnifying mirror. I took a course in art and had to close my eyes because I could not bear looking at lantern slides of landscape paintings, in the first place because they looked so big, and secondly, because of their being a little fuzzy and out of focus. This matter of being out of focus is just awful.

The meaning of this early memory of looking in grandmother's magnifying mirror is not certain. It fits into the context of the previous associations in that mirrors and looking at the self often symbolize insight. In this case it would involve an inward look at terrifying feelings, which might fit with the dream of sister coming to the window with hostile intent. But what is meant by the details of magnifying, the landscapes, and the being out of focus? Do these relate to the patient's size relative to her sister, to a setting on which she focuses to screen the terrifying feelings? Are they projections of the body? Mountains, for example, are often breasts or represent mother, mother earth, which would fit with the excessive dependent love needs to mother and also with repressed hostility to her. Is the fact that the mountains are seen as dangerous a feature of the common mechanism of hostility projected and turned on herself? Could the magnifying relate to phallic erection, also dangerous because of the patient's hostilities, which are part of her difficulties with men? Neither the ego nor the sexual meanings are clear enough for reasonable certainty. Hence it is best to say nothing and continue to wait watchfully.

PATIENT: As I think back, it seems to me that my anxiety increased so a few weeks ago because of breaking up with Tom. Perhaps I was guilty for breaking up with him. It was my fault because of my own hostility.

ANALYST: Possibly there was also some direct anger at him because you felt rejected by him.

PATIENT: That is certainly true and I felt it toward my

father and mother also because they sided with Tom. They have always said that Tom is so nice I should be nice to him.

At that same age, seven to ten, when I was so jealous of my mother's attention to anyone else, I got terrific crushes on mother figures, even on quite young ones like camp counselors. I can hardly express the intensity of these. They were more than crushes. They were obsessions. They were my whole life. As I got older, instead of getting better, they got worse. In fact, this is something that still bothers me. At age eleven I had one of these all absorbing crushes on a film actress. I always thought I was the only one for that person; that we belonged to each other; that we had a secret exclusive love, for me and not for anyone else; and I thought of nothing else. Then at twelve, what I had so long wanted happened. A friend came along and responded to me. She had been divorced. This crush lasted from age twelve to fourteen. Then I got a letter that she was remarrying, and I felt betrayed and lost, but then I met and got to know her husband and loved him. She is very different from my own mother. She is my ideal of womanhood.

These crushes sound like a clear, direct, continuation and transference to other girls and women, of the original overly strong dependent love needs toward her mother during earliest childhood It is as though there is promise in these women of all the patient yearned for but never had satisfied by her own mother. They may also present to the patient her own ideal for herself, the perfect woman she wants to be.

PATIENT: In my teens I got crushes on girls my own age, including a physical element. I was tomboyish, wore jeans, and felt masculine. A little of that still seems to be present and I do not understand this connection. Masculinity to me means aggressiveness, not hostility, but just aggressiveness. I am especially attracted to small, tiny, feminine girls because they make me feel protective toward them and also masculine.

Only a few moments of time now remained.

ANALYST: It may be that you saw life very much as a world of mother and child and mostly identified with the child. Perhaps the older women you had crushes on fit in as mother substitutes and this small, tiny, feminine girl is also in part a representation of yourself and you want to protect her as you have wished to be loved and protected.

She reacted to this possibility that the girl represented herself with another illumined expression as though this were a new, rather startling but true idea. She said she did not quite understand where the masculinity fit into this. There was no time to pursue this further, and we decided to let the matter go until next week. I did not feel on sure enough ground to interpret the possible transference meaning of the dream—anxiety about the analytic work. Since the patient had interpreted her hostility to her sister, I simply followed the material. Occasionally this sort of procedure is indicated, but basically it is better technique to discern and interpret the main underlying emotions that make the associations flow as they do.

The extent to which the small girl represented her sister, with the overprotectiveness and masculinity as possible compensation for hostility toward her, and also the role of masculinity in relation to mother, were not discussed with the patient. However, the possibilities were in my mind, as was the notion of the possible identification with the father, a rival for her mother. It also occurred to me that the mirror might represent a reflection of her own repressed unconscious impulses along with possibly symbolic implications of the magnifying. Here, although the associa-

tions lead into somewhat new material, the explanation of the data probably lies in the basic formula that was discerned in the preceding hour. The physical element in the crushes, the tomboyishness, and the masculine aggressiveness are not at all surprising. In fact, these details tend to confirm the formulation of the importance of an overstrong infantile attachment to the mother as a primary source of the whole problem. An overclose infantile attachment to the mother often has just this outcome in girls. The attraction to other girls is often a continuation and transference to them of the attachment to mother. The physical element may enter only because all strong feelings tend to mingle with the ever-present sex drives to seek sexual expression. The aggressive drives, which tend to masculine manifestations, are often in part an overcompensatory defensive reaction against regression to helpless infantile passive dependence upon the mother. Also, too strong wishes in girls for the mother's love often increase boyishness.

The technical handling of this session is open to criticism. The pressure of the associations was so strong, they poured out with such a rush, and their content itself was so important that I did not want to interrupt them. On the other hand, I sacrificed thereby getting associations to the specific elements of the dream and did not get to try to understand the dream in terms of all the other associations of the hour. Her sister's coming up the ladder, for example, might be a clue to the patient's fear of heights. If an hour contains a dream, the dream is usually its focal point, for it regularly reveals the main forces that direct the associations of the hour.

6th hour

The patient appeared the following week. She looked immeasurably brighter and happier but said that she was somewhat exhausted by the examinations she was taking and that these distracted her to some extent from her emo-

tional problem. But of course, she was quick to point out, it was still with her.

PATIENT: This is a continually revealing process. Now everything makes more sense.

This was probably not mere bland resistance. She was under severe emotional pressure and had proven herself very perceptive psychologically. My interpretations were designed to be acceptable and to arouse as little resistance as possible by enabling her to see the main issues as they appeared without having to use obstructing defenses.

PATIENT: One night my roommate was away, and I was alone and became very frightened. What usually happens happened: When I close my eyes, I see in my mind's eye pictures on the wall and then these disappear and there seem to be great vistas, and I become panicky. This does not bother me if someone else is present, but if I am tired and alone, I cannot stand it. Then I usually rush out and find someone to talk to. That night I left the light on all night. Sometimes when I am reading, I get the idea that there are pictures behind me. I know this is ridiculous but no matter how I fight against it, I have to look behind me frequently to be sure.

The intense emotional charge on pictures, which is so prominent in the patient's phobia, is also evident in her dreams and comes to expression in life in an interest in painting. Here, however, unlike the phobia, it is an enjoyable interest. Why this is so and what the psychological mechanism is are fine questions concerning the nature of a person's interest in art. The answers are not yet apparent but they have definite implications for treatment. Possibly the patient's painting and her interest in pictures has some connection with hostile feelings that generate guilt, for example as a way of winning parental favor over sister. But neither hostile nor libidinal roots have yet appeared in her associations.

PATIENT: I have decided about the summer. I want to go to school in Sweden. My sister will be in Holland, and I want to travel with her and go hiking with her at the end of the summer. But what will be the effect of being in the mountains alone with my sister? Sweden is, of course, mountainous. Beyond this I have no plans. There is no use considering them so far in advance. One girl went to France and became pregnant by a French fisherman and was disowned by her parents who are high up in Boston society. I hope you don't take me seriously.

ANALYST: I don't know whether I take this seriously or not. We know that much of your hostility and guilt are bound by your anxieties and phobias, but we do not know whether or not they may also find some outlet in masochism, in some form of self-punishing behavior.

I thought of the reference to pregnancy in her first memory, but decided to wait and not mention it now. Perhaps it would have been better to hold to the principle of silence during the hour, commenting only at the end; but I yielded to this opportunity to discuss the masochism. The infrequency of our visits combined with the intensity of the hostility and guilt made me fear acting out. The patient might not only have tendencies toward self-injury, but she might actually live these out without realizing what she was doing. For example, one person when angry does not show it, may not even feel it but gets a headache (psychosomatic); the next person has a tantrum (hysterical); another consciously plots revenge (criminal or criminoid); still another hurts himself by a physical accident or by behaving in a way that makes trouble for himself (masochistic); and so on. Hence this led me to take advantage of this opening to get the matter of possibly regrettable acting out frankly talked over at once. Nevertheless it is regularly very much better for the analyst to remain silent and hear the rest of the associations and not break in until near the end of the session.

PATIENT: I see what you mean. This connects with Tom. He was always having little accidents and these would make me feel enraged toward him. At his age (*twenty-five*) he should have learned better. I do not have accidents.

This shows that she grasps the concept of masochistic behavior. At least she sees it operate in Tom, if not in herself, and it is not yet clear to what extent it does operate in herself. Perhaps her phobia takes care of these motivations and is her way of draining them so she need not make added suffering for herself by self-injurious behavior.

ANALYST: But, there are other forms of making trouble for oneself.

PATIENT: Then I do have some. Something in connection with boys and sex. I used to be such a terrible prude about sex. If a boy tried to hold my hand, I would become all upset—or if I went out with a boy and thought he was going to try to hold my hand or try to kiss me. I went with one boy for a while and after coming home we used to sit in the car for over an hour. I guess my parents thought we were necking but actually we were only discussing my shyness, and it always ended with me in tears and not a single move toward me on the part of the boy. Both my sister and I are very, very inhibited about sex. At Christmas time I told my mother about this and blamed her for it, but she said it was not fair; it was not her fault. If it is not, then where could it come from? My sister never had a normal boyfriend, because she had the same attitude toward sex as I—just a great inhibition.

This fits. Such inhibitions may be because of direct repressive, puritanical training. They may also spring from too strong attachment to mother and fear of separation from her. Sexuality normally involves a thrust toward independence and maturity, which is a move away from the child relation to the parents. Also, such inhibitions are frequently caused by intense unconscious hostilities. Any physical contact, including sexual, can arouse them, but the person may feel only panic, not knowing what it is that he fears. However, if the hostility is not too intense and if it can be acceptable to the conscience and handled by the ego, then it may find expression as an exaggeratedly hostile aggressive component in the sexuality. It can heighten the sexuality. It can lead to rape or lust—murders or to insatiable sexual urges. In the right amount it merely heightens the excitement.

PATIENT: Then suddenly at college I lost *all* inhibitions. I had a wonderful relation to a boy for six months. In high school, if I were going out with a boy or thought he would want to touch me, I couldn't eat, got sick to my stomach, couldn't possibly let him kiss me.

ANALYST: What do you mean by losing *all* inhibitions?

PATIENT: No, I don't mean intercourse. I never considered that at all. I simply lost the inhibitions I had and could kiss and neck.

ANALYST: I asked this question about loss of all inhibitions and sexual relations for a very good reason, because sex, especially for women, can provide an excellent path for masochism.

PATIENT (*interrupting*): I see something. This reminds me of a story I read. There was an intense relationship between the hero and the heroine. In one scene she struck him in the face with a dog leash. That night he entered her room and raped her. I thought this was terrific. This is how sex should be. *(It was now evident that the patient was becoming more and more aroused emotionally with these thoughts.)* I get so I just want to hurt somebody badly and be hurt myself. Sex is the kind of thing in which I want to be attacked. I want the man to just about ruin me. I am simply exasperated with the nice, gentle boys. Sometimes I would hit Tom good and hard, trying to get him to hit me, but Tom was too normal; he just couldn't do it. He was simply too gentle. Then the fiasco with his friend Buff. Buff lacked culture but was a physical type. We had a date but what happened was a terrible anticlimax. He asked me to elope with him.

ANALYST (*smiling*): You mean instead of raping you?

PATIENT: Exactly. Then after that I had the best relationship with Tom I ever had. Perhaps because of guilt. Just before then, on my twenty-first birthday, my father gave an expensive party for me with twelve people present, but all I could do was flirt with Buff. I simply couldn't help myself. This infuriated my father and also Tom and wrecked the party.

ANALYST: Do you understand this?

PATIENT: Yes, I think so.

Because the time was getting short, I sketched what I thought was going on. If time had permitted, I would very much rather have elicited these points from her.

ANALYST: Your hostility, which we discussed in previous talks, plays a part in your sexual feelings. Therefore, probably, when you were very young and had less intense sexual feelings, the hostility in the form of attacking and being attacked was more prominent and you were afraid and therefore sexually inhibited. But your sexual feelings are now strong; you feel them reinforced by the hostility, both attacking and being attacked, and therefore they are even more intense. In other words, the hostility used to inhibit the sexual feelings but now it intensifies them.

PATIENT: Yes, and mother and father always said Buff looked so cruel. Could a girl find a man who was so sadistic in sex but not otherwise? I suppose probably not.

ANALYST: You see now the connection between the hostility and making suffering for yourself. We see it very clearly in your anxiety and phobia and also in your sexual feelings, but we do not know yet whether it comes out elsewhere.

PATIENT: Oh no, no, no! I hope not.

Because only a few minutes remained, it seemed well to discuss possible solutions in terms of known experience in other patients. This was done by some mutual discussion in which I did not hesitate to make certain main points. Again, because of the lack of time, it seemed better to do this than to have the patient go until the next interview, which could not be until two weeks hence, without some more constructive perspective upon her problem and how it might be solved. The following points emerged in the discussion.

Sex normally contains a certain amount of hostility. This aggressive, hostile drive, depending on how it is handled, can cause inhibition or intensification of the sexual feelings. What is also involved is the matter of whether or not the hostility is balanced off by other contents of the sexual drive, such as dependence or love. Sex itself is so strong a desire that it can be very intense and gratifying even without great reinforcement by hostility. It can be strengthened by other urges also—for example, by love—which can balance off the hostile components. It is conceivable that the hostility might come out in a person chiefly in sexual relations and that the individual might otherwise be loving. This we just leave as an open question.

PATIENT: I follow this perfectly. How many things there are in one person!

We did not have time to discuss the fact that the patient's aggressive hostility was probably also an important source of the tomboy, masculine trend she had noticed in herself. In all likelihood part of her wish to be overpowered and to be treated sadistically was a wish to be forced back out of a masculine position by being driven into a masochistic femininity. I did not remark that masculinity is also frequently a defense against feminine feelings that are too masochistic, that is, too filled with wishes to be hurt because of guilt and self-directed hostility.

This interview revealed why this girl was so arresting and attractive. Underneath a boyish, aggressive, and strong exterior, there is the challenge to male masculinity to conquer her and drive her into a truly feminine relationship. This she wants especially in the form of direct physical sexual contact. Actually her standards, ideals, and good sense as well as her anxiety have prevented her, as she said, from even considering actual illicit sexual relations. However, it is also obvious that she would in all likelihood succumb rapidly to a thoroughly virile onslaught by a man whose own masculine drives are intensified by a sufficiently sadistic component. Such a girl might well swing from almost total sexual inhibition to compulsive nymphomania.

All I said to her in the last minute or two that remained was that because of all these practically important things that needed working out, I thought that she should have some more systematic analytic work than she was getting under these very limited conditions. She replied, however, that she had completely dropped this idea. She would not sacrifice the trip to Europe and she could not possibly ask her father for money because, beside the fact that he could not give her money for treatment in addition to the trip, if she asked him for it, she would have to tell him all about the reasons she wanted it, including her hostilities. This latter, I said, would certainly be unnecessary. But she insisted that her relationship to him was such that she could not possibly ask him for money for treatment without telling everything. This provided me with an interesting observation on the type of relationship she had with him or at least thought she had.

PATIENT: Anyway, entirely apart from the money, the trip makes it impossible to come more than once a week, and as you know, I have this job on the side.

Behind the good reasons are often the real reasons. She may have had an emotional resistance against more intensive treatment. This may have involved anxiety about it or a masochistic desire to avoid what would better help her. But she showed no wish to discontinue. This might be acting out unconsciously in the transference to me part of the childhood pattern toward her mother. I suspect that she wants closeness but fears it because she fears rejection and the rage she feels in reaction to rejection.

As the interview ended, she asked if I had read a book about depth psychology, saying that she was fascinated by deep things. I agreed that "depth" was fascinating and that I had a similar interest but pointed out that for her purposes, this could also be a defense against seeing a simple reality. I went on to say that her hostilities arose out of the patterns of her emotional relationships established in childhood and could probably be best understood in simple terms. With this she concurred and added that she could see the importance of this kind of motivation in sociology and religion.

Important as the progress was in this hour, I do not like to have a patient go as long as two weeks with these insights and with these forces stirred up but not well clarified and worked over. I would have preferred that she return in a few days but since it was realistically impossible for her to arrange it, there was nothing to do but accede to seeing her two weeks hence. Thus far, with the discussion of the hostility, her symptoms had noticeably abated and she felt much more comfortable. Now, however, with the interview not coming to a good resolution, I would not be surprised if she suffered some increase of anxieties before our next visit. This was probably my own fault. I had succeeded in getting out into the open the topic of masochistic acting out, but by breaking into the associations, the common element running through them was to some extent lost. We consciously discussed a vital topic which, had it remained undiscussed, might have led at some point to self-injurious behavior. But, I sacrificed getting the full expression of her unconscious. To some extent then you could say that I sacrificed unconscious dynamics to content. Although I was confident that this was indicated, I still felt very uneasy.

It is also to be noticed that thus far I made no attempt to interpret the transference beyond repeated but very brief remarks to the patient that the emotional patterns toward the parents and siblings tend to repeat themselves toward the therapist, and that it is very important to keep these under frank, open discussion. Wherever possible, I like to bring the transference out in the open just as soon as possible in order to prevent these feelings from piling up in intensity. In general, whatever is kept out in the light and discussed becomes thereby more controllable. But in this particular case I felt that the time was not ripe and that we would have to wait until the transference showed itself more openly. I was not yet sure enough of the suspected pattern toward mother, and perhaps father also, of her fearing that her dependent love needs would make her too vulnerable and expose her to rejection. I was able, however, to let her know that any feelings about the treatment or toward me were of great importance and should be discussed as they arose, whether it was easy or difficult for her to do this. All strong feelings tend to become directed in some part in the transference, and unless they are discussed they affect everything else that the analysand thinks and says and can impair the progress of treatment.

Whether or not there is any risk of acting out or risk to the sister by having the patient alone with her in the summer in the mountains, is a question I will be alerted to.

By her past behavior, the patient's defenses are very powerful. The hostilities, as they have been revealed up to this point, have come out in directions other than toward her sister, and they should be appreciably diminished by our work before the patient's departure.

7th hour

Three weeks have passed since our last visit. The patient was obviously tense; she said so much had happened that she was unable to express herself. This was typically the case, with the patient when she had so much to say. It turns out that she met a boy, Ernest. He is her own age; not a man, she thinks, but a little boy. He is a chemist and the patient reveals that she never likes physical scientists because they are concerned with molecules and things that do not interest her. She feels they do not understand life or people. However, it turned out that Ernest understood her so well. Apparently he made a little speech, and she thought it was the most beautiful thing she ever heard. This was just last night. Now she is furious and does not know why.

I said I thought she did know why; that this is related to what had been discussed during the last visit. She agreed. I asked her what it was hard for her to say. She finally stumbled out with the fact that she finds herself hostile to those to whom she is close. At first the relationship to this boy was purely platonic, only to have somebody to go with. Now she has to fight against falling in love with him. She does not want to, and she does not want to marry a chemist.

PATIENT: I want to pick up this ashtray and throw it through that window. *(At the moment she looked as though she were going to do so.)* What do you do when you feel so enraged? Last night after my date I came back and threw things around the room and woke up everybody in the house.

I told her that above all we should try to understand why she was so enraged. She thought it was because she does not know what to do. She now feels close to the boy but that makes her feel furious. She does not want to be close and she does not want to be distant. She sees the connection with her sister. The patient wrote a little article on sibling rivalry, saying that it is unnecessary. She claimed that if parents would handle children properly, it need not be so intense as it is within herself. In this interview the patient is able to see the operation of her major dynamics—the intense dependency and the consequently overly intense sibling rivalry, the defenses against these, and the resulting hostility—in her reactions in a life situation with this boy. She also saw that it was no accident that this relationship to him occurred just as this material was being aroused and coming into focus in the visits with me. It is, of course, not unusual for a patient to act out some of these emotional patterns while they are emerging analytically. This is one of the difficulties in handling a patient of this sort with such infrequent meetings. Three or even two full hours a week would probably make it much easier to keep up with and analyze the outflow of material so as to make her not quite so impelled to act it out.

To help her handle her tension, we discussed as much as possible why she was so angry at the moment, particularly in reaction to this relationship to the boy.

During this hour much of my note taking had to be sacrificed to the difficulties of the discussion. What follows is a report, without the support of raw data, of what transpired. One thing we touched upon was that her hostility to Ernest was in part a defense against her becoming too close to him and too dependent upon him. The causes for this could be found in the intensity and nature of her needs for love, which were patterned upon those of her early childhood toward her mother, with all the risks of jealousy and frustration that she suffered during childhood after the birth of her sister. Her feelings toward him along the lines of the pattern toward her sister were less clear, but may have been mentioned. It is usually best to discuss motivations only when they have emerged rather unmistakeably and can be accepted smoothly by the patient.

It is a constant source of wonder to see directly the enormous and overriding power of dependent love needs. These are carry-overs from the infant's demands upon its mother. In infancy and early childhood the mother is in reality essential to the very survival of the young organism. The infant's dependence is abjectly and utterly real in the extreme. These dependent love needs continue with apparently undiminished force into adult life, in persons who, for whatever reasons of closeness or rejection, have not normally outgrown them to some extent. Such a person, like the patient, is apt to dread a close relationship. The sexual attraction has content—her hostility and guilt—and at bottom there lies the childish dependent love needs that were originally focused on mother. If she yields to her longings, she fears she will be hopelessly dependent upon Ernest, abjectly requiring his love, a sort of slave to him emotionally, and exposed and doomed to the frustration of these too intense, too childish longings. Hence she fights them off unconsciously, violently, with a rage she does not fully comprehend.

In this hour the patient's emotional involvement is with a boy her own age, and this is a healthy development away from the apparently excessive involvement with her parents and sister. Why her dependent love needs are so intensified is not yet clear. Perhaps this arises from overindulgence with feelings of rejection when she was pushed out of the position of only child by the sister. On the other hand, perhaps there was some actual lack of love that caused anxiety and intensified her clinging needs for love.

8th hour

PATIENT: Am I supposed to be mad at you?
ANALYST: Why do you ask?

PATIENT: Because I seemed to be for the past fifteen minutes before this hour.

ANALYST: Good for you to notice this. It is vitally important for us to discuss all feelings that you have in connection with treatment and with me. Why are you angry at me?

Mostly children are forbidden expression of anger and hostility in childhood. Parents generally punish them when they demonstrate hostile aggressive behavior. Instead they should realize that hostile behavior is always a reaction to something that threatens or frustrates the child and that therefore what is needed by the child is not punishment but understanding. If the threat or frustration is removed, the child will be sweet tempered and will mature properly with good human relations. If he is simply punished, he is thereby given an example of hostility by the parent. Consequently, his own resentment is intensified and driven underground to cause all sorts of anxiety symptoms and malformations of personality. To reverse this in treatment, the analyst therefore encourages the free expression of hostility, not in actions but in words, so that it can be understood and diminished at its source. Hence I immediately complimented the patient for recognizing her own anger and urged her to seek the reasons for it.

PATIENT: I can see why it would be important, for just as you told me (*this was discussed in the 6th hour*), it would influence everything I say, but I don't know why I have just been angry at you. After seeing you the last time I was in a terrible rage. I was in the kitchen of a friend's house and actually almost threw things. However I calmed down and was fine until three nights ago when I had the most terrible dream I have had.

In the dream I was so tense that I felt I was bursting. Father, mother, and sister were there. I became so enraged that I felt I was going out of my mind. Then I seemed to go out of my mind and had to be taken to a mental hospital in order to be safe and was cared for like someone completely dependent.

This dream is distressing when you consider that it is the nature of dreams to show what a person is capable of and tends to do. The anger we know is near the surface and this we can handle, analyze, understand, and thereby diminish at its source. But the regressive element is less auspicious, especially in this overt form of giving up by losing her mind and retreating to a mental hospital. However, it must be noted that losing one's mind and going to a mental hospital is also a favorite weapon that a patient may use against the analyst, for what can depreciate the analyst more than such a result in a patient. Also it can of course mean to the patient a way of being closer to him, more dependent on him in a helpless way, as of child to parent. We will see what the associations reveal about these two elements.

PATIENT: The boy I told you about last week, Ernest—I am afraid I hurt him. He wanted to go steady with me right away, but I said I did not feel ready for this. He said he could not stand going with me and having me around on any other basis, so I guess he is out of the picture. If I am nice to any boy, he seems to fall madly in love with me, but if I am not nice, then I am apt to be a bitch.

This fits with the fear of being too close. Apparently she is attracted to a boy who himself has excessively strong dependent love needs. This is not really unusual; we all respond to a trait in others that is similar to a fundamental one in ourselves.

ANALYST: What else do you associate to the dream?

PATIENT: The terrible tension in the dream was out of frustration at not being able to let off my anger. It was like being in a strait jacket. I have felt this way when not dreaming also, but never so completely helpless as in the dream after being taken to the mental hospital. I feel frustrated and tense when I lose my temper, which happens about once every three or four months. Then I must lock myself up until I cool down for fear I might actually hurt someone, like the experience with the little girl a few years ago. I was at camp. She lay on the floor reading comic books. I told her to pick them up and get up. She paid no attention to me and I became so enraged that I barely kept myself from kicking her in the head or strangling her. It was so bad that I had to rush out.

ANALYST: Why do you think you get so hostile as this?

PATIENT: For the reasons that you already told me in our previous talks.

ANALYST: Good, now you see the problem and you see the intensity of this hostility and rage. It is no wonder, then, that you have the phobia, which is the kickback of this hostility. If you can discuss this hostility with me freely and work it through here, it will relieve the pressure toward acting it out.

PATIENT: I think I can see that. There is something else I should say. I have had guilt all my life. Guilt that I have had everything so good; such good parents; such a good life. I feel I should make it up to others who are less fortunate and I fear that this good fortune of mine must be made up for; that my husband will be killed; that I will have idiot children; or that something else terrible must happen to me. Could this guilt be because I want my parents' love? I mean that wanting their love means that I must want to go back to the time before my sister was born and therefore wanting their love implies getting rid of my sister. I have had this so long it is like a dream.

This is a direct, simple statement of precisely how these psychodynamics work. Pride goeth before a fall, because pride is usually connected with hatred of rivals. The same with dependent needs for love—of which pride can be one form. They may well be, exactly as the patient put it, intimately associated with hostility to sister as rival, and to mother for a complex of reasons. First, hostility toward her as a defense against these needs, that is, against being too enslaved by the dependent love needs, and second, out of frustration of these needs in that they cannot be accepted and indulged because of the guilt for repressed hostility to loved ones. In addition, the hostility is related to fear of excessive regressive dependence and frustration themselves. But what part of this pattern is most centrally transferred to me? What is uppermost, the pattern to mother or to sister? Or, perhaps, is the later edition, the pattern to father, uppermost? This is not clear and definite enough.

The patient pauses, apparently asking for a comment, possibly as a reward for her insight. Probably I should have remained silent until nearer the end of the session, but the opportunity to discuss directly the hostile feelings toward me was ripe. I could do so now in a general way without knowing the precise aspect of the childhood pattern that was most centrally transferred to me, although most likely it is that toward her mother just as it seems to be this toward Ernest.

ANALYST: You have been sensitized by these experiences in relation to the members of your family and the patterns to them persist into your adult life. Therefore you tend to repeat them toward others, including myself. Perhaps this plays some part in why you have felt hostile to me although we do not know why it should occur just fifteen minutes before the interview. This tendency to repeat the pattern and the hostility to me is distressing; but also it can be most relieving and therapeutic insofar as you work it through and clearly discriminate me from your parents and your sister. If you get angry and hostile against them, you become shocked and guilty, whereas being angry at me is merely something that you and I can sit down and discuss and go into the reasons for and the consequences of.

Now we were getting over the hurdle of being able to discuss openly the transference of her feelings to me. By her expression and nod, the patient signified that she understood this well. I therefore asked her a question that I had no opportunity to ask in an earlier session; namely, whether her specific fear of mountains might be connected with her sister, for example to hurt the sister somehow when they were in the mountains together.

PATIENT: No, I thought of that, but my phobia is not only of mountains but of all open spaces and enlargements like enlargements in a shaving mirror. My father used to try to force me to face this. For example, he made me look at a picture in a magazine, a huge picture of the sky with a very large airplane. I hated him for making me do this. Mother was the same. She once took me to the museum to look at some underwater scenes. There were a lot of them. I was so panic-stricken, I rushed out. Then mother would say how disappointed she was in me. That was between the ages of eight and twelve when I did not get on with my mother very well anyway but had intense crushes on other mothers. I would viciously say to my mother, "I wish so and so were my real mother." This would upset my mother and make her weep. The first time I knew I was afraid was at age ten at camp. We slept on the top of a mountain on an overnight trip in the Rockies. There was a beautiful sunset, but the other mountains looked so black. I got out of my sleeping bag before dawn and the valley was full of mist like a sea of clouds. I was so panic-stricken I hid in my sleeping bag until they assured me that the mist had burned off.

The patient was being carried away by these memories. The time was short and I wished to emphasize the main issue.

ANALYST: I am sure this phobia is a kickback of this intense hostility that you describe and which you sometimes even have difficulty in controlling. Because of the hostility, you become very guilty and experience the phobia. The phobia is the same thing that you experience otherwise as a rage so intense that you need to be tied. Or at any rate, it is a combination of that with the guilt, which is also a result of this rage.

PATIENT: I can see that but will I not be in such a habit of being afraid of mountains and open spaces and so on that even if the rage is reduced, I might go on with this phobia?

ANALYST: Other experiences show that where the hostility is grossly diminished, the phobia is also. That is the force that keeps the phobia going. Moreover, you are so young that you have plenty of time to form a different habit over the next ten years, especially since you also love and enjoy the mountains as well as fear them.

PATIENT: Yes, like my trip to Sweden. I am so eager to go but what will happen to me there?

ANALYST: That depends upon how thoroughly we work through the hostility and its sources.

PATIENT: Another question. Do I and did I love my mother and father?

ANALYST: I am sure that you do and did, otherwise you would not have so much guilt toward them. We are guilty when we have anger and hostility toward people we love. Had they been nasty and mean to you, you probably would not feel the guilt nor would you have all the warm feelings and love in your make-up.

PATIENT: (*apparently much relieved*): I talked on the phone with my father for a whole hour last night. It was so loving and so wonderful.

ANALYST: Perhaps this conversation with much warmth and love and also hostility is the key to your remark earlier in our interview today in which you said you are either hostile to the boys or else, if you are nice to them, they fall madly in love with you. Perhaps they respond with love to all your own reactions of warmth and love and needs for love that exist between you, your parents, and your sister also.

She could see the possibility of this and the interview ended with a few minutes of further discussion about the importance of seeing the hostility in all its aspects. This meant very precisely recognizing it in her childhood pattern, in her present life, and in the transference to me. I explained that the aim was to get her so accustomed to seeing it and so able to discuss it freely with me, even to the point of boredom, that the pressure of it upon herself would be relieved.

It should be noted that in this hour, I did not stress the sexual meanings or aspects of the symptoms or material. This was avoided because I believed the hostility to be central in this patient and that the disturbance of the sexuality, the problems in relation to getting along with boys and other problems on the erotic side, exist chiefly because of the hostility. I think that if this hostility is resolved and grossly diminished, the girl will be able to have good relationships with boys and a normal sexual and love life. In other words, the disturbance in the love and sexuality is a result of the hostility. At a deeper level, it is a cause in the sense that the hostility arises from intensified libidinal demands upon the parents (for love of the kind the child needs from its parents, not for adult genital love) with consequent frustration and intensified rivalry with the sister. The analysis of the hostility involves understanding it and the reasons for it, which lie in these underlying childhood libidinal desires. Originally these were aimed at mother, but then they became exaggerated by the closeness of the family and the relative overindulgence of the patient. In addition, perhaps there was some rejection that heightened the patient's demands and the sibling rivalry and hence her susceptibility to frustration and rage. By focusing on the hostility, by analyzing its causes, the analyst deals with the libidinal situation; by dealing with its results, he deals with the symptoms—phobias, behavior in life, personal relations to others, sex, and so on. Thus, the hostility is central, and in analyzing its causes and its consequences the analyst deals with the central pathology of the case.

9th hour

The patient came to this hour obviously still tense but also bright and cheerful.

PATIENT: I have not been so happy for years. Last year especially I thought I was in the wrong university and wanted to leave. Two years ago I was in continual trouble but was kept on, so I guess that is flattering in a way. Today I got a letter from a man. I am the only one who writes him—because he is an underdog.

I told you everyone I was hostile to except I didn't mention one person; that is my roommate, Beatrice. I am so hostile to her and there is no reason for it. I dreamed that she came with me to where our family goes on the lake in the Rockies. It was as though we were on a big, exclusive oceanliner. I did not want Beatrice there and tried to avoid her, not exactly escape from her, but avoid her. I started upstairs in an elevator to a dance floor. There was a big picture window extending all the way from the floor to the ceiling, and as I went up in the elevator, the boat began to pitch and huge waves came against the glass window and I could not get out of the elevator. Finally at my floor, the elevator was separated from the shaft but I managed to leap across it to the floor. Then I went into a gift shop and saw Beatrice and tried to avoid her.

(*The patient went right ahead with associations without any word from me.*) I was crazy about Beatrice and she was about me until we took an apartment together a year ago. She had an unhappy home life and was rather cold and undemonstrative. I was warm and thought I could do a lot for her. I really loved her a great deal in a normal healthy way, but Beatrice was embarrassed by any show of affection and I was determined to make her change in this.

It seems possible that Beatrice represents to the patient part of her own unconscious, her own deep-seated needs for love, which she, like Beatrice, fears and defends against and is unable to gratify. She wants to give Beatrice what she herself craves.

PATIENT: She was never popular with boys and I always was—and then the tables turned. She began going with a boy of some status and began to gloat over me, although I did not want to go steady and simply wanted a number of dates, which I had. From that point on we grew apart because of constant jealousy and pettiness. I have never been petty like that with others. She made me feel that I had to compete with her in everything—boys, clothes, grades. This year another girl, Carol, is my best friend, and although I still room with Beatrice, she is so tied up with the boy she goes steady with that she is rarely there. When she comes in, she usually irritates me. For example, I will be quietly in my bedroom alone and she will barge in without knocking, which I resent, and then she'll talk in rasping tones. I try to ignore it and not express my feelings by being silent and reading. The relationship with Carol is constructive without any rivalry or jealousy, but with Beatrice each one of us is trying to get the best of the other. She is critical because my family has more money than hers and she is critical because I date a number of different boys and do not settle down and am not on the verge of being engaged as she is. Now why is this?

ANALYST: I will let you answer your own question and give you exactly one guess.

PATIENT: (*smiling*): Of course, the pattern is the one toward my sister, but why?

ANALYST: Probably because the two of you are similar and therefore you were attracted to each other, but now what attracted you, the underlying similarity of the craving for love, probably following the pattern toward mother, has turned to rivalry just as with your sister.

PATIENT: This is very true, and Beatrice has a younger sister exactly the age of mine.

ANALYST: This is one of the important sources of marital difficulty. The man and woman are attracted to each other because of the similarity of needs, but then they may become the objects of the hostilities in the other person's pattern, just as here. For example, they may be attracted to each other because they understand each other emotionally, and they are drawn ever the more closely together by an underlying internally frustrated craving for love. But then they may turn these cravings toward each other; or they may become rivalrous and jealous, following a pattern of sister or brother competition.

I pointed this out so that the patient would be alerted to acting out this pattern in her choice of a husband, a much more serious choice than that of a roommate. I hasten to note here that I would not have done this, in all likelihood, and not at this point, in an ordinary psychoanalysis. But here the pressure was great for we met only a half hour once a week, and the patient would soon leave for six months in Europe with her future plans uncertain. My remark aroused some anxiety in the patient, as could be expected.

ANALYST: I know that this is a disturbing thought, but it is much better to face the facts, to know what is going on. I feel safe in pointing this out because I know that we have the key to your difficulty and you should know it yourself so that we can work it out and resolve it all the faster. Also, it is a little bit more difficult to make a husband fit the pattern than it is another girl your own age.

Our interview was drawing to a close.

ANALYST: I have an idea about your picture window. Does this make you anxious?

PATIENT: No. It is interesting.

ANALYST: In the dream you want Beatrice with you. After all she was not there; it is only a dream. If you didn't want her, you needn't have dreamt her there in the first place and then tried to avoid her. I think partly you wanted her there but you also were hostile to her, and I think this hostility is represented by this huge, threatening wave. Is this not your own hostility to Beatrice; your own turbulent unconscious?

The patient immediately responded to this affirmatively, but this was not glib, superficial acceptance. She was usually able to see the point clearly, as the flow of material and the increasing insights showed.

PATIENT: And I must tell you something else about the pictures. Now if I go into a room that has pictures, I immediately look to see if there are any that might make me afraid, and if so, I say to myself: That is my hostility, I need not fear you. It is a wonderful feeling. Also, I tell myself that I do not care what anyone thinks of me. I do not feel so abjectly dependent any more. I do like boys better as friends than girls. In fact, I have always wished that I were a boy. Then I could be more aggressive and initiate things. I feel best when I am treated as one of the boys.

These observations of the patient confirm the suspicions that I mentioned previously. The patient consciously wished to be a boy. This would indeed have solved many of her problems. For example, she could then relate to boys without having her sexual feelings stir up her hostilities, guilt, and masochism. This would put an end to her seeing sex as an attack, a view that arose out of her own hostilities and guilt. She could enjoy boys on a boy-to-boy basis. Her closeness, originally to mother, which continued as crushes on girls, would be heterosexually colored and she would escape the feminine competition with sister.

Our time was at an end, and we could not follow up the connection of this line of association with the previous material. I did not, however, want the possible transference to go without notice or discussion. I therefore asked whether she also felt that she did not care what I thought of her.

PATIENT: Oh yes, I care very much. You are different from anyone else. In fact, it is as though you do not exist. You only exist on this day when I come to see you, but I do care very much indeed what you think.

This fits with the pattern of too strong childish dependent love needs transferred toward me and defended against by ignoring my existence between appointments.

ANALYST: I just wanted to make sure that we keep all references to the treatment and to me well out in the open. If you have the least concern that I might think less of you for anything you say, we should discuss this. The opposite is true because my opinion of you is unrelated to the content; it has to do only with your courage in being emotionally honest, with your ability to bring out and face your feelings, memories, wishes, and whatever else comes to mind.

PATIENT: I understand that.

The pattern of sister competition, which was so obvious in the material, did not seem clearly transferred to me. Hence, we see only the mother relation to the extent the analyst's good opinion was brought up, wished for, and defended against. It may seem that I am bringing in the transference more than is necessary and attributing to it considerably more significance than it warrants. But I must say that it would be almost impossible to overestimate the extraordinary importance of this aspect of psychoanalysis. As I have said many times throughout this book, it carries the analysis, the quintessence of which lies in isolating a laboratory sample of the patient's human relations. Sometimes the transference is rather on the surface from the beginning, but mostly it is hidden, and it can develop to great intensity in a very insidious manner. Therefore the analyst must lean far over backward in being on the look out for it.

The content of the dream that the patient brought to this visit might have additional meanings. The ocean and large ships are often symbols for mother and here a dangerous ocean may reflect hostility and guilt toward mother. However, the ship and ocean may relate more to the patient's wishes for the trip to Europe. Also a ship at sea very often represents the patient on the sea of his own unconscious and on the sea of life. Lacking further associations, I can say nothing concrete about it.

10th hour

When the patient arrived a week later, I observed that she appeared noticeably less tense, more calm, and generally healthy.

PATIENT: Why do you look at me that way? (*I asked her to explain but she went on as follows.*) You remember what I told you about my roommate, Beatrice? It is amazing but things are much better with her since we talked. She doesn't know why. I hope it lasts. After our talk, I became nicer to her and then she was nicer to me. There was something I could not tell you very well the last time, and I will try to do that now. That is my need for independence. I do not want to be involved with a boy unless it is the real thing and therefore I go out with several of them to show each one that he is not the only one.

Actually I feel sort of dead inside about men. I have not felt that way since high school. I can take them or leave them. This is not hostility; it is indifference. Not hostility, that is, except for one boy I knew last year quite well whom I still see. He makes grand statements about me, and I simply cannot stand this probing by him. In a way he has a right to say things about me since we know each other well, and I am sure he means well by it.

Also, and I don't know if this has any bearing on anything, sometimes I wonder about my feelings for my best friend, Carol. These feelings are everything all the other relationships are not. It is a wonderful thing but I am so intensely jealous of her, as a boy in love with her might feel. She is engaged and the boy is really worthy of her. At present he is in the Navy somewhere. Why am I so close to her? It has all the elements of heterosexual attraction, even some physical elements which I often feel toward girls but which I do not think is very important and which I do not think Carol would mind, but I am so jealous of any attention to her from anyone else—boys or girls. I am taking her to Wisconsin for skiing this weekend and will be so happy to be away with her alone. Is that unusual?

ANALYST: All love follows sexual patterns. Usually when the heterosexual drives become strong in adolescence, they lead the person to the opposite sex. Thus, a girl becomes interested in a man. But many of the childhood feelings—identifications, dependency, needs for love, and so on—follow the sexual feelings and form the psychological content of the sexual attachment, which is thereby transferred from the family to the man. This includes feelings toward mother or sister, which can also be transferred to the man. Therefore, in falling in love with a man, there may be much of the dependence, competitiveness, and so on from the childhood pattern.

PATIENT: I can see that. Carol is less this way than I. She is more feminine than I am. This relationship is just the opposite to that with my roommate.

ANALYST: Maybe the hostile competition toward your sister is directed toward your roommate, Beatrice, and the overcompensatory feelings, protectiveness, and love are felt toward your best friend, Carol.

Occasionally I make these tentative interpretations even when the evidence is only suggestive. I do this if I feel that it will help alert the patient to feelings I am reasonably sure she has, or if I suspect that it will at least loosen up her thinking and sharpen her observations. If I saw her more frequently, there would be time to get more adequate material. Alerting is basic to the analytic technique. The analyst really only tells the patient what to look for. It has meaning to the patient only when the patient is able to discover for himself emotionally what the analyst may have mentioned dozens of times.

PATIENT: I will see my sister this weekend. We are going to surprise her, taking Carol along. It will be an interesting situation. I was just thinking if much of the dependence on my father and mother gets into these relationships with boys and with girls. I want so much to be independent; but I feel as though I am extricating myself from something like Michelangelo's "Slave Coming Out of the Rock." Between semesters I had a tonsillectomy and my father and mother took me to the hospital. They didn't baby me really, but I felt as though I were a little girl and realized how terribly dependent upon them I am. I wondered what I would ever do without them. I should not be that dependent at my age. Maybe it was exaggerated in my mind, because I was depressed then as I always am just before my menstrual period. I became so angry at myself for being so dependent. I don't want to be so dependent on my husband; I want to depend upon myself. At my age I should be more free.

An individual usually resents being dependent and usually has an underlying resentment against the person he is dependent upon. I am pleased that the patient recognizes this in herself.

ANALYST: Seeing it is the first step toward solving it.

PATIENT (*smiling*): Last night I talked with my parents on the telephone and my roommate said what wonderful parents they are. It is gratifying to hear this from others. I do think they are the most wonderful parents but this wonderfulness does keep me awfully close to them. I see a boy twenty-five years old and when I am with him, I act so young. First I thought I was just acting a little peculiar and then realized that this amounted to my feeling and acting about age twelve. In other words, I acted instinctively as though he were a father figure and I can't stand it if he acts young. I can't stand being depended upon, at any rate by someone that I want to depend on. On a rainy night this boy carried me from a car to the door and this just made such a difference, because he showed he could dominate me. This means to me that I could be dependent upon him and not only the other way around. It is terrible to be so dependent—a menace.

In this hour the patient is working through: she is seeing in herself emotional patterns and motivations that we have already discussed as these appear in her everyday relationships. In such working through these insights become integrated and understood and applied realistically in her daily life. I therefore wanted to make a few comments near the end of the session to help this process.

ANALYST: I think there is something else in it besides the dependence. For example, I think you have a very strong reaction against being so dependent that makes you strive to be independent. In addition, there is the matter of hostility. I think the drive to become independent combined with the hostility makes a certain aggressive drive and therefore you like men to dominate you in order to force you into the feminine position.

PATIENT: And another thing that would make difficulty in adjusting to a husband. My father has long told me that I am so very critical of everyone. Why is this?

Since the hour was up, I explained that I could not answer this right off and that we had best wait until we got a little more material to see what it was. I told the patient that this hour had been quieter than most hours but good. To this she shrugged.

PATIENT: I feel discouraged.

ANALYST: Why?

PATIENT: Oh, probably my cold.

ANALYST: I hesitate at sudden physical explanations. Maybe you are disappointed in this visit.

PATIENT: Yes, that is true. I feel as though I am wasting your time.

ANALYST: Of course you are not and you did very well. Once we get the main issues, the main motivations, the less revelations occur in the hour and the more working through; the more you can see how these motivations in their childhood pattern enter into your relationship with boys, with your roommate, and with your best friend, Carol.

But beyond this, the unconscious wants gratification and not insight. The ego, the part of you that runs things, wants insight but after all, it wants that too for purposes of gratification. The greatest gratification comes in maturing well emotionally so that you marry and enjoy the right man and your friends and other human relations. Now, as we have mentioned before, any feelings about me or this treatment are of great importance. This is a unique relationship for it is the only relationship in which you can discuss everything with a person, including the feelings that come up in relationship to him. You can discuss lots of things with your family and your friends but not everything. Here you can.

In this way it was possible to mention the transference rather unobtrusively. It was evident that the patient well understood the meaning of the comment that unconsciously she looked for satisfaction in the hour and not only for what she wanted consciously, namely insight. We discussed this, but the nature of the satisfaction that she wished for was not brought out. Once the discussion of the transference has been initiated, it is easier to watch in succeeding hours and to deal with in ways that are not embarrassing or anxiety producing for the patient. Meanwhile the way is paved for discussion of her excessive, conflictful dependence in the transference to me. Perhaps with the dependence coming out so frankly my further comments were technically incorrect, and it might have been better to discuss only the dependence, its obvious importance, and its possible development in the transference to me. However, I was afraid of letting an erotized form of it develop. The discussion was also intended to lay the groundwork for going into this matter of the sexual coloring of her feelings.

The importance of this was revealed in the earlier part

of this session: the patient was able to handle her rivalry with Beatrice and her dependent love needs toward Carol, as well as the jealousy these latter generated around Carol. But her feelings about men were more difficult for her to deal with, if for no other reason than that the same underlying pattern of dependent love needs, which were defended against largely by hostility, were intensified by the sexual drives. The sex drive makes more powerful the dependence and love needs as well as the fears of eventual jealousy, rejection, and frustration. Further, the sex drive also turns the hostility to the man, both directly and also masochistically as fear of attack by him, upon herself. Gradually she will see all this, but at present it is not central and presenting specifically in the transference. Hence the technical task is only to lay the groundwork, to make the emergence easier for the patient, that is, easier to comprehend, control, work through, alter, and integrate.

11th hour

One week later, the patient rushed in ten minutes late, her first tardiness.

PATIENT: I feel awful. I have the flu. I haven't eaten for three days. I was at a horse show and was very bored and noted down some things I wanted to tell you. Now they seem silly. But there is a dream I must tell.

Like with most patients, dreams are brought in spontaneously. Patients sense the enormous importance of the dream and its relation to the unconscious. During sleep, with our consciousness mostly in abeyance and without the restraints of waking life, our deepest and most secret wishes, impulses, and feelings can come into our fantasying either freely or in disguised forms.

PATIENT: I had a dream when I was on the boat to Europe,

a dream which was so awful that it stayed with me for a week and after dreaming it, I was unable to go back into my cabin—managed to but hated to. This dream was that a teacher was a hermaphrodite and raped someone—raped a waitress in a restaurant who became pregnant. I got a scientist to change her into two frozen statues—one of a man and one a woman. I could not stand to look at them, but he made me. It was just horrible. When I worked in a mental hospital, I could stand everything except the sexual perversions. Simply couldn't stand dragging one old woman out of bed with another, nor could I stand the talk of homosexual men. Why is this?

I did not know how much anxiety might be stirred up by an attempt to interpret directly the homosexual tendencies at this point, or to discuss why the transference references (teachers) took this form. Consequently I decided to start with what we had already frequently discussed, material that I knew she could handle.

ANALYST: You torment yourself in these dreams, so certainly there must be some guilt, which you know comes chiefly from hostility. You know that everyone has bisexual trends—you, me, and everyone else. *(The patient smiled faintly and nodded assent.)* Why then do you take it so hard?

PATIENT: Why, Why? Once as a preadolescent I kissed a girl. She was like my present best friend now, Carol, quite feminine and I felt very protective toward her. Why? Why?

The patient's insistence upon an answer was not really like her and seemed to imply that she really did want to discuss the subject and that she was able to stand doing so.

ANALYST: We already have some idea why. There are

several possibilities, but I do not know how to weigh them. For one thing there is the very close childhood attachment to mother. This close attachment to mother is one of the bases of bisexuality in people. We all have a mother and a father. If we are attached to the parent of the same sex, then that is one line for the sexual feelings to follow, and if they do so, when they intensify at adolescence they can make a problem. Attachment to the parent of the opposite sex of course makes a channel in the heterosexual direction. So your close attachment to mother might play some role in this. *(At this the patient smiles, signifying understanding and assent.)* Probably, you also identify with her and therefore feel mothering and protecting as you did toward your adolescent girlfriend and with your present girlfriend, and as you probably feel toward yourself and your sister. Your sister is the second possibility. Your hostility to her involves you with her emotionally and might arouse overcompensatory protectiveness. Thirdly, apart from the objects, mother or sister, the hostility alone, as we have discussed in the past, makes you probably feel, as you once told me, that if you were a man, you could *do* something. There might also be some identification with your father.

PATIENT (*thinking*): This weekend Carol and I did not go to visit my sister and ski in Wisconsin; we went home instead. I had great anxiety about my father and mother. Father and mother always sleep in separate rooms. I once asked mother if they any longer had any sexual relations, but she did not answer me.

We went to a horse show. Coming back father was not drunk but he drove so fast that I was frightened and wanted to drive myself, but he would not let me. When he got home, he just collapsed into bed. Very soon he was writhing and moaning in his sleep. I thought he was awake; couldn't believe that he was asleep, but he really was and was snoring. I told mother I thought father was really very unhappy, but she said, with a laugh, he only becomes restless when he drinks too much. Actually it is very rare that he does. Sometimes I feel the same kind of anxiety about my mother. Probably it is my own overworked imagination.

ANALYST: Why would you have that?

PATIENT: Could it be that I am unhappy and want to get away by myself? Could it really be that? I don't know.

ANALYST: I don't know either. We have seen the hostility to your sister come out very clearly along with the identification with her, the love for her, and the overprotectiveness toward her, but the hostilities toward your parents have not appeared clearly at all. We don't know much about them. Maybe that has something to do with your anxieties about them.

PATIENT (*for the first time, silent a moment or two*): Do you remember when I spoke to you about Tom, my former fiancé? You said my feelings toward men in general were patterned partly on those toward my sister. I did feel toward Tom as I did toward my sister when I was a child. I felt that father and mother were forcing me to love Tom just as they forced me to try to love my sister, and I have a compulsion to resist them. I feel I have power over them if I can resist loving them.

ANALYST: What do you mean?

PATIENT: I mean a feeling that I can't trust any man enough to love him completely, even wonderful men like Tom who want to marry me. I feel that if I let go and love, if I once give in, then I am lost. If I do not, then I am safe.

ANALYST: Perhaps by loving, which is a broad term, you really mean your own needs to *be* loved because that is what we know about your childhood pattern. *(To this the patient nodded agreement with considerable feeling.)* Perhaps then you feel the intensity of your own needs for love because these were so powerful toward your mother and father, whether from overindulgence by them or from some feeling of some form of deprivation by them. Perhaps you feel that if you once let yourself go and need the other person's love so much as that, then you are too much in their power and therefore subject to possible frustration and jealousy and the consequent rage.

PATIENT (*smiling*): Yes, yes, yes.

The time was now more than up.

ANALYST: If we reduce the pattern, then you would not have to fear what is awakened when you want love.

PATIENT (*wistfully*): That would be good indeed.

I had let the transference meaning rest with the implications of our discussion. I did not feel that the possible transference to me of the dependent love needs had as yet emerged sufficiently for direct discussion. I decided to be cautious until these were worked over further lest the intensity of the patient's feelings make such a discussion upsetting.

This session confirms the comments at the end of the previous one. The patient cannot solve her difficulties by full acceptance of femininity nor by attempted flight into masculinity. What was said about the transference gains some support. It may well be that she is transferring the mother pattern to me with a strong heterosexual erotization. But, for reasons given previously, the heterosexual feelings are too powerful, conflictful, and tumultuous for her. She fears the dependence upon the analyst, the infantile wishes for his love and approval, the anticipated frustration, jealousy, rage, and guilt. If only the analyst were a woman, it would still be difficult but probably somewhat less so. If only the patient were a man, then she could be friendly with the analyst, without all the turmoil of dependence, love needs, frustration, jealousy, rage, and guilt.

12th hour

The patient entered the office a week later with a smile that was combined with a tense, scrutinizing gaze.

PATIENT: I'm having such awful dreams!

ANALYST: Good. I'm sorry that you are uncomfortable with them, but I think it means progress.

PATIENT: I'm so glad! The dreams are so bad I am afraid to go to sleep. I putter about until very late and have hardly slept. Friday night I dreamed I was at our place at the lake in the Rockies with my father and mother. I seem to have quite a lot of dreams of being there. They let my sister do some little thing, such as skiing, but they would not let me. I went into a fury. I felt as though I were paralyzed in a wet pack; it was just awful. The next day I thought that was just one nightmare and was over with but then that evening, Saturday, I had another dream that I drowned my mother in a bathtub while my father looked on. It was so awful; I never had anything like that. It was like the dream of going out of my mind and being taken to a mental hospital.

Here are two dreams. The first one reveals frank rivalry with sister, and again it is in the masochistic form of sister receiving some preference in the form of permission over the patient, with an ego reaction of intense rage. In the second dream there is direct hostility to the patient's mother, and this is acted out in the dream by the ego, by the patient in her own person. The themes are clear, but why did the patient dream these at just this time? Do these dreams express her current feelings about her mother and sister, or did she dream so frankly about them to avoid seeing the present objects of these feelings—are they toward other persons in life or are they toward me in the transference? Every-

thing must be watched in relation to the transference if only to be ruled out.

PATIENT: I think these dreams are connected somehow with Andy. He is a boy who said he thought he was in love with me, and I said I was not in love with him and that his being in love with me might not lead anywhere and that night I had a nightmare. That was about three weeks ago. Then last Friday before the nightmare I told you (*being at the lake*), there was the same situation with another boy, Brent. I wanted to tell him not to fall in love with me before he got so involved. I said to him, "I'm always saying no. It would be so nice to say yes." And then I felt I had revealed so much. I came home and felt awful and then had that dream.

The patient relates these dreams to the wishes of Andy and Brent for her love. But do they signify the patient's own wishes for love toward the analyst? Is this the involvement she is fighting off? It is not yet open enough in the material to discuss it bluntly. Instead, at this point it would be better to attempt to elicit the patient's own feelings and insights about it. Hence I move on slowly.

ANALYST: Why did you feel so upset?

PATIENT: Because I feel as though I am incapable of loving anyone. Each boy falls in love with me and then I must say I am sorry.

ANALYST: I think this is partly reality. A girl must say no she is sorry many times and say yes once. That is how it is with attractive girls. That does not mean that there is no psychological problem also, but I have seen this to be true. My own daughter is only a small child but that is what I expect. Boys begin to get involved with a girl, and then it is hard to keep a friendly, nice relationship without too much intensity and complications until the girl thinks she wants to be seriously involved and marry the boy.

In this statement I departed from my usual custom of bringing in nothing personal whatever. In the first place I wished to emphasize the reality and the in the second place, knowing the intensity of the patient's needs for love toward the members of her family and her intense jealousies, I thought that emphasizing the fact that I am married and have a small daughter would help her defenses against too intense a transference of these dependent love needs to me. It might also help as a defense against the erotized transference, which so readily skips the gap of years. In other words, this was a double dose of reality in relation to boys and in the transference. Probably this was a correct move, because she seemed noticeably relieved in connection with the reality of having to say no to boys and of all girls having to do this. Her next remark was illuminating.

PATIENT: Why I never thought of you as having a daughter.

This remark might confirm my suspicion that the patient had eliminated from her feelings and thinking the possibility that I had a wife and child. She probably did this because of her wishes for exclusive love, which it seems she had enjoyed in reality although perhaps not with full security, before her sister was born. Was her unconscious recognizing what I had conveyed? The gist of this was: We know the intensity of your demands for mother's exclusive love and the consequent violence of your jealousy and your rage when these are frustrated. I want to help you to defend against developing these demands, whether erotized or not, too powerfully toward others and toward me; but we must face them squarely and frankly in order to handle them so that they will yield satisfaction in real life and not neurotic difficulties.

After this brief interchange, she went on spontaneously.

PATIENT: I often wonder whether or not a person is good enough for me. I fear if I give in to something in a relationship, I will be lost. I will be flooded with feeling. Like when Tom, you remember Tom who was my fiancé when I came to see you, was affectionate, I was afraid I would be overwhelmed with emotion. I simply could not dare let myself go. Therefore I would become flip or else very vague as though I didn't hear him and that is horrible. Then I would feel so selfish; what an awful way to treat someone. I would fear to show my feelings and pretend that I had none. Why is that?

This seemed to fit in very well with what I thought was going on. Still preferring to elicit the insight and interpretation from the patient, I told her I thought I knew but made no further comment.

PATIENT: Please tell me again.

This was sufficient opening. I acceded to her request and reminded her of the intensity of her childhood feelings and even of her current feelings toward the members of her family. I discussed her rage when frustrated and the rage and jealousy she felt toward her sister. I also mentioned with some emphasis the fact that this pattern got transferred to other persons in life and to me.

Since the hostility was so central in the two dreams reported in this hour, it had to be gone into. If the patient were not so hostile, if her rage could be reduced by insight into it, making it fully conscious and then freely discussing it, it would be much easier for her to deal with the libidinal demands and fear of their frustration, which generated the rage as a defense. Therefore I took this opportunity to go further and point out that the reason I said in the beginning of the hour that the nightmares indicated progress was related to the fact that hostility plays a special role. When she came to see me, her hostility and rage were very thoroughly repressed and she was consequently not aware of the extent or significance of them. But now, however, they have come near enough to consciousness to trouble her in her dreams. It is progress because it is more open.

Progress is usually in three steps. The first is that the hostility is no longer so thoroughly repressed, and because its power to generate symptoms is lessened, it begins to show in the dreams. The second step takes place when the patient is thoroughly aware of the hostility, its consequences, and the guilt in connection with it. Then we can discuss it back and forth easily and the patient will not have to dream it. The third step involves a shift in the underlying attitudes generating the hostility that act to diminish it. Less intensely compelling demands for love means a lessened intensity in all its consequences.

PATIENT (*smiling*): I can see that. Sunday night also I had a nightmare; that all the girls in the dormitory hated me and were out to get me because of something I had done.

ANALYST: Good. What do you associate to something you had done?

PATIENT: Could it be me? Could it be a form of projection? I was out with Brent Saturday and made a confession that I never admitted before; that I am jealous of the girls I dislike. I mean that probably the real reason I dislike these girls is not that I am so superior to them as I tell myself, but because I envy them that they can love and I cannot. With Brent this was rather horrible, because my chief feeling for him is pity. He has heart trouble. He won't live long, but he cannot face this and talks big, tells all sorts of plans for the future, but actually he is only a lonely guy.

The attraction to Brent in the light of this information is probably in part identification, because underneath the patient feels that she also is handicapped—by her emotional difficulties—that she too is lonely. In part also, it may well be that Brent's weakness relieves the patient of her fear of strong men, whom she sees as dangerous chiefly because they stir up her tendency to regress to excessive dependence and because the sexual impulses arouse her hostility, guilt, and masochism, her unconscious wishes to be attacked. Handicapped or weak men may stir up a woman's sadism as well as her maternal protectiveness. These are my thoughts about a single association, but I recognize the importance of not letting these ideas throw me off the track of the dreams and the central, presenting forces.

There followed a very brief further discussion of the childhood pattern of excessive dependent love needs, of hostility and guilt, and of the effects of these and of the transference of them to others. It would seem that the patient's observation is probably correct that she is hostile to any girl and probably to anyone out of envy of their human relations, particularly, as she put it, their ability to love.

PATIENT: It is true, for I will admit now that if I see a young couple together, really getting on well with each other and happy with each other, my feelings become so unbearable that I cannot help weeping.

ANALYST: Our goal is rather clear, and we will certainly try to reduce the hostility and guilt and the demands that keep these going so that you can have good human relations yourself and free your own capacity to love.

The needs for love are not frustrated only because of their intensity and fear of the excessive dependence involved. What is also pertinent here is that the hostility to other persons prevents the patient from being free in her feelings toward others. This rage, and the guilt it engenders, disturb her relationships and especially makes her fear any physical expression, as in sexual feelings. This is a vicious cycle. The hostility and guilt cut her off from receiving love and because she cannot receive it, she craves it all the more and is all the more jealous, envious, frustrated, and further enraged. I still do not know whether in early childhood she felt that she did not get enough real love—or maybe too much—and therefore now feels that she is sure to get insufficient love in any relationship, thus making her crave it so desperately.

PATIENT: Not all girls who come in to see you are psychiatric problems as I am.

ANALYST: You are in part a psychiatric problem for very good reasons; namely, you have conflicts over your hostility. Whether you had too much love in early childhood or felt some deprivation and therefore now both crave it and dread frustration, we do not yet know. But there was so much love in your family and still is and therefore so much love in you that you cannot bear your hostilities and feel in conflict over them. This warmth and capacity for love is, of course, a very good thing, and it is certainly better to have it and to have the conflict. Probably it is this combination of warm love and repressed hostility that makes your relations with the boys so all or nothing as you describe. They respond to your capacity for love and your intense needs for love but then the hostility is also there and makes a problem. The hostility interferes with being loved and this interference frustrates you and makes you hostile. Hence the solution of the two emotional forces go together. We want to see frankly and clearly the hostility and also the dependent love needs—and also this interrelationship between them. The better your guilt and shame about these motivations are analyzed, the more readily you will see them and handle them.

13th hour

PATIENT: Oh, Dr. S.! (*shaking her head as though life were indeed difficult*).

ANALYST: What is it?

PATIENT: I guess I am just glad to see you each week. Such awful nightmares. I may have to resort to sleeping pills, but I have not minded the nightmares so much since you told me what you did. They are not quite so direct anymore. I cannot understand them.

Something preys on my mind but I must face it. I hate to. Last summer I took care of two little girls, age nine and eleven, and I think I really did all right. But I had and still have excessive guilt about it, about not trying hard enough, and I am afraid that perhaps I think of these little things because I can't face the main issue. But since a dream I had last week, maybe it begins to make a bit of sense. Before telling the dream, I must tell you a little about the situation. The children's parents were divorced. The father was nice to me but distant, but the mother was always critical of me, and I was under constant pressure to please her. Even if the matters were infinitesimal, if I forgot to empty a wastebasket, for example, the mother would hit the ceiling. I was under constant criticism. The girls were very competitive and the mother said I must try harder with May, the older one. I could not get on with the older one but loved the younger one. I could hardly wait for the end of the summer. What a tragedy it is for children to be brought up in such a family. The agency through which I got the job warned me it was a very neurotic family and if I took the job, I would just have to stand it.

By way of setting for the dream, we hear the familiar pattern—mother and two competitive sisters. Further, one sister is favored over the other by the patient and there is a struggle to please the mother. Of course there is no parallel history of the patient's mother being thus harshly critical. Happily, the content of the associations is rather consistently one of emotional investments and involvements in real life with exogamic persons and not with the family of childhood. This signifies a thrust toward mature independence and tends toward allaying fears of too great a fixation upon parents and sister. These emotional fixations adversely affect and inhibit her relationships with other people, but at least they do not prevent her from having real feelings for them.

PATIENT: The dream was as follows. May was away. I was with the younger child, Evie. We may have been playing cards or something and then in the dream six of my friends came. I had the right to have friends in and did have two but in the dream there were six. They took over the place, left dishes about, were completely obnoxious, and I knew I would get blamed by the mother. I tried to get rid of them. Then I put Evie to bed and tried to go down to clean up before her mother returned. Evie pleaded with me not to leave her. She said I did not love her, but I assured her I did, and as I was telling her how much I loved her, in came her mother, furious about everything, and I awoke simply overwhelmed with guilt.

ANALYST (*deliberately not picking any individual elements of the dream*): Now some associations.

Our time was short, and I wanted to see what further material the patient would bring and what she herself could make of the dream. My own thoughts were that the dream might be a reflection of her feelings toward her family, stimulated by her anticipated visit with them. I thought that the destructive behavior of the patient's six friends was a projection of what she herself wanted to do, her own hostile impulses and guilt toward the children's mother. I also considered that this might well be in the childhood pattern of her hostility and guilt to her own mother and that this in turn foreshadows what to expect in her feelings toward me in the transference. Evie probably is a representation of the little girl part of the patient herself, longing for assurance of being loved, basically in the mother pattern, and probably these childish longings are to some extent transferred and felt toward me. Evie's pleading with the patient not to leave her might refer to the plans to leave for Europe and anger because of this anticipated frustration. Also, there is probably direct hostility following the pattern to sister in May being away, that is, eliminated. Here the twist is that the older child is eliminated and the patient seems to identify with the younger one.

PATIENT: Even last summer I felt that Mrs. Q., the mother of the children, was somehow connected with my mother. I myself went through a period when I was petrified to tell my own mother things, even tiny things like forgetting to take the laundry off the line.

This is confirmatory. Why the fear of telling mother—fear of revealing hostility or sexual impulses or what? Psychoanalysis is telling. Following this pattern to mother, this is probably fear of telling me things, probably the very things I have suspected and that are now emerging, especially in the transference.

ANALYST: What do you associate to May not being there?

This was the first element in the dream, and it seemed like a simple wish to eliminate the rival sister. Hence I started off by asking for associations to this.

PATIENT (hesitating): I think of myself. Identification with May or could it be that I had done away with her in some way? *(Falling silent briefly.)*

Could this be hostility to the sister figure turned against herself?

ANALYST: Have you any notion why you have nightmares just now at this particular time?

PATIENT: Because of the hostility coming out. If I had been with a family with boys or only one child, it might have been different but the two girls made me identify too easily with my sister and myself in my family and these girls were so intensely jealous of each other all the time, just like my sister, Letty, and I. We are three and a half years apart and those children were only sixteen months, but I don't think that matters much. Yesterday was my sister's birthday; she was eighteen and in view of what has come out here, I actually celebrated. I felt that I was really glad that she was born.

Time was rushing on and we still had not come to the main issue of the dream although it sounded as though her suggestion of possibly doing away with May might touch on some of the hostility for which she was so guilty. This may have been stimulated by Letty's birthday about which, although consciously pleased, she may have been unconsciously resentful. I therefore asked where the hostility was in this dream.

PATIENT: To myself? To Mrs. Q.?

ANALYST: It seems to be hostility and also guilt, since you woke up feeling so guilty.

PATIENT: Yes, overpowering guilt that haunted me all during that month. I liked her as a person but as an employer, I couldn't stand her. She had been seeing psychiatrists for years.

ANALYST: Could this guilt to Mrs. Q. be because of your hostility to her and perhaps also to May, following your sister pattern? May is not present in the dream and you suggest that you might have done away with her. Or, could the hostility even be to Evie? *(The patient signified comprehension.)* Could it be something in the transference? Is there guilt for telling me these things, especially your hostilities? In the past the hostility made you feel guilty and now telling me about the hostilities may reawaken this guilt and therefore have something to do with the nightmares. Could this be guilt for hostilities to me following the mother pattern, guilt because there was love between you and your mother and sister and therefore guilt for hostile feelings to sister and to mother?

PATIENT: No, I have glad feelings because you are not only a person who listens but one who can actually help me. In my wilder moments I picture you as a wizard. Like the Wizard of Oz, I always think of wizards as good. I really feel there is nothing I cannot tell you.

ANALYST: Good, I am glad you see the difference between this situation and that one toward Mrs. Q. and even toward your mother, who might have been critical or shocked. In this situation it is good to verbalize your hostilities, it is analytic progress. You are no longer a child and the mature part of you works with me and is also the wizard, for it too sees the hostility, the guilt it causes, and other results and is learning to handle them. Is there anything else now that we should get from this dream?

The patient could see some of the hostility-guilt pattern in relation to her family, that is, the original edition of it and also as it appeared in current life toward roommates and in her reactions to the Q's household. We could discuss powerful component motivations, the dependent love needs, and the hostility. We could touch upon the erotized edition toward men and toward women. But, while I could mention the transference edition of it toward me, the patient could not yet quite see this, as her thinking of me as a wizard showed. The dreams show how directly she can see the main motivations, but she does not yet see them in the transference. This cannot be pushed. It will come with time. The analyst can smooth the way by mentioning what is to be expected and thereby through forewarning, forearm the patient and tone down the intensity. I therefore returned to discussion of the dream.

PATIENT: Yes. I was ashamed of my friends there. Last summer perhaps I was a little ashamed of my friends because the Q's are multimillionaires, and I did not want to impose upon them anything from my life. I wanted to maintain a certain standard for myself in front of them. Not that I really feel socially inferior actually but just superficially.

ANALYST: What do you associate to Evie saying you do not love her?

PATIENT: I don't know. You tell. Perhaps I identify her with my sister. I felt that I did love her. I was anxious to assert it. Maybe that means something. Maybe it means that I felt she was not mine and therefore I had no *right* to love her. Mrs. Q. was jealous all summer, and I could not be demonstrative with the children, although I could during the period we were with the father. Sometimes I would feel as though I would want to run away with Evie and keep her forever.

This might well be a turning of her love needs from the mother figure and in the transference from the analyst, over to the child. This is a mechanism by which a love-hungry mother so often hangs on to her children: the love-needy little child she is underneath identifies with her children and clings to them.

ANALYST: Possibly your friends in the dream are a representation of your own wish for unrestraint and rebellion against this authority.

PATIENT (*smiling*): It is true. You *are* a wizard!

ANALYST: We may see the jealousy triangle from a little different point of view. You probably turn to some extent from your mother to your sister and identify with your sister, with the feeling that if only it were not for mother, sister and I could go off together and could love each other.

There followed a brief discussion in which my goal was to relieve further the feelings of guilt about the hostilities, because next week the patient was going to be away to visit her home and we would not be able to talk then. I pointed out the following: first, that she already knew we were trying to understand the hostilities to mother and sister figures in the dream in order to relieve her guilt; second, that all children have hostilities to their parents and to each other, and that this is nothing to be upset about but simply, insofar as it is disturbing, to be treated as a problem; third, that if we understand the hostility, there would be no reason to diminish the hostility, the guilt, and the nightmares; fourth, that she is no longer a child and is capable of good loving relationships to the members of her family and to others on an adult basis; fifth, that Evie's pleading to her in the dream not to leave might refer to her own sense of frustration in leaving her family and perhaps myself next week when we cannot meet and in the future when she would be leaving for Sweden and that this might generate some anger, even though she was doing what she wished; and sixth, that some of this entire reaction may be stimulated by her reacting to the anticipated visit with her family. I have frequently seen such reactions in college students before they return home for vacation.

She left, obviously greatly relieved and smiling almost happily for the first time. She expressed her thanks with feelings of appreciation.

I feel gratified by the progress the patient is making in the course of these thirteen visits, but I must admit that I am not entirely at ease in one respect, and that is the transference. As was discussed in the chapter on transference, the patient tends to repeat toward the analyst the major features of the pattern in the family that causes the problem. Hence, in this case I can expect to have directed toward myself (1) the extreme dependent demands for love that the patient felt toward her mother and less so toward her father; (2) the hostility toward them as a defense against these enslaving demands, because of their frustration and because of jealousy of them in relation to her sister; (3) the closeness of identification with the parents and with her sister; and (4) all the guilt borne of the hostility toward those with whom she identified, whom she loved, and whose love she craved above all else.

Thus far none of these demands for love, nor the intense jealousy reactions, nor the hostility, nor the overwhelming guilt have appeared openly toward me. But, the patient does see them toward her family in childhood and also toward others in the past and in the present. The relationship to me is entirely friendly on the surface. Nor have the patient's dreams revealed clearly the development of ominous feelings toward me. In this last dream, am I represented as the mother of the two children? Am I a child to be sent away? Am I the child who wishes not to have the patient leave him? Or, is the transference tucked away in the patient with the younger child, Evie, who pleads with her not to leave? Is this the patient pleading with the analyst not to leave and to prove he really loves her? Is this plea stimulated by the fact that the patient herself is leaving for two weeks? While these possibilities are very much in my mind, it would be ill advised indeed to more than touch upon such interpretations in any way that might alarm the patient. In time I know that the pattern will certainly develop toward me; these dreams and associations forewarn me of what to expect.

Probably one reason why this emotional pattern has not yet come out in the transference is that the analysand is still so intensely involved emotionally with the actual persons of whom she dreams—with her actual mother, father, and sister in the original family pattern. Hence, for the present her strongest conscious reaction to the analysis is wonder and appreciation for the insight she has obtained into these feelings and into their connections with her phobia and with her difficulties in human relations, especially in making a suitable marriage. Some patients have positive therapeutic reactions, being able readily to use in life the insight they gain. Others react without such progress and even feel worse for a period. Fortunately this patient has thus far been able to gain great relief from the insight and has been able to apply it in life to a very considerable degree. She is learning to understand her own dreams and to see their relationships to her difficulties.

Meanwhile, however silently, the transference is certainly developing, or has developed but is defended against, following the childhood pattern. Doubtless the patient gains much emotional support from her visits, for, as she said in this hour, she feels she can tell me everything and that I will not simply listen but also be able to help her. As her analyst, I can offer her understanding without generating guilt or shame—an experience she has apparently not had with her parents.

The long intervals between sessions, while probably working to keep the transference at less intensity, makes the interpretation of it more difficult. The reason for this is that the interpretation must be carefully timed and the patient so prepared for discussion of it that she will not be upset by this insight but make the greatest possible therapeutic use of it. This session demonstrates something of the difficulties of short and infrequent sessions. There is not time, when the material is full, for adequate associations to all dream elements, nor, in other sessions, for getting the common element, the red thread, in all the associations.

14th hour

Two weeks later the patient returned looking a little bit quieter than usual.

PATIENT: How are you?
ANALYST: Fairly well, and you?
PATIENT: I'm not yet back in the spirit of things. I returned two days ago from spending Easter at home. I am

bored. I have exams coming up. However, happiness is in the mind.

ANALYST: I guess circumstances can play some part also.

PATIENT: Yes, but it is a matter of how the mind approaches the circumstances and reacts to them. Once I wanted to commit suicide. I went to see a woman doctor. She said it was because of menstrual tension. Some women have more and some women have less. She gave me some hormones, and I felt better and still do. *(The patient paused, then suddenly went on.)* I wish you could hypnotize me and then tell me that when I awoke I would not fear mountains. I am afraid. It is so near the summer and having to go to the mountains. You asked me to always tell you any feelings toward you. Now I feel it is not fair to you if I get discouraged.

ANALYST: How so?

PATIENT: I think that it is as though I were losing faith in you. Last evening I was thinking that you would like it if I had a good dream, and I hoped to have one, and it is amazing that I did.

There is much suspicion in the literature about the patient using dreams as a resistance, bringing them only to please the analyst. However, in my experience, if the analyst is well aware of what is going on, if he understands the tremendous role that the patient's needs for love play in the whole treatment, then he is able to utilize the wish to please him as a powerful instrument for cure. Furthermore, he can analyze it and reduce the patient's dependence upon him and attachment to him, making the patient wish to get well for his or her own sake and not just to please the analyst. He can make the patient turn to life for the satisfaction of needs for love instead of expecting this from the analyst.

At the same time, however, he understands that the patient is unhappy in part because of feeling unloved by the parents or undeserving of their love. This feeling is carried along within the patient's mind as the superego. The analyst must replace this feeling in the patient's mind by one of being understood and accepted, thereby providing the patient with the proper parental attitude and correction of the superego. Thereafter the patient should feel more secure and more adequate because he feels that this part of his own personality, taken over from the analyst, now understands him and approves of him and supports him.

Therefore, while alert to any possible difficulties or resistance, I saw no reason not to welcome the patient's dream with an open mind as an honest effort not merely superficially to please me but also to achieve cure by making analytic progress with those forces that were producing the symptoms. The dream, no matter what, is still the royal road to the unconscious and therefore must always be taken with great seriousness.

PATIENT: This was the dream last night. I was with Tom. You remember, the boy I was engaged to. It was natural to think of him because mother talked a lot about him during my time at home. In the dream Tom and I climbed a mountain together and then came down again. I was not afraid when we were climbing but after we were down from the mountain, I looked up and said, "I would be scared to climb that; it is so high." Then he said, "Why you did climb it already."

Here is a dream of mountains, which are so central in the phobia and feared in the dream also. Going up and down the mountain might refer to the treatment, which is frequently represented in dreams as a journey. The endings of dreams are always especially significant. The patient's fear of climbing the mountain combined with the thought, verbalized in the dream by Tom, that she has already climbed it, may suggest a feeling that she has already handled difficult and dangerous emotional forces. Does this relate to the transference? Mountains, as has already been noted, sometimes represent mother. If this were so, they would sym-

bolize in this dream the anxiety laden conflict over the feelings to mother, which we have repeatedly surmised.

PATIENT: Reaching the top of the mountain and not being scared seems to me to mean freedom. Before going to sleep I had thought deeply of Tom and of my relationship to him. In a sense I conquered my fear when I committed myself to him but then I backed down again. Tom told mother that sometimes I would love him and sometimes I would hate him and really I myself never knew from minute to minute how I would feel, but I could not commit myself fully. I tried but just couldn't.

This lends support to the possibility of the dream dealing with the patient's efforts to free herself from the conflict with mother, as developing toward the analyst.

ANALYST: What do you associate to the mountain in the dream?

PATIENT *(hesitating for some seconds)*: Freedom. Getting to the top means I am free. My dreams are often of freedom. Freedom through conquering my fear of mountains. Also in dancing. I have many dreams of dancing in a large room, leaping with nothing to hold me down. I become deliriously happy and sometimes I fly. *(Hesitating a moment.)* Mountains. The first mountain I ever climbed was at age ten. I was at camp. It was an overnight camping trip. I was aware that some things frightened me but it was only a reflex. It was not intellectual. On the top of the mountain there were no trees but my real fear was not of that mountain but of the *other* mountains. They were so big and black and the big dark clouds.

This may have some very specific significance. On the other hand, however, it may be the result of a very general mechanism, that is, that the reality of the solid ground she is on inhibits the unrealistic fear, which is more easily projected onto what is less immediate and more distant and vague.

PATIENT: In the morning I got up early and looked down on a sea of mist but simply could not stand looking at it and got into my sleeping bag. (*Apparently the patient did not realize she had told this experience in a previous visit.*) I have climbed many mountains but am always afraid. I do it as a matter of pride. With others there, it would look awfully sissy not to. It is much worse if somebody knows I have this fear. At age fifteen if no one knew about it, I could take someone's hand over the worst part and then no longer be afraid when we reached the top.

Does this mean that she managed to suppress the anxiety better out of shame of others knowing that she has it?

This dream dealing directly with mountains seemed like a fine opportunity to make some progress in understanding why the phobia attached to mountains specifically. I therefore interrupted this chain of thought by asking the patient to what she associated climbing. Doing this was no doubt a mistake. Since the transference is such a powerful and disturbing constellation of feelings, no digression from getting it into the open is justified. Interruption of flowing associations is usually only disadvantageous.

PATIENT (*thinking*): Nothing. I know what you want but I think of nothing. Now I remember another time. I was seven. It was not true that the first time I climbed a mountain was at ten as I just told you. At seven it was not an open mountain. Others climbed it and on top there was a fire tower. I was afraid to go up the fire tower although all the rest did. I have never been up one. I am also afraid of climbing ladders. I am afraid of all high places. When I was very little, three or four, we had a swimming pond with a diving board; not at all high, maybe three feet over the water. When father would be in the water and tell me to jump—he was a big strong man and could catch me—I was petrified. I simply could not jump.

Heights very often signify in the ego meaning, striving to be high up, to be above others, that is, strivings for prestige and superiority over others.

PATIENT: One of my earliest memories was of our big police dog pushing me into the water by mistake. The water was rather shallow. I went in head first. I was not hurt at all but I have always been afraid to dive. Sometimes in these freedom dreams, I am in a high place and do dive. I never could do that really unless maybe I were drunk.

This suggests that one thing heights mean to the patient is freedom, perhaps from the conflictual dependent love needs to mother and perhaps from submissiveness to her. Hostile rebellion against this emotional relation to mother might well generate guilt and anxiety. Feeling quite sure of the motivational forces behind this symptom, I continued.

ANALYST: These anxieties are common and usually spring from hostility and guilt and fear of punishment. But why just mountains? Could it be because the family often went to the mountains? Did you want to push your sister off a mountain? Or are the mountains only symbolic?

I mentioned the patient's sister in order to get the hostilities well verbalized and out in the open so she would not be afraid to mention and discuss any sort of impulse.

PATIENT: Symbolic. Because the anxiety began not with

mountains at all but with pictures and it is also about other things such as loud noises. I even feared to look into a microscope because of the enlargement and also because things are distorted and out of focus.

ANALYST: Where could this come from—this fear of what is enlarged, distorted, out of focus?

PATIENT: I have no idea. Could it be something I have forgotten? I wish I could ask my parents.

ANALYST: Why not?

PATIENT: Possibly I could ask my mother. I told her during my visit home that I was seeing you. She is with the idea. She is curious as to why. She suspects that it is because of my fear since that is what I saw the other psychiatrist about. He would scare me. He would ask me how I would feel if he told me that the next room was full of snakes. I was frightened to death. Then he would go and tell my mother that I was high-strung and nervous. He once told me I was afraid of my mother. He was a jerk. I saw him five times. He would stare and stare at me. He made me feel stupid, an absolute moron.

The references to size and enlargement might relate to the phallus—or they might not. If so, the anxiety about it would still be because of the underlying forces. Hence it seemed best not to risk mentioning this but rather to follow Freud's basic method of dream interpretation by getting chains of associations, by breaking the dream up into conceptual elements, and by being guided by the manifest dream. Therefore I did not hesitate to return to the question of the specific choice of mountains. My next remark, though based on experience, was probably unwise, a shot in the dark.

ANALYST: Symbolically, mountains are sometimes related, for one thing, to prestige, to climbing.

PATIENT: Of course. Why couldn't I see that?

I took this question literally and grasped the opportunity to inform her further of how the mind operates.

ANALYST: Because it is in your own mind and is a defense. Instead of seeing your hostility, guilt, and needs for punishment in relation to your mother and sister, you displace it all onto the mountains. That is why you speak to me; so I can show you what this looks like when someone else sees it.

PATIENT: That summer when I was ten, I was obsessed with a counselor and my sole object was to get her to acknowledge me and my existence, at least until she finally blew up at me. Then I wanted someone, it didn't really matter who, to like me better than anyone else. The other children teased me. They came after me with daddy-longlegs. They put brooms in my bed.

This is similar to the early memory of being pushed into the water by her dog. Those who should be her friends behave antagonistically toward the patient. Of course the dog did so only by mistake.

PATIENT: I don't know why they didn't like me, but that mountain trip was charged with competition with the other girls. In fact those two summers were.

Would this express a pattern of feeling insufficiently loved, originally by mother, and of competition with sister?

PATIENT: I recall a picture in my baby book of mother and me on a little hill in Wisconsin where there are no mountains, only little tiny ones, maybe two thousand feet high. You took an old road to get on top and up there it was very private and there was some view although not much of a view. This was before my sister was born, I think.

ANALYST: What is the connection?

I noted silently the association of mountains and views with sole possession of mother a connection previously noted as a common symbolization—mountain and mother.

PATIENT: That I wanted to be the only one. I was curious to see my sister this vacation after talking with you. My hostilities were near the surface, and I often thought of hitting her for no reason, and then I thought: How silly; you are twenty-one. Why do you want to hit your sister? She and I spoke of how we constantly fought as children. When I was fourteen and she was ten, I remember yelling at her, "You little bitch," and throwing a dish at her, and then I was petrified for fear of what might have happened if I hit her. And you know, I think my sister was more jealous and envious of me than I of her! *(This revelation burst out with much emotion.)* When I came home, sister was sitting with father. Father jumped up but sister froze as though now that I was home, she must take a back seat. I could intuitively see something drain out of her. She did not run up happily and spontaneously and kiss me but quietly said, "Hi." It was the same when an old flame of mine came over, older than I and no friend of hers. She sort of went dead inside and the same thing happened when a different friend came and do you know how I felt; that I must get rid of her jealousy. It was the greatest feeling. In talking with you, I see that. She must have had a worse time of it than I because I was older and was more to compete with.

This does not reveal with full frankness the meaning of heights and the fear of heights. However, it does strongly support the suspected connection with the excessive rivalry with the sister, perhaps to be above her, superior to her, par-

ticularly in the eyes of mother but also of father. The specific factor, why mountains enter the phobias, may be in part the time alone with mother, before sister's birth, on "the little hill" in Wisconsin. A little hill to an adult may loom large to a child. Many a grownup has been surprised on returning to scenes of his early childhood, at how small objects looked to him now that had appeared so large in his memory.

ANALYST: The mountain probably represents this competing—who is higher, who is better. It also has to do with mother—who is closer to mother, who is preferred by mother.

Mountains often symbolize the maternal breast, but as Freud advised, it is far better to wait for the associations than to jump in with unsupported symbolic interpretations.

PATIENT: I have gotten on much better with my roommate these last two weeks because of understanding the competition.

Only a few moments of the interview now remained and since the issues were now so open, I wanted to use these minutes to tie up loose ends and bring in various points that could not so readily have been discussed prior to this visit.

ANALYST: Are these connections clear?
PATIENT: Yes.

The transference had been mentioned but not directly interpreted, for reasons that were stated previously. This seemed like another opportunity to discuss it, especially as she had referred to it at the beginning of the session.

ANALYST: The transference has been no problem until now,

and I only mention it so we are both constantly forewarned in case you should fit me into the sister pattern as competition. Or, more specifically and more importantly, perhaps, you might fit me into the mother pattern and tend to have toward me such feelings as toward mother.

PATIENT: I don't feel that way. I might if you were in contact with my father and mother. Then I would have to fight you as well as them. What I like best about this is that I came to see you on my own entirely and no one except my roommate even knows about it. (*Earlier in this hour she said she had told her mother also.*) This is what I hated about the other guy. He would see me and then talk with father and mother, although I was the one who came to him for help.

It was possible that she was unwittingly acting out to some extent in the transference this very exclusive possession of mother that she once had and still so strongly longed for. She may have been acting it out by feeling that except for her roommate, she alone knew of her treatment with me.

Since this patient was under considerable tension and also could come only once a week and often for only thirty minutes at a time, interpretations involved unusual difficulties. This was the fourteenth interview. It seemed evident that she could face the hostility and guilt to her sister more easily than that to her mother. It was also clear that at this point she could not face the transference. Hence my further interpretation of the dream to her was entirely ego-syntonic.

ANALYST: The dream might refer to the analysis, equating the analytic task of the facing of your feelings with climbing up and down the mountain, where you also faced your anxieties successfully. These may be in part because of conflict over being close to anyone following the pattern toward mother.

Here there is a gap in the notes, and I do not know what led to the following, just as the time was up.

ANALYST: You wondered why the children at camp disliked you. I have an idea about that. Perhaps your wanting someone to like you better than any of the other children caused some intuitive reaction in them. Perhaps they reacted to your wish to be better than they and preferred to them as by mother over sister.

PATIENT: That could well be. This summer I have to take sister to her school, which is in high mountains. I am beginning to get scared. Would hypnosis solve it? Will I get over the phobia? Does anyone?

ANALYST: They do and I think that this is just a matter of time, of what we can accomplish before the summer comes. The phobia is a matter of the same kind of anxieties that everyone has; anxieties about heights are quite common, and it is a quantitative matter whether this is great enough to make you afraid to look at pictures. Hypnosis would be like taking aspirin to relieve a fever when you had an infection; you wouldn't be treating the cause, the infection itself. The phobia shows you that there is still hostility and guilt and that these need to be worked through and reduced.

PATIENT: Do mature people ever want to throw things or get so angry?

ANALYST: Yes. It is, as we have been discussing, a matter of degree. No one completely overcomes their childhood but the patterns that make the trouble can be reduced and we will do our best to achieve that so you will have a comfortable summer. But the important point is to make progress with these underlying feelings because it is these that affect your relations to other people and to the man you will marry.

This closing discussion is not in entirely accurate order. It evolved more smoothly than appears from the write-up which, however, is the best that I can reconstruct from the notes. It was designed not as further analyzing of her unconscious but rather to give some perspective and support to her ego in dealing with this pattern of motivation within her.

15th hour

The patient came in, looked at me, was silent for a few seconds and then said, "I have nothing to say." A few seconds later she went on.

PATIENT: I did have a dream though. It was terrible but I think it was a good sign. After I woke up, I laughed about it.

At this point the telephone rang—one of those rare emergency calls that cannot be entirely avoided and for which the analyst must accept an interruption, however much he dislikes to. I exchanged a few brief, noncommittal words. It often happens that these little real life incidents actually are advantageous to the analysis. The time will certainly come when we learn to use them and eventually create them for this purpose. For the present, however, I personally never do anything that is artificial but rather trust to real life to introduce little situations that usually produce very revealing material.

PATIENT: I'm jealous of whomever that was. Of course that is foolish. I cannot expect to have you all to myself. But that is me. That remark that I want you all to myself.

ANALYST: That is the first real transference manifestation toward me, the first direct connection of your childhood pattern with me, so let us make the most of it. Do not hesitate to go ahead and tell me more.

PATIENT: When I feel someone really understands me, they become precious to me. I would rather have a few real, good, close relationships than a lot of others. With Carol, my best girlfriend, too, I want a relationship that is too close, too exclusive, and this is making difficulties with her, and I know it is for this reason and it is my fault. I feel that if someone understands me, were with me, I could even climb the mountain without fear, and I feel I will miss you when I leave this summer. I will greatly miss having someone around who understands me. I feel secure with you, and I think the reason is because with you I can tell my hostilities freely, even ones toward you, and therefore they are sort of made impotent. Something like this dream, which was so horrible when I dreamed it, but when I awoke I could laugh at it and could even think it was good I dreamed it.

Now we begin to reap some reward for our efforts at interpreting the basic dynamics and especially the transference edition of them. The patient has been well enough prepared for these feelings of hers and also for their emergence to me, that she is able to speak of them with relative frankness and ease.

PATIENT: In the dream I poisoned my mother's two big Doberman Pinscher dogs. The female was already dead and the male was dying. Then I was overwhelmed by guilt and felt simply horrible. There were several people around, and they were shocked. Mother is crazy about these two dogs; she just loves them. You aren't going to tell me I am jealous of a couple of dogs are you? But I'm not so sure. How can you tell? Mother would certainly prefer me. I think both of my parents do a great deal of sublimating. If mother loves something intensely like dogs or if father loves something intensely like his hiking, I think there is much sublimating.

Here was a dilemma. I did not understand what she meant by her use of the word "sublimating," and to understand the meaning of this association seemed important. On the other hand I did not wish to interrupt the associations. Since she has never been really thrown off the track by a simple question, I risked asking.

ANALYST: What do you mean by sublimating?
PATIENT: I never discuss this with my parents and should not discuss it with you.

"Sublimating" meant to her something so charged emotionally and so secret that she never discussed it with her parents and hesitated to do so even with me. Now I have interrupted the flow of associations and face a second dilemma—to let her reluctance pass or again risk a few words. Here again I threw in a side remark, hoping it would not get her off the train of her associations—a side remark of great importance.

ANALYST: With me, as you know, you can and should discuss everything. You have already learned this; it is the only way to proceed.

In every case instructions must be given for free associating, and what must be emphasized is the fundamental rule of withholding nothing, no matter how anxiety producing or trivial seeming. Sometimes free associations can be discussed didactically and formally. With other patients, instructions are best imparted gradually in the course of their natural associating rather than formally at the outset. These patients are readily eased into the process—made just as thoroughly acquainted with and grounded in it as patients who are formally instructed. This patient had to be eased into the process for two obvious reasons. First, she spontaneously associated very well and freely, bringing really emotional material in the context of intelligible outpourings of associations and of unsolicited dreams. Second, she said at the beginning that she simply could not free associate.

PATIENT: When I was seventeen I asked my mother if she had slept with father for many years because they always had separate rooms. When we go away, we take two double rooms. Father and I share one and mother and sister the other, and I resent that they do not have a room together like other couples. I feel it is mother's fault. Can it be that she is not fair to father? She *is* delicate and father does snore like a moose and that would offend her. I can understand it at that level but down underneath I am upset. When I was about sixteen, I feared father would go off with another woman and I wanted him to hurt mother, but also I could not stand the idea of his hurting mother because she is so nice and so delicate. Sister and I said mother should have another child. This was mostly in fun but also we meant it. Later mother said that some years back she had wanted another child but that father had been against it. I don't know, but I seem to have resentment against mother sometimes and feel that I want to be very passionate and warm with my husband to make up for how mother has been to father, but I don't even know that she actually has been cold. Two years ago mother was away, and I ran the house for father; ran the house and cooked special dishes. It gave me the biggest thrill to show him that I could do it and that mother couldn't. I made snide remarks, disparaging mother like, "I cleaned the icebox today; it looks as though it hasn't been done for six months." I feel a woman's duty is toward her husband, and it is to create a beautiful home, and I resent the attitude that when a woman gets her man, then she can let

> herself go to the dogs. Mother really is not that way and yet I feel that she fails father. I have felt this less during the past year. Since the breakup with Tom, I have been close to father, who feels that because of my breaking up with Tom, there is something wrong with me. He gave me quite a pep talk. "Life," he said, "is a compromise. You can't live in a dream world. My marriage with your mother is a success because we have both compromised . . ." He went on and on. Later mother spoke to me and laughingly said she heard father had given me a pep talk.

This series of associations suggested a variety of possible interpretations, largely because the patient could be identifying variously with mother or with father, wanting love from one or the other and competing with first one, then the other. It would not be justified simply because we are familiar with the oedipus constellation to apply this knowledge deductively and uncritically, basing our understanding on using a cliché, rather than upon careful technical procedure to discern the psychic reality in this patient at this time. The procedure is to find the common element in all of the associations of the session, relying strongly on the dream, which we know selects and represents what is central and uppermost. At first came the incident of the phone call and the patient demurring against her wish for exclusive attention and possession. This was followed by the dream of poisoning mother's two dogs, which is hostility to mother and probably elimination of rivals, and perhaps something connected with sex difference. Then there came the adolescent memories. In these there seem to be shifts of wanting love from one parent and then the other, with the other as competitor, also identifying with one, then with the other. Here we can trust the dream to present what is central and ripe for interpreting. In the dream the hostility is directly to the rivals and indirectly to mother. It is still not clear just how the sibling rivalry enters the transference. Probably it is not urgent in the transference at present for the patient has no rivals when she sees me. But in these associations there seems to be direct competition with both mother and father in relation to the other. It is safest to stay as close as possible to the dream text, for this is what the ego accepts sufficiently to be able to dream of. Therefore the take-off point is what is most obvious in the dream text. We can go further if indicated, depending upon the patient's reactions to this and upon the remaining time of the session.

ANALYST: Because we have so little time left now, what does all this have to do with the dream?

PATIENT: I don't know.

ANALYST: The dream shows hostility—you poison the dogs. This hostility, whatever else it may mean, is certainly directed in part toward mother because, as you said, she loved the dogs. Therefore the dream seems to deal at least in this aspect, with hostility to mother. Then the associations about disparaging mother. Could it be that you feel mother has not been warm enough to you and you say she is not warm enough to father——

PATIENT (*interrupting*): You mean maybe this is a projection onto father? Maybe I was jealous of father even before sister was born. At age two and a half or three (*sister was born when the patient was a little over three and a half*) an incident occurred that I remember. I didn't tell you this as one of my earliest memories. I was in my crib and got out of it, which at that age was no small feat, and I cut off my hair, and father and mother were just furious. I cut out big chunks and ruined my hair. They were so mad, but I was glad. I must ask my parents whether this was before or after my sister was born. Do you ever get over this kind of thing or do you only learn to control it?

The patient responds with an illuminating bit of unconscious material, in fact with one of its most revealing expressions, an earliest memory. If this memory antedates the birth of the sister, it suggests hostility to both parents before her arrival. The form of the memory resembles strikingly the form of the dream. In the dream the patient expresses hostility to mother by killing her dogs; in the memory she vents the hostility, also indirectly, this time masochistically by ruining temporarily her own hair. The analyst wants good emotional responses but must also help the patient's ego to deal with the powerful emotional forces with which it struggles and which may be to some extent further mobilized by the analytic procedure. Therefore, since insightful and emotionally significant material has come out, and in intelligible form, it seems indicated to use the remaining minutes of the session to help the understanding and orientation of the patient's ego. For this reason I was very willing to answer her question directly, although under other circumstances it might have been proper to deal with it only as an association and not to take it literally, as I now did. It was particularly difficult here to record and recall the precise words of the discussion. It included the following points.

ANALYST: You can outgrow these difficulties, and insight is the first step toward doing so. We all operate on two levels, a mature and a childish. The little child persists in every adult. If your pattern has been to want the exclusive love of mother so strongly because of having had too much or too little or for other reasons, then you can transfer this wish for exclusive love, and the consequent jealousy and competition, to father, to your best friend, Carol, and to me, as was so evident when the telephone rang.

PATIENT: And I am afraid I transfer it to all men. I noticed it around here. I break dates. I won't kiss them goodnight. I don't want to become a man-hater. Will it be all right?

The main issues were now out in the open. There might be

various modifications, many details would be added, yet we could discuss the needs for love; the defenses against them; the dependence, jealousies, and frustrations resulting from them; the consequent hostility and guilt. Now we had out in front of us the main central motivations in the relationship to the patient's father, mother, and sister, where the pattern originated, and also to the people in her present life, and at least to some extent, in the transference. It would not be inappropriate to take advantage of the progress to make total or nearly total interpretations with reference to childhood, current life, and the transference. Whatever the transference battles still to come, the hurdle of discussability was now crossed.

ANALYST: If repression of the hostility eliminated the hostility that would be one thing, but as you know, it only comes out in your anxieties and symptoms and in disturbances in your relationships with men. You already had the trouble with Tom before you ever saw me. Therefore the best way to avoid being a man-hater, to really eliminate the hostility from the relationship, is to face it frankly, to understand its sources, and to make what shifts in attitudes are necessary to reduce it. We must discuss the solution a little more at length later, but it is obvious that you cannot behave toward a boy or toward your best girlfriend, Carol, with the same attitudes and feelings as you had toward your mother when you were a baby. The real life situation is now different. There is no better place to see how this works than toward me; therefore particularly watch for the hostility toward me. For example, in the matter of the telephone call, you expressed jealousy of who called but not hostility to me, so let us watch for that. This does not mean that you cannot get the love you want, rather, the opposite is true. At present you cannot get the love because it is too related to the child's wish for mother's love and too closely connected with frustra-

> tion, with excessive dependence, and with jealousy and therefore with hostility. By reducing some of the intensity and exclusiveness of the demands and thereby reducing your vulnerability, that is, your ready frustration and hostility, you will have better human relations and will actually be able to give and receive love more freely and more satisfyingly in real life. This is the goal of what we are doing.

This was said, of course, not at all as a promise, but merely as a way of elucidating the rationale and goal of our procedure. Making this clear has the advantage of winning over the patient's conscious ego to work with the analyst on the childhood pattern that causes the trouble, with the understanding that by resolving, reducing, and mellowing it and diminishing its power, she could reach a better, more mature, and more gratifying adjustment. This interpretation, in the tone of conversational discussion, aimed to bring out for the patient the major features of her emotional problem and of the process of treatment: (1) the central dynamics—the main emotional forces and their interplay; (2) confrontation of the childhood operation of these forces with current reality (for example, the feelings toward mother, father, and sister, exaggerated for reasons we still do not know with certainty, were the inevitable reactions of the tiny child, but are inappropriate and unworkable as transferred to persons in the patient's present life); (3) further forewarning of these feelings toward the analyst with the treatment situation as a laboratory sample of her human relations; (4) the technical importance of analyzing in the transference the exaggerated childhood pattern that causes the difficulties; (5) possible solutions to the problem, including hope and expectation, to provide a stimulus to analytic progress and maturing—to show that by quantitative shifts in attitudes, feelings, and demands, the patient can reduce her internal frustrating of herself and increase her satisfactions in real life.

16th hour

Today there occurred an hour that represented the crossing of a hurdle that is most important in every analysis. No analysis can be secure until the transference hostilities have revealed themselves. This does not mean that they need to burst forth violently against the analyst, but they must at least signify their presence sufficiently to allow recognition and free discussion. This serves as a forewarning against their becoming too intense later, and through this intensity, exacerbating the patient's symptoms, threatening the treatment, and perhaps generating so strong a resistance that the analysis of them becomes enormously more difficult. Moreover, if the hostilities pile up and the patient feels much guilt from them, then the patient may be plunged into a severely masochistic, self-punishing state of mind and may even go into a negative therapeutic reaction, becoming so guilty that he feels he does not deserve to be cured and relieved of suffering.

This is not meant to suggest that the hostile feelings are the only important ones. In fact, we have seen in this case that they arise chiefly from the dependent love needs, as a defense against them and because of their frustration. However, what is important in this context is that the hostile feelings do make for the greatest difficulty. Since we are not seriously threatened by regression, by giving in to a return to passive, helpless infantilism (as in the patient's dream of losing her mind and going to a mental hospital), the more the rage, hate, jealousy, resentment, and other hostile feelings are reduced, the easier it is to deal with the libidinal needs that underly and generate them. Analyzing the hostility leads directly to dealing with these underlying libidinal demands, which are too strongly infantile at present.

Today the patient entered noticeably more alert, more vivacious. She smiled pleasantly. She began by mentioning that she was a bit early, and this seemed to betoken a stronger wish to come. However, she then continued with some hesitation and reluctance.

PATIENT: Do you know what happened to me? I dream every night and in the dream I almost always think that I will be telling this dream to you, but then in the morning I forget it, so now I have no dreams and nothing to say to you.

Instead of making an issue out of this resistance, which I felt was superficial and a reaction to the fact that the dream of the last visit had revealed the transference to me of the mother pattern, I tried to pass it off in a casual way.

ANALYST: In that case simply associate freely.

To this the patient responded with a smile, which showed she knew what I was doing, and she continued after a little hesitation.

PATIENT: I am going home for a weekend; my parents are coming up; they are driving me back. Something great is happening to me. I feel wonderful about it. I am being confirmed in the Presbyterian Church. This means nothing to my mother but a great deal to my father. It is much better when something like this is done not just formally but as one's own decision.

This week for the first time I did not want to tell you anything. I thought, what business has he to know my private thoughts—and then I laughed. I feel that way about everyone. Maybe I am scared you will find out something or maybe it is something I do not want to say.

Here, as luck would have it, there came another very brief phone call, which was taken care of by just a few words.

ANALYST: I am sorry about this interruption.

PATIENT (*laughing*): I'm not even jealous. Something is making a demand on me I feel. I feel as though I should be less selfish, less jealous. Is that childish?

I followed along with her and reminded her very briefly of our discussion of last week about the two levels of the personality—the mature and the childish—and that the childish one, by being too strong or disturbed, is what causes the problem. Hence what disturbs her is, just as she said, no doubt childish.

As I have stressed throughout this book, interruption of the flow of associations is always to be avoided if possible, since the whole basis of this procedure is that contiguous associations are linked by a common emotional element. However there are no inflexible rules. This is especially evident when, as here, a patient is struggling to deal with powerfully disturbing motivations. In a situation like this it may be necessary, instead of treating the questions as associations and not answering them, to take the questions at face value. That is, the most appropriate technique in such an instance may be to answer them in a way that will help the ego understand the disturbing motivations, gain perspective on them and the whole process, and therefore make progress toward mastering and resolving them.

PATIENT: When with girls, I am always on the defensive. I was in a class with some girls. I wanted to show the professor that I was better than any of the other girls; that I was the great, sensitive soul who understood his every word. That is how it started, but now I like a lot of these kids. I am less competitive toward them, and I don't mind so much if what I say in class does not go over with the teacher. Last week he again assigned a paper that I wanted to do to someone else, I looked at him hard to let him know that I wanted the assignment, and when he gave it to her I was so furious I could not speak. I clenched my teeth; I was so mad. This lasted for ten minutes. The girl who got the assignment noticed this and offered to change with me. By then I had recovered and I said, "No thank you, I am quite satisfied with the one I have." After that I was proud of myself. I get so enraged. It's dumb.

Here we reap some rewards for previous work. The competition comes frankly out into the open. Here it is undisguisedly toward sister figures both for the teacher's preference and also perhaps independently from it. It is toward people in her own current life and is not fixated on her parents and sister. The childhood pattern disturbs *her current exogamic relationships, but does not* prevent *them. But how does this appear in the transference? If the analyst is the teacher, how does the patient bring in sibling figures as competitors? Is this still her reaction to the telephone call which fortuitously provides the competitor? In any event, it would seem that her hostility is directed in these associations more so to the sister figures than to the teacher, the parent figure. Not infrequently a child turns some of its hostilities against a parent onto a sibling, in addition to those originally felt toward the sibling.*

The sister competition, with the hostility and also with the patient's tendency to attack herself for her reactions as being silly, childish, and dumb was quite clear. But, I said nothing, waiting to see if this would not fit better into a more comprehensive interpretation, especially as these further associations confirmed the suspicion that she was reacting to the insight of the last hour into the mother transference to me and defending herself against these feelings in a healthy way.

PATIENT: A year ago another girl got the editorship, and I made such a scene. I cried and everything, and she gave it to me. I have been so ashamed of myself ever since. I used to be an awful show-off. I once told my father that and he said, "Do you know why?" "No", I replied, "Why?" He said, "You started to be that when your sister was born. You did it to get attention. You will outgrow it." He also told me I would outgrow my phobias about pictures. I would also do awful things at school. I ran around without clothes on. I took awful dares. I even got involved with a professor who got kicked out.

Here is more direct expression of sister rivalry, with a frank statement of the patient's demands for adulation and attention, and a bit of their history. And now comes mention of some acting out, which seems motivated by these demands and also by angry vengefulness that probably is masochistic because of guilt and shame. Here the patient obviously wanted me to ask what had happened, and I did, feeling that at this point and in her present mood, it would help, not hinder, the flow of her associations.

PATIENT: When I was thirteen, a girl whom I worshipped created a great scandal by becoming involved with one of the teachers who got kicked out. I resolved to create a great scandal too. When I was fifteen I flirted with a teacher twenty-eight years old and he was kicked out; not that anything happened at all. We used to walk and talk. I had just begun being interested in boys, and I was very physically attracted to him, but he never took advantage of this; but he was kicked out.

ANALYST (*keeping the conversational tone which made it easier for the patient to tell her thoughts freely*): For what then?

PATIENT: Well, he later got mixed up with some other girls too, and the school didn't like it. He wrote love letters to me and actually wanted to marry me, but I have never seen him since. On the walks, we used to beat each other.

The previous associations dealt with a recent teacher and other students, and what was central was the hostile, jealous, rivalry with the students. Now this leads, through the association of competing with the girl who created the scandal, to the patient's conflictful relationship with a teacher when she was fifteen years old. In all likelihood this is a further manifestation of the emerging transference to the analyst, probably of the pattern toward mother.

ANALYST: Verbally?

PATIENT: No, physically. Once I broke off a switch and beat him with it and he got mad. It is so silly of me to behave that way.

Here is direct acting out of first, the hostility (in a setting that signifies competing with the sister figure, that is, the other girl who created a scandal) and second, of wanting love and attention (from the teacher). The self-depreciatory remark about being silly probably is an invitation for encouragement in the difficult revealing of memories and feelings.

ANALYST: When you are fifteen, can't you sometimes be silly?

PATIENT: Yes, but I am still that way. There is a boy I have met recently who is interested in me, and I feel like hitting him, but he is too nice.

Again the same pattern emerges. With this remark, the patient fell silent. Such silence, especially when the material could apply to the transference, usually signifies that transference feelings have come into the patient's mind and are being defended against.

ANALYST: What else?

PATIENT: I don't know. Why do some people feel that others don't like them? I often feel that way, especially with girls. Is it a kind of projection? I feel insecure with girls, on the defensive. Why?

This sounds like simple guilt and retaliation fear, the reflection back upon herself of her own hostilities to the sister figures, which she has described so frankly in the earlier associations of this session.

ANALYST: You can, of course, answer that yourself.

It is usually more effective for therapeutic progress and for the patient's independence postanalytically to elicit interpretations from the patient rather than to just give them. The analyst can, of course, then supplement them with anything he sees that the patient does not.

PATIENT: Yes, I can, but I like to hear you tell me.

Here the archness, coyness, charm, and slight seductiveness were all very evident. Here was a plea for attention and good feelings. I still waited in hopes of being able to make a total interpretation of the central theme rather than have to fragment *the interpretation to apply, however, accurately, to various sub-themes.*

ANALYST: Why do you like to hear me tell you?

PATIENT: Because I expect it of you. Is it a sort of projection that I don't like them; like with my sister and the fear of competing with them and therefore I pretend I don't care?

This is a supplement to the way I saw it. It adds a different twist and a very good one indeed. The analyst alerts the patients to what to look for. The analyst can convey the main ideas of what is going on and sometimes, from a dream, can do so with precision. But when the patient sees and emotionally grasps, realizes, and appreciates emerging feelings and reactions, then the patient will formulate it and phrase it in his or her own individual, specific way.

The end of the visit was approaching, and I thought it best to begin to introduce the main theme. Interpreting from the top down is a principle with which I think all analysts agree. The best interpretation does not plunge blindly to the depths, but is almost a paraphrase of what the patient has said, focusing down on the major underlying motivations more sharply than the patient has been able to do. This makes known to the patient something more of the unconscious motivations, but in a way that is acceptable. This will lead to further expression and progress rather than stir up anxiety, increase resistance, and slow down movement. Here the main theme is almost in the open and needs only this sharpness of focus for the patient.

ANALYST: It is like conditioning. Like what your father told you—your reaction to your sister. A new baby apparently meant to you that you were no longer the only child and therefore you felt some resentment against her. Other girls perhaps remind you of this. They represent being pushed out of the position of being the only child; in other words, they are sister figures. You can think of it as simple conditioning.

PATIENT: Suppose I had a brother too, besides my sister. would this have been the same?

ANALYST: Of course it could have been, but perhaps you would then have been that much older, and might not have competed with him but might have tended to team up with him against your sister.

PATIENT (*smiling at the likelihood of this*): I can be crazy about someone and then turn completely against them. I used to be crazy about that teacher I told you about before, who gave the assignment to the other girl. He was to write a letter of recommendation for me. He did but I found out he waited until the last day before the deadline to do it. I went into a rage against him and have turned completely against him. That is foolish. Some people are lazy and not prompt and why should I mind.

This rage seems like a reaction simply to the feeling that she was not getting enough attention and interest—love in the broad sense—from the teacher in his waiting until so near the deadline to write the recommendation.

ANALYST: You raised a vitally important question. Why do you think you can turn so completely against someone? Is there any historical pattern in your childhood for this?

PATIENT: Only that I have felt so hostile to my mother all my life, or at any rate, since my sister was born.

The transference hostility to me was now near enough to the surface that it could be openly discussed. Now we would at least be able to watch it openly. I began by pointing out that when the patient says she is crazy about someone, this probably really signifies an intense wish that that person be crazy about her. I indicated that the pattern for this is probably her intense wish for love from her mother, which for reasons not yet apparent, was heightened during early childhood and caused to persist so insistently. In fact if it were not for this intense wish for mother's exclusive love, she would not have been so jealous of her sister whom she could in greater part have welcomed as a playmate. With this the patient agreed.

I went on to say that I felt good about her progress and relieved that she had brought this out so frankly because I thought this tendency to be hostile was also appearing in the transference. At first she was much distressed by this, but then agreed that it was so. She raised the question of why this must be bound to happen, and then at the same time she said that she had a presentiment that it would. I simply told her, without going into the theory of the matter, that it was an empirical fact that the most disturbing feelings tended to repeat themselves to the analyst according to the childhood pattern.

PATIENT: But what then, is the solution to this? What can I do if I am always crazy about people and then turn so violently and completely against them? I feel anxiety. I might come in here one day and go after you. How can I feel this way and yet get along with people?

ANALYST: The solution is really not so very difficult.

I told her about the little experiment in which the dog faces meat in a cage that is open at the back. If the meat is in the center of the cage, the dog goes around to the back and gets it, but if the meat is put just out of his reach at the very front of the cage, he is so close to it and so intent on getting it that he cannot tear himself away long enough to go around to the back of the cage. To this the patient replied with her quick smile of insight. We discussed the fact that an individual cannot expect love and attention of the same quality and intensity as what was demanded by the small infant of its mother, nor with the same impatience. This defeats its own purpose. Reducing the demand reduces the jealousy, frustration, and rage and the disruption in personal relationships and makes it possible actually to satisfy the needs for love by reducing them to workable proportions.

We then discussed the transference in some detail. We began by talking about her intense wishes for attention from me, such as she had described in relation to the two teachers whom she had spoken of in this visit, and then we traced the origin of these desires in her infantile demands upon her mother. The hostility that went with this was faced openly and that even made her fear she would attack me with a knife, disrupt the relationship, and deny herself the good opinion that she wanted. We discussed this hostility in detail, seeing it as directed to her mother as a defense against the childish needs for love. These needs make her feel too vulnerable, too much at the mercy of the other person's attention.

PATIENT: That is exactly why I run away when someone likes me. Just recently a boy showed that he liked me, and I froze up and almost fled in anxiety.

She could see that childish needs for mother love put her too much at the mercy of the person whose love she wanted. In addition, these needs placed her in a position in which her violent reactions of jealousy and frustration were inevitable. A second reason for the hostility to those whose love she craved too intensely was the expectation of the inevitable frustration of the desires and the inevitable little incidents that she was bound to take as rejection. Doubtless, the kind of love that she wanted—the exclusive love of the mother—could not be satisfied in a world of adults in this continuous fashion. We discussed a third reason for the hostility. This was probably the conditioning of it toward her mother. It was toward her mother that she had the deepest desires for love and also toward her mother that she has had the strongest unrelenting hostility because of feeling betrayed by the mother through the birth of her sister, and perhaps for other reasons.

PATIENT: That is what I came to ask and now I can see the solution. Without the infantile reaction in my relations with people, the ordinary pains and problems of loving and being loved would be nothing.

With this she really hit the nail squarely on the head. In saying good-by I complimented her on her ability to bring out and understand this pattern, especially the germ of the hostility to me which now, with her seeing it in advance and being able to discuss it freely, we would be able to handle. Complimenting her was meant as recognition and reward for progress and to demonstrate that my opinion of her was truly dependent, not upon her childish pattern of feelings, but upon her ego—her mature capacity to face and handle these feelings.

With this hour the analysis had crossed the second great hurdle. The first was for me to discern the childhood emotional pattern underlying the patient's emotional problem, to find the formula. The second hurdle was for the patient to understand this. The third hurdle was the achievement of the patient's insight into the operation of this formula in the transference to me. The fourth hurdle will be the development and living through of these emotional forces toward me. Their intensity will be palliated by the fact that we can now see the broad aspects of the pattern foreshadowed in relationship to me. The patient has already expressed her intensified needs for love in her childhood toward her mother and also her hostility toward the mother. The hostility arising from rivalry with her sister has not yet appeared in the transference, but the strongest forces, both libidinal and hostile, have declared themselves.

It may be well to recall at this point that this has been accomplished in sixteen interviews of thirty minutes each, on a once-a-week basis, which the patient has been unable to maintain with complete regularity. The work has extended over a period of approximately five months. These conditions were not deliberately set but were imposed by necessity. The choice was whether to do nothing at all or to do the best I could with what I had. The time relationships are noted here because they are so important in a procedure as protracted as analysis.

17th hour

The notes for this hour are only fragmentary, but there is a special reason for this. It was one of those working through hours in which it is proper for the analyst to discuss rather freely and very realistically with the patient what the patient has learned about the basic motivational forces, about the formula for his personality as it is expressing itself in his current thinking, feeling, and living. Such hours of discussion can be utilized by the patient as resistance (as can any other hours), but when they are not too frequent, then they serve an essential function—that of helping to make the unconscious motivations simple and realistic to the patient.

The previous session had eventuated in a total interpretation with special focus on the transference. One of the frequent and natural outcomes of such a session is that the patient feels some relief, anxiety, and resistance. At the same time, the patient gains improved perspective on these insights and the psychological digestion of them, which involves relating and connecting them with real life, both past and present, and with the transference. The discussion should help the patient integrate and assimilate what has been unearthed from the unconscious. This is one of the ways in which the analyst can and should help. Cure in psychoanalysis is a matter, in the end. of what use the patient is able to make of the psychoanalysis in his real life.

PATIENT: I went home last weekend and had a good time. Yesterday mother was here to visit and she enjoyed it. That seems to be about all I have to tell you.

This remark seems to say: "You see, I am making progress with my conflict with mother. She loves me in spite of my demands and hostilities toward her. Therefore you, the analyst, should be pleased with me." But of course I made no such interpretation. I'll wait and see if the further associations have the same meaning and how they fit together, what element they all have in common.

ANALYST: Then just free associate.

PATIENT: You mean to say just what comes into my mind? It might be boring, wouldn't it? I got confirmed Sunday.

ANALYST: Congratulations.

PATIENT: I think I'll write Tom (*her former fiancé, who had strong religious sentiments*). I'll see him this summer. After mother left yesterday I felt wonderful; as though I couldn't be afraid at all, but I couldn't test it so I pretended I was on a mountain but was not afraid. The wonderful feeling lasted only a minute—or could it be better even today? Do you think so?

It was becoming increasingly apparent that this was a visit in which the patient was not going to pour forth a continuous flow of associations. She was telling certain events and asking questions—asking them not in a hostile, challenging, resistive fashion, but apparently with sincerity. Behind it was probably a reaction to the last hour, to her confirmation, and to her mother's visit. I decided that it was indicated to take her questions literally and use the answers to help consolidate the insights we had achieved and to connect them with her symptoms and with her problems in relating to people.

ANALYST: Do you? And why? (*She did not answer.*) I do think so because now you face your hostility toward your mother, your sister, and me, and therefore you don't need these fantastic escapes about mountains, pictures, and the like. You now face the real issue.

I said this to keep her attention directed to the forces that caused her symptoms rather than to the symptoms themselves. In this way, when she felt fear, she would be trained to think about her hostilities, their sources in her needs for love and their consequences. Seeing these, she might the faster lose the anxieties.

PATIENT: I do have some fear of this new boy, Dwight. Why am I secure with people who are secure and not secure with those who are not? Dwight is shy and insecure, and I am scared when I am with him. I can't bear that kind of person for long. I've always been that way and don't understand it. Why?

ANALYST: Go ahead and we will find the answer.

Here I could get by without answering and could just keep her associations going, which is unquestionably far better. I was saving my ammunition until the end of the session, when all her associations would be in.

PATIENT: I fear they will demand something from me—some strength. I want to follow and not to lead. When I feel a guy is following me, I think he is weak and I have only contempt for him. I want him to resist me. It is just one big game, isn't it? I lead them on, and I think how long will this go on. Tom was different because he is older and wouldn't stand for it. Now I think it is childish. I feel incapable of committing myself to anybody or anything in the world. The minute I do, I feel trapped and run away from it. I feel I don't have to prove myself anymore, though, but I still do it from force of habit and I don't like it. I ought to have enough confidence by this time to know what I am doing. I like reserved men and they are usually shy and unsure of themselves.

This sounded like a further developing of transference feelings, a supposition supported by her initial hesitation in free associating, which so often represents repression of feelings about the analyst. The patient went on to mention the interruption during the previous hour and her tendency to jealousy. In this way she brought out her understanding of the fact that the component of the jealousy that has been hard for her to face and handle has been the hostility.

PATIENT: What would happen if I were in a situation in

which I had to face my symptom—a picture of height? What would happen?

My opinion was that the patient now saw her hostilities toward her parents, sister, boys, and feminine competitors at college, with sufficient clarity to be able to discuss them with me. Moreover, she also saw and was able to discuss the growing attachment to me in the transference. In accordance with the formula of her emotional life, the threat of increased dependence upon me was the emergence of hostility as defense against this and as a reaction to the inevitable frustration of this dependence and the needs for love. I realized that this hour had been full of questions to me and that such questioning usually signifies a resistance against expression of feeling that may take this form. The reason for this is that there is some underlying question that the patient is not quite able to formulate and ask.

With this in mind, I took advantage of her last question to discuss with her why it seemed to me that she would be able to handle her symptoms much more readily now. The answer to this involved the discussion of the basic dynamics of her personality toward her parents, in her life situation, and in the transference. As this discussion showed, most of these powerful feelings were well out in the open except for the full force of the potential demands and hostilities to me in the transference. The chief task before the summer's interruption, now only two months off, with her trip abroad including mountains, was to make her so familiar with the idea of her demands and hostility toward me in the transference, that she would no longer be threatened by these feelings. As is usually the case, the transference hostility is the keystone of the analysis. As I have noted, it most directly produces the symptoms, and the analysis of it leads directly to the underlying libidinal problem. Dependent love needs and hostility seem to be the two great central, emotional forces in every analysis.

As an addendum to the discussion of this hour, we

spoke of my having to be away the following week and so missing our next appointment. We talked about her reactions to this. We also covered some points about the patient's hostile, aggressive drives, which take the form of a feeling of masculinity. To avoid this, she wishes to be with stronger men and to be in the position of follower so as to achieve a feminine orientation. Largely because of the hostile components, to be feminine means to her to be attacked, to let herself go means she would become too dependent and love-needy toward the other person, whom she would then attack. This, in turn, she feels as aggressive masculinity. Hence she fears strong men but despises weak ones and consequently she has been unable to achieve a good relationship to any man.

18th hour

In this next visit, two weeks later, the hope of crossing the major hurdle of bringing the strong transference feelings out into open discussion was realized. It came about as follows. The patient, wearing an attractive new dress, looked a little tense as she began.

PATIENT: You look just the same.
ANALYST: You look rather better.

Behind my words was the realization that her opening comments probably meant that I had not sufficiently dealt, in our last interview, with her reaction to my having to be away and thus missing one visit. I took her remark as perhaps meaning: You have not changed even though you have been away and did not see me for the last regular appointment. In all probability she was highly sensitive to this and quite angry about it. However, I said nothing because the evidence was far from sufficient. She continued, this time without the questions and hesitations that marked the last visit and which were probably in part reactions to the prospect of my going away and her missing the interview with me.

Her questions of two weeks ago may also have marked a wish to ask where I was going. The fragmentary notes of the last visit do not show whether or not I went adequately into the patient's reactions to my being away. This must of course always be done insofar as the status of the analysis permits it. As I noted earlier in connection with telephone interruptions, these little real life situations provoke reactions that are usually highly revealing, largely because people are so extremely sensitive. We would certainly expect this to be so in a patient whose exaggerated dependent love needs transferred from mother, are only just emerging. They are extremely sensitive to frustration and, when thwarted, they generate intense rage.

PATIENT: I am not better. I am terribly discouraged. I don't know what to do. This dependence upon people seems to be the real crux of the situation. I understand it better now but don't seem to be able to do much about it. I have nightmares every night. Just now when I came to see you, I was upset because Mr. R., one of my teachers, passed by outside this building just as I was coming in and I did not want him to know I was seeing you. You remember, he was the one I was jealous about in class, the one I wanted so much to prefer me to the other students in the class. Last Thursday I went with him and the other students to the Art Institute on Michigan Avenue. I thought it was silly to be jealous in such a situation, and I had a good time but that night I had an awful nightmare. I was sleeping in the same, old, large house as Mr. R. was. He was somewhere in a different room. It was dark. I got up and went into the hall; I could not find the light. There were big pictures in the hall with scenes I could not stand to look at. I had to return to my room and then found there was a picture there, and I was petrified. My roommate was there—I don't know when she came into it—and she was going to turn on the light so I would see the picture. I felt then that I would see the picture and if I did, I would die, so I took off my clothes and hung them over the picture so as not to see it. I awoke petrified and felt terrible all day.

The connection with the symptoms is evident although the intermediate links are not quite so clear. The patient is discouraged and angry and here is a dream in which she is threatened and in which the anxiety takes the form of her phobia. In the dream the picture appears in connection with direct physical exhibitionism (taking off her clothes to hide the picture). This might be one form of expression of the original dependent love needs, the original desire to win mother's and father's special love, attention, praise, and admiration. Now, the patient being sexually mature, it is sexualized as being "in love" with the teacher, sleeping in the same house with him in the dark, and taking off her clothes. It could be in part genital sexual curiosity, but then why should this be so terrifying? Many children have anxieties and make an issue of the lights being on or off when they sleep. And much has been written on the child's interest in parental sexual relations (primal scene). Here it looks as though the pictures are in part a projection of the patient's own exhibitionism—she does not want the lights on to see them and even takes off her clothes to hide the pictures. The whole scene probably relates chiefly to the analysis and the transference. The light is probably light on the darkness of her hostile and sexual impulses. Children fear these impulses because, among other reasons, they get them into trouble with the parents. These initial suppositions occur to me as a result of past experiences, but I'm going to save them and wait to see if I can obtain associations to each element of the dream. This is the basic procedure for analyzing a dream, Freud's first method and still by far the best. It is not easily accomplished, however, with only thirty minutes for our session.

PATIENT: The following night I had a dream in which I was fighting with my mother. We were on the floor trying to kill each other. It was awful.

In this dream the hostility is only partly projected, mostly coming out very directly as the patient's behavior rather than being disguised as a phobic symptom. Possibly the hostility is so frankly expressed partly because the object is disguised, because it is largely at me, in the transference, but displaced to the original object, mother. I cannot leap to the conclusion that this is the oedipus complex, hostility to the mother because of sexual rivalry for father.

PATIENT: And the next night I had a similar dream about my sister. I was angry at you also.

ANALYST: Good. Tell it frankly. You know how important the transference feelings toward me are.

PATIENT: I am not angry at you any more, but I have the feeling that you cannot help me. I don't want to come any more. It is somehow mixed up with this boy Dwight. He was so dependent on me, but he beat me up this past weekend and now I am so meek I just follow him around. It's funny; he fights with *his* mother. I'm not really involved with him, but I hurt him and then feel so sorry that I can hardly stand it and I would do anything to make it all right, and he is the same with me. This is all just too much. I can't take all this and the final exams too. I'm afraid I might not pass this year. I didn't want to come today. There is no use bringing this all up and then nothing happens. Yet much *is* happening, of course. Also this is somehow tied up with my joining the Church. I don't know if I would have done that if I had not come to you and all this hadn't come out. I got a letter from Tom after I was confirmed, congratulating me, and I wrote him back how wonderful I felt.

This is the first expression of the flight side of the patient's fight-flight response. Apparently her main motivations are now nearer to her ego. She suffers less with her symptoms as defenses but struggles more in handling consciously the feelings that generate the symptoms. This struggle would not itself be so difficult at this point though, in all probability, if the hostility to me were not acutely intensified by my being away for the previous appointment. Now the mother transference to me, the dependent love needs and the rage at me as a defense and because I was away are probably what make the patient so uncomfortable emotionally that she would like to escape it all. But her unconscious does not show flight—therefore she will not leave. The dreams only show anger, fight, struggle, and, as in the first dream, the terrible fear of seeing something—no doubt something in her own feelings. The dreams are a reliable guide to what the patient will do or at least what she is capable of doing in waking life.

PATIENT: Last night I fought with my roommate because she had made a remark about Dwight. I wanted to lash back but then I just went off to my room and stayed alone. I did not want to come down to her level. I had an awful time controlling myself with her, although what she said was just a thoughtless, although destructive, remark.

More fight, this time with the roommate, eventuating in some flight—to her room to be by herself.

PATIENT: I have been getting along with girls much better, though, and I'm glad. I realized recently that the girls even like me and go out of their way to be friendly. It is simply amazing. It has changed my whole outlook.

The sweet with the bitter? This sounds rather typical. It is not at all unusual to hear about the benefits as well as the pains of this stage of the analytic treatment when the main issues are out intellectually but not worked through yet emotionally. Also, at this point the transference is still developing and not yet well worked over.

PATIENT: But the five people I run with are all boys and except for Dwight I have no involvement with any of them at all; they are just buddies.

Just to talk with someone sometimes helps. Like when I told Dwight of my own tendency to be destructive—to hurt people, to hurt him. Only now, as I said, I feel so guilty that I would do just anything to make it up to him. But I am not in love with him and after school closes this spring and he graduates, we will never see each other again. Is it just sex, or spring, or what? I would rather let him beat me up than hold my hand and if he tried to kiss me, I'd go all to pieces.

Probably the affection and sex stir up the deepest dependent love needs and hence the deep hostilities and guilts connected with these. The "beating up," however, is mostly hostility used at a more superficial level as a defense against these deepest involvements.

PATIENT: It's absurd, and it is all because he is shy and without much confidence in himself. If he were different, it would be all right.

This is a common and almost invariably a vain hope—if only the other person were different! But the fault is usually the beam in our own eye. How difficult it often is to untangle these issues between a husband and wife, each of whom sees their difficulties as arising in the other.

The time was beginning to run out and since dreams, more than anything else, point up the main issue of an hour, I thought it best to interrupt and get some associations to the elements in the first dream.

ANALYST: Let us go back to the first dream. What do you associate to sleeping in this dark house with Mr. R. in another room?

PATIENT: His remark at the art museum. I was very impressed with some monastic paintings and said, "If I were a man, I might be a monk," and he replied, "The monastic life has much to recommend it." It was nice because we understood each other.

This sounds like confirmation of the defense against affection and sex, probably because they are the erotized expression of the conflict over the dependent love needs with the resultant hostility and guilt. Why otherwise should she not simply be aware of her desires for love and sex? These are simply natural expressions of the mating instinct. Why shouldn't she be happy about them even under deprivation, until they can be more satisfied in marriage? Of course I now suspect and expect tranference feelings and references.

PATIENT: In the dream it was an old house, and I could not find the lights and I wouldn't turn them on anyway or else I would see the big picture.

ANALYST: What do you associate to the pictures element?

PATIENT: This summer when I go to Europe, I will have to look at pictures that are just the kind of pictures that scare me—big and vague. Mr. R. represents a father figure or something to me as you told me when he came up in an interview before.

ANALYST: Because the time is getting short I will interrupt with a question. Do you know any connection between pictures and fine arts and your sister, mother, or father?

PATIENT: No. I was scared of pictures long before I became interested in the arts.

I thought that she had some reaction during the previous visit and again during this one to my having been away, and that she was also reacting to the approaching interruption during the summer. Such reaction to the summer's interruption is, of course, the usual thing even though an analysand knows from the very beginning that there will be such an interruption. This is, of course, particularly the case with this patient since it will be occasioned by her going abroad.

ANALYST: I will again take a guess on the basis of this material, even though it is not yet adequate enough to be conclusive. In the first place, that nightmare may have some relation to the fact that there is still considerable attachment to Mr. R. as a father figure with jealousy of the sisters, but I doubt that that is the main issue. If you are so attached to him as a teacher, I think you must be at least as much attached to me and perhaps much more so, if only because of our discussions of these feelings, which are so vital to your life. You mentioned seeing dependence upon people just recently as the crux of the situation. Perhaps you have this dependence upon me like the dependence of a child upon its father or mother.

Here I purposely brought up the dependent element without referring to its erotization. The sexual feelings add another problem for the patient as we have seen; therefore, it is easier for her if we deal with the dependence, the original dependent love needs toward mother. As the patient understands and handles these, she will herself bring out the unsublimated sexual component. To put this another way, she will handle the sex if she has learned to handle its content, the infantile attachments and hostilities behind it. Also, it may be that her parents were strict and that she feared rejection if she revealed anything sexual. Further, sexual love is a powerful force toward separation from the mother and father. The patient seemed to follow the interpretation that I offered, and so I continued.

ANALYST: Therefore, probably with Dwight you fear the kiss more than the fight because the tenderness awakens these too intense needs for love, much as a child feels toward its mother or father. This would make you feel too dependent upon another person, too vulnerable. The fighting and the hostility serve as a defense against becoming too dependent. Therefore you would rather fight and be beat up than be so helplessly needy of love and dependence. This probably accounts for the hostility to me, that is, your not wanting to come in and continue the analysis. But this is a defense against wanting to do this too much. So I think you are angry at me because of being dependent and as a defense against it, but you are also angry at the idea of separation this summer when you go to Europe and will not be seeing me.

In order to end on a note of reassurance I added a few words.

ANALYST: It will probably be better, though, when you are actually away than when you are, as now, in the process of anticipating the separation in a few weeks.

PATIENT: I had feelings of questioning whether I should go to Europe at all, whether I could stand the separation from my father and mother, but now I see that to solve this dependence, going to Europe and being away is the best thing in the world; to go and be on my own, and now I see why I only kid with boys. I tend to feel nothing and that is because I am in transition in my feelings toward them. I feel that when this is solved, then I will be able to do what I have never been able to do and that is really commit myself permanently to another person. Now it would be impossible and ridiculous.

ANALYST: I do not see why you will not solve this very well, and the important point is to stay out of trouble while doing so. It is better to have some distance from people while solving this than it is to get into any irreversible difficulties.

These remarks sprang, of course, from my concern about acting out. She has already done some, such as the beating up of each other when with boys and the "scandal" at age fifteen with the teacher who was dismissed. Her hostility and guilt are discussable, but far from worked through. Her sexual and mating drives are at their height. In Europe she will be away from the restraining superego forces of her school, her friends, her parents, and the analysis. The analysis is a powerful superego force for many reasons, including simply the situation of telling someone everything. Also she will be alone and her dependent love needs less satisfied. If the result of all this is further mobilization of her nuclear pattern, I do not want her doing any self-injuring, masochistic acting-out, sexual or otherwise. I have not forgotten the friend of hers who took out revenge on her parents and punishment on herself by becoming pregnant by the French fisherman.

PATIENT: That I can well see. What is it that makes something inside of you aware of these things even though you are not quite conscious of it? It is a nice feeling that something down there knows more about this than I do. When I was thirteen, I did a series of about ten drawings. I never understood them. After a few months the inspiration left me, and I never did such a series again. I treasure them though more than anything I ever did. Now this business has come out. I will understand them. This means I must have understood them somehow at that time even though I was only thirteen. I want you to see them. One scene in them is hostility, and then there is my spiritual self and this hostility is pushing me off cliffs and doing all sorts of things to me. Just what we have seen. And there is another scene of either running away or trying to get out of something or escaping. There are imprisoned ones. The last painting is my secret. I won't tell you but I'll send for them and show them to you.

This is fascinating from the point of view of the emotional origins of interest in art and of artistic creativity. In the dream she was in a panic lest she see the painting—but now she offers to show me her own paintings, which reveal her deepest feelings. Are paintings connected with jealousy of her sister or mother? Did they paint? Or are paintings partial expressions of the basic conflict—the needs for exclusive admiration and all their connections and consequences? Because of the very stringent restrictions on our available time, I felt I could not be diverted from analysis of the fundamentals to an interest in specific symptoms.

There followed a little more discussion of the dependence upon me and the anger against me because of this dependence and as a defense against it and because of the anticipated separation for the summer. I made the following remarks to help her ego further and express appreciation for her progress.

ANALYST: We are over the worst hurdle because now we can see and discuss the transference openly. The nightmare probably referred directly to the analysis and to your unconscious. Considering your associations to your paintings, which expressed your inner problems at age thirteen, fearing to turn on the lights and see the pictures probably means fearing to face what is in your own unconscious. You are afraid to turn on the lights and see what these paintings really mean but now you are able to understand them and to face these feelings right here toward me.

PATIENT: Yes, yes, I didn't realize it. I didn't realize that I was dependent upon you and that I was so angry about it and about leaving. But this dependence upon you is not a threat because you don't make me feel like a nincompoop but give me confidence. And, that is why I didn't suspect that I was so dependent.

ANALYST: And here the dependence and everything else—the erotization of it, the hostilities, jealousy, and everything else is also less of a threat because we can discuss these things openly and use our insight, the relationship, and the situation to help solve these feelings.

I thought it best, as noted above, not to discuss the sexual feelings directly at this point. Although they were implied in the dream, they were not central and the problem in handling them arose from the forces upon which we were focused. I therefore referred to them only in terms of "erotization" of the trouble-causing motivations.

The patient left with the first signs of an expression of real happiness that I had seen. Naturally the whole problem was far from being resolved but a great hurdle had been crossed. We were now in the clear so far as being able to discuss these powerful feelings in the transference itself and therefore in a strong position for dealing with the emotional storm that would be bound to come before this pattern of powerful emotions could be sufficiently resolved and outgrown in favor of greater maturity and such tranquility as this brings.

19th hour

With her new freedom, the patient, who hitherto had been definite but restrained, almost burst into the office with the beaming expression of a little girl. She described a series of oil paintings she had once made. As she spoke about them,

I got the impression from the images she evoked that I was witnessing an unfolding series of dreams from a patient in analysis. Freud wrote in his preface to The Interpretation of Dreams, *that he realized afterwards that this book had been a piece of self-analysis. My impression was that these pictures were something similar for the patient. She never did anything like them either before or since. They were among her very first attempts.*

PATIENT: It was soon after this that I became deeply interested in religion. My mother was studying it.

Now she sees that the series of pictures represents almost everything we had discussed in her analysis, revealing with special clarity the hostilities toward her sister deflected back against herself.

The patient remarked that she had had a dream the night before, apparently precipitated by a fight with her roommate. She felt extremely guilty because of this fight. In the dream, they really hated each other.

I reminded the patient that our time was now rather short and that we would be meeting only one more time before she left for Sweden. Consequently, I emphasized that we must be sure to cover her reactions to the separation from me. Perhaps, I suggested, the hostility and fight in the dream were also related to her anger at me because of the prospective separation.

The patient has some understanding of the psychodynamics that are at the root of her phobias, anxieties, tensions, and difficulties with people, including sex and mating. She also has some slight insight into the transference of this interplay of motivations toward me. I cannot overemphasize the fact that it is the transference of feelings toward the analyst that carries every analysis. As a matter of fact, it is one of the basic criteria for distinguishing psychoanalytic from other forms of psychological treatment. So much of the neurosis (that is, the persisting, exaggerated, or otherwise disordered childhood feelings) focuses and concentrates on the analyst that it would be both missing a therapeutic opportunity and courting unnecessary turmoil in the patient, to allow her to leave without the fullest possible interpretation and discussion of her transference feelings. This was the patient's nineteenth visit of a series spread over about five months. This sounds meager but intense transference feelings can nevertheless develop, and they must be analyzed as directly and thoroughly as possible so far as it can be done ego-syntonically. This is essential to make the most of the treatment. The aim here is to ease the patient's reactions to separation and to being alone abroad. Further analysis of the transference is vital as a forewarning and preparation for what the patient can expect in her own feelings. The fact is that what the patient is conscious of, she can make some progress with while she is on her own. Therefore I put great emphasis on the transference in the interpretation.

PATIENT: All this week such wonderful things happened to me. I have been so different—so much better than I have been. All week I could not wait to tell you about them, but when I woke up this morning, I didn't want to. Perhaps this is because telling you would make me more dependent upon you. Now I feel indifferent about telling you.

These last three sentences unquestionably indicate progress, for the patient brings out spontaneously something of her dependence and her conflict over it. She wants to tell me something, while at the same time she resists doing this. She takes notice of this. Perhaps this taking notice is largely to please me, but if so, we will analyze that motivation, for it must be itself part of the conflict. However deep or superficial is the patient's insight and emotional realization, here she does take direct notice of a fundamental conflict, and what is of especial importance is that she sees it in relation to the transference.

PATIENT: One thing was about this boy Dwight. The axe had fallen. I was in doubt about becoming involved with him, but now I am involved because now I dare to. Before this I could not have done it, but now I feel so much better and more secure that I can. We talked. He has a very bad background; his parents were divorced; he has never been close to anyone. If I would be too dependent upon him and he on me, it would be a big mess but now I think we can be just friends. I feel so much more outgoing. I feel strong enough now to be dependent and to be giving.

This is further working over of the dependency conflict. This time it has to do with a boy and this would seem to indicate that the patient's insights into this conflict in the transference are more than superficial. She is beginning to see it in different directions and editions.

PATIENT: I used to only thwart people. We talked it all over; only we fight physically. He never told anyone about himself before and after telling me, he became very angry at me. He beat me up and twisted my arm for fear that I would use what he told about himself against him, and in the past I would have, but now I will not. This is a new thing for me but the end of the year is at hand and after another two weeks we will never see each other again. He asked me to trust him not to get too involved. I spiel off things about him that you tell me about myself.

Such identification with the analyst is a usual occurrence. It must be carefully watched, for identification is, like dependence, a way of relating to people. It can be used unconsciously to express various feelings and motivations.

PATIENT: For example, he asked what it was like to love someone and now I feel that I know and am amazed at myself. This is so different from what I ever was and yet at the same time it is so much more like me. I feel warmer, stronger, as though I can give without making demands.

This announcement by the patient of her sense of progress may be too optimistic, but it should not be summarily dismissed.

The time was up and I ventured no interpretation other than the remark about the dream. I could see various other possibilities to these associations. For example, there was the effort to tell me she was better and apparently thus to express her gratitude for the understanding and tolerance she had gotten from me. In discussing Dwight, she was perhaps also expressing a similar ambivalence toward me, a feeling that she could admit her involvement in the transference and yet handle it. It might well be defense also, especially because of her leaving soon, against the hostility to me that was expressed in the dream. The dream and associations might be to show that she could confess to me, as father and mother, her hostility to her sister. But these and other possible meanings were not clear enough for me to venture any further interpretation.

As she left, I reminded her again to watch carefully before the next hour for any further reactions to me, to the impending separation from me, and particularly for any hostile feelings toward me.

20th hour

Two weeks later, the patient arrived late for her visit.

PATIENT: I'm sorry to be late. Am I late because of hostility, because of trying to get back at you because I am leaving and will never see you again?

ANALYST: Why never?

PATIENT: Well, it might not be.

ANALYST: Anyway your interpretation may well be correct; namely that there is a strong attachment to me which, as you know, is basically the dependence of the child upon the parent. In yourself this takes the form of the wish to be the especially valued and preferred one, especially loved, and this becomes more or less erotized and romanticized. Hence the separation is painful and frustrating and arouses a reaction of resentment and anger. And some of the anger serves as a defense against this attachment, as we have seen.

PATIENT: I had another dream. I suppose in reaction to this. I am in my roommate's, Beatrice's, room, and I said to her, "Why are you so destructive and tear down things that belong to other people?" Beatrice replied, "I do not." I said, "You do. You make snide remarks about my things and so on."

That was the end of the dream and the patient went right on with the following spontaneous associations.

PATIENT: One of the magazines invited some of the girls to supper to choose models. Both Beatrice and I were invited. We each thought if one of us were chosen and not the other, we would not have been able to stand it. Then fortunately at dinner also, they chose both of us to be models, but then they took a picture of Beatrice in a group and of me alone and this was enough for Beatrice's attitude toward me to change. What terrible competitiveness we do have. If they had chosen Carol, my best friend, I would not have minded.

ANALYST: Why? Because of your identification with her, like identifying with your sister?

It was a question as to whether or not to interrupt the association by this remark of mine. On the one hand, since we would meet only one more time before the patient's departure, I wanted to get in the major interpretations. On the other hand, it was so important to hear what her unconscious was saying that I did not want to interrupt. I decided on this remark because it was only a single sentence, and I thought she would grasp it without the associations being thrown off. There did not seem sufficient evidence in the associations to suggest the possible direct transference meaning at this point. I was puzzled. The material was frankly competitive, but what could be the transference meaning in her feelings to me of this competition? Is she thus directly competitive with me also—and if so, how and for what? Or is she acting toward me as her mother or father, her competitiveness toward her sister? If so, why does it come up just now? Is it only because it was stimulated by the reactive situation the patient described? If this is so, has it no transference meaning beyond blowing off steam to a sympathetic ear? I have not yet felt satisfied that I understand how this frank competitiveness shows in the transference, except for those two interruptions by telephone calls. Hence I must wait alertly and watch the material.

PATIENT: Yes, that is how I understand it. I had another horrible nightmare last week about my father and mother. They were making me do something. Can I ask you a question about repetitive dreams I have had? Do they have any universal meaning? The one is about flying and the other about all my teeth dropping out. All during childhood I had dreams about flying. They were wonderful. When they stopped and I no longer had them, I was crushed. Now I rarely have them any more. They are pleasant but if I go too high, I become panic-stricken. Also I can fly up but not down. The other day I had a dream. I was walking with Dwight at the university and suddenly I was flying. Then I swooped back down at them—I guess there were some other people there also—like a bird. It was a wonderful feeling of liberation. It had something to do with Dwight. These days everything does. It seems I must prove all I have learned through you by living it, and I feel like a new person. The relationship to him is different than any I have ever had. It is wonderful. Did you know that a group climbed the tower of one of the buildings; I did not, but now I seem to be not really terrified but scared more out of habit. I could have climbed if it had meant enough to do so. I am not panicked any more.

ANALYST: Could these dreams have to do with the transference?

PATIENT: You mean because I dreamed of my roommate the night after seeing you? I saw a movie that night. It was all about transference, and I understood it. It was *The Secret Beast*. It was sort of corny but rather correct. I have had an ambivalence all year about trusting you. I mean because of telling you secret things. There were lots of things I was scared to tell but I told them anyway. Could this reflect a lack of trust in my parents? My mother asked me why I was seeing you. I said, "I will tell you some day," and she said, "Okay."

Thus far in the material the anger at me about the separation has not been expressed consciously. The one dream had dealt with intense competitiveness with a roommate, but the relationship of this to the transference was not clear to me. The flying was connected with a sense of liberation and this seemed to have an obvious transference meaning in view of the patient's imminent departure for a year; namely, her anticipated sense of liberation from her conflicting transference feelings. Now comes the theme of not trusting me. Again the question of whether to touch upon this point at once or wait. If the patient had not been leaving, I would certainly have waited. As it is, I again risked what I hoped would be a very brief interruption in order to call her attention to a mechanism that I have found to be extremely common in this connection.

ANALYST: Could this fear of trusting me also be a projection of your own feeling that in a way you do not trust your own feelings or something about yourself toward me? Could it also be that you fear some retaliation from me for your hostilities to me?

PATIENT: I thought I could not come again at all, but I might be able to come a week from today.

ANALYST: Could it be that, in addition to the transference of the father and mother pattern, which we have discussed, the sibling rivalry also plays a role toward me—because of the dream about your roommate? Is this rivalry with another girl for me after the sister model toward mother? Or, is it possible that there is also some direct sister rivalry toward me? The flying dream becomes intelligible if we recognize in it the sense of liberation from the attachment to me and also from the necessity for competition, from the frustration and the anger. But what about the sister rivalry dream?

Freud warned repeatedly against dream-book interpretation by simply applying symbols. Flying may well often be a phallic symbol, and it may be such here, but this need not exhaust the possibilities. Further, without associations, it is doubtful if such an interpretation, in terms only of infantile sexuality, is the whole story. In this context, the associations and the ego meaning seem to express a sense of liberation—and not simply of or from sexual feelings—from her conflictful dependent love needs toward Dwight and the analyst.

PATIENT: I don't know what more to say about it. I am worried though about what to do when there is no one to talk to as I have talked to you.

Here is the other side of the conflict. The patient wants to escape her dependent love needs in the transference and anticipates this with a sense of liberation. But, on the other hand, to be away does not solve the dependence nor the relief of feelings because then she will be alone. The only solution is for the child in the patient to resolve the conflicts with her parents and with her sister. She will have to outgrow these conflicts gradually and develop less childish and more mature attitudes and feelings. Only in this way will she move toward true liberation, that is, liberation from her own too intense childhood emotional pattern.

PATIENT: There are always two people in me and the one calms the other one down, but suppose I forget all that we have discussed. Friday I almost collapsed after the exams. I went to my room, locked the door, and had hysterics—the worst since I have been seeing you. I was so mad at myself to be so childish. *(There followed a brief passage for which, unfortunately, there are no notes.)* I don't know where I will be after returning from abroad. I will not return for over a year.

ANALYST: Can't we meet when you do return; can't you come in to say hello, and let us see how things are?

PATIENT: How can I handle the future when I am away? How does a person get over these things?

ANALYST: By counting on the pleasure principle. On the infantile level it operates the attachment to me and the wish to be the only one, with the frustration and anger, the rivalry with Beatrice and with me or others. But, as you see, rather than yielding peace and pleasure, this constellation makes you upset, gives you hysterics, anxiety, phobias, bad dreams, difficult human relations, and the like. As you gradually come to recognize this, you will learn that you can get much more pleasure in life by having adult attitudes in adult life, and you will grow out of the childish pattern and move into the mature attitudes.

The above is the gist of what I said. It is given here in the abstract, omitting the concrete illustrations from her own material that were used for the explanation, especially of the mature versus the infantile.

PATIENT: This talking to myself, these two people in me, probably they are the mature and infantile. This has become much clearer since seeing you. When I had hysterics, there was almost a voice in me saying, "Pull yourself together." It was like cracking a bull whip, a real thing, a projection of myself. It is good that it was there to crack down on me. I was in such a state I could have gone out and killed somebody. Then we had a wonderful talk. We even had a metaphysical discussion. I said, "Will you always be there when I need you?" The voice said, "Yes, but not when you don't." It even drew a picture for me. I asked it to stay until I went to sleep, and it did. Isn't that funny. Obviously it was me because it knew me so well. It was definitely a she, and it was so wise; it knew everything. It was like the little man helping me in the last picture only it was a she. It is sort of neat, isn't it. It is good to be on good terms with oneself. Everyone has this, don't they?

The voice seems to border on a hallucinatory experience. This need not be especially alarming, however, if it is viewed in the overall context and under the immediate and unusual emotional pressures of leaving home, friends, school, boyfriend, and analyst to be gone for many months. This seems to be in part an introjection—the mature part of everyone is largely the representation in his mind and personality of the adults who reared him. This is the essence of the superego. In this patient, the evidence suggests that it would be mostly mother. But this pattern to mother is transferred to others, hence her guide, mentor, and supporter can be a man. Originally it was mother, but now it seems to be also the analyst and the mature part of herself. The person who carries in his mind the good, supporting images of his parents and others, is less alone, less lonely. The dynamics here seem to be, at least in part, the effort to find in her own mind the support she has been having from others, especially from mother and analyst. She uses this to help control herself, that is, her turbulent, too powerful infantile feelings, which we have discussed so often and which are now intensified by the imminent departure.

ANALYST: Yes. Probably it is more intense in some than in others. Perhaps it is intensified in you now because of your leaving and wanting a substitute for me. When you want someone to talk to about your main feelings, then if I am not available, this probably means that you want to use this part of yourself—the part that has worked with me—on these reactions of yours in attempting to understand, control, resolve, and outgrow them. Being away from me, you will use the insight you have gained and the mature part of your own personality.

The nature of mature emotional attitudes was discussed with the patient, although the notes do not provide the details. The patient left saying she could not return for a week, but that she would do her very best to get in then so we could have one more visit before her departure.

PATIENT: My whole life is changed since seeing you. It is like being reborn!

All may not be so rosy as this statement, which probably expresses the patient's feeling at the moment, but neither can this feeling be lightly dismissed. It seems like an encouraging sign.

ANALYST: It remains to digest it, work it through, consolidate it. Once it is grasped, the process of growth goes on for years.

21st hour

The patient did manage to come for an interview one week later just prior to her departure. I made only scraps of notes because of wanting, in this last interview, to pay full attention to her, undistracted by writing. In addition I wanted this visit to be conversational in tone and devoted to integration of what we had learned. We needed to pick up loose ends, to discuss points that had gone before, and to gain further perspective on the problem. It would have been inappropriate at this time to again focus upon the current presenting emotional forces. In other words, in this final session I wanted to help the patient's ego to make the most of what we had already learned, and to prepare her for reactions to leaving and to the anticipated period of isolation and adjustment abroad.

The patient entered, punctual and a bit breathless. We exchanged a few words about the preceding visit. These touched upon her dream of flying and the sense of liberation and its reference to her attachment to me with the sense of being held emotionally, with consequent frustration and resentment. We talked briefly about the fact that in part she wants to hold onto the relationship, while at the same time she would feel it as a liberation to be free of it. Hence in the dream of walking with Dwight, she soared away, but then glided back. This mixture of attraction and escape probably prevented other relationships from being close and stable as is necessary for marriage.

PATIENT: I also felt that this flying was showing off; showing that I can really like someone. This is new and it is a wonderful feeling. *(There followed a passage for which no notes are available.)* I thought it would be easy to separate from Dwight, but it isn't. I don't want to be emotional about it. That does no good. I am the strong one and mustn't lose my head. Formerly I would have been afraid to be the strong one. Now I think I can be, but the separation is not easy.

In this last visit I did not hesitate to interrupt in order to deal with main points realistically even though this meant that we would lose the connecting red thread of the associations.

ANALYST: The separation from Dwight is probably intensified. Leaving the university, leaving your family, leaving me, leaving your country, with this in mind I can imagine it is also much harder to leave Dwight.

PATIENT: Yes, I know that.

Then came a brief discussion of her description in the last interview of the voice that spoke to her and had kept her in line, and with which she had held conversation. I pointed out again in connection with leaving that the voice also represented a substitute for myself. Having no one to talk to, she would talk to herself as an introject of me.

PATIENT: You know, I have not admitted it, but I have a secret dread of going abroad. To whom could I turn? I will be entirely on my own.

ANALYST: It seems to you like a void, because you have no idea in your mind as to how or to whom you will attach your needs for love. It is perhaps important that at first your needs for love do not attach to someone who is also a sexual object because we know how stormy a relationship can be when sex and romance enter into it. You need a backdrop of more sublimated platonic relationships such as you have here in relation to Dwight. You have in your contacts with me, with your family, with your friends, and with your school, all sorts of emotional supports that help you to handle the relationship to Dwight. Abroad, alone, without them, if all the needs for emotional support and love attach to the same person in whom there were also romantic and sexual interests, this might be stormy indeed. That is why so many girls who go abroad alone are anxious and then soon become rather easy targets for the first man who comes along.

PATIENT: Why that explains a lot, and of course, I have no intention of being a pushover.

What I said apparently had keen meaning for her and she spoke of it a little further. Then came the following.

PATIENT: Does stealing have anything to do with things like these? What has bothered me has not been the stealing itself, which didn't amount to anything at all, but my cold-bloodedness, my doing it without having any feeling about it.

Here is a good little example of how the analyst must, while alert to all he knows of the whole background and dynamics, nevertheless also keep an entirely open mind for current material as though he never saw the patient before. This last visit is devoted to an integrative, perspective-forming discussion of the patient's feelings and motivations in relation to the current reality, her trip abroad. In the midst of this, she throws in a totally new point, something about herself she has never even hinted at. It does not come up as an association in a train of associations because we are not using that technique in this final visit. Hence, it cannot be treated by usual proper analytic procedure. It must have some meaning coming up at just this point. Is it simply a last minute seeking for more answers from me while she is still here? Whatever it is, I cannot risk her feeling rejected in any way in this last hour, so I will respond to her question.

I said that it probably was connected with the emo-

tional constellation that we knew about, but I did not know just how. Perhaps it was related to her strong wishes to get love, possibly displaced onto things. Perhaps it was related to her sister and her sister's things and the rivalry with her. I added that if it were not the last interview I would not guess at this at all but would have waited until we had adequate material to understand it. I did not want to introduce any more guesses or symbolic suggestions so I asked if she could trace it back to any pattern in childhood. She thought of this and said that she could not.

PATIENT: My father, mother, and sister were very conscious of whose things were whose. I was spanked if I ever took anything of my sister's.

ANALYST: This shows there also might be some element of rebellion in it, and it also points up the risk of guessing without adequate material.

PATIENT: You know, I want to teach. When I was nine and my sister was five, I taught her and that was the only time I really loved her. When I was teaching her, I had a feeling of real tenderness for her and this was a great pleasure for me. It was then that I wanted to be a teacher. After that my sister went to school and did very well, and mother said it was because of my teaching her and that made me so proud. I felt that my sister was all mine, that she was dependent upon me, and I loved her and that is how I like to feel about little kids.

It is in just such gratifying situations in childhood that there is often formed the kernel of a future career. It will be of interest to see how the patient develops and what her interests and activities will be.

PATIENT: But if I only had people dependent upon me, if I had to be all alone with no one for me to depend upon, could I do it? I sometimes think if my husband died and left me with children, or if he were ill or worthless, if everyone were dependent upon me, could I do it. I think I could. This is related to Dwight. Not that he is so weak, although he does have problems. His parents are divorced, he is poor, has no money. He does not know what he wants to do.

Such a dependency conflict can influence all phases of a person's life, including career and choice of husband. It appears from what she is saying that she needs a strong person upon whom she can attach her dependent love needs. But, because she is so strong, these threaten excessive frustration and jealousy. Therefore she tries more or less unconsciously to escape all this by being with persons who are weaker than she and who are dependent on her. Her sister fits this role especially when the patient was teaching her; and Dwight also fits to a considerable extent. In these roles she can feel out from under, she is freed of her own conflictful dependence upon the other person—but to be so also means standing alone with her own dependent love needs unsatisfied.

PATIENT: The other night I was in a bad mood on the telephone with him and was angry. Dwight was very surprised. He said he always thought of me as a paragon of strength.

Sweden is in my mind just a big black nothing. I am afraid of being alone. I envy my sister for going to a small school. I envy her although in reality I absolutely would not go to such a place.

Then followed a short discussion of what we had already spoken of, namely Sweden being a void because the patient had not yet made any human contacts there. When she arrived, if she got to know people whom she liked at all, other students, teachers, local families, she would feel very different about it. She then brought up her fear of moun-

tains, which she said has been much better. I warned her to expect that anything that aroused her hostilities—loneliness, competitiveness, or whatever—could be expected to intensify to some extent her phobias. When she felt these irrational fears, she should ask herself what she was angry about. To this she replied that her fear of mountains has improved so much that she has even thought of taking a trip to the mountains with Dwight.

PATIENT: I would not go, but I am delighted that I could get such an idea and think about it.

This is a typical bit of self-testing, at first an idea is tried only by imagination. In this last hour when the matter of her fears of mountains in Sweden again came up, some of her material indicated that these fears were also related to her feeling very small as a child and afraid of what was very large. It was not possible, however, in this last meeting to clarify this any further, nor did it seem wise to make any sort of symbolic interpretation that might not be correct and that might upset her just at the point of departure.

The interview now ended. Although I did not interpret it, it seemed clear that she now no longer felt so strongly that she would never see me again, that this was an utter separation. We agreed that she would drop me a note occasionally about how things were going. This would maintain the contact and give her some emotional outlet and support in meeting her needs, in however slender fashion.

The analysis had to be interrupted without adequate working through, without her sufficiently understanding and dealing with the infantile part of her personality, that which caused her problems. Nevertheless we had come through an initial phase and had worked them over far enough so that the patient could achieve a tremendous sense of relief, release, and strength. It now remained to be seen what she could do with this when alone and on her own.

The judgment that we had come through an initial

phase is based upon the fact that both the patient and I had gained insight into the central emotional problem as seen in early childhood, in life relationships, and in the transference. Furthermore, it was certainly true that the main issues could now be discussed with considerable freedom and openness with the patient. The judgment that the working through was far from complete or sufficient was based upon the intensities of the patient's emotions. They are still a threat to her; they are not so thoroughly conscious and under such conscious mastery that they are no longer a danger. Also the transference feelings are not fully in the open and the reasons for the exaggerated dependent love needs to mother have not yet emerged. Although the phobias have improved, much general anxiety remains and the interpersonal relations are still stormy and so difficult that the patient can hardly be capable of enjoying them or of tolerating any close friendship, let alone marriage. She should be much further along the road to good, easy relations with herself and others before the analytic work should be properly interrupted.

Rather severe emotional bumps can be anticipated because of the separation coming without sufficient working through and because of the patient leaving the country to be entirely alone. However, it can also be assumed that the patient might surmount these difficulties, that she would make other contacts and make appreciable strides in progressing out of the childhood pattern toward maturity and therefore toward increasing satisfaction in her relations with other persons. If the treatment should be resumed later, this interruption then could be considered enforced fractionation of the analytic work. What she is unable to handle and make adequate progress with will remain as a residue to be treated analytically after her return. Meanwhile she has the formula for her problems and the key to their resolution, and hence she is able to work at them casually, at their roots.

What the above record probably does not convey adequately is the patient's emotional intensity, although this may perhaps be sensed from her various statements about her feelings and reactions. Every hour was so highly charged that this may have contributed to my inability to reach precisely what had been the treatment of the patient by her family prior to the birth of the sister that generated such strong dependent love needs toward her mother and the rest of the emotional constellation. Today my technique is, I hope, developed to the point where this would have been accomplished. I suspected that the intensity of the patient's reaction to the birth of her younger sister was probably determined by the strength of the patient's dependent love needs toward her mother. Therefore the arrival of the sister was so difficult to take. But what treatment or circumstances exaggerated in the patient her overly strong dependent love needs to the mother? It is really essential to proper psychoanalytic treatment to know the major injurious influences as well as the emotional pattern they formed in childhood. If at all possible, this should be known from the very first hour because the whole basis of analytic treatment is, as Freud put it, after-education to correct the aftereffects of this injurious treatment. Was it excessive spoiling and indulgence? Or, was it neglect or deprivation? Obviously the whole analysis proceeds much more in the light if this is known clearly. Except where there is physical impairment, every single case invariably betrays faulty conditioning during childhood, which warps the emotional development and produces the emotional problems.

Whatever the shortcomings historically, we did achieve a good beginning dynamically in bringing into consciousness the most disturbing motivations. The patient is well on the way to conscious comprehension of the results of these frustrations and defenses in the pressure of resentment and hostility that she chronically sustained. She is also coming to conscious awareness of her defenses against this hostility. All of this she saw with increasing clarity in relation to the original members of her family and as transferred to me. What still had not come out definitely toward me was the extreme competitiveness with her sister, which was, however, frank toward others. The result of her awareness was that, through it alone, the patient was exposing her most violent feelings to the highest powers of her ego so that they would be consciously dealt with. Prior to her achieving this awareness, they operated automatically and unconsciously with her at their mercy. By transferring them to me, they could be discussed openly and directly with the very person toward whom she felt them. In this way she could contrast her childhood reaction to mother and sister, and to father, with appropriate adult reactions to the analyst in a situation of professional understanding. With me she could tell everything and understand everything without the consequences that would have ensued in her early childhood. Thereby she could learn to handle these forces, not as she had done because of the personalities of her parents and the situation of her childhood, but in rational ways that would work and that could be arrived at through mutual discussion. In this way the automatic patterns of her id and superego became exposed to the mature parts of her personality so that she could handle them with the highest powers of her ego and thus outgrow them. Moreover, her automatic superego reactions were now also being made flexible by the replacing of her early images of her parents with a new analytic superego that was the result of understanding, tolerance, and free discussion. The automatic id and superego responses, through coming into consciousness and being openly discussed, were emerging into her ego, that is, into the conscious and most adaptive part of the personality where further development toward flexibility was begun. Where id and superego were, ego came increasingly to be. The task was not finished but a good beginning was made. The patient was released from the relentless automaticity of the childhood patterns, and so she could now be expected to learn from experience and gradually to mollify and alter these otherwise inexorable patterns. I have recently learned that the patient is married, has two children, and is doing well.

25 / WORKING THROUGH

The case that follows was conducted in a full-scale, five-day-a-week analysis. The details are, therefore, greater than what was presented in the previous case record, and the material is somewhat more complex. However, the way to understanding remains unchanged. As in all that has gone before, understanding comes only after the early injurious influences have been laid bare and their effects on the past and present of the patient have been revealed. Because this analysand's insight and psychological capacity are so definitely superior, the central theme, and the several interrelated themes of each session, usually come forth without it being necessary to identify the main elements common to each of the associations.

Unlike the previous chapter, which had as a primary focus the workings of the analyst's mind as he conducts each session of treatment, this chapter is concerned almost exclusively with raw data. What the analyst is thinking is not explicitly given here; but, of course, it can be deduced from the analyst's remarks to the patient. Where gaps exist and where the material, for one reason or another, is difficult to follow, notes are provided for the reader. Limitations of space made it impossible to include all the hours of this analysis in their entirety. The first few hours are presented in greatest detail, for it is here that the patient's history, main dynamics, and beginning attempts at working through emerge. Succeeding visits have been abridged, some more and some less so than others. In a number of instances, especially where the material was excessively repetitious and dull, entire hours were eliminated. The rule that governed the editing and paring down of the hours was that the chief aim of this chapter is to present a clear illustration of the process by which a patient works through the injurious aftereffects of faulty, early conditioning. Thus, the hours in this analysis, as they are presented here, should not be taken as models of the technique that is described in the preceding chapters of this book.

In this patient so much is close to consciousness that you will not see much of the process of digging for insight through many forms of resistance. Instead, a few questions by the analyst were usually sufficient for the patient to get the idea and find the childhood pattern and its operation in her present life. The record of this analysis shows how various facets of the pattern recur as the patient increases her emotional realization of them, recognizes solutions, and begins to outgrow them. Her struggles with the transference clearly reveal this process, which is also apparent in the dreams. In fact, reading through the dreams alone, without reference to any of the associative material, shows how lucidly the major themes and patterns emerge. The sexuality, infantile and adult, is obvious, but so are other forces—intense needs for love, inferiority feelings, hostility, and guilt, all the effects of early conditioning by training and identifications.

It may seem in this case that at times the transference was brought into the interpretations when there was insufficient supporting material. This may well be. For example, the associations and dreams may not directly indicate any reference to the transference, but the analyst nonetheless thinks of this and may even mention it. This is because the human relation of patient to analyst is a sample of the patient's human relations and the transference is so centrally important that the analyst must watch for it like a hawk, having it always in his mind lest he miss it when it appears. Taking notes is a very difficult task when you are trying to formulate an understanding of the central presenting material of an hour, when you are deciding whether to say little or perhaps nothing at all, when you are deliberating as to the appropriateness of a partial or total interpretation. Therefore, what the analyst said may not be recorded here with full accuracy. This probably makes little difference for the reader's comprehension in the long run, and unless the balance of forces in the patient is highly propitious for rapid change, the run is apt to be long.

All I knew of the patient before she entered my office some years ago was that she was a lawyer in her early thirties. What image or even stereotype that brings to your mind I cannot know; but for myself, when my secretary showed her in, I was surprised—strongly and pleasantly surprised. No eyeglasses, no aggressive intellectual, none of the rigidities that the formalities of the law seem to impress upon some of its enthusiasts. She is happily married and has four children.

Why does she come for analytic treatment? I think she was quite honest in trying to state her reasons. She complained of a vague anxiety and of a specific phobia of cats. The patient also had the idea that the insights she gained through analysis would be valuable to her in her profession. It was a number of months before she realized that she was plagued by some twenty symptoms, including the serious one of fear of losing her mind.

1st hour

Unfortunately, I did not record the first interview with the patient. However, her dynamics were elicited soon enough and I did record, after the first interview, the dream that she had the night before this first visit. Such dreams reveal a great deal about a patient's unconscious feelings toward analytic treatment, and therefore they tell much about the personality.

PATIENT: I had a dream last night. I was in the cellar of what looked to be our house. The cellar was clean except it had too many pipes. When I came down, I saw that some of the pipes were leaking, so I started to fix them with an instrument. A man was helping me fix them. We were doing all right but, to my consternation, when we finished with one, another pipe would start. Behind in the shadows, watching us, was my sister, Lois. She did not help us but watched. I looked at her as if I were saying, "Why don't you do something about it?" but she did not move. The feeling that I had in the dream was how surprised and somewhat disgusted I was to see Lois there, just watching, when I was doing this for her. At the same time I was upset having something like this happen when she was there.

The patient spontaneously went on to say that her sister Lois has been causing her a lot of trouble; doing a lot of distressing acting out. Lois has refused to see an analyst even though the patient has tried to get her to do so. The patient thinks that fixing the leaks sounds like her trying to help her sister.

It was too early in the analysis to dig for further associations. However, since the patient showed some anxiety about the dream, I decided it would be best to venture an interpretation in an effort to relieve this. I pointed out that the cellar of a house frequently refers to the unconscious. The patient saw the connection at once and said that the man who is helping her in the dream is probably me. I agreed with her and added that her sister may represent impulses that she acts out and which the patient also has but does not act out. Her sister's watching her may have to do with her anxiety about the impulses that she and I will see during the analysis. Again the patient saw the association and said that the leaks meant that even though she tries to hide her impulses from me, they keep leaking out.

As I noted above, this first interview was not recorded. What follows is a reconstruction, based on some rough notes, of the patient's personal history. We began with her chief complaints.

PATIENT: I have a fear of cats. When I was three, my sister accidentally kicked our tom cat. The cat scratched her and father shot the cat. I had a kitten as my own, and it was killed by a car. Then one of the cats got sick and father killed it. When I had my first baby, my cat was killed. My real complaint is the fear of cats. Why, when I go to a house, my first idea is this: Do they have a cat?

But, I also have a lot of fights with the children—really not with the younger ones, only with the oldest, Tom, nine, and I have a lot of guilt for this.

The patient then went on to describe her present life situation, including some remarks about her professional work.

PATIENT: The center of my life is home. I have four children. My husband is Will. We have a nurse, Annie, who has been with me for six years, and a cook who has been with us for two years—she's a case, but good with the children. Annie means a lot more to me than a nursemaid—it's not just that she takes care of the children, but she is nice looking, not very intelligent, but clever. She always takes the easy way, not the hard way. If we have an argument, she just tells me I'm upset and goes away. If Will and I fight, she comes in and tells us to stop because of the children and quiets it all down. She comes right into arguments between my husband and myself, and we don't resent it and she quiets things.

Tom teases her and she just laughs. Basically all is fine except Tom's fighting, really teasing, constantly with Annie, cook, me, and the other children. And he argues all the time. He teases his father, but less so. Mostly it's cute; others laugh but not the ones he does it to. He does it in the house only, not with friends. I talked with Tom about this and about his school troubles. I said we would not be here forever and that when he is grown he will be on his own. I said that he will be nothing and have only trouble if he does not study and behave. He listened very seriously, got very serious, and he has changed. I used to fight with my sister Lois and father and mother pressed me to help her, but I saw she couldn't be helped, but it was upsetting.

I love my job, but the problem is with my immediate superior, who has trouble with everybody. He is so rigid; he says no to everything. But I can manage. I get on fine with all the others.

ANALYST: Let's continue.

PATIENT: I get on fine with my husband. Of course we visit and go out with friends, and so on.

ANALYST: Community interests?

PATIENT: No time. Work and four children—that's the week. Friday we never go out but always take the children to the movies, and we take them out somewhere Sundays and Saturdays, except Saturday nights when Will and I go out. We love to go out by ourselves.

ANALYST: What about the parental family?

PATIENT: A problem. Father and mother and my sisters were no problem while we lived in San Francisco. Therefore we loved it, but they are a problem here. Lois, my sister, writes the family everything I do, even if I breathe she writes it. And they visit quite a bit. Mother came in the summer; one of my brothers came a few months ago; and my brother-in-law came one or two months ago. I want to be independent, left alone, and they want to know every time I draw a breath. It's not just my feelings. The nurse, cook, and my husband feel the same.

ANALYST: Cheer up, I'm on your side.

PATIENT: Ever since I decided to come and see you I've been depressed. And then a few nights ago I had an anguished dream that my husband was in love with another woman. In the dream this woman weighs three hundred to four hundred pounds, so there is no danger. In another dream later that same night, my husband fell in love with a friend with whom I grew up and who had three or four mental breakdowns.

ANALYST: Do you have any associations?

PATIENT: I might fall in love with someone else. My husband could leave me. Does it go back to sibling rivalry? We were all girls except for two boys who were much older. I was the youngest. There was great rivalry for my father.

ANALYST: Could these dreams have anything to do with your seeing me?

PATIENT: Sometimes I talk with myself as though I were seeing an analyst.

ANALYST: Is the sibling rivalry a father pattern to me?

PATIENT (*laughs hysterically*): Yes it is, because I want to cry and do not want to let myself. There is a guilt about going to talk with you. Mr. B. at work told me that I am so afraid of psychoanalysis—as though I were doing something wrong, but officially permitted.

ANALYST: Why do you have guilt?

PATIENT: Guilt about the pleasure, about letting someone know myself.

ANALYST: Why?

PATIENT: As though I am going to be naked.

ANALYST: Is there a sexual element?

PATIENT: No, although there must be. (*Thinking.*) I was so raised that father did not want to see pants near the house, not within one mile. Father was away a lot and so were my brothers, who were older. Mother, like father, thought something was wrong about talking with men. I was the only one of us girls who was allowed to have boyfriends. Therefore the others were jealous of me. I was pleased at this, but father was so strict with the others that I got a lot of the strictness too.

ANALYST: What about the sexual element? That is what father forbid, and perhaps that is why there may be rebellion.

PATIENT: That is exactly how it is; and the guilt toward my husband. I feel as though I am cheating him by coming here. I have never talked with anyone, not even with girlfriends. I must talk with someone so I've talked with my husband, and I tell him everything—my dreams—all—he knows me better than I do.

ANALYST: Is it the sibling pattern to father—fear of attachment to me? Do you want it, enjoy it? Is the father trauma the problem?

PATIENT (*laughing*): To have father alone is a pleasure, but I fear this is the last time I will have him alone.

ANALYST: Now you see what analysis is. You have basically a good, loving relation with father, but it is troubled by his too close watch over you and his forbidding you to talk with men and even with other women. You feel rebellion as a result of this, but you also feel your father's prohibition when you talk with me. It is forbidden, and it has sexual implications because this is why you were forbidden to talk with men. Hence, seeing me is against your training by your father and it is also felt as disloyalty to your husband. We must also watch out for your repeating toward me your pattern toward your father; that is, you wish for his love in competition with sisters, and now in the transference you have some fears, as toward father, of revealing yourself. You feel you are too closely watched and are rebellious. The task of analysis is to analyze out the disturbing elements. I'm not your father, and I'm not seducing and raping women. Equally important is the fact that you are not a little girl.

I wanted to return to getting the patient's history, So I paused a moment and then asked her if she was involved in anything other than her family and job.

PATIENT: Only reading—everything from novels to psychiatric literature—everything that is good. I have no time for other things or the community except what I have to do for the children, like the PTA.

ANALYST: Tell me something about the main emotional relationships from birth until age six, as nearly as you can sense them.

PATIENT: Chiefly father, mother, and sisters. I was always the favored one. I got everything I wanted from father and I was always very close to him. One of my earliest memories is that I had a toy doll and was masturbating myself with it and mother came in and said it was bad. I was very young then. It was in the first house we lived in, so I was three or not more than four, and I remember soon after that father shot and killed a cat. Roberta, who was two years older than I, kicked the cat's leg. It had a wound there, and it scratched Roberta. Mabel, another sister of mine, told father and he shot the cat. Father was very impulsive. He always carried a revolver. He doesn't act that way any more and, in fact, advises us not to be impulsive. At that time I used to get up early and go into father's bed until mother got mad and forbid it, and I noticed mother was jealous. I was the youngest and always was told, "You're not dry behind the ears yet."

I used to be fearful nights. I was afraid to have the light out. Because I was the last child, I felt mother never had too much time for me, although she is a sweet and understanding person; but she never thought too much about me while I was in school. If my grades were good, okay; if I had bad grades, that would be okay too. But I almost always did have good grades.

When I was older, I went with father wherever he went—hunting, everything. We had a maid at home who was very nice and told me that when I was born, father refused to see me because I was another girl. However, a few days later father came over and had some guilt about this and therefore was very protective of me. Mother told me that she wept when she was pregnant with me because she and father were not getting along, things were not good financially, and father had a mistress.

I was always on father's lap as soon as he got home. My sisters would say, "She's looking for something," meaning money or presents, but father always said, "No, she isn't."

Father was cruel with my first sister, Vivian, and also with Lois, the second girl. They had boyfriends and were always going steady. One day they were in the movies and father found out. I guess they were necking in the movie. I was always with father. He got out all their dresses to burn them; and he cut a stick. I went and told them. They came home, but he hit them with the stick. It was thin but flexible. It hurt terribly. Lois said, "You can kill me and I won't cry." He beat her badly and father said to the rest of us, "If you have a boyfriend, this will happen to you." I thought: I'll be a nun.

But I, and later my sisters, did go ahead and have boyfriends. I had a boyfriend at fourteen, and father liked him very much. My sisters married against father's will. There was a great difference in father's treatment of me and my sisters. I was still scared because I never knew when father would change and act in the old way.

When I was very young, three or four, the man who worked in the garden exposed himself to me. I was scared and ran but told no one. If I had, father would have destroyed the man.

Father had a mistress. But then, all the men of his generation were the same. They all had mistresses, were involved in politics, fighting and threatening to kill each other—just like the cowboys on the movies. I can't think of a man who did not have a mistress. As soon as I was grown, I knew about it because the men acted so openly, and it frequently came up in conversation in the house. But there were no divorces. Now it is the opposite—not mistresses but divorces. Now women count more; in those days women always were at home, never went any place.

ANALYST: Why more divorces, then?

PATIENT: Because women won't stand for it any more. They are educated, hold jobs, are independent, and parents now help the daughter get a divorce. It used to be that the poor people cared about the families and the wealthier didn't, and now it is the opposite. Now in the poorer classes, the women have children by different men.

ANALYST: Continue with your main emotional relations from birth to age six.

PATIENT: Mother was a quiet person, passive, sat with me when I was ill. I had good relationships with all the people in the house—three or four maids, cowhands, all. There was only one nursemaid with whom I did not get along. We were playing nearby and a man came and threatened the nurse and the nurse held me in front of her and said, "If you hurt me, you'll hurt this child and it's W's daughter and he'll kill you." I was scared.

I got on very well with Roberta until I started school at six, or maybe it was until I was seven or eight that we got along. Anyway, it was until she started to menstruate. Then she became close to Mabel, who is five years older than I, and I was left alone.

ANALYST: Were your sisters a great emotional influence on you?

PATIENT: Oh they were. They were all very good students, were very close, and I was always left out. I always had my friends outside of them, and they are the ones I shared secrets with. My sisters had outside friends too, but they were closest with each other. My sisters told mother everything, but I didn't, although mother had a way of getting it. I felt everything I did was wrong. I was guilty about something.

ANALYST: That is important.

PATIENT: It's still like that. If I receive a letter from mother, I think it's going to tell me something is my fault. My husband has helped me with this. The whole family except father never gave me the benefit of the doubt. I'll give an example. Recently my husband and I were in very bad shape financially. We had three children and were expecting our fourth. We were given some money by Lois and Mabel, and then later, after much struggle, we bought a house and they wouldn't come over to see it; no one except father came. Then when I visited mother, she said we had so much money! Annie, the nursemaid, had told mother that I had money. Of course it was borrowed from the bank. They knew Annie lied all the time, exaggerated, and so on, and yet they believed her and wouldn't even talk to me. They thought we had so much money and yet took money from them. I said they should feel guilty and that I would tell father. They were scared and begged me not to, so I didn't. Really, Annie thought the family would not let us buy a house unless they thought we had money, so she told mother.

The guilt—I don't know why I have it today. Maybe I wish that father would leave everyone for me.

ANALYST: Anything else?

PATIENT: For the hostility I have toward my family. I could talk about that for two years. I'm angry. My sisters say mother is a martyr, that father is a very cruel man, that father never worked, that all we are is because of mother. But I feel the opposite. If mother had married a different man, we'd be nothing. Father was hard on Lois, that's true; but they try to crush him all the way down. They say mother suffered so, all for nothing; but that is not true. She suffered because she loved him and didn't want to leave him; she didn't do it for us. I'm more hostile, at least consciously, to the women in the family. I can't excuse even one. My oldest sister is really very nice, but she is so identified with mother. They are hostile to each other also, but mother holds them together. My sisters found in me someone they could talk to who would not run and tell mother. Each of them tells everything to mother. We may as well have a circular letter. My husband and children and I should not be involved with father, mother, and my sisters.

ANALYST: Right—biological development—you are a wife and mother and should not still be fighting and struggling with your father, mother and sisters.

The notes do not indicate exactly how this hour was concluded. All that is clear is that we summarized the main points that had emerged, and I decided to complete the history during the next hour.

2nd hour

At the beginning of the second hour the patient related two dreams of the night before.

PATIENT: In the first dream I am at a zoo with a man. I am a teenager, about eighteen. The man is about the same age. We look at the animals, in cages, of course. It was pleasant until another man came along—a doctor—then you were your own age and went off with him. In the second dream a doctor is operating on me and a lot of pus comes out.

My impression of these dreams, supported by some associations, was the following. Being a teenager again is to be single, young, and free. The man is the analyst. Hence both are free for any relationship. The zoo is associated with former good times, also with the animal nature—free sexuality and hostility. The element of the cages has to do with being inhibited, restrained. The animals would rebel, break loose, if they could. My going away with the other man is a defense against the patient's becoming too attracted to me and against anything sexual. This is how the patient sees the analysis. She and I look at her animal impulses together, including at least, hostility, sex, and rebellion against feelings of being confined, restrained. Also implicit in the dream is the wish for the analysis to be like a date, but she defends against this by having me go away. This involves a sense of rejection and, because I leave with someone else, a sense of being left out. There is also probably some jealousy because of there being a third party.

In her associations to the second dream, the patient said that what is inside her is pus and this is bad. This dream, too, then refers to the analysis. At the end of the first dream I go off with someone else, and this should have made the patient feel anger, but she said nothing about it. Probably she repressed the anger, and it appears in dream two, in the form of being turned against herself. Here in this dream the analysis is not a teenage date with all kinds of possibilities for the future, it is an operation. The pus, the bad things, probably refers to guilt, which, however connected with sexuality, is usually also (and perhaps primarily, as Freud concluded) a result of hostility. Certainly she wants the analyst to relieve her of "badness" and guilt.

The early dreams regularly foreshadow the analysis. They show how an analysand sees it. These dreams show much frankness and insight, and they sound the main themes that underlie the patient's symptoms and problems and with which she has been struggling. The main points were all discussed with the patient in a friendly, easy way that she could take as not threatening but as understanding and helpful. After this discussion we continued the personal history.

PATIENT: When I left the last time, I felt everything I said was bad. Other times when I thought of these things, I would cry, but yesterday I didn't even feel like crying.

ANALYST: Good. I heard nothing that sounded so bad. It was more in your mind. It probably has to do with the guilt you told me about for talking with a man, that is, myself, as though it had forbidden sexual implications.

PATIENT: It's a pleasure to drive here, because all my life I've never been alone with myself. Now going by myself in a car is the only time I'm alone with myself and can relax. It's a transition time, before and after.

All of my friends know me as a strong woman with a lot of hostility; no one can put anything over on me, but it isn't true. It is fear. I try to be calm and just can't. I get upset, so I better just be the way I am. Then I am happier. Others don't notice it, but I do. I feel as though I let my emotions go, but I don't.

ANALYST: What about from the age of six to the present?

PATIENT: At six I started school and liked it very much. In school it was completely different than in the house. In school I was a leader, thought up everything, good or bad; but at home I was guilty about that. I got very good grades; I was second in the class. Once I said I wanted to be an actress and do acrobatics. Father was outraged by the idea and threatened me. But I did it anyway at school. Someone told father and he came and I fainted, my stomach was upset, and I gave up these ideas. But occasionally I've had these spells. But whenever I get some distance away from home, I am fine.

In school I fell in love with different boys; liked a lot of boys. I had a conscious fantasy when eight or nine that I, father, and the family would be driving home in the car and find the boy I was in love with, who in the fantasy was an orphan, alone. Father would stop the car and bring him with us, and I was happy. At other times I would fantasy that I was the orphan and other women picked me up. Father had a way of teasing women constantly and often it hurt and my sisters never forgave him, but either he didn't tease me that much or I didn't care as much. Father would ask me if I was sure that he was my father and mother my mother and not some other man or woman that he would name who was undesirable. Father would just keep this up.

I did fine in school until I started going with a boy father approved of. We went together for a year, and when I broke up with him in my last year of high school, I almost flunked. He went with other classmates of mine, and I was just wild, lost weight. I left him because I knew he would leave me, so I left first. Then I went away from home to college. I broke loose and started going with another boy. I later heard he hadn't married because he was impotent. I went with him for a year. He was very passive but used it so well. He knew how to involve a girl. The best girls got involved with him, but he never married them. I later told him that he must hate women. Then I had no interest in him; I still like him though and we have remained friends. He had to marry finally because he went with a girl for seven years who was just beautiful. Now she's the opposite. Most girls shine after marriage, but this girl gets worse and worse. Then I went with other men but there was no necking or sex.

That first year at college I didn't do well and the dean of women wrote my parents about the boy. The school was very strict, so father arranged for me to transfer to a more liberal one.

I don't like the ages seventeen to eighteen. I wish I could erase them from my history. I had no good relationships with any boy. I worked for a year in St.

Louis as a hostess. I lived with two girls and had a lot of trouble with them. They went out, and I was often alone nights in the apartment. I dated but avoided sex by making each one my best friend. A. R. had been in love with me since childhood, and I was attracted to him because of his looks, but he was so passive. But in St. Louis I was so miserable that when he came, I went out with him. His family bought a ring for me, and I got scared and after that I had a lot of trouble getting rid of him. He is very successful now, married, and has two children. The children have problems and go to a psychiatrist. I like his wife. She is upset when she sees me. I liked A. R., but he was just too weak.

When I met my husband, at first I liked him enormously but was guilty about going out with him while I was still seeing A. R. Will was very successful with women, and then I did not like him so much. He went away for a year and wrote to me to come. Mother said absolutely not and so did the whole family, but father said yes, so I went. A year later we were married and a year after that we had our first baby, and that was the happiest time of my life. It was so happy, not only because we were young, in love, married, and had a baby, but it was more than that. We were in San Francisco seven years, and I enjoyed everything I did, good or bad. I couldn't talk about it for years after coming back (*beginning to cry but smiling through the tears*) and still can't; it is too painful. After the first two years back home, if anyone mentioned it, I would leave. I can now talk of it superficially. but more than that I get too emotional. When we returned to Texas, we lived very near Will's parents and didn't get along with them and had a terrible time. I expected it, but we couldn't help it. A few months later we moved to Chicago. My mother-in-law kept criticising how I raised my children. When we moved to Chicago, we bought a small house.

After a brief pause the patient continued her history by opening up the issue of her feelings of dependency.

PATIENT: If mother was not around, I wouldn't flop to pieces. But, one day when I was about five or six, mother was away all day and I cried and didn't know why, but that was why. However I liked to be out of the house as much as possible, stay overnight with friends. And they never had to come for me. Mother was more dependent on us than we were on her. When I left home at age seventeen, I was very homesick and cried quite a bit. I found a girl from Washington who felt the same as I did, so we roomed together, and we didn't cry any more.

ANALYST: What did you miss?

PATIENT: The whole thing. I missed mother but at the same time didn't want her around. Father was not in the picture most of the time. One of my sisters wrote how much she missed mother, but she never wrote a word about father. Father was left out of everything, but I always wrote to both; I said very little about missing them. When mother came to visit us just before I had Barbara, I followed her around and then decided that was not good. At that time mother said she did not care for sex. How did we girls come out of it without being frigid? Father once told mother he was impotent, but he wasn't. He told her that because he had a girlfriend, only nineteen and beautiful, but then the family got together and made father send her off to New York City. Mother organized everyone against father and then put herself on his side. Father talks little but is very dramatic. One day he said he tried to commit suicide. He took two sleeping pills and mother saw him lying on the floor. He had a revolver and could have used that. My sister Mabel saw father and just said, "Get up!" and he got up. Father always said he was useless and that his daughters would have to take care of him or he would shoot himself. Until then they all thought he was so strong, but after that they didn't think so any more, although they still love him deeply. All this was when he had a girl friend and was breaking up with her.

The patient continues her history by describing her love needs and then her feelings of inferiority and guilt.

PATIENT: I need a lot of love. It is hard to explain. Maybe I was asking for too much that no human being could get. There were so many children, and I was the youngest, so I guess—I don't know—mother had to work her way with so many of us, so close in age, so different in personality. I couldn't show anything too much because every time we had a fight father would say, "You are going to kill your mother." He said mother had a heart condition although she didn't. I got a lot of love from the maids too. The others stayed close to mother, but I followed the maid (she was the cook's daughter and was only three years older than I) into the rooms, with the men, milking cows, etc.

A big problem with me is inferiority. I always felt inferior to all of them. At first I went to the same school as they and hated it. They were always comparing us. I can't get on with Roberta because she can't accept just human errors in anyone; she is rigid, most like mother. I was the most ugly of them. I was the most mischievous and the worst. I always felt this inferiority. The only thing that has changed is that I am a better mother than my mother. No, I don't want to put it competitively. I mean I try to be. When we were children, they idealized mother so that it was unreal, out of this world. We could never be like her. She gave us the idea that a mother must sacrifice everything, including the father, for the children; and two of my sisters have done that. But if the marriage is not happy, how can the children be happy?

My main problem is the guilt feeling—that I was bad, that everything I did was wrong, until I married and Will pointed out the opposite. Although I didn't know it at the time, I guess what drove me to study law was the fact that my sisters were in it. When I graduated, I was so happy to be a lawyer and they destroyed it in five minutes by saying, "You graduated from a second-class university." I guess I worked so hard the next two years to refute that. Two years ago a man helped me very much. He was my direct superior, but I realized I was getting a crush on him, getting too involved. My marriage was beginning to be affected so I quit and went to a different firm.

I guess I told you of father and mother. Everything that reminded mother of sex was bad. Mother was malicious, or what shall I call it? She knew what was often behind things and always suspected it; always said *derrières pensées.* Maybe that is right, but she never assumed that everything was normal, and this made me and the others guilty. For example, we could never stay overnight with friends and I would ask why and she would never tell. Later I found out it was because she feared that the father of the house would make some kind of sexual advances to us. She never let us go to the movies without her.

ANALYST: Tell me about the role of religion in your family.

PATIENT: Father did not believe in the clergymen, so he never went to church. As a result, they never were very strict about religion. I think the men of that generation drifted away from the church—whenever you went, you saw women but very few men. Now it is different; the girls now have more children again, and the men go to church, too.

The patient then went on to give a history of her conscious feelings of hostility.

PATIENT: I guess I'm a hostile person but I get along well with the people I should but not with the passive-aggressive type who tells you one thing and does the opposite, who doesn't have the honesty or strength to be direct. For example, my boss, L. B. wants to transfer someone with whom I am working well. L. B. smiles on the surface but goes behind your back to do it—he doesn't discuss it openly and directly.

I was often angry at mother but was not conscious of it until my teens. I probably was not conscious of it because I was too guilty. As a child I had more guilt than hostility, but as a teenager I was still guilty but also knew I was angry and this made me more guilty. One day I was in a car with mother and Vivian. I was so mad at mother who reacted by saying, "The only way is for you to marry and leave me and have your own house." I don't remember usually being mad at father, only when he punished me and when he killed the cat. My chief anger was at mother. To father it was only occasional. I had none with Vivian, the oldest, nor with Lois, the second, but had quite a bit with the third, Mabel. I got on fine with Roberta until she had her first period and then I was left by myself. Why was I angry at Mabel, I don't know, except that after Roberta menstruated, Mabel took her away from me. Now I have the best understanding with Vivian and second best with Mabel.

ANALYST: How about your feelings of hostility prior to age six?

PATIENT: I don't remember.

ANALYST: At mother?

PATIENT: Very little so early, except nights when I was afraid and wanted to get into bed with mother and she would not let me. So I went in bed with father, but I was angry at mother for this. In the morning when I awoke, I tried to get into bed with mother and she refused, so I gave up and went into bed with father.

They slept in the same room but had separate beds. Father would hug, kiss, and play around with me and mother did not do that. I felt some anger, but chiefly I felt that mother didn't love me. They told me I always liked to be close to someone, that I liked being fondled and kissed. Mother did not like that. Now mother complains when I see her that I don't kiss her. But with my children I'm affectionate all the time—they come in bed with me, jump on me, and all that. Will is the same with the children and with me. Will is happier in the house than I. He is always kidding, joking. I don't do that but not because I'm unhappy. I'm most happy when I'm with the children, especially when we're in the car going some place like to a picnic. These are the happiest moments. It's strange.

My chief hostility was to mother for the frustration that she did not love me enough or that she showed the love to the others—and still does. Not that she didn't love me; really she loved me very much. She's a very sweet person and our house was always full of teenagers because she is the perfect type to give advice; she's very intelligent and always knows how to say the right thing.

ANALYST: What was the form of the hostility?

PATIENT: As a child I never showed it. I was afraid to and felt guilty, so I lived my life outside my home.

ANALYST: Did you have temper tantrums?

PATIENT: Oh no, I was afraid to—but I had fears at night. As a teenager when I was angry, I would leave the house. Mother says I was a sweet and quiet child—just the opposite on the inside. As a teenager when I was angry at mother, I'd get bad marks.

ANALYST: And today?

PATIENT: I get mad but over the wrong things. I shouldn't. I should accept things the way they are. Last year we were all sick in bed with flu. I had 104° fever. Our cook phoned that she wouldn't come for fear of catching it, so I got up and cooked. I didn't get mad until I was well. Then I was depressed, crying, not mad. At home everybody would have been in helping and here for the first time, I had no help. Mother has a way of always making me and the others feel guilty by taking a martyr attitude. I know how easy it is to manipulate your children's guilt but that is awful.

ANALYST: What is it, especially, that you want analytic treatment to change?

PATIENT: The guilt. There's hostility and everything reacts to that. I know it but not emotionally. Why is the hostility so great? I feel very childish when I react by being mad. Will said he's happy when he can express what he feels. I'm the opposite. I mean that when I'm with people out of the family I want to be poised, controlled, not show anything. I admire such people. I want to keep a cool head, that is how Will is, the opposite of father.

During this hour we reviewed the patient's chief complaints.

PATIENT: I feel guilty and don't know why except that now, after giving the history I have some idea. I wish I could control myself better and express it in another way, like sister who can speak calmly and say the right thing at the right time and lets the other person feel upset. But I get mad, feel upset, say things I want to say, not the proper things, and I shake like a leaf. That makes me mad although no one notices it. It is all inside. Yet although this is aggressive, it has brought me where I am, so maybe I shouldn't be too controlled. Oh, I don't know how it is. It's the fear, even if I say the right thing, I'm so tense and so anxious.

ANALYST: Give me an example.

PATIENT: On Wednesday, L. B. gave a friend of mine some

advice, which she said she couldn't afford to act on. L. B. then replied something harsh in a very loud voice. She told him not to yell at her. Then he began to yell at me and I yelled back and I was so mad at him. I should have been calm and said I didn't want to be yelled at or criticized in front of others. If he has anything to say, he should say it politely.

Without too much supporting detail, the patient went on to offer the following additional complaints. She said that her fear of cats was somewhat improved since giving the history, but it had by no means disappeared. She is less afraid of small ones, and never afraid of her own cats. She continues to feel guilt toward her first son but not toward her other children. The patient also complains of occasional migraines.

Later in treatment, the patient confessed that her chief reason for seeking analytic help was a fear that she could barely admit even to herself—the fear of losing her mind. She said she feared that if she told me this, I would have found her unfit for analytic treatment.

In defining the main dynamics, the following points were discussed back and forth with the patient. To be sure, they were not stated dogmatically, as here. The description that follows results from trying to jot down the main points at the same time that I was talking to the patient. Typically, this kind of material is elicited from the analysand rather than dictated by the analyst.

ANALYST: You were the youngest child and did not get all the acceptance from mother that you wanted; but mother was so good that you could not get angry at her, which implies some hostility underneath and some guilt. The attitudes you identify with mother are: sacrifice for the children; men are everything, the center; indirectly women can get things out of men but with love. As a result of your feelings toward mother, you turned to father. He was accepting but only with you, not the other sisters. This made you feel guilty toward your sisters even though you were very happy about the special attention from father. This was somewhat erotized. Father was very strict with your sisters about sex and men, but he was less so with you. The attitudes you identify with father are: be aggressive and not well-controlled; shoot first, inquire after.

PATIENT: Exactly. Father would say, "Hit first—he who hits first hits twice."

ANALYST: All your sisters treat mother as an angel; they are so good, more than human. Toward your sisters you feel both a sense of guilt for being favored by father, and a sense of inferiority, which is now slowly disappearing. Guilt is a main issue; it is as though you have done something wrong.

PATIENT: Yes, father would say I was his weakness.

In response to questions aimed at eliciting the current main issue, the patient had this to say.

PATIENT: Mother controls everything, knows all the children so everyone knows everything about each other. But I have been very rebellious, always wanted to be out of this, never told mother about myself as the others did, but then I felt the guilt.

ANALYST: This much seems central and simple.

PATIENT: It is. From this I get the fear of loss of self-control, fear that I'll break completely with them, come out with all the hostility. Then I fear not what they would think but that father would get mad at me and that's what I care about most.

I still feel a little anxiety about coming to see you. Maybe I see you as though you were father; that if I come out with what I think, you won't like me.

ANALYST: I am glad you see that. It is an essential of analysis.

PATIENT: I have feared that I would not be right for analysis, fear I would not please you.

ANALYST: What would you say was traumatic for you in your relationship with your sisters?

PATIENT: Inferiority, rivalry, jealousy, wanting to get away from them. And if I went with a boy and they laughed at him, I wouldn't go out with him any more. I had this constant wish for their approval, and at the same time I felt rebelliousness against them because they were like mother. They were always trying to get me to break up with a boy; or, if I wanted a pair of shoes, mother would start them mocking me. I tinted my hair once and when I came home, they said I was ugly and should change it. But, in the end, they changed theirs. Since marriage I have been less afraid of them. I still care, but I used to care so much that I would not do the things at all. So the sister pattern is really mother and the sister trauma is mother trauma.

ANALYST: Mother trauma?

PATIENT: I can't identify you with mother (*laughs*); with father, yes, but not with mother. Mother always manipulates you with your guilt, and with you that would be too unrealistic.

ANALYST: Father trauma?

PATIENT: Not wanting father to know my faults would be the chief one. Father's approval counts more than anything.

ANALYST: The rest should be easy.

PATIENT: Not so easy. Many things haven't come up, and I'm afraid.

ANALYST: Of course, and we always feel the way gradually.

PATIENT: What I'm very afraid to tell you is about our son Tom. I feel so guilty. I've read of sons who kill mothers. The poor child is afraid at night now. For a while I feared I would be stabbed by him with a knife. This fear is relieved if he comes in bed with me or I with him. I don't know what started this. It's all gone now, but I lose my patience with him so easily and with the others I don't.

ANALYST: Why do you fear to tell me?

PATIENT: Because it sounds like craziness.

ANALYST: Anything else you fear to tell?

PATIENT: Yes, if I come out with both, I will feel easier. Six months ago when at home, I got thoughts of a breast of a woman. I get it when I'm anxious; and then it develops into genitals of a woman (*with this she begins to cry*).

ANALYST: Are you upset because you think they are crazy ideas?

PATIENT: Very much so. These two are what upset me, and I know they have a relation. With our son, I fear I have been too seductive; that is what I'm fighting; this is why I'm harsh with him. It started three or four years ago. He is a favorite of my mother-in-law. My husband was the only boy of four children. Mother-in-law is the most castrating woman I've ever seen. She is very seductive. She wears the pants; if she wants something, she gets hysterical, crying, screaming, and she is closer to Tom than to my other children. She complained that I didn't raise the others to love her enough. Will is safe only because he left her when very young.

ANALYST: Why do you fear to tell me?

PATIENT: Because you would think I'm crazy, no good. May I smoke?

ANALYST: We want to analyze the tensions in order to relieve them.

PATIENT: True. I wanted to have a cigarette and take my mind off these thoughts. When I was sixteen, I saw an operation on mother. It was the first time I had seen a woman's genitals, and I was shocked at the operation and fearful of mother having cancer. While at the hospital, I saw a woman with an ugly face but beautiful breasts. And with my son I fear that I would seduce him into being a mama's boy. I know I haven't but I'm guilty because of rejecting him to fight my own unconscious desire to have him right by me. But he's a boy through and through. I fear that I have him with me too much and that if I protect him too much, he will become a homosexual.

ANALYST: Where did you get all this?

PATIENT: I don't know.

ANALYST: Was it because you identified with your son? In childhood you wanted so much attention from mother but instead you got it from father, and so you followed him around.

PATIENT: Then I fight against that.

ANALYST: Behind compulsive ideas there is usually hostility, and with it goes guilt.

3rd hour

PATIENT: I don't know what to talk about. Have we finished the history?

ANALYST: Yes. Now you are up against free associating. I'll try to make it easier. Would a dream be easier?

PATIENT: Yes. I dreamed not of you but of Dr. C., and with considerable anxiety. In last night's dream I was at a table with a girl and Dr. C. was at another table with a woman. I said hello to him and he said hello to me but in a very cold manner. So I sort of showed off to get his attention, and he looked down his nose at me as though thinking: What's wrong with her? I was so mad for putting myself in that position and for his rejecting me. I woke up mad and then felt depressed.

Before I had a chance to ask for associations, the patient offered the following.

PATIENT: Could it be that Dr. C. represents the bad father? I don't show emotions to you; that is, it's less threatening to dream of him than of you. My being at a table with someone, I think a girl, suggests gossiping with a girl and wanting boys to be around.

ANALYST: What do you associate to Dr. C. and to his being at a table with another woman?

PATIENT: I wanted him to be with me or maybe I wanted to be in her place. But instead of going to talk with him, I started to act like a child. Am I acting in analysis like a child? Do I wish to be a child? If a child again, I would know better what to change, what I would do differently. At least I did not have sex relations before marriage. I wouldn't be so stupid as to do that. But no one told me anything. Could it be that I wanted sex relations with him in the dream! (*Laughs.*) It couldn't be, but then why did I flirt in the dream—so there must be something. I met Dr. C. a long time ago and thought him very cold. Maybe he represents my father. He knows what I do with my husband, so he judges me without my expressing myself, but with you I can express myself. Last week Dr. C. was at a party and a Mrs. L., a widow, was there. She was raving about Dr. C. Maybe I wanted to be her although I didn't think about it until now. Mrs. L. is crazy about Will. Could it be that I'm jealous of her, not about my husband but about Dr. C? My husband thinks Mrs. L. is more intelligent than I. She builds him up, and I think I should be that way but can't. She has two loves, my husband and Dr. C. She told me, "I can be very submissive to men if they are good, but I can't be submissive to women, can't work with a woman on a higher level." I am to work with her as my boss; I feel the same way. But she is easy to work with, so there is no problem, and I admire her. She is sure of herself, enough so as to have able people around. L. B. has no one.

ANALYST: What did the dream mean?

PATIENT (*laughs*): I can't say. I'm too embarrassed. I wanted you with me but acted like a child, probably because it was easier for me.

ANALYST: Is this the father pattern—the attachment to him? Only now you are grown and it is more erotized, and consequently it takes more of a sexual flirting form. Is this why you feel embarrassment—fear and expectation of rejection because father was strict about sex and beat your sisters? Also, is there a question of hostility and guilt? Could acting like a child be a defense against too much involvement with me, against falling in love with your analyst? Do you fear the attraction and all the jealousies involved? Do they carry over from father?

PATIENT: When as a child I was in bed with father, I had no guilt until mother began to react. Mother got mad and said, "Don't dress in front of him!" Not until then did I get any idea. Father was affectionate; he kissed me and carried me, but all very nicely, no overseductiveness. From then on when mother reacted, I felt that if I couldn't trust father, I couldn't trust anyone; but he never did anything. It must have been my own fantasies. It is the same with you now, as though mother were telling me to be careful.

It's childish—not realistic. Father always stayed with mother so I shouldn't want this. If I do everything to please him all my life, he still stays with mother.

ANALYST: So it isn't only whether you shouldn't want him, but that you can't entirely have him. Is this also transference feelings to me?

PATIENT (*laughs*): Make the most of what you have.

ANALYST: Yes, that's one of the secrets of life, instead of pining for what you don't have.

PATIENT: Is that also why I think of old boyfriends and of the parties here with open flirtation?

ANALYST: There is always a residue in everyone—if deprived or indulged—we always want more love and some of it in sexual form.

PATIENT: Even at home I thought I should not flirt so openly, but even if I act differently, I want to just the same.

I wonder if this has to do with my oldest son. I work so hard and enjoy him so much. They jump all over me; this morning all four of them were in bed with me. My husband was away overnight.

I had two martinis last night and nearly blacked out (*laughs*). That never happens to me. Last night I read a book. I liked the author's approach to suffering. I'm happy when melancholic. It's not unhappy, not masochistic. This is how my mother is. Why do I get so upset with my eldest son? Not yesterday. In fact, I have been very happy with him this week. He's always asking questions and then I get fed up. It doesn't happen with the others. Are they more obedient, submissive? It's my fantasies. I know I'm hurting him because he now has nightmares and doesn't want to be alone in his room. He was up last night until 2:00 A.M. and I said he could come in my bed and he did. I've been with him more than with any of the others. When he was a baby, I was constantly with him and gave him more than I gave the others. The first nursemaid we had, when he was about two years old, was very cruel with him. When he was five, I started working and wasn't home much. Now he asks, "Do you love me?" and I take him in my arms and say, "Sure I do." I'd never ask my parents that. I think you only ask it if you are sure your parents do. If there is any doubt, you don't ask. I wouldn't ask my mother. It would be too embarrassing. By asking she might think I was doubting. I *was* doubting (*chuckles*). That's why I didn't ask. It was too painful for me. What if she said, "No." Not by words. I know if I asked, she would cry and I'd feel guilty for asking. That's how I conclude Tom knows I love him (*laughs*). He gets childish, sits on my lap and asks so coyly, "Mother, do you love me?" He asks in a tone that shows he is sure.

Yesterday my five-year-old daughter, Beverly, said, "I'm the only one in the house who doesn't have a boyfriend. I want one like father, but there is no one like father." I told her certainly she'd find one to marry like father. Then she asked me, "When you die, can I have your pearls? When you die, can I have your dress?" So I said, "You can have them right now." Then I was guilty for making it so conscious. There was a twelve-year-old boy and Beverly put a cigarette in her mouth, walked slinkily, and said, "That's how I'm going to be when I grow up. I'm going to be just like you (meaning me) when I grow up." I love her so much. When she cries, I just melt. That's how I want to feel toward my oldest son. That's how I used to feel until three years ago.

The other day I was mad at Will. We had to be somewhere and I was late and he told me to hurry. I don't like that. I know when I have to hurry. And Tom is the same. If I tell him to eat he loses his appetite. I'm the same, but yesterday when I was angry at my husband, I took it out on Tom. Maybe that's what I do—displace hostility to him. When I'm angry at my husband, I used to show it plainly. We did not have real fights; we got on very well. The only time of tension in the marriage was before I was having our first son, when I foolishly went back home to have him. The only two deliveries that were any trouble were the two when I was at home. There I had anesthesia and I screamed. For the others, when away from there, I had no anesthetic and didn't suffer. Before we had our first son we fought over where to live—with Will's family or mine. I criticised my family but Will couldn't stand a word being said against his. The tension with Will was for the few months while we lived in a small house near his parents, which they had offered to us. We realized though that to save the marriage we couldn't live there. I always got along very well with my father-in-law.

I've always had migraines. They began when I had our second child and Will's parents were visiting, staying with us. There was much friction with my mother-in-law. Once a man came for packages and was directly insulting to me. I said, "I'm the lady of the house," and the man said, "What, you a lady!" My father-in-law just sat and didn't say a word. I said, "If you don't leave, I'll let this dog loose." The dog wouldn't have done anything but he looked ugly and the man left. That was the cause of the first headache. I thought my head would burst, and I had to go upstairs.

ANALYST: What do you think is the gist of this hour?

PATIENT: Based on the hostility to my parents?

ANALYST: Doesn't this relate to your love-needs, which we discussed in the last hour, and to me in the transference? Now you are concerned with my reaction. Will I love you? Can a child ask a mother if she loves him? You couldn't ask your mother this. Did mother love you? You want a man like your father, but if you are insulted or I don't help, like father-in-law, then you give me warning of your anger.

4th hour

PATIENT: Oh, I'm a living image of hostility. Before our last hour I had what I thought was a hangover but afterward, that afternoon and evening, I had a terrible migraine. My sister Lois invited me to dinner, my husband went to get the children, and they all ate there. I stayed home with Annie because I did not want to go there, especially with a headache. Lois has migraines too and has one every time father and mother come to visit; Lois gets sick, gets all upset, talks so much and so fast. Lois came over and told me about her husband, about father and mother coming in a few months, and I couldn't get a word in and was angry. I took a pill to sleep, thinking everything would be normal in the morning, but the headache was not gone on Saturday and I don't know what I did all day. Sunday I fought with everybody. We went on a picnic and my husband said, "Did we come for you or for the children?" The poor children. I was mad at you, mad at work, mad at everyone.

ANALYST: Let's go into the anger at me. What was your last hour?

PATIENT: I don't remember very well. I remember Beverly wanting to marry someone like her father and the man who insulted me and I threatened to unleash the dog. Why do I fight the transference so much? I'm always looking for excuses not to continue analysis and analysis is you, now. I guess I get mad when I realize you can't give me anything.

ANALYST: Meaning?

PATIENT (*laughs*): Love. I realize it but continue fighting it. I thought: What the heck is analysis for? This is all related to my son too. I haven't been so harsh with him as I was yesterday. I have the thought I shouldn't seduce my son as my father did me, meaning getting *too* close—although in a way it helped me. I can express the hostility to my mother. That is no problem. The problem is what I have to father. I can't even see it, but why else would I fight any relationship that could be close. Because I'm afraid of my fantasies? I was not afraid of father. It was that I was afraid he would leave me. The first time I saw mother and father in the same bed, after that I never went into that room. They slept in separate beds. I must have been about seven. Why do I remember now the one time he beat me up? Actually he hardly touched me, but I couldn't stand the others laughing. He was laughing himself. It was so ridiculous.

ANALYST: Why else do you fight the transference now?

PATIENT: For fear I would admire you so much that my husband would lose out, and I don't want that to happen. Or, maybe I'm afraid it's my father who would lose out, and I don't want that. That is the most, I think, father.

About two years ago I was working with someone and found I was comparing him with my husband, so I just left the job. I had found myself acting like a teenager. I quit the job I liked the most in my life. *(Weeps gently.)* I think since then I've been fighting everyone. *(A few more tears.)* My husband doesn't think so because I don't show it, but I'm more myself when I'm alone. With my husband, if I want to argue or say something, I'm always afraid of getting him into trouble. When alone, I can be definite, outspoken, but with my husband I wait for him to talk.

ANALYST: The problem of fighting the dependent love needs, which is now appearing in the transference to me, existed before you met me, so now it is a better situation because you can discuss it all. You are embarrassed to tell about it, and to do something about it is, of course, impossible. On the other hand, to do nothing is frustrating. Even the feelings, the trouble, the guilt regarding husband and father, you had before seeing me. You left a job you liked the best because of this.

PATIENT: I guess the migraines are a form of hostility to my husband. That is the right person; lots of times I am angry at him and can't express it.

ANALYST: Is it because as a child your father was a god but your husband is of your own generation and, like yourself, he has love needs?

PATIENT: Probably it is. Also I found out yesterday that all my free time is taken and Will and I have almost no free time together and this really made me mad. But, the migraine is when I can't get mad.

When I get mad, I don't show it, except maybe with our oldest son, poor soul. Otherwise I get along fine with everyone, but now I'm more relaxed, less hostile. This morning Tom got his marks, a new kind, no grades, only that he is not working up to his ability but is above average in sports. He knows if he doesn't work harder, he won't go to the next grade. He could go to summer school. This morning he cried; he didn't want to go to school, he doesn't like it. All my guilt was aroused. I took him on my lap and said, "What is it, dear? Is it the students? The teachers? What?" He just said, "No, no, no." But then he went. I guess he is resigned to staying in the same grade. All the others are doing very well. The first time I had problems with Tom was when I was working at the place I liked so much, two years ago, and where I liked that man. I've always had something strange with Tom. He looks so much like me. When I see him, it is like seeing myself. I thought it was only my imagination, but others have said the same. He has a way of looking and then people say he is exactly like me. I guess I should do as my father and mother did. If we got bad marks, they would just laugh and say, "Next time they'll be better." Yet with this attitude we all studied and did so well. In the mornings, from seven o'clock I try to get them up and off to school, especially the two boys and especially Tom. Beverly is always up; I don't have to tell her anything.

I had two dreams last night. In the first one I was married to Will but was in love with this boy whom I first liked and left. In the dream I thought: How can I leave my husband? M. H. was the father of my children, not Will. I was having sex relations with M. H., and Will and mother came in and said, "How can you do that? You're married!" But I just passed it off and they didn't seem to mind much. I just loved M. H. and had to go with him no matter what. I was embarrassed that they saw me, but so what.

The second dream was long, but all I can remember is my going to have sex relations with a man but his penis was cut or stitched somehow so he could not have an erection and somehow it was my fault. But I didn't have too much anxiety.

ANALYST: Associations?

PATIENT: M. H. is a boy I went with for three years, and it was all very innocent. When I didn't love him, he was in love with me, and when I began to fall in love with him, he withdrew. We were too young. He was my first love, and I haven't seen him since then.

ANALYST: Do you want to say right off what you think these dreams mean?

PATIENT: Yes. I think M. H. is really Will and that Will is you. You are the one who is watching.

ANALYST: So you were in love with M. H. and feel you must go with him no matter what?

PATIENT: That's my unconscious. That I love Will more than anything. I'd like to leave all the childish things behind and everything should be the way it should be. *(Laughs.)* Anyway, in the second dream I fix him, just in case, *(laughs)* so I know nothing will happen.

ANALYST: Freud said all dreams have "the mark of a beast." Is there any other possibility in the first dream?

PATIENT: Yes. M. H. could be you—with mother and father watching.

ANALYST: When you are a small child loved by father and by mother, they are apt to seem like gods. When you are grown and the sexual component is so much stronger, there is usually a residue of the wishes of the small child for the love of the great, all-loving parents, and these are intensified if there was too little or too much insecurity. Some of this gets transferred to the analyst.

PATIENT: Yes, and I don't lose the image. Even though father today isn't such a hero anymore. So I guess I can't really satisfy it. If I tried, I would only feel guilty.

ANALYST: Yes, as you said, it is a matter of enjoying what you have.

PATIENT: And not being too frustrated by the wishes and

images of childhood, I guess. I never thought I would be able to tell this at all. I felt myself blushing so, but not too bad. I wonder if I could have told anyone else? My feeling is I could not have; that is one reason I came to you.

ANALYST: You see how much better it is when it is all out frankly, and I hope you'll be the same with the guilt, the hostility, or anything else.

PATIENT: That doesn't worry me; the sex did, but if I'm angry at you or hostile to you, don't worry, I'll tell you and I suppose it will, as here, show in the dreams.

8th hour

PATIENT: This week I had a lot of feelings—I was happy, pleased, relaxed, nothing bothered me. But the other evening there was a small party and Will was in a side room with Mrs. L. and I walked in. She and Will were talking. I tried to show nothing. She looked apologetic that the door was partly closed. I guess she had her fantasies; and I had mine. Later Will said, "How can you be mad because I had the door partly closed?" I said, "You guessed it." I've been jealous of beautiful women, but toward Mrs. L. I never thought I'd be like that. I don't show it but inside I'm so mad my mind blocks; I can't think too well. Later I thought this goes back to jealousies with father about mother. I'm not jealous about the idea of Mrs. L. sleeping with him, because she is not attractive. If she were, I would be. But I'm jealous because she has a maternal quality and he talks to her—the same pattern I have toward him and his mother. The next day I thought it over but found I ignored Will and Mrs. L. Yesterday I had a virus and decided to stay home. For five minutes I had it all figured out and was relaxed, and then it was gone again.

ANALYST: Therefore you can see that insight alone in

analysis is not enough. Working it through is vital.

PATIENT: Could it be my own guilt? That I am guilty because of my fantasies about you, and I say they think that way when *I'm* the one who is. This is how I must have felt with my mother. Maybe that's why I get so mad—because I'm afraid it's not beauty that counts. No matter how attractive I was to father, there was something else, and I fear Will will find it in Mrs. L. just as father found it in mother.

ANALYST: Sometimes it is in part being a child and dependent versus being an adult and responsible—immature versus mature.

PATIENT: It could also be rivalry with my sisters. I know better, but it makes me mad to think she might think she could possess him, not physically but spiritually, like an office wife. It goes back to you *(laughs)*. It's a projection of what I feel about you. Let me see if I can explain it. I'm afraid of my own wishes. If I cannot have you sexually, then I want you intellectually, spiritually. That's it, because I feel more relaxed, but then it's gone. I can see it with father. I'll study more, be what father will admire, and still things remain the same between father and mother. Therefore the frustration and therefore the hostility. After all I've done, you and father have done nothing about it. Everything I try to do is to please you; and then I'm afraid I'll say something I shouldn't say; for example, the last visit I asked, in a disguised way, how I was doing, if I was pleasing you. That was after seeing the girl whose appointment is before mine. I guess you have her in analysis too. It left me with a bad feeling. I shouldn't have asked.

I think I don't get jealous with men; it's a female rivalry unless I feel someone is in a position better than mine. I get on best when I'm in the top position. I feel I know women and their reactions. I should, after living with mother and my sisters all my life and being the youngest and having to be careful and repress things, which I guess was bad. I'm so embarrassed about my feelings toward Mrs. L. although I never am about straight jealousy. I just tell Will openly.

ANALYST: Is there anything else about the girl you saw here? We want to be sure and have it out in the open.

PATIENT: Before I saw her I always felt that I should be cold and distant, just another patient, and so I controlled everything and acted that way. Until I saw her. Her car was parked next to mine and we passed each other and I felt funny and got back the same thought. I guess it goes back to feeling that I'm only another daughter. When I was home two years ago, they said that Roberta, my next older sister, has replaced me as father's favorite. She is very intelligent—there goes intelligence again. I would feel that if I asked mother to go shopping with me, she would say no and then I'd find her in the store shopping with Roberta.

ANALYST: Probably that childhood pattern is a little too strong. You want to be more mother's favorite than you feel you are, and you also want to stay father's favorite.

PATIENT: Am I jealous from frustration or from fear? From which do you lose more?

ANALYST: The simplest is historics—repetition of the pattern, the love needs, frustrations, jealousies.

PATIENT: I can see that.

ANALYST: Also dynamics. If you feel toward me as an office husband, then there is guilt and you expect your husband to have Mrs. L. as an office wife. Punishment fits the source. You are hostile because you are jealous and the punishment is therefore in the form of jealousy.

PATIENT: Now I see that when I was jealous as a teenager, I got revenge by going out with boys, doing what mother and father did not like.

ANALYST: Yes. But now you are a wife and mother and need not be so absorbed in how much mother and father love you and all the jealousies over them and your sisters.

We need to see the patterns clearly; only then can you outgrow them and reduce their influence on your present life as an adult.

PATIENT: I had a dream two nights ago that Will died. Then I saw one of our best friends. Her husband died leaving her with four children and she married her husband's best friend, *(laughs)* who is a doctor! *(Laughs.)* In reality one of our best friends had a husband who died. When she remarried, even though it was after two years, the community talked so, they destroyed her, and I sided with her and fought them. Well, in the dream, she told me my husband was dead. At first I felt anguish but not as I thought I would. I thought I could never stand it at all, that not the others, nor religion, nor anything could keep me from falling apart; but in the dream I took it nicely. It wasn't that bad, and I went to a party but didn't want people to know Will died.

ANALYST: Associations?

PATIENT: My childhood pattern must be strong. Here it is again. If Will would disappear, I could marry you. I wouldn't kill him (*laughs*); I only want him to disappear. But why wouldn't I want anyone to know? Because of guilt? I didn't want anyone to pity me or start attacking me as they attacked that friend of mine. They taunted her with incessant gossip: "Now she will remarry soon." She did, but after two years of hell. When I was thirteen, I went with a fellow and talked of my ideas for the future and he said, "Why do you have so many castles in the air? They never come true. If you want something, think of the opposite." I must have been just ripe for this because it made a great impression on me, and I did it. I always feared father or mother would oppose what I wanted. Before my marriage, I fantasied that Will would leave me, and later in marriage I imagined that he would treat me awful, and of course the reality is the opposite. But still

I fear that if I want something, I won't get it, so I do not dare wish for it. Is there a connection with fantasies I've had of being deserted, or finding my friend injured or dead on the road? I was a martyr; no one loved me or cared about me. Real life is just the opposite. This must be a way of punishing myself. If I want the love of father, I shouldn't think of it or God would punish me as if it were a sin. I had two uncles but mother said that it was a sin, that it was not nice to undress in front of them, when I was a child. By their telling me what not to do, I learned what went on and what I could do. At school I was reprimanded because once my brother picked me up at school and put his arm around me under an umbrella in the rain. Where sister went, you couldn't shower without a robe on. So we got ideas—everything made into sex by their telling us what to guard against.

Father saved me from mother with all the sisters around her, but he gave me a little too much. Father was better with me. I had a boyfriend when I was fifteen and my sisters could never have any males around the house and my oldest sister at that time, when I was fifteen, had to have a chaperone although she was going with her fiancé. At the same time father was so good to me, made more of a feeling of obligation and maybe guilt in me toward him. Once I went to a party and father objected because there was no chaperone there that he knew, but he let me go and gave hell to mother for not seeing that there was someone he knew at the party. If I felt hostile to father, I couldn't show it, and still can't, while to mother and sister I could show open hostility. But I pity him and would always find excuses for him. I can't see myself mad at him. I could be scared to death about what he would say to me.

ANALYST: In this dream there is a pattern that has appeared in your other dreams. There is always a triangle. If you have one, you must be rid of the other.

PATIENT: Yes, if I have one, someone else must go (*laughs*). So could my husband dying also be you? (*Laughs.*) That would be easier. Why wasn't I severely shocked? I guess I'm still fighting psychoanalysis. Maybe I don't want to lose the dependence on father. I feel wonderful after leaving you for a few hours and then get so mad—mad at being in psychoanalysis. Why am I so mad? Is it fear to leave all things behind? Fear to grow. Has it to do with hostility to father which I don't want to see? I always thought the relation to father was the only thing I had in life and I fear finding out that it was not as I thought. I don't want to see him as he is because I idolized him so, even though it is childish. That image I created isn't so.

13th hour

PATIENT: Yesterday I felt angry at father. Why did he have to be the way he was? How sadistic he sometimes was, even in games. Then I began to think that there was something behind this. I always talk of the same thing, and it goes back to resistance to going on with analysis. Father and mother were as they were. Why do I not want to go on? It comes back to the obsessive ideas of the breast and genitals. My fear is of saying that I'm afraid these mean I'm homosexual. I've thought of it so much. I can't even cry here. My family cry so easily, and I can't. (*Laughs.*) I know I'm not attracted to women. Of course I was around so many women in my family all the time. I didn't think much about it until I heard L. B. He talked about how a certain woman was really homosexual. He seems to think all women are lesbians. But why did I react to him?

The first time I knew about homosexuality was at college. I was sixteen and I gave a girl a ride home every day and she was mannish and then mother forbid me to see her, and I insisted that mother tell me why. So eventually she did, and then I became conscious of it. This girl later married, but she is the same in her manner, and she got control of her husband's business. Her husband is an alcoholic. She isn't actively homosexual—she is just so aggressive. She hides behind being a woman to do the most aggressive things—mostly to get money for herself.

I'm blank now. No. I've always said I pity men. At parties the women complain about being at home, the house, the kitchen, the children, the maids, and so on, while their husbands are free of all these things and are at the office. But it makes me mad. How do men feel to know that all the income depends on them? I'd rather stay home and not worry about where it comes from.

I had a dream last night. Will and I were in San Francisco and we went to visit a couple at their home. I said how happy we were to see them, and the wife said, "Oh, we were in Chicago a few weeks back . . ." and I was so mad and hurt that they were here and didn't call us.

ANALYST: Associations?

PATIENT: Sunday my brother was here in town and he didn't even phone, but I thought nothing of it. It never occurred to me that it would hurt me. It must be something else, but I can't see anything in the transference; can't place you in there.

ANALYST: What do you associate with San Francisco?

PATIENT: In San Francisco I was very happy away from everything, not working, doing nothing, enjoying myself, no problems with my husband or with the children. No problems.

ANALYST: What about the couple? Any associations?

PATIENT: All our happy times were with this couple. They had lots of money, a top position and family. Whatever we wanted their father would supply. Since we've left, they have suffered. They've lost all their money; had to live for a while in poverty; did not have enough food; she had an operation; they can't have children; she got T.B. We don't have the money or anything to help them. My wish is to have friends like them again. Everyone is so busy. If you visit someone here, you feel you are bothering them and must get baby-sitters and make all kinds of arrangements. You can't just ask someone over for a drink, so Will and I go out by ourselves.

ANALYST: What does this hour mean?

PATIENT: I don't know. I still want to leave analysis. I am fighting being here in analysis.

ANALYST: Why?

PATIENT: Fear of a change, fear of what I'll find out about myself—like that I'm homosexual. Father always said that if he had a homesexual in his family, he'd kill him, or rather he'd wish he were dead.

ANALYST: You are married and have a good sex life. Obsessive ideas usually come less from sex than from hostility. What is the connection between this and your resistance to analysis. Is it fear of being in love with the analyst? That is, are your dependent love needs, as to mother and father, now sexualized and transferred to me?

PATIENT: Yes, then to be homosexual would neutralize it!

ANALYST: Yes, like the dream you had in which the penis was stitched so there was no erection, just to make sure. (*Patient laughs.*) The dream you just told about is a defense by your being away in San Francisco. It also shows anger again at feeling not sufficiently loved, accepted. That the couple did not call means such frustration regarding me.

PATIENT: Yes. Yesterday I even thought I knew someone was coming here and thought: He sees him and not me. He doesn't see me enough!

What I told you about my sister Lois a few sessions ago—I've changed and my husband remarked on it and said I would have told her to leave or else been in tears. I was depressed when I told you, but after that the feeling was out and I no longer had it. I told the right person. It was like telling father.

ANALYST: I thought you were more angry than depressed.

PATIENT: True. I was angry. I used to be depressed.

For the first time in my life, for half an hour, I felt some hostility to father. I guess I couldn't allow myself to be angry at him because he is the only one who gave me security. Also everything I have done has been to please him. If I were angry at him, I would lose him and then have no one to please. Of course I shouldn't live just to please one person, like father. I should enjoy things for their own sake. Why do I begin to feel able to handle the hostility to father now? I think because now I have you, taking father's place in my feelings. I think you are so good. Your daughters are lucky to have you as a father. (*The patient weeps and smiles, then just weeps.*) As a child father kept asking me, "Are you sure you are my daughter?" Sometimes he would say he found me in the trash can. Sometimes he said I was the daughter of F. M. He was one of the hands, a huge fellow. He did it to all of us, not only to me. We are a very nice family and father would talk as though we, and our grandparents, were the worst trash. Mother's family was from a small town and made a lot of money and father lost all of mother's money in gambling and then father stopped gambling, drinking, and smoking. Father was constantly depreciating mother and mother's two brothers, although these uncles are really very nice. Once we were in a pinch financially, but whenever we had troubles or problems, they were always there helping.

As a child I saw so many things. When I was four, someone stole father's watch and father caught him and twisted his arm behind him and held a knife to his throat to make him confess. I would have confessed to anything if treated like that. How mother could let me see such things I don't know. I'm glad that generation is out. They all acted like dictators. The new generation is much different and better. Father used to threaten men with a gun to make them vote as he wanted; and I lived through others threatening father's life. A lot of father's friends were the same way.

I think of why I am as I am—because father always questioned my identity. I was too young to know. What I got as a child was only that I wasn't the child of any of them, and thank goodness I did not get father's implication that I was not his daughter. He really has a paranoid jealousy toward F. M., that big fat ranch hand, but thank goodness I didn't get that. This paranoid state has come and gone since I was a child. In fact F. M. was with father for forty-five years and father apparently was always jealous of him. (*Beginning to cry softly.*) He wouldn't let F. M. around if mother were there and father was away. F. M. is fat, heavy, has no teeth, and is really nothing to be jealous of. (*Crying.*)

ANALYST: You will have a better relation with father if you get this all out and resolved.

PATIENT: I know that but I could face the hostility to mother but not to father. I just got cold and shaky inside. Why I told this today—I'm not clear on the connection with today's material, except that I told Will how good you are, and I thought father was good too, but not all the way.

I feel very depressed (*tears still in her eyes*). I can't even talk . . . and I thought my problem was with my mother! I guess I repressed my hostility to my father very well, and Will comes up too. I guess I also repressed things that hurt in my marriage—that I suppose come up in every marriage. But now that I'm conscious of my hostility to Will, I feel less hostile to him. When I first met his friends, he told me to be careful of what I said. With my inferiority feelings, of course I said nothing. He used to tell me I was born lazy and had a relapse. It would make me so mad. He used to be excessively precise, fix everything in exact order, and I never noticed those things. Once we had guests and every time Will went to the kitchen for drinks, they would put a lamp out of position. They did it five times and five times he came in and straightened it. Now he is much better.

I told Will that things he told me hurt me and he stopped when I threatened to hurt him, but I can't deliberately hurt anyone. I *think* of revenge, but I can't *do* anything about it. I tried to help Will with his work, but he has to do everything so perfectly it didn't work out. I said I never would help again and haven't, and he's done much better.

But that is not why I felt depressed. I guess I am depressed because of the hostility to father, which I have hidden all my life. I always got mad when anyone of the family told me the truth about him. In my childhood it was not only father and mother. There was also a cook and her daughter, who was a few years older and we were very close friends. I have all good memories of all the hands, and I was always with them. I was close to father but closer to those hands than to my own parents. I followed father, but there was no sharing with him. He didn't know I was around. Father could never stand the smell of onions or garlic. When he was away, the cook would use onions or garlic and if father returned, everyone would fan, spray, try to get rid of the odors, but if father detected it, he would become furious.

Mother's side of the family is stable, not strange like father's side. My brothers are closer to mother's brothers than to father and this upsets father. Father is the kind that if he wants a car, he buys it whether or not he has the money for it. And then my brothers pay for it. I don't know how father ever paid for our education. When he needed money for our tuition, he would sell a few cattle and then in time replace them. When I was to leave for college, eighty cattle died and mother said I couldn't go, but father said I could and would go. Somehow he managed. We all worked summers. When Roberta wanted a dress, she'd give blood to get the money. This is why I feel guilt—to be hostile to father after all he sacrificed.

ANALYST: We'll have to work on getting rid of this guilt and hostility.

PATIENT: But why can't I be close to mother like the rest? I can't talk about things with mother. When I do, she tells everyone, brings it up at the wrong time, but she doesn't do that with the others. I didn't call her on Mother's Day; I didn't know what to say and then thought this was foolish, acting out, and so on. Tuesday I wrote her as though I started the letter on Saturday and finished it on Tuesday (*laughs*). That is just what mother does to me—starts a letter and then loses it for two weeks. When I write mother about my worries, she ignores them. I know it's childish of me to write her to get her attention but she doesn't write a word. I know it all goes back to looking for love, attention, protection. In writing I was testing them.

ANALYST: Let's discuss the depression. Is it a sense of loss that all is not so perfect with father as you fantasied?

PATIENT: Yes, I kept it from myself and others that he is not so perfect.

ANALYST: How do you solve this?

PATIENT: I don't know.

ANALYST: The first thing to realize is that no relationship is perfect. By analyzing the hostility and guilt you can make this relationship better. This is like with your husband; you said that when you faced the hostility, you felt it less. You also can be more on an adult-to-adult basis with your father.

PATIENT (*interrupting*): That's what I would like. It would be much better.

ANALYST: All the good was and is in the relationship and feelings. Therefore, do not be upset because there are other things too. Times have changed. You are no longer so dependent on father as when you were a small child. Now you have grown out of your parents' home and your emotional life must naturally shift its center to your husband and children, to your own life. You have repressed a great deal. Now, through analysis, it can all come out and you can develop better relations.

PATIENT: The family won't change, I know. But I suppose I can learn to be more at ease with them.

ANALYST: Looser, more adult-to-adult, less of the childhood pattern, as we have said.

PATIENT: The golden image of father is what I expect from men. I either admire them too much or despise them—all or nothing.

ANALYST: I'll be careful (*laughs*).

PATIENT (*leaving*): By the way, I had a dream a while ago that I haven't told you about. I'll tell you next time.

ANALYST: Tell me now, although we won't have time to analyze it.

PATIENT: I am necking like mad with a doctor, and I'm enjoying it! (*laughs*).

14th hour

ANALYST: We let you off from analyzing the dream you told yesterday.

PATIENT (*laughs*): I don't feel like it.

ANALYST: We'll get to it, and as we see all this worked over a little, it will be less embarrassing. Let's try and discuss it.

PATIENT (*after some hesitation*): I was someplace with Dr. R. and we were necking, kissing, and I enjoyed it very much but mother and all my sisters were watching me. I said, "That's your problem; I'm enjoying this." So I continued.

ANALYST: Associations?

PATIENT: This dream was the night of my party. Dr. R. was there and during the party I gave him a kiss on the cheek and my sister saw it and disapproved. I guess in the dream it was you. It's better; I don't mind it, but I hope I always displace it (*laughs*).

Last night I had two dreams. In the first one I was in a room with you and you were behind a desk. I was on a chaise lounge and I thought: Why am I sitting on this chaise lounge? I put you behind a desk as a defense. Suddenly my children were in the room, jumping and screaming around, but I thought: What can I do; that's how they are? So, I went on being analyzed. Will was there then, next to you and was mad at you. He said, "She has been seen by you a long time and isn't cured." You ignored him.

In the second dream I had a baby in my arms. We were in your office. You were there, and I was kissing and loving the baby. Then I went to a car where my family was, and I felt guilty, as though they would think I was doing something wrong in the office with you—wrong meaning sex.

ANALYST: Associations?

PATIENT: I've had guilt feelings all my life whenever I've had to face my family. Is it from the childhood pattern of wanting father and feeling guilty?

ANALYST: The last time the upsetting thing was your hostility to father, not the sex, as in these dreams.

PATIENT: Yes, then why is father not in the dream? The guilt could come from the hostility that I've been repressing. How can I face father after talking with you about my hostility to him? I still feel it is wrong to be hostile, even if unconsciously.

ANALYST: As it becomes conscious, it will reduce. What

about the transference. If you want the loving and kissing, as in the baby dream, from father, is it transferred to me?

PATIENT: If I want it, I must repress the hostility. Do I want to be a baby because I might lose father and your love if I'm not a baby?

ANALYST: You neck and the family objects, is it sex? Do you want father's love but also sex with others to spite father, rebel against him, be independent of him?

PATIENT: Maybe, but then necking was the feeling of being with a person one wants very much, like when I was seventeen years old and wanted the moment to last because I was enjoying it so. In the dream I don't see that I was necking because of hostility to father.

ANALYST: But we watch for the whole pattern to me, not just the love needs. The relation to me can be at least double: (1) wanting my love as though I were father, and (2) sexual interest in me, which is forbidden by father, mother, and sisters.

PATIENT: I don't think the necking was hostility because I was not tense, only happy.

ANALYST: Is the libidinal transference expressed frankly? Is your only reaction embarrassment?

PATIENT (*laughs*): Yes.

ANALYST: But the hostility to father made you cry and feel concern about seeing him. We want to relieve that.

PATIENT: I do feel much easier about the hostility to father. I can think of it now without it being upsetting. My husband told me three days ago that I've changed, and my maid told me that yesterday. She said now I don't get upset when women are angry at me; I just laugh or shrug it off.

The sex is not a rebellion against father. Maybe it is against mother. She is the one who was always telling me about being pure, chaste, and all that. Of course father did too. Maybe in the dream I used the word guilt wrongly; maybe it was embarrassment. Guilty that you should not do it. Embarrassment that you can; more freedom allows you to do it again.

ANALYST: Isn't the question of guilt always connected with punishment?

PATIENT: It was not guilt but embarrassment.

ANALYST: At the moment the associations are of hostility to father and guilt. The dreams show sex, love, and embarrassment, apparently in the transference.

18th hour

PATIENT: Will never voices any open hostility the way I do (*laughs*). When something happens, I get furious and Will says, "So what." But I say, "That's your problem; go and solve it." But I wish I were more like him—so controlled. He always says the right thing, and I get mad and say the wrong thing. Will has changed very much. We got a hostile letter and instead of ignoring it, he wrote a strong letter back. But, I think his problem is that he has a lot of hostility inside that he is not aware of. He is very good to me, never anything else. He couldn't be better. I'm guilty to Will for telling you this.

ANALYST: Why?

PATIENT: I don't know, but I have noticed a change in me since the hostility to father is coming out. For example, I don't argue with our son Tom, don't say nasty things to him any more, and don't feel guilty. He said yesterday, "Everyone in this house is against me," and I saw it was true and took him in my arms. I always used to say, "Don't hit sister or brother," and I guess I never saw it from my son's point of view. I'm much less afraid of cats; I'm still frightened some, but not so my knees shake as they used to.

Father was too freely aggressive and dangerous for me to dare to be hostile to him—like when he beat my sisters Lois and Vivian and they bled. Father said,

"Will you leave your boyfriends?" and Vivian replied, "Yes, right away!" but Lois answered emphatically, "No!" and father went on beating her even though she was bleeding. Father was never this way with me. My sisters married secretly and against father's wishes and are very unhappy in their marriages and are upset emotionally. There must be a connection with why every time I relate to a man, it must be sexually. Of course I don't show it at all. At first it's tense and later I relate very well, feel fine, and can say anything. This is when I see that I like him and he likes me and I needn't be afraid of him. That's why I get along fine with overt homosexuals and with real men, but when they don't have any real identity, then I'm uncomfortable. I can handle hostile men easily but not passive men. This is my problem with L. B. It shouldn't be. My father was hostile, and I learned to handle him.

ANALYST: This has to do with the imagoes you have formed. Probably everyone is easier in the relations they have learned to handle well in childhood. Father was the man in your childhood and you are accustomed to relating to this kind of man; however conflictful it is, you are accustomed to it.

PATIENT: Sure.

ANALYST: Earlier we remarked that your feelings of having to be sure you have father's love is probably a defense against fear of him and fear of losing him if you did not have it.

PATIENT: Yes. Let me just add that this first reacting sexually to men is more since leaving home.

ANALYST: Could this be because of feeling out from under the severe restraints imposed by your father and mother on boys and sex? Maybe this is some hostile rebellion against these restraints?

PATIENT: I thought I was getting so courageous and so much better, but this morning——. Well, it's a long story. I asked B. P. to be in his division, and he approved. Then at a meeting L. B. opposed it. Then R. B. was first flattering and then he opposed it too, saying it was giving too much privilege to make this transfer. It isn't at all. One man stayed three years where he wanted to. Then B. P. got mad and spoke for it. Anyway, this morning I got a letter of acceptance, but at a meeting with B. P. I got the feeling of fear I got with him about a month ago. I block completely—my mind goes blank. He is so protective toward me. I think he sees it—the whole thing back again. I can't think, can't talk. Then I feel I should speak without fear and get angry when he is protective. I think it's because I take him as a father figure, and he knew my sister Vivian, and I fear he will find me less than she. But if I know what it is, why do I have it? There must be something else.

ANALYST: There probably is, but insight alone cannot resolve everything.

PATIENT (*smiles*): Probably basically that is it. Of course now in his division I will see him every day, so I guess I'll solve it. *(Laughs.)* I like that aggressive type, but why did I get depressed?

ANALYST: Why do you think?

PATIENT: I know. I fear that he thinks so much of me and that I won't live up to it, and I'll lose him, meaning I'll lose my father. I don't really care about losing him. He defended me so aggressively, just like father used to. Then after the meeting B. P. asked me to stay and said I'd be seeing him in his division half the time and remain where I am the other half. Actually L. B. doesn't bother me so much any more, but when he makes people miserable, he really does. He got two of the men out, and when he hates someone, he really does. He is so childish. Now I get mad, blow my top in front of him, and leave. I no longer get upset by him inside.

Before all this about the change in the division—really all this happened today—I had a dream. Well, actually, it was two dreams. But first, why do I worry about losing father? I guess it's still the childhood pattern. I had been reading a book and fell asleep. I've been pitying Will so much for what he is going through. His boss is asking for reports on him by his superiors, I think this means something is wrong, although Will thinks it is good. I feel it means things are not going well, and I pity him. He was angry at me the other day; I never saw him so hostile and for nothing at all.

In the first dream I was seeing a client, a woman in a white coat, and I was talking on the phone to Will. I wanted sex with him and thought: Why doesn't the client go out? But Will did not get what I was trying to communicate about wanting sex with him and then a man came into the room and then went out. Then I was going upstairs thinking Will was in the room at the top; and on the way met my son and thought: Oh, he too! But in the room I found Will was not there, and I was mad. I went to bed and it was as though watching myself sleeping and watching myself dreaming. But at times it was just me, not watching myself.

Then in a second dream I was having sex with Will and enjoying it very much but also at the time I had the feeling that there was no one there, that I was alone and only sleeping and dreaming—as though saying to myself: There you are. How stupid can you be, dreaming of sex with your husband and he isn't here. Then Will did come in and I said to him, "She (meaning myself) is asleep" (*laughs*). Then the phone woke me up, and I was mad and said to the person on the phone, "Why call now? I was having a nice dream." The woman who phoned said, "What were you dreaming?" and I said very coyly, "Oh, nothing."

ANALYST: Associations?

PATIENT: Maybe I feel this is the only way I can give love. If Will needs me, I should be there trying to help him.

Yesterday I felt very close to Will, embraced him and didn't want the time to go. I hardly ever feel so close with anyone. Will never admits when he is worried, and so it is hard to comfort him. He covers up right away unless it's about money. And that I don't like, but he covers his personal feelings.

ANALYST: Is there any transference in this dream?

PATIENT: Sure! *(Laughs.)* I feel embarrassed. *(Laughs a little hysterically.)* I was taught as a child that a lady never takes the first step. I'm embarrassed about the urge.

ANALYST: Looking at yourself in the dreams sounds like analysis.

PATIENT: But I was not embarrassed in the dream, so I guess I don't intellectualize it now. No matter if you have the urge, a lady should not show it. That is, I'm embarrassed superficially but not underneath, as shown by the dream.

ANALYST: Again we see the sexual wish. Here it is very frankly expressed but also inhibited from full satisfaction at the last minute, so to speak. This could, of course, still be the defenses against erotic wishes in the transference. In the associations there is the wish to be close and also the wish to comfort Will. It may be that you want to be close to me and have me comfort you. I agree that you are less embarrassed about the erotic component and are handling it well. Also, by transferring the father pattern to me you are learning that you can tell me about sex with your husband without embarrassment, which you have felt toward father. I'm accepting of your sexuality where you felt father was not.

21st hour

PATIENT: Will told me that in our ten years of marriage I have never encouraged him as his boss and his mother have. The wrong examples. But it's true. I can't verbalize it, but I'm always there and when he needs it, I push him. I have a lot of conflict over it. It's sibling rivalry or jealousy or envy toward him. He says he has none to me, so I feel worse. Maybe that's why I don't encourage him, but he's so sure of himself. If we discuss something, and I have an opinion—for example, that he should talk to his boss about something—then if it goes badly, he blames me saying it wasn't the right time. If it goes fine though, he says nothing. He is too sure of himself, and I'm too insecure. Actually, as I told him when he says I don't encourage him, he doesn't tell me his worries, except financial ones, and when I do try to encourage him, he rejects me. When I'm angry at my family, I tell Will, but he goes to his mother, tells her how good I am, and then she gets jealous. Then he tells me about how good she is, and I get jealous. I tell him to let me find it out for myself. She *is* good, although I don't get along with her. Will can criticise my family, and I agree with him, but I can't criticise his, although he's better about it now. His mother writes me in such flowery style: My dearest, darling . . . I wrote her plainly that we would be away on the date that she and Will's father wanted to visit (we are planning a trip then), and Will was upset about what I wrote her.

My sister Mabel came. She said she wanted to go to a party with Lois. I didn't want to go because Lois always drinks, gets high, and winds up in a state. Lois had phoned that she would be here, but she wasn't. Mabel asked about Lois and her drinking. I gave in and said we would go see them at the party. Lois behaved very well. She did not drink, but she also didn't come near us. I think my jealousy is improving. Mabel's husband was dancing very close with a girl, a married woman, and Mabel said to my husband, "Why don't you cut in, Will?" Before I could say anything he did. Actually he was scared when the girl then danced so close to him, and he left her the instant the music stopped. I hardly reacted.

Mabel said all was fine at home. Once when the headlights of the car were not working, mother and two of Mabel's children nevertheless rode with father. Mother thinks father is a god; she said everything would be all right because father was driving. Mother sees father as a god and that's how we children always saw him. If mother was sick, when father came home, mother was well. If father did something to the children, it must be correct.

The big incident of the party occurred when someone asked me, "What do you think is the cause of mental illness?" Before I could answer, Mabel said, "Why parents of course; what else?"

After the party I came home and went to bed. I had two dreams. In the first one I was on a beach with my children and the nurse, Annie. I don't know whether or not Will was there. I saw a house—it was your house and a lot of people were there. We went in. Then it was dark and everyone left but I said, "This is Dr. S.'s house and he won't mind if we stay longer." Then you came in to see your family and you did mind and asked what we were doing there, so we left. I was mad and hurt, as though you didn't want me there because it was your family's place.

Then later that night I had another dream. You and I were working together and it was very pleasant—a lot of understanding and we got along fine.

ANALYST: In the first dream, what are your associations to the house with a lot of people there?

PATIENT: You weren't there! I didn't think of it that way (*laughs*). There is a place near home that Will and I thought of buying and mother wrote that Mabel and Jim were going to buy it but it was too expensive. Mabel always wants us to share and asked us to share it with them, and when it is not used, we can offer it to visitors. I wished you would come.

ANALYST: So the least I can do is invite you into my house.

PATIENT (*laughs*): But I still don't know why there were so many people, like a party, but not one. That is what you do, you see people during the day and are at home at night, so I wanted to belong to your family at night and not just come as a patient by day. But why did you reject me in the dream? Maybe it was because I feared I wasn't good enough and was punishing myself.

ANALYST: Why were you with the nurse and all the children?

PATIENT: We came for help. We were on a beach and were coming to get out of the sun. When I was a child, mother always said, "Don't go in the sun; you'll become an albino." This brought the hostility. Why did they tease that way? If father teases me now, I don't care, but a child doesn't know about teasing. Today I would say, "Whatever I am, you are." At least I could take teasing easier, but Vivian suffered under it.

ANALYST: What do you associate to coming in the house in the evening?

PATIENT: Both families were there. I'd like you to meet my family and then we'd be friends, but you didn't want to! *(Laughs.)* So what could I do?

ANALYST: But in the next dream you accept it; we are working together.

PATIENT: I would like to work with you. If I can't have the social basis, I can have the working basis.

ANALYST: In the dream there is the question of allowing the social basis. You think it consciously, so why not in the dream? Is that the punishment?

PATIENT: Yes (*laughs*). You didn't punish me, so I punished myself.

ANALYST: These manifest dreams fit the quite consistent pattern of your wanting to be close—sexually in previous dreams, socially and in working together here. But there is always a triangle situation in which there is jealousy and in which you feel not sufficiently accepted but somewhat rejected, and therefore you are angry. Why don't you permit this exclusive acceptance, without jealousy or frustration, in your dreams? You dream you want it but don't quite get it. Was this a pattern of childhood? And is it kept going at least in part by this guilt, which you feel is so important that it makes you think you deserve to be rejected? And if the guilt is from hostility, then is this a case in which the punishment fits the source? That is, does this mean that the childhood pattern was feeling not enough acceptance and therefore anger and guilt from the anger?

23rd hour

PATIENT: This morning I got angry again. Mabel phoned and asked about staying with us instead of with Lois, but we are painting and I hoped she wouldn't. When she found this out, she said she would stay with Lois, and then I felt rejected, left out, inferior, and angry. I get so mad at myself for feeling that, as though Mabel is mother (she is the most like mother) and that she prefers Lois to me. I try to bring myself back to reality by saying we are painting and she is trying to help me. I'm grown up; if she wants to go to Lois, let her go, and Lois would be more hurt than I if Mabel came to stay with us. I don't need the family and Lois does. I tell myself this all the time. Maybe a central reason I was so happy in San Francisco was that we were far away from the family. When I see them, everything comes out: jealousy, envy, hostility, and then guilt and depression. I guess it's easier than being directly hostile.

ANALYST: This is not really so complicated. This hostility is to members of the family whom you also love, and who also love you; and you are trained to love them, be close, stay together. The hostility goes against all of your training as well as your love feelings.

PATIENT: Yes, we are supposed to be a close family and a model family. I fear that they get together and talk about me as I sometimes talk about them (*laughs*), but it goes back to my childhood. Whenever I saw any of them talking, I would not enter the room. They might be talking about me or the others, but I feel it is mostly when mother is present. Mother is the one who really does. They gossip and have conferences about Lois, and sometimes they do it in front of her—discuss where she is wrong, whether or not she looked at another man five years ago, and so on. I said, "What's the difference after five years?" and then they attacked me, so I got up and left and never discussed Lois again. Lois was in tears.

ANALYST: Biology: all animals after adolescence leave their parents and make their own homes, their own lives. You can't serve two masters—that is, you can't be the child in the parental home and the wife and mother in your own home. The direction is toward independence. If you are emotionally independent of your family, then you can be friendly with them on an adult-to-adult basis. But if you are a love-needy child toward them, then all these problems arise of being loved enough, feeling jealousy, rejection, and so on. You are past thirty, you have a husband, children, home, profession, and friends. Yet, you can see from your associations how much of your emotional life is still occupied with these struggles and conflicts with your parents and sisters. Or, in another aspect, the manifest dreams show occupation with your present life, but they show how much these emotional patterns to parents and sisters since childhood affect your present relationships with people—including, as a sample, the transference to me.

PATIENT: Sure. Outgrowing this is what I've been striving for, but I have so much of the old pattern, of wanting to be back in the family. The family is too strong and always made such a point of being such a model family.

25th hour

PATIENT: All day before coming to see you, I think of what I will talk about and then in the hour I talk of something else. Then sometimes I have nothing to talk about. I guess I have a lot of things but don't want to talk about them.

ANALYST: Why don't you start with anything you want, but remember, just as you've done before, leaving nothing out once you begin.

PATIENT: The only argument I ever had with Vivian was in front of father. It was when Vivian said she had an I.Q. of 140. I was saying that a certain doctor at home was stupid because he could see nothing that was not organic, physical damage. And she said who was I to say that, and I said anyone, a simple cook, can see the importance of feelings in headaches, upset stomachs, and other things. Then Vivian said she herself had an I.Q. of 140 and knows. And I said she might have but she certainly wasn't using it. Later Vivian came into my room and asked why I was upset. I said that I never had taken a stand for my rights and privileges and from now on I would. She said we were all so good. But we always think everyone else is superior in every way to us, but it isn't real humility. Deep inside we don't believe it, and so we use it aggressively and it makes other uncomfortable. We are aggressive and not good. Vivian comes home and tells how stupid a man was not to see certain things, and it was really because he knows Vivian so well and doesn't want to hurt her.

Vivian and Roberta are my most intelligent sisters. Vivian did not study and did brilliantly and poor

Mabel slaved away to pass, but in real life it is the opposite. Vivian has all sorts of troubles while Mabel has a good husband and has accomplished much more although she was not good in her studies.

I get along with my brothers-in-law very well—much better than with my sisters, except for one.

When I was young, father and mother once drove two of my sisters somewhere and left me at home. I was nine years old then. Vivian was also at home with her husband and a friend of theirs, I had a crush on the friend but was young and didn't know it. I was in bed. He came into the room and tried to touch me. Of course I didn't let him at all. I told no one. It was good I didn't or father really would have killed him. I forgot that incident until I was married, and then forgot it again until I saw him. I was revulsed. It has also made me hate my brother-in-law.

I remember mother saying, "Don't trust anyone. Never take into your house any other woman." She had only the most ugly women for maids.

27th hour

PATIENT: I had a dream that two aggressive women were going to seduce father in a hostile way.

ANALYST: Associations?

PATIENT: Two of my sisters visited. Lois has the idea that psychoanalysis makes people hostile to their parents. She fears her hostility to father and mother and is so guilty about this because of the myth of our great family unity. Of course, some of my guilt is because I decided to get analyzed and have gone ahead with it independently of the family. So, it is a sign of my independence of them. Now I begin to see why I have felt guilty, because I see my own hostility to father, to mother, and to my sisters also.

29th hour

PATIENT: I've changed some already. Now I act the way I want to act. But, I don't feel yet the way I want to feel; that is, I don't feel the way I act. For example, at work if someone was mean to me or slapped me down, I used to be so friendly the next day, as though nothing had happened. And then they would slap me down again, and I stayed so smiling and friendly. I just had no respect for myself. Now I take it, say nothing, go on working with the person, but that is that. L. B. and R. B. both are always looking for something to criticize in everyone—all little, picky details. They're concerned with what time someone came to work, not with how well he does the job.

I had a dream last night. In the first scene I was to have an hour with you at a place that was sort of both a home and an office. When I arrived there, the maid said, "Dr. S. told me he had to go downtown on an emergency and you should go there, and he'll see you there." But I had no car and also you had another girl waiting there, so when you returned my time would be up. I chatted with the girl and I was mad, but she defended you and said you had the emergency. Then you returned.

In the second scene of the dream, I'm in the same place, but now I'm sitting on the floor. You were lying with your head in my lap, but I didn't like your face. It was a face I was afraid of because it implied sex—like those sharp guys who flatter you—not the gentle, loving face but completely different. I was afraid of what I saw. The eyes were like what girls call a wolf. It wasn't just the sex but sex was involved. In the dream I thought: I must be wrong; it must be me. Mabel was sitting on the floor and you were trying to convince her that birth control is not bad, that she is stupid to go on having children because she isn't well physically, and I felt it would do no good. Then Mabel went over to mother and said, "See, Mama, he is like that and she (meaning me) will change." I didn't want to argue and tell them you had a reason for saying this, so I just left. I walked down the road.

I'm depressed and I don't know why. You know the dream of two days ago—the aggressive women taking father away. Their hairdo was the kind mother used to have.

ANALYST: Associations?

PATIENT: There's an emergency and you desert me. It's what I want, but fear.

ANALYST: At our meeting yesterday I did have an emergency. We had the hour in the car at the last minute in preference to cancelling it.

PATIENT: Yes, that could be. It was a very good hour. But I had a lot to talk about and suppose I didn't? Now I think mother always told me not to ride in a car with strange men, Mabel asked me how old you were, and whether I was still going to church.

ANALYST: Psychoanalysis mobilizes the hostility and guilt to the family and also shows the sex, which was such an issue—so aroused and so forbidden. In the transference you are angry because you feel rejected, frustrated, and jealous. This shows in the first scene of the dream, which is in your usual pattern. In the second scene your sexual wish is projected onto me. This is consistent with wanting to be close, sexually, socially and in work. But here the sex has a most hostile element, not all love. You defend against the anger at me in the first scene by having the girl defending me, and in the second scene you do so by your own wish to defend me, though in the dream you said nothing. In this scene Mabel criticizes me, but of course that's you—it's your dream and she does your bidding. Probably you took riding in the car as a seduction situation, with the wolf theme and mother's prohibitions. You wish for me to be a wolf but also fear if I were one.

30th hour

PATIENT: At work I have only three more weeks under L. B., and then, thank goodness, I transfer to another department with a very nice boss.

I had a dream last night in which I am at my house, introducing my children to you. You were very nice to them, and I was very proud. Here comes sex, though (*laughs*). We were holding hands, just friendly, but there was also sex. I guess sex feelings must be my way of expressing myself, although in reality I don't express it this way except with my husband. Then we are on a couch and (*laughs with embarrassment*) you want a baby by me because your wife can't have one and you want one so much. I think this is a way to express love for you, but at that moment my psychoanalytic grandfather, Franz Alexander, who I know was your training analyst, came in and took me away with a very paternal attitude.

ANALYST: Associations?

PATIENT: In an earlier dream I tried to be in your house and you wouldn't let me, so here I have you in mine. I am really very proud of my children.

Holding hands is friendly, but there is also a sexual element. When I was a child mother and father always were suspicious of sex—they felt that everything having to do with a man must be sex. Once when I was about seven, Lois' boyfriend was waiting for her a few minutes, and I talked with him and laughed when he told me a joke. Father came in and asked why I laughed. I said I didn't know; then I told him the joke. Father said, "Are you sure?" implying that there was some sex. When I was eighteen or twenty, Mabel's husband picked me up in his car when I was waiting for a bus, and that night father was furious and said that would be the last time I was ever to get in a car with a man. My brother-in-law was always very nice to his children and to me.

ANALYST: What associations do you have to the element in the dream that I want to have a baby with you because my wife can't?

PATIENT: I don't know. I felt I loved you in the dream, but not sexually. I guess I attributed that to you because you wanted a baby. I guess love for me is sex; sex is the most I can give and the most I can get and the product is the child—concentration of two loves. But then I bring someone to rescue me. I can't go through with it although my wish in the dream was to do so. When Dr. Alexander came in, I couldn't and I was mad.

Dr. Alexander analyzed you and the implication is that if you want sex relations with me, Dr. Alexander didn't do a good job. Maybe my sadism is in it. I would destroy a man if the man is weak in his unconscious. It is now coming out. My wish is that I could seduce you, that you would not be as well analyzed as you are, that you would be a man and would feel something toward me sexually. But then I know if this happened, and if this goes back to father, it would destroy everything, as though my father tried anything sexually with me—no matter how many fantasies I must have had. I guess the bitterness I have had has to do with father being too protective and too seductive with me. But I didn't have any idea of what sexual relations were at the time. He gave me too much and too little, but if I gave too much, well, I might have been psychotic for he was all I had. But he let me grow up more than the others. The first boyfriend he allowed in the house was mine.

You know what helped me very much? I had no idea until I got married. Thank God I married the man

I did. Mother said I'd never understand men until I married. I did not have sexual relations as a teenager; and when I married and did, I felt I loved him so much and that what I can give him is sex. For me sex was the demonstration of love. I didn't realize that for many men sex was not love. So many teenage boys are that way. They only think: Did you have sex with her or not? That is why I liked Will so much. He was not that way; he was my friend. Oh, what helped me was this. After I was married and was pregnant, I started to work and had a man as a boss. This was the first man I had worked with. He was in his mid-forties and his wife was upset, so he never talked about her, so it had to happen. I liked him a lot and had many fantasies of rescuing him. Anyway, I openly expressed my liking to him, and he was gentle, smooth, and stayed friendly, but there was no sex. I learned you can be friendly with a man, can even like and be attracted to him, and he need not do anything or make me do anything.

ANALYST: If I understand, you are saying that during your childhood there was a lack of an easy, secure, friendly relation with a man. This was the trauma expressed in the negative. The corrective emotional experience, as Alexander calls it, is to learn that with all these feelings, love needs, sex, frustration, inhibition, jealousy, and so on, you can still have a secure, easy, friendly relationship. And one place you are learning this is in the transference to me.

31st hour

PATIENT: When I left the job with the man I liked, R. T., he should have given me a present, but I felt like giving him something so I did. It was a small thing. Anything expensive would have been out of place. I was angry that he never showed me he liked me. I knew he liked me. Vivian heard that he spoke highly of me and she said no man could speak so highly of a woman and not be in love with her. So there came the sex again and I was angry because it meant I really was not so praiseworthy in myself. But he only said these things because he was in love with me.

When I gave him the present, he said, "You are a sadist." That is the first time he ever said such a thing. Then I thought he was right. I was constantly seductive toward him and he was unhappy with his wife, but he respected me anyway because he knew I liked him too much. In fact, I liked him more than any other man, and I didn't want to upset my home so I left that job. He had the reputation of being a wolf, but he wasn't with me. Now the sexual attraction I had for him, which was so strong, is gone; but I care for him in a way I can accept—I just like him very much. I haven't seen him for two years. That was the first time I ever was attracted sexually to anyone except my husband, and I got scared and left quickly.

About men and sex, mother was more suspicious and malicious than father. As I told my girlfriends, when I never even had the idea, she put it in my mind. Between mother and father for a long time I didn't have a male friend. I realize now why my rebellion against mother and father took a sexual form. Sex was the path for the love needs and also for the rebellion. For everything. I also punished myself with it, feeling guilty. Now I don't feel too guilty. The first man I almost had sex with was because he said we would get married. But thank goodness we didn't have sex and didn't get married. He is so immature. He married a wealthy girl and both are very unhappy in the marriage, which is breaking up. He is full of fears and anxieties. When I saw him later, I'd say hello and did not feel guilty and I thought: How could I ever have been in love with him! He was so weak I felt I had to protect him. At home your past is always present.

They know your whole past but if it goes well with the family, the rest would be okay.

ANALYST: Is the pattern you described toward R. T. what is now in the transference to me? If he did not respond, love you, you are angry; but if he does, then he is taking advantage of you and you are more angry.

PATIENT: Yes, of course, that is transference.

ANALYST: And isn't the problem, then, how to have friendly, good relations despite sex?

PATIENT: Yes. If it were not for sex as rebellion and defiance, then sex alone would not be much of a problem. At the present you are not so much a mother or father figure in the transference, but the opposite. Being analyzed alone is a defiance and rebellion of father and mother; and of course in the transference the sex is also a rebellion.

ANALYST: If it weren't for this traumatic pattern toward father and mother, then there would be nothing to rebel against. It is no longer as it was in childhood. You are a wife and a mother; you have a husband and children and your own life; you have grown up and handle everything quite well. I have no dictates or restrictions as to what you should or shouldn't do, and therefore, there is nothing to rebel against.

33rd hour

PATIENT: I am much better in relation to Will and other men. I used to feel that I should not and could not even look at any other man and if I did, then I always compared him with my husband, and often this was to Will's detriment. Now I feel I can have sexual feelings toward other men without being disturbed by them and can like other men without comparing my husband with them. This probably goes back to father and even more to mother—all the pressure not to look at a man or be alone with one. When I was first married, a man asked me to dance and I did not want to. I thought: Why should he ask me when I'm not going any further than to dance with him, when I won't give him any more than that? Now I feel I can be friendly with you—friends without comparing my husband with you or disturbing my feelings toward him.

37th hour

PATIENT: I am taking part of my vacation time this week. I'm afraid if I stayed, L. B. might drive me really to jump on him or to do something I would be sorry for; so when Annie said she had to leave for a week, I took advantage of this. *(Beginning to weep.)* I've felt this way since yesterday. Why is this man, L. B., upsetting me so? I must find out because I'll meet many like him. I must solve it myself. I don't want help from anyone. I never felt like killing anyone, but I feel like killing him. With his horrible sarcasm, he tries to prod me in a meeting. Regardless of what I say, he does the opposite and the wrong action is taken and others suffer. So now I just won't give him my opinion on a decision that it is his responsibility to make. He gets so hostile and goads me. Doesn't he know that when he drives a person to be so tense that they could hit him? Then he asks an opinion and says, "What you say will not count against you." But whatever I say, he picks it up and attacks. Finally, yesterday, I began to cough, like in the first interview with you, and I went out coughing; I guess to throw him out of my craw. But I must find out why he upsets me so much. I feel like my daughter Barbara, she's three and a half. She's too small to hit back; she hides behind me and yells, "You are a queer and a sausage!" and then she runs off. She doesn't know what it means.

I was mad at you too yesterday. I told Will I was not going back to analysis with you any more.

ANALYST: Why?

PATIENT: I felt rejected yesterday. Don't ask me why! *(Angrily.)* I displace it to others, but it's you!

ANALYST: Why did you feel rejected?

PATIENT (*irritably*): I don't know! It's too much for me to be angry at you. More than I can stand.

ANALYST: I don't mind. I'm not your father or mother and you can be angry at me, and we'll just discuss it in a friendly way.

PATIENT: All my life, if anything like what happened with L. B. would have happened, my father would have gone over and that would have been the end of L. B. But I know that is wrong and he won't always be here, and it's time I learned to handle situations myself. That's how father has protected, not just me, but all of us. So I guess that is why I'm mad at you; because you are not helping me, but I don't want you to! I can accept it from father but from no one else.

ANALYST: You want either for father to beat him up or for you to do it. Is that it?

PATIENT: That is right. My pattern is to beat up. The treatment is that father should beat him up, or I should, or someone should, but my pattern is he should be beaten up. He is feminine and manneristic and looks me up and down, sensually, and I feel like saying, "Take your dirty eyes off me!" His hostility is mostly against women. Of course I don't show everything; I wouldn't give him the pleasure of knowing I'm upset.

ANALYST: One other thing. In the last hour we had some timing problems. I was late and then we couldn't run over at the end of the visit. Were you angry with me because of that?

PATIENT: I don't know. I wrote my father a birthday letter and hesitated to send it, but of course I did. I thanked him for all his help in my life and for being a model of what people can be, especially when there are troubles. But it is hard for me to write, because what

I say is always used against me. I try to be more loving to mother but can't. I love her very much inside but whenever I open myself to her, she hurts me. Maybe it is my fault because I expect too much. Mother has always loved me, and we are closer than a lot of other mothers and daughters, but we're not close compared with how she is with my sisters. Mother is neutral. For violence, I remember father; for love, I remember father. When I was four or five, I had a middle-ear operation and they gave me no anesthetic and when I cried, the surgeon slapped me. Father was outside and he rushed in and grabbed the surgeon. They told him to stop or the surgeon would not finish, so he quieted down. That's something they told me. My memory is of being in bed, propped up on pillows, and father being very attentive and loving to me.

When I was about eleven or twelve, I wanted to be a teenager and asked mother for high heels. Mother said I was too advanced in every way for my age, and I was. I was the last child and of course looked forward, and no one told me anything. Mother said no, but father would have the last word. So, I went to him and he said yes. Mother said father always said yes to me.

The time I nearly flunked in first year of college, I was scared to death. The dean of women wrote my mother. Among other things, she asked if mother knew I had a boyfriend. Mother did, and father said the dean should mind her own business. The dean said I must straighten out or I would be dropped. Father said I wouldn't go back there anyway, and he arranged for me to go away to a different college, and that is one of the things I am most grateful to him for.

Returning to the letter. I write to father but rarely write to mother. Before I was married it was almost the opposite. I guess before I had Will I was more dependent on mother. The feeling is that I don't want to find out that I love her very much. I'm afraid of it.

This way I can keep distant and don't let mother and my sisters affect me so much. If I open myself to mother, I fear being hurt.

ANALYST: There is a distinction between loving and being loved.

PATIENT: That's it; I'm afraid I won't be loved as much as I want. I felt I was and am loved by father, so that's no problem. So we're back at the beginning (*laughs*). I want to love father, to give him my love, and I want mother's love.

ANALYST: Father gave you his, so you want to give yours. Is it that mother never gave as much as you wanted?

PATIENT: Yes, and I'd like not to be dependent on her, to just love her.

ANALYST: Are the dependent love needs toward her the issue?

PATIENT: Sure. But do people change?

ANALYST: Quantitatively, and with time, experience, and practice, yes.

38th hour

PATIENT: Will and I are planning a two week vacation this summer at my parents' home. The children don't want to go in spite of the riding, the country, and many other things I'm sure they'll love. Annie doesn't want to be left alone with the children, but she would agree. I would feel guilty going without the children though, but we must get away. Otherwise Will will be working so hard on the house and I'll get caught up in it myself. And if we are here, even though we're on vacation, the office is sure to call anyway. And if we stay here, we will spend more than if we go away. We would not stay with the family but in a house that is on a nearby ranch. Will's parents are very devoted to us and to the children, and we could also stay with them.

On the way here I thought I would get angry at you. I don't know why. I suppose it is related to all I said yesterday about how much I love my father. Let me see if I can explain. Sometimes, like coming here today, I start to get mad at you. I think: I don't want to come. And yesterday, all I said about loving my father is a way to repress my hostility to you. If I love, I love; why must I say it? It must be a defense to convince myself, because there is hostility underneath. Really I feel both the love and the hostility, but when I start to get mad at you, I try to excuse you. I think how nice you are and all, but I feel some guilt.

ANALYST: Why then did you get angry at me?

PATIENT: I don't know. I'm afraid to go to work next year in the new division with people I don't know, and that you will find I'm not as intelligent as your other women patients.

ANALYST: What is the solution?

PATIENT: It is the pattern of my sibling rivalry.

ANALYST: But how can you solve it?

PATIENT: I don't know. I just see it. I don't know.

ANALYST: To see it is the first step; but now you need to correct it, to see that I am not like father and that to please me you need not be so intelligent. I don't watch for it, don't think of it, and don't compare you with my other women patients.

PATIENT: I know it.

ANALYST: But you didn't say it. We have to discuss it very openly, back and forth, to see the reality and correct the childhood pattern.

PATIENT: Why do I feel guilty and mad at myself when I tell you these things about this feeling of rivalry, of comparison with my sisters and with others? Mother and father said you shouldn't fight with your sisters, be jealous, and envy them. Not only did they say this, but father also said, "When I grow old and must depend on my children, I'll kill myself." And he said this many, many times.

ANALYST: What is the connection?

PATIENT: I don't know. I just thought of it. Maybe it is

that when we children showed rivalry and jealousy, mother felt like dying of anguish. They couldn't stand anything that is not love. Like when I openly said that Lois tried to destroy my way of life, and mother heard of it and hasn't written. I can't be honest.

ANALYST: Therefore your fear you can't be honest with me, and you have guilt because of this.

PATIENT: Yes, and it is related to death. If we argued, father would say, "Watch out, mother will have a heart attack. Watch out, you will kill mother." Mother actually has a perfect heart.

ANALYST: You were not brought up to see that everyone has sibling rivalries and that there is a difference between feelings and behavior. Could you ever discuss the sibling rivalry?

PATIENT (*laughs*): I sure couldn't!

39th hour

PATIENT: I took a vacation day today, and all day I feared that the phone would ring—from the company. L. B. thinks we are slaves, as though he is doing us a favor to let us work there. B. P. is obscene but without any feeling. It's just a mannerism, not like L. B. If they would lose B. P., I don't know what would happen. Thank goodness I'll be directly under B. P. soon. B. S., who is now assistant director, makes the craziest decisions and is so rigid. It may be partly because L. B. works people against each other. This is the first time in my life I've felt like fighting so much. I don't fight, but I feel like it. If it continues after I change to the other division in two weeks, I'll leave.

Yesterday when I left you, I continued to feel guilty for what I said about the sibling rivalry.

Maybe part of all these troubles are my fault because I expect too much from people. I mean, if I have a friend, he or she is always a friend. We can argue and squabble, but it doesn't affect the friendship. A friend once told me, "You don't want to know the people you work with too well; you don't want to know their limitations, to be too close." I can't work with people in an indifferent way, as though they are pieces of furniture. I want to know what they are like inside, even if I don't get along with them. I am friendly with everyone at work but I don't lose my authority. It is warmth. L. B. lacks warmth. But why can't I work with people who are not warm? That is my problem. L. B. attacks me for being warm to people, but that is how I am.

ANALYST: Is there a connection with your remark about being guilty for sibling rivalry?

PATIENT: Yes. But let me think what . . . something about telling you these things.

ANALYST: Telling me what is wrong with these others?

PATIENT: Yes, that's it. But . . .

ANALYST: Could your anger at how you are treated by L. B. and B. S. be part of the pattern of your telling me, father or mother, about your sisters, complaining that your sisters don't treat you well?

PATIENT: Yes, but if I told father, he would say, "They get along and you don't, so it must be your problem." I have no guilt regarding L. B. The only guilt is for my telling you about B. P. or about the woman I'm to work with next year. I should wait and see, but I fear you will think it's my problem.

ANALYST: We know it is your problem.

PATIENT: Yes. I saw the woman patient who preceded me and felt guilty because I realized I was jealous, but I have none of that with younger people. I only feel very protective and get along with them very well.

40th hour

PATIENT: I went back to work this morning. L. B. was all

right. Anyway I decided life is too short to be bothered with some people, and I'm going on and enjoy it as I have. Maybe that is why Will and I get along so well. We both try to enjoy every day and every minute. To do this one must learn not to worry about people and how they are.

I've also realized why I've been so upset about L. B. I think it is the rivalry—that I show you that he isn't much, that he is less good than I. When I saw this, I did not feel guilty, but I felt better. It's true though that he is not very nice to me in reality.

ANALYST: What about my having to cancel our hour yesterday and its being uncertain today?

PATIENT: That is the first part of my associations—that nothing matters enough to bother me. I lived all this far without you, so why be upset. Now I think I see that what I've been fighting is the dependency on you. I hate to be dependent on anyone, except Will, that's enough. Just as I hate to be dependent on father and mother because of the kind of people they are. I've tried every way not to be, especially to mother, not so much to father. I think it boils down to this: I want to be dependent on mother because I never had the security with her that I wanted and I fight this. I know father loves me, gave me all he had, so it's very different. I'm sure of him. I can be away from father for years, and I don't long for him; I don't care and I don't mind. I know that when I go back, he will be the same. He will never stop loving me, turn his back, or doubt me. I don't have to prove anything to him nor he to me. I am what I am because I owe it to him. I sometimes wonder what would have happened to me if father weren't as he has been. (*Beginning to cry.*) My children ask me if I love them. I wouldn't have dared to ask my mother that. Nor would I dare to now —I'd fear what she would say. When I realized mother was not as close with me as with the others (*crying freely*), I tried then to get close to father. Mother is good; she is considered the best mother. The house was always full of teenagers. She is sweet, but when I couldn't find in her what I wanted, I turned to him. When my sisters said I clung to him, I got mad, but I never sat on his lap after I was five. The others used to send me to ask him for money of permission to go to the movies. He used to call me his weakness, but I have never felt lonesome for him, although I have for mother.

ANALYST: So father is no great problem because you always felt so secure with him. You can take him for granted.

PATIENT: Yes. But it's not just my fantasy that mother did not care as much for me as she did for the others. Will thought it was obvious and was upset about it. I knew that the minute I left the house, they all started criticizing me. That's not paranoid; it's real because the others told me about it. They also talked about me and criticized me among themselves. Mother has been good to me but there has been something lacking, but I think she didn't love me enough. She didn't want to have me. She cried and cried when she found she was going to, she told me. There were many reasons maybe—there was some rumor that father was interested in another woman, the finances were going bad, and other things. Vivian is the one who took care of me, and I should feel to her as to mother, but I don't. I love her very much, but she has her problems. She tells everyone how intelligent she is, feels rivalry with me, and so on, but this doesn't upset me much.

ANALYST: Then the key is the feeling that mother loved you a lot, but she didn't love you enough?

PATIENT: Yes. But I feel so guilty to say that, to say that mother didn't love me. I say she did love me because she took care of me, and she suffered with me, especially when I was a rebellious teenager and I would keep a long face for five days and she would suffer. She loved me because she is human and had a child and loved me as she would have loved the neighbor's child. She isn't mean, never has been—rather it is a lack of enough love, enough warmth. Maybe that is my sensitivity to people who are not warm, and yet she is the warmest person I've ever seen with my sisters. If she could give me the benefit of the doubt, but she won't. She never has.

ANALYST: Very good. Maybe because of my having to cancel the last hour and my having to be away next week, we've come closer to the heart of the problem. Do you see much hostility to mother because of this?

PATIENT: Yes, very much.

ANALYST: I'm sorry about being away next week, just when this is so much clearer.

PATIENT: Maybe it is better. It helps me not to become too dependent on you. I don't want to be dependent on anyone. If I see you too often, the threat of the dependence is so great that I talk about extraneous things to avoid it, like about L. B. and B. S.

ANALYST: This dependence seems to be because of the insecurity of not feeling loved *enough.* And this has to do with the dependent love needs. We've mentioned them before and we will handle them by analyzing them. If the father pattern is not so threatening as the mother pattern, we must see the mother pattern too, see the whole childhood pattern clearly and how it can be upsetting still when you are a grow woman. The trouble you tell about in this hour seems to be in relation to mother and in the mother pattern to me.

PATIENT: Yes, I feel I can trust no one if I can't trust mother.

41st hour

PATIENT: The last time I spoke about my dependence on you and on mother, wanting it but defending against it, and for the first time I felt much more at ease. It bothered me from the beginning, and I was glad that I could bring it up. I thought I would miss you because of your being away this past week, but I didn't. I was at ease, at least until L. B. came on the scene again. T. H., who is a very rigid man, is such a perfectionist. He commented to L. B. about me, and L. B. tried to get one of my associates to give him complaints to use against me. The associate told me, and I grabbed the phone and blew off at T. H. I told him that no one is perfect and if I want to complain, I have plenty to tell about him, and that he should know how I am and where he stands. Later we met, and I told him I could have given L. B. fuel against him, which is true. L. B. is open for all kinds of poison. Since then, T. H. has been easier than ever, and we have been friendly for the first time. Then I met B. P. who said, "Don't talk about L. B. because everyone admires you for the way you have handled him." I answered that I wouldn't. Today is my last day in L. B.'s division but he won't let go and will keep after me if he can, but he may be transferred to an inconsequential position and relieved of his present job. I must be pretty good because he's been looking for ammunition against me and can't find any. You know he got two others—one a man and one a woman—fired. He gets mad and loses his sense of reality, not just getting angry for a few minutes but constantly trying to hurt, hurt, hurt, whomever he gets onto. I'm so glad I'm leaving his division. The replacements are mature, and he will have trouble.

Anyway, last night I dreamed that your secretary phoned that you were not back and would not see me today. I felt so mad, so rejected, that no one loved me, just depressed. It was so real that when I woke up I wondered if it were true. Then I thought I was losing my mind.

ANALYST: Associations?

PATIENT: It must mean I didn't want to see you. Maybe I feel guilty for blowing off at T. H. When I did, I thought: What will you think? Then I thought: To hell with you too!

You know why I felt so good since the last hour, because after it I felt I could not lose my mind. I'd still had some anxiety about that. I think it was because of discussing the dependence on you and the defenses against it. Mother would never let us be independent and it's as though if I were independent, I would go crazy, but you just analyze it and help me be independent. This week for the first time I no longer had the compulsive idea.

ANALYST: The last hour we talked about mother not loving you as warmly as you wished. Did this play any part?

PATIENT: Yes. I felt much better after telling that too. I was always struggling to change that. But, you can't change the past. That is what I didn't want to accept.

ANALYST: But she loved you enough to let you go.

PATIENT (*laughs*): Yes. Maybe it's better because the others can't live without mother and I can. Maybe she didn't love them as much as I thought either, or they wouldn't be so dependent.

ANALYST: But love and dependence can be different. You can love but make people independent too.

44th hour

PATIENT: Today was my first day at work in the new division. I enjoyed it but at noon I got anxious, as though something bad was going to happen. Then I realized that I was afraid I couldn't get off one of the afternoons I come for analysis, that he wouldn't let me. And I couldn't ask for a privilege. Then I thought: When I wait, things work out. It turned out that I can work overtime another time. Then the anxiety disappeared, but in this place after all that has happened,

I feel I have to be on guard all of the time, and I hate that. But nevertheless, I'm a new person already and it's like a nightmare looking back at what I went through with L. B.

I had a dream last night that I was in a place like a living room with a lot of doors. No one was in the room but a party was going on outside. I was naked. A man named J. T., whom I've met only twice, came in and I dashed for my clothes and pulled something over the front but nothing behind. Yesterday in reality, even though it was a holiday, I worked until 1 A.M. and forgot I had no girdle to wear this morning, which would be my first day at work. I have gained some weight. In the dream, J. T. said, "It's all right; no one will pay attention to you." He forced me to turn my back to the party but no one did pay any attention. In reality, next Sunday we are going to a family party, each family with all the children.

ANALYST: What associations do you have to being in the room alone and the party going on outside?

PATIENT: New job and for the first time in my life being afraid of people and of how I would react. I have two women superiors and a father figure, and with my sibling rivalry I'll have to solve my problems. One is M. L., whom I like the little I've seen of her. Everyone says she's nice. She has psychosomatic reactions and gets sick enough to be out often. The other is S. C. I don't know her.

ANALYST: Do you have any associations to pulling your clothes over the front with the back remaining exposed?

PATIENT: It was something like a big towel; I had nothing else. Women care about covering the front. I don't care too much about the back. I should always put up a front, no matter if the back is quite open. The back wasn't so bad when in the dream; I wasn't anxious. I'm not so bad inside. I was telling myself nothing is wrong in showing how I really am. I'm more sure of myself. I always thought I was worse than anyone else —more stupid, ugly, bad, more acting out of sex, but I'm not. So I guess I can show my back too.

ANALYST: The others paid no attention to your not being properly dressed. Any associations?

PATIENT: I don't know . . . no . . . I don't know. I am less conscious of what women might think of me than Will is. I can go out dressed any way and Will says, "How can you?" and I say, "If they know me, it doesn't matter and if they don't, it doesn't matter." Of course, it really does matter if people pay no attention to me. But I don't care so much now about showing how I really am.

ANALYST: Transference?

PATIENT: You were the one who helped me to come out of the room.

ANALYST: But why represent me as J. T.?

PATIENT: I tried to show all my faults and J. T. is just the opposite of you—big and fat and I hardly know him at all, but he comes to the office sometimes. So maybe it's a wish for you too—to work with you. I almost know, but can't quite understand it. If it had been you, I would have been more embarrassed, so I picked someone the opposite. I don't know J. T. so I don't care what he thinks, but I do care what you think. He's the most colorless person I could pick and therefore I would have the least reaction.

ANALYST: Do you think there is some sexual element in the dream?

PATIENT: No. It was a purely friendly approach; he was only trying to help.

ANALYST: What do you make of the dream?

PATIENT: For a while now I've felt much more at ease inside, and I can have feelings about you, like being glad to see you, without feeling guilty. I'm easier about my own feelings and more sure of myself.

ANALYST: Good. But why do you dream yourself into an embarrassing situation?

PATIENT: I don't know. Well . . . could it be a sort of punishment for fantasies, like being very fond of B. P., and of you but with sex in it too? I can think about it now, yet deep inside I must feel I should punish myself. One thing that amazed me: I used to like men, of course, but when I liked any man, even at a distance, I had fantasies about him but then rejected him completely. Even in fantasy I had to be a one man woman. Now I can fantasy but I love my husband even better. I needn't suppress my fantasies, feel guilty, punish myself, and reject Will.

ANALYST: Very good; and part is the reaction to the new job and what they will think, as you said earlier.

46th hour

PATIENT: I have so much to say I don't know where to start. I'll begin with the most painful. Both my mother-in-law and my mother are coming to visit us on our vacation and to a house where we are already overcrowded. You can imagine my hostility inside. Last night I cried so much about it. They have no consideration for the facilities, if you are tired, and so on. But mother is much more understanding than my mother-in-law. The point is that it comes after I've been through so much and I just wanted to let down completely. Now I'll have no privacy. I'll have to cook meals and show them around and everything. My husband tried to dissuade his mother on the phone last night, and she said we didn't want her and then Will said that that isn't so, and on and on it went. Mother-in-law interferes so with how we treat the children. They want to stay the whole month of our vacation. That's why I cried so much; it was anger. Just out of the blue this call last night saying they are coming. Now I know why I liked San Francisco so much because they came only once. They upset Will so he beat up on our son, which he never does. They upset the relation of Will to me and of both of us to the children, and they upset the maids. And they never even ask; they just phoned and said they would arrive in a few days by plane. My mother-in-law's idea of being happy is to be a martyr—she weeps in front of people about her past troubles, and she has the best time when she complains that she works so hard and that no one helps her. No one can help her. When you try, everything you do is wrong.

ANALYST: If you and Will were to make a decision about this and say you are not able to have them while on vacation, what would happen?

PATIENT: Then they would say it's all my fault, that I'm dominating and that I've influenced Will and the poor children. But I no longer care. If they disinherit us, it doesn't matter because if they did leave us anything, it would be when we didn't need it. It's now we need it and they give us nothing—thank goodness. Father always told us, "I will not leave you any money, but I will leave you an education. That is important all your life, and that's it. If money, then you'll wish for my death and fight among yourselves for the money, and that's not good." I think he is right. If you know you are getting the education and that's that, it helps you mature. My husband's father is attractive, but so egotistic. Will has more problems with him than I do with my mother. If Will tells his father he was promoted or something of the sort, his father looks at me and asks me if that is correct.

47th hour

PATIENT: I talked with Will about the visit from his mother and father, and I thought he'd share my view about protecting our relationship and our children but he said he couldn't tell them not to come, that I wouldn't tell my father or mother that. I told him that I would. And, I would. But I wouldn't have to because mother is considerate and wouldn't come if she thought she was a bother and father never visits his children, because he says he doesn't want to be a bother. Will said it is my problem, that I have trouble with people. I was surprised. That is the first time I was the calm one. I asked him what he meant and he said an example was L. B. I reminded him that once he was with L. B. for five minutes and that was more than he could stand. Will said I don't know how to handle people, so I asked him how he would handle the situation with his parents. He said we must have a relation. To this I agreed. Will was very mad, but he did write them that it was impossible to make arrangements to have them with us now. He said we would expect them in the fall when we are back in town in the larger house. In this struggle between mother-in-law and myself, Will said I had a fantasy of being a *femme fatale* because being sexually irresistible, a woman can handle men.

ANALYST: Is this struggle to separate Will sufficiently from his parents, to make him really put his wife and children first, what so many wives have?

PATIENT: Yes. Yes, that's it. My father and mother are excellent that way. They never come unless they are sure they are wanted. I think Will married me because his mother thought I was all right. If my parents had objected, I would have married him anyway. But, if his mother had said no, he would not have married me. Will's parents may come anyway in spite of his letter. I bet they will. But now my problem is to help Will. He feels so guilty toward his parents for sending that letter. Why did I react so calmly when he said it was my problem? That surprised me, but I think I know. We took a big step and it may cost us a lot—at any rate cost me a lot.

49th hour

PATIENT: My mother came and the others did not. I'm so guilty. My husband and I went to the station because we got no phone call from his mother, no letter, or wire or anything and so I said we'd better go to the airport in case they came. My husband was furious before we went to the airport, and he took it out by cleaning up the lawn and the house. But since mother arrived, he's been fine. Mother just has a remarkable quality. She was very nice. She reacted to the change in my attitude. I no longer felt I had to do everything to win her approval. I felt that I'm her daughter, and she must love me. And I felt secure. The greatest relief was freedom from guilt. She told me of talking with Lois, and instead of my feeling that they had been talking against me and that she loves Lois better than me and is closer to her, and my then feeling guilty, I was able to feel glad that they were together. It was a great experience. Mother changed in her attitude to me. She said Lois should live like me, and I told her to please not discuss me with Lois and to omit all mention and encouragement of comparisons and rivalries between us. So I don't feel guilty; in fact, now I feel happy and fine. I feel mother is fine without my having to feel guilt. I also discussed with her the idea Lois gave her that I was going crazy and that I hated mother. This is one reason mother came. I could talk about it freely and without guilt and mother and I understood each other very well.

ANALYST: This improvement of your relationship with your mother is important. You can see that you can actually have a good relationship with her if you give up the childhood pattern and move into a more adult-to-adult basis.

52nd hour

PATIENT: I feel like the day today (*dark and raining*) with your leaving and my leaving, I won't see you for weeks. I find I would like to talk about you all day. I start to say to mother, "Dr. S. . . . " and then I catch myself and don't. If I did, they would think it is nothing but sex, that there could be nothing else in the relation. I never told you but the family had a bad experience once with a psychiatrist. One of my sisters went to a poorly trained psychiatrist for years, and he made advances to her. Our whole family knew about it. He was crazy, had fights, threw things, beat his wife. So I don't talk about you at all. Now the physical attraction to you is no problem any more. It's hard to explain. The feeling is more something sweet, something dear. It has sex in it of course, but it's not like toward the boss I spoke of. There it was almost entirely physical attraction. With him I was only looking for something and with you I feel I can give, and I don't feel guilty. Now I can look at my feelings and at the whole depth of my emotions without any fear at all. I used to be scared to death of them. Maybe that's why I feel I'm going to miss you, but it's not that I fear missing you too much or that I fear being unable to function. I feel inside the security of your friendship and with that I don't have to miss you so much. *(Smiles as tears come to her eyes; cries a little.)* Maybe this is what I have lacked with mother. I should have felt like this with her. Of course I did, somewhat. She must have given me enough or I wouldn't be as I am, but if I'd had it, I would have felt more sure than I feel now. I realize she gave me a lot; she couldn't give more because there were too many things involved. The feeling of hostility that I had toward her has changed to gratitude for what she gave me. I look around me and thank God for the way I am. I pity my sister Lois, and I pity mother because she gave all she could and did the best she could and didn't know any better. She's gentle, smooth. Sometimes I wish I could be like her but I can't. My children are like lambs when they are with her. They argue with me about their bath until I grab them and put them in the tub (*laughs*) and mother just talks so quietly, and they do just what she says. This is the first time mother has been worried about me, because I'm working too hard.

ANALYST: You've talked of the libidinal part of the transference. Is there any anger at me for going away?

PATIENT: No. None.

ANALYST: But when you said you felt like the dark, rainy day, did you mean you felt depressed? Isn't depression partly anger?

PATIENT (*smiling*): I'm not aware of any. I'd tell you if I felt it, but if it's there, I'm repressing it. I have felt mad at you at times.

ANALYST: I just want to be sure we don't miss it if there is any anger. Did you dream last night?

PATIENT: No, I slept like a rock. I haven't been dreaming that much lately, although two nights ago I had a dream. It was sex and about you, but it wasn't you in the dream. It was a good and pleasant dream. At first in analysis I dreamed so much and recently so little, or rather I do dream, but then forget. Maybe now what I dream is not acceptable.

ANALYST: And maybe at first it was easier to tell dreams than to express your feelings.

PATIENT: That is true, and until today I could not tell you the feelings toward you I told you about today. I've felt that way for weeks now and yet never told you, and I guess I couldn't tell you . . . no . . . That's all.

ANALYST: Could you say you got some good superego from me?

PATIENT: I though this morning that I felt more secure. At first I was more secure being hostile—that feeling of:

If he tries to walk over me, he'd better watch out! Now I feel with other people that I don't have to retaliate any more, and I've asked myself why and why I feel more secure. It's partly because I feel secure with you, and I think you have a good opinion of me and therefore I can't be so bad. Maybe I can even be pretty good, and if you feel you are all right, then you don't have to be showing people that you are not bad and you don't have to be hostile.

53rd hour

This is the first hour after the summer vacation.

ANALYST: How do you do? I'm glad to see you. How are you?

PATIENT: The summer was good. We got a cat, but there were other changes also. I quit my job. I phoned you and wanted to discuss it but you were away and I had another job opportunity and couldn't wait to decide. B. S. was going to change the working schedules and when he did, I found out I would be working 8:30 A.M. until 9:00 P.M.! Mother said I was overworking and that she had never seen me so tired. She threatened to phone father. I laughed at that and said, "What can father do?" Mother said, "He can talk with your husband, and tell him we never made you work so much and so hard. You are neglecting the children." That point really got to me. Anyway I talked with B. P. and asked his advice. The company gave me a leave of absence for a year, which was very nice, and I'm glad to have it. I've taken a new job but I'm mad; I'm not happy. Although I'm happy at the new job, I'm mad at you for the first time. I'm mad at Will and worried about our debts. He says that all these years we've had worse debts and that now things are better. In the past the children pay for it when I feel this way but not this time. When your secretary phoned about an appointment, I was glad. I knew I would be glad to see you, but I'm also mad at you. I spoke with mother about you and also about L. B. and mother saw I would not give up the analysis and that the weakest point was the job, so she convinced me to quit the job. After I decided this, I felt better; I relaxed. Now I get home at 5:00 P.M. and the children are much better because now it's me who is with them and in charge of them. So everyone is happy except me. It's missing the experience at my other job that makes me angry. It was such good training.

ANALYST: What else makes you angry?

PATIENT: Having to sacrifice for my husband. This is the third time. Each time we needed more money and therefore I sacrificed my position. No . . . I guess I was mad at you because I was afraid and didn't want to show that I was afraid. It's only my fantasy, but the fear was that you would be like father and say, "Why do you do something like this?" My consolation is that I'm not losing anything, but I don't know. Everyone there said such wonderful things that I should resign everyday. I guess I'm angry at you because it's the analysis that is making me change jobs. I need the money to finance the analysis. It's not only you. It's my husband. I guess I'm just trying to find someone to put the hostility on because I blame B. S. for not leaving my work schedule as it was. B. S. never even answered my note, and this shows he doesn't like me.

55th hour

PATIENT: I don't know whether or not to be concerned about the sex interest of our two sons, Tom, nine, and Davey, seven. Lois says I only imagine it, but I had feelings at that age and knew more than they do, only I didn't show it.

I've been homesick for two or three weeks. I have a great wish to go back and visit the ranch. I didn't have it right after mother left but I did later. Just before your vacation, after I left here, I was crying and crying—for no reason—but after it I felt good and was not depressed. I felt good and did not miss you while you were on vacation except the last week, when I wanted to discuss with you the changing of jobs. But then I got a little depressed and edgy as it came nearer the time to see you and that is when I started to want to go home. Then I read about one of my favorite nieces back near home. She is a little withdrawn but still an all-around girl. I read that she had won a scholarship and also a prize for riding. Life is different there. All you do here is work and work and work. I shouldn't complain with all the help I have at home. It's not that I'm homesick for the family. I really think it's better to be away from them—the further the better. This same thing happened to me when I was in San Francisco, and then I went back home and after that I wasn't homesick. In fact, I was rather glad to leave home again. But it is a whole different tempo and attitude.

ANALYST: Is the homesickness partly a reaction to leaving your job and taking a new one but feeling unhappy about it?

PATIENT: I never thought that could be. In this new job I'm just locked in my office, while in the old job I was involved more with people and I was healthier. But I had to leave it.

59th hour

PATIENT: I've had the most terrible headache. I get them only rarely now; I get some, but none for the last few months. It started the day before yesterday, the same day I received a letter from mother that upset me so very much. I don't know why I didn't talk about it. But I do know—I didn't want to sound like a patient talking about mother and siblings and what they have and I don't have. I know my problem, so I shouldn't spend an hour on it, but it was more than I thought because the headache started. It was relieved at a party the other night. I took only two drinks because although they relieve my headaches, the next morning I have a headache and a hangover. Yesterday morning the headache was awful—a real migraine. I had my period, too. I couldn't work, took phenobarbital, and slept until dinner. I still had the headache so I took another pill and woke up this morning feeling fine. Last night I began to figure out why I had the headache and thought: Why didn't I realize how much I reacted to mother's letter? Yesterday morning when I couldn't work, Will said, "Don't worry; it's just because you are emotionally upset." I flared up and said, very angrily, "Just because I have a headache, why should you think it has anything to do with the emotions! You always have to look for that!" *(Laughs.)* Then I began to think about it and realized it was mother's letter and that he knew it because he had read it also.

ANALYST: Therefore, what do we learn?

PATIENT: That I am still the same in that relation. Why have I been associating so superficially since your return when I have much more important things to talk about? On vacation I had very queer dreams and this past week, since your return, I've had psychotic dreams, and I'm anxious when I awaken, but I'm not during the dream. If I had such dreams four or five months ago, I would have thought: That's it; I am going to go crazy. But now I know I'm not.

I'm even scared to get letters from mother. This one was about money. She wanted money from us. It is so hard for us and is nothing for my brother. What they do as a favor turns out to be hostile. My brother gave five hundred dollars to Lois although she and her husband have a quite big income. Then I hate myself for thinking this way. And the letter from mother was not only to ask for money, but it was filled with telling me I should do this, do that, and so on. I must face it: Mother just doesn't have the feeling for me that she has for the others. Well, that is what made me so mad and gave me the headache. Mother talks and talks with me, but she never comes out straight and tells how she suffers—she just goes on and on.

ANALYST: The other thing we learn is not to suppress and repress. What we must do is get it out here in the analysis—you may be angry and upset, but you may avoid the headache.

PATIENT: Yes, but it's the same old story.

ANALYST: How long do you think it takes to solve these things? You only faced it a few months ago.

PATIENT: Mother told me she came to visit because Mabel told her I was tired, and she was concerned about me. Of course she loves me and was concerned, but I don't believe this was the real reason. What it was that she came to enjoy seeing was Lois, who was here then. Of course it was to see me too, and to tell me not to work so much, but she knows that I'm not like Lois and that she could have written me or phoned me, and I would have done the same. She kept telling everyone here about Lois, only Lois, as though I didn't exist. Even Will got to the point of saying something to her. What I mean is that for a moment I had the feeling I had wanted so much all my life, and I thought things had really changed. But that isn't so; it's just the same (*tears*). I enjoyed it (*smiles*) when I thought that for the first time she was worried about me, and I felt good and didn't need you so much (*tears*). Since she left, she's written two letters, the first about money and the second about money. I don't know if I'm trying to console myself, but I think it's better she's like this for if she had always been so sweet, I would have been so dependent on her that I'd have no hope of freeing myself from this need.

ANALYST: The need is too great?

PATIENT: Yes. To want mother's love so much is unhealthy.

ANALYST: But she does love you in her way, and so does father in his way. When you are grown up, the chief love is, of course, with your husband and children.

PATIENT: Oh, yes (*smiles*). And father is no problem. He loves me, and I have no craving there. But with mother things like this make me bitter, and I stop writing, or I write very short, superficial letters. That's how I drifted away from her. I tried to get close to her. She has the ability to make people talk about their personal affairs, but then she uses this. I really broke with her when I was a teenager. I never sat until two in the morning with her like the others, telling her so freely and much about my dates and how I felt, as the others did.

ANALYST: Is this problem with your relation to mother solvable?

PATIENT: Yes. And it was all right before this visit, and it will be all right when I'm entirely independent financially.

ANALYST: It *was* all right?

PATIENT: In the sense that I was accustomed to the pattern until this visit when she tried to be different. I once read one of your books that you dedicated to your parents and I felt I couldn't do that. And then I thought I could to father, and then during the visit I thought I could to mother. Until that letter. But she's done so much for me and really given me so much love, more than many people have.

60th hour

PATIENT: Last night I had a dream. It was as if we had a

group of friends and went out with them, and I liked one man very much—the same man I dated and who later I heard was impotent. I was naked most of the time and wore very little. My great concern was what all those people would think, but no one paid any attention.

Now I remember why I had the dream. I read yesterday that a movie star was asked if she would appear in a play without any clothes, and her husband said, "If so, there will be only one spectator—myself!" I thought: She runs from one man and one husband to another, so why should she be so puritanical. But why should that little thing stick in my mind? Then I thought: I wish I were not in analysis with you; then I could see you outside. Then I thought about seeing you at parties but realized you don't go to the same parties I go to. There's no more rigid and puritanical people than psychiatrists, judging by the ones I've met. The ones I've heard talk try to show that they have what they haven't. Psychiatrists should be more broad-minded. They are the least so of the medical specialists. If a doctor has an affair with a nurse, no one cares; that is his business, but not if he's a psychiatrist. I can't figure it out, (*laughs*) unless I would like to be the nurse. (*Laughs.*) I realize it now, but it's still true about psychiatrists even if this is transference.

Could it be, in the dream, that I'm surprised and worried at myself, that the people are my superego and they are not as strict as I thought or want them to be? Why am I so worried in the dream that they don't pay any attention? Part of me doesn't worry about analysis any more, but another part does. I can't think any more.

ANALYST: Then just associate to the element in the dream of a group of friends.

PATIENT: I was at a party a few days ago and I had such a good time compared with parties I've been to where some psychiatrists were present. They have to drink to have any warm relationships. Of course not only psychiatrists do that. I've been to other parties where I've drunk a lot, where people don't know what to talk about. Normally at parties I only like talking with the men, because the women talk about their children and in fifteen minutes I'm tired of it.

ANALYST: What are your associations to having few or no clothes on?

PATIENT: That I haven't much to say here any more. On vacation I kept thinking of all the things I was going to tell you and now I don't have to say them, and it's none of your business. *(Laughs.)* I mean trivial things. I had so much to say and now I can't find anything. I do have quite a bit to say but don't. Yesterday I did but the two hours before that I got angry at myself for talking of things that didn't reach me inside.

There are those psychotic dreams. I better talk about them. In one of those dreams I was going to a party but was all in black. Someone said, "You look like a widow," but this dream was pleasant.

In the second dream I got close to the mirror and had blackheads at my nose and I squeezed them. Then to my horror they were not blackheads but were three or four long black hairs, and I had hair all over my cheeks. I thought if I go on looking in this mirror, I'll become a wolf, and I awoke in a panic. It was a nightmare. That was about two weeks ago. Another dream was about the little kitten we have. Will was hanging from a rope, head down from one ankle, but at the same time he was next to me watching this. The man hanging was hanging against a wall and I was horrified. Then a huge tom cat was there, threatening to scratch me and I had to get close to the man hanging. That was the worst nightmare.

ANALYST: That's quite a mass of dreams. Two themes are clear. The first theme has to do with how you look: undressed, in black, with hair on your face. Hostility is the second theme: directed to you with the cat threatening to scratch you, directed to your husband with you being a widow and with him hanging from the ankle.

PATIENT: That's right. I've had a lot of hostility to Will these past few weeks. I've sensed it.

ANALYST: Why the concern with how you look?

PATIENT: Maybe it's like a punishment, maybe for the hostility that I felt to everyone. After hearing from mother the first time, I got mad at Will. I don't know; maybe I'm too upset about things, like the money. Will knows how prompt I am with payments and if he'd sent the check, all this with mother wouldn't have happened and I wouldn't have to be hearing about it for the next months. Before this occurred, I thought Will was changing, growing, and I was respecting and admiring him more and more. Then it all went to pieces. I know it's my problem.

ANALYST: In the dream, you have anxiety over the fact that they don't notice you. Could that be a complaint that they don't pay enough attention to you, and that they wouldn't even if you were nude?

PATIENT: It must be. The people are my family. But no matter how much people tell you things, if you don't feel it . . . It's like at the last job. They thought I was the best they ever had, but I can't feel it inside. It's as though they were talking about someone else.

ANALYST: The people could also refer to me, the transference.

PATIENT: Yes, but do I put you with women or with family?

ANALYST: The dream must be, at least in part, a reaction to yesterday's hour when you came out and told the feelings about mother and that you were not loved as much as your siblings.

PATIENT: No . . . no . . . Yes, I guess I didn't want to. I thought things had changed, and they didn't. And, I didn't want you or anybody to know.

ANALYST: You were not going to reveal yourself, but you did.

PATIENT: I didn't want to expose the fact that what I thought could be true was not—that my love for mother was reciprocated. So I must accept it as it is and go on from there. It is a childish wish. I had enough.

ANALYST: You reveal yourself in the dream, but they pay no attention. Associations?

PATIENT: Oh, that could be many things. It could be mother, could be you, and that's it.

ANALYST: Meaning that you reveal these feelings and mother does nothing about it?

PATIENT: Yes, and you don't either. That's what worried me in the dream, or rather not worry, but I *suffered* in the dream.

ANALYST: But in reality I do do something. It may be somewhat abstract, but it is something important—I listen, understand, analyze.

PATIENT (*nods and smiles a little*): Yes.

ANALYST: It's very good that it's out in the open.

PATIENT: But why does it cost me so much to put it in the open?

ANALYST: Because it's painful. One other thing. You do not only suffer from it, but it must also make you very angry toward mother, although in the dreams you show it only to husband and to yourself.

PATIENT: Yes, very much. I didn't realize how much.

ANALYST: So you must see further the hostility to mother and if this is hard to face because it does not come out to her—

PATIENT (*interrupting*): Although she is the one responsible for everything that happened.

ANALYST: I think that as the whole thing, that is, all your feelings about it, including the anger, comes out toward mother, you will feel better and will be able to have a better relationship with her. Very good.

61st hour

PATIENT: We had a picnic yesterday and had a very good time. Usually I don't because by the time I get all the children dressed and everything ready and into the car for a long trip, I'm worn out and mad inside. Will is the one who is jovial and plays the games—games about what letters we see in advertisements as we drive and such. But yesterday, although it was a long trip, I enjoyed it.

I see now that there is more anger in me to my mother than I realized and it is more threatening than I thought. I'll tell you why I think that. Now I can feel much more anger than I could before, and yesterday I realized that I must have been displacing it onto my children. Then I get panicky as though my mind goes blank, and then I get scared. It's happened several times in the last two or three weeks. It happened a few times this morning, and then again I thought: Oh, I'm going to go crazy. And I felt that if I did, the first person I'd act out my hostility toward would be my mother. One of my father's aunts was in an institution although I never thought of her as mentally sick—only as sick. I punish myself by thinking this: If I'm hostile to my mother, God will punish me by making me crazy. Only I don't think about God in this . . . well . . . yes, I do. My belief has been that only crazy people express their real feelings. I've heard the question: "Why is it that when people go insane, they always hate the people they love the most?" Even now it is so frightening. I feel—not numb in any way—but sort of light, and that feeling is in my head. I can't think for seconds; I get panicky.

I thought I had all my neurotic symptoms under control when I was away from home, but when I returned and we lived again near my family, it brought everything back.

It's strange, now I'm this way consciously but my dream last night was pleasant. I forget it completely but I know I wanted to go on dreaming it when I had to get up, and I was not tired. But I remember none of it—nothing.

When I'm relaxed, the whole house functions so well as though I were the axis.

ANALYST: Of course, isn't that true of the wife and mother?

PATIENT: Yes, of course. For the past two or three years I have *not* been relaxed at home, but yesterday I was and we all had such a good time again. This was like when we lived far from my parents in San Francisco. When I was not close to them I felt entirely free.

Another thing, something I thought I would never get over, but now I have hopes. I mean the feeling I have when I'm close to my parents—that I can be hurt easily. I can sense all that is inside me; I think this fear will disappear, and I realized that yesterday when I felt so happy.

Something is bothering me inside. It's quite upsetting and probably more so than I'm conscious of.

ANALYST: Let's discuss what you are conscious of.

PATIENT: Mm-hm.

ANALYST: The most immediate is the conflict over the hostility to mother.

PATIENT: That's right.

ANALYST: And this is chiefly from guilt—for this hostility you may be punished.

PATIENT: Mm-hm.

ANALYST: Therefore, our job is to reduce the hostility and guilt.

PATIENT (*smiling*): Yes, yes it is. But how?

ANALYST: Partly by reason, common sense, exposing it to your ego, and partly by transference, by the effect of your childhood feelings to me, whatever authority I have, pointing out the reality. The reality is: Do not make a fuss about the hostilities. All children have some hostility to their parents and maybe there is always some hostility in the parents to the children.

PATIENT: There was hostility in mother to me and that is what I cannot face.

ANALYST: Maybe not.

PATIENT: Yes, there was hostility to me and father was the cause.

ANALYST: Still, now you are a grown, responsible adult, and you are out on your own. The task is for you not to be upset by it or by your hostility to her and the guilt—you are grown up. Now your life is your husband, children, friends, profession, and so on.

PATIENT: I know that, but inside I don't seem to know it.

ANALYST: So we get it out and talk about it and I say if anything does no good, like the guilt as well as the hostility, then don't be guilty. Step one is don't be guilty; step two is reduce the hostility. We try to work on both simultaneously.

PATIENT: Yes, but it's so deep-seated.

ANALYST: Another difficulty has to do with your needs for love toward mother since you are grown up.

PATIENT: Then why aren't they present when I'm away? I guess it's more the relationship. I'm not homesick when I'm away.

ANALYST: Right; it's not tolerating the sense of hostility from mother and her preference for the siblings.

PATIENT: That's it!

ANALYST: And that hasn't much reality any more either; now it's husband, children, friends, job, everything in your real, present life.

PATIENT: That's my consolation.

ANALYST: It's more than consolation—that is your mature life.

PATIENT: I'm striving to have it be more than consolation.

ANALYST: We have to get the mother relationship, which is so important when you are a child, from being so important in your feelings now that you are grown up, when it should be only a small part of your life.

62nd hour

PATIENT: Even at the new job there are fights and things going on as everywhere. I stay strictly out of it. It's so nice to be out of everything. But yesterday a man decided to resign, so I have to take over a lot of his work.

I had two dreams last night. In the first one we were at a small fair and at the same time it was not a fair but a store that gives premiums, gifts for stamps—the same idea—as though I were winning many things at the fair or getting them for stamps. I was so happy but still there were other things I wanted. *(Laughs.)* We had lots of packages and were putting them in the car. I had a small outdoor stove, but it was dirty and I was cleaning it. Will and I were very happy together.

In the second dream my sister Mabel had a baby girl, as she does in reality; and then someone came and told me there was a mistake. Her baby was not a girl. She had taken someone else's and her's was a boy, but Mabel said she was happy with the girl and would have nothing to do with the whole thing.

ANALYST: What are your associations to the first dream?

PATIENT: At the fair Will bought beautiful old tables, and I said we can't afford them but they cost only ten dollars each. We cleaned them and they looked very lovely. I get all these things, but there is more that I want. I'm happy but want to be happier. I have more than most people—I don't mean material things but healthy children who love me and I love them, and a good husband, and he and I get on much better than most. We depend greatly on each other. Will said a friend of ours told him he rarely saw a husband so in love with his wife. Will is more in love with me than I with him or rather he expresses it more. But I know I can be happier because I have been. Maybe Will and

I understand each other better now, but it seems we used to have more fun. We'd leave a party at midnight and then drive off someplace that was a twelve hour drive away. Of course then we had only one child and I was not working and did not feel guilty about leaving the baby because I was with the baby all the time. Now that I work, I feel guilty.

ANALYST: What are your associations to the second dream, to Mabel having a girl baby instead of a boy?

PATIENT (*smiles*): Maybe it's myself. I'd like another baby girl, but I have enough children. Then I think, we're young and I'm healthy, why not have another child. And here comes something neurotic—I have a fear that I would die in childbirth. I always knew I would have four children and that would be it. Barbara, my youngest, is just perfect, everything one would want a child to be. She is the only one with no problems at all. We tried nothing, just let her grow wild, and I'm crazy about her.

ANALYST: What are your associations to Mabel not changing the girl for a boy.

PATIENT: My father wanted only boys and got mostly girls. When I was born and he heard I was a girl, he didn't even want to see me. I guess mother liked me very much at that time. If I didn't have him then, I had her. Mother said she suffered with father but made up her mind that it would not interfere with her bringing up her children. And it's true. I remember her only as being in love with him, and she never criticized him, so in that I admire her. So that's the association. It's better to be a girl than to be a boy. I find it's easier to have daughters.

ANALYST: Do you have any idea that if you had been a boy that your father would have loved you even more?

PATIENT: No. Father isn't that way with my brothers. No, I never felt that. In fact, I always felt that by being a girl I could get closer to him.

ANALYST: Do you think it would have been any better with mother if you had been a boy?

PATIENT: Maybe. Maybe she would have thought she made father happier, but not for herself. She didn't want any more children, boys or girls. I've thought about this penis envy and think it's what goes with it. Take, for example, the freedom—boys are free to do things girls can't. If society were different, there would not be the envy. Women have something better though. Women can give birth. And as my sister said, we know it's our baby; men can never be sure (*laughs*).

ANALYST: What do you think these dreams mean?

PATIENT: I don't know. Could they be a reaction to yesterday's hour?

ANALYST: They could.

PATIENT (*laughs*): In yesterday's hour I was infantile in my approach—the dreams are a way of solving it by reality. I have enough to be happy.

ANALYST: More precisely, the dreams tell you to be satisfied with what you've got. You have plenty so don't insist on more. There is dissatisfaction and you tell yourself to be satisfied with what you have. The dissatisfaction is about mother—what you told about yesterday—not getting enough love from mother. That hurts. But then you tell yourself——

PATIENT (*interrupting*): You have enough, don't complain.

ANALYST: Yes, plus some current dissatisfaction with the set-up here, the job, way of life, and so on.

PATIENT: Yes.

ANALYST: So we should understand and try to help.

PATIENT: Yes, there is the frustration of not being able to go on at the other job.

63rd hour

PATIENT: Now I seem to be dreaming quite a lot. There were times when I didn't. In my dream last night, Will and I entered an inn; it was as though we were traveling. It was all right but not as nice as I expected. Next to it was a most beautiful house and the owners of the inn, a man and a woman, lived in this house. And I wondered how they could live in such a house when they had an inn which was not too good. Then I saw a lot of maids in uniform—four or five—enter the house and I thought: That is good; now Annie can have friends. Then someone told me the inn was not well taken care of because the lady of the house was sick. Then—— But first I must tell the reality that old friends of ours from near the border are coming here to visit next week. Now in the inn I said, "If you can't stay at the inn, stay with us." In reality they are to stay with us.

ANALYST: What are your associations to the inn?

PATIENT: I love to stay at inns. I prefer it to a fine hotel. It's warm, a better atmosphere, near the life of the townspeople. But this one was not so good as I thought. I don't know . . . No matter how bad they have been in reality I've always loved them.

ANALYST: What are your associations to wondering how they live in that house with that inn?

PATIENT: The inn is the inside. The outside looks good but the inside is sick. She can't take care of things as she should; that's myself.

ANALYST: Why?

PATIENT: I guess it's a continuation of yesterday's dream about how many good things I have but don't take care of them as I want to and should. Maybe I don't want to realize that I'm not taking care of things as I should. The children, mostly the children.

ANALYST: Anything else besides the children?

PATIENT: Yesterday the children were out when I came home. They returned and started to tell me where they had been. They had gone pretty far and I felt guilty, although if I were home, they'd have gone out anyway, but I made them promise not to go so far again.

ANALYST: Associations to the beautiful house?

PATIENT: If I have a good family, as I do, and all I have is good, it is because I made them good. But if I don't go on keeping them good, then—— Maybe I am exaggerating, but it seems whenever I talk with the boys, it's only to give orders: Take a bath, do this, do that, and so on. I found out yesterday that they play on the railroad tracks. It worries me.

ANALYST: How do they live in so beautiful a house when the inn isn't so good? Associations?

PATIENT: It's the opposite. Living in such a good house, why do they have an inn like that? The lady of the house didn't take care of the inn, just what I've been saying.

ANALYST: Could there be any transference meaning?

PATIENT: No. I don't see any.

ANALYST: Could the criticism of the inn be a criticism of treatment?

PATIENT: Yes, it could be. You are the big house, and I am the little inn. You are big in psychiatry and I'm in analysis with you. But, my feelings inside are still not as I want them to be.

ANALYST: If they live in the big house, why don't they take better care of the inn?

PATIENT (*laughs*): I told you. It's not—— The house itself is you; it's criticism, hostility. If you are so great, why don't you fix me up!

ANALYST: Good question.

PATIENT (*laughs*): It's I who must fix myself up. Actually I feel you are doing very well with me.

ANALYST: I think you are right about this dream. The dream continues what we did yesterday with the dissatisfactions and guilts. But before that, you mentioned envy of women with beautiful houses. Do you feel any to me?

PATIENT: There is envy of women with beautiful houses,

but I think it's a healthy envy. It's normal. If I didn't want to be like you, there would be something wrong with me. It refers to things in general. As you are with your children—that's how I'd like to be because I'm guilty toward my children.

66th hour

PATIENT: I'm so late. I was talking to a woman at work, very nice, and I was so interested in what I was learning about business matters from her and then I looked at my watch and was shocked at the time. I'll go right to one thing and that is a dream. I was going to marry my oldest brother and no one minded. He offered me a big house, everything, and we went out to parties and everyone was congratulating us, and I was very happy, pleased that everyone approved. Before they did, I had some guilt and shame and felt it wasn't right but when they all approved, I was relieved and happy. But then I preferred another man who was on a ship or train that was passing by. I saw him at a window among some people.

ANALYST: Associations?

PATIENT: Last night Will and I changed from twinbeds to a double bed for the first time. Actually when I was nine or ten, my brother went to the University of California to study engineering and he wrote me, and I was so pleased that he wrote me and sent a gift. It wasn't much, but for me to get the attention meant a lot, and I almost had a crush on him. Could it be that in the dream my brother is father, whom I loved so much and so would also be you? Therefore the dream doesn't end in marriage.

ANALYST: What about the other man on the ship or the train?

PATIENT: If it's you, I send you away, so at the end I'm by myself. But the dream was relaxing, no guilt. It was a happy dream, as though something had calmed down inside.

ANALYST: Why did you arrive so late today?

PATIENT: Because of the dream (*laughs*). Oh, now I remember. The dream continued and I was with my brother and also with the other man, but we were at a place where Catholics were persecuted. That was not relaxing, but it wasn't a nightmare either.

Maybe I came so late as a reaction against the transference. I told you the other day you were not doing anything for me, which isn't so at all; it was hostility. Coming late is a way of expressing hostility and has something to do with my talking with a woman. Last year I was so hostile at the company where I was, I had no normal relations with anyone. I guess I'm reacting to you the same as I did to mother. And, not you or mother or anyone can give me what I looked for as a child. I realize that but still I can feel frustrated.

ANALYST: As we said, all I do is analyze you.

PATIENT: That's right.

ANALYST: Therefore, that's all. You can't marry brother, and so on. Therefore, it might be better to talk with a woman. Is it mother?

PATIENT (*laughs*): It's a healthy reaction at least. But I never thought this could happen to me, to forget the hour!

67th hour

PATIENT: We went to visit the H.'s and I enjoyed them very much. They were homey, had unity, didn't care what others thought, and father is the boss. I think Jewish families are mostly like this. I've been thinking of why I had the end of that dream yesterday—prejudice against Catholics. I met a Jewish man who was just brilliant but keyed up, and he said that there have been three Jewish geniuses—Jesus, Freud, and Marx—and that we are waiting for the fourth to combine these three. I laughed with him and said he was thinking of himself. Anyway, about the dream I told you about last hour. If I think it's all right to marry my brother, I must punish myself, although in the dream they didn't persecute me for marrying my brother. After leaving the H.'s, Will and I discussed all the prejudice there is. I just can't think—the persecution was against a religion that permits brother and sister to marry. Maybe the religion is psychoanalysis; there is prejudice against it. If I told someone I dreamed of marrying my brother and that there was nothing in the dream against such a thing, they'd just drop. How careful I have to be at home—if I make a slip of the tongue that seems critical of religion or of anything at all around home. Now I think of L. B. He is very anti-Catholic, so against it that it's pathetic.

ANALYST: Is this like the dream at the party where you were without clothes and no one noticed? Here you marry your brother and no one cares. The first dream prompted your confession that you did not feel enough love from mother, and you did not want to face that.

PATIENT: Yes. It is transference. Just as then I said mother didn't care, in this dream it's that you don't care.

ANALYST: That I don't care enough about you to care if you are clad or unclad, or if you marry your brother or not, or——

PATIENT (*interrupting*): Yes, or if I stand upside down! That's what it is. That identification is there with others who are not loved socially, that is, the Jews. No one is loved enough, no matter how good they are.

ANALYST: If that's what hurts, we must get it analyzed. Yesterday's dream also shows the defenses against the wishes for love. I think this is particularly so in the transference. As in the dreams, you think of all kinds of solutions. If you want my love as a brother, isn't that the answer? But even then the wish goes too far—to marry brother. So, you turn to a stranger who is on a train with other people and thus defend yourself against this pattern of wanting the love so strongly that you feel too dependent, too jealous, too sure to be frustrated, not loved enough. You struggle with this old childhood pattern toward your mother and against repeating it with me. But this dream is happier, there is no jealousy. Apparently, the pattern of your love needs toward your oldest brother was much quieter and easier than the ones toward your father, mother, and sisters. And, you are unconsciously trying this out toward me. Can you get the love from me without all the complications if I'm seen as the rather distant but good brother?

69th hour

PATIENT: I'm blank and flat inside, feel nothing. Maybe I'm fighting the transference, but I don't feel as though I am. I feel as though everything is fine and maybe this is the time to stop. I accept that I like you very much, that there is a transference, but there is nothing to threaten me in it. I see the problem with my father differently now, and that is easier. I see the problem with mother, and it still hurts. It will take a little time. I still get mad underneath, but it is improving greatly.

Seeing my children grow up, my own childhood comes to mind and I think my parents were certainly rigid about sex and whatever relates to it. Yesterday we got a present from my mother-in-law and Beverly got a bathing suit and she danced something like a hula and I enjoyed so much just watching her. I remembered when I was a child, I used to say I wanted to be an actress and do acrobatics. Mother told father and he threatened he would beat me if he ever caught me. One day father saw me, and I felt sick and fainted. That was the only way I could escape a beating was to be sick. But I really felt sick, and to this day I have these sick dizzy spells.

The other evening I remembered an incident that happened when I was about in first grade. I was at home writing in my school book and father asked, "What are you doing?" I said, "Nothing," and Lois said, "That's what she always does." I was so scared that father would look in my book because I was drawing a sexy girl. I don't remember what happened but I always had this feeling of guilt, and when one of my sisters said something, I'd think: This is it! This feeling is now diminishing to the point where it's nearly gone. Some of it was guilt for masturbation and for anything else connected with sex. My children tell me all sorts of things, and I just say, "Uh-huh," or I talk with them about it. I was two different persons as a child. I don't know. I was guilty because I liked boys at age six. Once, when I was about three or four, mother caught me masturbating with a doll. I was trying to see how babies come out, and just then mother came into the room. Once at age about six I masturbated with another girl the same age. We both must have felt guilty. I didn't touch her; she masturbated me. That was age five or six, but nothing after that. After that I just liked boys.

ANALYST: In talking of guilt we must not omit hostility as a cause as well as sex. Some guilt could be coming from the hostility to mother, to sisters, and to father.

PATIENT: You mean it could be that the sexual behavior came in part from my hostility to them? Yes, it could be that because I always said, "No one understands me," which meant that I wanted more love and understanding, that I felt not loved enough and rejected by everyone. I was not thinking of sex but there was rebellion in the sex. But I didn't act out much as a child. It's normal to play doctor. The guilt about that hasn't lasted. I feel that the sex is much more accepted than my hostility to mother. Mother and God are the same thing. Hostility of any kind to mother will never be accepted in my family. If I ever said I'm a better mother than my mother, they would drop to the floor! But I think I am. That's why I have to be so careful at home.

76th hour

PATIENT: I had a very bad weekend. Now I know why; I wanted to quit analysis. I was defending myself. I have a terrific headache. Friday night Will was away overnight and I had a nightmare. I awoke at 1 A.M. and couldn't go back to sleep. I was scared to death, and it was just the same as when I was six years old. Like at six, I was afraid to turn from my left to right side because I had to watch the window to be sure no one was coming in. It was utterly unrealistic. I heard noises, was just scared, although when I went to bed, I just opened the windows to air the place. I couldn't even read as I usually do. So I called Annie and she came and slept in the next room. Then the fear disappeared completely, and I was able to go back to sleep. But by then it was 4.30 A.M. and Beverly came in for crayons at 6.30 A.M. and woke me up.

We had a party Saturday night and some people stayed on afterwards and didn't leave until 3 A.M. I wasn't especially tired and couldn't sleep much. Then last night we had company and they stayed until 1.30 A.M. I still didn't feel tired and I couldn't sleep, so I tried to read. Usually I am so tired when I go to bed, I'm asleep as soon as I hit the pillow. But this morning when I woke up—Oh, my! I felt awful and this headache.

ANALYST: What about the nightmare?

PATIENT: I was a patient in a mental hospital and I was

old. I was myself but at the same time I was also my grandmother. A friend, a woman, was there. A new patient came in and my friend said, "Now is the time to escape," but one of the patients who was short and thin, killed the guard. Another guard came in and I shouted at him that they were going to kill him, and he escaped, saved himself. We were all in the dark. The door was open and I escaped too because I thought that because I saved the guard, I betrayed the patients and they'd do something to me. I thought I'd be safer at home. I was telling this to an old, gray haired lady who was very protective of me and gave me her wallet with money in it. When I was talking with her, I was young but when I left the hospital and was looking for my house, I was old. I was my grandmother. I passed my parents' house. The mental hospital was the grade school I attended as a child. The street was the one I was so afraid of as a child. There were always some low class men on it who must have been perverts. They did some exhibitionistic things. In the dream I thought: If I go into my parents' house, they will put me in the attic because I am old and mentally sick and they won't want me to be seen. So I was looking for my own home, which I couldn't find.

Then I went back to sleep and had another dream, but it wasn't a nightmare. J. E., a man at work, was telling me about a woman client he was having a lot of problems with. I told him he wasn't handling the situation well, that he was reacting as though she were a sexual thing but really she is full of hostility.

ANALYST: Associations?

PATIENT: When I left you the last hour, I was not convinced about the hostility. I thought: No, it's the sex that causes me all the guilt. Then I thought: Of course it isn't; it's really my relation with the whole family—I still have more inside than I'm aware of. Maybe now it's not so much the hostility as the fear that I'll be punished. I feel I will be punished somewhere along the line. Now I feel sure that I am not going crazy, that I don't have to go crazy to show the hostility, to show my real feelings. But Friday night I felt exactly as when I was a child.

ANALYST: The last hour we discussed only the question of whether or not sex is the *sole* source of the guilt. We must look further. Last time we talked about the idea that hostility can cause guilt too. It may even be the chief source. You were strictly trained about sex; how you feel about it, about masturbation, boys, and so on went very much against the training. So, of course there was anxiety, guilt, and shame. But why more now?

PATIENT: I had the severe anxiety when I was closest to father and also the time I had a lot of hostility to mother. Since then I've never been close to mother. Of course I wasn't close to her before then either, but I wasn't so against her.

ANALYST: Could any jealousy of mother in relation to father have played a part?

PATIENT: Yes. When mother very often harshly sent me out of the bed when I was in with father, I thought: She's mad at me because father loves me. The way I felt toward her then, as the hostility was getting stronger and more conscious, is the same way that it is now.

ANALYST: Meaning what?

PATIENT: I was hostile to mother, felt she didn't love me, and therefore I feared that ghosts and robbers might come in the windows. All these things were the punishment.

ANALYST: Why is this pattern aroused now?

PATIENT: What keeps coming to my mind is that Will and I now sleep in the same bed. Why should I give any importance to it. It is as though, because it makes me self-conscious before the children, they know I belong to a man. They say nothing. If they thought anything, they would say it, so it's my own fantasy. I feel guilt, as though I'm doing something wrong sleeping with a man.

ANALYST: Where does the transference fit in?

PATIENT: I don't know. After Will and I got married, we lived far away from home for a long while. When we returned home for the first time, I was very pregnant and I felt embarrassed in front of my father. But I did not feel like that in front of mother. About mother I didn't care, but then father would know I'd had sex.

ANALYST: He'd trained you so strictly against sex?

PATIENT: Yes.

ANALYST: So my job is to counteract father and tell you sex with your husband is fine, sleeping in the same bed with him is fine, etc.?

PATIENT (*laughing*): That is funny. Just because we change from twin beds, that I should feel all the embarrassment, fear, as though I were doing something wrong, and after having four children! I do all right in reality.

ANALYST: You *do* all right but don't *feel* all right.

PATIENT: Correct.

70th hour

PATIENT: I had a dream. There was a war going on. I was supposed to have a romance, or sex, or marry a certain man. However, he was much older than I. There was no one in particular telling me I had to do this. I just had a sense of it, but I protested and said, "No, I need a young man, not an old man like that." Then there was a young man. There were a lot of wild things going on as there would be in war, bombs exploding and the like. Then I managed to handle things so that the young man and I left this war scene and came away. Then there were other people around and we were to be married and were on the way to being married and the dream ended very happily and pleasantly.

ANALYST: Associations?

PATIENT: We had visitors last evening from Texas. I thought that I would be very homesick; but it was just the opposite. To my surprise, I found myself showing them around the city and at one o'clock in the morning I suggested that we go to visit some of the parts of town that I particularly like. My husband gave me quite a look when I suggested the excursion at that hour. Nevertheless we all went.

ANALYST: What associations do you have to the older man?

PATIENT: Of course, he could be you, but he didn't look like you, and he was much older than you are. He reminded me more of father. He was rather sloppy; he was not at all well groomed or attractive. This and the war are how being at home seem to me. To go back home is to be caught in the war within the family. All my feelings about mother and the competition with my sisters and my not being loved enough by mother and my turning to father but feeling controlled by his wishes, which all of us are—all this comes forward. Very much of our whole lives are influenced by the wish to please father and, of course, mother too. I feel now that it is foolish to be involved in these family wars. Suppose my mother did not love me as much as I wanted when I was a child, what of it! I should get away from all that, feel free of it, and be able to love my own children and take care of them and detach myself from this whole family involvement.

I think the young man really is my husband. It means I can accept a younger man and separate myself from the family. Also, now that I have contacts here and feel more secure because of the analysis, I feel more able to be less dependent upon my parents.

ANALYST: Also, however, I might be the older man. The unattractiveness might be a defense against being too close to me and against any sexual or romantic elements in the attachment.

PATIENT (*laughs and shakes her head in affirmation*): I think that is right because the problem at home is that when I am around mother or father, I get to be not just close to them but too close. So, maybe I fight that off with you and also fight off the sexual element.

79th hour

PATIENT: I'm arranging to be home early three afternoons. This will allow me to be with Tom and help him. I hope this will relieve my guilt feelings.

Yesterday I got a letter that our two cats at the ranch died. I feel upset. I feel so silly to cry (*tears*). They are only cats, but in some ways they are better than people. That is why I hate to have cats. They die and you—— Since both died, they must have been poisoned, but they never went after any animals or poultry. They were good. The same thing happened with the last one we had. He fell in love and used to watch the female cat from our window.

The same feeling I have toward the cats I had toward my sons. I think it's easier for me to tell it about the cats. When we get a pet, I think: I don't want to get involved. (*Still occasional tears.*) I treat him very well, but I'm on guard emotionally not to get involved because I know he will die before I do. It was the same with my sons—I felt that if I got too involved, then when they left to get married, it would be too much of a loss for me. I never felt it about my daughters; I never had to be on guard toward them. I used to think only of "the children." Now I realize this was toward the boys and not toward the girls and that this was the beginning of the problem with Tom. I'm this way with the kitten we have now—a female—but I won't let myself go. By the time I was only seven, so many of my pets had already died that I decided: no more pets.

ANALYST: Can you make anything of this analytically?

PATIENT (*pausing reflectively*): Well, first that everything I loved got killed or died; so, love was dangerous. What I mean is, it's not that they died but that I was left alone. As a child all I had as a companion was a cat or a dog. I didn't play much with my sisters. They were different. Once I played dolls with Roberta and that is one of my earliest memories. So my love needs were toward animals, cats.

ANALYST: Is there any transference meaning in this?

PATIENT: I guess it's the same. If I tend to turn any love needs toward you, I'm afraid something might happen —not sexually—but losing your friendship, losing you.

ANALYST: Do you mean that analysis would end or do you mean something else?

PATIENT: It's that I don't want to place my happiness in someone else's hands. You must have it in yourself, not that you are pleasing someone else but that you are pleased with yourself. So, I'm still fighting the transference as I fight anything that makes me too close to someone. When I married, I resolved I'd never love Will more than he loved me. If I don't, then I'll control the situation. Real happiness is to give, no matter to whom or how the other person reacts.

ANALYST: Isn't this problem, this struggle because of the strength of the dependent love needs, quantitative? We know the source, that is insecurity about them, especially to mother.

PATIENT: Of course, but why does this come out today? I don't feel it to her nearly so much anymore, so it must be that I'm turning it to you. Of course I still feel that way to mother; it can't change quickly, but it's changing. I can just love her as she is.

ANALYST: Is it that if we could reduce the intensity of the dependent love needs, then you wouldn't have to fear them so, with mother, or with cats, or with me?

PATIENT: Yes. I'm displacing everything to you.

ANALYST: The advantage of doing that is that with me we

can discuss these feelings. You can't with mother or with the pets.

PATIENT (*smiles*): Or with the children.

ANALYST: This seems to be the core of the problem.

PATIENT: It is there; it's coming out.

80th hour

PATIENT: I have realized that I must go back to my old job. I owe them so much. I met my old boss at a party and he spoke about how much he wanted me, all the plans and arrangements he has been thinking about for me.

Something else I must tell you. I've changed in some ways. A complicated situation arose involving Lois and another girl. The big change in me is that I felt secure; I handled the situation quietly and for the first time I fought for something I wanted. Formerly I would have been so unhappy; I would have felt like a martyr and talked a lot about how Lois doesn't think about me, and so on. Now in this instance I felt that if she doesn't think about me, I should do something to see that she does. I phoned her for another reason, told her of the letter I just got from mother, and then brought up the issue very casually. And now all is very good and friendly with Lois. We are on very good terms; (*laughs*) we never see each other. Poor thing. Now she constantly talks about me. So it's reversed. When we first came up here from Texas, I feared being alone and thought I'd have her, a member of the family, relatively near. But she is lonely only because of her own personality.

I had a dream last night in which I am going to go off to have an affair with a married man. My family are around and they all object and argue against it, but I go off with him anyway.

ANALYST: Associations?

PATIENT: I think of wishes for love, which we have discussed toward mother, and my feeling that she did not love me as much as I wished or as much as she loved the other children. I sort of knew this, but I never realized that it was because of this that I turned so strongly to my father. But then I was afraid of wanting his love too much because he was rather strict and intimidating and also because I was afraid of the sexual element, not only toward him, but if I showed any interest at all in sex or boys.

ANALYST: Any transference references?

PATIENT: I don't think that the married man I'm having an affair with in the dream is you.

ANALYST: Do you see any hostile meaning?

PATIENT: No, I don't see any.

ANALYST: Could it be that having an affair with a married man is something your family would disapprove of?

PATIENT: And how!

ANALYST: And therefore, the dream could well have a meaning of defiance of the family and of revenge, as though you would say: If you do not give me all the love I want, or if you give more to the other children, then I will go off and disobey you and give my love to somebody else and get the love I want from somebody else. In other words, what we have here is definance and revenge.

PATIENT: That is certainly correct. I didn't realize it before, but now that you point it out, I can recognize the feeling and that may be the transference reference. The transference is a frustrating situation because I defend myself against being too attached to you because I know that I will not get all the love I want from you, either. And, if I get attached, the analysis will end anyway eventually or at any rate the love won't be satisfied. So maybe part of the anger that I feel because of this frustration takes the form of saying: All right! Then I'll go out with somebody else! And, his being a married man is a special defiance of my family who were, of course, so strict. Although father, as I told you before, fell in love with a number of other women.

82nd hour

PATIENT: Now I can talk about the relation between Will and me. I couldn't before because I was too involved. Now I see it more coolly. I see things also that I never recognized before. He has been selfish since we've been married. It's very hard to talk about my husband; it's much, much harder than about my mother or my son. Will never sees the end of my strength. In every role in life I must play it perfectly. As a mother, I must never tire, be perfect with the children, and all that sort of thing. As a wife, he wants me to act as though I had no children, didn't work, and as if he were the only one I lived for. What I mean is, he wants me to have my hair perfectly set from morning until night, but he doesn't want me to spend the money once a week in a beauty parlor. He wants me to be up with him until midnight or 1:00 A.M. every night, as though I had nothing else to do. I come home and the children want to talk to me, and he sends them away because he doesn't want to share me with anyone. If I'm tired around 7:30 or if I go to bed at 10:00, he makes remarks as though I had just been lying in bed all day. What hurts me more is his saying I'm lazy, when the truth of the matter is I'm on the go all day long. His mother is the kind who seems to be doing a lot of things, puffs and pants and moans and groans and does almost nothing; and she looks awful all day. I'm not going to kill myself. His mother changes the furniture arrangements every month or so and paints the rooms often, even though they don't need it. Then she gets sick. But when I am tired, I go to bed. I don't feel that it's my house; everything is where and how *he* likes it. People think he's such a help to me, but it's his compulsiveness.

Having it the way he likes it is the reason he does things, it's not to help me.

I realize now that he is very dependent upon me—like a helpless child. He can't live without me. If I am away for a week, he goes around helpless and confused. About the selfishness, when we needed a car for the family, he came home with a little sports car because he wanted it. When we talked about getting a car, I spoke up and he listened and seemed to agree. Then he came home with his little car. He listens, but he really pays no attention because he knows I can take care of myself, that nothing will happen to me. He's losing his control of his hostility, gets angry so easily. I hope it's for the good.

ANALYST: These things that you're telling about, we should see them as problems and consider what, if anything, can be done to be constructive and not disloyal. We should also discuss why it is so hard to talk about these things.

PATIENT: I know that. In him I found the love I want and need and I should be grateful. I don't want to lose him.

ANALYST: But we can still understand the irritants, which are in every marriage, and see how best to handle them.

86th hour

PATIENT: I'm tired. We went to see some classic dancers last evening. It was very good. Today is one of the days I feel like not working any more. I feel as though I'm working so hard for the two maids, so they can have a nice house, a nice kitchen. We don't have time to enjoy our house. One thing for sure, wherever I live I want to have a place far away from people. We used to rent a small house where we could go for weekends, no phones; we couldn't be reached.

This morning I had an argument with my son

Tom. I don't feel too guilty, but I shouldn't have said what I did or been like that. I just didn't control myself again. Last night, because we weren't home, Tom didn't come home until 8:00 P.M. He was at a friend's house. He did nothing wrong, but he had no dinner and the mother of the friend had to bring him home. This is the fourth time he's done this, and I never said anything nor punished him before. I just said that I'm home early afternoons and would like him to be there so we can be together. But this morning I got so mad! I told him he couldn't stay out after school for the rest of the week and that he couldn't go camping with his father this weekend. He says nothing but looks so hurt. Of course he's going with Will this weekend. I knew he would and he knows it too. I wouldn't keep him from that pleasure. That's what's wrong.

ANALYST: Why is it so wrong? You blow your top and then you turn out not to be really mean and disciplinary. He learns from this that you get angry but quickly get over it and are reasonable again.

PATIENT: I feel less guilt, but he went to school feeling bad.

ANALYST: Your anger was enough punishment. Could it be partly that you were tired this morning?

PATIENT: Ninety per cent of the time that Tom and I have trouble is because Annie tells me something about him. She has to though, it's her job. He's at an age when he wants to be a grown man. If one of the other children brings home a paper from school with a good grade and I praise it, Tom depreciates it. He says he sees nothing good about it at all. I don't see how they can like him. But now I am much more at ease with him and can express warmth and love without being afraid to. I must have had the same relation to him that I've had toward all males. I have it to Davey, his younger brother, also. Namely, I think that if I got too close, I'd fear the sexual element. And, not only do I fear being too close, but I fear making him too close, not sexually.

ANALYST: Sounds a little like your problem of closeness with mother and with father.

PATIENT: Before starting this analysis, I used to fear that Tom would come at night and put a knife in my back. It got to the point where I couldn't sleep. I had to take sleeping pills to get any sleep. And, the poor child was afraid of me! I feared to tell my husband because I thought I was going crazy. Ever since I can remember, whenever my sons approached me, I felt there was a sexual element. This was before I ever heard of psychiatry. At first I thought he wanted to kill me, but I thought somehow it was related to sex. At other times I thought I was so hostile to him in the day that at night he would come for revenge.

ANALYST: If it is sex, then why should sex take the form of being killed by a knife in the back?

PATIENT: I must have identified with him as when I was a child. I must have felt that hostility to my parents when I was a child, especially to mother. Not, of course, to the extent of really getting up with a knife; but the idea of retaliation was there. Father always slept with a revolver under his pillow. My conscience wouldn't let me think about these things, but I certainly felt the anger underneath. My relations with Tom are much better than those between mother and me, although not on the surface. Mother thought I was one of the best children she'd ever seen, but the war went on inside of me. I would have felt better if mother had blown her top. Then I would have hated her more openly, but she never did. She would just say, "I'll tell your father when he comes home." And did that even scare me! I knew she wouldn't, but was I scared that she would. Now I know that even if she had he wouldn't have paid any attention to it. Father spanked me only once; he never punished me and never called me in for a reprimand. If he had, I would have died. Maybe I was so scared he didn't need to punish. Maybe I thought I would have disappeared, like the tom cat he shot. And, I've seen him be very cruel to human beings too. When I was four, a fellow stole father's watch and father twisted his arm and held a knife to his throat until he told where it was hidden. I saw that at four, and I never dared move. I get scared and shake even now to think of it.

ANALYST: Perhaps you took it all even worse because of your own hostility and guilt to mother. And, because of all this you didn't dare express it—you had to repress it.

PATIENT: Tom has never seen what I saw by the time I was four, nor has he felt such fear. Men would lie in wait for father and try to kill him. But the relation with mother was good, because in spite of going through all this, I'm okay—neurotic, but that's all. She gave me enough security. The big thing is certainly the relation to mother.

87th hour

PATIENT: I'm mad at you and at everybody.

ANALYST: Just so you understand it and analyze it, that's good; especially if we see and discuss the hostility to me.

PATIENT: I'm mad because everyone is a conformist and, of course, coming from a big family, I can understand that. You either are a conformist or a rebel and if you are a conformist, you don't enjoy life.

ANALYST: Usually, like this, one sees only two possibilities even though there are others.

PATIENT: Yes. I got to the office late this morning—an expression of rebellion. Someone came in with a pile of work and I said, "Take it away; I just don't want to work today." He looked at me. Of course I did it, but I thought: Why am I doing this? Just because my parents got me started and wanted me to. In San Francisco, when we were first married, Will and I would dash off, do some wild or crazy things for two days and then come back to work. I want to argue with someone and can't. One thing I envy about Tom is that he doesn't care about anyone; he laughs at everybody and enjoys life. Last evening Tom said, "I told a friend that I can't go camping with father." I said, "It's good you did." He said, "I didn't, though." I said, "Why not?" and he said, "Because I know you'll let me go." I then said, "You know me too well." He went off laughing.

I never felt that I wished I wanted to be a man except for one thing. If I were a man, I know I'd get to the top because I wouldn't have the ties and responsibilities and demands of the home and the children. A man is free to make his job his chief concern, but I have responsibilities that are more important than my job. (*Sighs.*) Let's go to the dream I had last night.

In the dream mother looked young, she had short hair and was sloppy. She's really the opposite—thin and very neat. Mother, Will, myself, and some of the ranch hands were all walking together to our house—our present house. It was a shack, dirty, only one room, no furniture. Mother went to the only room with a bed, and I sat down in another room that had no bed and no place to sleep. I came out a few times and every time I did one of the ranch hands came out of mother's room as though afraid I would catch him there. The third time this happened the ranch hand was upset and said, "Why don't you say you are coming!" At that point the hate for my mother was so great. I thought she was a whore. She always said, in reality, that she didn't like sex with father, she thought it was dirty. And here she was having sex with the help. Then we were again walking down the street and Will was with mother, telling her that Lois' husband said she was a whore. I was so mad at Will because if he were telling her what Lois' husband said, he must not have believed it, and if he didn't, he was a fool. Then I went for my analytic hour. I had it with you first and with T. H. later. The place was packed with people, his whole family was there and he said, "Do you mind? This will be the hour." What he meant was that the whole family would be there. I said, "No," but I did mind. Then I realized that I'd had my analytic hour with you already at 1 P.M., now it was 3 P.M. Then Lois came in, she looked very nice and I was proud of her. I introduced her to T. H., but she was hostile to me and to him. So, when she left, I was relieved. Oh, yes, when I told Will mother was sleeping with a ranch hand, he said, "No, there is a yacht through that door and he's only helping her with it."

ANALYST: Associations?

PATIENT: T. H. wants to analyze me with all his family present. This has to do with my hostility to you, like when I meet other people coming to their sessions with you. It's the same problem with mother. I just wanted her for me alone. Anything that interferes with the time I have with you, I reject. Though in the dream I said I didn't care, I really did. Very much. Now I don't so much. I'm able to talk about it. (*Angry.*) It goes back to my mother and I can't help it! I can't now but I will! (*Still angry, but smiling.*)

ANALYST: In the dream there are two analysts. Associations?

PATIENT: If there are two, then the relation is not so close as if only one. When there is just one, all is concentrated on you. And, if I have only one, I might lose that one, but if I have two, there is always at least one.

ANALYST: What are your associations to mother being a whore?

PATIENT: (*laughing outright*): If mother ever knew I dreamed that, she'd drop dead. It must be me.

ANALYST: Do you have any associations to all of you walking to the house, which is a shack?

PATIENT: I think that is what father and mother think of Will and me, that we are rebellious, independent, do as we please, live like Bohemians.

ANALYST: The yacht—associations?

PATIENT: The house was a shack, but we had a yacht! It was just an excuse—a way of going places.

ANALYST: Is it possible that mother was really very indulging and loving toward you during your babyhood and then, only when you were older did you find you had to share this love and attention with all the older ones? Could this be the case instead of a lack of love from mother?

PATIENT: Why, it could be true. Yes, it could. It must be related somehow to not conforming also.

ANALYST: Is it possible that you felt special so long as you were the baby of the family, but that when you grew up a little, you didn't want to be only one of so many?

PATIENT: Of course it's possible. Why shouldn't it be. (*Angry.*) I'm beginning to realize that I have too many jobs to get anywhere, and I know which I am going to choose: Mother!

ANALYST: Why do you want to get anywhere?

PATIENT: Why! Of course, for my sisters' sake. To beat them. But now I realize that I don't care about doing that in business. The only way is with my children.

ANALYST: But you don't want your children to mature well just so you can beat out your sisters?

PATIENT: Oh, no! For them.

ANALYST: Isn't beating your sisters simply a way to establish the original pattern, that is, in the eyes of your father and mother?

PATIENT: Yes, of course. I'm tired of all this stuff, but it really has been strong.

ANALYST: And the envy of the man is that he's free to be the best in one job, in his work, to be the preferred baby of the family.

PATIENT: Yes. And remember, my brother, the oldest one, he never had to do anything. He never had to compete, except perhaps with father.

ANALYST: Watch the envy toward me, then. The pattern

repeats toward me, toward anyone. The whore element is partly the revenge again. If I don't love you enough, you'll sleep with your help.

PATIENT: I can see it.

90th hour

PATIENT: Yesterday Lois phoned and I told her I thought we should stop the relationship. She doesn't understand and I couldn't explain. She is just so upsetting that I can't stand it any more. She has been upsetting me so much that it interferes with my relations with Will and the children. Lois wrote mother all sorts of things against me. Mother doesn't write me about it, but she just believes it and then the family believes it and then the whole community knows it. If I return, Vivian and Mabel can make or break me, and that is all controlled by one person—mother. So it has a lot of reality and not just my emotional reactions. Some years ago when I didn't have a proper dress and wanted to borrow money to put down on a house, they thought I had twenty-five thousand dollars. Therefore they wouldn't lend us any money nor would they even sign a paper saying that we were reliable. As a result, the banks wouldn't lend us the money. So, without saying a word to mother, we went to uncle, and he immediately signed the paper and the bank gave us the money without mother's knowledge. I'll rise in mother's esteem again when I have money to give her. When I was a child, I rebelled not against all the siblings but against her trying to control me completely. Vivian is completely identified with mother, and she married a man just like father. Vivian can't live her own life at all. I asked her if she were happier when away from the family and she said yes, but she refused to discuss it. Vivian thinks it's father and doesn't see mother's control. The family accepts anything, any acting out, like Lois, even sex, but what it will not accept is emancipation. Mother writes Lois what are almost love letters. Mabel is the only one who stands up to mother. I pity father. Mother controlling the daughters and there's no place for him. Mother the heroine and father the cause of all the trouble. Father is just outside, except for Mabel and me. The fear I've always had all my life and the hostility to mother is the idea that she could destroy me. It's not that I would lose just her love but everything. I have felt too terrible and too guilty for so long to say it, but I think that if mother were dead, I would get on better with my sisters. I'm sorry I had to say that. When I heard someone say that only crazy people hate the ones they most love, I took it to mean that those who hate the ones they love must go crazy, because God punishes them. It's hard to confess this hostility to mother. It's not hard to say it to you, but to myself it is very very difficult. I never believed one could change, but it's true, and I never had any hope for me; but now I see that one *can* change, and therefore I've been so relaxed for two days. I don't care about pleasing people so much any more.

93rd hour

PATIENT: I had a dream last night that I was at home with my sisters. We heard that Lois was here and that she was psychotic and had just had a baby. Vivian passed it off, said there was nothing we could do anyway. But I felt terrible and took a plane here. Once I got here I found it wasn't Lois, it was Mabel. She was in an awful state hospital. I tried to have her moved. I felt terrible.

ANALYST: Associations?

PATIENT: Today I punished myself, little things. I had a slight tiff with Will, then went through a yellow light as it turned red and in the mirror I saw a policeman writing down my number. The psychosis—I take that as punishment, as I told you. If a person is hostile to loved ones, he loses his mind. Fear of losing my mind was my main reason for coming to you for analysis. Did I tell you that?

ANALYST: Yes, but not at first.

PATIENT: And, if I had not come to you and if I had had the kind of analysis I hear about—I am scared to even think of it—I would have lost my mind. Or, maybe my self-preservation would have made me stop, and this isn't just transference to you. I can give you lots of examples. With me, for example, there is my fear of Tom coming in with a knife. If we had gotten into all kinds of sexual symbolism, the oedipus complex, and the like we might not have seen the hostility and guilt, which almost immediately relieved the symptom. And we haven't missed the sex either.

Mabel is me. I identify with her. I suffered so much when I saw it was Mabel in the dream, and I pity her so much.

ANALYST: Is this, perhaps, the guilt for the break with Lois?

PATIENT: That is right. Mostly I have difficulty remembering dreams, but this one I tried to forget. I wanted to go back to sleep, but the image stayed with me. Especially of Mabel.

ANALYST: Mabel is half way between Lois and you, isn't she? Hostility is not turned entirely on you out of guilt but only on the one you identify with.

PATIENT: Yes. A friend of ours died last week. He was a very prominent, successful, nice, and truly beloved man. But he had so many problems. Three of his children are in psychiatric treatment and his teenage son tried to kill the mother (the man's wife). The man and his wife were also in treatment. The psychiatrists made the most unbelievable mess of it.

ANALYST: Made it or only failed to cure it?

PATIENT: They made it worse. That whole family was much better off before the psychiatrists. The wrong interpretations and treatment can confuse a person terribly.

ANALYST: Why were you at home in the dream?

PATIENT: That is what I'd fear most now after breaking with Lois. I'd be more guilty.

ANALYST: Or the opposite—back with them and they would love you in spite of it.

PATIENT: Yes, that too.

96th hour

PATIENT: I'm depressed weekends. I think it's partly because I don't see you. And also, I'm jealous of a beautiful new secretary who does some of Will's work at his company.

Last night I had a dream. I was with my sisters and they were accusing me of having masturbated as a little girl, and I kept saying, in a very anxious way, "I didn't do it; I didn't do it." Then Tom called me to the phone. He said it was a woman who said she was just a friend. I knew it was Lois and it was. She asked me for some directions, something inconsequential. Later a big box of things arrived for my daughter. It's so childish. And she heard my toaster needed repairing and left a toaster for me. It is childish and I am too. That's how she handles her guilt. She dashed in, left the toaster, and dashed out. Now it's something forbidden and she's enjoying it.

I thought I couldn't be so jealous of a secretary. I'm not that abnormal, so I thought of the transference. I must be jealous of all the women you treat. But why this dream at this time? I'm even guilty about masturbation, but I've had dreams of intercourse with other men and I didn't feel as scared, embarrassed, and ashamed as I do in this dream. I don't know. I don't know.

ANALYST: The dream is of guilt and shame toward your sisters. Could this be in reference to cutting off contact with Lois and then she sends gifts, etc., not only because it is forbidden, but probably as a plea for love?

PATIENT: But they have the opposite effect. It could be the guilt for breaking with Lois. I don't know. All I know is I wish they would leave me alone. Lois phoned and asked Annie if I go to church every Sunday. Then mother wrote and said she hoped I was going and taking the children. All I want is for them to leave me alone.

ANALYST: What are your associations to masturbation?

PATIENT: As a child mother once saw me masturbate with a doll. I told you that memory. I thought I didn't have dolls, but I did.

ANALYST: What else do you associate to masturbation?

PATIENT: Only the wish for them to leave me alone with my husband and children.

ANALYST: Could the masturbation symbolize rebellion against control and interference?

PATIENT: It could. As a child I heard that masturbation was terrible, that one should never do it alone or with someone else. But I didn't know what the word meant. (*Laughs.*) I was so innocent. No one ever explained, so it was always a puzzle to me.

When I grew older, I realized my sisters were as human as I was, sexually I mean, and it was a great relief, but I didn't see that they were also so human in their emotions, in love and hate. They still don't show they are human in their feelings and never will. If mother dies, Lois will go into a depression, superficial I hope, but maybe severe. That's the dream.

ANALYST: What is? Why the guilt, shame, and embarrassment?

PATIENT: Maybe the masturbation is like psychoanalysis—masturbation is by yourself, and in analysis you find out things about yourself.

ANALYST: But why the guilt and shame?

PATIENT: In both you find things that are considered to be wrong—sex and hostility. I acted out my guilt for this hostility to Lois and I broke off with her; and you act out when you masturbate. I feel trapped, I feel that I want to break off and no one lets me. But how else could I end it. I broke off, but I've not achieved it.

ANALYST: This has actually mobilized the guilt you've felt all your life to mother and your sisters. And, you may be correct in equating the analysis and masturbation—like analysis and sex—because as we've often discussed, your parents and sisters oppose your being in analysis. They take it as a forbidden sexual situation, and insofar as you have any sexual feelings in the analysis or even enjoy talking to a man, you feel it is against all your training, against your superego.

97th hour

PATIENT: For the last few days I have been afraid of losing my mind, also of losing control and yelling and screaming, or something of the sort. This is a terrible feeling. Then, when it passes, I wonder how I could feel that way; but it makes me very much afraid. It must be connected with the old fear I had that if you are hostile to someone you love, you will go crazy. At work one of the men said, "What is the matter with you?" I said, "Nothing." He then said, "You are not having any of that psychoanalysis are you?" I guess the analysis has helped because if someone had spoken to me like that a year ago, I would really have blown my top at him. My husband noticed my mood and he also remarked upon it, as though it were your fault. But I said to him, "It's *your* fault," and then I finally told him that I was jealous of the beautiful new secretary who is doing some of his work.

At home mother and my sisters discussed everything but father never knew what was going on in the family.

ANALYST: This seems to relate to your jealousy in relation to your husband's secretary, and last hour you also expressed jealousy in relation to other patients that I see.

We can therefore expect that the material of this hour relates to me also, even though it is in the form of other people's comments about analysis. Before we come to the transference, however, we should raise the question of how much of this is a reaction to your having broken off with your sister.

PATIENT: In the past I have withdrawn also, but always I did this without feelings of losing my mind.

ANALYST: But, as I understand it, you never directly rejected any member of your family before in this way, actually telling them that you did not want them to phone you.

PATIENT: That is true.

ANALYST: Therefore, considering that one of your chief complaints was a sense of guilt (and we have found how much guilt there is toward your mother and sisters) we really shouldn't be surprised if it takes a while to digest this direct rejection.

PATIENT: With that I agree.

ANALYST: However, in this acting out we must also look for a transference meaning. You brokc off with Lois before you mentioned it to me. Why this haste? Why not follow what you know is the best policy, that is, of analyzing pretty thoroughly any acting out that you consider rather than doing it impulsively. Could this, in the first place, be related to what you told me about father not knowing what went on in the family because no one ever told him anything?

PATIENT (*chuckles a little*): That seems to be correct.

ANALYST: Perhaps your needs for love toward your mother and maybe toward father also, made you feel that you had to do exactly what they wanted and therefore you rebelled against this. Perhaps this is why you wanted to act on breaking off with your sister rather than discuss it with me. In other words, this behavior was not only a rebellion against the submissiveness to your family and the wish to break away, but it was also the same pattern transferred to me. It was a rebellion against being dependent and submissive toward me, and this would make for fear of my reaction and this present anxiety that you feel.

PATIENT: Yes. I hate to be dependent on you. I feel though that if I let myself go, I would be too dependent and want your love too much and have to do too much as you want me to.

ANALYST: But I am not your mother or your father. This is rather simply anxiety, chiefly I think because of your repeating the pattern of rebellion, because of the dependent love needs, toward me. I think there is no danger of your losing your mind.

98th hour

PATIENT: I had a dream last night about you and for the first time it was in a very nice way, a happy dream. I saw you as you are. I didn't have to distort the image.

You and I were home and my husband was there too. Everybody was there but only in the background, so it was only you, Will, and I. You had papers, like a manuscript in your hand, and were teaching me; and I was learning very much and felt very close to you. It was not hard for me to understand what you were saying and teaching me, although before that I had the impression that it was difficult. Then I told Will that he should learn from you because you were teaching me so well. Will came, and you taught him too. You were sort of in a bed or on a couch, and I had no place to sit, so I sat down and put your feet on my lap (*laughs with embarrassment*). I thought: What will people think. Then I thought: I don't care what they think. It was so late that I told you that you should stay overnight, and I tucked you in bed as though you were a child, with much love for I was taking great care of you. Then I went off with Will, very happy.

ANALYST: Associations?

PATIENT: All the analysts I have seen are so hostile, and they cut people down so. But last evening I met an analyst who was so feminine and so human. I don't know how she really is, of course, but everyone felt she was so nice. I know now that I could have been analyzed by a woman, if it were one like she.

I think this is the first dream I had of you that is a nice dream. At the same time I think that I like you in a more relaxed way. When I left yesterday, it started—I got a very sharp headache. I thought: Something in the hour made me mad, but what? It could be that I can't do things without consulting you, just because reality tells me I shouldn't. I had a headache, but I was relaxed. I guess I was fighting what came out last hour. I said yesterday that I didn't want to be dependent on anybody, and I don't have to be, just because I like them. I think so many things I just can't say.

ANALYST: Like what? (*Patient laughs.*) All right, why can't you say them?

PATIENT: Because I feel embarrassed. I do know that my relation with you can get better in that I needn't just look for something but that I can give too. It can be a mature relation. Yesterday you said you were not my mother or father, and I've been thinking about that. At least I can like you without being scared. If you don't like me, that's your problem. It won't keep me from liking you. Two patterns are there: on the one hand I like and love my mother without looking for what she and no one else can give me, and, on the other, I can be attracted to you without being afraid that my wish will come true.

ANALYST: Meaning the sexual wish?

PATIENT: Sure, that's the only thing I'm afraid of.

ANALYST: Of course, as you know, that is impossible in a professional situation. Let me make a few points by way of explanation. First, because of mother and father transference, wishes are intensified but also incestuous.

Second, the aim of psychoanalysis is to help people get satisfactions in real life. Third, all the hostility and anxiety in relation to mother and father would also be intensified. Perhaps you will take this as rejection, but these are the facts.

PATIENT: No, now it relieves my fears, but it is true. If you said it to me even a month ago, I would have felt very rejected, but now I feel I can like you without having bad feelings. So it came out.

ANALYST: What you were embarrassed to tell?

PATIENT (*laughs*): No, no, no. I told you the point but not the specific fantasies. It's a very big change for me that they don't embarrass me to have them but they would to tell them to you.

ANALYST: Don't I know them from the dream?

PATIENT: Sure. No, no. (*laughs.*)

ANALYST: I mean being on the couch and you tucking me in like a child.

PATIENT: (*interrupts*): Yes, so you couldn't move, that was the defense.

ANALYST: Is this a reaction to yesterday's hour?

PATIENT: Yes, all of this. And yesterday's hour was a defense against what came out today.

ANALYST: One last thing is about the rebellion against telling me everything, the submissiveness.

PATIENT: Yes, I have wondered why I like you so much now. I thought: He's controlling me. No, not that, but that you are stronger than I.

ANALYST: We'll have to straighten this out too. I refer to yesterday and your remark in this hour. If you have a problem, talking it over is usually good, but you feel that doing so impairs your freedom. You can't just act, but you must tell me.

PATIENT: I said that when I was hostile, but I'll tell you tomorrow.

ANALYST: Your defenses in this dream against being too close and too submissive, and your defenses against the sexual element are that you relate to me as though I were a teacher and as though I were a child. Then you can relinquish the mother-father attachment to me enough and the sexual transference as rebellion against them enough to go off with your husband and be happy with him.

103rd hour

PATIENT: I had a dream last night. I was at my parents' home. They were all off at a party. It was something like a store. I was left at the store and a man we know, S. M., was there. He is a very pudgy, babyish, and unattractive man. He kissed me and I took that all right and he left. But then I saw him there taking his pants off and I got scared that he was going to rape me. I thought: Why this? Why not try for sex in the usual way? Why must it be rape! I screamed for help and my mother and sisters came and then I was afraid they would think that I had done something to encourage this.

ANALYST: Associations?

PATIENT: I've never spoken to S. M. except for a few words, and he seemed friendly to me. I always had that fear in the dream that they would think I was bad. When I was twelve or thirteen, I was out with a fellow who was seventeen. Mother and my sisters were along and he couldn't even touch my hand, and he didn't. We only looked at each other. But Lois said he could have done anything he wanted to with me. I didn't defend myself against her attack, and I guess the reason was that I believed he could have too. I thought I knew a lot then and I knew nothing. If he had touched my hand, that would have been to me like intercourse. But as long as I can remember, I've heard the family say no one could trust me with boys, and I didn't do a thing. I just liked boys in a normal way. Why couldn't they take it as normal; why did they have to take the attitude that I was doing something wrong? That's what makes me mad. I thought I was solving the problem, but it's right here. It's too deep. Why can't a man flirt with me or just be nice to me without my feeling guilty? (*Tears.*) With you I don't feel that way, unless it's unconscious. Why can't I be the way I was as a teenager?

ANALYST: What do you associate to being back in your parents' home?

PATIENT: When I was nine or ten, this friend of my brother-in-law made a pass at me when the family was away. Nothing happened at all, but I felt as guilty as if something had.

ANALYST: What are your associations to your parents going off to a party?

PATIENT: They've left me alone, and that's what I want. But at the same time I get afraid.

ANALYST: Associations to the house being like a store?

PATIENT: Hm! (*Laughs.*) I'm for sale (*head in hand, sighs*). Why do I get so scared in class or in a small meeting? My heart just pounds and if I want to talk, I hardly can, my heart pounds so. It is worse now than it used to be. Of course this is all transference. Why do I have to feel that you will rape me or get mad at me?

ANALYST: Any clue in the mother pattern to me? Could it be anger that you did not have enough love? The jealousy and revenge is to go out and get raped. Couldn't the sex be the way of acting out the wishes for love and the rebellion and hostility?

PATIENT: Could it be that I want to make you jealous? But the jealousy is not in reference to mother. I'll show you that if *you* don't want me, other men do.

ANALYST: That could still be to mother. The jealousy could then be directed to her over your sisters and not be anything sexual. But now you can act it out in sexual form. If it's rape, it's hostile, it's punishment, and it's not your sexual wish—it's forced on you.

PATIENT: It's almost conscious that I do want to make you jealous. This is so infantile. I felt I wanted to be a *femme fatale*. I guess every girl wants to.

ANALYST: Any connection with the heart pounding in the meetings?

PATIENT: I fear that they will find out what I want to do. It will take a lot of time to find out. It's a main complaint, and I never told you.

ANALYST: Why? Whether needs for love, jealousy, or hostility—these tend to be acted out via sex. Sex is the pathway, so if you are mad at a father or mother figure and you feel guilty, this shows up when in a public situation.

PATIENT: But also I want to please my father.

ANALYST: That is the conflict. You want to please him and fear what he'll see, that is, the very things you don't want him to see. And, these are chiefly your own hostility and guilt as well as the sexual feelings, which are connected with these.

104th hour

PATIENT: Since yesterday I've felt that something is in me that has been dormant and is awakening, and I never thought it would. It's only in dreams. Last night I had a dream. I think of these things clearly when I'm on the way here and when I'm here, it goes. I feel that I want to act out sexually and I'm mad that I can't. This is how I felt always, but when I married I had to keep it so thoroughly under control that I couldn't even allow myself to think a man was nice looking. I could say so, but with no emotion at all. Every time—well, it happened twice—that if I liked someone, it would interfere with my life, with everything. The first time was with someone who didn't know I was married and when he found out, that was the end. I liked him but I felt guilty. Once at a party, while dancing, he tried to kiss me, and that was really the end for me. He kept trying to see me, but I didn't like him any more. He was single. Later I saw him occasionally and I liked him but had no sexual feeling, no guilt—completely dead. The second one, R. T., was a physical attraction, and I didn't like him so much. But he feared anything physical. I feel guilty about it. His wife was upset emotionally. Now as I look back, I think: Thank God that it was someone like that. He liked me a lot but avoided anything physical. He reminded me of father. I guess that is why he attracted me. He was strong like father and had some of the same interests. What I don't like are the consequences in me. What I mean is that then I become critical of Will, don't enjoy sex with him, and that's the beginning. Then Will gets mad. That's why I quit that job where R. T. was.

In last night's dream I was in St. Louis studying. In reality I was there when I was seventeen or eighteen and it was the worst time of my life. I was nothing. I could have died in the street and no one would have cared. Anyway, in the dream I was there and as lonely and as miserable as I was in reality. A man appeared and I tried to attract him. Then I thought he thought: This is another one of them.

ANALYST: Meaning?

PATIENT: Not that I was a prostitute. He seemed to know me. More that I was fresh, fast, on the make. But days later he returned because he was lonesome and missed me.

Then I had a second dream. Why do I dream so much of yachts and water? Well, in this dream I was poor but on the yacht of rich friends. In reality I do have rich friends and I have been on their yacht. In the dream I felt poor and inferior. On the yacht was E. V. In reality he once wanted to marry me. I was so lonely and he was too; so I thought I'd go around with him again. Then I thought I didn't want to hurt him just because I was lonely, but I did go out with him.

As I understand the dreams, you are the man in the first dream who rejected me. You just think: Here is another hysterical patient. Then I think: If I can't act out in reality, I will in dreams. Then I think: I have a storm in me. A storm of passions, all kinds. They serve me well sometimes but badly other times. Could all this be brought on by breaking off with Lois? Because members of the family have written her two letters, and I have not gotten one letter from anyone.

ANALYST: Yes, indeed! Although you are a wife and a mother, nevertheless, just like everyone else, the needs for parental love remain powerful.

PATIENT: And now Will is having problems and I have to be the strong one and support him and keep the marriage and family going well. When he is upset, I suggest we go out to dinner and eat and chat.

ANALYST: And, as you see, the impulses to sexual acting out are in reaction to feeling lonely and rejected—sex is the pathway.

PATIENT: When I was younger and felt lonely and rejected, I though that if I could have sex relations with a boy, I would be less lonely and rejected, and maybe I could love him.

ANALYST: Yes, only don't miss the hostility that makes the guilt and masochism, and therefore, the masochistic dream. Instead of a simple wish-fulfilment to correct the reality, you dream that you are lonely and rejected and not that the family write and come to see you and tell you they love you.

111th hour

PATIENT: I got another ticket. A car with two girls in it cut in on me, and I go so mad and went through a light. During the past months I've been stopped three times and this is the second ticket. Someone stopped the first ticket for me, but I can't go on this way or they'll take my license away. Actually if I'd talked nicely, I could have gotten away without this ticket, but I was mad and didn't. Maybe this is the way I've taken to rebel, instead of sex. I'd rather have sex. You don't get into so much trouble and you have pleasure. What pleasure do I have going to court? It must be against you that I'm rebelling; there is no one else. You don't care if I act out with sex, so I'll find something else. (*Laughs.*) I don't feel mad at you. Maybe I do because of the money. I have to pay you every month. (*Laughs.*) Recently I've been taking charge of all the bills and the first of the month I get depressed, especially when I get letters demanding payment within ten days. I get several of those. I dread seeing the mail. (*Weeps and then smiles.*) I don't know why this never came out. I just couldn't tell it. I get mad at Will too. We barely have enough and then Will goes ahead and spends money foolishly. I'm getting so accustomed to those letters. (*Sighs sharply.*) Well, that's my problem.

ANALYST: Does your budget balance?

PATIENT: Will would pay you and let other things go, and I never knew where we stood. But no, we do not live within our income. We've just been lucky—had money returned on our income tax. The budget will balance soon.

ANALYST: Do you mean when analysis is over?

PATIENT: No, Will is expecting to get a raise very soon. But I'd rather be the one to worry and so keep Will alive. He might have a heart attack like a friend of ours did. He was only thirty-eight years old. Will works a lot harder than I. I won't have a heart attack. I blame Will. When I say no, it should mean no. But we bought the house when we couldn't afford to. Oh, we'll get back the money we put into it and with a big increase, but not for some years. I just realized my tendency is to act out with tickets from policemen and with sex;

and Will's acting out is with spending, not for himself though. He runs around in old clothes although he's always worn fine ones. What he bought was a cover for the bed for nearly one hundred dollars. It was my fault too. I should have said, "Get the twenty dollar one." Will likes to spend; I'm tight. I won't leave money in the bank, because if I do, we'll spend it. Since I took over two months ago we've been paying off what we owe piecemeal. Will is embarrassed but that's what I have to do. He spends almost nothing for himself.

ANALYST: Very good. Get out all these facts and feelings about the money problem.

112th hour

PATIENT: I must be acting out in other things too. I don't want to do a lot of the work. I must be mad. Could I be trying to test you? My fantasies are about other men, but could they be to make you jealous? You don't react and then I get a ticket for going through a light and you still don't react. So now I feel I won't work. This has been going on a whole week and my conscience is bothering me more.

I had a dream four nights ago. I don't know why I haven't told it. I was on a beach with mother and my sisters and I had on a white bathing suit. In reality I never had one like that. I looked so well, had the figure I had at eighteen, and mother thought I was the best—in intelligence, appearance, everything. But I kept looking at myself thinking: My God, I don't have this figure any more.

I think this dream was the night last week that I slept well and slept late. I enjoyed the dream.

ANALYST: What are your associations to the white bathing suit?

PATIENT: I never had one because when you go in the water, it becomes almost transparent. But the dream shows

I can wear it, that I'm no longer afraid to show my emotions. I don't care if people see through me any more.

ANALYST: The beach—associations?

PATIENT: Vacation. The next vacation is at Christmas, and I'd like to go home to the ranch. Yesterday when I was complaining that we were ruined financially, I was still planning how we could fly home to the ranch for Christmas.

ANALYST: Any associations to mother and your sisters being there?

PATIENT: Well, father was not there. I was not so mad at mother. If I have maternal feelings toward you, I can see her more clearly. I'm like a teenager who goes away to school: if she doesn't get a boyfriend soon, she will soon be back home. That was my pattern. I never thought I was better than my sisters, no matter how many times Will told me so. I don't want to feel better or worse. I only want to be myself.

ANALYST: Good, that's what we are after.

PATIENT: I can get along with two of them like friends, very well, but not with Lois or Roberta. I can though with Vivian and Mabel, except that I have to be careful. But then, I don't tell personal things to friends, either. If I tell my sisters, they will tell mother; they can't help that, mother is too strong.

ANALYST: What are your associations to mother saying you are the best.

PATIENT: I can't see her saying that. If she did, I'd just drop. But this not working can't be acting out the mother pattern to you because she never cared. At school I never showed her my marks. She would tell me not to study late, and then she'd say that if I was doing poorly, then I should just relax and take the subject again next year.

Father wanted only sons but had mostly daughters. He said we should be independent, like men, and be able to take care of ourselves in the world. I certainly don't expect my daughters to work. Father would constantly ask us as children, "What do you want to be when you grow up?" Once I asked mother what she was and she said, "Mother of a family." Then I ran to father and told him that that was what I wanted to be and they all laughed. Why did they laugh? It's not so abnormal. That's what I should have been. I thought that father, in a way, wanted us to be lawyers and businesswomen—career women.

ANALYST: I've wondered about last week, about whether my being sympathetic and permissive didn't sort of uninhibit some of your rebellion in various ways, like breaking with Lois, feeling that you don't have to return to Texas, and feeling that you don't have to be a career woman. Has there been an undercurrent of rebellion that you now begin to act out?

PATIENT: It was there, and very strong. I have to go through this.

ANALYST: You don't have to act out; just analyzc.

PATIENT: Don't worry. In reality I am well controlled.

ANALYST: Good. In the dream you wish to be the best of your sisters in mother's eyes. The usual pattern of sex, which is forbidden, is there by allusion in the white bathing suit. In this dream you permit yourself more satisfaction: Mother thinks you are the best of the sisters, you wear the white bathing suit, and you have a figure of an eighteen-year-old. The only bit of masochism is in thinking you don't have that figure anymore. This probably comes from remaining hostility and guilt that derives from competing with your sisters for mother. Here the sexuality is part of this competition. Probably the same pattern exists toward me in the transference. I think you are right about the ego meaning too. That is, you are less concerned about being transparent, about seeing and having me see your love needs, sexual wishes, competitiveness, hostilities, and so forth. Also, you see that life is much easier if you just enjoy your own life and don't always compare and compete with your sisters.

114th hour

PATIENT: I have been recalling good memories about my mother! (*Laughs.*) This is the first time I've ever have had good memories about her. It has usually been either "I can't live with her" or else "I never want to see her!" Another thing is that I realize that I've changed. I don't know if it's for the better! (*Laughs.*) A lot of what I had done before getting married was rebellion against my family. For example, I tried to go out with every man, even if he was dating one of my girlfriends. I'd flirt with everyone, except if he were married. Then it was as if he was dead. But after my marriage, it was what father taught us: One man and just put on blinders, like a horse.

ANALYST: Then it was the marriage that changed you?

PATIENT: Yes. I grew so much after I was married because Will let me do anything I wanted. If I wanted to dance all night long with someone, he'd let me. So, the whole responsibility was on me. He is jealous but doesn't show it. Sometime I even get mad about it. He didn't protect me. One night Will was flirting at a party with another girl and I was watching him. I was chatting with a very egotistic man. I left him to go over to Will as I always would when I thought it was time, and this woman got angry and said, "All women are prostitutes at heart." I said, "I don't know what kind of a mother you had; of course, you are including her!" And then I dashed to the ladies room for fear he would hit me.

ANALYST: Flirting with everyone could have been competition with your sisters as well as rebellion.

PATIENT: I couldn't figure out why I liked you right away. I thought you reminded me of father, but you don't;

you are the opposite in looks and feelings, except you both have a certain gaiety. But now I realize that you remind me of my mother (*smiles*) because she always took my side, excused me, calmed me down. I can't find another word; just the simple word: Good. Mother was good, as you are. I can say the same about father but not so deeply. In the important problems of my life father helped me, superficially, and I always had him to back me in the sibling rivalry and with mother, but I felt that he always needed me. He needed someone in the family. I don't think I'm hostile to him. I couldn't be. I don't really know. I never took a big problem in my development to him. For example, when I was sixteen and realized I should break with the boy I was seeing or else he'd leave me, I never talked it over with father. I never let anyone leave me; then your pride is hurt, too. It was mother who told me, "So long as your pride is intact, you are all right." The boy was going out with other girls. Mother cried with me. Mother lived all our lives with us. She cries easily.

This week, for the first time, I felt lost, confused, as though all my defenses were breaking down, as though the little child in me was gaining control. It's happened before, but never so strong. So yesterday I said, "This can't go on. I'm losing reality. I'm going back to what I was."

118th hour

PATIENT: I had a dream I was walking with father, but he was old and something was wrong with him so that he could not walk fast. We were going to something like a fair. I felt sorry for him, but I had to get there. So I went on ahead a little, and once father saw I could walk faster he told me to go on. At the fair was a big waterfall with stairs under it, and I had to go up those stairs. I was on a tricycle, but I managed. Then I was without the tricycle and came down a very narrow path to find it, but it was gone. Father watched me going up and down in a friendly way.

ANALYST: Associations?

PATIENT: Walking with you. It's hard for young people to get places, but we are doing very well. What is worse: to be young and immature or to be old and filled with so many traumatic experiences that you are therefore afraid to do anything? I'm a lot more at ease now when I'm mad at you than I was at the beginning. Then I used to get headaches. But you are not the only one I am mad at. I get mad at mother when she writes letters. She doesn't write me; she writes Lois. I wish they'd leave me alone. She always writes something that upsets me.

ANALYST: Why doesn't mother write you?

PATIENT: Because I write her very little, and even when I do, I tell very little about our family. I don't tell her everything the way my sisters do, and I protect my children. If Tom doesn't do well in school, I protect him and don't tell it, or else they would all gossip about it.

ANALYST: What are your associations to the fair and the waterfall?

PATIENT: That's what my life has been like—hard, climbing up, not only up stairs, but against the current.

ANALYST: What has been so hard?

PATIENT: My own feelings! The tricycle is my childhood. I never had a tricycle.

ANALYST: What do you associate to the element in the dream where you go up and then you come back down?

PATIENT: That's the analysis: I'm going back through my life, down into my unconscious. Going up is leaving people behind, leaving my family; and when you get up there, you are up there. But, you are not happy. I'm going up, with all my childhood still in me and a great drag on me, and I get there. But when I get there, I realize that it's not it. I don't find what I was looking for, that is, my parents' love. So, I come down again to get it. In the dream father stayed down, but I couldn't find the tricycle.

ANALYST: Meaning?

PATIENT: I don't know. Then I look for it elsewhere.

ANALYST: Could it be what you said, that is, your childhood?

PATIENT: Yes.

ANALYST: Do you see life as climbing up and losing father, being alone, or else coming down, wanting childhood but at the same time not wanting it? Do you represent life with climbing up and coming down?

PATIENT: Yes. All weekend I thought that I don't want to talk about my childhood in analysis any more. Without my childhood as a drag, it is much easier. I'm not living my childhood any more; now it's time to leave it behind. You let me be unrealistic this last week! You should repeat: "You are married and you have children!" That makes me mad, but it brings me back! Isn't it that to leave childhood means to diminish gradually the attitudes and wishes of childhood?

ANALYST: So it's a matter of which specific attitudes and wishes of childhood are a drag on you.

PATIENT: I'm lost. I'm mad.

ANALYST: In the dream father is old and not well and you can and do go on without him. You go to the fair and find that you can enjoy yourself without him. There may be some competition with him (and in the transference with me) but I think it is more a dawning insight to you that now he is old, while you are still young and strong and can live your life without him. Only in the dream you can not quite relinquish the wish to be the child, to have the tricycle, to which you associated not having one. This probably means all the love you wanted but felt you didn't get enough of. In the transference, this is the wish for love from me with which you have been struggling so long. You have been troubled by the problem of how to get into a relationship to me that works. One as with mother wouldn't do because it's too frustrating, homosexual, and fraught with jealousy of your sisters; one as with brother wouldn't do because although good, it's too distant; one as with father also wouldn't do because it's too submissive and also intimidating. In this dream you try it with father, but he is old and not well. Then you can leave him, but you still keep him there watching you in a most distant, fatherly way. The reality, though it makes you angry for me to say it, is that you have everything of maturity—a fine husband, children, friends, profession, health, everything—so the problem is to enjoy this present reality and not to pine for the love you didn't get enough of in childhood from mother. And in the transference the solution is the same—you need to relate to me as adult to adult and not as in childhood wanting from me what you wanted as a child from mother.

123rd hour

PATIENT: (*looking better than ever before*): The vacation was fine. The ranch was never more beautiful, and that whole area was simply glorious. It's too bad I have family there.

There are several points though. The first is that mother is really and truly hostile to me. In a way I am relieved to see it. I mean it's good to know that it is not all my fault and all my feelings but that she really is this way. She never really said one word to me the whole visit that was not critical. When I called her from the station on our arrival, the first words she said were, "Your father and I think that you and Will are crazy to make this trip down here."

The whole family were really very cold to me, except Mabel. She was very warm and friendly. She is the one who is able to fight back against this hostility, and I think this time she sided with me because she identified with me. In the past when I was attacked, I would only say I'm sorry and feel terribly guilty inside. Now I realize what is going on and I am able to fight back. I really snapped back frequently. This is not ideal and it is not what I want. I would much rather be unaffected by it and just stay calm and pass it off.

Actually I am really that way with father. Mother asks me how I could do such and such and I flare up and become very angry. Of course there is no real clash with her beyond this because she won't clash; but if father says the same thing, I merely say that I don't know or I ask what he means, and there really isn't any hostility between us. However, father, as I now see, is also quite hostile himself. Like the rest, he was only critical of me and of what I was doing and during the entire visit he never gave me one word of support and approval. So they are cold and they are hostile and very difficult and very bitter. Nothing like my husband's parents, who are warm, friendly, and easy and supportive.

Now I am no longer so dependent upon mother although, of course, down underneath I do still so much want her love and I still deep down feel guilty. But, now I realize that the only solution to this is to grow up to the extent that I do not need her love so much. But I am tied to her and therefore involved in this way with the family. It just upsets all the rest of my life.

ANALYST: Of course, this is one of the most difficult steps in growing up. I think you are right that the goal is to put the relationship on an adult basis. You are now a wife and mother yourself and, of course, what you say is true. You cannot enjoy your own husband, children, friends, and so on if you are constantly kept upset by the involvement with your parental family and by feeling that you have to have mother's love but find that she is always somewhat hostile and unsupporting to you.

It is a bitter pill for everyone to learn that to be adult is to be alone.

PATIENT: Nevertheless, it was a very successful vacation and I feel that I have made great progress with this. I now see so much more of the reality of what is going on and I'm sure that I can get this solved. I do not think we will ever be close and warm and friendly on an adult-to-adult basis because, unlike my husband's parents, father and mother are too bitter and too hostile and too difficult. In fact, I think father, although he will not break down, still has a quite delicate adjustment to life. But I think I have been making great progress with it and toward being much less upset by it.

125th hour

PATIENT: I didn't tell you the good things of the vacation. In the first place, I didn't have my phobia of cats. There was one at our good friend's house. That cat always jumped on my lap and I used to be terrified of it and begged them to keep her locked up. This trip I feared to go over there. In the past I'd about given up going for fear of that cat. But after all my fear of being afraid, before I even got out of the car I already felt different. I had no fear. When we went in and sat down, the cat immediately jumped up on my lap. They all exclaimed in astonishment, "What's the matter with you, you've changed! You're not terrified by her." I smiled and told them I was being analyzed; that's all.

Then there's the poise. We visited a very grand old southern family, extremely rich, but the wife is really a crook. She got her money by getting a man to sign a contract of some sort, which she then told him she had to show to her husband. Of course, the man thought she was a lady and signed, she added something over his signature that he didn't notice until later. We were supposed to visit them, and Will asked if we should. I said, "Why not? They've done nothing to us." We went and visited them, and all I felt was pity. I was surprised at my own poise.

I realize I can only relate to mother superficially. We went around visiting every day, and the only time mother asked me to visit with her was when she wanted to hear the gossip. It was so transparent and Will got very mad about it.

Much of my life is built around jealousy. I saw it. Vivian's daughter, four years old, my niece, a beautiful little girl, sat next to my father, and he kept saying to her, "You know, I love Dolly more than I do you. I'm going to take her riding. I'm going to give her a horse of her own . . ." He went on and on. I told him that was no way to talk to a child and I asked who this Dolly was. He knew no Dolly. He just made up the name. And I remembered that's how he was with me. I was the youngest, but he would always say he was going to bring home another baby—a big, big, plump baby boy and so on and so on. I don't know, father and mother are both so bitter. How can they live together? Our friends were really glad to see us, much more so than my family.

Last evening I had a fight with Will because of this jealousy I have. It was because before we left for vacation he spoke to a secretary on the phone and called her by her first name, and I said this was not businesslike. Then at the ranch, I said to Will, "The hell with everything, including Dr. S." (*Laughs.*) I felt that now we were away from everything. I don't mind your hearing everything; you are not a foreign body in my life. I don't know why. Then last evening there was a message for Will from the secretary signed by her first name. I got angry. Will then got angry and said I should work it out with you in my analysis, but he insinuates that analysis isn't doing anything for me, but he doesn't put it so plainly. I got mad and then he got mad and I said, "All right, I will, and it will cost you a lot of money." Then he got mad and said nothing. My only problem in the marriage is this guilt. Will has a lot more problems. I help him so much in his emotions and he helps me in other ways but not in my feelings. There is only this one thing, this jealousy, and he could help me with it so easily by just avoiding these little things.

127th hour

At the time I conducted this analysis I was beginning to find it therapeutically helpful to review the analytic situation every half year or year for clarification and perspective. I thought this hour would be a good time for a review because the patient had spent a few sessions telling of her vacation and we had not yet resumed regular analyzing. However, this turned out to be an error in judgment and timing. The patient wanted to tell a lot more about the visit home, she wanted to express more feeling and insights about it all. Hence, there was at this time an undercurrent of resentment against this whole procedure of stock-taking.

ANALYST: With what symptoms or complaints did you come?

PATIENT: My chief complaint was guilt without knowing what I was guilty for. Also, I lacked confidence and had fears—I was terrified of cats. Really I had fears of everything, I think—fears at night, fear that someone would break into the house, fear of being left alone in the house, fear that I was not raising my children properly.

ANALYST: Any other fears?

PATIENT: Well, specifically, I had fears because of the problem I had with my son Tom. I also had hostility to the whole family except father, only I had a lot more hostility than I thought I had when I started the analysis. I had insight only into a little bit of it. And I had jealousy. I was aware of it, but I didn't know why I felt it. I was over-jealous of my husband and of my children, but that was all I knew about at the start. I didn't know I was jealous of mother and my sisters. I was not even conscious of how severe the fear of cats was.

ANALYST: Any other complaints?

PATIENT: No.

ANALYST: How about the fear of losing your mind?

PATIENT: Oh, God, yes! Fear of losing my mind was the worst! and I had the fear that my marriage would break up. Of all of this, the most important one was the one I forgot: the fear of losing my mind!

ANALYST: Anything psychosomatic?

PATIENT: Oh, yes. There were gall bladder problems that I don't have any more. Also migraines, very severe migraines, but I haven't had any for a long time. I even have an allergy, it's to face powder. I don't know if it's psychosomatic, but I don't have it anymore either. There was also fear of talking in a group, and that is gone also. I no longer have those palpitations. I just feel ordinary in the group both when I'm quiet and when I talk.

ANALYST: Anything else?

PATIENT: Yes, sometimes I feel quite depressed. I've been that way all my life. I still have this but it is much better. I think that's all the complaints. If I go on, I'll write a book. Oh, but there is something else. I had obsessive thoughts about seeing the female organs. And there was also the fear that Tom would come and kill me with a knife at night. These I knew, but didn't want to say, but I won't hold back anything else. Going to personality, I thought every man who came near me had sex on his mind. Remember how afraid I was of coming to your office? I felt I was doing something wrong sexually.

On vacation last week I thought: I've gone

through a lot with Dr. S. How could he have stood it, and with all the patients he has?

ANALYST: Anything else?

PATIENT: No.

ANALYST: Anything else about personality?

PATIENT: People thought I was aggressive and independent but inside I knew I wasn't. I felt very passive, very dependent, and very insecure.

ANALYST: Anything else?

PATIENT: No. Oh, yes! I thought I was dumb. I was scared to death a few years ago to take an I.Q. test. I thought I'd get 90 or, with luck, 100. Now I think I'd get 110 (*laughs*). It's that now I don't put so much importance on the I.Q. I told Vivian on vacation, "You may have a 140 I.Q., but you're not using it. I may have only 100, but I use it all."

ANALYST: Anything else?

PATIENT: No. My whole relation to my husband, including sex, is really no problem.

ANALYST: Poise?

PATIENT: Yes. Yes in that it is really a lack of self-confidence more than a lack of poise as I always called it. Oh yes, and I dislike dominating women. I know why now after this vacation. That's how all the women in my family are.

128th hour

ANALYST: Are there any more symptoms?

PATIENT: Haven't I given enough? Actually there is another and in all this time I haven't told you of it. I pick a spot on my right hand and I'm worried that I might get cancer there but I can't help myself. I resolve, I try my best, but I can't stop it. Vivian does it too—that's where I got it. I never do it here when I'm with you, but this is the only place I don't. Or, maybe I don't do it in the movies. I'm so worried about it, so afraid of cancer. It's been since I was a teenager, but it's been much worse for the past four years. Often I meant to talk with you about it, and I just didn't. I don't know why. I'd forget and then blame myself and determine to tell you the next time.

ANALYST: Why don't you have it here?

PATIENT: I'm doing the talking; and I don't want to show it.

ANALYST: Are there any other reasons?

PATIENT: I don't know. This started when I was young because a doctor told me when I was sixteen I might get cancer, but I couldn't stop.

ANALYST: Is there any connection with your not having it when here and the fact that here you have undivided attention in contrast to the situation in life where there are constant demands being made on you? Might this be an angry protest?

PATIENT: I do it more when I'm nervous. For example, in school before I took an exam, or more currently, when going through a bad experience.

ANALYST: What did you hope to achieve by being analyzed?

PATIENT: It's strange. I don't remember. It's gone. I have to think all the way back there. It's hard. To get rid of the guilt and not to feel inferior. I wanted to be more secure in myself. I wanted to have poise. I mean I had poise, but it was put on, forced. Most important of all, I wanted improvement with Tom.

ANALYST: What did you find were the emotional forces that underlay and caused these symptoms or complaints?

PATIENT: First of all, my relation to mother. That is the most important. On the one hand I wanted to be dependent on her and on the other I had to give up too much to get what I wanted from her. My love needs were never satisfied by her so I kept looking for more. It could have been because I was the last of many children. One day at the ranch father came in and said, "Women should be submissive and passive toward their husbands." Roberta laughed and said, "You've always taught us to be strong and aggressive in case our husband should turn out to be an s.o.b." Father laughed then. All this caused the hostility, which I couldn't show toward mother, or, for that matter, toward father either. I couldn't toward mother because father said if we did, mother would die of a heart condition, which she really never had; and I couldn't toward father because he was all I had. Mother did love me but father gave me a personality among so many of us. He individualized me. That's all.

ANALYST: Do you see any connections or patterns formed by these forces?

PATIENT: All that I've said. Always looking for approval, trying to please, scared to death that someone would reject me. At the same time my relation to father was so close and he was so seductive I was afraid, and he made me suspicious of the opposite sex.

ANALYST: Were there certain main influences upon you during childhood that resulted in these reactions, problems, and difficulties later?

PATIENT: I was the last of many children and this made for unending comparison and competition. We all went to the same school, all had good marks, and all were girls. Of course, there were my two brothers, but they were much older, these were not important for me. Father didn't want girls, and that's why he tried to make us aggressive, not sexually but in other ways. Father would say, "I'll make my girls not dependent on men." And then there was the relation between father and mother. They were going through economic stress and father was sometimes interested in other women. Father wouldn't let any boys in our house, even when we were small children. Mother and father didn't actually want any more children when I came. I think father was very jealous of mother.

129th hour

ANALYST: What were the most important influences and what were your reactions to them?

PATIENT: Most important was mother and the rejection. Mother is not the kissing type; she doesn't like to be close physically. For example, when I had my baby in my arms, she couldn't stand it and said, "Wouldn't it be better to put him in the crib?" At that time I interpreted this as her not loving me, thinking I was not good enough.

When mother became pregnant they wanted a boy so much and here I came along. If I approached her to kiss her—and I'm the opposite of her in that if I love someone, I want to be close—she wouldn't let me touch her beautiful hair, never let me come into bed with her. But when I was sick and needed her, she was warm and she was there. So, deep down I know I can count on her. I know if I ever had a divorce, she would be the first to understand things. Really I can't exactly say why I felt rejected by mother. I got it from small things. At age six I was in a Christmas play and she came, but late, and someone else had to dress me for it.

Mother is very domineering in a passive way. She is always saying what you have to do and what you shouldn't do. As for my reactions to mother, father always told me not to fight with her. He warned that I'd kill her because she had a heart condition, which she did not and even now doesn't have. But I always felt I could kill her. As a result, I felt guilty.

The past few months Beverly has been saying, "Mother, please don't die." *(Laughs.)* I could never have said that to my mother. Mother controlled me by playing on my guilt, and the more she did, the more hostile I became and the more guilty I felt.

I was never praised as a child. On the contrary,

although they never said exactly that I was ugly, they would disguise it and say, "She'll change!"

The main problem is that we were too many and I got lost. I can't put it concretely, but it still hurts. When I came to analysis, I was submerged in it. Now I can see it, but I can't write it down as a book. I'm still afraid of my mother, not nearly so much as before, but still some. Now I know it and I don't act out with others, but mother is still too powerful for me. There's much I haven't told you yet. There was an incident with my second brother, Sam, who paid for something for us and mother found out and she called and insisted I write Sam, apologize, and say I will do this and change that and so on. She tells me these things, and I can't even answer. I can only say, "Yes, mother" and hang up. This involved a very small amount of money, but when Sam gave Lois a really large amount, mother supported it. Sam has plenty and when we are in need, why shouldn't we help each other?

Another problem is jealousy of my sisters in relation to mother, but this is made by mother. Really it is mother's hostility to me. She goes out of her way to make me feel bad and increase my guilt instead of trying to alleviate it. Now I really don't have the jealousy any more. I don't even have that depressive feeling any more. I don't want mother; let them have her. Yet even while telling you of mother's hostility to me, I feel guilty and suspect that maybe it was all my imagination. But, when I went home to visit and saw mother's hostility was actually there, then I knew it was real and in her and I didn't blame myself and the depression left.

130th hour

PATIENT: I have recognized that I've been angry at you for the past week. I find myself saying, not only to myself, but to others as well, "Why do I have to go to the store?" "Why do I have to do this?" "Why do I have to do that?" I'm being generally irritable. I do not clearly understand this, but I now realize that it is anger, chiefly. As I see it, it is because after my return from the vacation visit with the family, I was bursting to tell you all about it, and although you gave me a number of hours to do so, I felt that this was not sufficient. Then, instead of allowing me to proceed spontaneously and listening with interest, you initiated the stock-taking review. This pattern I see relates directly to that in the family where I felt I could not talk freely and spontaneously to mother or father, and where I felt, as my deepest hurt, the lack of a warm personal interest.

ANALYST: Thus, it seems that what you said in the review about this being your main hurt was actually mobilized largely by the stock-taking and by the conflict it generated with what you wanted to talk about during the hour.

131st hour

PATIENT: I don't know what I'll do to you if I get any more hostile to you. I wasn't so mad until the review. Yet what we did with the stock-taking was what I did myself anyway. It was only the *timing* of bringing up the review. I think one month sooner or later would have been okay. But, it's good you brought it up, because this is a reaction I've always seen in me. If someone rejects me, I take it, but then I go into flight; I cut off every tie, like with my first boyfriend. When I sensed I was more interested in him than he was in me, that was the end! It shouldn't be so.

ANALYST: How is it that you take my going into every detail with you, as in the stock-taking review, as a rejection?

PATIENT: I can tell the answer, but let me tell a dream. My

whole family said they wanted to get rid of father but mother defended him. We said, "How can you! He had love affairs while married to you." And then I said, "If he doesn't go, I will!"

So you can see my mood is mad, and I have never been so mad at my father. It's not the stock-taking itself, it's that it puts me back into reality. No matter how I feel at present, we still have to do this review. So, it is analysis and not friendship. You didn't give me time in a friendly way to tell all the things I thought and felt about the vacation. It was something like what happens after an analytic hour: I leave here elated but then get back to home or work. Here I returned from vacation and you bring me back to realities here, so you are the one who gets the anger.

ANALYST: I calculated wrong and didn't give you enough time to abreact the vacation.

PATIENT: That's right. That's it, but the anger is still there. So now (*laughs*) I won't say anything about the vacation. Like when Beverly comes home from school and follows me around to tell me things and I'm busy and then she cries and I realize what it is. I talk with her, but then she won't tell me; anyway, not until later.

ANALYST: Apart from this, do you think that also it is more fun, more gratifying, to free associate than it is to do the stock-taking?

PATIENT: Maybe, but I think the review was interesting and I would have done it gladly a month before or later. I've been so hostile, and now I see how hostile I was. I wish I could feel as angry as I am toward you to my father. I know this is a healthy anger at you. When we started, I couldn't have been angry; I just thought: You are so good; I never met anyone who was so good. This dream is the first time I've ever had hostility to father. Why do I have father in the dream and not you?

ANALYST: What do you associate to this?

PATIENT: I don't know. I'm sick and tired of everything. My ambition is gone. Now I know I'm better off than my sisters. Why prove anything? Why am I sacrificing myself? For what?

ANALYST: For father?

PATIENT: Could be! But if I wanted to retire, father might be the first one to say it was the best thing.

ANALYST: Lifelong conditioning doesn't disappear quickly.

PATIENT: Yes, it could be. I don't know.

ANALYST: Maybe you take out on me some of the anger you feel at being back here with all your responsibilities again.

PATIENT: It could be. It's not the place—it's the work. I hate work. I hated to study. All I wanted was to have a house and to cook, but with help. I don't envy men. Since working like them I see what it's like.

ANALYST: It sounds as though there might have been rebellion against father for pushing you into working.

PATIENT: Yes! My children won't. *(Mockingly.)* They'll do as they please. Maybe I don't want to be a housewife either because then there are more things I have to do: go to PTA, be a den mother, and so on. Someone told me I was like a gypsy, wanting to change all the time, and it hit me because it was so.

ANALYST: There is much in this hour and I hesitate to say more, but could the review also have felt like something you *have* to do?

PATIENT: Yes. It could be.

ANALYST: Maybe the rebellion is against what you feel you *have* to do—return from vacation to work, to analysis, to the review, etc. Is this the main theme?

PATIENT: It wasn't just father. It was the whole family, the whole attitude, my sisters too. You have to go to church, you have to be somebody, why don't you cut your child's hair—all this, all my life. You have to, you have to, you have to.

135th hour

PATIENT: Last night I had a dream I didn't like. This morning I had a feeling of fear. All I remember of the dream is that there was a house with a ditch around it. We were on the other side of the ditch—we meaning Will, my daughter Barbara, and I. Barbara was visiting at the house which belonged to my sister Vivian, whose husband I really hate. When I was nine, a friend of his made a pass at me, and I didn't want Barbara to go there for fear he would do that with her. Actually his friend didn't do anything at all and neither would he. Now I remember more of the dream. Barbara expelled some flatus and laughed, so cutely, just as she does in reality. I said, "If you do that, you will have to stay there." Then the dream changes and I am in a supermarket buying food. It is a dirty supermarket. I am with Will. I felt such anxiety and on leaving I felt I'd forgotten something. The ground was full of holes and I could fall in and get full of mud. There was a little walk of boards to go through. Will said, "I can go through it all right." He wasn't afraid and just jumped from spot to spot, and he did get through.

ANALYST: Associations?

PATIENT: Will says that they say in the period of the oedipus, girls get more attached to the father, but he plays rough with Barbara and then she doesn't want to have anything to do with him. She is kicking and pokes him, and he gets mad. I say, "That is how she flirts with you." Last Saturday evening we were at the G.'s. The three daughters and the elder Mr. G. were there. The girls treated their father as a friend, laughing and joking with him. And the girls had an easy relation with their brothers-in-law, kidding around—just the way my sisters and I are to our brothers-in-law. One of the daughters said, "This guy is my father, can you imagine that!" And it was all in fun. I couldn't imagine any of us saying that about my father.

In the dream I was the one in danger at that house. If mother hadn't been malicious about my relation with father, then my relation with father would have been all right. When I was very little, long before five, mother would say, "Don't get into bed with father. Don't go near father. Put more clothes on, here comes father." It could have been my own fantasies, but I don' think so. Mother always has in mind guarding against sex. When I was eight, a lady said father was a lady-killer, and I was furiously mad at her.

All this has something to do with my boys too. I had no problem with them until they got big enough that I sensed there was sex involved.

ANALYST: Is the sense of this—the ditch, flatus, holes, mud—that sex is dirty and is always to be looked for and guarded against? Does this idea carry from mother?

PATIENT: Oh yes, and also that all men think about or want is sex.

ANALYST: How do you correct that?

PATIENT (*laughs*): By . . . (*Laughs.*) This is what I've been saying for the past few days—coming to the answer—that I can let myself have a close transference to you and know for sure nothing will happen. The only way I can get this out of me is to come out with all the wild things I think when I'm in love this way, go through all the emotions and feel sure that nothing will happen. Last week I said I thought I was pregnant, and you know, every time I felt fear, I would become pregnant. Then, with a big tummy, that was that; then I'm a mother and pregnant by my husband and then all the other fantasies disappear. This was true of all the pregnancies except the one with Tom. That was the last one, I did it consciously; it was unconscious. I mean I didn't get pregnant consciously to get rid of the fantasies. But I noticed that when I was, the fantasies left.

ANALYST: Could sex be dangerous because mother was so against it? And, therefore, could it be used as rebellion against mother and defiance of her?

PATIENT: Of course.

ANALYST: Then, if sex means hostility to mother, can't the anxiety be gotten rid of by analyzing the hostility to mother? Through this as well as what you've said about learning you can tell all and yet feel secure, you might also be able to shift to the view that sex is not dirty.

PATIENT: True, and father also implied sex was dirty, not only mother. I do feel that if I enjoy sex, get pleasure from it, and do not think about it as being dirty, then that is defiance. This is the main problem I have with mother since I've been married. She talks constantly, whenever I see her, about sex being repulsive. I ask how father is doing and mother goes right to sex. "He goes to bed with me and you know I don't like that. I don't know how women can stand that!"

ANALYST: Therefore, part of the corrective is for me to make it clear to you that I don't see sex that way, as you know. It's important for us to discuss it so you can see it, feel about it, and handle it realistically as something clean, good, wonderful. In this way you can learn not to use it for rebellion, hostility, and masochism.

136th hour

PATIENT: It's been a week. I've missed you a lot, more than I realized. I began to notice that I had dreams of T. H., and of four other men and then I realized that it was really you. It is strange why I should substitute other men.

ANALYST: Dreams take your mind off problems of reality.

PATIENT: These have been pleasant dreams, though. In one I'm at a table and the men there comment on how beautiful this woman is who approached the table, especially her eyes. I looked and thought she had the most beautiful eyes I ever saw. Then the man with her said I had beautiful eyes too. I didn't want to show that he was saying this about me. I was embarrassed.

ANALYST: Associations?

PATIENT: I've no idea. None.

ANALYST: He says you have such beautiful eyes too. Do you have any associations to that?

PATIENT: It could be, not beauty in itself, but good, balanced, all round virtues—not just physically. It must have to do with my inferiorities to my sisters. But all the other dreams this week have had to do with how good I am, with people liking me and being pleased to meet me. They have been pleasant dreams in which I'm being praised—my vanity. But I superficially felt slightly depressed. I realized that I wanted to see you and never really accepted that before this. I still have the feeling that if I need you, that then I have a dependency on you, which, for my entire life, I never wanted to have on anyone. I've been fighting it, from the beginning. And when I meet T. H., I like him but not that much.

ANALYST: Could that be a defense against becoming too dependent on me?

PATIENT: Oh, yes!

ANALYST: Then that is one reason you have other men in the dreams.

PATIENT: Yes, and the eyes must be some jealousy that comes with being attached. And I don't want that. If I like you, then I have all these other kinds of emotions, and I don't want that to happen.

ANALYST: That's a large part of the problem. It's not only liking me; it's the wish to *be* liked, loved, that brings in the dependence and thus also, by the childhood pattern, the jealousy.

PATIENT: I feel that everyone says that a mother's love for her son is the most beautiful, but I think it is the son's love for the mother. And, if a son doesn't have it, it's because the mother didn't have it for the son. They tell you, "You only have one mother so take care of her." But I feel it isn't so.

Although I missed you all this week, I behaved better toward my children, especially toward Tom, than I have in a long time. I realized that he loves me more than I love him. I mean that I have contaminated it, not he.

ANALYST: But why do you treat him better when you do not see me?

PATIENT: I have no idea, but I'm more relaxed because I repress better—all my emotions—I'm myself.

ANALYST: Is this because not seeing me doesn't stir up everything, but especially the dependent love needs to me? Therefore, do you feel you don't have to fight off these and the jealousy?

PATIENT: Yes, it could be. I can have pleasant dreams and not have to fight off too strong an attachment. If I don't depend on mother, then she can't hurt me. If I don't like you too much, you won't hurt me, and it is the same with my son. If I keep the relation to him superficial, he won't hurt me so much. I always felt I shouldn't love my children too much because in the end they leave you.

ANALYST: Here again isn't it the need to be loved and the dependence that makes trouble?

PATIENT: Yes, if I love, then I want to be loved and I open myself too much to being hurt.

138th hour

PATIENT: I am getting along worse with my husband and he's hostile to me also. He's the only person I have and he loves me and therefore I feel guilty. All the past week I've felt fed up. I wanted to act out—sleep with anybody, get drunk, fight with people. I don't know what it is. I wish I were a hysterical woman like J. R.

Everyone forgives her because they know she's hysterical. I drove an old car in awful shape and Will does nothing to be of any help, because he knows I can take care of my self. They told me a tire was so worn that it was dangerous, but Will wouldn't get another and didn't know what kind to get. I handled it and went and got one and then he complained that I was spending money. I handle all the bills and he looks at my desk and says, "Why do you have your desk in such a mess!" I guess he has toward me the pattern toward his mother. For example, if Will says to her as a joke, "I saw father with a girl," then she gets hysterical, cries out, and recalls every flirtation of his, although he never really had any. Once Will had a drink and his mother came over and started in that he mustn't drink, and that's how people become alcoholic, and on and on. They had a big fight and Will left and I tried to comfort her. She wept and wailed and said how much she loved Will, and she asked why he was upset by what she said. My mother never expresses emotion.

ANALYST: Why have you been in a different mood this week?

PATIENT: Because I haven't been seeing you. Will said, "You're as bad as you were before analysis." I said, "You lived with me for ten years before analysis and if you don't like it, there's the door." I'm angry at not seeing you for a week, but also I have a lot of hostility to Will. He controls his emotions so. I'm too much the opposite. I'm very informal. If we have close friends over and have a bite in the breakfast nook and the ketchup is on the table in a bottle, I don't mind, but he's all upset because it isn't strictly proper.

Maybe I'm hostile because I have to swallow hurts to my pride and have to go on giving and supporting. I do something good and he takes the credit, and I must swallow my pride about it. He takes credit for everything. He must always be the first one. I learned this about him as soon as we were married, and I thought about it a lot. I thought: I can defeat him if I study him; or, I can help him to be something very good. Of course, I decided to help, but I don't mean that he himself isn't good—very good. He's the only person other than you I would go to for help. He is warm, he has understanding, and he is human.

ANALYST: So we must analyze your hostilities to him.

PATIENT: Yes, but also we must finish the stock-taking. I haven't forgotten it.

139th hour

ANALYST: To continue the review, let's go on with the childhood pattern. How would you describe the general characteristics of your family?

PATIENT: Altogether I would say, taking the whole family as a group, that the central problem was sibling rivalry. In reality, because we were many, sibling rivalry had to be there. But also, both my parents made use of the rivalries to play one child against another. For example, father would threaten that if you didn't love him, he would love so and so more. With our studies he made each one feel he should be better than the others. My parents used the rivalries for everything, not only love and studies, but also for intelligence, beauty, and who was the best behaved. I was a very good child, believe it or not, and I was never a problem of any kind until I was a teenager.

I don't know if it belongs in here but mother and my sisters had this attitude of being so humble—too much of a show of modesty. For example, Vivian would say, "When I got there, everybody knew more than I." Then she mentions big names and then goes on to show that she knew more than any of them. I have some of this too.

ANALYST: How about the pattern to father?

PATIENT: Father never wanted girls. God, no! Therefore, he made us so aggressive.

ANALYST: In what ways?

PATIENT: I don't know exactly but I think he has a problem with women—a sex problem. I think there is also hostility to women because he was hostile to his mother. Therefore, he has tried to make us the opposite of what we should have been, that is, feminine, good housewives who take care of their husbands. He encouraged aggressiveness of all kinds. For example, if I had a fight at school, he would enjoy it if I won. He taught us to hit first, saying, "He who hits first hits twice." Father made me be the winner in any kind of encounter. I had a clash with a policeman once and father kissed me. Now he's changed. Also, he wanted us all to have professions, careers.

For him, sex and anything connected with it was a sin. That's too mild a term—he considered it much worse than a sin. I thought if a boy looked at me, he'd lock me up in jail. The good thing was that he was away much of the time while I was a child.

He was very cruel with my two oldest sisters. He called each of us by names that were not nice, and he did it in front of everyone.

Father showed much hostility to mother and to mother's family, and we all felt this.

ANALYST: How did this affect you?

PATIENT: We did not see a good example of marriage. Instead of being encouraged to admire my mother and my uncles, I was told not to; although, reality told me I should. Also I rather enjoyed his being hostile to mother because I was hostile to her too, but I couldn't show it.

ANALYST: Did this also show that mother, the woman, is rather beaten down psychologically by the man?

PATIENT: Yes, it did, but I never accepted that. Anytime I

ever got in that relation to a boyfriend, I quit. Some girls fearfully wait for the boy to phone, but not me. Or, some husbands come home at 3 A.M., or come home drunk, or go out with other women, but I just could never put up with that. In other words, I can never be as masochistic as mother was. Although some people admire such a woman and consider her a saint. So I'm wrong according to mother's pattern.

I was father's favorite, but I wanted him although he didn't want me. I must have sacrificed a lot to win him over to my side. Hostility to father was allowed but not to mother. I sacrificed my wishes to be a housewife and a mother and that's all. I had a deep hostility to him. I couldn't quit studying law because I felt he was the only one who believed in me. I guess I didn't sacrifice for him when I was little. Being so close to him I was scared also because he was seductive with me. I was often in bed with him. He carried me around always. I was always on his lap.

ANALYST: That scared you?

PATIENT: Yes, it did; it was too close. Maybe it would not have been if mother had not given me the idea. He really was not too seductive with me. It isn't so; that was mother who implied that something was wrong in the relation. Otherwise it would have been like any other relation.

I identified with father and not with mother because I went everywhere with him—to rodeos, race tracks, everywhere.

My chief memories of father are that I loved him and that I feared him, especially if I would be interested in any boy. I feared him not for what he did to me but for what he did to others. He beat Lois until she bled, killed a cat and also a dog in front of me, and twisted a man's arm and held a knife to his throat.

My chief fantasy in childhood was that I would have lots of money and pay all father's bills and then when he would go to pay them, they would say, "Somebody has paid them." He would not know that I did it. I still have this fantasy.

140th hour

PATIENT: Yesterday my boss told me it was perfectly all right to take the same time off that others do, but this morning he blew up and said in a nasty way that it was impossible. If I told him I wanted the time to come to see you, he would be even worse because he is rabid against analysis. Of course he was against long lunch hours from the beginning. He had to admit that I turn out more work than anyone there. I have really been mad. I think I will go back to the firm I was with before as soon as they can take me. I have a call in to them now and should hear this afternoon. But I want to leave where I am in a very friendly way if things don't work. M. T., the boss, has been nice most of the time.

ANALYST: Now, back to the review?

PATIENT: Yes. I thought yesterday that I told you mostly the bad things; there was much good also.

ANALYST: That's good therapeutically, for then we see which of the old patterns make trouble for you today. We want to see what works well also, but that is what we have to change.

PATIENT: Father, in his own way, was very warm and still is. Also he was a person any child would admire. (*Chuckles.*) He is really insecure but gives the impression of being very secure, of being able to do things very well. He reads a lot and knows about a lot of things. I guess it's that he gave the impression that when he was there, nothing bad could happen. If I were sick and he came, I knew I wouldn't die. If you had any problem and he took over, you knew it would be solved for your own good. If you did something he didn't like, he would handle it and tell you not to do it again. But then he would forget it and never reproach you with it later. Mother was the opposite. I think all the security I got was from him, not from mother. She was so insecure. Even the bad things about father didn't matter so much because he gave me such a sense of security.

I wanted to tell the good things about father, because I just can't see good things in mother or tell them. Yet, she must have them. But I don't even know how to start with mother.

ANALYST: What is most outstanding when you think about her?

PATIENT: Rejection (*sadly*) rejection.

ANALYST: You've discussed it often but let's again see what you mean by that.

PATIENT: I've always had the feeling that I was left out, left out of something, out of the group, that I was not given the importance that was given to the others. Mother was warm toward me because she is a warm person, not because I was her daughter. If I wanted to get in bed with her, she wouldn't let me. If I wanted to approach her and kiss her, she wouldn't allow it. So I always felt she didn't care.

Mother was malicious. If any of us, but this was especially the case with me, stayed out with a boy until midnight, she treated it as though we had gone to bed together. She always said, "Don't trust men; all they come for is sex." So, since I've been a child I've thought men could be controlled by sex. Like, "She's a prostitute but she can control him; he's crazy about her." Also, sex was taboo—not just outside marriage, but even in marriage. She said she hated it. One day after I was married, she said that to me and I said, "I think it's wonderful," and she nearly fell over. She was the only girl with three brothers and very puritanical parents. Her mother didn't even want me to wear short sleeves when I was single. So mother has broadened a lot. She didn't enjoy her youth, but she did want us to enjoy ours. She took us anywhere; I guess she enjoyed her youth through us.

She didn't care much about grades and marks in school. She didn't have much ambition for us; that was father's thing. She covered up for us many times. She could never control me as she could the others. I guess she wanted to live her own life again through me, and I wouldn't let her. I told her very little—unless I had broken up with a boy and was suffering and then I'd talk with her and she'd help me.

When the others were grown and away at school and I was about fifteen, I was the only one left with her and I didn't like it because she wanted to dominate me and find out every thought I had. I resented that and liked being independent. Then we had a lot of clashes, and she showed open hostility. So in this sense, it's not so bad being one child of many; it's better than being alone with mother. I don't remember much about trouble with father at that time. Emotionally I had problems with mother. With father I did what he wanted; but also, without his knowing it, I did what I wanted. But I had no guilt. I knew he couldn't be changed but also I had to find out my own way of living. But, because of the problems with mother, I had only one aim: to get married and get out.

141st hour

PATIENT: Yesterday, I talked about my very deep feelings that I was always left out and that I did not get enough love from my parents, particularly mother. Now in my life I find that I still always feel I want more, that I am not getting enough. For example, I feel at work that the boss gives more appreciation to someone else and not enough to me; and I kill myself working, trying to get more. That is why I studied so hard as a child and then went into law. If I'd been secure in the love of father and mother, I don't think I would have gone on with law at all. At the same time, this feeling that I must overexert myself to get what no one can give me anyway makes for hostility. In my marriage, I've tried to change completely to be what Will is, in order to be sure to be his only love. But I also feel frustrated and hostile because I also want to be myself. I'm working very much because of Will. He wants me to go on, just like father and mother, so I feel too bad about quitting working. If Will didn't want me to continue, I wouldn't feel I had to, and maybe then I'd go on on my own. To get the love from him, I feel I *must* do it, and this makes me frustrated and angry. If I didn't have to work to get the love, I might enjoy it.

Recently I've felt so tired. I go to bed tired; I get up tired. It's such a sacrifice to go to work. I don't care about talking with anyone. I used to be more outgoing at the old job and restrained at home. Now I'm better, more relaxed at home, but I don't like the job. Last evening I was so mad at Will that I said, "I'm so tired and don't feel well physically or mentally and you don't help me at all!" He said, "I don't want to support your neurosis." That is what made me mad. I replied, "Don't be an amateur analyst to your wife. Just treat me as your wife. I gave you what you needed when you had need and that was love. Just treat me as a person, as your wife, who is feeling sick. Leave my neurosis to my analyst." I was never cold to him this way.

ANALYST: Never mind the review for the time being. Let's concentrate on why you don't feel well. Is it largely emotional?

PATIENT: Yes, I think 90 per cent. It's that Christmas visit at the ranch that stirred up all these feelings. The pattern is toward mother, but it was the relation with my oldest sister, Vivian. I expected to talk with Vivian, to tell her about our experiences here, to open my heart to her. I had hoped to talk to her as one talks to a very good friend. But the first day I saw her she didn't even look at me, and then later she felt guilty. I realized it was her problem, but I'm still upset. They put me on the defensive right off. That was the chief hurt. Long ago I gave up expecting anything from mother. She gave me whatever she had long ago. But with Vivian I had that kind of communication in which you don't even have to talk, and it's that which was broken—not just broken but turned against me. She actually attacked me, more than any of them.

ANALYST: But is this permanent? Do you think, do you want the relationship reestablished?

PATIENT: Oh, it will be; she'll come back. It's her problem: she felt guilty. Before I left she was getting ready to be more friendly. She feels threatened by my own training and experience, but she pretty much controls the family.

Yet I feel worse now than I did three weeks ago when I returned, so it can't be that alone. It could be the work.

ANALYST: Could it be the analysis?

PATIENT: It could. If I were not in analysis, I could take life easier and not have this present job. I could take an easier one. The difficulties at this job and the uncertainty of how soon I can change are troubling me. It's not the analysis itself, but the mechanical problems it makes. But why the depression?

ANALYST: Maybe all work and not enough love, libido, fun, recreation, the difficulties of all this snow and bad weather?

PATIENT: Yes! I'll feel better when I can get outdoors and be mobile and have some expansion.

143rd hour

ANALYST: To continue the review, let's begin this hour by talking about how the pattern to mother operates in your present life.

PATIENT: I thought that my cat phobia was all related to father, but now I think it is to mother because since we've gone into the feelings toward mother, it has greatly decreased. I think I was hostile to mother, not to father; and when father shot the tom cat for scratching Roberta, I thought: That is how one gets punished for hostility. The cat scratched Roberta and Mabel was the one who told father about it. She told him the cat had nearly killed Roberta, but actually the cat hardly even touched her. The poor cat. He had an open wound on his thigh and Roberta stepped on it accidentally. The cat's reaction was only natural. Afterward, father was angry at Mabel. Roberta has often been scratched by cats, three or four times, so she fears them too. So I think the cats represented my hostility to mother. They probably represent this today also and maybe all my hostilities. But, I also like cats, I displace all sorts of emotions. I couldn't show mother much love and affection either, so I showed it to the cats and dogs and somewhat to the horses. So if I put so much emotion into an animal, my love needs were more satisfied by the animals than by my mother. I was constantly with them. The ranch was big, and I had no playmates except the animals. If I went any distance, mother thought I would be raped, so I had no playmates until I went to school at the age of six. But Roberta and I played together. She was only two and a half years older. The relation was good; it had to be because there was only the two of us. Although I was more outgoing, I was with the men for milking the cows and I was never in the house, I didn't like it. She was mostly in the house. She sews well, cooks well, and so on. I was the opposite. I did follow the cook, who was like my second mother. She would tell mother that she was going shopping and take me and give me candy and tell me not to tell mother that she was drinking. Mother knew anyway, because she could smell it on her breath. So I was always looking for something outside the house, although Roberta and my other sisters, except for Mabel, were also inside with mother. Today I have many contacts outside and my other sisters are all still in the family circle with father and mother. The only times Vivian goes out is with mother. She has no outside friends or interests. She even says her only happiness is to be with the family. She rarely goes out with her husband—he is so jealous of her that she doesn't like to. Her husband is the image of father, only he's less intelligent and more paranoid. One day Vivian, who is very naive and says things out of the blue, told father that he looks like her husband. Father hates him and since then father hasn't talked with Vivian except for occasional things that have to be discussed. It ended their relationship.

I felt that no one understood me and so I kept looking outside the family for friends and people to get along with. I found many, more than my sisters, as I said. Today I have enough outside of father, mother, and my sisters so I don't look so much any more. Of course, I have all the professional work and interests and contacts outside of my home. So the childhood pattern of being outgoing and having all the interests and contacts outside of the home continues just about as it was.

The same feeling of going out of the closed family circle to find friends made me feel guilty because mother always said, "Your only friends are your family. There are no friends, only the family. You can't trust anyone." So my pattern of going out and finding friends was not supported as a good thing. Instead, it was condemned as not right, and so it still is. Therefore, all my life I thought I was bad and doing the wrong thing by not having as my only and best friends mother and my sisters. But now I find that I'm right and that I have been right all along. One fortunate thing as a child was that there were lots of help at the ranch that I could relate to who were not mother. This accustomed me to relating to people.

It has to do though with my resistance against meeting new people; for example, if I am invited by new acquaintances to dinner, I feel guilty about it because it is not doing what mother told me.

ANALYST: And this sounds like an additional source of guilt for being analyzed and for feeling a friendly relationship with me.

144th hour

PATIENT: As soon as I heard it would be 60° today, I felt so much better. I have owed invitations to dinner for weeks and just couldn't do anything, but today was so beautiful, I went ahead. Yesterday I didn't finish about mother. She also said, "You only have one mother, so treat her well because if she dies, you'll never have another and the mother's love is the purest and the best." This made guilt for me because if you are taught from the beginning of life that mother's love is for you and that it is perfect, then if you feel that it is not perfect because she gets mad at you, ignores you, rejects you, even if all these are normal reactions, then you think it is you who is at fault, you who is bad, and it's all your fault. Then you feel guilt for even having a thought that mother was not all good toward you. And if, on top of that, you have three sisters who all say mother is perfect, what can you do but feel guilty.

I think none of us had a real problem with father because we could express our hostilities to him—not directly to him but to mother and my sisters. He was good and when he was mad and we got angry at him, we didn't have to keep it in, we could all talk with each other about it. But I have never, never, never heard anyone complain about mother. With father, we knew he wouldn't die if we showed hostility. This was not like mother who said, "You are going to kill me." I did show hostility toward her, answered her back, but not much, certainly not like Tom does to me or anything near to that. One day when I was twelve or thirteen, I said jokingly, "Are you crazy?" and she slapped me with all her strength across the mouth. I rarely answered back. My way of showing hostility was to have a long face and not talk all day.

ANALYST: Does all of this pattern to mother continue toward her? Does it continue to other people?

PATIENT: Yes, it does. I still can't show hostility. I shake inside and can't talk. I wish I were like Mabel. She expresses it openly and directly and like a whip, but at the same time she is smiling and pleasant, so at the end you are still friends. She controls her emotions, but my emotions control me, and I'm still afraid and that is the pattern toward mother.

ANALYST: Does this pattern still hold toward mother?

PATIENT: Gosh, yes! She never gives me any alternative. I can never sit down with her and say I'm angry at her about anything. If I should make her cry, my sisters would descend on me and kill me. If I get angry at someone, I want to go and talk it over and clear it up. But I can't, I just shake all over. I wanted to discuss things with my present boss and couldn't. My hands get cold, my feet get cold, and I shake.

ANALYST: Can you with me?

PATIENT: Yes, I think so, because for me you are a friend. I always could talk things out with my girlfriends, but I can't with authority figures. I first thought it was the pattern toward father, but I'm sure it's much more toward mother.

ANALYST: Could you talk with father?

PATIENT: No. So, it is both.

ANALYST: With whom could you talk?

PATIENT: Not to any of the family, but I could talk to the

cook and the help and all those toward whom I felt superior. Maybe I can somewhat with Vivian. She's the only one. I don't why, but I get afraid, scared to death. If I have to talk with a superior, what I want to do is just talk objectively not hostilely, not emotionally, and I can't. I'm so scared, so if it's a man, I flirt a little and this and that and I may get my way. But I hate myself for making use of my femininity this way. I never liked myself. Now maybe I'm starting to like myself.

Maybe another reason I've been depressed for these last two weeks is that C. L. is away and he was my right-hand man at work; he took care of more for me than I realized. That's how mother is. When she approaches a problem, she is very passive. She doesn't come out forthrightly. She smiles a little, cries a little, and circles you with a ring of emotion.

Another example of this pattern at present is my panic at talking with the principal of Tom's school. I couldn't; I got Will to. I never show this to anyone. Will and you are the only people in the world who know it. I show just the opposite, but what it costs me! And out of the fear, I get very aggressive. If I need a favor, then I go like a little child, or else I get on the defensive. That's like two weeks ago when I said I was thinking of quitting. Another example is the last visit home. I should have sat down and talked with Vivian, but I had the same guilt as I did as a child; it was as though I were doing something wrong.

148th hour

PATIENT: If I could only, just once, feel that I had the love I wanted from mother, then I'd know that it existed and that nothing could take that away from me. And then I could go on.

ANALYST: In a way you do. In the transference you can

tell everything and get sympathetic understanding and now you are an adult, a mother, a wife, a woman with a professional career and not a helpless small child.

PATIENT: I'm depressed today. I always feel depressed when we discuss transference. I feel that these wishes for mother's love will come out to someone and I'd rather have them come out to you than like a few years ago when there was the man who was my boss. I had to leave that job. Of course now it has sexual implications.

ANALYST: Yes, being adult, it takes a sexual form.

PATIENT: When I have these strong feelings toward someone, all my neurotic symptoms disappear—the fears, the insecurity, everything—because I get what I want from the person.

ANALYST: Now?

PATIENT: No, because with you, now, I don't let myself go. I did let myself go, though, when I was a teenager. Even with Will, I wasn't that crazily in love. The transference is like with Will, well under control. I don't want to let myself go for then I'd be putting myself in the position of being in the hands of someone else.

ANALYST: Why?

PATIENT: I'd be too dependent on you for love, and it's even the same with my two sons, but not with the girls. I've realized now that I have the same pattern with you as with Tom. I'm afraid to get too close because I'm afraid I won't get enough, but I don't have this with the girls. I guess I identify more with them, especially with Beverly. I guess it makes her more secure and able to give more. She is very close to Will, but I have no jealousy. Of course she is very close to me also. She has a good normal, healthy relation with both of us. She likes to go with me when I go, like to a shop or to the beauty parlor.

ANALYST: But I cause you more trouble and problems?

PATIENT: Yes (*laughs*).

ANALYST: Let's talk them out.

PATIENT: Yes. I don't know why I tend to get closer to the girls than to the boys. I feel more threatened with the boys. As a child, I never had normal relations with anyone of the opposite sex! Even with father, it was not so normal. There was something threatening in the relation to father. I don't know what. I think even the relation with mother was less threatening—more secure. My relation with father had some flavor I didn't like. I don't know; it will come out.

ANALYST: Can't you define it now?

PATIENT: Well, I was always aware of the difference in sex. Maybe it's different, but I have a memory, very early, about three and a half. I was very close to a window and everyone was saying, "Look what is going on outside." I thought: Why do I have to be so small that I can't see it. And another early memory at about the same age was that mother left the house and didn't take me with her. I cried and cried. The cook came over, and I sat in the corner crying. I was so very angry at mother that she didn't love me. No, not that she didn't love me, but that she didn't love me *enough.* I cried loudly so mother would hear me as she drove out past the house. I'm talking about mother, and I guess I don't want to talk about father. I'm getting very anxious.

ANALYST: Could it be that you came to terms with the relations to mother and then turned to father with the notion that if mother doesn't love me enough, I'll win father. You are his favorite and if you lost that, you'd have nothing.

PATIENT: No, not that. Father's love had a flavor of danger that mother's love didn't have. It wasn't the danger that he would stop loving me, it was that the love was too seductive sexually. Maybe it was my own fantasies, maybe it was vengeful fantasies toward mother, but there was a sense of danger in it for me.

ANALYST: A number of sessions ago we talked about your cat phobia. This is what father could do to you if you were hostile to mother. Could——

PATIENT (*interrupting*): Yes, that's right. That was in it.

ANALYST: Fear of punishment in father's love?

PATIENT: Yes, because I saw how he beat my sisters. But it wasn't only that. It was also because I felt that he showed preference for me, and I thought that was my fault because I was seducing him. This is like the experience I had with that friend of my brother-in-law's who made a pass at me. All my life I thought it was my fault when it wasn't. Where did I get the idea?

ANALYST: When we talked about your cat phobia, you said this is what father could do to you because of your hostility to mother. Could this now be what he could do if you are hostile to your sisters and win out over them, that is, do better than them? Is this connected with your feelings of jealousy, envy, and hostility to them?

PATIENT: Yes! It was my own fantasies as to how I got to be father's favorite that made me feel guilty. It was the sex in it.

ANALYST: So the two forbidden components are hostility and sex.

PATIENT: I hear girls say how their fathers made sex advances and how they hate them. But, I have a good relation to father. I loved him and gave him more than the others, and he loved me more. I think the sex was more in me, not in him. I had very strong sexual feelings, stronger than my sisters.

ANALYST: It seems father was the punishing figure, and if you showed hostility or sex feelings, then you would catch it.

PATIENT: That's right! Mother would withdraw, but father was the one who killed the cat and beat my sisters.

152nd hour

PATIENT: My hostility to my sisters made me closer to father. It was as though I felt: See, I have him and you don't. I think some of my fears at night come from this. It's like my fear that Tom will come and hurt me, and it's also like the dream I had two nights ago that people were going to kill me by stabbing me in the heart. I think my fears in childhood must have been related to my sisters also. I had intense hostility to them, but I could never show it because I felt I was the only one with any hostility. I felt that you should love all members of your family and that I was abnormal because I had this hostility. And about this dream. I remember that whenever we children fought, father would say, "Stop it! You will kill your mother, she will have a heart attack." The dream was that they would stab me in the heart.

I was so hostile to my sisters because I was never included; I was never in the group. They always had this air of superiority over me and they showed it. I was the youngest, the most ugly, the least intelligent, and the most awkward. I didn't know how to say things. I was in all ways the worst. Mother says I changed so much at sixteen, but I don't think so. I think I was a cute child, but it is how they saw me. And they would say that all I thought about was sex and all I talked about was boys, and it wasn't so. But I certainly felt inferior in all ways, completely, and of course this made me mad. And the way they treated me. I was too small to hear this, too small to do that, always too small for everything. I am the youngest, so this war I know I can't win. For example, only a few months ago Vivian said, "You don't know what life is like, you are too inexperienced, too immature." Her idea is that to be mature is to be masochistic, to go through all kinds of suffering. She believes that I'm immature because Will is so good to me that she thinks I don't know what suffering is. This pattern toward my sisters continues today just as it used to be. Lois is the only one of my sisters who doesn't think this way. Because of this pattern to my sisters, I have much of my insecurity and feelings of inferiority. I probably learned a lot in trying to adapt to them, but I got oversensitive, which isn't good. For them suffering meant suffering from father, because he was so hard on them. But, because he was so much nicer to me, they say I didn't suffer and that I am immature. What they could never imagine is that I suffered because I didn't get enough love from mother. They see mother as a saint and would never believe that she didn't give me enough, but I think their problem is more with mother than with father. I think they didn't get enough either. But mother is very domineering in a very passive way. Since the only person they had was mother, they couldn't see the situation. I had father too, which was healthier. I was more distant and all my life I have craved to be close. But they were close to mother in an unhealthy way, and mother would not let them get close to father.

154th hour

PATIENT: Whenever mother writes she asks how my new maid is. This is the girl I brought back from the ranch after the Christmas visit. Mother was sure she would never work out. I've been afraid to write back how good she is for fear something will go wrong with her.

In changing back to my old company from the present one, I tried to be very man-to-man about it but it didn't work. I went back to the old pattern and was emotional and joked, and I guess I was flirtatious. L. B., my old boss, just softened up and so did my present boss and they were as nice as could be. They offered me whatever I wanted. Now I don't want to change my ways and be cold and matter-of-fact anymore. I'm satisfied with this old pattern. I developed this pattern toward father and it worked, and it works with other men too, and now I'm satisfied with it, to be as I am.

I always expect you to be like father or mother and when I see that you are just quiet and interested in my welfare, that you are good, then I can't be sure of it. I'm not accustomed to it. It's new, and I am afraid of it because I want it so much. I always thought I was an extrovert, but I guess I do keep my real feelings to myself. People say I keep things pent-up. I think so much about what you think of me, whether you think I'm worth anything.

Last night's dream was not bad. Dr. C. and I were dancing. There was another girl and myself, and you had to choose between us. It was you because I always put in Dr. C. when I mean you. You chose me, and I looked so nice and had on a beautiful dress.

ANALYST: Associations?

PATIENT: Being too close to you threatens me, my love needs are too great. But then it gets like childhood, and I want to be the only one but know there are others, other patients. I'm not the only one, and then I get jealous. And you've been looking tired and I'm mad that you have to work so hard. I wish I could help you and now, I don't know why, but I feel like crying. (*A few tears.*) My feelings toward you are close, like toward Will, but at the same time they're not so altruistic. For example, I feel that if you got sick my thought would be: What will happen to *me*? (*Laughs.*) I guess I'm too dependent on you and that's what I've been fighting. I want this to be a personal relationship and not just analytic treatment. When you point out the father or mother pattern to me, I get mad. I get furious. If you feel you are in love and then find these feelings are like those toward father, then it's as if you, the analyst, are nothing and it's all just my problem. You have no reaction to me and my feelings to you really are only to my father. Then the whole thing disappears and I get mad. I get so mad at you that you won't let me get romantically attached to you. Then I think, I'm not the only one he's analyzed. He's gone through this a thousand times. I'm not the only one. Now don't tell me that is my mother or father pattern! (*Laughs.*)

ANALYST: Does it have to be one extreme or the other?

PATIENT: No, no, I know it doesn't.

159th hour

PATIENT: Yesterday the boys were fighting in the bathroom where everything is so hard and they could fall or hit something and hurt themselves. I pushed Tom out and accidentally scratched him a little. So then I had to throw Davey out a little roughly too. Tom made a big fuss and put on a bandage to show what I'd done to him. I felt terribly guilty. Will came home and Tom showed him the bandage before I could say anything. Then I told Will what had happened. Tom went to his room without my telling him to. I felt awful, went up, caressed him, and told him how very sorry I was. All Tom said was, "Go away." Then I couldn't sleep and had the fear again of Tom coming after me during the night.

Then, thank goodness, I had this dream. I was talking in a friendly way with mother, who changed back and forth with being you. So, it was you and mother.

When I awoke this morning, I felt different. I felt more calmness and love toward Tom and the children, and I realized that I had a lot of tension and hostility. I saw that I had taken it out on them and had not had enough real love toward them recently. (*Continuing but gently crying.*) Then I saw that it is true. I long for my mother's love. Last week it was more father transference to you and it had sexual elements. But I saw clearly this morning that what I really have wanted is mother's love. You've been telling me that for the past week or so.

ANALYST: Much longer?

PATIENT: Yes. You even told me that yesterday, and I've always only gotten very angry at you. But this morning I could see so clearly that it is true—the sex, the flirtatiousness, the turning to father—all this is the longing for mother. But now it is more the longing of the grown-up daughter for her mother. Before going to sleep, because I couldn't sleep, I turned on the radio and in a commercial or something I heard a daughter phoning her mother to chit-chat with her and to tell her mother she had new furniture. That is what I long for but I know I will never have it. If I told mother something like what the girl on the radio told her mother, she would just answer, "How much did you spend on it?" (*Crying quietly while talking, no sobbing, just tears.*) Mother has such a negative attitude toward me, but if in the middle of a conflict one of my sisters come, then mother changes. I always think that a woman—I don't know how to put it—you never stop growing, but a girl still wants to be able to turn to her mother. It's so nice to have someone you can trust, who will enjoy your happiness, who will give you advice in this and that. I've tried, but it's not my part of it. It's hard. When my daughters grow up, they will know that they always have me if they need me.

Maybe some of this came about because Lois phoned me last weekend. I was so upset. I said yes and was interested and supportive about everything she said. Maybe this stirred it all up again. It's not that I long for the kind of relation Lois has with mother. That kind of relationship I don't want.

It's many things. I don't think I have ever gone through the amount of stress I have now—the analysis, all the financial stress. I get one bill paid and two more come, and the work at the office is more than I can keep up with, and then there's the responsibility of my home and children.

I'm trying to say my whole concept——Or, maybe it's only that I realize it emotionally now. I was going to say that my whole concept of the relationship to mother has changed. Before it was: I don't want any part of it. It was I who decided to leave because I felt they didn't want me. But it isn't that. Well it *is* that, but different. I left because they didn't want me, but I wanted so much to be with them.

I don't know why I'm more at ease now.

ANALYST: As you know, the course of development is to grow up and leave the parental home—all animals do this.

PATIENT: Yes, but when you want to, not when you are forced to.

ANALYST: Of course, but still it's better than your sisters, who are held and didn't leave.

PATIENT: Yes, but not so good as a good relation with mother.

ANALYST: Right, but once you are grown up, you have to be alone anyway, although to have a good relationship with mother all your life is, as you said, very nice.

PATIENT: I was just thinking (*laughs*), it's too bad you're not a woman.

ANALYST: No it isn't. The transference to me of the wishes for mother's love are plenty strong enough as it is. For you, it's better to have a man for an analyst, not a woman.

PATIENT: I wish I could continue to feel this way and thus keep from feeling hostile. The dream made me feel better because the fulfilment was there. I don't want to accept it, but I do come to talk to you about my children, as I want it to be with mother, but something is lacking. It will come up. I always picture your wife with your daughter. Your daughter has a better time of it with your wife than I had with my mother. People who enjoy their children and grandparents who are interested in their children and their offspring enjoy so much but take it for granted because they have it. But when you don't, you appreciate it. I have it somewhat, though, with mother. I see it not in an infantile way of dependence, but more as a mother guides you with your child from her experience with her child.

ANALYST: Good for you. This longing was lurking there and is much better faced. Now you will be able to handle it well.

PATIENT: Yes, as soon as you accept it. Well, before I thought: They don't love me. I didn't see it as a real need of mine.

ANALYST: Very good. If you don't see it, you are always fighting it and are tense; it is frustrated and you become hostile. But, now that you see it, I'm sure you will handle it well.

164th hour

During this session, I used the couch with this patient for the first time. It seems to me to be rather poor technique to have a patient use the couch before a very clear understanding is gained of the patient's dynamics. Upon seeing, early on in this analysis, the patient's immediate struggle with intense transference feelings with needs for love, her dependence and guilt, all of which was highly sexualized, the use of the couch seemed strongly contraindicated. Even now there was not much reason to introduce it because all was going well. However, I thought she would want to try it just for the experience; and also, it would be a small test of ego strength and would probably yield some illuminating material. Therefore, I considered it worth trying, but I remained cautious because it was certainly not worth sacrificing any of the good analytic progress that had already been achieved.

PATIENT: I had a dream last night, but I have forgotten it, except that I was fighting all through it. I like to fight. I think that it is a most healthy thing. For three or four days I've been trying to get someone to fight with me and no one does. (*Chuckles.*) I complain to you of the bad things my sisters and mother do to me, but I never seem to tell the good things. Maybe the one I want to have a fight with is you.

ANALYST: Why?

PATIENT: You didn't see me last week, but you saw other people. When I heard about it, my reaction was depression, not too much but some. Then I thought: Why should I be depressed? I should be hostile. Then I felt better. I talked with your secretary and I thought: If he stays here and doesn't go away, he should see me. If he needs a vacation, he should go away! So there goes my sibling rivalry. I guess if I put all the feelings onto you, it would be the safest thing; at least I could talk about them. This is a very difficult hour.

ANALYST: Why does it seem so?

PATIENT: Because of the couch. I don't like to talk to the air. I don't like it. I can't even talk although I'm thinking, but I can't say what I'm thinking.

ANALYST: And what are you thinking?

PATIENT: That I don't like it. It's too . . . I can't even explain. It's too isolated. This is how a child must feel when very young and it doesn't have control of its muscles so it can't turn around and look at its mother the way it wants to. It's frustrating. It's too much. I like to see your face. (*Laughs nervously.*)

ANALYST: Why?

PATIENT: So I can have a reaction to what I'm saying. I'm getting hostile to Freud (*laughs*) because I'm thinking how selfish he must have been. I read that his main reason for using the couch was that he didn't want to be looked at. So actually he thought of himself first and only second about his patients. I never thought the couch would be so difficult. I can't find anything to say and the hour isn't nearly over yet! (*Laughs.*)

ANALYST: Let's go thoroughly into why it is difficult.

PATIENT: I thought the couch would threaten me sexually, but I'm not. Or, if I am, I'm repressing it beautifully. It's that I'm lost. This is like talking to yourself. I once did that and thought I was going crazy. I had a funny sensation doing it, so I stopped. I don't know. I don't know what else to think about.

ANALYST: Just associate.

PATIENT: I can't! I'm thinking of a girlfriend who just started analysis. She is seeing Dr. G. once a week and says she's on the couch. I wonder what her reaction is. When she told me she was on the couch, I said, "Oh, that's easy." (*Laughs and turns around and looks at me. Laughs again.*) I can't think of anything. I'm thinking of that cloud I see out there.

ANALYST: So we have a problem. Why is the couch so difficult for you? Some people love it.

PATIENT: If they do, I think they must be quite withdrawn or schizophrenic. I feel guilty about talking so much about me, and this is the essence—talking to yourself. When I was about seventeen, I read that life would be better if people talked less about "I" and more about "you" or if they just listened.

165th hour

PATIENT: I had a wild dream Saturday night. I saw Will having sexual intercourse with another man. I was so nauseated. I always say I have a small fire burning here (*points to heart*), but once it's out it's out. Of course after seeing this, it was out. Will tried to explain but it was no use. Will said, "It takes all kinds of women." And then he said, "In some places in the world boys can do this and no one thinks anything of it." I said, "Yes, and the one who plays the woman's part is the one I'm sorry for." I also said, "How can I have relations with you, but how can I when your organ has been in such a dirty place?"

ANALYST: Associations?

PATIENT: I've never talked like that in reality! Except in one way: I can't understand how a woman can sleep with a husband who has been to prostitutes. Maybe I'm too narcissistic about my body. Will's mother doesn't wear panties and that disgusts me. I told her about a couple who always go around naked with their children. The children turned out to be homosexual. How could it be otherwise? After hearing this, my mother-in-law became more modest. Of course she has a smell, while my mother is so clean, meticulously so. So I think the man in the dream is my mother-in-law. When we were first married, I thought Will was sort of feminine because he was so precise about arranging things in the house, about how I looked before leaving for a party, and so on. Father was nothing like that. Father was a man on a horse—he never even remarked that I had on a pretty dress. His only interest in women was for sex. He never fussed about the house. Then I thought: Why does it bother me so much if a woman smells? Why does it make me so hostile? I think it is because father was in the saddle so much and perspired and had an odor. That's it! The other man is my mother-in-law and Will has relations with her and I don't want him.

ANALYST: What do you gain by that?

PATIENT: I don't know, or does this have to do with wishes toward father. The dream does have to do somehow with my mother-in-law and with Annie and all these old women who are on top of me. Yesterday we all went for a drive, and I kept saying it was too cold to go driving to see the country, but they insisted on going. Annie is managing everyone and mother-in-law is doing the same, so I just was silent and didn't say a word.

ANALYST: If the hostility is to the old women, why take it out on Will in the dream?

PATIENT: Will looks so much like her. I used to think: How can a woman not get along with her mother-in-law if she looks like her husband. Of course my mother-in-law is really a good person and this is my problem. It was such a clear dream.

ANALYST: Any other ideas about the dream?

PATIENT: No. Well, there must be a homosexual problem somewhere. Do you remember I once said I thought I had a homosexual trend as a defense against the transference? Yesterday I could see that that could be a defense related to father, not to you. But now I don't see it. This is somehow part of my reacting to using the couch the last visit for the first time. This has stirred up sexual feelings in the transference again or at least the fear anyway. But why dream that way? I should have dreamed that father is homosexual or that you are, and therefore you can't do anything sexual to me. Oh (*laughs*), maybe in the dream you are one of the two men, and then I don't have to have intercourse with you. The wish fulfilment in the dream is *not* to have sex with you, then I won't have sex with you. I trusted you and wanted you for my analyst because you are so different from father, and that's also why I married Will. If I'd had a very aggressive analyst, it would have been too incestuous. I don't know why I should dream this now though, because I've known for some time, at least since I began analysis, that men like you and like Will are the real men and that men like father are defending themselves against their own passive feminine trends. They do this by being so aggressive. Or else, why is father so afraid of being just normal? I know all this, but the little child in me often reacts differently. The day before the dream Will said, "I'm going to rape you." I was scared, panicked. I knew he was only joking and it was my husband and I thought: Poor women!

ANALYST: So if you were a man, you wouldn't have this problem.

PATIENT (*smiling*): Yes.

ANALYST: Father, and mother too, may have given you the masochistic concept of sex. Mother hated it, and father had no interest in women except for sex.

PATIENT: Yes (*tears*), but more than that. (*Laughs through the tears.*) Mother says, "Sex is the cross that women have to bear." Mother also says, "Men like dirty things." But Will and I are the opposite. We like to be clean and we like sex.

ANALYST: One last idea about the dream. Could it also have been anger, not only as a defense but out of frustration? You lie down, and I don't respond.

PATIENT (*laughs*): Yes, yes. If you don't react to me sexually then you are a homosexual. That's father. If father ever knew I were on a couch in a room with you, he'd be sure I was a prostitute or that you were a homosexual. He'd just flip to the floor. What a puritan Freud must have been not to have considered any of this.

ANALYST: Before you go, one last thought. The homosexuality is pretty surely a defense, but why is Will in it and not only me? Could this be because if he is a homosexual, then this would justify a sexual reaction in the transference?

PATIENT: Maybe. I can see that.

166th hour

PATIENT: It's a nice day. Since the day before yesterday I've had a rash all over—on my arms, legs, body, everywhere. I thought it might be from something I ate, but I don't know what. Some friends kidded me that it might be emotional. I began thinking about it. Why did it start the day before yesterday? That is when I started work again back at the old company, although now I'm in a new position. Anyway it was better this morning. I felt no anxiety at all at this change to the new job; maybe I had more anxiety than I felt. (*Long pause.*) I don't know. I've been feeling quite hostile the whole week. The other morning while I was getting ready to go to work, I told Will that the job I had just left already seemed like a bad dream. Will said, "That's just what you said when you left the previous place." That made me angry. I said, "That's not true. There is only one man there whom I don't like." Will insisted. I said to him, "You don't realize that I am the one who made the sacrifices to leave that place I liked for the new one. I did it only because we needed the money." This blew things wide open. He said that this was the first he'd heard of that. He said he didn't know that I was playing a martyr role and that he thought I changed jobs because my mother told me to. Why didn't he just say he was glad I was back at the old company and that he hoped all would be happy? This is the first time that I realized that there was any problem in our marriage. I've always been afraid to look at or face it. I said, "Whenever you have taken a new job, even when it's for less money, I only encourage you." He asked me what I thought of S. G. and I said I liked him. Will looked at me and said there was something wrong with me. I'm supposed to change and not say critical things; but when I don't then he reacts. He is accustomed to hearing me say outspoken things, and now if I don't, he feels that he will have to say them himself and then he'll explode because he has been so controlled. I told him he was hostile to me. He acted as though this was impossible. I said he should face it and that if he did we'd get on better. He has called me lazy in spite of all I do. Thank goodness I hear things from other people that are complimentary. Someone from my last job, which I just left, told me that my associates over there are depressed because I left. I need to hear things like that. I think the rash was emotional, but I'd rather have a rash than feel tense. There's a girl at my present job that Will has met and thinks is so attractive, so poised, so controlled. I feel so mature, so old. And then I saw Will looking at her in a very sweet, approving way—the way he used to look at me. I have a feeling down inside that I don't like—that the relation with Will has changed into something I don't like and I can't stop it. I used to take him as mother, father, husband, everything; now I don't. Maybe it's more mature, but I was happier the other way. Maybe my love needs have changed. I don't know. I'm confused.

ANALYST: You sound a little depressed. Why?

PATIENT: I don't know. I thought about the transference and wondered if that had anything to do with it. I feel worn out, old, ugly, tired, and on top of that, people tell me I've lost a lot of weight. Maybe it's the new job, something that I'm not experienced in, and I'm scared.

ANALYST: Could it be the couch or the difficulty now in arranging times to see me?

PATIENT: I don't feel it about the hours, but I lack something. For the past few days, I lack a spark, (*laughter.*)

ANALYST: Could it be using the couch?

PATIENT: All I can think about is that it has to do with mother. I can't even think.

ANALYST: Could this be physical, this thing with the rash?

PATIENT: It could be, but I don't feel sick. I do feel tired.

ANALYST: You are barely over three weeks of virus infection, with fever, and now you have a rash. Don't you think you should get a medical opinion on it?

PATIENT: I guess so. One thing is good. I do have back again the interest in my work; I like my whole profession again and I enjoy studying.

ANALYST: Are you taking any drugs?

PATIENT: I'm taking something for the rash.

ANALYST: I think you should see your doctor. At the same time, we can question if your feelings are partly because using the couch seems to be like losing your mother.

PATIENT (*laughs*): That is what I was thinking when I mentioned mother just now. When I first used the couch I said that it was like the poor baby who can't turn around and see its mother. Only I didn't want to say it.

167th hour

PATIENT: I think I'm getting worse. Have you ever felt you aren't where your body is? You know what you are doing but it's like being an automaton. You laugh and say things but the other part of you feels differently. I'm not afraid. It's not scary and it's not depressing. I always picture emotion as rays coming out from you that you can feel and detect. Now I feel as though the rays are not as sharp. No matter how much stimulus I get, I'm blunt. I laugh, I react, I smoke, I say whatever I have to say, but it isn't me. Of course it's me, but I don't feel it deep inside. I've had this feeling often before, like when we went to cocktail parties for celebrities and you had to say hello to everyone and act so stupidly. But that was only at a party and this is all day long. And I felt like this as a teenager. I used to just sit and stare out over the land and gradually the feeling would go away. Sometimes I would ride out all alone, and I was never afraid. Other times I would take the car and drive and drive, and when I came to my senses if you had asked me what I saw, what roads I'd crossed, I couldn't tell you, but at least I was myself again and could face mother and the family.

ANALYST: You said you could return and face mother again. Is this some transference reaction? Do you take the couch as distance, as a rejection, as only being treated like a patient? Do you feel a loss of rapport, a loss of closeness?

PATIENT: I don't know. Maybe not sitting up so I see you. I don't know why I can't say it. I think that's it. I feel threatened—that this relation to you will have an end.

I don't like things to end. I told you I didn't want to come to see you, that money is more important and all that, but I could say it because I knew I'd be coming. But now that I know that sooner or later I won't see you any more, I'd at least rather have you where I can see you.

ANALYST: So, depersonalization may be a defensive reaction. You feel I withdraw, and when we are not face to face, you are withdrawn inside about your feelings and also about ending seeing me. You withdraw your feelings so you won't be hurt.

PATIENT: That's what it is! I thought of it but in relation to returning to the old firm in a new job. So many women I know are so highly charged emotionally; my response is to be dull, not to react. But now I see it's more likely to be in the transference. I never want to think about the transference. I don't want to think about it because if there is transference there are dependent love needs, and if there are love needs, I get hurt. If I don't attach them to anyone, then no one can hurt me. I guess it's a reaction to the couch. I never thought it would be so strong, but it is strong because on the couch, when I don't see you, I don't know what I should say to please you, so that you'll love me.

ANALYST: It's easy now. You say everything that comes to mind, anything at all. Do it as freely as you can. You will learn gradually that you can do that and still get from me love in the broad sense of acceptance, sympathetic understanding, and interest in your welfare. As a child you had to be careful of what you said. Now you can and should say anything and everything. You get the love in this sense anyway. If you had felt free and easy and secure about it in childhood, you wouldn't feel so insecure and anxious about it now. And, the relationship really continues after the sessions stop and the experience should leave a modification of your superego as well as ego. The experience becomes the memory, which is internalized, of a kindly understanding attitude. Also, we must move toward correcting the anxieties of the past toward mother, father, and your sisters.

168th hour

PATIENT: I have so much to say that I don't know how to start. When I left yesterday, that feeling was gone. I was my old self again. I was so glad to be myself again; it was as though the cloud in my mind had lifted. I have changed quite a bit. Yesterday you talked about love and if you had done this before, even in this broad sense, I would have been severely threatened. But yesterday I wasn't. I think my transference to you is as toward mother, and therefore I am not threatened. I hadn't played with the children in a long time but when I got home yesterday, I did. I showed them how I could wiggle my ears. They tried it, and we had a fine time. How I hope I can stay that way.

At work I spoke with the boss and my heart didn't even pound. But when I started to come here, that feeling returned of the cloud descending and of being sleepy. But it was not one-fourth as bad as it's been. Then, on the way here, I saw a church and had the impulse to go into it for five or ten minutes. I didn't stop, but it was as if——I've done this before. I've often not gone to church for long periods and then I go in just to sit. Since childhood what father has said has stuck in my mind, "If I were God, I couldn't stand hearing all these old ladies saying these prayers." So I just go in, am silent, and free associate to God. So I still must fear the transference. I want to go to church and I suppose thereby leave a real man for help from an abstract being.

When I'm very anxious about the analysis, it seems I don't dream. But when I come here and see something clearly, then I dream, but it's a bad dream and as such the opposite of my waking mood.

Last night I dreamed about an earthquake. I was in a house, or an office, not my house. Then the earthquake started. Will was there. My first thought was the children. I ran outside and the building was crumbling. People said, "Don't go, stay here." I said, "I must find and save my children." I went toward my house. Everything was crumbling. On the way I saw a cat with a wild look. I thought she would attack me, but she was scared and didn't notice me. I got home and got the children, who were waiting outside. We went into the house and we waited and were safe. It was a nightmare, but it ended well.

Then I had a second dream. My menstruation was a hemorrhage but not a miscarriage. In this dream too, the emotion was fear.

ANALYST: Associations?

PATIENT: The first dream. Well, that is how I've been feeling, but not yesterday. I felt everything was crumbling, and I couldn't do anything about it. I think my children, whom I save, are myself. It was the street that was dangerous. In the house it was safe. Once when I was little and was on a street, I saw a man exposing himself. Mother and father said streets are dangerous. A girl on the street is looking for danger. Last evening we had friends over and the man said, "A mother who spanks a child for going into the street, spanks him because she loves him." I said, "Not to the child; love is not a spanking. Of course, you must be realistic and not let small children run into the street." But, if I spank, I know it is because of my own needs.

ANALYST: Anything else about the street?

PATIENT: Yes. When I think of street, I picture a small girl about six years old, and I see a man exposing himself. I think this is the first time I've dreamt about a cat. I think of the second dream that when I had my first period, I was only ten. I was the first one in my class. I felt so out of place. I felt the way I did for the past week, so old, knowing things others didn't, knowing that curiosity is pleasurable and I didn't have it anymore because I knew, and I told no one because mother had told me not to. One day I had a big fright with my sister Roberta. She was older, but heavier, and I was thin and could always get on top of her, poor thing. She raised her leg and I saw blood and got so scared and thought it was something that I had done. That evening was the first and last time father spanked me. Father wasn't mad but I was furious and the rest looked on and laughed. Mother's passivity—why she would just sit there. How could she just sit when father was cruel to the others? I would have saved my children. I had to get along with father. I had no one else to defend me. I guess the others hadn't either.

I don't know what I associate to the earthquake. I'm getting anxious. The earthquake has a feeling with it that nothing else has. It's that somebody has such power and you are so weak and somebody can decide your life for you. Maybe the earthquake in the dream is you. Yes, it is, because yesterday I thought: I was so sick and with one word he brought me back to emotional stability and that word is love. If I had known the meaning of that word since childhood, without fears, without needing to please, if I had just understood love without all the attachments to it, then I would be a very happy person today.

ANALYST: And the feeling is of helplessness related to being on the couch.

PATIENT: Yes.

ANALYST: The earthquake and the hemorrhage also—is that anger?

PATIENT: Yes. But for what? I guess for being so helpless.

ANALYST: On the couch is it that it's more like being in someone's power?

PATIENT: That's it.

ANALYST: And maybe there is also defensiveness against the sexual elements, that is, the associations about the street.

PATIENT: Maybe.

ANALYST: Unfortunately, time is up and we can't put all this together in order now. But anger on the couch seems to be there, and just why it is present we are now getting to see.

PATIENT: Yes, and it's coming out better than I thought.

176th hour

PATIENT: The whole weekend was like a storm—inside me—not outside. I guess it happens whenever I get an insight. Like when I realized how much I wanted and needed my mother after having fought against it for so long. I cried most of the weekend.

I think it was Saturday I had this dream. Will and I were at a convention. There were two rooms, one for the men and one for the wives. I was with the wives and looked into the other room. S. G. was there. I think he's an alcoholic. Will says not, but I know he drinks some everyday. S. G.'s wife also drinks a lot. S. G. and Will are old friends. In the dream Will was calm, talking with S. G., but he was not getting emotionally involved. In reality they often argue heatedly. I felt I belonged with the wives.

ANALYST: Associations?

PATIENT: Sunday morning I was so depressed, more than I have ever been. Will saw it and he came over to me and said, "Are you afraid of losing me? Nobody will ever take me away from you." That did it. I started to cry hysterically and couldn't stop. Then everyone went somewhere and I was alone. I felt that was one day they shouldn't have left me alone. I had ideas of suicide although I knew I'd never do it. I started to try to figure out why I felt this way. I thought of the storm that went on inside me when I saw how much I needed mother. Then I thought Will must have hit the spot—that I was afraid of losing him. And then I realized how much I needed him—and you—both. Then I felt calm, as if I didn't have to fight any more. Now I feel that I know what I'm fighting. Maybe it's a coincidence that my mother-in-law is here and this makes things worse.

Remember that dream I had of Will having sexual relations with a man? In that dream I left him. That's what I always do when I feel my love needs are not satisfied, when I feel I'm not given what I want. Then I want to just let it all go. Leave. It's not that I'm afraid Will will leave me. I know darn well he won't. It's that I'm afraid I'll leave him because of his not giving me what I want. Why have I calmed down? I crave love so much and don't have it, and then I get hostile and want to go. And, if I go, then I punish the other person. He won't have me. I punish myself because I won't have him. You know that time I realized how much I needed mother, I still couldn't picture myself being nice to her, giving her anything. And now I think I'm beginning to realize how much I need you, and therefore, I feel I don't need mother so much. As a result, I can be nicer to her. I feel that I must go through the same thing with my sisters and my children. I need them. I must realize that to need someone doesn't necessarily mean that you will get hurt. You've discussed this with me.

Two things happened. Yesterday we got a letter from a man in St. Louis. He and his wife are old friends. Last year when we were there we found they were divorced. This letter said she committed suicide, and the man wrote that he was glad to be rid of her paranoid jealousy. I identified with her and thought: Thank God, I've had this help! While waiting for you, I got the feeling, not of losing my mind, but of going blank. You came late, and in those five minutes I thought: Maybe your secretary phoned to cancel. Did she? Didn't she? This is the right day, isn't it? I even looked at the paper to check the date. I thought of phoning you. Then I thought: How absurd. If you don't come, I'll find out why. Then a moment or so later I thought: If you don't come, is it because you are angry at me?

Another thing. About a month and a half ago I ordered some things for knitting, and I haven't had time for it. I thought: I want to do this and get work, books, psychoanalysis, and everything out of my system.

ANALYST: We do not have time to discuss all this. Is it the pattern to mother? Is it that since you didn't get enough love from her, you feel that way now to Will, me, and others? Is it that you need the love so but fear you won't get it?

PATIENT: Yes. I did think that way, but I don't now. I think that now I'm not so hostile to mother. I can identify with her and in the dream I accept being with the wives.

ANALYST: And, you let Will talk with S. G. and you don't feel you are losing him.

177th hour

PATIENT: I've been hostile to you for the past few weeks. I think it's because this is the second time I've been so dependent on someone that they could destroy me. The first was to mother and now it is to you. Now I feel better toward mother. You wrote a book and dedicated it to your parents. I used to feel that if I wrote a book I never could dedicate it to mother, or even to father. But now I could because now I feel so much better toward mother and also, now I see the dependence and I'm handling it better. Since I see it, she can no longer destroy me. The same is toward you. I was so hostile to you because I didn't want to realize this.

ANALYST: Now that you see in the analysis this dependence on me, you can begin to try to reduce it and work it through and thus have less to fight.

PATIENT: I see mother as domineering because I want to, and I suppose I want to because that is the childhood pattern. I can feel as I did in childhood.

ANALYST: You don't have to see her as domineering. You see her as such because of the childhood pattern, as you say. Part of you gave in to this. What is the importance of this in the transference to me?

PATIENT: It's not that you are this way or that you are dominating, but when I got love this was part of it. I see this must be corrected. My fantasy is: He's good. I've never seen anyone so good, but he's strong and therefore if I want his love, I must get dependent on him. But then I see that I'll be dominated. Just a few days ago I realized that this need not be so. And I even see that I don't have to do anything to please you. I can even tell you to go to hell and you won't do anything to me. You won't react. You'll be good to me no matter what I do. I don't mean good, or bad, because of course you'll have feelings, but you won't go away. You'll be here. It's hard to express.

ANALYST: Is it? Isn't it availability and also security—feeling the interest I have in you? So, if you tell me to go to hell, I'll say, "This is interesting. It is the first hour you've told me that. Why is it?"

PATIENT: Yes! It's that you will listen, be here, be interested, and that we'll find out why.

ANALYST: Yes, the patient attributes to the analyst attitudes and feelings of patients, parents, and other childhood figures. But then the patient also introjects the analyst's attitudes as a new superego—tolerant, accepting, approving, available, and secure. This is what the parents' attitudes would have been ideally. In one case, the analyst was critical and depreciatory in his tone to a patient and the patient took over these feelings toward himself. As Freud pointed out, the analyst's attitudes must correct the parental ones that made the problems.

178th hour

PATIENT: I had a dream last night. It was you, but you were so ugly, looking uglier than anyone I've ever seen. You were conducting a meeting and my whole family was there to see what you were like. They had a very critical attitude. I looked at you and thought: My God, what happened! Your eyes were displaced, you had a hunchback, and you sat all curved over and crumpled in a chair. You were physically abominable. Mabel said, "How can you fall in love with anyone like that?" And I answered, "That's what you always say."

ANALYST: Associations?

PATIENT: In reality that is true. When we were younger and any of us went with a boy and the family wanted to break it up, they would talk against the boy. Only, if mother had talked against a boyfriend who was going with one of my older sisters, my sister would have done the opposite and just married the boy right off. Mother usually attacked a boy's looks, his physical appearance. I paid little attention to that, and I was much more concerned about his mind, his intellect, his accomplishments.

ANALYST: How about his personality, his emotional make-up? Didn't that enter in much?

PATIENT: I thought that if you are intelligent, you know how to handle your emotional life. Now I know better. Of course, I never could go out with hostile boys or boys who acted out a lot. I couldn't be so masochistic. I never could see how anyone could be happy when suffering. Everyone in our group of girls was the same. If one of us heard that a boy who was dating a girl in the group was also going out with another girl, we'd tell our friend. She would then tell the boy that she knew about the other girl and that she refused to be second. So, the boy would be forced to choose between them.

The son of a very wealthy family married the daughter of a wealthy family, but the girl is so withdrawn, so fragile. We were out with them and another couple, and I couldn't make her at ease or get her talking in the group, although we've known her husband a long time. She admitted that she was too shy to talk in company. I thought: With all that wealth, why should she be shy? Now I know that wealthy women can also make mistakes in rearing their children, just like anyone else.

But in this dream, why did I make you so ugly? My brother-in-law said to me before I started analysis, "You are a tough case and not everyone can handle you." I liked his saying that, but I got scared too. But I still don't see why this dream.

ANALYST: Is it partly from yesterday when you said you felt you could be as hostile to me as you liked and still feel secure that I'd be interested in you and that we'd analyze your feelings in a friendly way?

PATIENT: No, but it is still the defense against the attachment to you. I think the associations show this. Mother and my family are trying to break up the relation, the analysis. Now I'm getting mad. I don't know why. Yes, I do know. Because you treat it as though it is not important. I mean my thoughts about the dream. I think I feel threatened if I like you. Why should I be so threatened? I feel that it's something wrong, that something will happen to me. All I can think is that we talked yesterday of my taking you over, analytically, as a new superego, and I take this as being disloyal to my family. If I paid any attention or felt love to another child, I felt disloyal to my children. I feel bound in this way to my parents. Oh, now I see why I've had all the guilt. Because they trained me to stick to my parental family, and I've gone out and met other people. I've done it, and I'm even being analyzed. But, I've felt it was disloyal—not so much to father but to mother and my sisters. I always thought it was to father! No wonder it never left, because it's basically to mother and my sisters. That's why you threaten mother and my sisters so much, because you know this now and can see how mother really is. We are all scared to see how she really is. Although she's a good person, she has defects and we don't want to see them.

ANALYST: Why?

PATIENT: Because she has made us feel that we are all she has. This is how she feels. Father wasn't in it.

ANALYST: The time is up now, but next session we must go further into this matter of attachment, obligation, and loyalty to mother. You can have better relations if you are more on a free adult-to-adult basis rather than being as a child who feels not enough love and too much attachment and obligation.

183rd hour

PATIENT: I feel fine. I love the hot weather. I don't know if it's worth it, but there is something I should talk about. The other night we went to a party at T. S.'s. He's a writer. I was talking about paintings. Some of his are very good. Suddenly T. S. said, "Could I ask you for lunch? Would you go?" I hadn't been paying any real attention. I sensed danger, but I said, "Why not?" as though there were nothing to it. But I could tell by his voice there was more behind it. I left him and went over to talk to someone else, but wherever I went T. S. came over, and I couldn't get rid of him. I was uncomfortable. After the party I wondered if I should tell Will. I did. At first he wouldn't believe it. Then he angrily said, "The s. o. b.!" Mother said that if a man makes a pass at a girl it is because she has somehow invited it. At work he phoned me and asked me to lunch. I said I was sorry that I was busy. He said he phoned because I told him that he could. I said "I'll phone you if I have the time." He was so egotistic that he thought I would call him. This isn't like a friend asking me to lunch; this is an invitation with an intention behind it—first lunch, then tea, then dinner, then something until midnight. I tried something that has worked before. I've invited two other couples and T. S. and his wife for dinner in the hopes that he can see the relation as friendship and not as conquest. Will had a good reaction—he laughed. T. S. is so egotistic I find him very unattractive. The secretary said I should be flattered by his invitation to lunch, but I was mad that T. S. would think I was that kind of a woman.

I've changed. If this had happened a year ago, I would have been frightened and depressed because I would have thought: My gosh, he thinks I'm a prostitute! I'm not so Victorian that I don't go to lunch with a man who is a friend, but this is different. Will has helped me a lot with it. He jokes about it. When I said I felt guilty that maybe I'd done something to invite it, he said, "No, there are men like that."

Last night I had a dream. I had on a mask—the tragic mask you see in a theatre. It has something to do with you, with taking off the mask. Under it was beauty. Not that I'm beautiful. My skin was like that of a mature teenager.

ANALYST: Associations?

PATIENT: For the past three days I haven't had the sense that I could feel wrinkles at all. I feel like my old self again. I'm back in life again. I don't worry about problems; I feel I can meet them. Could this dream possibly be connected with T. S. phoning yesterday morning. Not because of T. S. himself, but because I don't want people to see the mask that I wear at parties and get the wrong impression, that is, that I'm a prostitute.

How can I think that! Have I such a conscience! I think I'm better, but it's the opposite of what I do. At parties they say I'm charming and in life too, that is, I have a nice face and at home I'm bitter—the opposite of the dream.

ANALYST: This guilt—let's look at it realistically. You are a very attractive woman, and handling passes that are made at you is just part of life. There is no need for all this guilt, conscience, and the like.

PATIENT: Yes, the others have kept it on the level of flirtation. If they ask me to lunch, I say, "Of course, anytime." They know not to phone. But this confused me because T. S. misunderstood and did phone. But I do have too harsh a superego about it instead of just being realistic.

185th hour

PATIENT: I'm trying to think of last night's dream and another one keeps coming to mind. It's an old dream in which I'm abandoned in the town near our house in Texas, and I keep looking for Will and a doctor friend, B. L. I can't find them. There are soldiers who come over and ask me if I need help. I say yes. It was three or four in the morning. I think I was going with Will and the doctor to a party and they left me and I was scared.

Last night I had a dream about R. T. and about an old boyfriend I had of my own age. R. T. was trying to get me to be with him and I was attracted to him but felt I should go with the boy of my own age. R. T. was giving a party for me.

ANALYST: What was the tone of your feelings?

PATIENT: Confused, ambivalent, I didn't know what I wanted. Then the dream changed. In reality we got a letter that was not for us. We must return it today to the postman. In the dream I went to this woman's house to give her the letter, and I tried to explain that I wasn't the person to whom it was addressed.

ANALYST: Associations?

PATIENT: R. T. wanted everything—for me to go with him, be with him, live with him, everything. Maybe I'm having resistance and there is transference. That's why I worried so as to whom to go to as my analyst. I didn't know how strong my needs were, but I sensed it. I just can't say how I feel. I realize how much I've been fighting all my life against this strong feeling in me of needing somebody. When I feel that way, I feel it from head to toe. It's true that you get better, but on a false basis because it's not realistic. If the dream is a wish, how do I explain that it shows ambivalence but that I don't have any? In the dream I go with the young boyfriend.

ANALYST: You didn't tell that part.

PATIENT: Yes, I went with the young boyfriend. But, I knew that the feeling I had with R. T. couldn't be had with the young man. I once told you that when I was a teenager, at times I felt the world should not go on. I used to think: If it would only stop right here so I could go on living this moment. That's not quite true. I also felt it later with B. L., although not so deeply. I also felt it yesterday in the analytic hour. I thought for a moment: If life would only stop right here. I don't know. Yesterday when I left I felt fine, like my old self, but now I feel depressed, although not too much. Right now I feel very anxious.

I knew the transference would be very difficult, that it would get me better but that inside I would have a storm—a storm that stays inside and that I never show. *(Tears.)* I thought yesterday that it can't be my needs for father. They couldn't have been that strong. It must be more to mother. Of course sex is now part of it. I'm a woman now. I feel embarrassed. *(Tears.)* It has to do with the feeling of closeness—that much I know. Twice before I've felt this way. The most important thing for me is to be close, close physically. You see, mother could be close spiritually, but not physically. Only once that I can remember did she ever take me in her lap. That was when I felt sick while driving to my grandparents. In the car mother took me on her lap. I would approach her much as my children approach me. When you are small you are like a little kitten that wants to come and brush against you and be close and then it goes out again. The children come in and give me a big kiss and I kiss them, and they go on. But mother said, "The best place for the baby is in the crib." I said to her, "No, in the arms." Mother said, "In mother's arms he's uncomfortable." And then I answered, "No, in his mother's arms he can feel good."

I'm going through this with you. It's massive. I think of you all the time—morning, noon, and night. I don't mean I go around like a ghost, but everything reminds me of you. You know why I feel better? It's because I know it and don't have to fight it, and I feel that you will protect me.

I have a feeling that the second dream is connected with the first. The business about the letter is like I want to change my name and address, or that I'm trying to find myself, that I'm telling myself: This is your name and this your address.

Yesterday I thought: I wish I could take care of you and make you healthy and fat.

ANALYST: During the last three hours we've been discussing material regarding ego identity. As an adult your first love and your first responsibility is to your husband and children. Home is now husband and children, not parents and siblings. To be adult is to be alone, but also it is to be free to love and to be loved with husband and children, and with friends. Everyone, though, has a residue of the child's needs for parental love that is not satisfied. You must be free to satisfy it as best you can as a responsible adult, and you should not feel that all other relations to friends, and even to husband and children, are disloyalty to father and mother. If you feel disloyal you will be guilty and not free to handle the residue of love needs, which are a hard enough problem anyway for everyone.

PATIENT: Yes, and feeling that being independent and that every contact except with father and mother is disloyal to them makes me mad and rebellious.

ANALYST: Exactly.

186th hour

PATIENT: I had a dream last night. There was a fight of rebels for freedom against a tyranny. I wasn't fighting, but I sympathized with the rebels. There was a man with four children, and he didn't know what to do with them to protect them.

ANALYST: Associations?

PATIENT: That's what I've been doing—fighting for my own freedom from too much dependence on you and on my parents.

ANALYST: What are your associations to the man and four children?

PATIENT: It can't be that I don't know what to do with my children! I met this nine-year-old boy whose mother restricts him so. She doesn't let him play ball or do other things with the boys, and I thought of my children. I'm not controlling like that. They do everything. No matter what happens in life, if you really love your children, nothing will happen. I mean *love* them; not *need* them. Fighting! Oh yes, last night Tom mentioned fighting and his father thought he meant him and myself, but Tom said he meant Will and himself. He said it all with a kidding tone.

ANALYST: The dream looks like a defense against hostility. You are the onlooker while the rebels fight and want to protect the children. Why are you hostile and to whom? How about in the transference?

PATIENT: I'm fighting for my freedom. From what? From you? It could be. No, it *is*. I know it is and there's hostility or I wouldn't be fighting. It has to do with my infantile dependence on you. In reality, yesterday I was thinking that I wish I could see you outside of only analyzing for then I could see you more realistically.

After yesterday's hour I felt depressed, alone, as though I was going to lose you somewhere, somehow. I don't feel hostile. Well, maybe I do. Yesterday I met another patient leaving and maybe it was sibling rivalry—that I'm not the only one, that I'm only one of a lot of children. I think I don't know what I'm talking about. All these silly things. Maybe because today is Friday, I don't want to get into deep things. I *do* have hostility to you, because I have to handle my own problems over the weekend until I can see you again.

ANALYST: So you are mad in part because you don't see me and in part because you want to see me.

PATIENT: Yes, but if I saw you more, I'd be more dependent. But then I'd solve it. Or. maybe it's only that I want to see you more (*laughs*).

ANALYST: But the dream?

PATIENT: The dream shows I'm fighting my own wishes.

ANALYST: Could yesterday's hour have anything to do with it?

PATIENT: It could, but I'm in a much better mood today. Today I can take the transference with humor.

ANALYST: During yesterday's hour we talked about being free of parents, about not having to feel disloyal. It is okay to be independent, for your first responsibility is to husband and children. It is also quite all right to have love needs and to satisfy these so as not to make trouble, that is, with husband, children, friends, and work. We also talked about ego identity and that the next step is to have independence and freedom by shifting your attitudes and not having to fight. You can become independent of parents by relating on an adult-to-adult basis and by not being bound, dictated to, and held like a child.

PATIENT: Yes, and I think I've found I wasn't fighting their domination but my own needs toward them. I covered up my own needs by thinking it was mostly their domination.

ANALYST: Yes, if you want the love so strongly, you must please them, be submissive. Then, of course, you will feel dominated, but you may also exaggerate what control and holding there is. The same is true with feeling held by them, which arises from your own needs.

189th hour

PATIENT: Only in the last few days have I felt that I could plan for the future. I've always felt that if I planned it, it would not work out. The other day we were drawing plans for a house for us for the future. That night I had a dream. Three or five people were in conversation. One man seemed to be you—sometimes he was and sometimes he wasn't. He said to me, "Can you describe what pain is?" I said, "No, I can't. It's a feeling, and if you don't know it, no one can tell you." As I spoke I felt pain, knew what it was, but I couldn't say. He said, "Well, you have pain, then you don't, then you have it again." That is, he meant a repetition of painful experiences. And I said, "My gosh. That's masochism. You don't have to live through pain again and again to know what it is." I thought: He is masochistic if he has to go through pain repeatedly to know what it is.

ANALYST: Associations?

PATIENT: I had another dream the night after this one. No, I think it was the night before it. In the dream I was in the backyard and the neighbor is a nice man, but he never talks with anyone. To my surprise he came over to talk to me instead of to some other neighbors who were also in my backyard. I was looking at him with such loving eyes. I was so absorbed by his presence that I didn't realize that I'd walked too far from our house. I stopped and turned and saw the house, and it was so beautiful. Now I think I had this dream the same night as the other one. I thought it wasn't my house and I wanted to return to it and I wanted him to go back with me, but I knew he couldn't because he had other responsibilities. So I left him, with some pain in me, and I saw some pain in him too. I returned to the house and in the yard I saw Annie planting some twisted vines in a huge hole. I got so mad and I picked up a log and said, "That's not right, it won't grow. It won't give shade so plant this (the log)." We did and Will helped; and the other logs, which had nothing growing on them, I put in the house.

I think the second dream is clear. The walking with the neighbor is analysis with you and how absorbed I've been. The dream is my wish to come back to reality. You've been pointing out about the wish to be with the parental family, but I know that my home, husband, and children are my real life now. So although I was unhappy leaving you, it was a kind of pleasurable pain in that I was giving up something for something else that is most worthwhile. Planting the log is maybe the wish to have my own roots in my own home and not be like the vine that Annie was planting. I mustn't go all over here and there like a vine, but I must give my family stability and shade. And I want solid roots, but I shouldn't let Annie plant it for me. That is my problem now.

There followed a period of open conscious hositility against me for which, unfortunately, verbatim notes are not available. The deepest source of this was the pattern toward the patient's mother, which was transferred to me. This is shown in the following dream pair.

PATIENT: In the first dream I am in bed with my mother. she puts her arms around me and touches my genitals. I get up thinking that this is rather revolting and that I am going away and find a man. In the second dream my husband is leaving me for another woman.

ANALYST: Associations?

PATIENT: I have been thinking of paying my mother a visit but I'm rather afraid to. Also I was afraid to come to see you this hour, and I must admit I've been rather anxious over the past weekend about seeing you. Also I no longer have any warm feelings for you. I am just terribly hostile to you although I do not why. I can guess however what you will say. I think that I feel that the analysis is beginning to come to an end and that I will be separating from you since we plan to go to the west coast. I think that I am furious with you because I do not want to leave and you do not insist I stay. And I do not want to admit to myself that I have become this attached to you. I am so angry at you because I am so dependent on you. I want to be rid of you because of all my dependence on you, all my wishes for your love. Also I am angry at you because of the prospect of leaving and no longer having you.

Somehow I must be guilty toward you for being so angry at you and the prospect of leaving you because in the second dream I go back to my old pattern of my husband leaving me. In reality it is I who am leaving you, but maybe I am so guilty for being so hostile to you that I think that I deserve to have my husband leave me. It is partly the fear that if I get angry at you, you will not love me any more; in other words, you will leave me. And then if you leave me I don't have to struggle with my feelings about leaving you. My father was important in my growing up but the reason

I was so strongly attached to him is because I felt that I did not get all that I wanted from my mother. My mother really loved me but you know somehow I felt that it was not quite personal enough and that somehow I was on the outside and she was closer to the older children, especially my sisters. Of course I see in the second dream what has so often come up, namely that my husband is going to another woman. It seems as though everything leads back to the strongest force in my life, which is the wish for mother and my jealousy of her being closer to my sisters. This wish for a more personal love from mother has remained so strong in my adult life because I have not been as secure in it as I have wanted to be. If I were absolutely secure in having all of the real personal love that I wanted while growing up, I am sure that I would simply take it for granted now.

This is only part of a single hour out of the period of months of hostile transference. Fortunately the hostile transference, indeed the whole childhood pattern toward mother, was now out in the open. As the patient points out with tremendous insight, she now feels secure enough with me to be able to feel and express freely the hostility and all the rest of the pattern consciously and directly. Without this, no analysis can be worked through. The analysis continued for a time. We did reduce the intensity of the transference by analyzing it. And, we did succeed in working it through and finally resolving it. Gradually the frequency of visits was reduced and then they were tapered off until termination. The patient, together with her husband and children, returned to San Francisco to live. She did very well except for a few brief episodes of conflict with her mother and sisters.

Appendix

APPENDIX
A REVIEW OF RESEARCH EVIDENCE*

Today few students of behavior question the concept that early experiences, particularly interpersonal ones, have profound and permanent effects upon animals and humans. But what is the actual evidence for this? Since the understanding of the personality and its pathology as well as the methods of treatment delineated in this volume are all based upon this concept, the reader might find it interesting and useful to have at hand a review of pertinent research evidence. The studies mentioned in this chapter reflect a variety of developmental research methods.

Freud opened many more fields of exploration in human psychology than could be cultivated in his lifetime. One of these was the lifelong effects of injurious emotional influences during early childhood. With its relation to the dynamic unconscious it was one of his greatest discoveries; yet only now is this fundamental area receiving concentrated research attention. The manifold findings are of great importance for the theory of personality, for the etiology of neurosis and all other psychopathology. They also have practical significance for therapy and prevention and may pro-

*The material in this chapter was originally gathered and prepared in collaboration with Solveig Wenar, Ph.D.

vide the key to understanding various sociological problems, the most outstanding of which is the infantile, libidinally fixated, hostile behavior with which man threatens man. This chapter offers a representative sample of research findings, organized under the headings of eight hypotheses that are central to Freud's concept of the lasting effects of early influences on adult personality.

Analysts reach their conclusions primarily through work with patients. They see evidence in each patient that symptoms, values, conflicts, and personality characteristics can be traced back to his reactions to his unique constellation of childhood experiences. The details of the whole process are many and involved and have given rise to a vast psychoanalytic literature. The very fact that the data of psychoanalytic observation are confidential, associative, and diffusely bulky makes difficult their treatment within strict research methodology. For adequate research review, we therefore include other fields related to psychoanalysis. No science stands alone; strength and healthy expansion are derived from interchange with related disciplines. While psychoanalysis has stimulated much of the research in all the behavioral sciences, it still seeks to learn and incorporate what is relevant to it from all sciences. Many problems appear in fresh perspective and can best be solved through other knowledge: for example, through extrapolation from the observation of animal behavior, through information gained from the psychology of learning and Gestalt psychology, and from experimental studies of conditioning and imprinting.

The following review of the literature is organized around some of the hypotheses implicit in the concept of the aftereffects of early influences. Eight hypotheses and their implications will be examined in detail after surveying the literature; also, only such discussion of research as is essential to this review is included.

To help clarify the main principles, it is well to first delineate the variables (Siegel, 1956). This is attempted here in the single area of childhood trauma. The comprehension of the aftereffects of early influences is essential to the understanding of fixation, regression, introjection, superego, transference, and other psychoanalytic concepts.

DEFINITIONS, ASSUMPTIONS, AND HYPOTHESES

In formulating a rough working concept, "personality" can be defined as a pattern of basic motivations and reactions. Each pattern for the individual is unique although its elements are common to all. The individual pattern represents one of all possible variations in quantity and combination of the basic elements, which are comparatively few. They can be conveniently grouped under the familiar headings of id, superego, and ego. In oversimplified form they are the biological needs, drives, and reactions of the id; the internal representations of identifications and training of the superego; and the defensive, perceptive, integrative, and executive activities of the ego.

Motivation is conceptualized as an inner variable. It prompts overt behavior, also modifications of it, and inhibitions. Overt behavior includes verbal responses and all behavior that is in some way observable by others. It is assumed that the behavior caused by any particular motivation is identifiable as such, at least by experienced clinicians. The clinician bases his diagnosis and treatment on his ability to identify his patient's behavior in terms of motivations.

Admittedly, these definitions are general and imprecise and would not suffice for specific research studies (Lindzey, 1958). However, they are adequate for this general survey of the relevant literature.

In the development of personality it appears that two broad classes of variables determine the pattern of motivations. The first of these is the class of inherited variables, including maturational and constitutional factors. The second of these is the class of external variables. In the first of these classes, the maturational factor is the force that impels each individual toward maximal growth and development. It proceeds, within certain variations, according to a biological timetable. Constitutional factors are described in the literature in two senses: (1) to signify inherited or gene-determined potentials, and (2) to signify gene-determined potentials present at birth that are modified by influences in utero and during the birth process. The term is used here in the first sense, while uteral conditions are considered among the external factors. (Whereas many studies indicate that constitutional factors play a considerable role in the development of temperamental and other personality aspects, they are not generally found to have great influence in the etiology of psychopathology. For this reason they are not of prime relevance in this chapter.)

External factors provide the conditions that determine to what extent and in what respects an individual's genetic and maturational potentials are realized. These factors appear to play an important role in forming personality and to be the critical factor, that is, the one having the greatest weight, in producing the distortions of personality that underlie all familiar forms of psychopathology. We are concerned with the operation and effects of these external influences from the conception of the individual.

In the interest of clarity, the view of personality development to be scrutinized in this chapter is presented in the form of eight hypotheses, each more or less subject to testing.

The first found hypotheses of personality development all bear time relations.

Hypothesis *A*: The earlier an influence impinges upon the developing personality, the more pervasive and significant are its effects.

Hypothesis *B*: Exceptions to hypothesis *A* concern functions that are most susceptible to influences during critical periods, which occur most frequently early in life.

Hypothesis *C*: The fundamental characteristics of

the personality are established by the age of approximately six years.

Hypothesis *D*: Once formed, the personality pattern remains fairly constant throughout life.

The next two hypotheses have to do with relevant influences.

Hypothesis *E*: Given adequate conditions for physical survival, the most important external influence is the emotional relationship between a child and his parents (or parental substitutes).

Hypothesis *F*: The most relevant aspects of the child's emotional milieu are parental warmth, parental control in accordance with his needs, and stability in his relationship to his parents.

The final two hypotheses have to do with the effects of relevant influences.

Hypothesis *G*: To the extent that ideal conditions prevail, maturation proceeds to the fullest and the individual eventually develops a mature personality, that is, he becomes a responsible, productive adult of good will.

Hypothesis *H*: Any deviation from ideal conditions is necessarily detrimental, and the greater the deviation, the more thwarted the maturation will be and the more intensive and extensive becomes the pathology of the personality.

METHODOLOGICAL CONSIDERATION

The task of reviewing research involves weighing the evidence against the adequacy of the methods used. To date there is no flawless procedure for the study of the development, consistency, and pathology of a personality during a lifetime (Dennis, 1955; Garn, 1957; Harris, 1960; Martin, 1960). Hence, caution is required in drawing conclusions.

Methodological flaws do not necessarily produce unreliable or invalid results, but they do limit the scope of conclusions that can be drawn from them. Whenever similar results are obtained by different investigators using different procedures (with different flaws) and few or no studies contradict these results, the chances that the hypothesis tested is valid are greatly increased. Even conflicting conclusions may yield important clues.

To facilitate the reader's evaluation of the studies to be reported, the advantages and disadvantages of the most common developmental research methods will be discussed briefly.

THE LONGITUDINAL APPROACH

This method studies the same subjects over a protracted period of time, observing them at frequent intervals in a systematic fashion. It has also been called the prospective method (Bell, 1960). Many advantages derive from the availability of firsthand observations by trained observers during the whole developmental sequence studied. Such observations are often more reliable and more complete, and they offer better comparability of subjects than data from other studies. The longitudinal approach makes possible the direct observation of changes in the personality as they occur, and thereby of factors related to, or causative of, the changes. Thus it offers a unique opportunity for describing effects of different combinations of variables. The method is suitable for predictive studies (Kris, 1957) and for studies of time relations in development.

Kagan and Moss of the Fels Research Institute (1963) point to the value of the longitudinal approach for studying the emergence of "derivative behaviors" and the "sleeper effect." By derivative behaviors is meant the behavior forms occurring at successive phases of development, representing modifications of the original primitive expression of a motivation; for example, verbal sarcasm may be a derivative of early forms of hostile physical aggression. Kagan and Moss state that "adult behavior is a complicated code in which certain responses bear a lawful relation" to early behavioral patterns. This code gives important clues to understanding human development, and it enhances the ability to predict adult reactions from behavior in childhood.

What the Fels group calls the sleeper effect represents delayed results of early environmental influences on the functioning of the personality. As an example, "maternal acceleration" of the child's external development (that is, efforts to push the child ahead) shows the highest correlation with school age achievement when the measure of maternal acceleration is obtained during the first three years of life. When maternal acceleration is measured at the same time as the child's achievement, the correlations are much lower (cf. Sontag and Kagan, 1963).

The longitudinal studies in the literature are relatively few, their combined number of subjects amounting to only several hundred. The disadvantages are apparent: spans of twenty years or more of work; financing; the long wait for results; the processing of many data; the difficulty of incorporating new scientific findings and techniques; and others. A few research groups have carried out major longitudinal studies in which personality functions are included (Anderson, 1963; Klatskin and Jackson, 1955; Kodlin and Thompson, 1958; Schaefer and Bayley, 1963; Skard *et al.*, 1960; Nashbum, 1959).

THE FOLLOW-UP APPROACH

The follow-up approach, which is closely related to the longitudinal method, consists in studying adults for whom detailed histories of their childhood are available. Usually the person studying the adult subject is not the same as the one who recorded the data. Typically, the procedure follows these steps: (1) to start with a group whose members have some common characteristics; (2) assemble all data available during a given time period; (3) relocate and study anew each of the subjects; (4) look for correspondence between the childhood and the later status of the subject. Often the common feature of the subjects was that they had been observed in child guidance clinics (Frazee, 1953; O'Neal and Robins, 1958, 1959). This choice of subjects has, of course, been determined by its advantages from the researcher's point of view, that is, the particular behavioral problem and the availability of records.

There are evident methodological defects. To begin with, data taken from clinical records not intended for research are generally inadequate (Grinker, 1961). Further, a common criticism of this approach is that it is limited to a population that is characterized by early gross disturbances. While this opinion is generally correct, it carries no great weight; what is important is that the conclusions match the premises. Without a control group, conclusions must be stated as hypotheses subject to subsequent testing by other methods. Control groups need not be "normal"; subjects with different types of early disturbances may serve as control groups, one for the other. Indeed, much interest inheres in comparisons of adaptation among adults who had exhibited different types of disharmony with the environment in childhood.

THE CROSS-SECTIONAL APPROACH

This is the follow-up method in reverse. It also starts with a group that has certain common characteristics; but, in contrast to the follow-up method, this procedure traces the development of the subjects back to childhood. An example is the comparison between delinquents and "normals" with respect to the incidence in early life of broken homes, ordinal sibling position, socioeconomic condition, and the like. Considering the difficulties in obtaining unbiased accounts of personality variables in retrospect, it is an advantage, from the point of view of reliability, that only rather gross factors have been isolated by the cross-sectional approach. Both this approach and the follow-up methods have been criticized for their poor techniques of sampling. In this respect they contrast sharply with the longitudinal method, which has been praised for its good sampling and valid data. The merits, however, are more evenly distributed, at least in studies of personality disorders (Bell, 1960).

The cross-sectional method is comparatively easy and quick and therefore useful in the early phases of a research program for the identification of relevant variables and the formulation of hypotheses.

THE EXPERIMENTAL APPROACH

Experimental procedures are variations of a basic model. Subjects known or assumed to be equal in relevant respects are assigned at random to an experimental and a control group. The former is subjected to the influence of the variable under study and the latter is not, but in all other respects the groups are treated equally. Both groups are measured subsequently and the effects of the experimental variable are assessed.

Were it not precluded by humanitarian considerations, many questions about human development could be answered by assigning children at random to various types of controlled environments and comparing the different groups at intervals. "How," asks Shakow (1959), "can one study human psychological phenomena scientifically . . . with a minimum of distortions . . . and ethically . . . with a minimum of inevitable trespasses?" Animal experimentation, therefore, is increasingly resorted to in studying emotional development. The subjects have a short life span, are easy to care for, and control groups are readily available.

To generalize from animals to humans requires great scientific caution. Animal experimentation is not a substitute for the understanding of humans, but it nevertheless furnishes excellent models and is a fertile field for developing and testing hypotheses. With respect to the question of the effects of early experience upon adult personality, research with animals is becoming increasingly important as a basis for hypotheses about human behavior. The variables involved are being systematically tested on a large scale; the adult consequences are being more carefully specified and measured. The rat and the monkey are now joined by many other species in the laboratory, and correlations with humans are being evaluated. Direct observation of various species in nature and in approximately natural settings is also casting much light on human behavior (Lorenz, 1935, 1952; Ostow, 1960).

THE CROSS-CULTURAL APPROACH

This approach to the problem of early influences on adult behavior consists of a comparison between different cultures or subcultures. Different cultures may be regarded as experiments in the problem of the nature of human development. They may furnish invaluable information about the ways in which widely varying early experiences affect later personality.

Specific childhood variables are selected and correlated with differences in the adult personality predominating in the different cultures. The uncontrollable variables—geographic, social, political, cultural, genetic, and others—are many. The diversity itself, however, may prove to be fruitful for the understanding of the laws of human behavior. The anthropologist, Whiting, states: "The advantages of the cross-cultural method are twofold. . . . First, it ensures that findings relate to human behavior in general rather than being bound to a single culture, and second, it increases the range of variation of many of the variables" (Whiting and Child, 1953).

THE RECONSTRUCTIVE APPROACH

Although the cross-sectional method may use reconstructive data, the term has commonly been reserved for the clinical method of psychoanalysis in which adult patients give data about their childhood as they remember it, and in which dreams, associations, feelings, and behavior reveal emotional patterns that can be traced to childhood.

Commonly listed as weaknesses of the method, from a scientific point of view, are the subjective nature of the data, the fallacies of human memory, and the difficulties of obtaining independent data to validate the statements made. The psychoanalytic situation nevertheless has a number of unique advantages that are apt greatly to reduce bias in the data and to offset the weaknesses. First, the verbal communications given in therapeutic sessions that are contaminated by such factors as defensiveness, carelessness, and distortions of memory are less likely to go undetected as such than are the responses given in the questionnaires or in the single interviews on which many research projects rely. It is also probably true that statements made in the psychoanalytic situation are generally less likely to be contaminated. Psychoanalysis can reasonably be expected to reflect more accurately a person's actual subjective feelings and attitudes as well as his otherwise unobservable behavior. Furthermore, as the treatment usually lasts for months or years, the therapist gets to know his patient's personality extremely well and, if he is of a scientific mind, he has many opportunities to make and to check predictions.

The psychoanalyst usually sees a select group of patients in terms of educational and socioeconomic conditions. Admittedly, his research population is restricted. Actually, he should therefore confine his conclusions to the same restricted population. On this point the temptation to err is great and many fail because of the consistency of the findings. In case after case, without exception, unfortunate early experiences are found to characterize patients with adult difficulties. The rigorous scientist may challenge the psychoanalyst's claim that the former lead to the latter without establishing that persons free of the symptoms are also free of the damaging early experience. The psychoanalyst, however, sees more than simple correlations between childhood and adult disturbances. He can trace, in great detail, patterns of specific disorders in the adult back through the years to specific origins in childhood which, moreover, not infrequently can be confirmed from other sources. These are only a few points in the evaluation of psychoanalysis as a research tool (cf. Alexander, 1948; Waelder, 1960).

RESEACH REVELANT TO HYPOTHESES A and B

> Hypothesis *A*: The earlier an influence impinges upon the developing personality, the more pervasive and significant are its effects.

> Hypothesis *B*: Exceptions to hypothesis *A* concern functions that are most susceptible to influences during critical periods, which occur most frequently early in life.

In reviewing studies of factors that determine the effects of early experiences upon the behavior of mature animals, King (1958) lists seven important variables: (1) the age of the animal when the early experience occurred; (2) the age of the animal at the time of the test; (3) duration or quantity of the early experience; (4) type or quality of the experience; (5) type of the performance task required by the adult animal; (6) methods for testing persistence of the effects; (7) relation of the experience to the genetic background of the animal. The approach demands that the researcher first try to predict the effects of each of these variables separately, and then try to unravel the interactions between them. King concludes that ". . . until the effects of the seven variables are analyzed further, it is possible to accept only the general hypothesis that early experiences affect later behavior."

Recent systematic studies pose the following questions: (1) Is there a relationship between age and the effect of an influence? (2) If so, is this relationship a monotonic function compatible with *A*? (3) Or is it a more complex function that might fit the critical period of *B*? (4) Does it fit neither hypothesis?

Among many studies under each of the following headings, only those are discussed that dwell specifically on the variable age of the subject at the time of the influence studied.

IMPRINTING

Imprinting refers to a certain type of study of critical periods in the early development of animals. Its relevance to human development has not been established. Lorenz (1935) introduced the term to designate the infant bird's early ability to recognize and to follow its parent. Psychologists in studying the phenomenon have varied the age of the bird at the time of exposure to its parents and to other objects. These studies have been extended to other animals and to a variety of substitutes for parents, including parents of other species as well as inanimate objects. They invariably show that the age of the imprinted animal at the time of exposure to the object of imprinting is of paramount importance (Frisch, 1957; Gottlieb, 1961; Gray, 1963; Gray and Howard, 1957; Hess, 1958, 1959a, 1959b, 1959c; Jaynes, 1957; Moltz, 1960). Without exception, imprinting can take place only during a specified time, very early in the animal's life. This period varies from species to species. The results, in so far as they are applicable to hypothesis *B,* are in accordance with it.

Tests of imprinting were initiated at various hours after hatching in neonate chicks (Jaynes, 1959). The imprinting object in this study was a green, seven-inch cube, which was presented to the subjects for a thirty-minute period. At the age of ten days, the animals were given a retention test. The results showed that the percentage of animals imprinted declined steadily from ninety percent, one to six hours after hatching, to zero, fifty-four to sixty hours after hatching. Other studies that have used a finer scale for the time variable find that imprinting often fails to take place in the very first hours of life. Hess (1958) reports that some imprinting occurred immediately after the birth of mallard ducks but that it was most effectively acquired at about sixteen hours after hatching. Many studies on different species give comparable results.

Two explanations have been offered to account for these effects. One holds that the critical period for imprinting is determined by the animal's perceptual development. According to this view, the critical period coincides with the earliest age at which the animal is perceptually capable of recognizing an object and able to remember it. It is a common finding that the older the animal (within the critical period), the more vigorous is its response and the greater its degree of retention. This finding has been considered to support the theory of minimal perceptual development. The second explanation assumes that the end of the critical period corresponds to the age at which the first emotional response occurs (Hess, 1959a, 1959b, 1959c). Moltz (1960), however, reasons that during the early hours of its life—when the animal imprints or becomes aware of a close object in its environment—fear reactions are minimal. This desirable state of freedom from anxiety becomes associated with being near the object. When, later, unfamiliar conditions arouse anxiety, the animal reacts as if the imprinted object is reassuring. To remain close to the object, the animal may have to follow it, as it does with a "following response" as soon as it becomes mobile.

These explanations are of special interest for those who find in them implications for human behavior as well. Gray and Howard (1957), for example, speculate that imprinting may prove to have conditioned those who later become criminals because of formative negative experiences during a few weeks of infantile fearfulness. They also speculate about the influences that may make adopted children wild and incorrigible when taken from institutions to private homes.

SENSORY DEPRIVATION AND RELATED STUDIES

Studies of sensory deprivation illustrate dramatically that even basic perceptual development, rather than being solely maturational, is significantly influenced by early environmental stimulation. For example, Riesen (1960) subjected chimpanzees and kittens to total darkness, varying the duration of the deprivation. He reports chemical and atrophic changes in the retina that were not only pronounced but also irreversible in those cases where the deprivation extended from birth throughout infancy.

Nearer to our interest in personality development are time studies of food deprivation. In Hunt's study (1944), which is the classic, two hereditarily equal groups of rats were observed; one half of each group was subjected to deprivation while the other half was used for control purposes. The deprivation consisted of fifteen days of very restricted feeding. For one group this started on the twenty-fourth day of life; for the other, it began on the thirty-second day of life. Control animals from both groups were freely fed. Following the experiment, all rats were allowed free feeding for five months during which time Hunt measured the amount of food hoarded by the now adult animals. The rats that had been part of the twenty-four-day-old group hoarded approximately two and a half times as many pellets as the controls. The rats that had been in the thirty-two-day-old group hoarded approximately the same amount as the controls. These results neatly confirm hypothesis *A*, that the earlier the influence, the more powerfully effective it is.

HANDLING AND SHOCK

In a contrasting type of study, animals are stimulated either by handling or by electric shock. The shock, usually from a wired floor, is always unpleasant although entirely harmless. Handling consists of holding the animal, stroking it, or otherwise touching it. The handling or, as it is sometimes called, gentling, illustrates a point made earlier in the discussion of the applicability of animal studies to human functioning. What it means to a rat to be handled by human hands is questionable, but experimenters who are particularly fond of rats tend to interpret it as pleasure and comfort, whereas others think it must be dreadful for the rat. Possibly these different feelings and interpretations may in part be responsible for the different results that have been obtained in studies of time factors in handling as related to later behavior.

Gertz (1957) handled rats at various early ages and later tested them for emotionality. As adults the rats failed to show significant differences. Gertz concluded that there is no evidence for either the earliest age or any other critical age at which handling is influential in later behavior. A study by Denenberg and Karas (1959) yielded different results. They tested both rats and mice. One group was handled from age one to age ten days, another from eleven to twenty days, and a third group from one to twenty days. For each time group there was a corresponding control group. The adults were tested for weight, mortality, and resistance to stress. Results showed that the group handled from first to tenth day survived stresses better than the other two groups. Among the rats, the one-to-twenty group weighed the most and lived the longest. However, the one-to-twenty group of mice had the shortest life span of all the mice.

If the results of these studies are valid, a great many variables need further exploration before the results can be meaningfully compared. For instance, aspects that vary without being controlled in the two studies are duration of periods of handling and the effect variable chosen for adult study; also the differences of species in the second study need further exploration.

In an earlier well-known study, lambs were raised exclusively on a bottle by Scott (1951). He varied the time of initiation and the duration of the bottle feeding, which also involved handling. The adult test consisted in observing the lamb's social behavior in its own flock. All the experimental lambs showed some indifference to the flock and even to their own baby lambs. The timing of the initial period away from the flock made a significant difference; the most profoundly affected lambs never learned to adapt socially to the flock nor to relate to its movement. Since the most effective time period was not the earliest but rather an intermediary one, Scott found his results to speak strongly for the existence of a critical period. Meier and Stuart (1959) report concordant findings in their experiments with Siamese kittens (cf. Meyers, 1962).

Two well-designed studies (Brookshire *et al.,* 1961) explored the age at the time of a shock trauma in rats as related to adults' escape learning and shock avoidance.* One of the studies compared adult performance in rats who had been shocked at twenty and thirty days of age, respectively. The other study did a similar comparison on rats shocked at twenty and one hundred and twenty days of age, respectively.

> With regard to the notion of critical periods our data are essentially negative. We may answer the question of age at time of treatment by comparing experimental groups A (traumatized at one hundred and twenty days of age) and C (traumatized at twenty days of age), since these groups were equated with regard to

*Escape learning here means being trained to run across charged flooring to escape further shock. Shock avoidance, or avoidance learning, refers to learning to avoid shock altogether by changing location on signal.

all other significant variables. . . . In both escape learning and avoidance learning no differences were found. It appears then that age is not an important factor. The hypothesis that infantile traumatic experiences more severely affect an organism was not substantiated in this experiment.

Denenberg and Bell (1960) report a similar study except that mice were used as subjects. Their findings give a possible clue to the variable most responsible for the results of the above studies, namely, the voltage. They varied the age at which different levels of shock (i.e., different voltages) were administered to baby mice. They found that mice shocked during infancy had an easier time mastering avoidance learning as adults if the magnitude of shock had been low. An intense shock, however, produced an interference so that all experimental subjects did more poorly than controls in adult avoidance learning. In terms of the effect of age at shocking, there was some evidence of a critical period at low shock levels (cf. Denenberg, 1963).

INSTITUTIONALIZATION AND MATERNAL SEPARATION

In the 1940s, Goldfarb (1943), Ribble (1943), and Spitz (1945, 1946) published studies documenting the pervasive and permanent ill effects of inadequate mothering during early infancy. The impact of these studies was considerable and led to the establishment of a new branch of scientific inquiry, commonly termed maternal deprivation (Glaser and Eisenberg, 1956). Two independent surveys of the literature on maternal deprivation have been published, one by Yarrow (1961), the other by Casler (1961). Both authors comment that the concept of maternal deprivation is a mixed one. Yarrow observes that at least four quite different conditions of abnormal mothering have been included under this heading: institutionalization; separation from a mother or mother substitute; multiple mothering (several persons at the same time or in quick succession); distortions in the nature of mothering in terms of domination, indifference, and the like. A further complication is that few studies have been confined to the main variable under study. Separations, for example, are often a consequence of distorted mother-child relationships; institutionalization often involves multiple mothering; distortions of the normal mother-child relations occur much more frequently in institutions.

A number of other factors compound the complexity of the details. Conditions in institutions vary greatly; without adequate description in these studies, their effects cannot be appraised. Casler observes that reasons for maternal separation from a child similarly cover a wide range. The separation from a loving but physically fragile mother may mean something very different than separation from a neglectful mother. Genetic or constitutional factors may also interact with aspects of mothering. To a higher degree than in the general population, childen in institutions are in some way defective at birth, or they are the offspring of parents who are unable to care properly for them, be it for mental, physical, or economic reasons. Page (1955) voices the same thought in his discussion of Spitz's work: "The absence of adequate experimental controls leaves room for doubt. Might it not be that infants kept in institutions for long periods are biologically less favored than infants who are adopted or placed in foster homes after a brief stay in an institution?" Casler suggests that " . . . women in our culture, unless they be unwed mothers, do not ordinarily yield their babies to institutions. Children who are in institutions cannot, therefore, be regarded as comprising a random sample from a larger population." One possible effect of the mother's unwed status is a greater intensity of anxiety during pregnancy. That anxiety during pregnancy may have an adverse effect on the offspring is suggested by numerous studies (Ader *et al.,* 1963; Ferreira, 1960; Kaplan and Thompson, 1957; Mintz, 1958; Montagu, 1962; Norris, 1960; Pasamanick *et al.*, 1956; Sontag, 1958; Stott, 1957).

The problems of research design, choice and suitability of measuring instruments, selection of samples, statistical methods, and so forth, enter into the comparisons of studies of maternal deprivation as they do in other comparisons of research work. It is nevertheless possible to make comparisons and draw tentative conclusions on the basis of these studies, particularly with the help of the contributions furnished by Yarrow and Casler.

In studies varying the age factor, the age of six months emerges repeatedly as a crucial period. Spitz (1946) and Bowlby (1956) have both observed that it is at approximately six months that the infant first appears capable of distinguishing the mother from other persons. In one of his earlier studies on "affectionless thieves," Bowlby (1944) notes: "In practically all these cases, the separation which appears to have been pathogenic occurred after the age of six months. This suggests that there is a lower age limit before which separation, while perhaps having undesirable affects, does not necessarily produce the particular results we are concerned with here—the affectionless and delinquent character."

Other investigators have explicitly or implicitly (by choice of ages studied) confirmed the importance of the six-months stage (Beres and Obers, 1950; Bridges, 1932; Drever, 1955; Schaffer, 1958). Schaffer and Callender (1959), investigating effects of early hospitalization, report a related finding:

> Two main syndromes, each associated with a particular age range, have emerged from this study of the effects of hospitalization in infancy. The findings parallel those of Spitz and suggest two developmental stages: a global and a differentiated. The latter, centering around the differentiation of self and environment, appears to be essentially continuous with the adult

> form, and only when it has been obtained can object relations by specific persons be established. The global stage . . . is quite different and certain life experiences may have quite a distinct meaning according to the developmental phase of the individual. The present study . . . suggests that the crucial factor in hospitalization at the differentiated stage is maternal deprivation, whereas, at the global stage, it is perceptual deprivation.

Beres and Obers (1950) report that of four cases that showed mental retardation, all were admitted to the institution before six months of age; four children who developed schizophrenia were admitted to the institution at a later age. Despite serious methodological flaws, particularly that the selection of subjects was not random but was biased in a pathological direction, the findings are suggestive in that they confirm a hypothesis that may easily have been derived on the basis of Schaffer's results. This hypothesis might be framed thus: If it is true that institutionalization before the age of six months constitutes perceptual deprivation and after six months maternal deprivation, and if it is true that early institutionalization constitutes an experience significant enough to inflict lasting effects, then institutionalization prior to six months of age might be a factor in causing mental dullness or perceptual distortions, whereas after age six months it would produce interpersonal difficulties.

The first six months having thus been confirmed as a sort of critical period, what then are the relationships of institutionalization and maternal separation to the age of the child after six months? Yarrow (1961) sums up the situation: "Psychoanalytic theories regarding the significance of early experience for later development have often been interpreted as postulating that the younger the organism, the more severe and fixed the effects of an environmental impact." Only limited data are available on human subjects. Ribble (1943) tends to interpret her data on maternal rejection as supporting this point of view. The retrospective studies of Bender (1945, 1947) and Goldfarb

(1945) suggest that the younger the child, the more damaging the effects of deprivation and stress. Some animal research supports this hypothesis (Seitz, 1959); other studies do not (Beach and Jaynes, 1954; King, 1958). A more refined hypothesis regarding the significance of the timing of experiences is the critical phase hypothesis. This theory holds that there are points in the developmental cycle during which the organism may be particularly sensitive to certain kinds of events or most vulnerable to specific types of deprivation or stress. Several animal studies (Moltz, 1960; Scott, *et al.,* 1951; Tinbergen, 1954) support the general outline of the critical phase hypothesis. It could be added that the studies by Liddell (1961) and Freedman, *et al.* (1961) also belong in this group. Both used isolation as the experimental variable (with or without extra stress introduced) to study the time factor in the development of relationships with members of the same species. Both studies confirm the hypothesis of a critical period.

Yarrow makes the following key points.

> Although the general consensus in the literature is that maternal separation which occurs before the child is five years of age is likely to be most damaging, the findings are not sufficiently clear to pin-point any one age as being most vulnerable. . . . One might postulate differing vulnerabilities at different periods of development. The developmental level of the child is likely to influence the significance of deprivation for the meaning of a separation experience for him. With regard to separation, the period during which the child is in process of consolidating a relationship with his mother may be an especially vulnerable one. Also significant may be the developmental stage with regard to memory functions. After the point in development at which the child can sustain an image of the mother in her absence and can anticipate her return, the meaning of a brief separation may be less severe than at an earlier developmental period.

Yarrow also suggests that the degree of autonomy the child has achieved, his ability to talk, and other such capacities, may affect the degree of severity that institutionalization or separation imposes on the child.

> There may also be age-linked effects of different types of deprivation. Some animal studies suggest that a minimal level of stimulation may be necessary to produce the biochemical changes for the development of the underlying stress structures. Deprivation in certain sensory modalities may be more significant at one age than at another . . . social deprivation may be most damaging during the earliest period of the development of social responses.

Unfortunately there are almost no data available on the effect of institutionalization and separation at different ages, systematically varied. A publication of the World Health Organization (1964) offers further pertinent discussion on maternal deprivation and its effects.

DISTORTIONS IN MOTHER-CHILD RELATIONSHIP

There have been numerous studies of mother-child interaction, but few have explored the effect of certain patterns of mothering at different ages of development.

Studies by a group conducting research on animals are relevant to the present topic (Ader, *et al.,* 1960). These authors found that rats were more susceptible to ulcer if they were separated from their mothers at fifteen days of age rather than at twenty-one days. Another study has more the character of distortions in mother-child relations in that the conditions consisted of interruption in the mother-child interaction. These interruptions consisted in one-half hour to five and one-quarter hour periods in which the mother was not present. Two sets of experimental and control groups were used. One set was submitted to the interruption during the first ten days of life and the second set during the second ten days of life. The results showed that the former group was significantly more resistant to gastric ulcers than animals experiencing the same interruption during the later period.

Some authors distinguish an autistic phase of development in human beings. During this period of time the newborn child is not yet psychologically very different from his prenatal state. This is followed by a symbiotic phase beginning at about three months (Mahler *et al.*, 1959). It may be, however, that one or two weeks after normal birth, the infant begins to relate to the mother. This may well be the beginning of imprinting for the human young and there may be serious consequences if the child becomes ready to relate to and attach himself to his mother and is prevented from doing so.

To summarize the material reviewed under hypotheses *A* and *B*: drastically withholding food from experimental animals and depriving others of sensory stimuli gave results compatible with hypothesis *A* (the earlier the influence, the greater its effects); and studies of imprinting have yielded results supporting hypothesis *B* (there are critical periods of special vulnerability). Handling of animals and moderate shock sometimes supported hypothesis *B*, but negative findings were not uncommon. Institutionalization and separation of human children from their mothers showed the first six months as a critical period that affected later social development. Studies of mother-child relationships reported that the first year was critical for the development of psychosomatic traits. Whenever critical periods were found (hypothesis *B*), these occurred early in life (cf. Meyers, 1962).

Hypothesis *A* (the earlier the influence, the greater its effects) is the general concept; hypothesis *B* (there are critical periods of special vulnerability) is a refinement. It might be that the closer an influence on the personality coincides in time with the early emergence of the function affected by the influence, the more pervasive are its effects. The greatest effect will ensue if an influence impinges upon a function just as it is becoming established. This formulation encompasses both *A* and *B*. Results compatible with either of these seem also to be compatible with this formulation. It also would relate to the idea of specific emotional vulnerabilities (Saul, 1960).

RESEARCH REVELANT TO HYPOTHESES C and D

Hypothesis *C*: The fundamental characteristics of the personality are established by the age of approximately six years.

Hypothesis *D*: Once formed, the personality pattern remains fairly constant throughout life.

By "fundamental characteristics" of the personality is meant the main basic motivations. (These have been discussed in some detail in chap. 3.) "Personality pattern" refers to the individual constellation or patterning of these motivations.

The longitudinal approach has great advantages for testing these hypotheses. A careful study using this method was done by the Fels Research Institute. Originated and directed by Sontag, the Fels group during its more than thirty years of operation has studied a variety of developmental variables. Of special relevance to hypotheses *C* and *D* is a project reported by Kagan and Moss (1960, 1963) on the stability of certain behavior over a period of time. In addition to the constancy or stability of motivations or, as the authors express it, "motive-related behavior," the study also investigated sources of anxiety, defensive responses, and modes of personal interaction from earliest childhood through young adulthood. The specific variables measured were passivity and dependency, aggression, achievement and recognition, heterosexuality and sexual identification, tendencies to withdraw, and maternal treatment of the child.

The Fels investigators defined motives as a variable intervening between an identifiable class of stimuli (incentives), on the one hand, and overt goal-directed responses, on the other. The desire for recognition from the social environment; naturalness and affection from friends, parents, and love objects; mastery of attack; sexual stimulation; coactivity with peers; and perception of a state of injury or anxiety in others (aggression) are the major motivational systems studied in the present research. The investigators concentrated their efforts on quantifying overt goal responses and in most cases avoided placing themselves in the position of assessing motive strength.

The subjects were eighty-nine white middle-class children who, with their parents, had been enrolled in the Fels longitudinal program from birth during the period 1929 to 1939, and who continued the contact with the Institute until early adulthood or longer. The data in childhood were collected in interviews with the subject and with the mother, by observations of them in their homes and in school, by school grades, and by a variety of tests. The childhood period was divided into four parts: birth to three, three to six, six to ten, and ten to fourteen years. On the basis of the data, each subject was rated on forty-eight variables for each of the four age periods. To illustrate the nature of these variables, it may be noted that in the area of aggression some of the variables were "aggression to mother," "physical aggression to peers," "indirect aggression to peers," "behavioral disorganization," "conformity," "competitiveness," and the like. The data for assessment during adult life were obtained by interviews and by extensive testing. Ratings of test results were organized into the same categories as the childhood data except for maternal treatment and physical fear. The numerical data thus consisted of the ratings of forty-eight variables for each of four time periods.

In summarizing their conclusions, the authors found that the most consistent finding of the entire study was that much of the behavior exhibited during the age period six to ten, and some during the age period three to six, provided moderately good predictors of theoretically related behavior during early adulthood. Passive withdrawal from dreaded situations, dependency on family or love objects, ease of arousal to anger, involvement in intellectual tasks, and the pattern of sexual behavior in adulthood were related to the child's behavioral disposition during the early years. These results thus give strong support to the concept that the adult personality begins to take form during early childhood. The Fels investigators sum up their findings this way.

> However, the degree of continuity of a class of responses was intimately dependent upon its congruency with traditional sex role values. The differential stability of dependency, aggression, and sexuality for males and females emphasizes the importance of cultural roles in determining both behavior change and stability.
>
> Passivity and dependency are subjected to cultural disapproval for men; aggression and sexuality are disproportionately punished for women. School-age passivity and dependency were related to adult withdrawal and dependent behavior for women but not for men. School-age aggression and preadolescent heterosexual behavior predicted corresponding adult dependencies for men but not for women.
>
> Intellectual mastery . . . which was rewarded for both sexes, showed continuity for both males and females from the early school years through adulthood. Social class membership is an additional variable relevant for particular sex role values. Certain behaviors (e.g., interest in art and music) would be more acceptable to middle class than to lower class males, and vocational aspirations are, of course, highly dependent upon social class position. Thus knowledge of the sex and social class of a child allows one to make an unusually large number of predictions about his future interests, goals, vocational choice, and dependent, aggressive, sexual, and mastery behaviors.

Further studies should uncover variables, other than social class and sexual traits, that effect changes in behavior. In this way, the accuracy of the predictions that can be made on the basis of childhood behavior will increase.

As mentioned, the Fels group did not measure motives, which they defined as intervening variables not directly measurable. They dealt instead with what they termed motive-related behavior. The variables classified under each main heading in the Fels material appear to fit well with accepted definitions of motives in the psychoanalytic sense. It can therefore be concluded that the findings reported by the Fels group on the whole confirm the constancy hypothesis on selected aspects of aggressivity, passivity, dependency, involvement in intellectual tasks, social ambitiousness, and patterns of sexual behavior and identification.

During the years from six to ten, the child exhibits behavior that is significantly related to his behavior as an adult. With some variables this also held true for the second age period, from three to six years. For instance, the sex-role content of boy's play during ages three to six was predictive of their adult sexual interest. Competitiveness and involvement in grossly mechanical motor and aggressive games during the preschool years were sensitive indicators of sex-role behavior twenty years later. Choice of vocation was also roughly predictable from the activities of children three to six years old. Another motive established very early in both sexes was social anxiety.

> Inhibition and tension with peers during early school years was predictive of social anxiety in adulthood for both sexes. For boys, the continuity of this anxiety was traceable to the first three years of life. Inhibited and nonspontaneous approach to strangers during the first three years was significantly associated with social anxiety in adulthood. For girls, the same relationship was not established until age ten.

As mentioned, most of the significant variables were stabilized by six to ten years of age, the behavior shown by then made it possible to offer fairly reliable predictions of a similar adult pattern. It should be noted that behavior that establishes this high coefficient of stability between childhood and maturity does not emerge suddenly at the age when it becomes significantly evident. It grows steadily, especially from the three-to-six period. In almost all cases there are high correlations between ages three to six and between the latter and the ten-to-fourteen period.

Tuddenham (1959) reports a more dynamically oriented follow-up of constancy in personality. At the early part of the study his subjects were teenagers for whom extensive personality ratings were available. Nineteen years later he had them rated again. He then correlated the two ratings on each variable to estimate stability of the variables. The results differed for the sexes in that, for example, the aggressive ratings were more constant for men and the desire for social prestige topped the list for women. That the subjects were adolescents when they were first tested detracts from the value of the study; however, it is noteworthy that the results agree very closely with those of the Fels group.

Another follow-up study (O'Neal and Robins, 1959) compared the rate of adult deviance among those who, as patients in child guidance clinics, had been "runners away" with those who had committed other offenses. As adults those who ran away had far higher rates of arrests and incarceration, of divorce, and of the diagnosis of sociopathic personality. The data give little information about precisely what personality variables in childhood are related to adult functioning. No doubt the nature of the data made difficult the task of determining variables. There are, of course, many reasons for running away, for arrest, divorce, and other deviations; but you may safely generalize that there was continuity of maladaptation (cf. Gesell and Thompson, 1941; Gregory, 1958; Kuhlen and Thompson, 1963; McKinnon, 1942; Mussen *et al.,* 1963; Neilon, 1948).

In summary, although not all variables measured by

these studies showed childhood-to-adulthood continuity, the bulk of the data do support hypotheses *C* and *D*. Thus, certain functions of personality are definitely formed in early childhood and certain social and cultural traits and maladjustments tend to remain constant in the personality. Of course, this does not mean that alterations cannot take place through inner growth and development, from remedial experiences in living, and as a result of treatment.

RESEARCH REVELANT TO HYPOTHESES E and F

Hypothesis *E*: Given adequate conditions for physical survival, the most important external influence is the emotional relationship between a child and his parents (or parental substitutes).

Hypothesis *F*: The most relevant aspects of the child's emotional milieu are parental warmth, parental control in accordance with his needs, and stability in his relationship to his parents.

Rigorous scientific evidence, as opposed to clinical observation, that bears down upon the above two hypotheses is scanty. Our discussion will therefore have to be fairly brief and speculative.

Studies of imprinting have relevance to hypotheses *E* and *F*. In simplest terms imprinting means the formation of an attachment. This attachment is normally to the mother. If the young animal is removed from the mother during the critical period, it still can attach itself to substitutes, even inanimate ones. If no substitute is provided, the young animal may die. Liddell (1961) separated one of twin kids from a mother goat. The one died, while the other twin, left with its mother, thrived. In another experiment a litter of puppies is left in a field with the mother and kept from any contact whatever with humans. If they are so kept for fourteen weeks, they permanently lose their capacity to become attached to human beings (Lorenz, 1952). Ducklings and goslings separated from their mother during the critical period attached themselves to Lorenz if he squatted as they followed him; but if he stood, they then attached themselves to his boots only.

When normal imprinting is disrupted, the animal's capacity to attach itself and relate to its own species is disordered as are many of its physiological functions.

It is characteristic of psychotic children that they are unable to establish attachments to anyone. It is not known whether this is a result of some form of mistreatment or gross neglect during the period when infants are normally helplessly dependent on their mothers, or whether this arises from some other cause. Spitz, in addition to his writings (Spitz, 1945, 1951, 1954, 1955; Spitz and Wolf, 1946), made a film showing that children separated from their mothers at five months and placed in foundling homes where they had excellent physical care but no love developed severe depressions and physical disorders, a considerable number ending in death. Bowlby (1944, 1956, 1957, 1960, 1961; Bowlby *et al.*, 1956; Bowlby and Cantab, 1953), who has studied the reactions of infants and young children to separation from their mothers, distinguished three states: protest, despair, and withdrawal. These likewise demonstrate the vital importance of the natural biological need for a mother and the dire, irreversible effects that you would reasonably expect to find when such a necessity is withheld or otherwise interfered with.

The fact that the helplessly dependent infant is biologically conditioned to such completely symbiotic attachments leads parents, whose biological instincts may have become attenuated or perverted, to treat their young in ways that are injurious to them. Their infants may be made to become too dependent, may be coldly neglected, may be abused by threats and punitive discipline, or they may be exploited in other ways that are directly or inferentially observed by psychoanalysts. It seems likely that a healthy attachment, responded to by love and disciplinary guidance, may perhaps determine the difference between neurosis and psychosis.

Harlow's experiments are now famous (1959a, 1959b; Harlow and Harlow, 1962; Harlow and Zimmerman, 1959; Seay *et al.,* 1962). Baby monkeys who were separated from their mothers were exposed in a small enclosure to a nearly vertical role of chicken wire with a milk-yielding nipple protruding from the center. Next to it was another roll, identical except for being covered with terry-cloth toweling. Given a choice, each baby monkey clung to the latter cloth-covered roll. Varying the nipple showed that it played no part in the choice. In another experiment, baby monkeys who were separated from their mothers and apparently handled very little by humans, were frightened by a mechanical face with flashing lights for eyes and grossly flapping parts. A baby monkey with no previous cloth "mother" ran as far as it could from this contraption and buried its face in its hands; but a baby monkey accustomed to a cloth "mother" rushed to it and clung to it. All of these baby monkeys showed severe disorders when they became adults: they were unable to relate to other monkeys or to the group, and their sex lives were deranged. When attentions of normal males were forced upon the unwilling females, the latter turned out to be sterile, only four out of forty-six becoming pregnant. Here the profound permanent effects of early maternal deprivation are dramatically demonstrated.

This type of study is a step toward achieving a detailed evaluation of hypothesis *F,* concerned with the most important elements in mothering for the child. It shows that sensory comfort in a "mother" is more important to the baby monkey than the feeding function, but that the properties of being alive and belonging to the same species are immensely more important than the sensory comfort alone. What particular aspects of the natural mother are crucial still remain to be established.

Perhaps the three best known principles of learning theory are those of frequency, primacy, and motivation. All seem to combine to make it likely that the parent's (or substitute's) influence on the small child is very great. The parent is usually the child's first or primary contact; the parent, usually the mother, is the most frequent one in the early years; and the parent is the one whose approval the child is most highly motivated to obtain. Under the combined impact of these three principles, the child can be expected to learn very well what the parent teaches him. What the parent teaches him is done partly consciously, in terms of skills and controls, and partly unconsciously and involuntarily, in terms of emotional interrelations. Moreover, the child tends to be like the parent, to take over his attitudes and feelings, to identify with him. The parents may, of course, not be the only influence on the child's learning and so ultimately on his personality. Siblings and other significant persons can also be important, but the parent appears to be the most important influence.

RESEARCH REVELANT TO HYPOTHESES G and H

> Hypothesis *G*: To the extent that ideal conditions prevail, maturation proceeds to the fullest and the individual eventually develops a mature personality, that is, he becomes a responsible, productive adult of good will.
>
> Hypothesis *H*: Any deviation from ideal conditions is necessarily detrimental, and the greater the deviation, the more thwarted the maturation will be and the more intensive and extensive becomes the pathology of the personality.

Traditionally there has always been a relative lack of interest within the field of personality study in what makes people healthy as compared to what makes people sick or maladjusted. Recent trends have shown a modification of this attitude. Considering first the dimension of warmth versus hostility, the publication by Bayley and Schaefer (1960) on the results of the Berkeley Growth Study is relevant. They found that early warmth and affection in mothers are associated with calm, happy, cooperative behavior in boys at most of the preadolescent age levels. For girls, the correlation between early maternal affection and friendly cooperative behavior tends to decrease with age. It is curious that the strongest relationship between maternal warmth and friendly behavior in girls occurs at the age when the same relationship is smallest in boys. There were no data on the influence of fathers on later behavior. A different pattern emerges when the mother's behavior is assessed during the child's adolescent period. These data show that hostile mothers have unhappy and hostile daughters and sons.

Slocum and Stone (1958), in a study of factors associated with family affection patterns, gave a questionnaire to more than two thousand teenagers in order to determine possible relationships between the subjects' perception of affection in their families and present behavioral variables. No striking relationships were found except that, on the whole, more benefits were shown to come from living in affectionate families than in ones where warmth is low. With respect to the autonomy-control variable, the findings appear even more consistent. Tsumori and Inage (1958) interviewed and observed mothers and children. They found that infants tend to show better development under permissive mothers who are in frequent contact with their infants than under autocratic mothers (cf. Hernstein, 1963). Of course, mothers showing different attitudes on strictness and frequency of contact may also have differed in other respects. However, the fact that alternative causation is possible does not detract from the significance of the relationship demonstrated between strictness and permissiveness and favorableness of development. Peck (1958) and Peck and Havighurst (1960) compared four dimensions of family interaction—consistency, democracy, mutual trust, and parental severity—with six dimensions of children's personality—ego strength, superego strength, willing social conformity, spontaneity, friendliness, and a hostility-guilt conflict. The results showed ego strength to be significantly correlated with stable and consistent family life in which there is mutual trust and approval between parents and child. Superego strength was related to ego strength and was associated with the same family factors but was not associated with severely autocratic rearing. Friendliness and spontaneity seem to arise from a lenient, democratic family atmosphere. The importance of stability and consistency was also reported by Scarpitti, *et al.* (1960), who found that boys originally selected as "good boys" in an area where the delinquency rate was high were found to continue to be good after several years, both in terms of their self-concept and their attitudes to parents and school. What particularly characterized the environment of these boys was a stable home life with few moves and few divorces or other destructive influences.

Baldwin, Kalhorn, and Bresse (1945) showed a very clear relationship between democratic child-rearing attitudes in the parents and psychological health in the offspring. Similarly, Watson (1957) found that greater freedom in the parental discipline was clearly associated with more initiative and independence, socialization and cooperation, less inner hostility and more friendliness, and a higher level of spontaneity and originality.

Thus, there is remarkable concordance among the studies in support of hypothesis *G*. Research relevant to hypothesis *H* (concerning the effects of various deviations from ideal conditions) is too extensive to be covered adequately. Only a small sample of studies can be considered here. As an aid in organizing the presentation, Schaefer's circumplex model of maternal behavior will be utilized. Its two perpendicular diameters consist of love-hostility and autonomy-control (approximately, permissiveness-domination). Other dimensions can be described in terms of their relation to the other two. For instance, indifference falls in the quadrant bordered by permissiveness and hostility; overprotectiveness falls in the quadrant limited by warmth and domination. The following parental influences will be discussed: parental rejection, overdomination, indifference or underdomination, overindulgence, and overprotection. Inconsistency will be treated separately.

PARENTAL REJECTION

Studies of maternal separation, which have been conducted with institutionalized children, may be grouped under rejection. As noted earlier, many investigators have reported extensive detrimental effects (Bowlby, 1957, 1960, 1961; Bowlby *et al.,* 1956; Bowlby and Cantab, 1953; Dennis and Najarian, 1957; Goldfarb, 1943, 1955; Maas, 1963; Spitz and Wolf, 1946). Bender's (1947) general conclusion is representative: "We found that children who had been emotionally deprived (usually by hospitalization) in the first several years showed personality damage beyond repair."

A great many studies of existing (not disrupted) parent-child relationships yield results that show that parental rejection without actual separation is also a strong determinant in the behavior of the child. Some investigators (Baldwin *et al.,* 1945; Radke, 1946) found that rejection in childhood leads either to shy and submissive qualities in the child or to aggressive, quarrelsome traits. These and other effects have been confirmed by Levy (1943). Redl and Wineman (1951) found that children who experienced extreme rejection and abuse show fear and anxiety, low frustration tolerance, irresponsibility, panic in novel situations, and great difficulty in reacting to failures. Symonds (1949) found rejected children to be fearful, hostile, overaggressive, and exhibiting antisocial behavior such as lying and stealing. Lewis (1955) found a particularly strong relationship between parental rejection and unsocialized aggression in the child. The findings of Redl and Wineman concerning difficulties in handling novel situations have been confirmed by Shirley (1942) and Heathers (1954). Peck (1958) found hostility and guilt in children to be associated with an unloving atmosphere in the home. Glueck and Glueck (1950) found, as have many others, that a high perecentage of juvenile delinquents come from homes lacking in parental warmth. A growing number of studies emphasize the importance of the father (Baker *et al.,* 1961; Hjelholt, 1958; Hoffman, 1960; Leichty, 1960; Mussen and Distler, 1960; Payne and Mussen, 1956; Sears *et al.,* 1957; Vogel, 1960).

Baker (1961) and Sears (1957) have also shown that there is a close relationship between hostility in the parents and aggression in the child. They have made particularly careful separate analyses of girls and boys in relation to the father and mother separately. Quantitative factors, of course, enter into whether a child responds with shyness and timidity or with overaggressiveness, or in other ways.

OVERDOMINATION

A great deal of research has been devoted to the results of domination. In terms of the child's behavior, it commonly leads to the constellation of shyness, submissiveness, dependency, difficulty in establishing friendships, self-consciousness, and dependability (Baldwin, 1948; Radke, 1946; Symonds, 1949). Mussen and Kagan (1958) demonstrated the submissiveness and conformity in an actual experimental situation. Using twenty-seven male college students, they first elicited TAT stories from them and then observed them individually in the Asch conformity situation. The results showed that a greater proporion of extreme conformists rather than independents perceived their parents as harsh, punitive, restrictive, and rejecting. It is suggested that tendencies to conformity are manifestations of basic personality structure and are influenced by early parent-child relations. Lewis (1955) found that strict and constraining parental behavior led to inhibited, neurotic behavior in the children seen in a clinic. Similarly, Peck (1958) found a hostility-guilt complex in the children of severely autocratic and disapproving parents.

In contrast to these studies, other investigations show

positive relationships between severity of strictness and aggressive, controlling behavior in the child. Bayley and Schaefer (1960) report that controlling mothers have sons who are rude, irritable, impulsive, and independent. In an experimental situation in which he allowed male college students to give him electro shocks, Hokanson (1961) found that the frequency of shocking was related to reported severity of punishment by parents during early life. In the same vein, Madoff (1959) reports that mothers of delinquent children are more primitive, more controlling, and more authoritarian than mothers of a group of control subjects. Bandura (1959) compared the family relations and child training practices of thirty aggressive and thirty withdrawn boys. Parents of the inhibited boys were shown consistently to deny the child an overt outlet for aggressive and dependent behavior. On the other hand, the parents of aggressive boys would not allow aggressive acts toward themselves but encouraged and reinforced aggression outside of the home. Another difference between these two types of parents was in their disciplinary methods, the former using guilt to enforce obedience and the latter directly punitive discipline.

Most studies of parent-child relationships of children or adults who are mentally disturbed, alcoholic, or criminal report some combination of rejection and untoward discipline (Abbe, 1958; Andrey, 1960; Becker *et al.,* 1959; Bethell, 1958; Brody, 1958; Cameron and Margaret, 1951; Caplan, 1961; Cline and Wangrow, 1959; Davits, 1958; Edel, 1962; Epstein and Westley, 1960; Finney, 1961; Frankel, 1959; Haley, 1960; Havighurst, 1963; Jenkins, 1960; Kagan, 1958; Kohn, 1963; Mohr, 1940; Monkman, 1958; Mussen, 1960; Palter, 1960; Pascal and Jenkins, 1960; Pringle *et al.,* 1958; Pulver, 1959; Reiner and Kaufman, 1959; Rosenthal *et al.,* 1959; Sears *et al.,* 1957; Slater, 1962; Sontag, 1952, 1955; Thompson, 1955; Wenar *et al.,* 1962; Winder and Rau, 1962).

The opposite poles from rejection and overdomination may be considered to be warmth and permissiveness or autonomy. These two have already been discussed under hypothesis *G*. Three additional parental attitudes occupy intermediate positions in the circumplex model: the detached or underdominating parent, the overprotective parent, and the overvaluing parent. The first of these belongs in the quadrant bordered by hostility and autonomy; the second two belong in the opposite quadrant bordered by warmth and control.

INDIFFERENCE OR UNDERDOMINATION

Insufficient control may be a manifestation of passive rejection and have undertones of neglect, but this is not always true. Bayley and Schaefer (1960) found some detached, ignoring mothers to have reserved, timid, polite sons, while Ausubel (1958), Levy (1943), and Cameron (1947) found a quite different clinical picture. The mothers studied by Bayley and Schaefer seem to be more indifferent, negative, and colder than those described by Ausubel. This, as well as other differences, may account for the differences in the children.

OVERINDULGENCE

According to Ausubel (1958) the overindulged child may be very much like the underdominated child. However, he is more used to dealing with adults and will modulate his behavior to obtain what he wants from them as well as their approval. His relationship with his peers is precarious, partly because he has not learned to compromise with their need satisfactions. Few studies have been done on the overindulged child. On the circumplex of parental behavior, overindulgence would be closer to warmth than to control. Extrapolating from the findings of the effects of warmth on the one hand and overdominance on the other, you would expect the indulged child to be considerably better off than the overprotected child, who more closely resembles the overdominated child.

OVERPROTECTION

Levy (1943) and Radke (1946) both describe overprotected children as lacking in skill, apprehensive, shy, anxious, and submissive. Ausubel adds that they are unable to defend their rights, are fearful, and tend to withdraw from peer relationships to the company of parents and adults. In novel situations or under stress, they feel and act inadequate (Shirley, 1942). It may be noted that in the descriptions of the overindulged and the overprotected child, there are no references to hostility, although clinical experience clearly shows that the overprotection and overindulgence produce attitudes and feelings that cause a strong sense of inferiority, making frustration inevitable; both the sense of inferiority and frustration produce hostility (Saul, 1960).

INCONSISTENCY

In the study by Peck (1958) stability and consistency in the family life were found to be significantly correlated with ego strength in the child. In a similar vein Scarpitti (1960) found, as mentioned, that the boys who stood out as "good" in an area with high delinquency, characteristically had very stable home environments. Inconsistency in parental attitudes has frequently also been held to be one of the determining factors in the etiology of schizophrenia (Bateson *et al.*, 1958; Haley, 1960; Reichard and Tillman, 1950). Eells (1960) has reported disturbances in animals as a reaction to inconsistent treatment.

Most studies support hypotheses *G* and *H*; that is, the more parental attitudes are characterized by love, warmth, permissive and democratic discipline, stability, tolerance, and security, the more emotionally healthy and well-adjusted is the child. Conversely, deviations from these ideal conditions result in various maladaptive attitudes on the part of the child and in failures and warpings of development that constitute and produce psychopathology, including man's hostility to man.

In sum, it seems unmistakable that the varied evidence supports the essential validity of the eight hypotheses described above and of the clinical formulation that the child he once was lives on in every adult. The long-range challenge to the behavioral sciences is to make a better world through avoiding the abuses in child-rearing, which make men of cruelty and violence instead of mature adults of good will.

REFERENCES

Abbe, A. E. (1968), Maternal attitudes toward children and their relationship to the diagnostic category of the child. *J. Genet. Psychol.,* 92: 167–173.

Ader, R., Beels, C. C., and Tatum, R. (1960), Social factors, affection emotionality and resistance to disease in animals. 2. Susceptibility to gastric ulceration as a function of interruptions and the time at which they occur. *J. Comp. Physiol. Psychol.,* 53: 455–458.

Ader, R., and Conklin, P. M. (1963), Handling of pregnant rats: Effects on emotionality of their offspring. *Science,* 142: 411–412.

Alexander, F. (1948), *Fundamentals of Psychoanalysis,* 23–33. New York: Norton.

Anderson, J. E. (1963), *Experience and Behavior in Early Childhood and the Adjustment of the Same Persons as Adults.* Univ. of Minnesota: Instit. of Child Development.

Andrey, R. G. (1960) *Delinquency and Parental Pathology.* London: Methuen.

Ausubel, D. P. (1958), *Theory and Problems of Child Development.* New York: Grune & Stratton.

Baker, J. W., and Holzworth, A. (1961), Social histories of successful and unsuccessful children. *Child Dev.,* 32: 135–149.

Baldwin, A. L. (1948), Socialization and the parent-child relationship. *Child Dev.,* 19: 127–136.

Baldwin, A. L., Kalhorn, J., and Breese, F. H. (1945), Patterns of parent behavior. *Psychol. Monogr.,* 58: no. 268.

Bandura, A., and Walters, R. H. (1959), *Adolescent Aggression: A Study of the Influence of Child-training Practices and Family Interrelationships.* New York: Ronald.

Bateson, G., Jackson, D., Haley, J., and Weakland, J. (1958), Toward a theory of schizophrenia. *Behav. Sci.,* 1: 251–264.

Bayley, N., and Schafer, E. S. (1960), Maternal behavior and personality development data from the Berkeley Growth Study. *Psychiat. Research Rep.,* 13: 155–175.

Beach, F. A., and Jaynes, J. (1954), Effects of early experience upon the behavior of animals. *Psychol. Bull.,* 51: 239–263.

Becker, W. C., Peterson, D. R., Hellmer, L. A., Shoemaker, D. J., and Quay, H. C. (1959), Factors in parental behavior and personality as related to problem behavior in children. *J. Consult. Psychol.,* 23: 107–118.

Bell, R. Q. (1960), Retrospective and prospective views on early personality development. *Merrill-Palmer Quart. Behav. Dev.,* 6: 131–144.

Bender, L. (1954), Infants reared in institutions: Permanently handicapped. *Bull. Child Welf. Leaque Amer.,* 24: 1–4.

——— (1947), Psychopathic behavior disorders in children. In *Handbook of Correctional Psychology,* ed. R. M. Lindner and R. V. Seliger, New York: Philosoph. Libr.

Benjamin, J. (1961), The innate and experiential in child development. In *Lectures on Experimental Psychiatry,* ed. H. W. Brosin. Pittsburgh: Univ. of Pittsburgh Press.

Beres, D., and Obers, S. J. (1950), The effects of extreme deprivation in infancy on psychic structure in adolescence: A study in ego development. In *The Psychoanalytic Study of the Child,* vol. 5. New York: Internat. Univ. Press.

Bethell, M. F. (1944), Restriction and habits in children. *Z. Kinderpsychiat.,* 25: 264–269.

Bowlby, J. (1961), Childhood mourning and its implication for psychiatry. *Amer. J. Psychiat.,* 118: 481–498.

——— (1960), Symposium on psychoanalysis and ethology. 2. Ethology and the development of object relations. *Internat. J. Psychoanal.,* 41: 313–317.

——— (1957), An ethologic approach to research in child development. *Brit. J. Med. Psychol.* 30: 230–240.

——— (1956), Mother-child separation. In *Mental Health and Infant Development,* ed. K. Soddy. New York: Basic Books.

——— (1944), Forty-four juvenile thieves. *Internat. J. Psychoanal.,* 25: 1–57.

Bowlby, J., Ainsworth, M., Boston, M., and Rosenbluth, D. (1956), The effects of mother-child separation: A follow-up study. *Brit. J. Med. Psychol.,* 39: 211–247.

Bowlby, J., and Cantab, J. (1953), Some pathological processes set in train by early mother-child separation. *J. Ment. Sci.,* 94: 265–272.

Bridges, K. M. B. (1932), Emotional development in early infancy. *Child Dev.,* 3: 324–341.

Brody, S. (1958), Signs of disturbance in the first year of life. *Amer. J. Orthopsychiat.,* 28: 362–367.

Brookshire, K. H., Littman, R. A., and Stewart, C. N. (1961), Residua of shock-trauma in the white rat: A three factor theory. *Psychol. Monogr.,* 75: no. 514.

Cameron, N. (1947), *The Psychology of Behavior Disorders: A Biosocial Interpretation.* Boston: Houghton Mifflin.

Cameron, N., and Margaret, A. (1951), *Behavior Pathology.* Cambridge, Mass.: Riverside Press.

Caster, L. (1961), Maternal deprivation: A critical review of the literature. *Monogr. Soc. for Research in Child Dev.,* 26: no. 80.

Cline, V. B., and Wangrow, A. S. (1959), Life history correlates of delinquent and psychopathic behavior. *J. Clin. Psychol.,* 15: 266–270.

Davits, J. R. (1958), Contributions of research with children to a theory of maladjustment. *Child Dev.,* 29 : 3–7.

Denenberg, V. H. (1963), Early experience and emotional development. *Scient. Amer.,* 131 : 227–228.

Denenberg, V. H., and Karas, C. G. (1959), Effects of differential infantile handling upon weight gain and mortality in the rat and mouse. *Science,* 130 : 629–630.

Dennis, W. (1955), Scientific models for the investigation of child development. In *Psychopathology of Childhood,* ed. P. H. Hoch and J. Zubin. New York: Grune & Stratton.

Dennis, W., and Najarian, P. (1957), Infant development under environmental handicap. *Psychol. Monogr.,* 71.

Drever, J. (1955), The concept of early learning. *Transactions N.Y. Acad. Sci.,* 17 : 463–469.

Edel, R. R. (1962), A study of the relationship between certain overt behavior difficulties in children and covert areas of personality in their mothers. *Dissertation Abstr.,* 23 : 1780–1781.

Eels, J. F. (1960), Inconsistency of early handling and its effect upon emotionality in the rat. *Dissertation Abstr.,* 21 : 1259.

Epstein, N. B., and Heider, G. M. (1959), *Prediction and Outcome: A Study in Child Development.* New York: Basic Books.

Ferreira, A. J. (1960), The pregnant woman's emotional attitude and its reflection on the newborn. *Amer. J. Orthopsychiat.,* 30 : 553–561.

Finney, J. C. (1961), Some maternal influences on children's personality and character. *Genet. Psychol. Monogr.,* 63 : 199–278.

Frankel, R. V. (1959), *A Review of Research on Parent Influences on Child Personality.* New York: Family Serv. Assn. Amer.

Frazee, H. E. (1953), Children who later become schizophrenic. *Smith Coll. Studies in Soc. Work.* 23 : 125–149.

Freedman, D. G., King, J. A., and Elliot, O. (1961), Critical period in the social development of dogs. *Science*, 133:1016–1017.

Frisch, O. (1957), Mit einer purpurreiher verheiratet (Married to a purple heron). *Z. Tierpsychol.*, 14:233–237.

Garn, S. (1957), Research in human growth. *Human Biology*, 29:1–11.

Gertz, B. (1957), The effect of handling at various age levels on emotional behavior in adult rats. *J. Comp. Physiol. Psychol.*, 50:613–616.

Gessel, A., and Thompson, H. (1941), Twins *T* and *C* from infancy to adolescence: A biogenetic study of individual differences by the method of co-twin control. *Genet. Psychol. Monogr.*, 24:3–121.

Glaser, K., and Eisenberg, L. (1956), Maternal deprivation. *Pediatrics*, 18:626–642.

Glueck, S., and Glueck, E. (1950), *Unraveling Juvenile Delinquency*. New York: The Commonwealth Fund.

Goldfarb, W. (1955), Emotional and intellectual consequences of psychological deprivation in infancy: A revaluation. In *Psychopathology of Childhood*, ed. P. H. Hoch and J. Zubin. New York: Grune & Stratton.

——— (1943), Infant rearing and problem behavior. *Amer. J. Orthopsychiat.*, 13:249–265.

Gottlieb, G. (1961), Developmental age as a baseline for determination of the critical period in imprinting. *J. Comp. Physiol. Psychol.*, 54:422–427.

Gray, P. H. (1963), Checklist of papers since 1951 dealing with imprinting in birds. *Psychol. Rec.*, 13:445–454.

Gray, P. H., and Howard, K. I. (1957), Specific recognition of humans in imprinted ducks. *Perceptual Motor Skills*, 7:301–304.

Gregory, I. (1958), An analysis of familial data on psychiatric patients. *Brit. J. Prev. Soc. Med.*, 12:42.

Grinker, R. R., Sr., *et al.* (1961), *The Phenomena of Depressions*. New York: Hoeber.

Haley, J. (1960), Direct study of child-parent interactions.

3. Observation of the family of the schizophrenic. *Amer. J. Orthopsychiat.*, 30:460–467.

Harlow. H. F. (1959a), Love in infant monkeys. *Scient. Amer.*, 200:68–74.

——— (1959b), The development of learning in the rhesus monkey. *Amer. Scientist*, 47:459–479.

Harlow, H. F., and Harlow, M. (1962), The effect of rearing conditions on behavior. *Bull. Menninger Clinic*, 26:213–224.

Harlow, H. F., and Zimmerman, R. R. (1959), Affectional responses in the infant monkey. *Science*, 130:421–432.

Harris, D. B. (1960), Conceptual and methodological developments in parent-child research. *Child Dev.*, 31:817–822.

Havighurst, R. J. (1963), Psychological roots of moral development: Discussion. *Catholic Psychol. Rec.*, 1:35–44.

Heathers, G. (1954), The adjustment of two-year-olds in a novel social situation. *Child Dev.*, 25:147–158.

Hernstein, M. I. (1963), Behavioral correlates of breast-bottle regimes under varying parent-infant relationships. *Monogr. Soc. for Research in Child Dev.*, 28: no. 88.

Hess, E. H. (1959a), The relationship between imprinting and motivation. In *Nebraska Symposium on Motivation*, ed. M. R. Jones. Lincoln, Nebraska: Univ. of Nebraska Press.

——— (1959b), Two conditions limiting critical age for imprinting. *J. Comp. Physiol. Psychol.*, 52:515–518.

——— (1959c), Imprinting, an effect of early experience. *Science*, 130:133–141.

——— (1958), "Imprinting" in animals. *Scient. Amer.*, 198:81–90.

Hjelholt, G. (1958), The neglected parent. *Nord. Psychol.*, 10:179–184.

Hoffman, M. L. (1960), Power assertion by the parent and its impact on the child. *Child Dev.*, 31:129–143.

Hokanson, J. E. (1961), The effects of guilt arousal and

severity of discipline on adult aggressive behavior. *J. Clin. Psychol.*, 17:29–32.

Hunt, J. M., ed. (1944), *Personality and the Behavior Disorders,* vols. 1 & 2. New York: Ronald.

Jaynes, J. (1957), Imprinting: The interaction of learned and innate behavior. 2. The critical period. *J. Comp. Physiol. Psychol.*, 50:6–10.

Jenkins, R. M. (1960), The psychopathic or antisocial personality. *J. Nerv. and Ment. Dis.*, 131:318–334.

Kagan, J. (1958), Socialization of aggression and the perception of parents in fantasy. *Child Dev.*, 29:311–320.

Kagan, J., and Moss, H. A. (1963), *From Birth to Maturity.* New York: Wiley.

——— (1960), The stability of passive and dependent behavior from childhood to adulthood. *Child Dev.*, 31:577–591.

Kaplan, A. R., and Thompson, W. R. (1957), Influence of prenatal anxiety on emotionality in young rats. *Science,* 126:73–74.

King, J. A. (1958), Parameters relevant to determining the effect of early experience upon the adult behavior of animals. *Psychol. Bull.*, 55:46–58.

Klatskin, E., and Jackson, E. B. (1955), Methodology of the Yale rooming-in project on parent-child relationship. *Amer. J. Orthopsychiat.*, 25:373–397.

Kodlin, D., and Thompson, D. J. (1958), An appraisal of the longitudinal approach in studies of growth and development. *Monogr. Soc. for Research in Child Dev.*, 23: no. 1.

Kohn, M. L. (1963), Social class and parent-child relationships: An interpretation. *Amer. J. Sociol.*, 68:471–480.

Kris, M. (1957), The use of prediction in a longitudinal study. In *The Psychoanalytic Study of the Child,* 12:175–189. New York: Internat. Univ. Press.

Kuhlen, R. G., and Thompson, G. G. (1963), *Psychological Studies of Human Development.* New York: Appleton.

Leighty, M. M. (1960), The effect of father absence during

early childhood upon the oedipal situation as reflected in young adults. *Merrill-Palmer Quart.*, 6:212–217.

Levy, D. (1943), *Maternal Overprotection.* New York: Columbia Univ. Press.

Lewis, H. (1955), Unsatisfactory parents and psychological disorder in their children. *Eugenics Rev.*, 47:153–162.

Liddell, H. (1961), Sheep. In *Lectures on Experimental Psychiatry,* ed. H. W. Brosin. Pittsburgh: Univ. of Pittsburgh Press.

——— (1956), *Emotional Hazards in Animals and Man.* Springfield, Ill.: C. C. Thomas.

Lindzey, G., ed. (1935), *Assessment of Human Motives.* New York: Holt, Rinehart and Winston.

Lorenz, K. (1952), *King Solomon's Ring.* New York: T. Y. Crowell.

——— (1935), Der kimpan in der unwelt des vogels. *J. Ornithol.,* 83:137–273, 289–413.

Maas, H. S. (1963), Long term effects of early childhood separation and group care. *Vita Humana,* 6:34–56.

Madoff, J. M. (1959), The attitudes of mothers of juvenile delinquents toward child rearing. *J. Consult. Psychol.,* 23:518–520.

Mahler, M. S., Furer, M., and Settlage, C. F. (1959), Severe emotional disturbance in childhood: Psychosis. In *American Handbook of Psychiatry,* 816–839. New York: Basic Books.

Martin, W. E. (1960), Conceptual and methodological developments in parent-child research. *Child Dev.,* 31:123–126.

McKinnon, K. M. (1942), *Consistency and Change in Behavior Manifestations as Observed in a Group of Sixteen Children During a Five-year Period.* New York: Teachers Coll. Bur. of Publ., Columbia Univ.

Meier, G. W., and Stuart, J. L. (1959), Effects of handling on the physical and behavioral development of Siamese kittens. *Psychol. Rep.,* 5:497–501.

Meyers, W. J. (1962), Critical period for the facilitation of exploratory behavior by infantile experience. *J. Comp. Physiol. Psychol.,* 50 : 1099–1101.

Mintz, B., ed. (1958), *Environmental Influences on Prenatal Development.* Chicago: Univ. of Chicago Press.

Mohr, G. J. (1940), Influence of mothers' attitude on mental health. *J. Pediatrics,* 16 : 641.

Moltz, H. (1960), Imprinting: Empirical basis and theoretical significance. *Psychol. Bull.,* 57 : 291–314.

Monkman, J. A. (1958), The relationship between children's adjustment and parental acceptance. *Dissertation Abstr.,* 19 : 1117–1118.

Montagu, M. F. A. (1962), *Prenatal Influences.* Springfield, Ill.: C. C. Thomas.

Mussen, P. H. (1960), Effects of parental behavior and attitudes on child personality and behavior. *Annual Rev. of Psychol.*

Mussen, P. H., Conger, J. J., and Kagan, J. (1963), *Child Development and Personality,* 2nd ed. New York: Harper & Row.

Mussen, P. H., and Distler, L. (1960), Child rearing antecedents of masculine identification in kindergarten boys. *Child Dev.,* 31 : 89–100.

Mussen, P. H., and Kagan, J. (1958), Group conformity and perception of parents. *Child Dev.,* 29 : 57–60.

Neel, J. V., and Schull, W. J. (1954), *Human Heredity.* Chicago: Univ. of Chicago Press.

Neilon, P. (1948), Shirley's babies after fifteen years: A personality study. *J. Genet. Psychol.,* 73 : 175–186.

Norris, A. S. (1960), Prenatal factors in intellectual and emotional development. *J. A. M. A.,* 172 : 413–416.

O'Neal, P., and Robins, L. N. (1959), The adult prognosis for runaway children. *Amer. J. Orthopsychiat.,* 29 : 752–761.

——— (1958), Childhood patterns predictive of adult schizophrenia: A thirty year follow-up. Presented at Annual Mtg. of Amer. Psychiatric Assn.

Ostow, M. (1960), Psychoanalysis and ethology. *J. Amer. Psychoanal. A.,* 8: 526–534.

Page, J. D. (1955), Review of *Depression,* ed. P. H. Hoch and J. Zubin. *Psychol. Bull.,* 52: 354.

Palter, G. H. (1960), A study of the relationship between the child's pattern of adjustment and the mother-child interaction. *Dissertation Abstr.,* 20: 4723.

Pasamanick, B., Rogers, M. E., and Lilienfeld, A. M. (1956), Pregnancy experience and development of behavior disorder in children. *Amer. J. Psychiat.,* 112: 613–618.

Pascal, G. R., and Jenkins, W. O. (1960), A study of the early environment of workhouse inmates (alcoholics) and its relationship to adult behavior. *Quart. J. Alcoholism,* 21: 40–50.

Payne, D. E., and Mussen, P. H. (1956), Parent-child relations and father identification among adolescent boys. *J. Abn. Soc. Psychol.,* 52: 358–362.

Peck, R. F. (1958), Family patterns correlated with adolescent personality structure. *J. Abn. Soc. Psychol.,* 57: 347–350.

Peck, R. F., and Havighurst, R. J. (1960), *The Psychology of Character Development.* New York: Wiley.

Pringle, M. L., Kollner, E., and Bossio, V. (1958), A study of deprived children. *Vita Humana,* 1: 65–92.

Pulver, U. (1959), Mutter irritierbarer sänglinge (Mothers of irritable infants). *Schweiz. Z. Psychol. Anwend.,* 18: 133–143.

Radke, M. J. (1946), The relation of parental authority to children's behavior and attitudes. *Univ. of Minnesota Child Welfare Monogr.,* vol. 22.

Redl, F., and Wineman, D. (1951), *Children Who Hate.* New York: Free Press.

Reichard, S., and Tillman, C. (1950), Patterns of child-parent relationship in schizophrenia. *Psychiatry,* 13: 247–257.

Reiner, B., and Kaufman, L. (1959), *Character Disorders in Parents of Delinquents.* New York: Family Serv. Assn. of Amer.

Ribble, M. (1943), *Rights of Infants.* New York: Columbia Univ. Press.

Reisen, A. H. (1960), Brain and behavior: Effects of stimulus deprivation on the development and atrophy of the visual sensory system. *Amer. J. Orthopsychiat.,* 30: 23–36.

Rosenthal, M. J., Finkelstein, M., Ni, E., and Robertson, R. E. (1959), A study of mother-child relationships in the emotional disorders of children. *Genet. Psychol. Monogr.,* 60: 63–116.

Rutter, M., Korn, S., and Birch, H. G. (1963), Genetic and environmental factors in the development of "primary reaction patterns." *Brit. J. Soc. Clin. Psychol.,* 2: 161–173.

Saul, L. (1971), *Emotional Maturity,* 3rd ed. Philadelphia: Lippincott.

Scarpitti, F. R., Murray, E., Dinitz, S., and Reckless, W. C. (1960), The "good" boy in a high delinquency area: Four years later. *Amer. Sociol. Rev.,* 25: 555–558.

Schaefer, E. S., and Bayley, N. (1963), Maternal behavior, child behavior, and their intercorrelations from infancy through adolescence. *Monogr. Soc. for Research in Child Dev.,* 28: no. 87.

Schaeffer, H. R. (1958), Objective observations of personality development in early infancy. *Brit. J. Med. Psychol.,* 31: 174–183.

Schaeffer, H. R., and Callender, W. M. (1959), Psychologic effects of hospitalization in infancy. *Pediatrics,* 24: 528–539.

Scott, J. P., Fredericson, E., and Fuller, J. L. (1951), Experimental exploration of the critical period hypothesis. *Personality,* 1: 162–183.

Sears, R. R., Maccoby, E. E., and Levin, J. (1957), *Patterns of Child Rearing.* New York: Harper & Row.

Seay, B., Hansen, E., and Harlow, H. F. (1962), Mother-infant separation in monkeys. *J. Child Psychol. Psychiat.,* 3:123–132.

Seitz, P. F. D. (1959), Infantile experience and adult behavior in animal subjects. 2. Age of separation from the mother and adult behavior in the cat. *Psychosom. Med.,* 21:353–378.

Shakow, D. (1959), Research in child development: A case illustration of the psychologist's dilemma. *Amer. J. Orthopsychiat.,* 29:45–59.

Shirley, M. M. (1942), Children's adjustment to a strange situation. *J. Abn. Soc. Psychol.,* 37:201–217.

Siegel, I. E. (1956), The need for conceptualization in research on child development. *Child. Dev.,* 27:241–252.

Skard, A. G., Inhelder, B., Noelting, G., Murphy, L. B., and Thomae, H. (1960), Longitudinal research in personality development. In *Perspectives in Personality Research,* ed. H. P. David and J. C. B. Brengelmann. New York: Springer.

Slater, P. E. (1962), Parental behavior and the personality of the child. *J. Genet. Psychol.,* 101:53–68.

Slocum, W., and Stone, C. L. (1958), Factors associated with family affection patterns. *Coordinator,* 7:21–25.

Sontag, L. W. (1958), Maternal anxiety during pregnancy and fetal behavior. Alternations in intelligence quotient in relation to personality variations. In *Physical and Behavioral Growth,* 26th Ross Pediatric Conference. Columbus, Ohio: Ross Laboratories.

——— (1955), Psychodynamics of child delinquency—further contributions. *Amer. J. Orthopsychiat.,* 25:254–261.

——— (1952), A differential study of psychopathic behavior in infants and children. *Amer. J. Orthopsychiat.,* 22:223–228.

Sontag, L. W., and Kagan, J. (1963), The emergence of intellectual achievement motives. *Amer. J. Orthopsychiat.,* 33:532–535.

Spitz, R. A. (1955), The influence of the mother-child relationship and its disturbances. In *Mental Health and Infant Development,* vol. 1, ed. K. Soddy. New York: Basic Books.

——— (1954), Infantile depression and the general adaptation syndrome. In *Depression,* ed. P. H. Hoch and J. Zubin. New York: Grune & Stratton.

——— (1951), The psychogenic diseases in infancy: An attempt at their etiological classification. In *The Psychoanalytic Study of the Child,* vol. 6. New York: Internat. Univ. Press.

——— (1945), Hospitalism: An inquiry into the genesis of psychiatric conditions in early childhood. In *The Psychoanalytic Study of the Child,* vol. 1. New York: Internat. Univ. Press.

Spitz, R. A., and Wolf, K. (1946), Anaclitic depression. In *The Psychoanalytic Study of the Child,* vol. 2. New York: Internat. Univ. Press.

Stott, D. H. (1957), Physical and mental handicaps following disturbed pregnancy. *Lancet,* 1: 1006–1012.

Symonds, P. M. (1949), *The Dynamics of Parent-Child Relationships.* New York: Teachers Coll. Bur. Publ., Columbia Univ.

Thompson, W. R. (1955), Early environment—its importance for later behavior. In *Psychopathology of Childhood,* ed. P. H. Hoch and J. Zubin. New York: Grune & Stratton.

Tinbergen, N. (1954), Psychology and ethology as supplementary parts of a science of behavior. In *Group Processes,* ed. B. Schaffner. New York: Josiah Macy, Jr. Foundation.

Tsumori, M., and Inage, N. (1958), Maternal attitude and its relationship to infant development. *Japan J. Educ. Psychol.,* 5: 208–218.

Tuddenham, R. D. (1959), The constancy of personality ratings over two decades. *Genet. Psychol. Monogr.,* 60: 3–29.

Vogel, E. F. (1960), The marital relationship of parents of emotionally disturbed children: Polarization and isolation. *Psychiatry,* 23:1–12.

Waelder, R. (1960), *Basic Theory of Psychoanalysis,* 3–35. New York: Internat. Univ. Press.

Washburn, A. H. (1959), Annual report to the board of the Child Research Council. (Unpublished.)

Watson, G. (1957), Some personality differences in children related to strict or passive discipline. *J. Psychol.,* 44:227–249.

Wenar, C., Handlon, M. W., and Garner, A. M. (1962), *Origins of Psychosomatic and Emotional Disorders.* New York: Hoeber.

Whiting, J. W. M., and Child, I. L. (1953), *Child Training and Personality.* New Haven, Conn.: Yale Univ. Press.

Winder, C. L., and Rau, L. (1962), Parental attitudes associated with social deviance in preadolescent boys. *J. Abn. Soc. Psychol.,* 64:418–424.

World Health Organization (1964), Deprivation of maternal care: A reassessment of its effects. WHO Publ. Health Papers, 14.

Yarrow, L. J. (1961), Maternal deprivation: Toward an empirical and conceptual re-evaluation. *Psychol. Bull.,* 58:459–490.

INDEX